CONTEMPORARY AMERICAN WOMEN FICTION WRITERS

An A-to-Z Guide

Edited by Laurie Champion and Rhonda Austin

Emmanuel S. Nelson, Advisory Editor

GREENWOOD PRESS
Westport, Connecticut • London

Library of Congress Cataloging-in-Publication Data

Contemporary American women fiction writers : An A-to-Z Guide / edited by Laurie
Champion and Rhonda Austin.
     p. cm.
Includes bibliographical references and index.
ISBN 0–313–31627–9 (alk. paper)
   1. American fiction—Women authors—Bio-bibliography—Dictionaries. 2. Women and
literature—United States—History—20th century—Dictionaries. 3. American fiction—20th
century—Bio-bibliography—Dictionaries. 4. Novelists, American—20th
century—Biography—Dictionaries. 5. Women novelists, American—Biography—Dictionaries. 6. American fiction—Women authors—Dictionaries.
7. American fiction—20th century—Dictionaries. I. Champion, Laurie. II. Austin,
Rhonda.
PS374.W6 C66 2002
813'.5099287'03—dc21
[B]   2002067825

British Library Cataloguing in Publication Data is available.

Library of Congress Catalog Card Number: 2002067825
ISBN: 0–313–31627–9

First published in 2002

Greenwood Press, 88 Post Road West, Westport, CT 06881
An imprint of Greenwood Publishing Group, Inc.
www.greenwood.com

Printed in the United States of America

The paper used in this book complies with the
Permanent Paper Standard issued by the National
Information Standards Organization (Z39.48–1984).

10 9 8 7 6 5 4 3 2 1

CONTEMPORARY
AMERICAN
WOMEN FICTION WRITERS

CONTENTS

PREFACE

This collection of essays contributes to the ongoing celebration of women's achievements. It adds to the continuing attempt to recognize women artists generally and American women writers specifically. These writers have benefitted from the struggles of their predecessors, writers who broke through barriers that denied women opportunities to express themselves. Although significant advances have been made toward gender equality in the United States, the battle for such equality is far from finished. Since the 1970s, when the second wave of feminism occurred in the United States, women writers who had been ignored have been added to the American literary canon and contemporary women have been given more opportunities to publish their works. This volume highlights American women writers who continue to build upon the once male-dominated American literary canon.

As its title suggests, *Contemporary American Women Fiction Writers: An A-to-Z Guide* provides overviews of American women writers who wrote or published their most significant works since 1945, the end of World War II and often cited as the end of Modernism. Most of the writers represented here are still alive and are continuing to write and publish. Each essay about a specific author consists of four sections: Biography, Major Works and Themes, Critical Reception, and Bibliography, which include both primary and secondary sources. Each essay offers biographical information about the author, an analysis of the author's major works, an overview of the critical reception of the author's works, and a bibliography that lists works by the author and introduces readers to works that have been written about the author and her works.

Writers who have received a considerable amount of critical attention in recent decades such as Toni Morrison and Joyce Carol Oates are included, as well as those such as J. California Cooper and Melanie Rae Thon, who deserve more critical recognition. Also, the authors represented here represent diversity in terms of ethnicity. Although not as blatantly as before the end of World War II, many of these authors have been ignored by critics, not only because of gender bias but also because of ethnic bias. In spite of this two-fold bias, women of color continue to contribute significantly to the American literary canon.

Adding to the growing body of women's works that are included in the literary canon, as well as to anthologies and scholarly studies that recognize women's contributions to literature, this anthology seeks to continue to challenge attitudes that underestimate artistic contributions of women and stereotype their social roles.

Working on this anthology has been professionally rewarding as well as personally fulfilling for the editors. We would like to thank all the scholars who contributed to this volume. Without their cooperative spirit, time, and effort this anthology could not have been completed. We also appreciate the encouragement and efforts of Emmanuel S. Nelson, the Advisory Editor of this anthology, for wisdom expressed in his solicitation of manuscripts that recognize women and minority writers. Thanks also to George Butler of Greenwood Press for his instrumental role in overseeing the preparation of the manuscript.

INTRODUCTION

Laurie Champion

The turn of the twenty-first century has proved a flourishing time for American women writers. Although historically women have been denied opportunities and silenced in many ways, they have overcome obstacles and made significant contributions both to society at large and to literature specifically. Historically, American women writers have struggled to overcome gender biases in order to become successful: Initial struggles for a voice during the later part of the eighteenth century and throughout the nineteenth century continued through the 1960s and 1970s, which marked the second wave of feminism in the United States. These battles for gender equality are occurring still, but more than ever, women currently experience more opportunities for artistic expression. Fortunately, since the civil rights movement, which parallels the Chicano/a movement, the black arts movement, and the second wave of feminism, American women and minorities gradually have been given more opportunity to publish their works and to succeed as writers.

The writers in this volume have all made significant contributions to the contemporary literary scene, and some have already joined the women writers who have established themselves among writers of works firmly established in the American literary canon. Many have won prestigious awards for their accomplishments, both nationally and internationally. Among the great achievements of contemporary American women writers was the awarding of the Nobel Prize for literature to Toni Morrison, the first African American woman to be distinguished with the highest recognition for literature.

Many of the authors discussed in this reference present themes and subjects that defy traditionally prescribed roles for women. The women characters perform roles that defy stereotypes. They are political leaders, pillars of their community, and spokeswomen for women's rights. Many face challenges such as divorce, balancing motherhood and career, and trying to maintain self-respect.

Patterns of strong female characters emerge through the works written by the women represented here. One excellent example of the ways contemporary American women writers defy stereotypical roles for women can be found in Gayl Jones's *Mosquito*. The novel centers on the African American narrator, Sojourner Nadine Jane Johnson, who is known as Mosquito, her Chicana friend, Delgadina, and her childhood friend, Monkey Bread, who works as a personal assistant for a famous movie star in California. These three women are strong, intelligent, and independent. Other characters also challenge stereotypes, and the narrator often speaks directly to readers about ways minorities and women are stereotyped. Although Mosquito claims that she is somewhat uneducated, throughout the novel, she makes powerful political and socially charged speeches that celebrate her African American and female identity. Another example can be found in Alice Walker's *The Color Purple*, which is set in the early part of the twentieth century. The protagonist, Celie, overcomes incest, domestic violence, and degradation because of prejudices concerning her ethnicity, her economic status, and her gender from society in general and from those close to her. She fights to find her identity and build her self-esteem in spite of perpetual physical and emotional abuse. She overcomes all of these obstacles to build a successful business that affords her economic freedom and allows her to comfort and provide for herself and for others in need. Also, Terry McMillan's characters are strong women. The four women in *Waiting to Exhale* find comfort in each other as they struggle with careers, romantic relationships, and raising children. Typically, McMillan's women do not depend on men to take care of them emotionally or financially. Her characters form a true community of women and create a strong sense of sisterhood.

Other writers depict characters who are so affected by an oppressive society that they cannot survive. Some of Toni Morrison's works come immediately to mind. *The Bluest Eye* shows how definitions of beauty determined by a white- and male-dominated society are detrimental to minority women. The protagonist, Pecola, believes that if she had blue eyes, she would not be poor or abused. Nobody can help Pecola overcome the lack of self-worth she experiences. Unlike women who can overcome oppression, Pecola is led to insanity by the oppression that stems from not being able to satisfy the demands of the empowered. Like Morrison, many of the ethnic writers presented here demonstrate ways in which American minority women have been two or three times jeopardized: victims of various combinations of gender, ethnic, and class biases.

Sometimes in addition to showing these types of oppressive social systems, sometimes aside from that issue, many contemporary American ethnic women writers celebrate their cultural heritages. Generally, their works present tributes to the myths, the folklores, and the beliefs of their cultures. Many of these authors present folk sayings, recipes, jokes, and spiritual lessons that have been passed from generation to generation to shape habits, customs, and traditions. These writers pay homage both to mythical figures and to real-life heroes and heroines that have inspired and encouraged their people. Reading this culturally rich literature reveals the polyethnicity apparent in contemporary American literature.

A subject that recurs frequently in literature by contemporary American women ethnic writers is the complex issue involving dual identity. For example, Maxine (Ting Ting) Hong Kingston's female characters struggle to find identity as Chinese Americans, and most are debased because they are female in a patriarchal culture. Ana Castillo's *Mixquiahuala Letters* is an epistolary novel that consists of letters written by Teresa to her friend, Alicia. Throughout the letters, Teresa tries to explain to Alicia the complexities of being a Mexican American. The letters reveal both to Alicia and to readers the plight of women in a sexist, racist, and classist society.

Some writers represented here blend feminist ideology with regionalism to express ideas about a specific region in the United States. The twenty-first century marks the continuation of the women's Southern literary tradition. Bobbie Ann Mason, Harper Lee, Gail Godwin, Alice Walker, Lee Smith, Jill McCorkle, Alice Adams, Toni Cade Bambara, Gayl Jones, Beverly Lowry, Jayne Anne Phillips, Anne Tyler, and other contemporary Southern women writers remind us that the Southern literary tradition for women is alive and well after the Southern renaissance that brought us such notable women writers as Eudora Welty, Carson McCullers, and Flannery O'Connor. Different from their literary predecessors, contemporary Southern women writers present a South with modern technology and pop culture. Building on their predecessors' achievements, these contemporary Southern women writers demonstrate complicated social systems and complex personal dilemmas.

Like some of their male cohorts, some of the women writers here use postmodern writing techniques in their works. They challenge linear plots, disrupt boundaries between reality and fiction, and blur distinctions between truth and fallacy. For example, Cynthia Ozick frequently invites multiple readings of her texts that disrupt each other. She also employs meta-fictional elements in her narratives. She explores the artistic process itself in ways that develop self-reflexivity.

This reference acknowledges and celebrates the achievements of contemporary American women fiction writers. In spite of a long history of attempts to silence them and to deny them opportunities to express themselves artistically, American women writers have proven that they are able to excel in a once-male-dominated profession. Rising above references such as that of "a mob of scribbling women," as Hawthorne once described them, American women writers have created their own voice. Contemporary American women writers continue to add to those voices, both building on the tradition developed by their forerunners and departing from that tradition to break new ground for women writers.

ALICE ADAMS (1926–1999)

Julie S. Amberg

BIOGRAPHY

Alice Boyd Adams was born in Fredericksburg, Virginia, on August 14, 1926. Her father was a professor of Spanish at the University of North Carolina and her mother a failed writer whose dreams for a writing life probably inspired Adams to her own career. Originally a poet, when Adams entered Radcliffe College at age sixteen, she enrolled in a short story writing class taught by Kenneth Kempton. Though Adams received little encouragement from Kempton, who suggested she marry instead of write, she later found support in a summer creative writing course in North Carolina taught by Phillips Russell. Russell taught a five-act formula for writing stories—ABDCE: action, background, development, climax, ending—which she used throughout her subsequent career.

After graduation from Radcliffe in 1946, Adams moved to New York, where she worked for a publishing firm but was fired after a few months owing to her frequent absences to visit Mark Linenthal, Jr., at Harvard. She and Linenthal were married in 1947 and moved for a year to Paris, where Linenthal studied at the Sorbonne. In 1948 they returned to the United States and moved to San Francisco, a frequent setting for many of Adams's works. In 1954 Linenthal joined the faculty at San Francisco State University and earned his doctorate in 1957 from Stanford University. By that time, the couple had had their only child, Peter Adams Linenthal, born in 1951. Adams remembers the 1950s as a time of frustration and denial. She was writing only infrequently because of the demands of childcare and was suffering a loveless marriage. In 1958 she divorced Linenthal and the next year published her first story.

During the next decade, Adams supported herself and her son through bookkeeping and clerical jobs, while continuing to write. Her first published novel, *Careless Love* (1966), is based upon one of several affairs Adams engaged in during this time. The novel's dry humor made it a popular work in England, but it did not sell well in the United States. Meanwhile, Adams continued to write short stories, publishing them in popular magazines such as *Cosmopolitan*, *Redbook*, and *McCall's*. Her first major literary achievement came in 1969 when the short story "Gift of Grass" was published in the *New Yorker*. Praised by critics for its subtle interpretation of family relationships in the 1960s, "Gift of Grass" (*Beautiful Girl*) was included in the 1971 *Prize Stories: O. Henry Award*.

During the 1970s, Adams published two novels and a collection of short stories. One of these novels, *Families and Survivors* (1975), chronicles the life of a woman who is born in Virginia, moves to San Francisco, gets married, divorces, remarries, and eventually becomes a successful artist. The novel contains situations that prevail throughout Adams's writing career—the precarious position of women who focus solely upon love and relationships only to have their lives shattered when romantic relationships fail—and the provocative suggestion, for its time, that women need interesting and engaging work to feel fulfilled.

Adams received a John Simon Guggenheim Memorial Fellowship in 1978 and that same year published *Listening to Billie*. Adams's last published work of the decade was her first collection of short stories, *Beautiful Girl*, published in 1979. Half of the short stories in this collection had previously won O. Henry Awards, and reviewers commended their spare style and fine, penetrating portrayal of human weakness, desire, and pain. Adams was awarded a fiction grant from the National Endowment for the Arts in 1979.

In the 1980s, Adams published prolifically, producing more award-winning stories, collected in *To See You Again* (1982), *Return Trips* (1985), and *After You've Gone* (1989), as well as three novels, *Rich Rewards* (1980), *Superior Women* (1984), and *Second Chances* (1988). *Superior Women*, a long novel that covers the lives of five Radcliffe girls from 1943 to 1983, became her first best-seller. In *Second Chances*, Adams chronicles the lives of sixty- and seventy-year-old friends who have many of the same concerns of Adams's earlier younger characters but who now confront these through the experience of aging. In an interview with Kim Heron, Adams says she is interested in exploring in the novel themes of sexuality, sickness, and friendship in older age. These themes perhaps concerned Adams herself: By the late 1980s, she was in her sixties and had experienced a cancer scare. She had also been in a long-term relationship with Robert McNie, a San Francisco interior designer, for more than twenty years.

In 1990 Adams published a non-fiction work, *Mexico: Some Travels and Travelers There*. She had been vacationing in Mexico for over twenty years, and it had often served as the setting for her short stories. She followed this with the novels *Caroline's Daughters* (1991), *Almost Perfect* (1993), *A Southern Exposure* (1995), and *Medicine Man* (1997). A final collection of short stories, *The Last Lovely City*, was published in 1999. Adams died on May 27, 1999, in San Francisco. Her final novel, *After the War*, which she completed before she died, was published in 2000.

MAJOR WORKS AND THEMES

Alice Adams's work belongs in the modernist tradition of fiction that features characters searching to create meaning in their lives within the context of social and personal barriers to knowledge. Adams's characters ask enduring questions in this search for meaning, yet they are very much shaped by their particular experience at the end of the twentieth century. Reviewer Molly Haskell describes Adams's style as a "mix of old-fashioned story telling with a modern sense of the elusive perplexities of identity" (16).

Adams's heroines often make realizations and life changes after suffering painful relationships with men. *Careless Love* (1966), *Families and Survivors* (1975), *Listening to Billie* (1978), *Rich Rewards* (1980), and *Almost Perfect* (1993) concern themselves with their protagonists' devastating affairs; yet, always careful to explore the nuances of personal relationships, Adams does not portray the histrionics of these love relationships but rather the quiet after-effect of their conclusions. Adams depicts the private, interior world of her characters with subtlety and precision and has been praised by critics for her irony and narrative control.

The importance of work in gaining an understanding of oneself is another common theme of Adams's fiction. Her protagonist in *Rich Rewards*, Daphne Matthiessen, is a middle-aged woman who has been through a string of affairs only to be disappointed by the inevitable loss of passion as each progresses. When Daphne, who is an interior designer, finally decides to concentrate on her work, she becomes happier and fulfilled and, though still interested in men, less likely to let her affairs control her completely. Similarly, *Listening to Billie* concerns the poet Eliza Quarles's slow development toward independence through a series of damaging personal relationships. Eliza overcomes depression caused by failed relationships once she focuses upon her art. The music and lyrics of Billie Holiday are weaved throughout *Listening to Billie* as a musical emblem of Quarles's pain.

In addition to her close examination of men's and women's relationships, Adams explores in her fiction the connections between family members and between friends. Her most popular novel, *Superior Women*, chronicles the lives of five college students during their years at Radcliffe and beyond. Adams renders the conventional characteristics of female friendships—loyalty, sympathy, understanding, cattiness, and jealousy—with convincing detail and complexity. Adams's novel *Caroline's Daughters* depicts a year in the life of a family of five women who reach varying levels of fulfillment in their quest for self-identity. Successful interpersonal relationships, as well as rewarding work, are the keys to their happiness.

The significance of family connections becomes foregrounded in two of Adams's novels set in the South. Despite her antipathy for Southern culture (Feineman 29), Adams is able to use what she remembered of her early life to write *A Southern Exposure* (1995) and its sequel, *After the War* (2000). The first novel is the saga of transplanted New Englanders, the Baird family, to the small southern town of Pineville during the American Depression. Adams wittily renders both the ordinary and the exceptional events of their lives against the backdrop of Southern social convention. In *After the War*, Adams continues the family's story. Haskell notes Adams's success in the novel in being able to write about the "dark events and emotions" that surge around events in these characters' lives, without breaking up the "flow of life" (16).

CRITICAL RECEPTION

Criticism of Adams's writing has come principally in the many reviews of her work, spanning more than thirty years. Excerpts from the major reviews are gathered in *Contemporary Literary Criticism*, Vols. 6 (1976), 13 (1980), and 46 (1988). Although there exists no book-length critical study of Adams to date, the following major reference works give extensive overviews of her life and writings: *Current Biography*

Yearbook 1989, *Contemporary Authors New Revision Series*, Vol. 26 (1989), and *Contemporary Fiction Writers of the South: A Bio-Bibliographical Sourcebook* (1993).

Interviews with Adams have revealed her thoughts on her life and work. In a 1980 interview with Neil Feineman, she discusses her earlier writing, while shorter interviews that discuss specific works appear in the following: *Superior Women* in Deidre English's interview for *Mother Jones*, *Second Chances* in Kim Heron's "Horror and Romance," and *Almost Perfect* in Lynn Karpen's "Poor Richard!" Biographical information is found in the *People Weekly* interview "Out of the Pages" with Nancy Faber.

Reviewers have generally praised her short stories, Adams's own favorite genre, while giving more mixed reviews of her novels. Writing in the *New York Times Book Review*, Benjamin DeMott suggests that the short story may be a better form for Adams's plots, which generally feature "moral vacancy, nervous shuttling in and out of relationships, weightless life commitments and plans" ("Stories of Change" 7). In a review of the short story collection *To See You Again*, Robert Phillips praises Adams's ability to shift point of view from character to character with "economy," thereby allowing the reader to make the associations between character and situation (189). In his essay-review of recent short story collections, Greg Johnson praises Adams for deftly portraying a combination of strength and vulnerability in the heroines featured in *After You've Gone* (283).

Critics of Adams's novels generally praise her spare, concise language and skill in depicting contemporary American relationships realistically, without sentimentality or nostalgia. At the same time, some reviewers have faulted Adams for her characters' lack of introspection and bloodlessness of heart. Writing about *Superior Women*, for instance, John Updike wonders if Adams's eye for detail and nuance suffers as she describes the events of many lives extended over the expanse of a novel. In this novel, Updike writes, the plot becomes almost "actuarial," and a "certain bleakly notational texture overtakes the survey [of characters and events]" (160). Another critic thought *Superior Women* a bad use of the formula Mary McCarthy introduced in *The Group*, the contemporaneous narratives of several college-aged women (Yardley 3).

A total of five critical articles that consider Adams's work have been published. Cara Chell, in "Succeeding in Their Times: Alice Adams on Women and Work," argues that Adams breaks with modernist and postmodernist traditions by creating new kinds of "happy endings" to her novels. Larry T. Blades in "Order and Chaos in Alice Adams' *Rich Rewards*" explores the "uneasy peace" between the ordered world of the heroine's life and the outer, chaotic world of her society. In "Changing the Past: Alice Adams' Revisionary Nostalgia," Lee Upton writes that heroines in Adams's short fiction often enter into nostalgic reflections of the past to negotiate their current situations. Upton suggests this nostalgic look becomes risky when it challenges the reality of past times. In her study of aging in contemporary literature, *From the Hearth to the Open Road*, Barbara Frey Waxman discusses Adams's stories "Lost Luggage," "To See You Again," and "A Wonderful Woman," all of which feature middle-aged women in the process of constructing new identities. Finally, in an essay-review of new works by women authors, Greg Johnson discusses stories in Adams's collection *After You've Gone*, placing them within the tradition of women's writing, as currently defined.

Adams's last novel, *After the War*, was published posthumously in 2000. In reviewing the book, Molly Haskell laments the passing of an author who so sensitively renders a sense of place (16). A review in *Publishers Weekly* notes the novel contains those perennials of Adams's fiction: hardhearted yet well-intentioned people and revelations about the complexities of love (329).

BIBLIOGRAPHY

Works by Alice Adams

Careless Love. New York: New American Library, 1966. Republished as *The Fall of Daisy Duke.* London: Constable, 1967.
Families and Survivors. New York: Knopf, 1975.
Listening to Billie. New York: Knopf, 1978.
Beautiful Girl. New York: Knopf, 1979.
Rich Rewards. New York: Knopf, 1980.
To See You Again. New York: Knopf, 1982.
Molly's Dog. Concord, NH: Ewert, 1983.
Superior Women. New York: Knopf, 1984.
Return Trips. New York: Knopf, 1985.
Roses, Rhododendron: Two Flowers, Two Friends. Minneapolis: Redpath Press, 1987.
Second Chances. New York: Knopf, 1988.
After You've Gone. New York: Knopf, 1989.
Mexico: Some Travels and Some Travelers There. New York: Prentice-Hall, 1990.
Caroline's Daughters. New York: Knopf, 1991.
Almost Perfect. New York: Knopf, 1993.
A Southern Exposure. New York: Knopf, 1995.
Medicine Man. New York: Knopf, 1997.
The Last Lovely City. New York: Knopf, 1999.
After the War. New York: Knopf, 2000.

Studies of Alice Adams

"Adams, Alice." *Contemporary Literary Criticism.* Ed. Carolyn Riley and Phyllis Carmel Mendelson. Vol. 6. Detroit: Gale, 1976. 1–2.
"Adams, Alice." *Contemporary Literary Criticism.* Ed. Dedria Bryfonski. Vol. 13. Detroit: Gale, 1980. 1–3.
Rev. of *After the War. Publishers Weekly* 14 Aug. 2000: 329.
"Alice Adams." *Current Biography Yearbook.* Ed. Charles Moritz. Vol. 50. Bronx: H. W. Wilson, 1989. 6–10.
"Alice (Boyd) Adams." *Contemporary Literary Criticism.* Ed. Daniel G. Marowski and Roger Matuz. Vol. 46. Detroit: Gale, 1988. 13–23.
Blades, Larry T. "Order and Chaos in Alice Adams' *Rich Rewards.*" *Critique: Studies in Modern Fiction* 27 (1986): 187–95.
Chell, Cara. "Succeeding in Their Times: Alice Adams on Women and Work." *Soundings: An Interdisciplinary Journal* 68 (1985): 62–71.
DeMott, Benjamin. "Stories of Change." Rev. of *To See You Again. New York Times Book Review* 11 April 1982: 7ff.
——. "Elderly Lives and Lovers." Rev. of *Second Chances. New York Times Book Review* 1 May 1988: 11.
English, Deirdre. "Interview with Alice Adams." *Mother Jones* Nov. 1984: 41.
Faber, Nancy. "Out of the Pages." *People Weekly* 3 April 1978: 48ff.
Feineman, Neil. "An Interview with Alice Adams." *Story Quarterly* 11 (1980): 27–37.

Haskell, Molly. "Southern Dish." Rev. of *After the War. New York Times Book Review* 15 Oct. 2000: 16.

Herman, Barbara A. "Alice Adams." *Contemporary Fiction Writers of the South: A Bio-Bibliographical Sourcebook*. Ed. Joseph M. Flora and Robert Bain. Westport, CT: Greenwood Press, 1993. 11–21.

Heron, Kim. "Horror and Romance." *New York Times Book Review* 1 May 1988: 11.

Johnson, Greg. "Some Recent Herstories." *Georgia Review* 44 (1990): 278–89.

Karpen, Lynn. "Poor Richard!" *New York Times Book Review* 11 July 1993: 7.

Phillips, Robert. "Missed Opportunities, Endless Possibilities." Rev. of *To See You Again. Commonweal* 25 March 1983: 188–90.

Prescott, Jani, and Jean W. Ross. "Adams, Alice (Boyd)." *Contemporary Authors New Revision Series*. Vol. 26. Detroit: Gale, 1989. 1–3.

Thornton, Lawrence. "This Is No Fine Romance." Rev. of *Almost Perfect. New York Times Book Review* 11 July 1993: 7.

Updike, John. "No More Mr. Knightlys." *New Yorker* 5 Nov. 1984: 160ff.

Upton, Lee. "Changing the Past: Alice Adams' Revisionary Nostalgia." *Studies in Short Fiction* 26 (1989): 33–41.

Waxman, Barbara Frey. *From the Hearth to the Open Road: A Feminist Study of Aging in Contemporary Literature*. Westport, CT: Greenwood Press, 1990. 75–94.

Yardley, Jonathon. "That Old Gang of Hers." Rev. of *Superior Women. Washington Post Book World* 2 Sept. 1984: 3

JULIA ALVAREZ (1950–)

J. Elizabeth Clark

BIOGRAPHY

Julia Alvarez was born in New York City on March 27, 1950, but her family soon moved to the Dominican Republic. Fleeing political reprisal for her father's participation in a failed coup against the Trujillo government, in 1960 they returned to the city, which would come to play a central role in all of Alvarez's work. Much of her writing is semiautobiographical, based on the experience of growing up with a bicultural heritage. The history and present of the Dominican Republic and the struggles of Dominican American immigrants, particularly women, figure prominently in her work.

Much like the characters in her breakout novel *How the García Girls Lost Their Accents* (1991), Alvarez was raised with the expectation that she would grow up to assume responsibilities for a home and family; her education in the United States created an alternative future for her as she studied the lives and works of many women writers. Accustomed to living away from home, having attended boarding school for much of her childhood, Alvarez attended Connecticut College (1967–1969), where her writing career began. At Connecticut College, she began to succeed in creative writing, winning the school's creative writing award two years in a row. In 1969 she transferred to Middlebury College and received her BA, summa cum laude (1971). She earned an MA in creative writing from Syracuse University in 1975.

Alvarez's entire career has focused on two pivotal roles: teaching and writing. Beginning in 1975, she worked as part of the Kentucky, Delaware, and North Carolina "Poet in the Schools" programs. In 1978 she received a National Endowment for the Arts grant to lead a workshop for senior citizens in Fayetteville, North Carolina. The culmination of this work was Alvarez's first book, an anthology of workshop participants' writing, *Old Age Ain't for Sissies* (1979).

In 1979 Alvarez accepted the first of several institutional teaching positions at Phillips Andover Academy in Massachusetts. She moved to the University of Vermont in

1981. While in Vermont, she created an exhibit of poems illustrated and printed by women artists. The illustrated poems were displayed in the Vermont State House and later toured throughout the state. This early public success was followed by Alvarez's first commercial poetry publication, *Homecoming* (1984).

Alvarez's early publishing career focused exclusively on poetry as she moved to two more institutions as a professor. She taught at George Washington University as the Jenny McKean Moore Visiting Writer (1984) and at the University of Illinois (1985–1988). In 1988 she worked as the resident writer at Altos de Chavón in the Dominican Republic. In the same year, she returned to her alma mater, Middlebury College, as a professor of creative writing, where she still teaches today. *My English*, the result of several years of work, appeared in 1990.

While the 1980s proved to be Alvarez's decade of poetry, the fiction work she published in the early 1990s established her as an important literary figure. *How the García Girls Lost Their Accents* was an enormous success. Alvarez followed this with the more controversial *In the Time of the Butterflies* (1994).

In the mid-1990s, Alvarez returned to poetry again with *The Other Side/El Otro Lado* (1995) and a reprinting of her 1984 *Homecoming* with new work added (1996). In 1995 she was honored at a dinner at the State Department for her contribution to the Dominican community in both the Dominican Republic and the United States. In 1996 she received two additional public recognitions for her work: a citation by the borough of Manhattan that recognized her achievement "in presenting issues in contemporary life in the United States" and an Alumni Achievement Award from Middlebury College. These events, along with many others, demonstrate the very public nature of Alvarez's work and life.

The end of the 1990s and the turn of the century were productive times for Alvarez. Seven books appeared in five years: the critically acclaimed ¡*YO!* (1996), *Something to Declare* (1998), *Seven Trees* (1999), *In the Name of Salomé* (2000), *The Secret Footprints* (2000), *The New Family Cookbook: Recipes for Nourishing Yourself and Those You Love* (2000) (a book co-authored with her husband, Bill Eichner), and most recently a novel for young adults, *How Tía Lola Came to Stay* (2001). In addition to her publications during this time period, in 2000 she received significant public attention for her work. She was chosen by the White House as part of the U.S. delegation to the inauguration of the new president of the Dominican Republic, Hipolito Mejia. She received a Woman of the Year Award from *Latina Magazine* and also was honored by the New York Historical Society with a dinner in celebration of her work.

A popular speaker, Alvarez has given talks and interviews at venues as varied as National Public Radio's "Face the Nation" (November 23, 1994); the New York Public Library, Celeste Bartos Forum (February 18, 1997); a keynote address, "Language as a Moral Force," to the National Council of Teachers of English (November 22, 1997); and a reading at the National Museum of Women in the Arts in Washington, D.C. (May 19, 2000).

Alvarez is widely published; her work has appeared in magazines such as the *High Plains Literary Review*, *New York Times Magazine*, *Allure*, *Helicon Nine*, and *New Yorker*. Her fiction has appeared in anthologies such as *The One You Call Sister: New Women's Fiction* (1989), *Mondo Barbie* (1993), and *New Writing from the Caribbean* (1994).

MAJOR WORKS AND THEMES

While Alvarez's poetry and fiction deal extensively with the immigrant experience and the struggles of bicultural identity, her work appeals to a large audience. She seeks to connect the experience of cultural dislocation to the larger experience of American living, realizing that the source of her own writing is a powerful site of inspiration for writing. She writes, "I came into English as a ten-year-old from the Dominican Republic, and I consider this radical uprooting from my culture, my native language, my country, the reason I began writing. 'Language is the only homeland,' Czeslow Milosz once observed, and indeed, English, not the United States, was where I landed and sunk deep roots" (http://www.middlebury.edu/~english/alvarez/Alv-autobio.html).

Alvarez's fiction has been cited for her portrayals of strong women characters and her use of beautiful language. Her stories present American dreams contrasted with American realities. Far from appealing only to a Dominican audience, Alvarez uses this discordance in American life to reach out to readers from a variety of cultural backgrounds. Inherent in her own writing of dislocation is a desire to write characters with whom her readers can connect. Alvarez also writes to connect to history. Through her stories and novels, she creates an alternative historical reality in which unpopular or unrecognized characters speak, coming alive on the page. Her fiction falls into three categories: literature of immigration, historical fiction, and children's fiction.

How the García Girls Lost Their Accents is loosely autobiographical. Like many writers, Alvarez uses her personal history and experiences as a source of inspiration. This collection of fifteen linked short stories follows the history of the García sisters—Carla, Sandra, Yolanda, and Sofia—through their immigration and assimilation to American life. As the title suggests, the longer they remain in the United States, the less Dominican they become; the loss of their accents is a method of representation of the complex, changing, and sometimes temporal nature of cultural identity. Like Alvarez, the girls leave the Dominican Republic because of their father's involvement in a plot against Trujillo. These stories offer a dark look at adolescence and adult life as the sisters struggle with Dominican cultural expectations in the context of living in the United States. Told backward, we meet the adult sisters with their very adult problems, including addictions and relationship strife. The novel ends in a more idyllic Dominican Republic during the girls' childhood. In the stories, the United States serves as a representation of the loss of innocence, while in the Dominican Republic, the girls' lives revolved around family and play. Life in the United States, however, brought with it multilayered complications. To date, *How the García Girls Lost Their Accents* continues to receive the most critical attention of any of Alvarez's novels. It invites comparisons with other Latina *bildungsroman* like Sandra Cisneros's *House on Mango Street* and Cristina García's *Dreaming in Cuban*.

¡YO!, Alvarez's third novel, continues to explore these complications. The novel is told by sixteen different narrators reflecting on the life of Yolanda García, who has become a successful novelist. Through the different narrators, the reader comes to understand different parts of Yolanda's personality, from her intimate, personal relationships to her business relationships to her family relationships. This novel answers some of the criticisms of *How the García Girls Lost Their Accents*, delving more fully into the life of one of the characters and moving away from some of the plot sequences considered clichéd and convenient.

In the Time of the Butterflies and *In the Name of Salomé* depart from Alvarez's other works. Both of these novels delve into the history of the Dominican Republic. *In the Time of the Butterflies* is told in four parts that explore and reimagine the history of the Mirabel sisters, Minerva, Patria, and Maria Teresa, who denounced the Trujillo government. The story is told by the fourth surviving sister, Dede, who did not become involved in the underground movement against Trujillo. *In the Time of the Butterflies* presents the sisters as butterflies born to a privileged lifestyle; they are unlikely revolutionaries. This novel is Alvarez's foray into the political novel: The Mirabel sisters are unpopular historical figures in the Dominican Republic. In the retelling of the story, Alvarez has rescued the Mirabels for an American audience, making their deaths tragic and uncomfortable for the reader; the novel is sympathetic to their positions. In *In the Name of Salomé*, Alvarez again returns to the historical, exploring the fictionalized life of Dominican poet Salomé.

Recently Alvarez has ventured into children's fiction with a children's book, *The Secret Footprints*, and a young adult novel, *How Tía Lola Came to Stay*.

CRITICAL RECEPTION

Alvarez's critical reception can be divided roughly into two categories: responses by academicians and responses by critics of popular literary fiction. The academic world of literary critics has celebrated Alvarez's work, comparing her with other Latina writers like Cristina García and Ana Castillo; Alvarez's work fits into the now-well-established canon of multicultural women writers of the United States and into the burgeoning subgenre of Latina literature. Literary critics have been fascinated by the emergence of a Dominican American writer, tracing thematic and metaphoric patterns in her novels to dominant Latin American literary giants like Gabriel García Márquez and Carlos Fuentes.

Critics of popular literary fiction have offered a more mixed response to Alvarez's work, evaluating it less for its place in the multicultural literary canon and more for its perceived literary merit. Donna Rifkind of the *New York Times Book Review* argued of the main characters in *How the García Girls Lost Their Accents* that "because their adult preoccupations are by now such clichés—the staples of women's magazines and pop fiction—these chapters are by far the book's weaker half. Much more powerful are the rich descriptions of island life and the poignant stories detailing the Garcías' first year in the United States" (14). Rifkind isolates an important criticism of Alvarez's first novel, the reliance on what are now perceived as clichés in immigrant literature. While for Rifkind this becomes a flaw, for academicians, it becomes the crux of Alvarez's connection to other Latina writers and the articulation of commonalities in the experience of characters' arrival and assimilation to the culture of the United States.

In the Time of the Butterflies offers another interesting split reaction. Reviewer Robert González Echevarría, also writing for the *New York Times Book Review*, argues, "Serious historical fiction establishes links between individual destiny and pivotal political events. It shows either the disconnection between the individual and the larger flow of sociopolitical movements or, on the contrary, the individual as a pawn of history. In either case there is irony, but in this novel the reader is not made aware of a broader, more encompassing political world" (28). González Echevarría's review focuses on a critique of the novel's historical element, comparing it with the documented official history of the Trujillo years.

Two other reviewers, however, celebrate the novel for its foray into the Latin American literary tradition of the political novel. In the *Progressive*, Elizabeth Martinez offers unmitigated praise for the novel, noting that she believes the negative reviews the novel garnered were based on its political theme: "To write a book about such icons could mean trouble, controversy. Sure enough, some Dominicans have berated Alvarez for daring to humanize the sisters. . . . Reviewers in this country have displayed similar emotions, as in the major *New York Times* review, which bristled with hostility and leveled absurd criticism like 'There is indeed much too much crying in this novel' " (39). Ilan Stavans of the *Nation* echoes Martinez's review: "By inserting herself in the cast as *la gringa norteamericana*, Alvarez links the old and the new. At a time when many Latino writers seem so easily satisfied exploring the ghetto, in fictional terms, of drugs, crime, and videotape, Alvarez, a writer on a different kind of edge, calls attention to the Latin American foundations of Hispanic fiction in English and dares once again to turn the novel into a political artifact" (556). Both Martinez and Stavans demonstrate an interest in understanding Alvarez's work as part of a literary continuum within the Latin American and United States literary traditions.

Alvarez has received many awards recognizing her achievements in both fiction and poetry. Typical of her career, she has received awards that honor her innovation as a Latina writer in the United States and awards that recognize her achievements in the literary community. Alvarez shows a sustained pattern of excellence in writing; through her award history, one can trace her development as a young, unknown writer to being a well-established literary figure. Among other awards, she has been recognized with an Academy of American Poetry Prize at Syracuse University (1974), a John Atherton Scholar in Poetry Award from Bread Loaf Writers' Conference (1979), a Kenan Grant for short stories from Phillips Andover Academy (1980), a Yaddo residency in fiction (1981), La Reina Creative Writing Award (poetry) from La Reina Press (1982), a Bread Loaf Scholar in Fiction Award from Bread Loaf Writers' Conference (1983), a General Electric Foundation Award for Younger Writers (1986), a First Prize in narrative from Third Woman Press (1986), a Robert Frost Fellowship in Poetry from Bread Loaf Writers' Conference (1986), a National Endowment for the Arts Grant (1987–1988), the Sixth PEN Syndicated Fiction Prize (1987), an Ingram Merrill Foundation Grant (1990), a Notable Book Award from the *New York Times Book Review* for *How the García Girls Lost Their Accents* (1991), the Pen Oakland/Josephine Miles Award for *How the García Girls Lost Their Accents* (1991), publication of the poem "Bookmaking" in *The Best American Poetry* (1991), a Notable Book Award by the American Library Association for *How the García Girls Lost Their Accents* (1992), a Reader's Choice Award for "Coco" (1994), a Notable Book Award by the American Library Association for *In the Time of the Butterflies* (1994), a Book of the Month Club choice for *In the Time of the Butterflies* (1994), a nomination (and ultimately finalist) for the National Book Critics' Award for *In the Time of the Butterflies* (1995), selection as "Best Books for Young Adults" by the Young Adult Library Services Association and the American Library Association for *In the Time of the Butterflies* (1995), an exhibit at the New York Public Library in New York City titled "The Hand of the Poet: Original Manuscripts by 100 Masters, from John Donne to Julia Alvarez" (December 1995 to April 1996), the Jessica Nobel-

Maxwell Poetry Prize awarded by the *American Poetry Review* (1995), an "Homenaje a Julia Alvarez" in Santiago, Dominican Republic (1996), the Dominican Republic Annual Book Fair dedicated to Alvarez's work (1997), election to the National Members Council of the PEN American Center (1997–1999), a Literature Leadership Award by the Dominico–American Society of Queens (1998), selection of *How the García Girls Lost Their Accents* by New York Librarians as one of twenty-one classics for the twenty-first century (1999), selection of *In the Name of Salomé* as one of the top ten books of 2000 by *Latino.com* (2000), and the Woman of the Year Prize by the *Semana Cultural y Festival Dominicano* in Boston in recognition of her writing (2000).

BIBLIOGRAPHY

Works by Julia Alvarez

Ed. *Old Age Ain't for Sissies*. N.p.: Crane Creek, 1979.
Homecoming. New York: Grove, 1984.
The Housekeeping Book. Illus. Carol MacDonald and Rene Schall. Burlington, VT: n.p., 1984.
My English. Chapel Hill, NC: Algonquin, 1990.
How the García Girls Lost Their Accents. Chapel Hill, NC: Algonquin, 1991.
In the Time of the Butterflies. Chapel Hill, NC: Algonquin, 1994.
The Other Side/El Otro Lado. New York: Dutton, 1995.
Homecoming: New and Collected Poems. New York: Plume, 1996.
¡YO! Chapel Hill, NC: Algonquin, 1996.
Something to Declare. Chapel Hill, NC: Algonquin, 1998.
Seven Trees. North Andover, MA: Kat Ran, 1998.
In the Name of Salomé. Chapel Hill, NC: Algonquin, 2000.
Julia Alvarez and Bill Eichner. *The New Family Cookbook: Recipes for Nourishing Yourself and Those You Love*. White River Junction, VT: Chelsea Green, 2000.
The Secret Footprints. Illus. Fabian Negrin. New York: Knopf, 2000.
How Tía Lola Came to Stay. New York: Knopf, 2001.
"A Brief Account of My Writing Life." Middlebury College Department of English Home Page. 7 November 2001 (www.middlebury.edu/~english/alvarez/Alv-autobio. html).

Studies of Julia Alvarez

Bados Ciria, Concepcion. "*In the Time of the Butterflies* by Julia Alvarez: History, Fiction, Testimonio and the Dominican Republic." *Monographic Review/Revista Monográfica* 13 (1997): 406–16.
Barak, Julie. " 'Turning and Turning in the Widening Gyre': A Second Coming into Language in Julia Alvarez's *How the García Girls Lost Their Accents*." *MELUS* 23 (1998): 159–76.
Gomez Vega, Ibis. "Metaphors of Entrapment: Caribbean Women Writers Face the Wreckage of History." *Journal of Political and Military Sociology* 25 (1997): 231–47.
——. "Hating the Self in the 'Other'; or, How Yolanda Learns to See Her Own Kind in Julia Alvarez's *How the García Girls Lost Their Accents*." *Intertexts* 3 (1999): 85–96.
González Echevarría, Robert. "Sisters in Death." *New York Times Book Review* 18 Dec. 1994: 24.
Luis, William. "A Search for Identity in Julia Alvarez's *How The García Girls Lost Their*

Accents." *Dance Between Two Cultures: Latino Caribbean Literature Written in the United States.* Nashville: Vanderbilt University Press, 1997. 266–77.

Lyons, Bonnie, and Bill Oliver. "A Clean Windshield: An Interview with Julia Alvarez." *Passion and Craft: Conversations with Notable Writers.* Chicago: University of Illinois Press, 1998. 128–44.

Martinez, Elizabeth. "Of Passion and Politics." *Progressive* 59 (1995): 39.

Martinez, Elizabeth Coonrod. "Recovering a Space for a History between Imperialism and Patriarchy: Julia Alvarez's *In the Time of the Butterflies.*" *Thamyris: Mythmaking from Past to Present* 5 (1998): 263–79.

Mitchell, David T. "The Accent of 'Loss': Cultural Crossings as Context in Julia Alvarez's *How the García Girls Lost Their Accents.*" *Beyond the Binary: Reconstructing Cultural Identity in a Multicultural Context.* Ed. Timothy B. Powell. New Brunswick, NJ: Rutgers University Press, 1999. 165–84.

Rifkind, Donna. "Speaking American." *New York Times Book Review* 6 Oct. 1991: 14.

Rosario Sievert, Heather. "Anxiety, Repression, and Return: The Language of Julia Alvarez." *Readerly Writerly Texts: Essays on Literature, Literary Textual Criticism, and Pedagogy* 4 (1997): 125–39.

Stavans, Ilan. "Las Mariposas." *Nation* 259 (1994): 552, 554–56.

Stefanko, Jacqueline. "New Ways of Telling: Latinas' Narratives of Exile and Return." *Frontiers: A Journal of Women Studies* 17 (1996): 50–69.

TONI CADE BAMBARA (1939–1995)

Catherine Cucinella

BIOGRAPHY

Toni Cade Bambara, activist, short story writer, novelist, screenwriter, and filmmaker, was born March 25, 1939, in New York City. Her parents, Walter Cade II and Helen Brent Henderson Cade, named their daughter Miltona Mirkin Cade, after Walter Cade's employer. By kindergarten, however, Bambara rejected "Miltona" and renamed herself "Toni." In 1970, while searching for a name for her child (Karma Bene Bambara), she added "Bambara."

In interviews, Bambara attributes her activism to her Harlem childhood and her writing to her "mother's respect for the life of the mind" (*Deep Sightings* 212). Helen Cade encouraged her children to daydream and to create, and she provided them "access to material, to libraries, to parks" (*Deep Sightings* 213). Bambara grew up listening to Harlemites proclaim at the Speakers' Corner, "the outdoor university . . . in front of Micheaux's Liberation Memorial Bookstore." In addition to women from the sanctified churches, the Mary McLeod Bethune clubs, and the Ida B. Wells clubs, these speakers included trade unionists, Harlem communists and socialists, Rastas, and Muslims (*Deep Sightings* 250). Because Harlem fostered communal and political involvement, Bambara saw "an active political life [as] a perfectly normal thing" (*Deep Sightings* 207). Bambara's fiction echoes the multiple voices of the Speakers' Corner, depicts the energy of matrilineal connection, and presents the power of community.

Always keenly aware of the people and conversations surrounding her, Bambara realized the importance of voice(s). From "overheard" conversations, she learned "standards of sexual behavior, sexual politics, and, most important, race issues" (Chandler 345). The women of Harlem—the church women, the club women, the tap dancers, the be-bop musicians, "the black slip mamas," "the beauty parlor" women, and her mother—taught Bambara the importance of doing, of speaking, of thinking, of writing, of learning, and these women both people and propel her fiction.

In 1959 Bambara graduated from Queens College with a BA in theater arts/English and with the John Golden Award for Fiction and, in the same year, won the Pauper Press Award for nonfiction. In addition, she published her first short story, "Sweet Town," in *Vendome* magazine. After her graduation from Queens, Bambara worked as a social worker and continued her education, pursuing a graduate degree in modern fiction at the City College of New York. In 1961, freelancing as a writer, she studied at Commedia del'Arte in Milan. Between 1962 and 1965, Bambara completed her master's degree, worked at Colony House in Brooklyn and in the psychiatric division of a metropolitan hospital, and served as director of various local community programs. During her years teaching at the City College of New York (1965–1969), Bambara served as advisor to various publications sponsored by the college's SEEK program. She spent the next five years (1969–1974) teaching at Livingston College in New Jersey. In 1974 Bambara and her daughter moved to Atlanta, and between 1974 and 1977, she became the writer in residence at Spelman College and a founding member of several cultural groups such as the Southern Collective of African-American Writers.

Bambara's first short story collection, *Gorilla, My Love*, appeared in 1972, *The Sea Birds Are Still Alive* in 1977, *The Salt Eaters* (her first novel) in 1980, and her second novel, *Those Bones Are Not My Child* (published posthumously), in 1999. In addition to her fiction, Bambara edited and contributed to two anthologies, *The Black Woman: An Anthology* (1970) and *Tales and Stories for Black Folks* (1971). In 1970 Bambara began studying film editing, thus initiating her commitment to independent filmmakers and filmmaking. Bambara's engagement with film manifests the same political and social concerns seen in all of her work. She sees in independent African American and Asian films a "striking out . . . for socially responsible cinema" (*Deep Sightings* 244), a responsibility that drives Bambara's own film and television writing.

Always insistent on political and social involvement, Bambara continued her activism throughout her life, traveling to Cuba, Sweden, Vietnam, Laos, India, Nigeria, Jamaica, and Barbados as a member of various delegations. Consistent with her belief in the reciprocity of the personal and the political, Bambara listened to the stories of the peoples of these counties: "I was always interested in the personal stories and I would ask, 'Who were you [before the Revolution] and who are you now?' " (*Deep Sightings* 233). This concern with the individual's relation to social change remains a consistent theme throughout Bambara's work. Toni Cade Bambara died of cancer in 1995.

MAJOR WORKS AND THEMES

Bambara ties the seven primary themes that dominate her work to both an African American consciousness and an African American activism: importance of community, construction of selfhood in relation to community, convergence of past and present in order to ensure a future, acknowledgment and employment of nontraditional ways of knowing, significance of learning, recognition of multiple voices, and imperative for social activism. These concerns merge and reconfigure within individual stories, and they splinter into subthemes throughout all Bambara's work.

Eleanor Traylor asserts that Bambara's fiction "fixes a view of ancestry as the single most important inquiry of personhood and of community life" (65–66), and both short story collections, *Gorilla, My Love* and *The Sea Birds Are Alive*, as well as *The Salt*

Eaters, investigate the self, the community, and history. Bambara makes clear that in order to situate oneself as a community activist and to displace racial and gender oppression, one must rediscover and understand the past. In *Gorilla*'s opening story, "My Man Bovanne," Hazel, the narrator, explains her invitation to a fundraiser for "this Black party somethin or other": "Grass roots you see. Me and Sister Taylor and the woman who does heads at Mamies and the man from the barber shop, we all there on account of we grass roots" (4). However, the black power movement has displaced these "grass-roots" folks. Bambara's narrative reestablishes their importance by recognizing that what Hazel, Bovanne, and the others know about the past proves crucial to understanding the present, and by acknowledging their ability to actively participate in community projects, "Bovanne" reinscribes "old folks" into the rhetoric of the black power movement: "Cause old folks is the nation" (10).

Throughout her work, Bambara insists that "every generation (and every individual in it) has to be nurtured and educated, has to be taught the old stories all over again" in order for lasting social change to occur (Alwes 360). This care, this education, and these stories rest with the old folks, who continually give meaning to the present. While navigating her students through a crumbling urban environment, the narrator of "Broken Field Running," from *Sea Birds*, reminisces, which leads her to stories of flying Africans and salt eaters. These tales presented within a call-and-response framework function to explain the urgency of political activism and the significance of black nationalist ideology: "Always talking about how we got to rise above this mess and don't tarry so long in the wilderness we forget how to fly. . . . 'You know it's the truth. We salt eaters' " (53, 56).

The Salt Eaters contains and expands the thematic concerns of the short stories. The importance of an organic, cohesive black community, the interweaving of past and present, and the absolute necessity of self-construction within a community coalesce in this novel. *The Salt Eaters* opens with a question: "Are you sure, sweetheart, that you want to be well?" (3). The question directed to Velma Henry, after an attempted suicide, suggests that healing depends on individual choice; however, Velma's recovery depends upon her understanding that she functions as part of a community and that she must "draw up the powers from the deep like before" (44). In other words, the narrative links the individual, as well as social change, to the community and to ancient communal rituals. These links, however, also generate forward movement or, as Traylor expresses it, "the rhythmic movement toward . . . destiny" (60). This movement toward destiny involves an engagement with personal and social histories in order to make meaning of the present. *The Salt Eaters* presents this movement in its narrative structure—the flashbacks, the jumble of voices, the fragmentation of time, and the overlapping of stories.

CRITICAL RECEPTION

The scholarship on Bambara's work clusters on her dominant themes, specifically voice and language, the community and the individual, and activism and social change. Regardless of individual focus, the conversation surrounding Bambara's work always acknowledges her commitment to social activism. In her investigation into the incongruity of language in Bambara's fiction, Ruth Burks observes that "Bambara perpetuates the struggle of her people by literally recording it in their own voices" (48). The voices in Bambara's fiction emerge as multiple, overlapping, and, as Mick Gidley points out, notable for their "vibrancy and verve" (71). This jumble of voices resonates with the utterances of the Harlemites on Speakers' Corner; thus, Bambara's multi-voiced narrative strategy employs the orality and musicality of African American storytelling.

Traylor suggests that the "improvising, stylizing, re-creative" aspects of jazz parallel the narrative qualities in Bambara's fiction (59). Burks rightly notes that "the plaintive voice of the spiritual" in *Gorilla* gives way to "the more upbeat, modernistic cadences of blues and jazz" in *Sea Birds* (52). Whereas Burks perceives an individual charac-ter's move to action in *Sea Birds* as analogous to jazz stylizing (52), Traylor aligns the movements of jazz with Bambara's examination of the "present moment while simultaneously exploring the re-creative and transformative possibilities of experi-ence" (65). Thus, for these critics, the cacophony of voices in Bambara's fiction works as a call to action and as a method to understand the meaning of the present through a (re)presentation of the past.

This understanding depends upon voice and language, and it proves crucial both to the individual and to the community. Traylor argues that "the community must engage its history in order to decipher the meaning of its own rituals" (60). The community in Bambara's fiction, particularly in *The Salt Eaters*, according to Derek Alwes, man-ifests as the site in which, against which, and through which self-construction and social change occur (355). Martha M. Vertreace's work on Bambara furthers the di-alogue regarding community and the individual, and she, too, makes clear the cen-trality of the community in the construction of personal identities: "The community helps or hinders the maturational process but is never merely a neutral background" (162). In Bambara's fiction, community becomes an active character that neither read-ers nor critics can ignore. Susan Willis points out that in *The Salt Eaters*, "the meta-phor of the individual's relationship to the community could not be more explicit," and she identifies the community as the cacophony of voices that both surround Velma and structure her memories (131). However, as Willis notes, in *Salt Eaters*, both the community and the individual emerge as fragmented, confused, and disjointed, and thus resolution, recovery, and cohesion depend upon making sense of a muddle of voices and the disparate memories of individuals. In addition, both individual and community must participate in this process, and all community members (medical doctors, female healers, relatives, and folks) must come together to enact the healing.

This coming together, however, demands that the institutions of patriarchy—mar-riage, medicine, religion, education—must acknowledge, recognize, and access alter-native epistemological and ontological paradigms. These paradigms most often align with women through the voices of Bambara's narrators and in the carefully crafted community of women that appear throughout her fiction. Elliott Butler-Evans argues that "revolutionary consciousness for Bambara, then, involves a struggle against rac-ism . . . and sexism" (11). Butler-Evans further argues that Bambara's fiction calls for a restructured male-female relationship that rejects existing masculine and feminine constructions, thus allowing for a "construction of Selfhood/Blackhood that displaces gender differentiation" (11). This displacement enables the " 'Black community' to move in unison against racist oppression" (11). Bambara's fiction, as Toni Morrison tells us, "had work to do"—revolution (*Deep Sightings* ix).

BIBLIOGRAPHY

Works by Toni Cade Bambara

Ed. *The Black Woman: An Anthology*. New York: Signet, 1970.

Ed. *Tales and Stories for Black Folks*. Garden City, NY: Zenith, 1971.

Gorilla, My Love. New York: Random House, 1972.

The Sea Birds Are Still Alive. New York: Random House, 1977.

The Salt Eaters. New York: Random House, 1980.

"What It Is I Think I'm Doing Anyhow." *The Writer on Her Work*. Ed. Janet Sternberg. New York: Norton, 1980. 153–68.

Deep Sightings and Rescue Missions: Fiction, Essays and Conversations. New York: Random House, 1996.

Those Bones Are Not My Child. New York: Pantheon, 1999.

Studies of Toni Cade Bambara

Alwes, Derek. "The Burden of Liberty: Choice in Toni Morrison's *Jazz* and Toni Cade Bambara's *The Salt Eaters*." *African American Review* 30 (1996): 353–78.

Burks, Ruth E. "From Baptism to Resurrection: Toni Cade Bambara and the Incongruity of Language." *Black Women Writers (1950–1980): A Critical Evaluation*. Ed. Mari Evans. Garden City, NY: Anchor-Doubleday, 1984. 48–57.

Butler-Evans, Elliott. *Race, Gender, and Desire: Narrative Strategies in the Fiction of Toni Cade Bambara, Toni Morrison, and Alice Walker*. Philadelphia: Temple University Press, 1989.

Byerman, Keith E. "Healing Arts: Folklore and the Female Self in Toni Cade Bambara's *The Salt Eaters*." *Postscript* 5 (1988): 37–43.

Chandler, Zala. "Voices beyond the Veil: An Interview with Toni Cade Bambara and Sonia Sanchez." *Wild Women in the Whirlwind: Afra-American Culture and the Contemporary Literary Renaissance*. Ed. Joanne M. Braxton and Andrée Nicola McLaughlin. New Brunswick, NJ: Rutgers University Press, 1985. 12–22.

Collins, Janelle. "Generating Power: Fission, Fusion, and Post-Modern Politics in Bambara's *The Salt Eaters*." *MELUS* 21 (1996): 35–47.

Gidley, Mick, "Reading Bambara's 'Raymond's Run.' " *English Language Notes* 28 (1990): 67–72.

Guy-Sheftall, Beverly. "Commitment: Toni Cade Bambara Speaks." *Sturdy Black Bridges: Visions of Black Women in Literature*. Ed. Roseann P. Bell, Bettye J. Parker, and Beverly Guy-Sheftall. Garden City, NY: Anchor-Doubleday, 1979. 230–49.

Hargrove, Nancy D. "Youth in Toni Cade Bambara's *Gorilla, My Love*." *Southern Quarterly* 22 (1983): 81–99.

——. "The Comic Sense in the Short Stories of Toni Cade Bambara." *Revista Canaria de Estudios Inglese* 11 (1985): 133–40.

Hull, Gloria. " 'What It Is I Think She's Doing Anyway': A Reading of Toni Cade Bambara's *The Salt Eaters*." *Conjuring: Black Women, Fiction, and Literary Tradition*. Ed. Marjorie Pryse and Hortense J. Spillers. Bloomington: Indiana University Press, 1985. 216–32.

Kelley, Margot Anne. " 'Damballah Is the First Law of Thermodynamics': Modes of Access to Toni Cade Bambara's *The Salt Eaters*." *African American Review* 27 (1993): 479–93.

Kolmar, Wendy K. " 'Dialectics of Connectedness': Supernatural Elements in Novels by Bambara, Cisneros, Grahn, and Erdrich." *Haunting the House of Fiction: Feminist Perspec-*

tives on Ghost Stories by American Women. Ed. Lynette Carpenter and Wendy K. Kolmar. Knoxville: University of Tenessee Press, 1991. 236–49.

Korenman, Joan S. "African-American Women Writers, Black Nationalism, and the Matrilineal Heritage." *CLA Journal* 38 (1994): 143–61.

Lyles, Lois F. "Time, Motion, Sound and Fury in *The Sea Birds Are Still Alive*." *CLA Journal* 36 (1992): 134–44.

Morrison, Toni. "City Limits, Village Values: Concepts of the Neighborhood in Black Fiction." *Literature and the Urban Experience*. Ed. Michael C. Jaye and Ann Chalmers Watts. New Brunswick, NJ: Rutgers University Press, 1981. 35–43.

Porter, Nancy. "Women's Interracial Friendships and Visions of Community in *Meridian, The Salt Eaters, Civil Wars*, and *Dessa Rose*." *Tradition and the Talents of Women*. Ed. Florence Howe. Urbana: University of Illinois Press, 1991. 251–67.

Rosenberg, Ruth. " 'You Took a Name That Made You Amiable to the Music': Toni Cade Bambara's *The Salt Eaters*." *Literary Onomastics Studies* 12 (1985): 165–94.

Stanford, Ann Folwell. "He Speaks for Whom? Inscription and Reinscription of Women in *Invisible Man* and *The Salt Eaters*." *MELUS* 18 (1992): 17–31.

——. "Mechanisms of Disease: African American Women Writers, Social Pathologies, and the Limits of Medicine." *NWSA Journal* 6 (1994): 28–47.

Tate, Claudia. "Toni Cade Bambara." *Black Women Writers at Work*. Ed. Claudia Tate. New York: Continuum, 1988. 2–38.

Traylor, Eleanor W. "Music as Theme: The Jazz Mode in the Works of Toni Cade Bambara." *Black Women Writers (1950–1980): A Critical Evaluation*. Ed. Mari Evans. Garden City, NY: Anchor-Doubleday, 1984. 58–70.

Vertreace, Martha M. "Toni Cade Bambara: The Dance of Character and Community." *American Women Writing Fiction: Memory, Identity, Family, Space*. Ed. Mickey Pearlman. Lexington: University Press of Kentucky, 1989. 155–71.

Willis, Susan. "Problematizing the Individual: Toni Cade Bambara's Stories for the Revolution." *Specifying Black Women Writing the American Experience*. Madison: University of Wisconsin Press, 1987. 129–58.

ANDREA BARRETT (1965–)

Ernest Smith

BIOGRAPHY

Born in Boston on July 17, 1965, Andrea Barrett burst onto the literary scene by winning the 1996 National Book Award for *Ship Fever and Other Stories*. But Barrett's diverse range of interests had already been displayed in her four preceding novels, the first of which appeared in 1988. Barrett grew up on Cape Cod, within walking distance of the ocean, and water figures prominently in most of her work. She began applying to colleges during her junior year of high school, and when accepted by Union College in Schenectady, New York, she left high school without a diploma at the end of her junior year. By the age of nineteen, she had graduated from college with a degree in biology and then entered graduate school at the University of Massachusetts at Amherst to study zoology. Although she did not receive a zoology degree, this discipline, along with others she subsequently studied, informs her detailed and thoroughly researched fiction. Within a few years, she had reentered the university to do graduate work in medieval and Reformation theological history. Although she had yet to begin writing fiction, the process of researching subjects such as the Inquisition and the founding and later conflict of the Franciscan order not only provided material that would later serve her writing but also suggested to her that her true calling was not as an historian or scholar but rather as someone interested in stories and naming.

In order to be with her husband, the structural biologist Barry Goldstein, Barrett moved to Rochester, New York, in the mid-1980s, when Goldstein was completing his graduate work. Over the next several years, she held down what she has termed "a seemingly endless series of jobs" (Donohue 1), including receptionist, billing clerk, customer service representative in a box factory, and greenhouse technician. In addition, positions as secretary to a biophysicist and as a freelance medical editor furthered Barrett's background in biology and medicine. During this period, Barrett was also writing fiction, composing at least one novel that was never published. While she never formally attended a writing program, she paid to attend the Bread Loaf Writers' Conference, where she worked with Nicholas Delbanco and Thomas Galvin. She credits Delbanco with helping to launch her career, by reading the unpublished novel and encouraging her to continue writing. He told her that while she had taught herself to write by working on and completing the novel, she should turn aside from it and begin anew. Barrett has said, "It was the best thing anybody ever did for me. I cried for a day, and then I threw it out, and then I wrote *Lucid Stars*," which was published by Dell in 1988 (Baker 363). Barrett's second novel, *Secret Harmonies*, followed quickly in 1989.

After the appearance of Barrett's third novel, *The Middle Kingdom*, in 1991, she was awarded a creative writing fellowship from the National Endowment for the Arts (NEA) in 1992. During the period of the fellowship, Barrett began researching natural science, medicine, and history in the seventeenth and eighteenth centuries and trying her hand at short stories, drafting some of the work that would appear in *Ship Fever and Other Stories* in 1996. A fourth novel, *The Forms of Water*, was published in 1993, and following *Ship Fever and Other Stories*, Barrett published the novel *Voyage of the Narwhal* in 1998. In addition to the NEA Fellowship, she has been the recipient of a Guggenheim Fellowship and is on the faculty at Warren Wilson College's master of fine arts program.

MAJOR WORKS AND THEMES

Readers may be tempted to divide Barrett's work into two groups. One would be the first four novels, centering on fractured families and the spirit of individual endurance and survival. The second group would include her latter two books, *Ship Fever* and *The Voyage of the Narwhal*, historical fictions with a focus on science and naturalism. While acknowledging that the setting for the first four books is contemporary and for the latter two historical, Barrett has commented that she sees all of her work connected by the extensive research involved in creating both the plot and the background material that shapes her characters' lives. All of Barrett's work centers on the interpersonal relationships of people and the psychological interworkings of individual personalities, meaningful friendships, and family conflicts.

The first three novels, *Lucid Stars*, *Secret Harmonies*, and *The Middle Kingdom*, all present strong female characters who find ways to come through difficult circumstances and refocus their lives. *Lucid Stars* is set in Barrett's native New England and spans the years 1955–1978. The narrative traces the lives of two families, both estranged from the main male character, the real estate developer and womanizer Benjamin Day. An expert skier, Ben meets and marries Penny Webb, who works in a Vermont ski lodge. Together they have two children, the talented and intellectual Cass and the quieter, sensitive Webb, before Penny leaves Ben after he establishes a pattern of betrayals. Although they are raised by their strict father and his new wife, Diane, the children remain loyal to Penny and further separate themselves from their father when they leave home to live on their own.

After Ben leaves Diane for yet another younger woman, the two families begin to establish bonds. Jordan, the vivacious daughter of Ben and Diane, enchants both Webb and Cass, while Diane begins to form something of a friendship with Penny. Diane summons Cass back home to help her overcome a depression and eating disorder, and by the end of the novel, there are signs that each of these characters will survive the psychological damage inflicted by Ben's selfishness. Nearly all of them are interested in studying the stars, via either astronomy or astrology, and the reconciliation of these opposing approaches is paralleled by the reconciliation of the two families. Late in the novel, Diane's mother, Sal, whom Cass had originally detested, offers a key to overcoming the various levels of conflict within the family by announcing, "The stars are just a guide, you know—it's all in how you read them" (229). Growth of independence among the women characters is the most striking aspect of the novel, along with the memorable character of Cass. When Diane tells Cass to look at the man in the moon, Cass answers, "My mother taught me to see that as the face of a woman" (259).

Secret Harmonies focuses on another New England family, the Dwyers of western Massachusetts. We follow Reba Dwyer, the oldest of three children, from her teen years through an unfulfilling marriage and eventual emergence as a self-sufficient woman. Reba's parents are a rural farm couple who "dealt out pleasure and approval, permission to do certain things one day and denial of that permission another, punishment and anger and coldness as well" (71). The family's existence is meager, and Reba's attempt to leave home and graduate from a music school in Springfield ends unsuccessfully. After her father leaves the family, she returns home to help support her mother and sister, and Reba's eventual marriage to her best friend from childhood, Luke Wyatt, seems like a concession. They live in a ramshackle house with Reba's brother, Hank. When the couple's twins are stillborn, Reba withdraws from Luke, although the couple continues occasionally to communicate in their secret pattern of musical notation. Much as the stars function in *Lucid Stars*, music becomes the novel's central metaphor, the "secret harmonies" of the title suggesting life's intricate but often unseen patterns.

Early in the novel, it becomes apparent that Reba is musically gifted, but neither her family nor her husband recognizes or nurtures that gift. *Secret Harmonies* is very effective in showing the limitations of class and circumstance, especially the narrow choices available to Reba as she continues to search for both authentic interpersonal connections and the freedom to make time for her music. At the same time, Reba does demonstrate the imaginative capacity and sense of self that enable her to take risks and make decisions without being in any way certain of their outcome. Her recovery from the devastating loss of her twins, repeated attempts to restore her marriage despite a pattern of flight and unfaithfulness, and the active relationship she maintains with her three immediate family members all show the strength to endure difficult times. The end of the novel finds her continuing the effort to weave these threads together, even as memories, knowing "it would take her years to learn all she needed to write the music she meant" (245).

Barrett's third novel is something of a breakthrough in terms of setting and point of view. While the middle section of *The Middle Kingdom* shares the New England setting of her previous two books, the action takes place primarily in China during the years leading up to the cultural revolution and the Tiananmen Square crackdown of 1989. Grace, the novel's heroine, has gone to Beijing with Walter, her well-regarded scientist husband who is twelve years her senior. Grace's friendship with the family of Dr. Yu Xiaomin, a Chinese biologist, coincides with her decision to break off her marriage. Dr. Yu, a quiet, dignified, but very strong woman, helps enable Grace to obtain a framework in which she can measure the choices she has made.

Narrated in first person by the protagonist, Grace's story is told through a series of flashbacks, framed by the passages set in China.

As Grace's past is filled in, it becomes apparent that she has spent much of her life "watching" the lives of others, as Dr. Yu comments, rather than making her own life choices. Despite two marriages and various friendships, the only person other than Dr. Yu to ever understand and appreciate her was her late Uncle Owen, whose own trip to China years ago serves as a sort of beacon for Grace in her own journey. Grace's life adrift is countered by that of Dr. Yu, whose family has struggled through political oppression over the years, emerging intact but with a talented and thoroughly Westernized son, Zaofan, who will never be allowed to fulfill his potential because of his family's political resistance. Grace shares a single night of intimacy with Zaofan and later gives birth to their son, Jody, but only after arranging with Walter to help Zaofan escape to America.

The Middle Kingdom is memorable for its evocation of Chinese culture and the spirit of political resistance and for the friendship that develops between Grace and Dr. Yu. Like the women characters in Barrett's previous novels, Grace comes to a deeper awareness of herself and her ability to thrive on her own, without a husband and in a foreign land. As the novel ends, she is set to become a research assistant with Dr. Yu and to continue pursuing her fascination with a new country and culture.

The Forms of Water again focuses on a broken family whose members are trying to bring some semblance of order to their everyday lives. The story centers on Brendan Auberon, an eighty-year-old former monk who spent time in China during the Japanese occupation of World War II. Now confined to a wheelchair and a nursing home in his native New England, he longs to revisit the 200 acres of land he owns near a large reservoir. The Stillwater Reservoir was created in the late 1930s to provide water to the city of Boston, drowning several small villages and displacing local families, including that of Frank Auberon, Sr., father of Brendan and Frank, Jr. The elder Frank's letters to the editor of the local paper protesting the seizure of land for the reservoir serve as a haunting backdrop to the contemporary narrative, which is driven by Brendan's journey to see the piece of land he wants to leave to his brother's children, Henry and Wiloma. Henry has botched his life through a series of personal and professional failures, while Wiloma has embraced an eccentric new age religion.

Brendan tricks his nephew, Henry, into "borrowing" one of the nursing home vans and driving to the tract of land near the reservoir. After he is found missing, two other parties set out for the same destination in search of Brendan. One is Wiloma and her former husband, and the other is a band of teenagers including Wiloma's two children and Henry's two children, who live with their mother and despise their estranged father. When all these characters come together at the end of the novel, the result is an unexpected tragedy, one that ends up serving as a catalyst for redirected lives. All of the people in the novel are attempting to make peace with the past, most poignantly Brendan, who has always felt the lack of a home amidst his world tour. Ultimately Barrett shows how even a splintered family has profound ties to the past, a family history shaping lives in the present, whether the characters involved realize it or not.

Barrett used her NEA Fellowship to begin working in the genre of the short story, and the result was her most acclaimed book, *Ship Fever and Other Stories*. Most of the stories are set in the seventeenth and eighteenth centuries, and most concern naturalists and scientists. The theme of close friendship between women is carried on by "Rare Bird," which demonstrates how an independent, scientifically oriented woman can help a woman with similar interests escape the constraints of a patriarchal household. The process of reshaping or rebuilding lives, another consistent theme in Barrett's work, is at the heart of stories such as "Soroche," in which a widow has to decide how to use the large sum of money left to her after her husband's death. In "The Littoral Zone," two people begin an affair amidst their shared work as naturalists, each ending a marriage so that they can be together. The great achievement of the collection, however, is the novella that concludes the collection, "Ship Fever."

Set in the Quebec region of Canada in the middle of the nineteenth century, the novella focuses on the great wave of Irish immigration during the potato famine to Grosse Isle, essentially a Canadian version of Ellis Island. A Quebec doctor serving the upper classes, Lauchlin Grant is prompted to go to the island by a challenge issued by an absent friend's wife—the woman he loves. Susannah's journalist husband, Arthur Adam, is covering the Irish crisis from abroad, in England and Ireland. When Grant professes a dissatisfaction with his daily life over lunch one day with Susannah, she spurs him by responding, "So *do* something." The account of his time tending the sick and dying aboard the ships coming into Grosse Isle is compelling. Amidst filth and disease, readers watch Lauchlin's spiritual and emotional growth. He saves the life of a young woman named Nora Kynd (one of her lost brothers, Ned, appears in *The Voyage of the Narwhal*), who stays on the island to nurse the sick. Her debt to Dr. Grant is repaid when she tends to him during his own fatal bout with the ship fever, typhus, which has ravaged the immigrants coming to the island.

Grant's self-effacing heroism and personal growth also form a theme in *The Voyage of the Narwhal*, particularly in the central character, Erasmus Darwin Wells. Both an adventure story and a historical novel, the book follows a fictitious voyage of rescue undertaken in 1855 by an egotistical young commander, Zechariah Voorhees (Zeke), and his crew as they set out in search of the lost British explorer Sir John Franklin. Zeke is engaged to Lavinia Wells, daughter of the Philadelphia family largely responsible for his upbringing; Erasmus, one of Lavinia's brothers, is the naturalist aboard the *Narwhal*'s crew. Erasmus, much more of a thinking man than Zeke, feels shortchanged by life. An earlier voyage under an exploitative captain ended in disappointment, and he agrees to journey with Zeke primarily out of a sense of obligation to Lavinia. The conflict between the two men and Erasmus's voyage of consciousness form one of the principal threads of the narrative.

But, as in all her novels, Barrett weaves a plot revolving around several human interactions, including that of the ship's crew. Erasmus makes his first close friend on the trip, a Swedish doctor named Jan Boerhaave, and their friendship and debates over man's evolution are among the most memorable scenes in the book. Ned Kynd, a young Irish immigrant, is the cook, who forms a bond with Erasmus and Boerhaave. After several instances of unwise, selfish choices on the part of Zeke, the ship ends up stranded in the northern ice, and several members of the crew die, including Dr. Boerhaave. After Zeke insists on leaving the stranded ship to seek fame in charting further northern territories and coastline, the remaining members of the crew talk Erasmus into leading them on a difficult journey back home.

Erasmus returns to scorn and disappointment in Philadelphia but forms a working friendship with Alexandra Copeland, who has been left in charge of his sister, Lavinia. It is Alexandra who in this novel represents the strong, independent woman common to Barrett's work. She has learned to engrave during the ship's long absence, working anonymously for a man whose book made use of her work, and it is she who, through intellectual curiosity and her own naturalist's talent, succeeds in convincing Erasmus to work on his book with her assistance. When Zeke finally makes his way back to Philadelphia, he has brought along a woman and child, two members of the Inuit people from the north, and his exploitation of the "Esquimaux" for his own reputation and financial gain results in the woman's death. Disgusted by Zeke's actions, Erasmus and Alexandra sneak off with the young boy, and, after marrying, successfully return him to his family in the Arctic.

The book is striking on several levels. As with the *Ship Fever* stories, the book is carefully researched, and the description of the northern landscape, its weather, plants, and animals, is stunning. While Erasmus is clearly the protagonist, more than in any other of her books, Barrett creates several strong, memorable characters, even the despicable Zeke. The psychological aspect of the interactions of these characters, especially the crew during the voyage, is rendered with a depth and sensitivity reminiscent of some of Henry James's work. As with the novella "Ship Fever," the book has a deep emotional resonance, capturing with authenticity the heroic endurance of the individual spirit.

CRITICAL RECEPTION

Barrett's fiction has garnered very positive reviews from the outset. Critical attention certainly increased after the National Book Award for *Ship Fever and Other Stories*, with that collection and the subsequent novel, *The Voyage of the Narwhal*, more widely reviewed than the preceding four novels. In characterizing her style, reviewers have used terms such as "luminous" and "crystalline" and with each of her novels have consistently mentioned the memorable and authentic characters. The *Washington Post Book World* calls her first novel, *Lucid Stars*, "elegant" and notes that "Barrett's prose is clear and lyrical, and her characters are vividly drawn and neatly contrasted" (Osborne 6). The character of Reba is singled out in reviews of Barrett's second novel. Terming *Secret Harmonies* a "superior novel," Ellen Bilgore notes that while Reba and the other characters are essentially "simple people," the protagonist "is elevated above the commonplace by her ability, at critical moments in her life, to see herself absolutely clearly" (3). Bilgore also praises Barrett's ability to use music as an analogy for the complicated rhythms and themes of life itself, quibbling only that at times, in instances such as an allusion to Emma Bovary, "Barrett steers her reader a bit too carefully toward what she wants us to think" (3).

Barrett's subsequent novels, *The Middle Kingdom* and *The Forms of Water*, began to garner praise from fellow writers such as Amy Tan, Anne Tyler, and Francine Prose and were reviewed more widely. The cultural backdrop of China and the structural technique of unfolding flashbacks are focal points in reviews of *The Middle Kingdom*, while with *The Forms of Water*, Barrett's handling of generational layers of family conflict and her evenhanded treatment of the novel's varied characters are singled out for praise. Pinckney Benedict found *The Forms of Water* "intelligent and elegiac," a novel dealing with major American themes such as religion and the "appetite for land" (2).

Reviews for *Ship Fever and Other Stories* poured in, particularly after Barrett won the National Book Award against fellow nominees much better known. Writing in the *New York Times Book Review*, Thomas Mallon praises the "complex, crystallized stories," calling the overall effect "quietly dazzling" (24). Not all reviews were as enthusiastic. Molly E. Rauch complains that "the stories that take place in the past—half of this collection—suffer from stumbles into prissy formalism" (32). On the whole, however, most reviewers concur with Mallon in noting Barrett's gift for exploring "ways in which the sciences offer an even richer stock of metaphor for human contention" (24). The connection with the sciences is also a feature often discussed in reviews of *The Voyage of the Narwhal*. Margaret Walters notes in the *Times Literary Supplement* that "Barrett re-creates the intellectual universe of the mid-nineteenth-century naturalist as brilliantly, as convincingly, as she conjures up the heart-breaking northern landscape. . . . [H]er writing is at once erudite and evocative, dense with period and geographical detail" (24). Annette Kobak writes in the *New York Times Book Review* of how "Barrett's marvelous achievement is to have re-imagined so graphically the cusp of time when Victorian certainty began to question whether it could encompass the world with its outward-bound enthusiasms alone" (11).

Barrett's growth and development as a writer over the last decade are striking. Presently she is working on her seventh book. Given the consistently evolving reach of both her imagination and her talent for researching specific periods and people's lives within them, Andrea Barrett promises to be one of the major voices in American fiction for years to come.

BIBLIOGRAPHY

Works by Andrea Barrett

Lucid Stars. New York: Dell, 1988.
Secret Harmonies. New York: Delta Books, 1989.
The Middle Kingdom. New York: Washington Square Press, 1991.
The Forms of Water. New York: Washington Square Press, 1993.
Ship Fever and Other Stories. New York: Norton, 1996.
The Voyage of the Narwhal. New York: Norton, 1998.

Studies of Andrea Barrett

Baker, Samuel. "Andrea Barrett: Images of Science Past." *Publishers Weekly* 10 Aug. 1998: 363–64.
Benedict, Pinckney. "Collision of Dreams." Rev. of *The Forms of Water*. *Washington Post* 7 June 1993: D2.
Bilgore, Ellen. "One Family's Symphony." Rev. of *Secret Harmonies*. *Washington Post* 26 Sept. 1989: D3.
Donohue, Keith. "Andrea Barrett: Perseverance." Interview with Andrea Barrett. *National Endowment for the Arts: Art Forms* (http://www.arts.endow.gov/Artforms/Lit/Barrett.html).
Kobak, Annette. Rev. of *The Voyage of the Narwhal*. *New York Times Book Review* 13 Sept. 1998: 11.
Kurth, Peter. "The Salon Interview: Andrea Barrett." Interview with Andrea Barrett. *Salon* 2 Dec. 1988 (http://www.salon.com/books/int/1998/12/cov02.html).
Mallon, Thomas. "Under the Microscope." Rev. of *Ship Fever and Other Stories*. *New York Times Book Review* 28 Jan. 1996: 24.
Osborne, Linda Barrett. Rev. of *Lucid Stars*. *Washington Post Book World* 4 Sept. 1988: 6.

Rauch, Molly E. Rev. of *Ship Fever and Other Stories*. *Nation* 29 Jan. 1996: 32.

Ryan, Marian. Interview with Andrea Barrett. *The Writer's Chronicle* 32 (1999): 4–9.

Walters, Margaret. Rev. of *The Voyage of the Narwhal*. *Times Literary Supplement* 5 Mar. 1999: 24.

ANN BEATTIE (1947–)

Claudia Milstead

BIOGRAPHY

Ann Beattie was born Charlotte Ann Beattie on September 8, 1947, in Washington, D.C., where she grew up in a middle-class suburb. Her father, James A. Beattie, was an administrator for the Department of Health, Education, and Welfare. Her mother, Charlotte (Crosby) Beattie, was a homemaker. An only child, Beattie has said she was brought into the world of adults at an early age and spent hours observing adults, an early training that shows in the minute details revealed in her otherwise spare fiction.

Although a bright child and a reader, Beattie did not do well in the public schools she attended, graduating in the bottom 10 percent of her class at Woodrow Wilson High School in 1965. Nonetheless, she was accepted by American University, where she briefly considered a career in journalism and then changed her major to English, earning her BA in 1969. In college she edited the literary journal and was a guest editor for *Mademoiselle* in 1968. Beattie, who first began writing short stories about 1965, says that she never had any career plans and stayed in school because she did not want to go to work.

In graduate school at the University of Connecticut, she took literature courses and started writing seriously. Creative writing professor J. D. O'Hara, who heard about Beattie's writing from his students, stopped her in the hallway one day and asked to read her work. He became her mentor, writing comments on the stories she left in his faculty mailbox and sending some of them out to small literary magazines. Beattie earned her MA in English in 1970 and then began working on her PhD while continuing to write. Her first published short story, "A Rose for Judy Garland's Casket," appeared in *Western Humanities Review* in 1972, the same year she withdrew from graduate school.

Beattie became a frequent contributor to the *New Yorker*, but only after twenty of her stories were rejected by the magazine. Her submissions were unsolicited, sent through the mail in a manila envelope without the help of an agent, although O'Hara had suggested she submit her stories there. In 1976 Doubleday published both *Distortions*, a collection of short stories that had appeared in the *New Yorker* and other periodicals, and *Chilly Scenes of Winter*, her first novel. Beattie was immediately established as an important writer, drawing comparisons with Salinger, Cheever, and Updike. Since then, she has published seven collections of short stories, five novels, a book on artist Alex Katz, and a children's book. She also has written introductions to books of photographs and various magazine articles, including one for the October 1999 issue of *Bon Appetit* entitled "My Life as a Closet Cookbook Reader."

Beattie was a visiting writer and lecturer at the University of Virginia from 1975 to 1977 and a lecturer at Harvard from 1977 to 1978. Except for these two positions and her stint as a graduate teaching assistant, she has always earned her living by writing.

Beattie was married in 1973 to David Gates, a fellow graduate student at the University of Connecticut. They separated, painfully, in 1980, with the divorce final in 1982. Beattie has acknowledged Gates's ability to accurately assess her writing, crediting him with retrieving from the garbage "Snakes' Shoes" (*Distortions*), a story that was eventually published in the *New Yorker*. She is now married to Lincoln Perry, an artist. They met in 1985 through mutual friends after she moved to Charlottesville, where he was a visiting professor at the University of Virginia. They married in 1988 in an informal ceremony performed by a justice of the peace at their rented summer house in Maine. Adamantly childless, the two spend their time in Maine, Charlottesville, or Key West, Florida. Perry, who originally found Beattie's stories grim, has learned to appreciate them so well that Beattie now considers him a good editor and asks for his help with titles.

Beattie initially tried to keep regular writing hours but found the practice counterproductive. She writes frequently but may go as long as six weeks without writing anything. She does not keep a journal and says she does not remember her dreams. Beattie begins her stories with an image or a line of dialogue in mind, having no idea where the story is going, refusing to outline a plot. In spite of this lack of planning, her early short stories were often written in just a few hours. "Skeleton" (*Where You'll Find Me*) was written on an air sickness bag while Beattie's flight to Florida waited in a long queue at the end of the runway for permission to take off. The first draft of *Love Always* was written in the summer of 1984, in less than six weeks, while Beattie was visiting friends in Vermont. The writing no longer comes so rapidly, however. The 1989 novel *Picturing Will*, for instance, took three years, undergoing five major changes and scores of lesser ones. She scrapped the book that became *Another You* (1995) and started over after writing 350 pages and realizing that it was not working. Beattie says that over the last fifteen years, she has seldom written a short story in one afternoon.

Beattie remains an avid reader, not confining herself to the usual list of fine literary fiction that is sent her way. Intrigued by the mysterious, Beattie likes to read cookbooks. "I find it very interesting to see the six steps of putting something together," she says, "and I don't know what that something is because I haven't read the preceding ingredient list" (Montresor 243). Conversely, she likes to read medical journals because of the "very forthright way" they are written (Montresor 244).

Beattie has won numerous honors, including the 2000 PEN/Malamud Award for lifetime achievement in the short story form. She was awarded both a Guggenheim Fellowship and an award in literature from the American Academy and Institute of

Arts and Letters in 1980 and an honorary doctor of humane letters degree from American University in 1983.

MAJOR WORKS AND THEMES

Beattie's reputation as an important voice of her generation was established with the publication in 1976 of both her short story collection, *Distortions*, and her first novel, *Chilly Scenes of Winter*, a love story set in the 1970s. That she remains, nearly thirty years later, strongly identified as the literary spokesperson for the disaffected and disengaged Woodstock generation is testament to the power of her spare, minimalist fiction. Beattie acknowledges that she writes about people who, like herself, grew to young adulthood in the 1960s, their lives shaped by the music and drugs of the counterculture. However, because she believes that her work transcends its setting, she dismisses as reductive the label of spokesperson for her generation. The label is inaccurate for her later work because those stories address larger issues and explore a wider range of characters.

In an interview with Mervyn Rothstein, Beattie explains that she is "interested in the price people pay" for not doing well at leading conventional lives (C17). In other interviews, she has said she likes to write about the things that trouble her, the things that seem mysterious. Frequently her stories center on relationships in the process of breaking down. Her characters are cynical, detached, and apolitical. To portray them realistically and to build tension, she reveals the small details of their lives—what kind of camera a minor character uses, the decoration on an old coffee tin, the glass prisms hanging from a fishing line in the bedroom. In the context of stories in which the action is so subtle as to seem nonexistent and in which much goes unsaid by characters who are emotionally distanced, these details assume a disproportionate importance. Further, her attempt to avoid intrusive narration results in a style often described as emotionless, flat, or deadpan but that perfectly mirrors the detached demeanor of her characters. In a review of Beattie's third collection of short stories, the critically acclaimed *Burning House* (1982), Margaret Atwood praises this style, remarking that "the evenness of tone used to describe both horrific event and trivial observation alike . . . accounts perhaps for the eerie, shell-shocked effect of Miss Beattie's prose" (34). The title story of this volume, the last in the book, closes with one of Beattie's most haunting lines. At the end of the day, when she has gone to bed, the narrator asks her husband if he is "staying or going." After explaining to her that men, unlike women, think they're "going to the stars," he takes her hand. "I'm looking down on all of this from space," he whispers. "I'm already gone" (*Burning House* 256). Here, we see the economy that makes Beattie's prose so powerful.

Beattie's economy works on several levels. Her descriptions, both of characters and of settings, reveal only what is necessary to the point of the story. What goes unsaid, by both characters and author, is at least as important as what is said. Her oblique endings, prone to being misunderstood by readers and critics alike, hinge upon the type of understated epiphany that Joyce uses in *Dubliners* and yield to interpretation through a reading of symbols. For example, in the short story "Janus" from the collection *Where You'll Find Me*, the bowl with which Andrea takes such care can be understood as a symbol of Andrea herself: empty, unilluminated, and with one small flash of blue vanishing on the horizon. Whether Andrea understands herself to be like the bowl goes unstated, leaving the reader with the uneasy feeling of holding key information that may remain hidden from the character.

In *Picturing Will*, Beattie consciously moves beyond the narrow world of her usual characters to explore the nature of the parent-child relationship. Although some characters in the novel, particularly the mother, remain self-absorbed and Beattie retains her spare prose style, she breaks new ground for herself in her touching portrayal of the nurturing stepfather, Mel. Indeed, it is her stunning character portrayals that mark Beattie as a significant writer, whether she is writing about alienated middle-class young adults adrift in a meaningless world or characters for whom the world has gained meaning through emotional connection.

CRITICAL RECEPTION

Beattie's initial two volumes, the novel *Chilly Scenes of Winter* and *Distortions*, her first collection of short stories, are still considered among her best work. Beattie's ability to capture minute details that marked her as a talent to watch soon developed into an uncanny talent for choosing the perfectly significant detail that delineates a character. This ability is particularly evident in *The Burning House*, a collection of sixteen stories recognized as her best to date. A 1998 collection, *Park City: New and Selected Stories*, contains twenty-eight of the best stories of Beattie's career since 1976 and eight new stories. Well received, the volume provides an overview of Beattie's career as a writer of short stories. Christopher Lehmann-Haupt, reviewing *Park City* for the *New York Times*, approvingly notes a trend in Beattie's later short stories toward moral commitment that "contrasts sharply with the irritating moral passivity of her earlier work" (E8).

Picturing Will is generally recognized as Beattie's most successful novel. Described by Judith Timson as "a brilliant meditation on the paradoxical aspects of the parent-child relationship" (157), it attracted readers who criticize Beattie's customary shallow, self-absorbed characters. That Beattie's short stories are better received than her novels may say more about readers' (and critics') reception of minimalism than about Beattie's talent. Chilly, alienated characters delineated by the spare details of their shallow lives may wear better in short works than in long ones, and a master of any form runs the risk of self-parody. *Publishers Weekly* called *Love Always* a "self-parody," faulting Beattie for "relentless reuse of her now familiar stylistic idiosyncrasies" (Montresor 111). The most scathing review Beattie has received to date is Michiko Kakutani's *New York Times* review of *My Life, Starring Dara Falcon* (1997), tellingly titled "Swapping Family Tedium for Ruthless Narcissism." Significantly, in a later essay, Kakutani characterizes minimalist writers as "withdrawing, turtlelike, inside their own homes and heads," creating characters with "spiky, anorexic narratives" ("New Wave" B11), suggesting, on the critic's part, a weariness with minimalism.

Publication of *Perfect Recall* in January 2001 was timed to coincide with Beattie's 2000 PEN/Malamud Prize for lifetime achievement in the short story form. In the eleven short stories, characters come to terms with altered circumstances, whether success or failure, and the legacies of long-held family myths.

BIBLIOGRAPHY

Works by Ann Beattie

"A Rose for Judy Garland's Casket." *Western Humanities Review* 26 (1972): 147–52.
Chilly Scenes of Winter. New York: Doubleday, 1976.
Distortions. New York: Doubleday, 1976.
Secrets and Surprises. New York: Random House, 1978.
Falling in Place. New York: Random House, 1980.
Jacklighting. Worcester, MA: Metacom Press, 1981.
The Burning House. New York: Random House, 1982.
Love Always. New York: Random House, 1985.
Spectacles. New York: Workman, 1985.
Where You'll Find Me. New York: Linden Press/Simon & Schuster, 1986.
Alex Katz. New York: Abrams, 1987.
Picturing Will. New York: Random House, 1989.
What Was Mine. New York: Random House, 1991.
Another You. New York: Knopf, 1995.
My Life, Starring Dara Falcon. New York: Alfred A. Knopf, 1997.
Park City: New and Selected Stories. New York: Knopf, 1998.
Perfect Recall. New York: Scribner, 2001.

Studies of Ann Beattie

Atwood, Margaret. "Stories from the American Front." *New York Times Book Review* 26 Sept. 1982: 1, 34.
Centola, Steven R. "An Interview with Ann Beattie." *Contemporary Literature* 31 (1990): 405–22.
Clark, Miriam Healy. "Postmodernism and Its Children: The Case of Ann Beattie's 'A Windy Day at the Reservoir.'" *South Atlantic Review* 61 (1996): 77–87.
Epstein, Joseph. "Ann Beattie and the Hippoisie." *Commentary* March 1983: 54–58.
Getlin, Josh. "Novelist Focuses on Childhood Isolation." *Los Angeles Times* 18 Jan. 1990: E1.
Hill, Robert W., and Jane Hill. "Ann Beattie." Interview. *Five Points: A Journal of Literature and Art* 1 (1997): 26–60.
Iyer, Pico. "The World according to Beattie." *Partisan Review* 50 (1983): 548–53.
Kakutani, Michiko. "Swapping Family Tedium for Ruthless Narcissism." *New York Times* 24 Apr. 1997: C16.
——."New Wave of Writers Reinvents Literature." *New York Times* 22 Apr. 2000: B9, B11.
Lee, Don. "About Ann Beattie." *Ploughshares* 21 (1995): 231–35.
Lehmann-Haupt, Christopher. "Books of the Times: Dissecting Yuppies with Precision." *New York Times* 8 June 1998: E8.
Mangum, Bryant. "The World as Burning House: Ann Beattie and the Buddha." *Notes on Contemporary Literature* 20 (1990): 9–11.
McKinstry, Susan Jaret. "The Speaking Silence of Ann Beattie's Voice." *Studies in Short Fiction* 24 (1987): 111–17.
Montresor, Jaye Berman, ed. *The Critical Response to Ann Beattie.* Westport, CT: Greenwood Press, 1993.
Murphy, Christina. *Ann Beattie.* Boston: Twayne, 1986.
Plath, James. "My Lover the Car: Ann Beattie's 'A Vintage Thunderbird' and Other Vehicles." *Kansas Quarterly* 21 (1989): 113–19.
——."Counternarrative: An Interview with Ann Beattie." *Michigan Quarterly Review* 32 (1993): 359–79.

Porter, Carolyn. "Ann Beattie: The Art of the Missing." *Contemporary American Women Writers: Narrative Strategies*. Ed. Catherine Rainwater and William J. Scheick. Lexington: University Press of Kentucky, 1985. 9–25.

Rich, Frank. "Chilly Scenes of Summer." *New Republic* 15 and 22 July 1985: 42, 44–45.

Rothstein, Mervyn. "Ann Beattie's Life after Real Estate." *New York Times* 30 Dec. 1985: C17.

Scarf, Michelle. "An Interview with Ann Beattie." *Writer's Chronicle* 33 (2000): 38–44.

Schneiderman, Leo. "Ann Beattie: Emotional Loss and Strategies of Reparation." *American Journal of Psychoanalysis* 53 (1993): 317–33.

Timson, Judith. "Little Boy Lost: Exploring Childhood's Rough New Landscape." *The Critical Response to Ann Beattie*. Ed. Jaye Berman Montresor. Westport, CT: Greenwood, 1993. 156–57.

Wyatt, David. "Ann Beattie." *Southern Review* 28 (1992): 145–59.

JUDY BLUME (1938–)

Austin Booth

BIOGRAPHY

Judy Blume is an extremely popular, award-winning author of juvenile and adult literature. She is also one of the most censored authors of our time, due to her realistic portrayal of the social and sexual lives of young adults. Blume's work has been translated into over twenty languages and has sold over 65 million copies. While Blume has written three novels for adults—*Wifey* (1978), *Smart Women* (1983), and *Summer Sisters* (1998)—it is her novels for young adults, notably *Are You There God? It's Me, Margaret* (1970), *Then Again, Maybe I Won't* (1971), *Deenie* (1973), *Blubber* (1974), and *Forever* (1975), that have brought Blume both success and controversy.

Blume was born February 12, 1938, in Elizabeth, New Jersey. She was very close to her parents, especially to her father, Rudolph Sussman, a dentist. When Blume was in the third grade, she, her brother, and her mother moved to Miami for the summer in order for her brother to recover from a kidney infection. This separation from her father had a large emotional impact on Blume and proved to be the ground for her later writings on the psychic as well as geographic separation of children from their parents. Blume attended an all-girls school, Battin High School, which fostered a sense of independence and strong female identity at the same time as exposing Blume to anti-Semitism on a personal basis for the first time. Upon graduating from high school, Blume began Boston University, but unfortunately she contracted mononucleosis and had to drop out. She later returned to college, attending New York University and graduating with a BS in education in 1961.

She married a lawyer, John Blume, in 1959 and had a son and a daughter with him. Blume began to write in the late 1960s. After several rejections, Blume published *The One in the Middle Is the Green Kangaroo* (1969) followed by *Iggie's House* (1970). After writing these two somewhat conventional children's novels, Blume decided to write an account of a young teenage girl's experiences. With the publication of *Are You There God? It's Me, Margaret*, Blume immediately became a controversial figure. That book revolutionized children's literature, introducing realistic first-person narratives on taboo topics into young adult literature. Although critics gave mixed, heated reviews of the novel, young readers responded in incredible numbers to the novel's story of Margaret's conflicting feelings about menstruation, breasts, bras, and religion. Blume received hundreds of letters from young readers who identified with her heroine. When the book was published in a paperback edition in 1972, the letters began to number in the thousands. Both *Are You There God? It's Me, Margaret* and Blume's next novel, *Then Again, Maybe I Won't,* were concerned with the social and sexual realities of growing up: For Margaret, these realities include beginning to menstruate; for Tony, the hero of *Then Again, Maybe I Won't*, they include the difficulties of hiding an erection when standing up in front of his class.

Blume's next three novels, *Freckle Juice* (1971), *Tales of a Fourth Grade Nothing* (1972), and *Otherwise Known as Sheila the Great* (1972), focused on younger children and were lighter and more humorous in tone. With *It's Not the End of the World* (1972), Blume returned to the problems of young adolescents, writing about a sixth grader's attempts to understand her parents' divorce. In 1973 Blume again courted controversy with the publication of *Deenie*, a novel about a young teenage girl with scoliosis, criticized by many for its frank description of Deenie's masturbating. *Blubber* also shocked many adult readers because of its depictions of the cruelty of children toward each other.

Fans who were young teenagers when they read *Are You There God? It's Me, Margaret* welcomed Blume's next novel, *Forever*, because it featured an older teenage heroine. The first line of *Forever* is one of the most often quoted, and most controversial, of Judy Blume's sentences: "Sybil Davison has a genius I.Q. and has been laid by at least six different guys" (4). The novel goes on to compare Sybil's inability to conduct smart relationships with boys, despite her "genius I.Q.," with the ability of Katherine, the heroine, to conduct mature and honest sexual relationships, but many angered adult readers never got past that first sentence. *Forever* turned out to be one of Blume's most popular works, though, gaining Blume a whole new audience of older teenage readers. As Blume's career grew more successful, however, her marriage grew less so. She divorced in 1975, remarrying Tom Kitchens, a physicist in 1976. This marriage ended in 1979.

Blume's next novel, *Starring Sally J. Freedman as Herself* (1977), is her most autobiographical. The novel features Sally, a ten-year old Jewish girl living with her mother in Florida at the end of World War II; the story deals extensively with the separation of a daughter from her father, an event that carried much emotional significance in Blume's own life. Although Blume published a book for adults, *Wifey*, in 1978, she quickly returned to children's literature, publishing *Superfudge*, one of her most popular titles, in 1980. A sequel to *Tales of a Fourth Grade Nothing*, *Superfudge* focuses on the humorous aspects of sibling rivalry.

In 1981 Blume published *Tiger Eyes*, generally admired by critics as Blume's best work, despite its lack of popular attention. Nominated for an American Book Award, *Tiger Eyes* is narrated in the first person by a teenager, a fifteen-year-old girl named Davey. The social reality that Davey encounters, however, is more complex than that faced by many of Blume's earlier characters. In *Tiger Eyes*, Blume tells the stories of Davey's move from Atlantic City, New Jersey, to Los Alamos, Texas, and the murder of Davey's father.

Smart Women, Blume's second novel for adults, focused on the difficulties of single motherhood and life after divorce. In 1984 Blume wrote *The Pain and the Great One*, a picture book for younger children. From 1984 to 1986, Blume worked on compiling *Letters to Judy: What Your Kids Wish They Could Tell You*, a collection of the letters Blume had received from her young readers throughout her career. In *Just as Long as We're Together* (1987), Blume returned to stories about younger adolescents, writing about three junior high girls and their complex friendships. In 1987 Blume also remarried, marrying George Cooper, a nonfiction writer.

Blume then wrote two sequels, *Fudge-a-Mania* (1990), which continued the story of Peter and Fudge from *Superfudge*, and *Here's to You Rachel Robinson* (1993), which revisits the group of seventh graders introduced in *Just as Long as We're Together*. With *Summer Sisters*, Blume returned to fiction for adults, although much of the story concentrates on the adolescence of the novel's two heroines, Caitlin and Victoria.

In 1999 Blume put together a collection of original stories by censored writers, including Katherine Paterson, Walter Dean Myers, Paul Zindel, and Norma Klein, entitled *Places I Never Meant to Be: Original Stories by Censored Writers*. The collection also contains pieces by writers concerning their experiences with and feelings about censorship. Blume has been involved in the National Coalition against Censorship for many years, vocally advocating for the rights of young readers.

MAJOR WORKS AND THEMES

Blume is known for realistically treating the concerns of her audience, children and teenagers. Her books for children (*Tales of a Fourth Grade Nothing*, *Blubber*, *Otherwise Known as Sheila the Great*) treat social and familial issues that children face, including ostracism and social groups, the formation of self-confidence, and sibling rivalry. Similarly, Blume's books for older adolescent readers (*Are You There God? It's Me, Margaret*; *Deenie*; *Just as Long as We're Together*; *Forever*) treat concerns such as divorce, menstruation, masturbation, sexuality, and religion. All of Blume's work, whether for younger children, adolescents, or adults, treats issues of self-identity, confidence, romantic relationships, and family strife.

Many of Blume's books examine common teenage problems such as conflicting feelings over sexuality and puberty and discord with or between parents. Blume's fiction for adults also concentrates on common problems: In *Wifey*, Blume examines a suburban homemaker's desire for more meaning from both her daily activities and her marriage, and *Smart Women* examines the difficulties of single motherhood and beginning new relationships after a divorce.

Blume's young adult novels explore the pressures on teenagers to adhere to codes of normality. She details the overwhelming sense of insecurity many teenagers have as well as the relative lack of power they possess to deal with their own fears and desires. Despite Blume's accurate portrayal of the powerlessness of children and teenagers, however, many of her characters—Davey and Deenie, for example—learn to negotiate complex social and familial circumstances and to embrace their identities as "different," multifaceted people.

Although many of Blume's books treat the social pressures of early adolescence, *Blubber* most distinctly treats the cruelty of children toward other children who are labeled different. Blubber is not a didactic treatise on the morality of treating others kindly; instead, it is a novel without a simple, clear resolution. Indeed, *Blubber* models the importance of observation and independent decision making, attributes that Blume hopes her readers acquire through the act of reading itself.

As both Blume's fans and her critics vociferously point out, one of the major themes of Blume's work is teenage sexuality. Her novels imply that teenage sexuality is central to her work simply because it is central to teenagers' lives. Blume's realistic depictions of teenage sexual desire are not part of a lesson in the dangers of teenage sexuality but rather an accurate portrayal of teenage concerns, including how to obtain birth control or how to ask a boy to use a condom.

Blume's novels are about more than sex, however: They are also about how to negotiate romantic and sexual relationships. A major concern for many of Blume's heroines is responsibility in relationships. In *Forever*, for example, Katherine must and does accept responsibility not only for her own sexuality and birth control but, in the end, for breaking off the relationship with her boyfriend, for his feelings as well as her own. Many of Blume's works, including *Deenie, Starring Sally J. Freedman as Herself*, and *Are You There God? It's Me, Margaret*, stress honesty as the means to a successful relationship. Indeed, many of her child and teenage heroes and heroines criticize the adults in their families for their lack of honesty, and it is adults' reticence to admit or discuss the realities of their family lives that create many of the problems the teens and children experience. Several of Blume's works, including *It's Not the End of the World* and *Just as Long as We're Together*, treat divorce and again emphasize the importance of parents being honest in communicating their own problems to their children.

The dynamics of family relationships are a major theme in Blume's work. Although Blume does portray the detrimental effects of adult dishonesty on children, she also shows family as a source of rich and supportive relationships, as people who help each other, especially among siblings, such as those in *Just as Long as We're Together, Tiger Eyes*, and *It's Not the End of the World*. Extended families are very supportive and important in Blume's works. In many of her stories, for instance, grandmothers not only are able to provide needed information (such as information about Planned Parenthood) but are also the receptors of their grandchildren's secret feelings and desires, thoughts the children cannot or do not wish to share with their parents.

As noted above, many of Blume's works focus on the powerlessness of children and adolescents. Compounding this sense of powerlessness for many of Blume's characters is their actual or imagined isolation. *Then Again, Maybe I Won't*, for example, compares the isolation of youth (Tony) with the isolation of the old (his grandmother). In this novel as well as numerous other works, Blume uses the geographical relocation of a family as a device that allows her to explore the general sense of being social "outsiders" shared by many of her characters.

Blume's writing is marked not only by its realism but its humor as well. While her plots are not overly complex, they provide detailed, nuanced accounts of her characters' lives. Her books are generally told as first-person narratives, a device that allows the reader to identify even further with her characters. By having her characters speak directly to the reader, Blume creates not only a confessional intimacy between her characters and her readers but a more realistic narrative as well. Perhaps even more important, the Blume first-person narratives consist of a child speaking to a child reader as an equal rather than a superior adult speaking to an inexperienced child reader. Blume also avoids the tendency, present in much young adult and children's literature, to tell the reader at the end of her books what the book's meaning was. It is a sign of Blume's devotion to realism that her books frequently lack neat conclusions.

CRITICAL RECEPTION

Generally, Blume's books have met with positive critical reception: *Are You There God? It's Me, Margaret*, for example, was chosen as a *New York Times* Best Book of the Year. Dissenting critics, however, find Blume's characters overly self-interested and her straightforward writing style uninteresting. Furthermore, some critics have charged Blume with classism, not only because she portrays largely, almost exclusively middle-class worlds but because her characters seem unaware of realities beyond their own affluent suburban lives. Both *Are You There God? It's Me, Margaret* and *Forever* have been critiqued for their lack of perspective on their own middle-class milieu and their tendency to universalize or generalize from middle-class experience. Despite the fact that many of Blume's major characters are girls, Blume has also been criticized for not promoting feminism because her books do not examine the relationship between her heroines' problems and the construction of girlhood itself. On the other hand, many critics have pointed out that Blume's honesty about and advocacy of teenage girls' sexuality are themselves feminist in their acknowledgment of girls' sexual desire as a positive and healthy force. Indeed, many critics admire Blume's frank writing about teenage sexuality and teenage anxieties. It is Blume's honesty, after all, especially about teenage sexuality, that has led to both the popularity and the censoring of her works. Blume herself has become a spokesperson for the anti-censorship movement in the United States, writing frequently about the dangers of refusing to give children choices, not only about what they read but also about how they live their lives.

BIBLIOGRAPHY

Works by Judy Blume

The One in the Middle Is the Green Kangaroo. Chicago: Reilly & Lee, 1969.
Are You There God? It's Me, Margaret. Englewood Cliffs, NJ: Bradbury, 1970.
Iggie's House. Englewood Cliffs, NJ: Bradbury, 1970.
Freckle Juice. New York: Four Winds, 1971.
Then Again, Maybe I Won't. Scarsdale, NY: Bradbury, 1971.
It's Not the End of the World. Scarsdale, NY: Bradbury, 1972.
Otherwise Known as Sheila the Great. New York: Dutton, 1972.
Tales of a Fourth Grade Nothing. New York: Dutton, 1972.
Deenie. Scarsdale, NY: Bradbury, 1973.
Blubber. Scarsdale, NY: Bradbury, 1974.
Forever. Scarsdale, NY: Bradbury, 1975.
Starring Sally J. Freedman as Herself. Scarsdale, NY: Bradbury, 1977.
Wifey. New York: Putnam's, 1978.
Superfudge. New York: Dutton, 1980.
Tiger Eyes. Scarsdale, NY: Bradbury, 1981.
Smart Women. New York: Putnam's, 1983.

The Pain and the Great One. Scarsdale, NY: Bradbury, 1984.

Ed. *Letters to Judy: What Your Kids Wish They Could Tell You*. New York: Putnam's, 1986.

Just as Long as We're Together. New York: Orchard Books, 1987.

The Judy Blume Memory Book. New York: Dell, 1988.

Fudge-a-Mania. New York: Dutton, 1990.

Here's to You Rachel Robinson. New York: Orchard, 1993.

Summer Sisters. New York: Delacorte, 1998.

Ed. *Places I Never Meant to Be: Original Stories by Censored Writers*. New York: Simon & Schuster, 1999.

Studies of Judy Blume

Brancato, Robin F. "In Defense of: *Are You There, God? It's Me, Margaret, Deenie*, and *Blubber*—Three Novels by Judy Blume." *Censored Books: Critical Viewpoints*. Ed. Nicholas J. Karolides, Lee Burress, and John M. Kean. Metuchen, NJ: Scarecrow, 1993. 87–97.

Egoff, Sheila. "The Problem Novel." *Only Connect: Readings on Children's Literature*. Ed. Sheila Egoff, G. T. Stubbs, and L. F. Ashley. New York: Oxford University Press, 1980. 356–69.

Goldberger, Judith M. "Judy Blume: Target of the Censor." *Newsletter on Intellectual Freedom* May 1981: 57.

Krutz, Mel. "Censoring Judy Blume and *Then Again, Maybe I Won't*." *Censored Books: Critical Viewpoints*. Ed. Nicholas J. Karolides, Lee Burress, and John M. Kean. Metuchen, NJ: Scarecrow, 1993. 471–75.

McNulty, Faith. "Children's Books for Christmas." *New Yorker* 5 Dec. 1983: 191–95.

Rees, David. "Not Even for a One Night Stand: Judy Blume." *The Marble in the Water: Essays on Contemporary Writers of Fiction for Children and Young Adults*. Boston: Horn Book, 1980. 173–84.

Weidt, Maryann N. *Presenting Judy Blume*. Boston: Twayne, 1989.

RITA MAE BROWN (1944–)

Roxanne Harde

BIOGRAPHY

Born November 28, 1944, and abandoned at an orphanage, Rita Mae Brown was adopted by Ralph and Julia Brown of York, Pennsylvania. When Brown was eleven, the family moved to Florida, where she excelled academically and athletically. Brown's secondary education began at the University of Florida, from which she was suspended for civil rights and feminist activism and for open lesbianism. In 1968 Brown earned a BA in English and classics at New York University and a cinematography degree from the School of the Visual Arts. Brown's activism continued in New York; she became involved in gay and feminist issues and helped to found a student homophile league and a women's center. An early member of the National Organization for Women (NOW), Brown resigned over NOW's "sexist, racist and class biased attitudes" (*Plain Brown Rapper* 91) and went on to join several more radical homosexual and feminist movements. Chief among these was the Furies Collective, to which Brown belonged as she finished her doctorate in English and political science in 1976 at the Institute for Policy Studies in Washington, D. C.

While in Washington, Brown began her career as a prolific author of primarily fiction by publishing essays in feminist journals and a collection of poems on lesbian activism, *The Hand That Cradles the Rock* (1971). Encouraged to write fiction by actress Alexis Smith, Brown drew heavily from life experiences to write *Rubyfruit Jungle*. Rejected by mainstream publishers, the novel was issued by Daughter's, a small feminist press, in 1973, the same year Brown published *Songs to a Handsome Woman*, a collection of erotic poetry dedicated to Smith. After becoming an underground bestseller, *Rubyfruit Jungle* was republished in 1977 by Bantam, whose advance for the novel allowed Brown the freedom to write full-time. In 1976 Brown published a collection of feminist essays, *A Plain Brown Rapper*, and *In Her Day*, a novel concerned with polemical feminism. Brown's third novel, *Six of One* (1978), began a series that includes *Bingo* (1988) and *Loose Lips* (1999) and features characters based on Brown's mother and aunt. *Six of One* brought Brown mainstream success and the offer of screenwriting work in Los Angeles; she continues to write for television and film.

In 1978, in the midst of her clandestine affair with author-actress Fannie Flagg, Brown relocated to Virginia. In 1979 Brown began an affair with tennis star Martina Navratilova that lasted three years and ended painfully and publicly. She next published *Southern Discomfort* (1982), a novel set in the early 1900s, which weaves together subversive plot lines that involve different social strata and sexual pairings— none of which are lesbian. Brown's following novel, *Sudden Death* (1983), sets a lesbian relationship within the world of women's professional tennis.

Brown then turned her attention to American history, which, she notes, "is never dead for me; it rides on my shoulder like a becapped and jeweled monkey" (*Rita Will* 283). A novel of the Civil War that explores cultural definitions of gender, *High Hearts* (1986) features Geneva Chatfield, who disguises herself as a Confederate soldier and joins her husband on the front. Brown followed this novel with the nonfiction *Starting from Scratch: A Different Kind of Writer's Manual* (1988), an autobiographical writer's manual. She then combined her knowledge of the classics with the problems of coming out; set in contemporary Charlottesville, *Venus Envy* (1993) makes clear the importance of openness, honesty, and passion. Brown returned to historical fiction with *Dolley: A Novel of Dolley Madison in Love and War* (1994), which features one of Brown's earliest heroes and one of America's great first ladies. *Riding Shotgun* (1996) combines both contemporary and historical issues in a narrative that involves time travel.

After publishing her autobiography, *Rita Will: Memory of a Rabble-Rouser* (1997), Brown returned to the Runnymede novels with *Loose Lips* (1999). In 1990 Brown co-authored, with her cat, Sneaky Pie Brown, the first of the Mrs. Murphy mysteries. Together they have written several novels in the Mrs. Murphy series and one cookbook, *Sneaky Pie's Cookbook for Mystery Lovers* (1999). Brown's use of animals as characters and narrative voices makes the series of murder mysteries notable, and she uses the device in *Outfoxed* (2000), which features a Virginia fox hunt, a murder, and several species. Brown has been a visiting instructor at the University of Virginia in Charlottesville (1992) and a writer-in-residence at Cazenovia College in New York (1977–1978). She is currently president of American Artists, which options novels for television and film. Fluent in Greek and Latin, Brown has been a reviewer of translations and fiction for several major newspapers. She has been honored with honorary doctorates from William Woods University (2000) and Wilson College (1992) and has received several achievement awards, among them outstanding alumna awards, Emmy nominations, and fiction grants. She won the New York Public Library Literary Lion Award in 1987 and has been recognized by the International Academy of Poets. She has served on the Emmy jury and on several panels for the National Endowment for the Arts. Brown currently lives on a farm outside of Charlottesville. An avid animal and sports enthusiast, Brown is the master of the fox hounds of the Oak Ridge Fox Hunt Club and a member of the Farmington Hunt Club, Glenmore Hunt Club, and Middlebrook Hounds. She also plays polo with the Blue Ridge and Piedmont Women's Polo Clubs.

MAJOR WORKS AND THEMES

In her autobiography, Brown writes that she found her milieu in fiction, particularly in the "comic vision, which entails an entire worldview incorporating pain and tragedy" (*Rita Will* 275). While Brown's forthright, utilitarian prose is a sterling example of the maxim that novelists should write what they know, it is her habit of discussing the painful with humor, honesty, and openness that makes her work successful in all senses of the word. Since *Rubyfruit Jungle*, which became a manifesto for both the lesbian and the feminist communities, Brown has provided women with alternative ways of being in the world and of articulating their world view. In it, the young Molly Bolt claims the right to be and to speak as a woman and a lesbian. While Molly and several other of Brown's early characters are larger-than-life protagonists, moving through their world but separated from it as they set forth lesbian and/or feminist polemics, they serve the function of teaching other women to claim the right to their own voices. Whereas the first-person narrative of Molly Bolt is concerned largely with the sexual preference that sets her apart from mainstream society, the third-person narrative of *In Her Day* sets forth each woman's right to her own type of feminism. In particular, the novel's protagonist, an older academic named Carole, criticizes the stereotyping committed by her younger lover Ilse's radical feminism and points out that each woman is an individual, with the ability and the right to think and act on her own. Ilse counters with the need for women to act as a cohesive unit for feminism to succeed. In *Six of One*, Brown widens her array of women's voices with the aging Juts and Wheezie, elderly women blessed with energy, resilience, creativity, ego, and idiosyncrasies. These sisters openly claim their rights and freedoms, including sexual freedom. Brown continues their story in *Bingo*, which expands the array of alternative families and lifestyles and lays claim to humor and honesty as essential to happiness. Brown's own bisexuality becomes more clearly figured in these novels, as her male and female characters engage in various pairings.

Like *Bingo*, Brown's next novels feature more human and fallible protagonists as they criticize the boundaries and limitations set by sexism, classism, and racism. In particular, the fear shown in *Southern Discomfort* by Hortensia, who cannot leave her social position to be with her black lover, heralds the maturation of Brown's art. Where characters like Molly Bolt claimed their difference with almost total fearlessness, Brown's insistence on individual freedom is clear as she allows Hortensia to conform and Carmen, the tennis star of *Sudden Death*, to remain in the closet. However, given her autobiography, the honesty and openness of Brown herself come through in her most vivid and appealing characters: Nickel from the Runnymede novels, Harriet in *Sudden Death*, and Frazier from *Venus Envy*, who accidentally outs herself after being told in error that she is dying. The plot involves a number of liberatory devices: the medical mistake that gives Frazier a new lease on life, her coming out, and a dream vision featuring erotic mythology. Brown's use of the classics is notable and Daniel B. Levine has done an exhaustive study of allusions in *Southern Discomfort*. These devices involve Frazier more closely with her emotional and sexual life than ever before, and her responses are warm and honest.

Aside from featuring the themes of feminism and lesbianism that Brown insists be dealt with openly, *Venus Envy* takes place in Brown's own Virginia. A thoroughgoing regionalist, Brown writes that "Virginia, then as now, nurses its own peculiar vision of world events" (*High Hearts* 2). While she began moving her protagonists south early on, in her later novels, Brown turns her attention to her home, including her historical fiction. Her Civil War novel, *High Hearts*, is set on the Virginia battlefronts and is a thoroughly researched look at that portion of history. Her next historical novel, *Dolley*, also makes clear Brown's "southern worldview, with its emphasis on honor in capital letters" (*Rita Will* 286). *Riding Shotgun*, Brown's third foray into historical fiction, features time travel back to colonial Virginia and the contemporary Virginia fox hunt.

Brown's most recent novel, *Outfoxed*, is a murder mystery set in Virginia and also features the fox hunt. *Outfoxed* combines the best of Brown's thematic concerns—feminism, freedom, honor—with her interest in and affection for animals. In the novel, foxes, hounds, and horses have voices; the killing of a fox is seen as horrific as the murder of a human. Brown's commitment to animals became apparent in 1990, when she published the first of her Mrs. Murphy Mysteries, *Wish You Were Here*. Aside from acknowledging her cat, Sneaky Pie Brown, as co-author of the series, Brown's mysteries feature the pets of her protagonist, detective-postmistress Mary Minor Haristeen (Harry), and give voice to other domesticated and wild animals who take an active role in helping Harry solve murder mysteries in the small town of Crozet, Virginia. Throughout the series, Brown's cast of players develops, becoming richer and more interesting with each novel. The catalyst is Harry, whose interaction as the central character often initiates and always displays changes in human and animal characters. Drawn as hardworking, forthright, anti-materialist, and animal loving, Harry is also shown in all her flawed humanity: angry over her failed marriage, critical of the shortcomings of others, afraid of close relationships. Harry's animal friends are entertaining and whimsical; they clearly have their own agenda, and they maintain a steady commentary on the failures of humanity. Their dealings with other species are memorable and thought provoking; the regular appearance of Simon the Possum is a case in point, as he learns to get past some of his prejudices against humans after Harry treats him with respect. The primacy of the animals to the series becomes most clear in *Cat on the Scent*, where only the animals know the truth and the murderers go unpunished. The charming combination of animal protagonists and Brown's moral and political concerns, set amidst Virginian history and local color, ensures the continued popularity of the Mrs. Murphy series.

CRITICAL RECEPTION

Aside from book reviews, critical attention to Brown's large body of work remains relatively scarce. The reviews make clear that Brown's work remains well received and popular, but critical interpretations of her work are widely diverse. *Rubyfruit Jungle* has been examined both as a lesbian feminist manifesto and as not being feminist or lesbian enough. Leslie Fishbein argues that the novel works against lesbian feminism as it reduces lesbianism to sexual activity alone and has a flawed feminism that shows "no genuine affection for women" (155). Similarly, while James Mandrell sees the novel as a watershed in the development of lesbian fiction (150), he goes on to claim that the novel changes nothing, "but rather, acquiesces to and confirms the marginality experienced by those who are not straight, white middle-class males" (163). Conversely, Jonathan Dollimore calls *Rubyfruit Jungle* "both a measure of and a polemical contribution to the lesbian feminist consciousness of the early 1970s" (184–85), and he finds it memorable and affirmative, notable for its humor and for carrying its agenda without apology to a wide audience. In her discussion of Brown's early fiction as lesbian *bildungsroman* that represents the protagonist as the quintessential outsider, Judith Roof also finds that Brown articulates the feminist lesbian voice. Similarly, in her discussion of Brown's ethic of nonviolence in *Six of One*, Kathleen Martindale regards Brown as a voice of feminist vision.

While Martha Chew also discusses Brown as lesbian and feminist, she finds Brown distinctly Southern, as she connects Brown's political writings to her early fiction: "It is in Brown's portrayal of the rebelliousness of her heroes that we can see how her concerns as a lesbian feminist underlie and inform her portrayal of Southern women and link her political visions with her imaginative vision as a Southern novelist" (79). Doctoral research by James Justus and Jonathan David Little places Brown within a new movement of Southern women writers who rescue a tradition of female honor and construct alternative communities and within a contemporary movement of black and white authors who find new directions for American miscegenation fiction, respectively. Overall, while there are readings of Brown's fiction using theories of gender, race, and genre, there seems a good deal of critical work left undone.

BIBLIOGRAPHY

Works by Rita Mae Brown

The Hand That Cradles the Rock. New York: Bantam, 1971.
Rubyfruit Jungle. Plainfield: Daughters, 1973.
Songs to a Handsome Woman. Illus. Ginger Legato. Baltimore: Diana, 1973.
In Her Day. Plainfield: Daughters, 1976.
A Plain Brown Rapper. Illus. Sue Sellars. Oakland: Diane, 1976.
Six of One. New York: Harper, 1978.
Southern Discomfort. New York: Harper, 1982.
Sudden Death. New York: Bantam, 1983.
High Hearts. New York: Bantam, 1986.
Bingo. New York: Bantam, 1988.
Starting from Scratch: A Different Kind of Writer's Manual. New York: Bantam, 1988.
Rita Mae Brown and Sneaky Pie Brown. *Wish You Were Here.* Illus. Wendy Wray. New York: Bantam, 1990.
———. *Rest in Pieces.* Illus. Wendy Wray. New York: Bantam, 1992.
Venus Envy. New York: Bantam, 1993.
Dolley: A Novel of Dolley Madison in Love and War. New York: Bantam, 1994.
Rita Mae Brown and Sneaky Pie Brown. *Murder at Monticello, or, Old Sins.* Illus. Wendy Wray. New York: Bantam, 1994.
———. *Pay Dirt, or, Adventures at Ash Lawn.* Illus. Wendy Wray. New York: Bantam, 1995.
———. *Murder She Meowed.* Illus. Wendy Wray. New York: Bantam, 1996.
Riding Shotgun. New York: Bantam, 1996.
Rita Will: Memoir of a Literary Rabble-Rouser. New York: Bantam, 1997.
Rita Mae Brown and Sneaky Pie Brown. *Murder on the Prowl.* Illus. Wendy Wray. New York: Bantam, 1998.
———. *Cat on the Scent.* Illus. Itoko Maeno. New York: Bantam, 1999.
Loose Lips. New York: Bantam, 1999.
Rita Mae Brown and Sneaky Pie Brown. *Sneaky Pie's Cookbook for Mystery Lovers.* Illus. Katie Cox. New York: Bantam, 1999.

Outfoxed. New York: Ballantine, 2000.

Rita Mae Brown and Sneaky Pie Brown. *Pawing through the Past.* Illus. Itoko Maeno. New York: Bantam, 2000.

———. *Claws and Effect.* Illus. Itoko Maeno. New York: Bantam, 2001.

Studies of Rita Mae Brown

Boyle, Sharon D. "Rita Mae Brown." *Contemporary Lesbian Writers of the United States: A Bio-Bibliographical Critical Sourcebook.* Ed. Sandra Pollack and Denise D. Knight. Westport, CT: Greenwood Press, 1993. 94–105.

Chew, Martha. "Rita Mae Brown: Feminist Theorist and Southern Novelist." *Southern Quarterly* 22 (1983): 61–80.

Dollimore, Jonathan. "The Dominant and the Deviant: A Violent Dialectic." *Critical Quarterly* 28 (1986): 179–92.

Fishbein, Leslie. "*Rubyfruit Jungle*: Lesbianism, Feminism, and Narcissism." *International Journal of Women's Studies* 7 (1984): 155–59.

Irwin, Edward E. "Freedoms as Value in Three Popular Southern Novels." *Proteus* 6 (1969): 37–41.

Justus, James H. " 'Old Ways Not Forgotten': Cultural Revisions in Contemporary Southern Fiction." Dissertation, Indiana University, 1989.

Ladd, Barbara. "Rita Mae Brown." *Contemporary Fiction Writers of the South: A Bio-Bibliographical Sourcebook.* Ed. Joseph M. Flora and Robert Bain. Westport, CT: Greenwood Press, 1993. 67–75.

Levine, Daniel B. "Uses of Classical Mythology in Rita Mae Brown's *Southern Discomfort.*" *Classical and Modern Literature* 10 (1989): 63–70.

Little, Jonathan David. "Definition through Difference: The Tradition of Black-White Miscegenation in American Fiction." Dissertation, University of Wisconsin at Madison, 1989.

Mandrell, James. "Questions of Genre and Gender: Contemporary American Versions of the Feminine Picaresque." *Novel* 20 (1987): 149–70.

Martindale, Kathleen. "Rita Mae Brown's *Six of One* and Anne Cameron's *The Journey*: Fictional Contributions to the Ethics of Feminist Nonviolence." *Atlantis* 12 (1986): 103–9.

Roof, Judith. " 'This Is Not for You': The Sexuality of Mothering." *Narrating Mothers: Theorizing Maternal Subjectivities.* Ed. Brenda O. Daly and Maureen T. Reddy. Knoxville: University of Tennessee Press, 1991. 157–73.

ANA CASTILLO (1953–)

Laurie Champion

BIOGRAPHY

Ana Castillo was born on June 15, 1953, in Chicago, where she grew up living with her parents, Raymond and Raquel Rocha Castillo. She attended high school during the civil rights movement, which also included the beginnings of both the Chicano movement and the second wave of feminism in the United States. In addition to more direct benefits of these politically charged movements, they helped raise consciousness about issues concerning gender and ethnicity. Throughout her writing career, Castillo has remained true to this raised consciousness, always unyielding in her plea for equal rights for Mexican Americans and for women.

After graduating from Jones Commercial High School, Castillo attended Chicago City College for two years. She received her BA in liberal arts in 1975 from Northern Illinois University. After receiving her degree, she moved to Sonoma, California, and taught ethnic studies at Santa Rosa Junior College from 1975 to 1976. Soon afterward, she returned to Chicago, where she served as writer-in-residence for the Illinois Arts Council between 1977 and 1979. During this time, she returned to college, earning her MA in Latin American and Caribbean studies from the University of Chicago in 1979.

During the 1970s and 1980s, Castillo taught Mexican American history and Mexican history classes at several community colleges in both the Chicago and the San Francisco areas. In 1983 her only child, Marcel Ramón, was born. From 1986 until the present, she has taught feminist courses and creative writing courses at several universities. She received a PhD in American studies from the University of Breman in Germany in 1991. She later returned to Chicago, where she lives with her son.

Considered a prominent Chicana writer, Castillo recently was featured in *Vanity Fair* along with Sandra Cisneros, Julia Alvarez, and Denise Chávez. She co-founded the literary magazine *Third Woman*, and she has spoken for both national and international engagements, including a reading tour in Germany sponsored by the German

Association of Americanists. She continues to be invited by prestigious universities to teach creative writing courses. She has been the recipient of many prestigious literary awards, including the Carl Sandburg Literary Award in Fiction, the Mountains and Plains Bookseller Award, the Before Columbia Foundation's American Book Award, and a National Endowment for the Arts Award.

MAJOR WORKS AND THEMES

Politically charged in terms of social and cultural ideas and celebrating Mexican American heritage, Ana Castillo's fiction and poetry are firmly established in the tradition of Chicana literature. Her works, however, take a specific feminist approach that examines the role of women in Mexican American culture. In fact, in her collection of essays *Massacre of the Dreamers: Essays on Xicanisma* (1994), she coins the term "Xicanisma" to signify Chicana feminism. Illustrating the politics of Xicanisma throughout her works, Castillo celebrates Mexican American culture and female identity as well as critiquing oppressive social systems. *So Far from God* (1993), Castillo's third novel, is most representative of her work. *So Far from God* centers on Sofí and her four daughters, La Loca, Esperanza, Caridad, and Fe. Married to an alcoholic gambler, Sofí assumes full responsibility for caring for her family. The novel traces the daughters' development as they struggle with romantic relationships, seek careers, and search for personal and cultural identity. Through her daughter Esperanza's wisdom, Sofí comes to learn that she deserves a life outside of caring for her children and cleaning the house. This wisdom inspires her to run for mayor of Tome, a position to which she is elected. After La Loca, Sofí's last surviving daughter, dies, Sofí founds and presides over the M.O.M.A.S. (Mothers of Martyrs and Saints) organization, which celebrates women and their daughters, both those alive and those who are resurrected during the organization's annual conference.

Women also exchange recipes and share healing techniques and folk wisdom throughout *So Far from God*. In the chapter "Doña Felicia Calls in the Troops Who Herein Reveal a Handful of Their Own Tried and Proven Remedios; and Some Mixed Medical Advice Is Offered to the Beloved Doctor Tolentino," various *curanderas* and a medical doctor examine La Loca, who has AIDS. The *curanderas* discuss various means to cure La Loca's sore throat, such as giving her "a drop or two of kerosene in a teaspoon of sugar" (233); we are told that "most had learned their remedios from grandmothers who had learned from grandmothers. And all who had lived on that tierra of thistle and tumbleweed knew that every cactus and thorn had a purpose and reason, once put into a pot to boil" (233). At the end of this chapter, Doña Felicia gives Doctor Tolentino a remedy for his baldness. This serves to show that the *curandera* knows more than a trained doctor. It also gives more credibility to a woman who is a natural healer and whose skills have been passed down through generations of women than to a male doctor whose knowledge has been passed down through male privilege.

As in *So Far from God*, criticisms of patriarchy abound throughout Castillo's first novel, *The Mixquiahuala Letters* (1986), an epistolary novel that consists of letters written by Teresa, a poet in California, to her friend Alicia, an artist in New York. In a brief passage at the beginning of the book, Castillo invites readers to read the letters in sequences from three perspectives—conformist, cynic, or quixotic—and lists the order in which to read the letters for each perspective. All the readings reveal the plight of women in a sexist, racist, and classist society. For example, in "Letter Thirty-Two," Teresa outlines the roles prescribed to married women in a sexist society: "A woman takes care of the man she has made her life with, cleans, cooks, washes his underwear, does as if he were her only child, as if he had come from her womb. In exchange, he may pay her bills, he may not. He may give her acceptance into his society by replacing her father's name with his, or he may choose to not. He may make her feel like a woman, or rather, how she has been told a woman feels with a man or he may not" (118). This letter shows that while a man chooses whether he will provide his part of the exchange that has occurred within the relationship, a woman is conditioned to perform her roles as prescribed by a male-dominated society. Teresa tells Alicia that this relationship, this unfair exchange, is a "deathtrap" (118). Similarly, in "Letter Twenty-Two," Teresa recalls when Ponce had asked her if she was a liberal woman. She had responded to him by saying his perception of "liberal" is her "independence to choose what I do, with whom, and when" (79). She also tells him it means she may choose what she does not do. Castillo's point, of course, is that what is considered liberal by a male-dominated society is merely making choices for oneself. Women who do not prescribe to the "deathtrap" are considered liberal rather than simply women who make decisions for themselves.

In addition to criticizing patriarchy, *The Mixquiahuala Letters* explores a strong bond between two women who struggle with racism and classism. Unfortunately, after Teresa's sister leaves her husband, Teresa tries to enlighten her; however, Teresa is unable to make a white-dominated society accept her sister, which ultimately leads her sister to return to her husband. In another letter, Teresa tells Alicia that her own anger is directed at the "white," the "privileged," and the "unjust" (50) and that the reason she hates white women and sometimes Alicia is because "society had made them above all possessions" (49). Ironically, the same sexist society that prevents Teresa's intimate love for Alicia also inspires Teresa's resentment of her: The male-dominated society prevents Teresa from becoming Alicia's lesbian lover, yet it also privileges Alicia because of what she might offer men. As Teresa teaches Alicia about the evils of racism, classism, and sexism through her letters, Castillo teaches the reader through the text that is made up of the letters: Both Teresa and Castillo are inscribers on crusades for social justice.

Castillo's second novel, *Sapogonia: An Anti-Romance in 3/8 Meter* (1990), reveals some of the same ideas found in *So Far from God* and *The Mixquiahuala Letters*. Within the first few pages of the narrative proper, we are introduced to Mamá Grande, who has told the narrator "stories that related to her people, their history, and her own ideas about their traditions, all of which are really quite entertaining and which I may somewhere along this discourse share" (12). Told from the point of view of a male narrator, Máximo Madrigal, *Sapogonia* concerns his obsessive love for Pastora. Máximo might be considered a hero if defined by Western white literary standards. However, he becomes an anti-hero, for Castillo mocks his sexist attitude and the traditional Western white story of the man who pursues a desirable female. Like the traditional Western white hero, Máximo separates himself from society, goes on a journey, and even searches for his father, actions representative of mythical archetypes. If, by Western white definitions, Máximo is the hero, then Pastora becomes the antagonist who challenges him. Castillo reverses the roles of hero and heroine found in traditional white literature to characterize a weak man who promotes sexism, classism, and racism and a strong woman who is able to make choices for herself and pursue goals without a significant man in her life.

Similar to Pastora, Carmen Santos, the heroine of Castillo's most recent novel, *Peel My Love Like an Onion* (1999), emerges as a woman who defies traditional stereotypes of women. The victim of polio when she was six years old, poor, a minority, and a woman, Carmen is four times jeopardized. She enrolls in a school for "cripples," as her condition was then called. Miss Dorotea encourages the students that they can do anything they want despite their handicap. Carmen heeds well the message and learns to dance flamenco. When she is eighteen, she meets Agustín, who becomes her dance partner and then her lover; however, Agustín is married and returns to Spain each summer to stay with his wife. Coincidentally, after seventeen years of being Agustín's mistress, Carmen begins an affair with his young godson, Manolo. Manolo has a conflict between his romantic feelings for Carmen and his loyalty for Agustín.

Although *Peel My Love Like an Onion* offers a more straightforward, linear, and realistic plot than some of Castillo's earlier novels, she brings forth through this narrative style the same political issues revealed in her earlier works. For example, Carmen recalls that she could not afford to go to the doctor when afflicted with polio. Also, she is "forced to make tortillas. It is the penance of the prodigal daughter, I'm sure. Sons inherit acres and wealth. Women get to make bread, pick up where they left off if they keep a low profile and don't remind anyone of their big adventure" (32). Later, she is told that if she had a man, she would know how to iron and cook and do laundry. The title of the novel derives from Castillo's poem "Peel My Love Like an Onion" (*I Ask the Impossible*), in which she describes love as consisting of infinite layers of emotion. *Peel My Love Like an Onion* also connects intertextually with *Sapogonia*: References to Máximo Madrigal appear in *Peel My Love Like an Onion*. Máximo's appearance in *Peel My Love Like an Onion* is important because it shows how Carmen and her friend, Vicky, react to him. They celebrate not Máximo's return but the exit of Manolo's ghost. They celebrate a man leaving, not a man entering their lives. Although she is still desired by both Manolo and Agustín, she is free from emotional need for either. She explains that literally she "was no longer obsessing over Manolo" and vows to explain to him why she is no longer obsessing by using a proverb she learned, ironically, from Agustín: "A dog and a wolf don't make a good household" (212). The last sentence focuses on her energy, independent of Manolo or Agustín: Having succeeded as a singer, she plays one of her recorded CDs and says, "I dance and dance and dance" (213).

Similar to Carmen, many of Castillo's women characters find independence and develop a strong sense of personal and cultural identity. As demonstrated in the ways that Castillo's women overcome obstacles and defy oppressive social prescriptions, Castillo's works exemplify a specific form of Chicana that blends ethnic pride with feminism, all the while providing readers with stories that, like the ones about the characters in her works, pass down from generation to generation, entertain, inform, and document, and preserve cultural history and pride.

CRITICAL RECEPTION

Although considered an important contemporary Chicana writer, Ana Castillo has received only moderate critical attention. Most of this critical attention concentrates on her poetry and fiction, specifically as Chicana works. Within this framework, many scholars discuss political issues addressed in Castillo's writings. Ralph E. Rodriguez considers *So Far from God* exemplary of what he terms "contestatory literature," a work that "fundamentally opposes the deprecation of an individual or a group based on race, class, gender, or sexuality" (3). Similarly, Theresa Delgadillo says that *So Far from God* "expands our definitions of what constitutes 'resistance,' of what is 'political,' and of who is capable of effecting social change by focusing on the defiance that characterizes the family of woman at its center and the insurgency that erupts as they engage in ongoing battles" (893). Kamala Platt, looking at *So Far from God* from an eco-feminist perspective, says, "Castillo situates environmental justice issues within the larger field of race, class, and gender justice, thereby embracing the 'virtual realities' encountered by a Nuevo Mexicano community" (139).

Some scholars concentrate more precisely on feminist issues raised in Castillo's works. Carmela Delia Lanza looks at the "home space which bell hooks would define as a 'site of resistance' " that Castillo establishes in *So Far from God* (" 'New Meeting with the Sacred' " 660). Several scholars point out the feminist ideology expressed in *The Mixquiahuala Letters*: Yvonne Yarbro-Bejarano argues that sexism, classism, racism, and homophobia complicate the relationship between Teresa and Alicia; Heiner Bus points out that Teresa's letters in *The Mixquiahuala Letters* inform both Alicia and readers of the struggles and oppression experienced by Chicanas in a society dominated by white males; and Tanya Long Bennett demonstrates that although Teresa's and Alicia's status as women unites them, it also prevents them from becoming "*completely* synchronized because of tension between them with regard to men" (465).

No doubt, scholars have offered some insightful assessments of Castillo's works. As demonstrated in these appraisals, Castillo's works continue to raise consciousness about social oppression and to break new ground for Chicana writers. Much like Teresa, who mentors and guides Alicia through her letters, Castillo, through her insights about the struggles caused by racism, classism, and sexism, has become a true inscriber for social justice.

BIBLIOGRAPHY

Works by Ana Castillo

Zero Makes Me Hungry. Chicago: Scott, Foresman, 1975.
i close my eyes (to see). Pullman: Washington State University Press, 1976.
Otro Canto. Chicago: Alternativa, 1977.
Women Are Not Roses. Houston: Arte Publico, 1984.
The Invitation. San Francisco: La Raza, 1986.
The Mixquiahuala Letters. Binghamton, NY: Bilingual Press, 1986.
My Father Was a Toltec: Poems. Albuquerque: West End Press, 1988.
Ana Castillo and Cherie Morag, eds. *This Bridge Called My Back*. San Francisco: ISM Press, 1988.
Sapogonia: An Anti-Romance in 3/8 Meter. Tempe, AZ: Bilingual Press, 1990.
Ana Castillo, Norma Alarcon, and Cherie Morag, eds. *The Sexuality of Latinas*. Berkeley: Third Woman Press, 1993.
So Far from God. New York: Norton, 1993.
Massacre of the Dreamers: Essays on Xicanisma. Albuquerque: University of New Mexico Press, 1994.

Ed. *Goddess of the Americas: Writings on the Virgin of Guadalupe*. New York: Norton, 1996.
Loverboys. New York: Norton, 1996.
Peel My Love Like an Onion. New York: Doubleday, 1999.
I Ask the Impossible. New York: 2000.

Studies of Ana Castillo

Baker, Samuel. "Ana Castillo: The Protest Poet Goes Mainstream." *Publishers Weekly* 12 Aug. 1996: 59–60.

Bennett, Tanya Long. "No Country to Call Home: A Study of Castillo's *Mixquiahuala Letters*." *Style* 30 (1996): 452–78.

Bus, Heiner. " 'I Too Was of That Small Corner of the World': The Cross Cultural Experience in Ana Castillo's *The Mixquiahuala Letters*." *Americas Review* 21 (1993): 128–38.

Curiel, Barbara Brinson. "Heteroglossia in Ana Castillo's *The Mixquiahuala Letters*." *Discurso Literario* 7 (1990): 11–23.

Delgadillo, Theresa. "Forms of Chicana Feminist Resistance: Hybrid Spirituality in Ana Castillo's *So Far from God*." *Modern Fiction Studies* 44 (1998): 888–916.

Evenson, Brian. "Book Reviews." Rev. of *Loverboys*. *Review of Contemporary Fiction* 17 (1997): 201.

Fernandez, Sandy Michelle. "Reviews: Books." Rev. of *So Far from God*. *Hispanic* Sept. 1993: 102.

Ibis, Gómez-Vega. "Dubunking Myths: The Hero's Role in Ana Castillo's *Sapogonia*." *The Americas Review* 22 (1994): 244–58.

Hampton, Janet Jones. "Painter of Palabras." *Americas* 52 (2000): 48–53.

Lanza, Carmela Delia. "Hearing the Voices: Women and Home and Ana Castillo's *So Far from God*." *MELUS* 23 (1998): 65–79.

——. " 'A New Meeting with the Sacred': Ana Castillo's *So Far from God*." *Romance Languages Annual* 10 (1999): 658–63.

Mermann-Jozwiak, Elisabeth. "Gritos Desde La Frontera: Ana Castillo, Sandra Cisneros, and Postmodernism." *MELUS* 25 (2000): 101–18.

Milligan, Bryce. "An Interview with Ana Castillo." *South Central Review* 16 (1999): 19–29.

Platt, Kamala. "Ecocritical Chicana Literature: Ana Castillo's 'Virtual Realism.' " *Ecofeminist Literary Criticism: Theory, Interpretation, Pedagogy*. Ed. Greta Gaard and Patrick D. Murphy. Urbana: University of Illinois Press, 1998. 139–57.

Rodriguez, Ralph E. "Chicana/o Fiction from Resistance to Contestation: The Role of Creation in Ana Castillo's *So Far from God*." *MELUS* 25 (2000): 63–82.

Saeta, Elsa. "A MELUS Interview: Ana Castillo." *MELUS* 22 (1997): 133–49.

Seyda, Barbara. "Massacre of the Dreamers: An Interview with Ana Castillo." *Sojourner* 20 (1995): 116–17.

Sirias, Silvio, and Richard McGarry. "Rebellion and Tradition in Ana Castillo's *So Far from God* and Sylvia Lopez-Medina's *Cantora*." *MELUS* 25 (2000): 83–101.

Socolovsky, Maya. "Borrowed Homes, Homesickness, and Memory in Ana Castillo's *Sapogonia*." *Aztlan* 24 (1999): 73–94.

Stavans, Ilan. "And So Close to the United States." Rev. of *So Far from God*. *Commonweal* 14 Jan. 1994: 37–38.

Walter, Roland. "The Cultural Politics of Dislocation and Relocation in the Novels of Ana Castillo." *MELUS* 1 (1998): 81–97.

Yarbro-Bejarano, Yvonne. "The Multiple Subject in the Writing of Ana Castillo." *Americas Review* 20 (1992): 65–72.

DENISE CHÁVEZ (1948–)

Beverly G. Six

BIOGRAPHY

Denise Chávez was born August 15, 1948, in Las Cruces, New Mexico, to attorney Ernesto Epifanio "Chano" Chávez and Delfina Rede Faver Chávez, a teacher. When her parents amicably divorced when she was ten, Chávez remained close to her father, but her mother was the primary parental influence. Chávez grew up surrounded by women. From mother, sisters, grandmothers, and the household helpers, she developed the finely honed sense of women's issues and values that later became major themes in her writing. Currently, she resides in her childhood home in Las Cruces, New Mexico.

At Madonna High School in Mesilla, New Mexico, a private interdenominational school, Chávez discovered her love for acting. In college, she began writing award-winning plays; the New Mexico State University Best Play Award in 1970 was only the first of a continuing series of awards for her work in all genres. She earned a BA in drama from New Mexico State University (1971) and an MFA in drama from Trinity University in San Antonio, Texas (1974). She gained theater experience at La Compañía de Teatro de Albuquerque, the Dallas Theater Center, and Theater-in-the-Red, Santa Fe. Always an avid reader and writer, Chávez combined acting and writing and earned an MA in creative writing from the University of New Mexico in 1984. She married photographer and sculptor Daniel Zolinsky on December 29, 1984.

Chávez's employment as a waitress in college and her varied work and volunteer experience later as performer, teacher, workshop leader, and storyteller provide themes and material for her writing. Chávez has led workshops for prisoners, schoolteachers, and senior citizens and has been an artist-in-the-schools for New Mexico (1977–1983), artist-in-residence with the Arts for Elders Program, Santa Fe and Las Cruces, and senior citizen workshop director for Las Cruces Community Action (1986–1989). She has been a visiting lecturer at the American School in Paris (1977), Northern New Mexico Community College, Española (1977–1980), and the University of Houston

(1988–1991). Chávez is co-founder and artistic director of the annual Border Book Festival in Las Cruces, New Mexico, and an assistant professor at New Mexico State University, the first Chicana to teach in the English department there (Brown-Guillory 40). As professional storyteller and performance artist, Chávez presents readings, workshops, and lectures across the United States and Europe.

Chávez has received numerous awards and honors for community service and literature, including grants from the New Mexico Arts Divisions (1979–1988), National Endowment for the Arts (1981–1982), and Rockefeller Foundation (1984). Other awards include the Steele Jones Fiction Award, New Mexico State University, 1986 (for "Last of the Menu Girls"); Premio Aztlán Award, American Book Award, and Mesilla Valley Writer of the Year Award, 1995 (for *Face of an Angel*); New Mexico Governor's Award in Literature, 1995; Luminaria Award for Community Service, New Mexico Community Foundation, 1996; writer-in-residence, Lannon Foundation, Marfa, Texas, 2000; and the Lila Wallace-*Reader's Digest* Fellowship, 2000–2003, to lead memoir writing workshops for older adults. She was a delegate to the Forum for US-Soviet Dialogue, Moscow, USSR, 1989, and is a charter member of the National Institute of Chicana Writers.

MAJOR WORKS AND THEMES

Chávez writes plays, short stories, poetry, essays, and novels. She is also a performance artist; her one-woman performance piece, *Women in the State of Grace*, is a celebration of the Latina woman's enduring love and beauty. Her plays have been produced throughout the United States and Europe; *Plaza* was performed at the Festival Latino de Nueva York (director, Joseph Papp) and at the Edinburgh, Scotland, Arts Festival. She has written more than twenty plays; many have been produced across the United States, but few are published. Two are accessible: *Plaza* in *New Mexico Plays* (1989) and *Novenas Narrativas y Ofrendas Nuevomexicanas* in *Chicana Creativity and Criticism* (1996), which also contains a collection of her poetry. Chávez's poetry and short prose appear in noted journals and anthologies, including *Americas Review*, *Journal of Ethnic Studies*, *Mexican American Literature*, *Cuentos Chicanos*, *Infinite Divisions*, and the *Norton Anthology of American Literature*. Many short stories have later become parts of her novels and performances. Chávez's overlapping of prose fiction and drama makes her dramatic presentations convincingly real and her fiction enthrallingly dramatic, reinforcing her claim that she is "a performance writer" (Duarte 51). Her major prose works are *The Last of the Menu Girls* (1986), *Face of an Angel* (1994), and *Loving Pedro Infante* (2001).

Because she blends forms to create new genres, Chávez's work is hard to classify. Chávez says that *Last of the Menu Girls* is "like a series of scenes more than short stories; it's not a novel. Maybe dramatic vignettes is a better description" (Gray 2). In writing *Face of An Angel*, she experimented with form, "bending the space . . . [in order to] combine dramatic scenes with poetry within the structure of a novel" (Gray 2). Two striking examples of Chávez's bending of emotional and literal space are in the excerpts from Soveida's *Book of Service* interspersed between narrative chapters and in chapter 5 where the double-columned text illustrates in form the simultaneous yet uncommunicative husband-wife monologues in a miserable marriage (*Face* 23–27). In breaking the boundaries of genre, Chávez invites her readers to become interactive theatrical audiences, drawn into her characters' broken relationships.

All Chávez's work concerns relationships—to land, community, individuals, self, and spirituality. Dominant themes include service, male-female relationships, cultural and personal identity, and love, and the dominant images are geographical, cultural, and spiritual borderlands. Chávez's narrative rests on a framework of Chicano/a folklore, folk customs, gender roles, and language.

Chávez excels at the seamless blending of Spanish and English that characterizes the Mexican American culture of the Southwest and insists that publishers not italicize the Spanish and imply a separation of cultures. In *The Last of the Menu Girls*, Braulia thinks, "Enough you have a man, his children. What more? Let that puta desgraciada sin vergüenza chorreada vividora see if her flowers can hold him" (166); in *Face of an Angel*, Mamá urges Soveida to be a nun because "they don't have no one belching and scratching and making pedos, you know, farts, on the way to the you-know-what, el escusado" (59); in *Loving Pedro Infante*, Tere says of her visit to the New Age Full Moon Lodge, "Wirms and I did get a good laugh out of it, two stupid Mejicanas going to an albino gabacha witch" (204). Chávez's argument against italics is that "when you italicize you separate. I don't want that membrane of separation" (Duarte 46). This is a critical linguistic decision, for the blended language illustrates precisely the bicultural nature of the Southwest.

Central to the portrait of Southwestern culture is Hispanic folklore; all Chávez's work is permeated with saints' days, folk beliefs and speech, legends, and traditions. For example, in *The Last of the Menu Girls*, Rocío has to understand that her culture's *compadrazgo* code means that one is "bound by the higher laws . . . having to do with the spiritual well-being and development of one of God's creatures . . . to be unrelated and yet related" (168), and in *Loving Pedro Infante*, Tere finds analogues for the relationships in her life in the movies and legendary life of the Mexican movie star and visits a *curandera* (196). *Face of an Angel* provides the greatest number of examples: Mamá's didactic tale of the devil man with chicken feet who seduced a maiden at a dance (156); Oralia's healing herbs and *dichos*, "one for every event in life" (104); Soveida's reflections on La Llorona, La Sebastiana, the boogeymen El Coco and El Cucui (49), and the saints of the Catholic Church (55–58); and Soveida's Chicano folklore class. The characters' cultural heritage binds them to each other, to community, and to God as the women help each other heal and endure.

Women are of central importance in Chávez's work. A self-proclaimed feminist writer, she explores women's role in a male-dominated social, economic, and religious culture. That role is to provide service to men, to other women, and to God, as seen in their occupations: wife, mother, daughter, housekeeper, waitress, nun. Their love makes service sacramental. Cleaning house, Chata becomes "[a] woman in a state of grace" (*Face* 217); serving food, Soveida is connected to "a divine, preordained belief in individual service" (*Face* 171). The service to men crosses generations. Repeatedly, Chávez's characters experience profound disappointments in their relationships to men, and when husbands and fathers beat them, have multiple affairs, desert them, her women are sustained by their *comadres*, healed with stories, laughter, and love. Speaking for all women, Tere says, "I knew where my place was in that long line of women that stretched into an eternity of loving" (*Loving* 249).

Woman's relationship with the masculine God of the Catholic Church is problematic. In a culture that places them "either on the altar or in the gutter" (*Loving* 230), Chávez's female characters confess their sins to each other and pray to the Virgin Mary and to "the Mother God," who is "a God of possibility and Hope" (*Face* 445).

Noting that her grandmother and mother never escaped their slavery to men's needs, Soveida sees her sister Lizzie, the lesbian feminist nun, as the only woman who is "truly free to love" (*Face* 446). Through their connections with the feminine in the Divine and with the strong female influences in their lives, Chávez's characters discover that their strongest assets are themselves. As they take their places in a never-ending line of service to others, Chávez's women forge a continual chain of love across generations. Chávez is undoubtedly one of the premier feminist writers of modern literature, but those who may relegate her to this role alone are in danger of missing some of her greatest gifts as consummate storyteller, poet, and humorist. Among all Chávez's literary gifts, the greatest is her unerring ability to speak the truth about life, love, and human needs and disappointments.

CRITICAL RECEPTION

Criticism of Chávez focuses primarily on four major areas in her work—feminism, Chicano/a culture, characterization, and narrative form—with the major emphasis on Chicana culture. María Herrera-Sobek lists two contributions to Chicana literature for Chávez: creation of new genres and "her skill in the elaboration of well-delineated, believable women characters" (34). Herrera-Sobek's insistence that being Chicana is central to everything Chávez writes is echoed by other critics; many discuss Chávez strictly within the context of other contemporary Latina writers.

Chávez's work consistently receives favorable reviews. Although some reviewers approach her innovations in narrative structure with caution, Robert Houston's assessment of *Face of an Angel* as a collection of raw, unedited material with "confusing dialogue" and "occasionally strained monologues" is an exception. In striking opposition is William Nericcio's assessment of the same innovations as evidence of the maturation of Chávez's narrative range. Nericcio praises Chávez's "eclectic and experimental" narrative techniques and sees them as graphic representations of the "expressionistic gap" between men and women and between Mexico and the United States. Nericcio feels the book is a "literary tribute to servants," Chávez's "*Odyssey* for the working poor." He sets the work firmly in the American storytelling tradition, among such icons as Twain, Toni Morrison, and Alice Walker, and equates Chávez with Laura Esquivel and Sandra Cisneros for her strong Latina women characters.

Other reviewers admire Chávez's powerful Latina feminism. Laurie Muchnick examines male-female relationships in *Face of an Angel*, calling it a study of the strength of women waiting on and for men. Susan Miller praises Chávez for giving voice to the dignity and worth of Latina women "in a macho culture." Reviewing *The Last of the Menu Girls*, Tomelene Slade says Chávez helps redefine Latina womanhood and joins other contemporary Latina writers in providing the growing numbers of young Hispanic girls with new Latina role models. Irene Campos Carr sees women's stories as the center of *Face of an Angel* and highlights Chávez's storytelling skills.

Reviews of *Loving Pedro Infante* address both women's issues and culture. Robert Con Davis-Undiano calls the novel Chávez's "own version of a women's movement" (88) and concludes that it is further proof that "Latina writing is becoming indispensable to contemporary culture" (89). Maggie Galehouse praises Chávez's strong women but finds the "cultural specificity" the most striking element of the novel. Galehouse feels that Chávez's Southwestern "atmosphere" takes precedence over characterization but adds that the English/Spanish code-switching intrinsic to the Southwest and to Chávez's narrative poses difficulties for the "gringo readers."

Scholarly attention to Denise Chávez's work is sparse. Martha E. Heard's article, "The Theatre of Denise Chávez," provides comprehensive discussion of her drama, but scholars have not adequately examined Chávez's prose fiction beyond *The Last of the Menu Girls*. Debra A. Castillo's "Daily Shape of Horses: Denise Chávez and Maxine Hong Kingston" (1991) examines the play of language and symbol in *Menu Girls*; her "In a Subjunctive Mood: Denise Chávez, Maxine Hong Kingston, and the Bicultural Text" (1992) expands the "Daily Shape" article to include the grammatical constructions in bicultural texts. Douglas Anderson's "Displaced Abjection and States of Grace: Denise Chávez's *The Last of the Menu Girls*" (1995) examines feminine divisions of body/self in *Menu Girls*.

Anderson asserts that menu girl Rocio's most important work in the hospital is to confront human mortality, accept her own body as Self rather than Other, and integrate the multiple selves whose disassociation keeps her from being "balanced in what Chávez calls a 'state of grace' " (236). In confronting the body's vulnerability to illness and death, Rocio learns that she lives in a society "in which disempowerment or marginalization are equated with the abject body's vulnerability or passivity" (242). As an Hispanic woman, Rocio is doubly "disempowered" by a society constructed in the image of male hierarchy. When Rocio chooses "a Chicana acceptance of the body in its sensuality and vulnerability to abjection" (247), she empowers herself to move beyond the marginality of ethnicity and gender forced upon her by society.

In "The Daily Shape of Horses," Castillo also focuses on the dilemmas of "the ethnic minority woman . . . in a dominantly white, . . . dominantly male, society" represented in *Menu Girls* (30). Using Derridian theories of signifier/signified and Whorfian hypotheses that the perceptions of one's language construct one's realities, Castillo concludes that Rocio and her student, Kari Lee, are made inarticulate and shapeless by societal constraints, so that Kari Lee's ambiguous turkey drawing in "Space Is a Solid" becomes the articulation of their means to empowerment. In her examination of the shape of darkness, Chávez confronts the issues of biculturalism, multiple perceptions of time and language, and the empowerment of "an undervalued gender" to "forcefully suggest new kinds of feminine difference" by naming, and thus claiming, the darkness imposed by society (42).

Castillo's "In a Subjunctive Mood" reiterates her theory that cultural and gender-based differences are central to Chávez's *Menu Girls* but adds an examination of the "double-voicing" found in Chávez's use of subjunctive mood in the Spanish constructions. Noting that the subjunctive "has no independent existence in standard grammar," Castillo insists that Chávez's Spanish subjunctives mirror the subordinate roles Hispanics are forced to play in dominantly Anglo societies (263). The subjunctive disrupts the narrative structure, making it subordinate to "mood," thus challenging the dominant position and restructuring boundaries. Castillo insists that Chávez's "looping plots of endless self-exploration and self-interpretations" (270) are necessary to effect the liberation and empowerment of her female characters.

Castillo notes that Chávez "has not yet been so fortunate in academic circles" ("Subjunctive Mood" 284) as other contemporary women writers of color, but that oversight will soon be redressed as more and more readers discover the beauty and truth in her work. In her insistence that we break down society's artificial boundaries between genders and cultures, Chávez enables individuals to integrate their own Self/

Other dichotomies and become authenticators of their own existence. This task is the responsibility of both enfranchised and disenfranchised in American culture, Chávez insists, and it must begin with an unflinching look at the truths of our society and an uncompromising insistence on the necessity of love. Denise Chávez challenges the hierarchical conventions of structure, genre, and society with evocative images, lyrical prose, and delightful humor. There can be no doubt that she is a major figure in modern American literature.

BIBLIOGRAPHY

Works by Denise Chávez

The Last of the Menu Girls. Houston: Arte Público, 1986.

"Lagaña of Lace," "Ya," "Mercado Day," "Purgatory Is an Ocean of Flaming Hearts," "For My Sister in Paris," and "Birth of Me in My Room at Home." *Americas Review* 15 (1987): 48–59.

"The Train Whistles," "The Space Between," "This River's Praying Place," "Our Linkage," "Progression from Water to the Absence," "Lagaña of Lace," "Worm Child," "Sisters, Sisters, Sisters," "On Mama Toña," and "Missss Rede." *Journal of Ethnic Studies* 15 (1987): 48–67.

"Denise Chávez." *Literature and Landscape: Writers of the Southwest.* Ed. Cynthia Farah. El Paso: Texas Western Press, 1988.

"Heat and Rain (Testimonio)." *Breaking Boundaries: Latina Writing and Critical Readings.* Ed. Asuncion Horno-Delgado et al. Amherst: University of Massachusetts Press, 1989. 27–32.

Plaza. New Mexico Plays. Ed. David Richard Jones. Albuquerque: University of New Mexico Press, 1989. 79–106.

The Flying Tortilla Man. Mexican American Literature. Ed. Charles Tatum. New York: Harcourt, 1990: 644–683.

"On Meeting You in Dream and Remembering Our Dance." *Infinite Divisions: An Anthology of Chicana Literature.* Ed. Tey Diana Rebolledo and Eliana S. Rivero. Tucson: University of Arizona Press, 1993. 138–39.

Face of an Angel. New York: Farrar, 1994.

"La Pesadez," "I Am Your Mary Magdalene," "This River's Praying Place," "Tears," "Cloud," "Artery of Land," "Silver Ingots of Desire," "The Study," "Starflash," "Saying 'Oh No,'" "Everything You Are Is Teeth," "Cuckoo Death Chime," "Door," "Chekhov Green Love," "The State of My Inquietude," "The Feeling of Going On," "This Thin Light," and "Two Butterflies." *Chicana Creativity and Criticism.* 2nd ed. Ed. María Herrera-Sobek and Helena María Viramontes. Albuquerque: University of New Mexico Press, 1996. 77–97.

Novena Narrativas y Ofrendas Nuevomexicanas. Chicana Creativity and Criticism. 2nd ed. Ed. María Herrera-Sobek and Helena María Viramontes. Albuquerque: University of New Mexico Press, 1996. 149–63.

"Crossing Bitter Creek: Meditations on the Colorado River." *Writing Down the River: Into the Heart of the Grand Canyon.* Ed. Kathleen Jo Ryan. Flagstaff, AZ: Northland, 1998. 109–19.

Loving Pedro Infante. New York: Farrar, 2001.

Studies of Denise Chávez

Anaya, Rudolfo A. Introduction. *The Last of the Menu Girls.* By Denise Chávez. Houston: Arte Público Press, 1986.

Anderson, Douglas. "Displaced Abjection and States of Grace: Denise Chávez's *The Last of the Menu Girls.*" *American Women Short Story Writers.* Ed. Julie Brown. New York: Garland: 1995. 235–50.

Brown-Guillory, Elizabeth. "Denise Chávez: Chicana Woman Writer Crossing Borders—An Interview." *South Central Review* 16 (1999): 30–43.

Carr, Irene Campos. "Life Was, and Is, Service." Rev. of *Face of an Angel*, by Denise Chávez. *Belles Lettres* 10 (1995): 35.

Castillo, Debra A. "The Daily Shape of Horses: Denise Chávez and Maxine Hong Kingston." *Disposito: Journal of Comparative and Cultural Studies* 16 (1991): 29–43.

——, ed."In a Subjunctive Mood: Denise Chávez, Maxine Hong Kingston, and the Bicultural Text." *Talking Back: Toward a Latin American Feminist Literary Criticism.* Ithaca: Cornell University Press, 1992: 260–292.

Clark, Beverly Lyon. Rev. of *The Last of the Menu Girls. New York Times Book Review* 12 Oct. 1986: 28.

Clark, William. "Denise Chávez: 'It's All One Language Here.' " *Publishers Weekly* 15 Aug. 1994: 77–78.

Davis-Undiano, Robert Con. "Denise Chávez: Her New Book, *Loving Pedro Infante*, Again Shows Her Love of Characters." *Hispanic* April 2001: 88–90.

Degliantoni, Lisa. Rev. of *Face of an Angel. Library Journal* Aug. 1994: 124.

Duarte, Gloria. "A Discussion with Denise Chávez." *Concho River Review* 14 (2000): 40–56.

Eysturoy, Annie O. "Denise Chávez." *This Is about Vision: Interviews with Southwestern Writers.* Ed. William Balassi, John F. Crawford, and Annie O. Eysturoy. Albuquerque: University of New Mexico Press, 1990. 157–69.

Galehouse, Maggie. "*Loving Pedro Infante.*" Rev. of *Loving Pedro Infante. New York Times Book Review* 13 May 2001: 17.

Gray, Lynn. Interview. *Short Story Review* 5 (1988): 2–4.

Heard, Martha E. "The Theatre of Denise Chávez: Interior Landscapes with 'Sabor Nuevomexicano.' " *Americas Review* 16 (1988): 83–91.

Herrera-Sobek, María. Introduction. *Chicana Creativity and Criticism.* Ed. María Herrera-Sobek and Helena María Viramontes. Albuquerque: University of New Mexico Press, 1996. 1–41.

Houston, Robert. Rev. of *Face of an Angel. New York Times Book Review* 25 Sept. 1994: 20.

Joyce, Alice. Rev. of *Face of an Angel. Booklist* 92 (1994): 110–11.

Miller, Susan. "Family Spats, Urgent Prayers." Rev. of *In the Time of the Butterflies*, by Julia Alvarez, and *Face of an Angel. Newsweek* 17 Oct. 1994: 77.

Mintz, Gwendolyn. "Denise Chávez Writes Her Way to National Prominence, but Stays Committed to Her Home Town." *Bulletin* [Las Cruces, NM] 16–22 March 2000: 1ff.

Muchnick, Laurie. "*Face of an Angel* by Denise Chávez." *Village Voice* 8 Nov. 1994: SS18–SS19.

Nericcio, William. Rev. of *Face of an Angel. World Literature Today* 69 (1995): 792.

Ott, Bill. "Chávez, Denise." Rev. of *Loving Pedro Infante. Booklist* 15 Apr. 2001: 1535.

Paredes, Raymund A. Rev. of *The Last of the Menu Girls. Rocky Mountain Review* 41 (1987): 124–28.

Rivera, Rowena. "Denise Chávez." *Chicano Writers: Second Series.* Ed. Francisco A. Lomelí and Carl R. Shirley. Detroit: Gale, 1992. Vol. 122 of *Dictionary of Literary Biography.* 70–76.

Saldivar, Jose-David, and Rolando Hinojosa, eds. *Criticism in the Borderlands: Studies in Chicano Literature, Culture, and Ideology.* Durham: Duke University Press, 1991.

Slade, Tomelene. "Growing Up Hispanic: Heroines for the '90s." *School Library Journal* Dec. 1992: 35–36.

Soete, Mary. Rev. of *The Last of the Menu Girls. Library Journal* July 1986: 106.

Zaleski, Jeff. Rev. of *Loving Pedro Infante. Publishers Weekly* 26 March 2001: 60.

ALICE CHILDRESS (1920–1994)

Joelle Biele

BIOGRAPHY

Born October 12, 1920, Alice Childress was the great-granddaughter of Annie Camp-bell, a slave who was freed in the city streets of Charleston, South Carolina, on "Juneteenth," one year after the Emancipation Proclamation. Childress was raised by Campbell's daughter, Eliza White, named by Campbell for the character in Harriet Beecher Stowe's *Uncle Tom's Cabin*. When Childress was five years old, she and her grandmother migrated to Harlem, New York. The moments Childress and her grand-mother shared had a profound effect on Childress's writing. White had attended school through the fifth grade and was an avid reader throughout her life. She shared her love of books with her granddaughter and gave the young Childress her first writing lessons. White encouraged Childress to observe the world around her and to put her stories to paper.

White's writing lessons included sampling the city and watching people go by their apartment on 118th Street. She took the young Alice to Italian neighborhoods and asked her to describe the smells drifting out shop doors. As they examined swatches of fabric, she asked her granddaughter what she would make from this piece of tweed or that bolt of silk. White and Childress put on plays with friends; they danced and sang at home. They often spent time looking out their window. White would ask what her granddaughter thought a passing man was thinking; that would be followed by questions about how many children he had and what his wife was like. Once they were done, White would say, "Now, write that down. That sounds like something we should keep" (Brown-Guillory 66). They went to testimonials on Wednesday nights at Salem Church, and Childress listened with rapt attention to women telling their troubles: " 'My son's in jail,' or 'My daughter's sick,' or 'I don't have any money, and my rent is due.' Everybody rallied around these people," she remembered. "I couldn't wait for person after person to tell her story" (Brown-Guillory 66). It was here, listening to these women, that Childress learned to be a writer, and with her grandmother serving as inspiration, she learned to write "without false pride or shame" (Childress, "Knowing" 10).

Childress is known primarily as a playwright, and her years in theater shaped the fiction that was to come. Childress joined the American Negro Theatre (ANT) in 1941. Founded by Abram Hill and Frederick O'Neal, the group met at the Shomburg Library in Harlem. Company members like Ossie Davis, Ruby Dee, Earle Hyman, and Hilda Simms participated in every aspect of the theater: putting together mailings, selling tickets, making costumes, designing sets, cleaning the theater, along with acting, writing, and directing. Childress performed in the company's productions of *Natural Man* (1941), *Anna Lucasta* (1944), and *Rain* and *Almost Faithful* (1948). With *Anna Lucasta*, the group went to Broadway, and Childress was nominated for a Tony Award for her portrayal of Blanche. Of that time, Childress says, "Radio and television work followed, but racism, a double blacklisting system, and a feeling of being somewhat alone in my ideas caused me to know I could more freely express myself as a writer" ("Candle" 115). She wrote her first play, *Florence, A One Act Drama* (1949), in one night as part of a bet between herself and other company members, among them Sidney Poitier, who believed that in a play about blacks and whites, only "a life and death thing like lynching is interesting on stage" (Abramson 189). *Florence* is the story of two women, one black, one white, waiting at a southern train station. Separated by a low railing, "Colored" and "White" signs hanging above them, Mrs. Whitney and Mrs. Carter talk about Mrs. Whitney's daughter, Florence, an actress in New York who is trying to break out of the stereotypical "maid" roles to more fulfilling parts. Shedding stereotypes was to become the major theme of her later plays.

Childress devoted the first half of her career primarily to plays; however, in the second half, she gave more time to fiction. After working at the ANT, Childress went on to write *Trouble in Mind* (1955), *Wedding Band: A Love/Hate Story in Black and White* (1966), and *Wine in the Wilderness: A Comedy-Drama* (1969), among other plays. Her first book of prose, *Like One of the Family: Conversations from a Domestic's Life*, appeared in 1956, followed by *A Hero Ain't Nothin' but a Sandwich* (1973), *A Short Walk* (1979), *Rainbow Jordan* (1981), and *Those Other People* (1989). She collaborated with her husband, Nathan Woodard, a musician, on pieces like *Sea Island Song* (1977), which she later retitled *Gullah*, and *Moms: A Praise Play for a Black Comedienne* (1986). She also wrote essays on African American theater and scripted the screenplays for *Wedding Band, Wine in the Wilderness*, and *A Hero Ain't Nothin' but a Sandwich*. Her plays and fiction have received numerous awards, including an Obie in 1956 for *Trouble in Mind* as best original Off-Broadway play, outstanding book of the year from the *New York Times Book Review* for *A Hero Ain't Nothin' but a Sandwich* and *Rainbow Jordan*, and a National Book Award nomination for the former. In addition, she was a member of various artistic and scholarly communities, often participating in panel discussions. From 1966 to 1968, she held a fellowship from the Radcliffe Institute for Independent Study (now the Mary Ingrahm Bunting Institute), and during the 1970s, she traveled to the Soviet Union, China, and Ghana. She died in 1994, at work on projects about her great-grandmother and Paul Laurence Dunbar.

MAJOR WORKS AND THEMES

As in her plays, Alice Childress concentrates in her novels on breaking stereotypes. Childress is particularly interested in creating complex portraits of the working class, "those," she says, "who come in second, or not at all." As her grandmother taught her, Childress writes about the people who inhabit her world. When she was a schoolgirl, her teachers encouraged her to write about blacks who were "accomplishers." They told her that her papers should serve as inspiration and help readers become "winners." Yet, Childress says, she went against this advice and decided to "interpret the 'ordinary' because they are not ordinary" ("Candle" 112). Childress creates characters with great sympathy and depth. *Like One of the Family* has spunky Mildred, who shares stories about working for white families with her friend, Marge; *A Hero Ain't Nothin' but a Sandwich* has thirteen-year-old addict Benjie Johnson and Butler Craig, Benjie's stepfather, a maintenance worker. Then there is *A Short Walk*'s Cora James, who performs in minstrel shows and runs a profitable gambling house, and fourteen-year-old Rainbow Jordan and her foster mother, Josephine Lamont, a dressmaker. Trudier Harris believes that Childress's handling of the poor and her writing philosophy come from her upbringing and the time she spent as an assistant machinist, photo retoucher, domestic worker, saleslady, and insurance agent (*Dictionary* 69). Indeed, chapters from *Like One of the Family* like "The Health Card" and "The Pocketbook Game" stem from Childress's own experiences working in the homes of wealthy whites. Childress considers it to be a "serious self-deception" of black writers to concentrate on those who have overcome great odds. "Black writers cannot afford to abuse or neglect the so-called ordinary characters who represent a part of ourselves, the self twice denied, first by racism and then by class indifference" ("Knowing" 10). She rejects the idea that characters should be used for image building since those images are for "others to measure our capability, acceptability, or human worth" ("Candle" 113).

Along with portrayals of the working class, Childress argues for more complex female characters. Spanning the twentieth century, Childress's women cover a wide range of African American life. Some characters are part of the Great Migration, like Cora who leaves the South Carolina lowlands for Harlem, while others, like Etta, Cora's adoptive mother, return to their sea island homes on Edisto. They are involved in the political movements of their day (Cora participates in the Marcus Garvey movement), and they listen to street corner speakers. Like Benjie's grandmother, Mrs. Ransom Bell, Childress's characters attend church services and pray for a better world. Childress gives us glimpses of traditional female healers, who offer blue potions to heal Benjie of his addiction, and of the rising middle class in Mrs. Anderson in *Rainbow Jordan* and the Tate family in *Those Other People*. Like Mildred, who serves as a counterpoint to the stereotypical "faithful servant," Childress writes against the popular media's portrayal of blacks. Childress wages a war of images in her writings and urges other writers to do the same. "The Negro woman will attain her rightful place in American literature when those of us who care about truth, justice, and a better life tell her story, with the full knowledge and appreciation of her constant, unrelenting struggle against racism and for human rights" ("Negro Woman" 19). As she is against characters being used for image building, Childress is against the idea that women "must be portrayed in an ideal light." She believes that this kind of writing "prevents us from discovering each other" (*Interviews* 74). And so her characters struggle with what the world has dealt them. Before Butler Craig came along, Rose Johnson worked alone to support her son, Benjie, and her mother in a small apartment. Kathie Jordan, who had her daughter, Rainbow, when she was fourteen, lives on unemployment and Aid-to-Dependent-Children checks between jobs go-go dancing while her daughter grapples with her sexuality. Childress says, "I concentrate on portraying have-nots in a *have* society, those seldom singled out by mass media, except as source material for derogatory humor and/or condescending social analysis" ("Candle" 112).

What gives Childress's characters their depth is her consistent use of the first person. Instead of being objects acted upon, they act. Each chapter is a soliloquy, a single character narrating past events as if speaking to a friend or writing in a diary. Mildred narrates all of *Like One of the Family*, each scene taking place at the end of a different day. Multiple characters narrate *A Hero Ain't Nothin' but a Sandwich*, *Rainbow Jordan*, and *Those Other People*, lending shifting perspectives to each of these stories. *A Short Walk* is the only novel in which Childress uses a third-person omniscient narrator, but this narration switches into Cora's voice. Childress's writing celebrates the oral tradition. She brings out the richness of Southern folk idioms and the rhythms of Harlem's streets. Seldom does any action unfold before the reader's eyes, and then only in very tense situations like Benjie's fall from the apartment roof. Childress writes in the present tense because she feels it is more "theatrical" and "more interesting" (*Interviews* 69). Her approach gives her novels the feeling of plays. She acknowledges that her books read this way because theater has been such a big part of her life. "When I'm writing a book, I visualize it all on stage," Childress notes. "I act out all the parts" (*Interviews* 67). The use of the first person invites the reader to participate in the story in a kind of call-and-response. In *Like One of the Family*, Marge's reactions to Mildred's tales are in the form of ellipses, and we can, as Harris points out, insert our own agreement at these moments (" 'I Wish' " 25). La Vinia Delois Jennings argues that Childress's satire "is designed to prick the conscience of her white readers while exorcising the anger of the black maids and butlers who have been victimized by similar dehumanizing acts" (40). In fact, all of Childress's novels can be read in this way. By putting her characters physically before the reader and using the first person, Childress gives her characters their fullness and their humanity.

CRITICAL RECEPTION

Although Childress has had a broad and active career, her work has not received much attention. As Harris notes, Childress receives only glancing notice in theater histories, despite the fact that she was a pioneer and responsible for many important developments in that medium. Even less consideration has been given to her prose. Harris believes one possible reason that *Like One of the Family* has been overlooked is because the stories originally appeared in Paul Robeson's magazine, *Freedom*; some critics considered this to be "an unfortunate publication because of Robeson's connections with the Communist party and his ensuing difficulties with the US government" (*Dictionary* 68). The book fell out of print, and Harris, after meeting Childress in 1978, worked to see it republished. One possible reason that *A Hero Ain't Nothin' but a Sandwich* and *Rainbow Jordan* have not been written about, despite their critical success, is that they are labeled "juvenile fiction." These books were classified this way since Coward, McCann & Geoghegan editor Ferdinand Monjo approached Childress about writing a young adult book on children and drugs. "Why should it be a young adult book?" Childress asked him about what would become *A Hero*. " 'It seems to me it should be an adult book that may be about a child.' 'It's a young adult book because I'm vice-president of the young adult division,' " Monjo replied (Maguire 63). Since *Rainbow Jordan* and *Those Other People* followed from Coward, they were also labeled this way. As with the others, the writing about *A Short Walk* came mostly in the form of book reviews. Though the reaction was generally positive, some believe that a negative review by Alice Walker "carried the day" (Jennings 15). Childress often noted in her writings and in interviews the difficulties African American writers face in finding an audience for their work. "Regarding the Black experience, we are on particularly shaky ground, since no major Black critic has the power to place a play, movie, book or other art work in the winner's circle" ("Knowing" 9). Despite the lack of critical response, Childress was writing up until her death. A remark she made to Doris Abramson in the 1950s could easily apply to her entire career: "Am working on two new plays. Why? Why? Why? I can't stop and the market being what it is—I should—How I wish I could stop. But there is an inner clock that keeps ticking away and running the works in one direction" (259).

BIBLIOGRAPHY

Works by Alice Childress

Florence, A One Act Drama. American Negro Theatre, New York. 1949. *Masses and Mainstream* 3 (1950): 34–47.
Just a Little Simple. Club Baron Theatre, New York. 1950.
"For a Negro Theater." *Masses and Mainstream* 4 (1951): 61–64.
Gold through the Trees. Club Baron Theatre, New York. 1952.
Trouble in Mind. Greenwich Mews Theatre, New York. 1955. *Black Theater*. Ed. Lindsay Patterson. New York: Dodd, Mead, 1971. 135–74.
Like One of the Family: Conversations from a Domestic's Life. Brooklyn: Independence, 1956.
"The Negro Woman in American Literature: A Woman Playwright Speaks Her Mind." *Freedomways* 6 (1966): 14–19.
Wedding Band: A Love/Hate Story in Black and White. University of Michigan, Ann Arbor. 1966. (Play). New York: French, 1973. (Television script)
"The Black Experience: Why Talk about That?" *Negro Digest* 16 (1967): 17–21.
"Black Writers' Views on Literary Lions and Values." *Negro Digest* 17 (1968): 36, 85–87.
"But I Do My Thing." *New York Times* 2 Feb. 1969: D9.
The Freedom Drum. Music by Nathan Woodard. Retitled *Young Martin Luther King*. Tour 1969–1972.
String. Saint Mark's Playhouse, New York. 1969. (Play). 1979. (Television script)
Wine in the Wilderness: A Comedy-Drama. New York: Dramatists Play Service, 1969.
Mojo: A Black Love Story. New Heritage Theatre, New York, 1970.
Ed. *Black Scenes: Collections of Scenes from Plays Written by Black People about Black Experience*. New York: Doubleday, 1971.
Mojo and String: Two Plays. New York: Coward, McCann & Geoghegan, 1971.
"The Soul Man." *Essence* May 1971: 68–69, 94.
"Tribute—To Paul Robeson." *Freedomways* 11 (1971): 14–15.
A Hero Ain't Nothin' but a Sandwich. New York: Coward, McCann & Geoghegan, 1973. (Novel). 1977. (Screenplay)
When the Rattlesnake Sounds. New York: Coward, McCann & Geoghegan, 1975.
Let's Hear It for the Queen. New York: Coward, McCann & Geoghegan, 1976.
Sea Island Song. Charleston, South Carolina. 1977. Retitled *Gullah*. University of Massachusetts, Amherst. 1984.
A Short Walk. New York: Coward, McCann & Geoghegan, 1979.

"Knowing the Human Condition." *Black American Literature and Humanism*. Ed. R. Baxter
 Miller. Lexington: University Press of Kentucky, 1981. 8–10.
Rainbow Jordan. New York: Coward, McCann & Geoghegan, 1981.
"A Candle in the Gale Wind." *Black Women Writers (1950–1980): A Critical Evaluation*. Ed.
 Mari Evans. Garden City, NY: Anchor Press, 1984. 111–16.
Moms: A Praise Play for a Black Comedienne. Music by Nathan Woodard. New Lex Theatre,
 New York, 1986.
"Alice Childress." *Interviews with Contemporary Women Playwrights*. Ed. Kathleen Betsko and
 Rachel Koenig. New York: Beech Tree Books, 1987. 62–74.
Those Other People. New York: Putnam, 1989.
"Alice Childress." *Speaking for Ourselves: Autobiographical Sketches by Notable Authors of
 Books for Young Adults*. Ed. Donald R. Gallo. Urbana, IL: National Council of Teachers
 of English, 1990. 39–40.
"Keynote Address." *International Women Playwrights: Voices of Identity and Transformation—
 Proceedings of the First International Women Playwrights Conference, October 18–23,
 1988*. Metuchen, NJ: Scarecrow Press, 1993. 11–14.

Studies of Alice Childress

Abramson, Doris. "Trouble in Mind." *Negro Playwrights in the American Theatre 1925–1959*.
 New York: Columbia University Press, 1969. 188–205, 258–59.
Brown-Guillory, Elizabeth. "Alice Childress: A Pioneering Spirit." Interview with Alice Chil-
 dress. *Sage: A Scholarly Journal on Black Women* 4 (1987): 66–68.
——. "*A Hero Ain't Nothin' but a Sandwich*." *Masterpieces of African-American Literature*. Ed.
 Frank N. Magill. New York: HarperCollins, 1992. 193–96.
Bullins, Ed. Rev. of *A Hero Ain't Nothin' but a Sandwich*. *New York Times Book Review* 4
 Nov. 1973: 36ff.
Curb, Rosemary. "Alice Childress." *Twentieth-Century American Dramatists*. Ed. John
 MacNicholas. Detroit: Gale, 1981. Vol. 7 of *Dictionary of Literary Biography*. 118–24.
Davis, Helen. "Laughter and Anger." Rev. of *Like One of the Family: Conversations from a
 Domestic's Life*. *Masses and Mainstream* 9 (1956): 50–51.
Govan, Sandra. "Alice Childress's *Rainbow Jordan*: The Black Aesthetic Returns Dressed in
 Adolescent Fiction." *Children's Literature Association Quarterly* 13 (1988): 70–74.
Harris, Trudier. "Alice Childress." *Afro-American Writers after 1955*. Ed. Thadious Davis and
 Trudier Harris. Detroit: Gale, 1985. Vol. 38 of *Dictionary of Literary Biography*.
 66–79.
——. "Beyond the Uniform: Alice Childress, *Like One of the Family* (1956)." *From Mammies
 to Militants: Domestics in Black American Literature*. Philadelphia: Temple University
 Press, 1982. 111–33.
——. " 'I Wish I Was a Poet': The Character as Artist in Alice Childress's *Like One of the
 Family*." *Black American Literature Forum* 14 (1980): 24–30.
Hill, Elbert. "A *Hero* for the Movies." *Children's Novels and the Movies*. Ed. Douglas Street.
 New York: Frederick Unger, 1983. 236–43.
Holloway, Clayton. "The Alembic of Genius: An Interview with Alice Childress." *Xavier Re-
 view* 17 (1997): 5–22.
Jennings, La Vinia Delois. *Alice Childress*. New York: Twayne, 1995.
Maguire, Roberta. "Alice Childress." *The Playwright's Art: Conversations with Contemporary
 American Dramatists*. Ed. Jackson Bryer. New Brunswick: Rutgers University Press,
 1995. 48–69.
McLellan, Joseph. "Harlem in the '30s: A Society in Flux and a Heroine Standing Firm and
 Taming the Fury." *Washington Post Book World* 28 Dec. 1979: D8.
Ortiz, Miguel A. "The Politics of Poverty in Young Adult Literature." Rev. of *A Hero Ain't*

Nothin' but a Sandwich. Lion and the Unicorn: A Critical Journal of Children's Literature 2 (1978): 6–15.

Richardson, Eni Carol. Rev. of *Rainbow Jordan. Black Books Bulletin* 7 (1981): 65.

Rogers, Norma. "To Destroy Life." Rev. of *A Hero Ain't Nothin' but a Sandwich. Freedomways* 14 (1974): 72–75.

Shepard, Ray Anthony. Rev. of *A Hero Ain't Nothin' but a Sandwich. Interracial Books for Children Bulletin* 6 (1975): 4.

Sloan, James Park. "Three Novels." Rev. of *A Short Walk. New York Times Book Review* 11 Nov. 1979: 14.

Strang, Robert. Rev. of *Those Other People. Bulletin of the Center for Children's Books* 42 (1988): 117–18.

Tait, Marianne Pride. Rev. of *Those Other People. Booktalker* 1 (1989): 14–15.

Troutman-Robinson, Denise. "The Elements of Call and Response in Alice Childress' *Like One of the Family.*" *MAWA Review* 4 (1989): 18–21.

Tyler, Anne. "Looking for Mom." Rev. *of Rainbow Jordan. New York Times Book Review* 26 April 1981: 52–53.

Walker, Alice. "A Walk through 20th Century Black America: Alice Childress's *A Short Walk.*" *Ms.* Dec. 1979: 46, 48.

Wilson, Geraldine. "A Novel to Enjoy and Remember." Rev. of *A Short Walk. Freedomways* 20 (1980): 101–2.

——. Rev. of *Rainbow Jordan. Interracial Books for Children Bulletin* 12 (1981): 24–25.

SANDRA CISNEROS (1954–)

Joy Castro

BIOGRAPHY

Sandra Cisneros was born in Chicago in 1954, the only daughter and the third of seven children of a middle-class Mexican father, Alfredo Cisneros Del Moral, who became an upholsterer after moving to the United States, and a working-class Mexican American mother, Elvira Cordero Anguiano. Cisneros's childhood was marked by poverty and instability. At regular intervals, her father took the family back to his parents' home in Mexico City for visits that lasted months at a time. When they returned to Chicago, they moved inevitably to a different house or economically depressed neighborhood. The frequent moves and new schools were disruptive for young Cisneros, who explains, "They caused me to be very introverted and shy. Because we moved so much, and always in neighborhoods that appeared like France after WWII— empty lots and burned out buildings—I retreated inside myself" (Sagel 74). Literature turned out to be a saving grace: Her mother took Cisneros to the library every week, and she became an avid reader. In high school, where a female teacher encouraged her talent, Cisneros edited the school literary magazine.

Cisneros attended Loyola University, where she graduated with a BA in English in 1976. She continued her literary studies at the University of Iowa Writers' Workshop, from which she received an MFA in 1978. Although as a Latina, Cisneros felt alienated there and believed that diversity and difference were discouraged, her breakthrough as a writer nonetheless occurred at Iowa.

Discussing the images of home in Gaston Bachelard's *Poetics of Space* in a seminar, Cisneros realized that her experience had been excluded from traditional narratives of artistic development. For Bachelard—and, according to Cisneros, for the professor and other participants in the class—the symbol of the house represents safe, secure space that offers pleasant seclusion to the dreamer and untroubled leisure time for creation. Frustrated and uneasy with a metaphor that conflicted with her experience, Cisneros determined to write against the assumptions of class privilege that informed

Bachelard's book, deliberately exploring in her work issues to which her peers and instructor seemed to have little access: poverty, sexual violence, racism, and the spectrum of Chicana experience. *The House on Mango Street*, the linked collection of stories and prose poems that emerged as her response to Bachelard's nostalgic utopia, was published in 1984 in an edition of 500 copies by Arte Público Press. Lyrical and moving, the semiautobiographical *Mango Street* is shaped by Cisneros's struggle to define her own ethnic, class, and gender identities. Cisneros reflects, "That's precisely what I chose to write: about third-floor flats, and fear of rats, and drunk husbands sending rocks through windows, anything as far from the poetic as possible. And this is when I discovered the voice I'd been suppressing all along without realizing it" ("Writer's Notebook" 73).

After graduating from Iowa, Cisneros taught for three years at an alternative high school for Latino youth in Chicago, where she became involved in Latino activism. With the publication of *Mango Street* in 1984, Cisneros's career skyrocketed. *Mango Street* was followed by two books of poetry, *My Wicked Wicked Ways* (1987) and *Loose Woman* (1994), and a collection of short stories, *Woman Hollering Creek and Other Stories*, whose publication by Random House in 1991 coincided with the printing of a Vintage edition of *Mango Street*. An illustrated children's book, *Hairs/Pelitos*, based on one of the *Mango Street* vignettes, appeared in 1994. Cisneros has received, among other awards, a MacArthur Fellowship, two National Endowment for the Arts Fellowships, the Lannan Literary Award, the Before Columbus American Book Award, and the Dobie-Paisano Fellowship. She lectures extensively and has taught at institutions across the United States.

Cisneros, who moved to San Antonio in 1984 to become the director of the Guadalupe Cultural Center, continues to make her home there in a border zone of the historic King William district that straddles poor and wealthy neighborhoods. Currently at work on the long-awaited novel *Caramelo*, she remains, as she famously puts it in the biographical note of *Mango Street*, "nobody's mother and nobody's wife" (111).

MAJOR WORKS AND THEMES

Issues that preoccupy Cisneros's work are the achievement of identity within community and the negotiation of cultural borders. Her fiction and poetry explore what it means to be a Chicana feminist in a white, male-dominated society: to function both within a patriarchal Latino culture that insists upon women's subservience and within the mainstream US culture, which has traditionally excluded Latinos and the poor.

A series of forty-four linked vignettes narrated in the first person, *The House on Mango Street* describes a pivotal year in the life of an adolescent Mexican American girl. In a pure, lyrical voice, Esperanza Cordero registers her keen apprehension of the ethnic tension, economic division, and gender injustice that surround her. The titular house functions as the key metaphor in the narrative, for Esperanza's hardworking parents have promised their children "a real house that would be ours for always so we wouldn't have to move each year," a white house "with trees around it, a great big yard and grass growing" (4). The cramped, dilapidated house on Mango Street deflates Esperanza's expectations. Observing family, friends, and neighbors, she bears witness to the thwarted lives around her, develops a sophisticated understanding of her complex social location, and constructs a definition of her identity that both critiques and embraces her community. Esperanza's given name means "hope" in Spanish (her surname comes from Cisneros's mother's name); as she matures in the *barrio*, her development of identity coincides with her growing willingness to bring hope to her community by speaking for it as the writer she becomes during the course of the narrative.

Esperanza defines her identity in opposition to that of the Latina women she sees around her who have pinned their hopes on heterosexual romance and now suffer spousal abuse or abandonment, the burdens of rearing children in poverty, and the creativity-crushing demands of traditional femininity. In an echo and expansion of Virginia Woolf's private room, posited as a prerequisite for the flourishing of women's creativity in *A Room of One's Own*, Esperanza discovers and articulates her desire for a house of her own: "Not a man's house. Not a Daddy's," but a space for reading, writing, and solitude, "a house quiet as snow, a space for myself to go, clean as paper before the poem" (108). Alarmed and instructed by the lives of the women around her, she rejects the traditional feminine role within Mexican American culture, stating, "I have begun my own quiet war. Simple. Sure. I am one who leaves the table like a man, without putting back the chair or picking up the plate" (89).

Mango Street functions also as a *kunstlerroman*, for Esperanza's development of identity is intimately linked to her growing recognition of herself as a writer. Her poetry writing is nurtured by women in her family and neighborhood; she is encouraged by her Aunt Lupe and trades poems with her friend Minerva. Moreover, through her own creativity, Esperanza fulfills the unmet creative promise of her mother, whose artistic abilities and desires—she can sing an opera and used to draw—have been subsumed by childcare and housework. Esperanza's mother offers her own life as a cautionary tale for her daughter, encouraging her to choose not romantic love, but education and the fulfillment of her talent: "Esperanza, you go to school. Study hard. That Madame Butterfly was a fool" (91). In the final story, Esperanza imagines neighbors wondering, "What happened to that Esperanza? Where did she go with all those books and paper?" (110). Esperanza's ambitions, however, become rooted in a moral commitment to Mango Street's less fortunate inhabitants.

The book's genre has been variously described as a novel, a short story cycle, and a series of prose poems or vignettes. The lyric quality of the voice is striking, and the narrative does describe—if loosely—the rise-and-fall trajectory of the traditional novelistic structure. Read this way, the climax of the work is formed by Esperanza's bitter passage into maturity, via her expulsion from an Eden of childhood innocence in "The Monkey Garden" and the betrayal and sexual assault that occur in the following chapter, "Red Clowns." After this assault, Esperanza resolves not only to escape Mango Street, as she has always dreamed of doing, but also to return—at the urging of "The Three Sisters," mysterious older women whose prophetic wisdom suggests that of the Fates in classical mythology—in order to help "the ones who cannot leave as easily" (105). The final story, "Mango Says Goodbye Sometimes," repeats verbatim the book's opening sentences, providing the narrative with a powerful sense of formal closure. Its circular structure thus echoes its content, for one of the sisters exhorts Esperanza, "When you leave you must remember to come back for the others. A circle, understand? You will always be Esperanza. You will always be Mango Street. You can't erase what you know. You can't forget who you are" (105). For Esperanza, the sister's words offer a model for relational identity and a strategy for the simultaneous affirmation of self and community.

In many ways, *Mango Street* is an autobiographical work of fiction—a portrait of the artist as a young woman of color. Cisneros gives voice to a dramatically expanded range of perspectives in her subsequent fiction collection, *Woman Hollering Creek*, which attempts to address the diversity of Latino experience. In "Never Marry a Mexican," one of the book's most powerful pieces, the young Latina mistress of a white man realizes that she has been exploited and takes an unusual revenge. Another story, "Eyes of Zapata," set in early twentieth-century Mexico and narrated from the point of view of revolutionist Emiliano Zapata's common-law wife, traces the political back to the personal: "Don't you see? The wars begin here, in our hearts and in our beds" (105). Loneliness and poverty inform several of the stories, such as "Los Boxers," in which a lonely widower chats with a young mother in a laundromat, and "There Was a Man, There Was a Woman," in which a lonely and compatible man and woman long for companionship but, owing to their different work schedules, never meet. Stories like the frequently anthologized "Eleven" and "Barbie-Q" explore Latina childhood and are similar in tone and structure to the vignettes of *Mango Street*.

The title story, "Woman Hollering Creek," examines the seductive, destructive promise of traditional heterosexual romance and the redemptive possibilities offered by female solidarity and the liberated imagination. It tells the story of Cleófilas, a young Mexican woman filled with dreams of romance from movies, *telenovelas* (Spanish-language soap operas), and tabloids. She comes to Texas as a bride, only to find herself isolated and lonely in her husband's house as their relationship deteriorates: He begins to hit her; she becomes pregnant; he philanders. Since the narrative focuses closely on the young woman's subjectivity, the reader does not realize the severity of the domestic abuse until, pregnant with her second child, the protagonist visits a clinic. A female staff member calls her friend, Felice, to help Cleófilas, explaining, "This poor lady's got black-and-blue marks all over" (54). Felice drives the young woman and her son to San Antonio, where they can catch a bus back to Cleófilas's family in Mexico. Border-crossing organizes the story: crossing from Mexico to the United States and crossing Woman Hollering Creek, the narrative's key image. When she first crosses the bridge over the creek that borders her married home, "pain or rage" are the only alternatives Cleófilas can imagine as reasons why a woman might holler. Yet, when driving Cleófilas and her son across, Felice "open[s] her mouth and let[s] out a yell as loud as any mariachi." Cleófilas is shocked, but Felice— who drives a pickup and is unmarried—redefines the possible for her: "Makes you want to holler like Tarzan, right?" (55).

Cisneros is as well known for her poetry as for her fiction, and the same themes echo through both. The collections *My Wicked Wicked Ways* and *Loose Woman* explore Chicana girlhood, brashly independent female sexuality, and the challenges of overcoming obstacles to make a space for creative expression. Here, as in her fiction, genre is challenged and redefined, for much of Cisneros's poetry is driven by a strong narrative impulse. In all her work, Cisneros explores the multiple marginalization of Latinas, who must face a larger culture that fails to corroborate their experience— they are neither white nor middle class—as well as male dominance within their own culture. Her powerful poetics of identity blends English with Spanish to tell stories of bright, rebellious girls coming of age and women bonding to help one another. "I'm trying to write the stories that haven't been written," Cisneros explains. "I feel like a cartographer; I'm determined to fill a literary void." Charting the *barrios* and borderlands of Mexican American experience, she revels in challenging mainstream assumptions: "I'm the mouse who puts a thorn in the lion's paw" (Sagel 74).

CRITICAL RECEPTION

The work of Sandra Cisneros broke crucial ground in American literature. Until the 1980s, the only Chicano writers who had crossed into mainstream literary culture were men such as Rolando Hinojosa and Rudolfo Anaya. As the first Chicana writer to make that transition, Cisneros became the predominant figure in a group of Latina writers—including Julia Alvarez, Ana Castillo, Denise Chávez, Christina Garcia, and Helena María Viramontes—whose work was embraced by a mainstream U.S. audience. Praised widely by critics for its lyricism, experimentation, and exploration of Latina experience, Cisneros's oeuvre is represented in numerous anthologies, and *Mango Street* is a frequently assigned text in classes from the junior high level to graduate school, in subjects from literature to sociology to psychology. Though no book-length scholarly studies of Cisneros yet exist, citations for over 100 articles about her work—focusing primarily on the fiction—occur in the bibliography compiled by the Modern Language Association, a good indicator of scholarly interest.

BIBLIOGRAPHY

Works by Sandra Cisneros

Bad Boys. Chicano Chapbook Series 8. San Jose: Mango Press, 1980.
The House on Mango Street. Houston: Arte Público, 1984. New York: Vintage, 1991.
"From a Writer's Notebook." *Americas Review* 15 (1987): 69–79.
My Wicked Wicked Ways. Bloomington, IL: Third Woman Press, 1987.
Woman Hollering Creek and Other Stories. New York: Random House, 1991.
La Casa en Mango Street [*The House on Mango Street*]. Trans. Elena Poniatowska. New York: Vintage, 1994.
Hairs/Pelitos. New York: Knopf, 1994.
Loose Woman. New York: Knopf, 1994.
El Arroyo de la Llorona y Otros Cuentos [*Woman Hollering Creek and Other Stories*]. Trans. Liliana Valenzuela. New York: Vintage, 1996.

Studies of Sandra Cisneros

Allison, Dorothy. Interview with Sandra Cisneros. *Sandra Cisneros.* Videocassette. Dir. Dan Griggs. Santa Fe: Lannan Foundation, 1996.
Doyle, Jacqueline. "More Room of Her Own: Sandra Cisneros's *The House on Mango Street.*" *MELUS* 19 (1994): 5–35.
——. "Haunting the Borderlands: *La Llorona* in Sandra Cisneros's 'Woman Hollering Creek.' " *Frontiers* 16 (1996): 53–70.
Ganz, Robin. "Sandra Cisneros: Border Crossings and Beyond." *MELUS* 19 (1994): 19–29.
McCracken, Ellen. "Sandra Cisneros' *The House on Mango Street*: Community-Oriented Introspection and the Demystification of Patriarchal Violence." *Breaking Boundaries: Latina Writing and Critical Readings.* Ed. Asuncion Horno-Delgado, Eliana Ortega, Nina Scott, and Nancy Saporta-Sternbach. Amherst: University of Massachusetts Press, 1989. 62–71.

Olivares, Julian. "Sandra Cisneros' *The House on Mango Street*, and the Poetics of Space."
    Americas Review 15 (1987): 160–70.
Rodriguez Aranda, Pilar E. "On the Solitary Fate of Being Mexican, Female, Wicked and
    Thirty-Three: An Interview with Writer Sandra Cisneros." *Americas Review* 18 (1990):
    64–80.
Sagel, Jim. "Sandra Cisneros." *Publishers Weekly* 29 Mar. 1991: 74–75.
Valdes, Maria Elena de. "In Search of Identity in Cisneros's *The House on Mango Street*."
    Canadian Review of American Studies 23 (1992): 55–72.
——. "The Critical Reception of Sandra Cisneros's *The House on Mango Street*." *Gender, Self,
    and Society*. Ed. Renate von Bardeleben. Frankfurt: Peter Lang, 1993. 287–300.
Wyatt, Jean. "On Not Being *La Malinche*: Border Negotiations of Gender in Sandra Cisneros's
    'Never Marry a Mexican' and 'Woman Hollering Creek.' " *Tulsa Studies in Women's
    Literature* 14 (1995): 243–71.
Yarbro-Bejarano, Yvonne. "Chicana Literature from a Chicana Feminist Perspective." *Chicana
    Creativity and Criticism: Charting New Frontiers in American Literature*. Ed. Maria
    Herrera-Sobek and Helena María Viramontes. Houston: Arte Público, 1988. 139–45.

J. CALIFORNIA COOPER (19??–)

Michelle L. Taylor

BIOGRAPHY

Joan California Cooper, or J. California Cooper, as she is known to her readers, intensely guards her private life. Very little is known about Cooper's personal life, including her birth date, which is absent from all material about her life and work. What we do know about this native of Berkeley, California, is that she was born to Maxine Rosemary and Joseph C. Cooper and that she has one daughter, Paris Williams, to whom she dedicates many of her works. The link between family and artistic production is an important one because, as she comments in an interview in *I Know What the Red Clay Looks Like: The Voice and Vision of Black Women Writers* (1994), her mother's influence was crucial to her own development as a writer: "My writing is an accumulation of information from things I've read, things I've seen and observed. My mother used to tell me: 'Any fool can get some fun, you need to get some sense.' My love for reading came from her, because her head was always in the books" (Carroll 66).

Cooper's inherited love of reading quickly translated to a love for writing, and she began writing and performing plays for family and friends at an early age. Again, Cooper attributes her craft to her mother: "When I turned eighteen, my mother made me stop playing with paper dolls, so I started to write down their stories, then I began writing plays" (Carroll 65). The plays that Cooper initially performed for family and friends later received both critical and popular praise. Cooper's play *Strangers* earned her the Black Playwright of the Year Award in 1978. By the mid-1990s, Cooper had written over seventeen plays. One of her most well-known plays, *Loners*, is anthologized in Eileen J. Ostrow's *Center Stage* (1981). Cooper's plays caught the attention of acclaimed writer Alice Walker, who encouraged her to begin writing prose. Walker's influence proved to be instrumental to Cooper's career. Walker's publishing company, Wild Trees Press, published her first collection of short stories, *A Piece of Mine*, in 1984, and Walker also wrote the foreword to the book. *A Piece of Mine* is a collection of twelve short stories that introduce the reader to Cooper's folk-inspired storytelling. This collection, like many of her later collections, is narrated by women and focuses on love, betrayal, and spiritual renewal. Cooper returns to these themes in her second collection of short stories, *Homemade Love* (1986), which won the 1989 American Book Award. By 1987 Cooper had published a third collection of stories, *Some Soul to Keep*, which was also praised for its conversational, folksy rendering of life's trials and tribulations. Cooper again garnered national recognition when she received the James Baldwin Writing Award in 1988. During the years following the Baldwin Writing Award, Cooper published two texts, including her first novel, *Family* (1991). Unlike her short stories, *Family* is a neo-slave narrative that tells the story of a family's struggle for freedom and dignity in antebellum America. Cooper quickly returned to short stories in that same year, with the publication of *The Matter Is Life*. She revisits familiar territory in this collection through her focus on women's triumph over abuse and victimization. By 1994 Cooper published her second novel, *In Search of Satisfaction*. Based in the fictional town of Yoville, a town reminiscent of William Faulkner's Yoknapatawpha County, the novel continues themes first introduced in her short stories. In 1995 Cooper published her fifth collection of short stories, *Some Love, Some Pain, Sometime*. Three years later, Cooper published her longest novel, *The Wake of the Wind*. Like *Family*, *The Wake of the Wind* explores the effects of the slave past through one family's development/transition from emancipation through the turn of the century. Cooper's most recent collection of short stories, *The Future Has a Past*, was published in 2000 and examines the ups and downs in the lives of ordinary women.

MAJOR WORKS AND THEMES

Cooper's work has found a receptive audience among readers of popular fiction. In many ways, her writing bears a striking resemblance to nineteenth-century popular fiction and sentimentality, as seen through her use of direct address, improbable co-incidences, and emotionally stirring monologues. Importantly, Cooper revises these tropes by examining key social issues such as drug abuse and domestic violence and by placing the narrative action within an African American cultural framework.

Cooper is best known for her short stories, which convey messages that concern self-love and self-reliance. Perhaps the most notable aspect of her stories is the folk-inspired/vernacular language that she uses. In many cases, the language sounds more like a conversation between friends than a short story. But the simplicity and com-monsensical approach to storytelling should not obscure the seriousness of the issues that Cooper depicts. Alice Walker comments on the folk wisdom of Cooper's work: "In its strong folk flavor, Cooper's work reminds us of Langston Hughes and Zora Neale Hurston. Like theirs, her style is deceptively simple and direct, and the vale of tears in which some of her characters reside is never so deep that a rich chuckle at a foolish person's foolishness cannot be heard" (ix). Cooper's use of humor is apparent in her first collection of short stories, *A Piece of Mine*, a collection of twelve stories that are narrated by an assortment of colorful characters, ranging from friends and relatives to neighbors. All of the stories share the common theme of finding a sense of inner peace and personal resolve. For example, "Sins Leave Scars" tells the story of Lida Mae, a young girl born to an overburdened mother who has little time for her nine children. Like many of the characters in Cooper's stories, Lida Mae is beautiful, which leads to all-too-often abusive relationships with older men. After a violent encounter with her married lover's wife, Lida Mae is left with both physical and emotional scars. Although Lida Mae never acknowledges the effect of her abuse, her best friend, and the narrator of the story, realizes that outward beauty offers no protection against emotional and physical abuse.

Cooper's success with short stories continued with *Homemade Love* in 1986, a collection of short stories that revisits many of the same themes first introduced in *A Piece of Mine*. In 1987 Cooper published *Some Soul to Keep*, a collection of five long stories that focus on the enduring power of the human spirit. In particular, "Feeling for Life" examines the life of a young woman, Christine, blind since birth, who has to learn to live on her own after her mother's death. After being forced to live alone and enduring a series of devastating events, she manages to find happiness in her adult life that includes a happy and healthy relationship. By the end of Christine's story, she has come to terms with her life, as indicated by the closing lines of the story: "We eat, we laugh, we play, we fuss together. We are a family. . . . I been blessed! I can't see a thing . . . but I got feelings you wouldn't *believe!* Well, I have told you all the things I do and all the things I have done. You know I am tired. Happy tired" (211). The final lines of the story serve as a testimony to Christine's personal journey that could also be applied to many of Cooper's other stories.

The interrelated themes of happiness and personal satisfaction are also important to the plot of Cooper's first novel, *Family*. *Family* is narrated by Chlora, a former slave who committed suicide rather than endure a life of enslavement. The novel follows Chlora as she watches over lives of the children she left behind. Ultimately, the novel reinforces Cooper's commitment to creating stories that reconstruct the African American experience and affirm the power of the human spirit.

Only a few months after the publication of *Family*, Cooper published her fourth collection of short stories, *The Matter Is Life*. Told in the same conversational tone that Cooper is known for, the stories in this collection return to familiar territory. Cooper's second novel, *In Search of Satisfaction*, is set in a fictional segregated town of Yoville. The novel focuses on the lives of two sisters, one white and the other black, and the struggles they endure as they attempt to come to terms with the complicated nature of their family relationships.

Cooper returned to short stories in 1996 with the publication of *Some Love, Some Pain, Sometime*. As the title of the collection suggests, the stories focus on love, happiness, and ultimately personal satisfaction. One of the most memorable stories in the collection, "The Way It Is," examines love and relationships in the lives of older women. In the character of Melly, Cooper creates a self-assured older woman who refuses to allow her age to hinder her chances for love. By the end of the story, Melly finds love and happiness with her high school sweetheart.

The themes of love, pain, and hardship are also well served in Cooper's third novel, *The Wake of the Wind*. This novel traces the lives of two families as they build a life for themselves in post-Emancipation Texas. In a sweeping tale that follows the family up to the turn of the century, along with Cooper's usual affirmation of the human spirit, the novel also chronicles the challenges faced by many African Americans after emancipation.

Cooper's latest work is a collection of four novellas, *The Future Has a Past*. Here, she examines the vexed relationship between choices and consequences. Cooper returns to the personal, conversational tone for which she is known as she tells stories of love and betrayal. Among the best in the collection is "A Shooting Star," which tells the story of Lovene, who "was the kind of girl who was so happy to have a vagina she didn't know what to do" (3). Though Lovene has a good heart and gentle spirit, her misguided search for love leaves her empty and alone.

CRITICAL RECEPTION

In many ways, Cooper's stories are modern-day cautionary tales meant to warn her readers of the dangers of a lack of self-respect. Despite the didactic tone of some of her stories, Cooper has become a favorite among readers of popular fiction. Rebecca Carroll's interview in *I Know What the Red Clay Looks Like* addresses Cooper's popularity. Her interview also explores the importance of Cooper's work in the black woman's literary tradition. The interview is particularly focused on exploring the dynamics of being a black female writer in America and delves into a discussion of Cooper's creative inspiration and creative models. Both Barbara Marshall's "Kitchen Table Talk: J. California Cooper's Use of Nommo: Female Bonding and Transcendence" and Madlyn Jablon's "Womanist Storytelling: The Voice of the Vernacular" take a more critical approach to Cooper's work. In particular, Jablon's essay places Cooper in the womanist literary tradition of storytelling that privileges the folk tradition and the vernacular. Jablon argues that Cooper's work "demands to be read aloud" (50). Jablon also argues that Cooper's stories "channel the didacticism of the sermon to recognition of women, their work, music, and pleasures" (54). Although Cooper has yet to receive substantial critical attention, the universality of her stories and novels appeals to a wide cross-section of readers who have supported her over the years. Cooper's provocative exploration of the lives of black women will certainly inspire increased critical attention.

BIBLIOGRAPHY

Works by J. California Cooper

Loners. Center Stage. Ed. Eileen J. Ostrow. Oakland: Sea Urchin Press, 1981. 17–27.
A Piece of Mine. California: Wild Trees Press, 1984.
Homemade Love. New York: St. Martin's Press, 1986.
Some Soul to Keep. New York: St. Martin's Press, 1987.
Family: A Novel. New York: Doubleday, 1991.
The Matter Is Life. New York: Doubleday, 1991.
In Search of Satisfaction. New York: Doubleday, 1994.
"Vanity." *Sisterfire: Black Womanist Fiction and Poetry.* Ed. Charlotte Watson Sherman. New York: Harper Perennial, 1994. 64–90.
Some Love, Some Pain, Sometime. New York: Doubleday, 1995.
The Wake of the Wind. New York: Doubleday, 1998.
The Future Has a Past. New York: Doubleday, 2000.

Studies of J. California Cooper

Carroll, Rebecca. "J. California Cooper." *I Know What the Red Clay Looks Like: The Voice and Vision of Black Women Writers.* New York: Carol Southern Press, 1994. 63–80.

Jablon, Madelyn. "Womanist Storytelling: The Voice of the Vernacular." *Ethnicity and the American Short Story*. Ed. Julia Brown. New York: Garland Press, 1997. 47–62.

Marshall, Barbara. "Kitchen Table Talk: J. California Cooper's Use of Nommo: Female Bonding and Transcendence." *Language and Literature in the African American Imagination*. Ed. Carol Aisha Blackshire-Belay. Westport, CT: Greenwood Press, 1992. 91–102.

Walker, Alice. "Foreword." *A Piece of Mine*. California: Wild Trees Press, 1984. vii–ix.

Yohe, Kristine. "J. California Cooper." *The Oxford Companion to Women's Writing in the United States*. Ed. Cathy N. Davidson and Linda Wagner-Martin. New York: Oxford University Press, 1995. 218.

ELLEN DOUGLAS (JOSEPHINE AYRES HAXTON) (1921–)

Elizabeth J. Wright

BIOGRAPHY

Josephine Ayres Haxton, the second of four children of Richardson and Laura Davis Ayres, was born on July 12, 1921, while her parents were visiting family in Natchez, Mississippi. A descendant of families that had lived in Mississippi since the eighteenth century, Haxton spent part of her childhood in Hope, Arkansas, where her father worked for the state highway department. The family remained in Arkansas until 1931, when they moved to Alexandria, Louisiana, where Haxton's father took a job building levees. Although conflicts with the Huey P. Long administration would later force Richardson to end his career as an engineer, the family remained in Alexandria throughout Haxton's childhood.

After graduating from Bolton High School in Alexandria in 1938, Haxton attended college, first for a year at Randolph-Macon Women's College in Lynchburg, Virginia, and then at the University of Mississippi, from which she graduated with a double major in sociology and English literature in 1942. During this time, she met her future husband, Kenneth Haxton. Following her graduation, she did brief stints at radio stations in Alexandria and Natchez, where working as a DJ permitted her time to write short stories while songs played. Haxton would become further entrenched in the literary world in 1944 when she moved to New York City and found work as a clerk at the legendary Gotham Book Mart. While living in the city, she was reunited with Kenneth Haxton, who had joined the navy and was temporarily stationed in New York City.

On January 12, 1945, Josephine married Kenneth Haxton at her grandparents' home in Natchez. Following their wedding, Josephine lived with her parents in Mississippi while Kenneth returned to naval duty. In November 1945, Haxton gave birth to her first child, Richard. Shortly afterward, she was reunited with her husband after he was discharged from the navy. The young family moved to Kenneth's hometown, Greenville, Mississippi, where he went to work at Nelms & Blum, a family clothing store.

Haxton gave birth to two additional sons during the next few years—Ayres in 1948 and Brooks in 1950. As the mother of three young children, Haxton found little time to write until her youngest child entered nursery school.

In August 1961, Haxton published her first short story, "On the Lake," in the *New Yorker*. The story would later be collected in the *O'Henry Prize Stories* for 1961. Because this story, like much of Haxton's fiction, draws from actual events and people, she adopted and continues to use the pen name "Ellen Douglas," a moniker intended in part to show homage to her paternal grandmother, Ellen, who also wrote stories. Haxton would publish her first novel, *A Family's Affairs*, in 1962. This well-received novel, which traces the lives of three generations of white women, gained mention in the *New York Times* list of the year's five best novels. In 1963 Douglas published *Black Cloud, White Cloud*, a collection of related stories that focus in depth upon the intersections of race, class, and gender. Among the stories contained in the volume is "Hold On," a longer version of "On the Lake." Once again, Douglas's work was named by the *New York Times* as among the year's best fiction.

Douglas's next novel, *Apostles of Light* (1973), was named a finalist for the National Book Award. In 1976 Douglas received a National Endowment for the Arts Fellowship to begin work on the novel *The Rock Cried Out*. Published in 1979, *The Rock Cried Out* was named an alternate Book-of-the-Month selection and won the Mississippi Institute of Arts and Letters Literature Award. With her reputation as a novelist growing, Douglas continued to serve as an important critic of Southern literature. Delivered at the Faulkner and Yoknapatawpha Conference in Oxford, Mississippi, in 1980, her lectures on the famous Southern writer William Faulkner, "Faulkner's Women" and "Faulkner in Time," were collected in the published proceedings of the conference. Douglas also continued to write fiction, publishing *A Lifetime Burning* in 1982, a work that again earned her the Mississippi Institute of Arts and Letters Literature Award.

During the late 1970s and 1980s, Douglas taught at several colleges and universities while continuing to write fiction. Serving as writer-in-residence at Northeast Louisiana University from 1978 to 1982, she occupied the same position at the University of Mississippi from 1983 to 1991. After divorcing her husband in 1983, Douglas served as visiting writer at the University of Virginia in 1984. She received a second National Endowment for the Arts Fellowship in 1985, the year she began work on her most famous novel, *Can't Quit You Baby*. During this same year, the Ellen Douglas archive opened at the University of Mississippi. Having published a children's book, *The Magic Carpet and Other Tales*, in 1987, Douglas published *Can't Quit You Baby* in 1988.

In 1990 Douglas was featured in *Southern Women Writers: The New Generation*, along with fourteen other Southern women writers including Maya Angelou, Doris Betts, Nikki Giovanni, Lee Smith, and Alice Walker. That Douglas would be included with such company points to her growing prominence. Indeed, Douglas has received a number of literary honors in recent years. In both 1992 and 1999, she held the Welty Professorship at Millsaps College. In 1995 *Southern Quarterly* dedicated an entire issue to her work. In 1996 "Grant" was published in the *O. Henry Prize Stories*. Douglas's most recent book-length work, *Truth: Four Stories I Am Finally Old Enough to Tell* (1998), represents the first time the author has felt able to tell her family's stories in a nonfiction collection. The collection was a finalist for the Robert

F. Kennedy Book Award. Douglas's most recent honor came in 2000, when she was awarded an honorary PhD from the University of Mississippi.

MAJOR WORKS AND THEMES

Similar to other Southern literature, including that of William Faulkner and Eudora Welty, Douglas's novels are intricately tied to the spaces in which they are set. Like Faulkner, who used Yoknapatawpha, a fictional county based upon the area surrounding Jackson, Mississippi, for his fiction, Douglas sets much of her fiction in Homochitto and Phillippi, fictional towns based upon Natchez and Greenville, Mississippi, respectively. In her fiction, Douglas tends to focus on how white middle-class families respond to the major political, social, and economic events of the twentieth century. Her families must deal with war, the Depression, changing social expectations for men and women, modernization, and, most significantly, integration of Euro-Americans and African Americans.

Although each of Douglas's novels is set in the South, the writer hesitates to label her writing strictly Southern. Indeed, many of Douglas's novels focus on themes that are anything but strictly Southern, as she tends to write about white middle-class women and their families. In *A Family's Affairs,* for example, Douglas tells the story of the Anderson family. With her description of three generations of white women and their marriages, Douglas is able to illustrate how gendered expectations have shifted since the beginning of the twentieth century. Douglas continues to explore family issues in *Apostles of Light*. In this novel, Douglas focuses on the politics of elder care. When an extended family must come together in order to devise a care plan for their elderly aunt, they are unexpectedly forced to confront their assumptions about family.

Douglas continues to explore the subject of marriage in *A Lifetime Burning*. After Corinne's forty-year marriage is threatened owing to her husband's affair with another man, she finds solace in writing a journal detailing her experience. Intended to be given to her children after her death, Corinne's journal is more than a lament on the state of her own marriage; rather, she uses the journal to explore her own sexuality, as she writes of her affair with another woman. Although Corinne uses her writing to explore how marriage restricts the lives of white women in general, she also suggests that white women may find new authority by bonding together.

Almost always white, Douglas's protagonists must repeatedly consider the complicated legacy that influences race relations in the South during the twentieth century. For example, in "Jesse," published in *Black Cloud, White Cloud*, Douglas writes about Anna, a young white mother who hires Jesse, an aged African American man, to teach her son how to play guitar. After Anna discovers that Jesse has taken to drinking before teaching his lessons, she fires the man. Only then does she learn the tragic story of his childhood, in which he tells of the deaths of his mother and baby sister. Overcome by guilt, Anna wonders how she ought to deal with the situation. "Who is to absolve us?" she wonders. "And do we expect by our confessions miraculously to relieve the suffering of the innocent?" (117).

Douglas's fiction also examines the complicated relationships between white and African American women. "Hold On," published in *Black Cloud, White Cloud*, tells the story of a white woman who offers to take an African American woman along on a fishing trip. After the African American woman comes close to drowning during a sudden storm, the white woman is besieged by guilt stemming from her inability to help the woman. With "The House on the Bluff" and "I Just Love Carrie Lee," also published in *Black Cloud, White Cloud*, Douglas illustrates how white women systematically deny African American women their subjectivity. In each story, the white employer simply cannot comprehend that her loyal African American servant might have a life beyond the spaces of her employer's house. In "The House on the Bluff," Douglas writes of how a white family's love for Tété, their African American servant, blinds them to her own life. In similar fashion, "I Just Love Carrie Lee" focuses on a white woman's recollections of Carrie Lee, an African American woman who once worked for her family, to illustrate how white women rationalize their poor treatment of African Americans. These stories, written early in Douglas's career, also illustrate how white Southerners use their African American servants to shield them from the outside world.

Douglas continues to examine the relationship between white women and African American women in *Can't Quit You Baby*, a novel in which Douglas describes how white women take the emotional and physical needs of their African American female servants for granted. After fifteen years of conversation in Cornelia's kitchen, Cornelia depends upon Tweet to listen daily to her problems. The relationship continues until Tweet suffers a stroke, an event that forces Cornelia to leave her home to travel to Tweet's. While helping Tweet to recover, Cornelia comes to realize how absolutely one-sided their friendship has been after Tweet tells her, "You ain't got *sense* enough to know I hated you. I hate you all my life, even before I know you" (254). In spite of her anger, Tweet knows that she, like Cornelia, depends upon the other woman's friendship. The novel illustrates the complexity of Douglas's fiction: Although Tweet and Cornelia become friends, their friendship is complicated both by the South's history of racial segregation and, as Douglas notes, by the lies that Cornelia tells herself about their relationship (Feddersen 147). For the women to become true friends, they must first acknowledge the complex history they have inherited. Seldom able to solve such problems, the women of Douglas's fiction are at least able to acknowledge them.

Douglas's fiction also examines the impact that the civil rights era had upon white middle-class families living in the South. With *The Rock Cried Out*, Douglas creates the character Alan McLaurin, a young white man who returns to his family's farm in Mississippi during the 1970s. A poet, Alan wants only to escape the outside world; however, Douglas uses the novel to again suggest that racial division and prejudice may not be avoided. As Panthea Reid Broughton and Susan Millar Williams note, "Alan wants to return to a simple and elemental existence, but he can escape neither the past nor the present" (59). For Alan, the past entails dealing with two pivotal events that happened seven years earlier: The Ku Klux Klan's burning of an African American church near his family's farm and the death of his girlfriend in an automobile accident. As Alan discovers that the two events may be related, he is also confronted by the knowledge of his aunt's lengthy, yet secret, affair with the African American man she employs to take care of the family's land. Alan's discoveries force him to acknowledge, like so many Douglas characters, that issues of race and gender may not be displaced.

Her interest in the intersections of race, gender, and class notwithstanding, Douglas's novels often examine the permeable boundaries separating truth from fiction. In *Can't Quit You Baby*, for example, the writer becomes a visible presence in the novel as she wonders how to tell the story accurately. "Whose story will she choose to tell?" Douglas writes. "It's her prerogative to decide" (38). Similarly, the narrator/writer of *A Lifetime Burning* often tells a story only to admit that she invented it in a desperate attempt to make sense of her life. In one memorable sequence, she describes how her great-grandmother's suicide was brought on by the discovery of her affair with another woman. Only later does the narrator admit that what she presents as truth is, in fact, fiction. Of her storytelling, the narrator explains, "I invented it all. A plausible—what seemed to me plausible—explanation of the mystery of her death" (151). Douglas continues to consider how fact morphs into fiction in her latest work, *Truth: Four Stories I Am Finally Old Enough to Tell*. With this nonfiction book, Douglas tells four family stories. In the final story of the book, "On Second Creek," for example, Douglas attempts to piece together documents recounting the 1861 execution of over thirty slaves accused of planning to revolt against their masters. As she begins her retelling of the events, Douglas notes, "All history and all fiction is a tangle of truth and lies, facts and purported facts, imaginary and real events" (135). Douglas's writing attempts to do more than simply distinguish truth from lies; rather, she uses her writing to reveal that successful stories always rely upon a strange—and yet also wonderful—combination of the two.

CRITICAL RECEPTION

Since the publication of her first short story, "On the Lake," in 1961, Douglas's writing has been received with critical acclaim. Susan Isaac's 1982 review of *A Lifetime Burning* is representative of the positive reception Douglas's work has received. Isaacs writes, "Ellen Douglas has all the qualities a reader could ask of a novelist: depth, emotional range, wit, sensitivity, and the gift of language" (11). Until the 1988 publication of *Can't Quit You Baby,* which seems to have inspired new critical interest in Douglas's writing, most of the analysis of the author's work took place in dissertations. By the 1990s, however, she had gained recognition as one of the "new" Southern writers. In 1990 Panthea Reid Broughton's and Susan Millar Williams's essay on Douglas's life and writing was included in *Southern Women Writers: The New Generation*, edited by Tonette Bond Inge. Carol S. Manning's entry on Douglas also appears in *Contemporary Fiction Writers of the South: A Bio-Bibliographical Sourcebook* (1993).

Critical essays on Douglas have tended to focus on the way the author examines issues of race in her fiction. For example, Minrose C. Gwin's 1992 article, "Sweeping the Kitchen: Revelation and Revolution in Contemporary Southern Women's Writing," focuses on the politics inherent in the conversations held between Cornelia and Tweet in *Can't Quit You Baby*. Carol S. Manning's 1993 article on Douglas examines the novelist's use of realism in her works as well as her attempt to interrogate some of the more pressing moral issues that trouble the South.

In recent years, Douglas's work has gained even further critical attention. In 1995 an entire issue of *Southern Quarterly* was devoted to this author (vol. 33, no. 4). The issue includes interviews with Douglas, a reprint of a speech Douglas gave entitled, "I Have Found It," and critical studies of the writer's fiction. For example, Jan Shoemaker's essay, "Ellen Douglas: Reconstructing the Subject in 'Hold On' and *Can't Quit You Baby,"* explains that Douglas "has always been interested in the difficulty of telling (and even of knowing) the truth" (84). More recent scholarship includes

Nancy S. Ellis's 1999 article, "Ellen Douglas the Storyteller: Both Bearer and Barer of Truth," in which she describes how Douglas uses her fiction to interrogate the meaning of truth. In 2000 many of Douglas's interviews were collected in a single volume.

BIBLIOGRAPHY

Works by Ellen Douglas.

A Family's Affairs. Boston: Houghton, 1962.

Black Cloud, White Cloud. Boston: Houghton, 1963.

Where the Dreams Cross. Boston: Houghton, 1968.

Commentary on Walker Percy's The Last Gentleman. New York: Seabury, 1969.

Apostles of Light. Boston: Houghton, 1973.

The Rock Cried Out. New York: Harcourt, 1979.

"Faulkner in Time." *'A Cosmos of My Own': Faulkner and Yoknapatawpha.* Ed. Doreen Fowler and Ann J. Abadie. Jackson: University Press of Mississippi, 1981. 284–301.

"Faulkner's Women." *'A Cosmos of My Own': Faulkner and Yoknapatawpha.* Ed. Doreen Fowler and Ann J. Abadie. Jackson: University Press of Mississippi, 1981. 149–67.

A Lifetime Burning. New York: Random House, 1982.

The Magic Carpet and Other Tales. Illus. Walter Anderson. Jackson: University Press of Mississippi, 1987.

Can't Quit You Baby. New York: Macmillan, 1988.

"I Have Found It." *Southern Quarterly* 33 (1995): 7–13.

"Proust, Ava Gardner, and the Last Frontier." *Southern Review* 32 (1996): 310–14.

Truth: Four Stories I Am Finally Old Enough to Tell. New York: Plume/Penguin, 1998.

Studies of Ellen Douglas

Broughton, Panthea Reid, and Susan Millar Williams. "Ellen Douglas." *Southern Women Writers: The New Generation.* Ed. Tonette Bond Inge. Tuscaloosa: University of Alabama Press, 1990. 46–69.

Brown, Laurie Lew. "One Fragment in a Mosaic: From 'Interviews with Seven Contemporary Writers.' " *Southern Quarterly* 21 (1983): 3–22.

Dean, Michael P. "Ellen Douglas's Small Towns: Fictional Anchors." *Southern Quarterly* 19.1 (1980): 161–71.

Ellis, Nancy S. "Cornelia and the Corpse: Ellen Douglas's Use of a Hindu Tale in *Can't Quit You, Baby.*" *Notes on Mississippi Writers* 23 (1991): 67–73.

——. "An Interview with Ellen Douglas." *Notes on Mississippi Writers* 24 (1992): 1–23.

——. "Ellen Douglas the Storyteller: Both Bearer and Barer of Truth." *Publications of the Mississippi Philological Association* (1999): 65–70.

Feddersen, Rick. "An Interview with Ellen Douglas." *Conversations with Ellen Douglas.* Ed. Panthea Reid. Jackson: University Press of Mississippi, 2000. 140–49.

Gwin, Minrose C. "Sweeping the Kitchen: Revelation and Revolution in Contemporary Southern Women's Writing." *Southern Quarterly* 30. 2–3 (1992): 54–62.

Hood-Adams, Rebecca. "An Interview with Ellen Douglas." *Conversations with Ellen Douglas.* Ed. Panthea Reid. Jackson: University Press of Mississippi, 2000. 31–47.

Hunter, Lee, and Leanne Benfield. "Selective Checklist of Ellen Douglas Materials." *Southern Quarterly* 33 (1995): 149–51.

Isaacs, Susan. "Not Going Gentle at All." Rev. of *A Lifetime Burning. New York Times Book Review* 31 October 1982: 11.

Jones, John Griffen. "Ellen Douglas." *Mississippi Writers Talking II*. Jackson: University Press of Mississippi, 1983. 47–73.

Manning, Carol S. "Ellen Douglas: Moralist and Realist." *Southern Quarterly* 21.4 (1983): 117–34.

——. "Ellen Douglas (Josephine Ayres Douglas)." *Contemporary Fiction Writers of the South: A Bio-Bibliographical Sourcebook*. Ed. Joseph M. Flora and Robert Bain. Westport, CT: Greenwood Press, 1993. 91–99.

McCord, Charline R. "Interview with Ellen Douglas." *Mississippi Quarterly* 51 (1998): 291–332.

McHaney, Thomas L., and Noel Polk, eds. *Ellen Douglas. Southern Quarterly* 33.4 (1995).

Reid, Panthea, ed. *Conversations with Ellen Douglas*. Jackson: University Press of Mississippi, 2000.

——." 'I'm Writing This': A Conversation with Ellen Douglas." *Conversations with Ellen Douglas*. Ed. Panthea Reid. Jackson: University Press of Mississippi, 2000. 206–23.

Sarthous, Sharron Eve, and Thomas M. Verich. "The Ellen Douglas Manuscript Collection at the University of Mississippi." *Southern Quarterly* 33 (1995): 131–47.

Shoemaker, Jan. "Ellen Douglas: Reconstructing the Subject in 'Hold On' and *Can't Quit You Baby*." *Southern Quarterly* 33 (1995): 83–98.

Speir, Jerry. "Of Novels and the Novelist: An Interview with Ellen Douglas." *University of Mississippi Studies in English* 5 (1984/87): 231–48.

Tardieu, Betty. " 'I'm in That Secular World, Even Though I Keep Looking Around for Someplace Else to Be': Interview with Ellen Douglas." *Southern Quarterly* 33 (1995): 23–29.

Tardieu, Elizabeth Wilkinson. " 'All This World Is Full of Mystery': The Fiction of Ellen Douglas." Dissertation, Louisiana State University, 1996.

Tate, Linda Kay. "Southern Women's Fiction, 1890–1990: Traditions and Revisions." Dissertation, University of Wisconsin, 1991.

Uhry, Alfred. "Where's There's Water There Are Snakes." Rev. of *Can't Quit You, Baby. New York Times Book Review* 10 July 1988: 13.

Williams, Susan Millar (with Henry Wiencek). "Publishing Scoundrel: 'I'm a Writer Instead of a Southern Lady.' " *Conversations with Ellen Douglas*. Ed. Panthea Reid. Jackson: University Press of Mississippi, 2000. 191–205.

Wilson, Christine. "Interview with Ellen Douglas." *Southern Quarterly* 33 (1995): 15–21.

Wilson, Deborah. "Patterning the Past: History as Ideology in Modern Southern Fiction." Dissertation, Louisiana State University and Agricultural and Mechanical College, 1991.

LOUISE ERDRICH (1954–)

Ann Engar

BIOGRAPHY

Louise Erdrich was born June 7, 1954, in Little Falls, Minnesota, the eldest of Rita Joanne Gourneau and Ralph Louis Erdrich's seven children. She grew up in Wahpeton, North Dakota, where her parents taught in the Bureau of Indian Affairs boarding school. Her paternal grandparents were German and ran a butcher's shop in Little Falls; her maternal grandparents were Ojibwe (Chippewa) and French. Her grandfather, Patrick Gourneau, beader, storyteller, and powwow dancer, served as tribal chair of the Turtle Mountain Reservation. Erdrich was raised Catholic; this tradition, in addition to the Native American tradition, figures prominently in her works.

Erdrich's parents encouraged her as a small child to write. Her father paid her a nickel a story, and her mother made covers for her completed books. Her family continues to be supportive and close. Her father copyedited *The Antelope Wife* (1998), and she wrote an article with her sister Heid.

In 1972 Erdrich was among the first group of women admitted to Dartmouth, where she met Michael Dorris, head of the new Native American Studies Program and her eventual husband. She majored in English and creative writing, published a poem in *Ms.* magazine, and became interested in her Ojibwe background.

After graduation, Erdrich returned to her home state of North Dakota to work for the North Dakota Arts Council as visiting poet and teacher. She taught in the Poetry in the Schools Program and presented workshops in prisons and hospitals. She also worked at various other jobs, including sugar beet weeder and flag signaler at a construction site. In 1978 she entered the Creative Writing Program at Johns Hopkins University and, with the submission of poems (later to appear in *Jacklight*) and part of a novel, received her MFA the following year.

After graduate school, Erdrich took a job as communications director and editor of the *Circle*, a publication of the Boston Indian Council. In 1979 she returned to Dartmouth to give a poetry reading, spoke with Michael Dorris, and began writing to him.

In 1980 she served as a fellow at the MacDowell Colony in New Hampshire. In 1981 she again went to Dartmouth, this time as writer-in-residence of its Native American Studies Program, married Dorris, and became mother to his three adopted Native American children.

Erdrich and Dorris became literary as well as marriage partners. They began by writing romance fiction under the pen name Milou North to earn extra money. Later, they collaborated on *The Crown of Columbus* (1991). Their collaborative process on their individual works included editorial teamwork: One would think up an idea, write the draft, and then give it to the other for editing and revision suggestions. They would discuss characterization, syntax, and word choice and would reach agreement before submitting the work for publication. Dorris also served as Erdrich's agent.

Erdrich's first success was winning the prestigious Nelson Algren Fiction Award in 1982 with "The World's Greatest Fishermen," a story that later became the first chapter of *Love Medicine* (1984). In 1983 Henry Holt and Company published her book of poetry, *Jacklight*. Dorris suggested that Erdrich's independently published short stories "Scales" and "The Red Convertible" might fit as part of a longer novel and helped her arrange the eventual sequence of narratives that became *Love Medicine*. *Love Medicine* received the National Book Critics Circle Award for fiction and many other awards. It was followed by *The Beet Queen* (1986); *Tracks* (1988), her first manuscript, which she had started in graduate school and continually reworked; and *Baptism of Desire: Poems* (1989).

In addition to writing and mothering the three adopted children, Erdrich gave birth to three daughters. In the 1990s, she continued to publish—an expanded version of *Love Medicine* (1993), *The Bingo Palace* (1994), the autobiographical *Blue Jay's Dance: A Birth Year* (1995), *Tales of Burning Love* (1996), a children's book entitled *Grandmother's Pigeon* (1996), and *The Antelope Wife* (1998)—despite personal tragedy. Her oldest son, Abel, was struck and killed in an automobile accident; another of the older children was imprisoned for violent threats against his girlfriend and his parents; Erdrich and Dorris separated in 1996; and Dorris was charged with child sexual abuse and committed suicide in 1997. Erdrich later said that her husband had suffered from depression and sleeplessness for many years and had been suicidal since the second year of their marriage.

Erdrich now lives in Minneapolis with her three daughters by Dorris and a new daughter whose Native American father she refuses to name. She continues to write; her most recent novel was *The Last Report on the Miracles at Little No Horse* (2001), which further deepens the stories of the Lamartine, Pillager, Morrissey, and Kashpaw families. Another new book, *The Master Butcher's Singing Club*, about her German heritage is not yet published. In 2000 Erdrich opened a store, Birchbark Books, which features books by Native American writers, crafts, foods grown by Ojibwa farmers, jewelry, and CDs of Native American music. The store serves as an outlet for grass-roots native organizations.

MAJOR WORKS AND THEMES

N. Scott Momaday's *House Made of Dawn*, which was published in 1968 and received the Pulitzer Prize in 1969, ushered in what some have called the "Native American Renaissance" with a substantial body of fiction, autobiography, and poetry that has gained both critical acclaim and popularity. Louise Erdrich has taken an important role in this renaissance with her short stories, poetry, essays, and especially her novels, which have been called some of the most significant novels of the twentieth century.

Besides their Native American roots, Erdrich's novels bear evidence of the influence of postmodern and Euro-American authors, particularly William Faulkner. Like Faulkner, Erdrich creates her own region, hers centered around an Ojibwe reservation and the small town of Argus, North Dakota. This area provides the setting for six of her seven novels. Also like Faulkner, Erdrich creates family sagas; in her case, the stories of the Kashpaw, Lamartine, Morrissey, and Pillager families and their relatives interweave through the six novels. Other similarities to Faulkner include the use of multiple, conflicting voices (sometimes first person, sometimes an omniscient narrator), nonlinear narratives, a sense of the past weighing on the present, the effects of race, and intersections of the comic and the tragic.

These connections with Faulkner illuminate important themes in Erdrich's novels. One is the importance of home and place, finding and returning to the place where one belongs. William Bevis has identified an important distinction between Euro-American fiction, which often emphasizes leaving home to gain freedom and opportunity and to escape the past (as in novels such as *Adventures of Huckleberry Finn* and *The Great Gatsby*), and Native American fiction, which features stories of coming home to a society, past, identity, and place (used by Momaday, Leslie Marmon Silko, and D'Arcy McNickle). Erdrich's *Love Medicine* begins with June Kashpaw walking through an Easter snow, which she walks over like water in an attempt to come home, and ends with her son, Lipsha, crossing the water of a river and "bring[ing] her home." In her 1993 revision of the novel, Erdrich associates the image of a figure crossing the water with a woman's laboring to give birth—the formation of life and beginning of identity. In Lipsha's case, he is bringing himself home in that he has discovered who his parents are and now he must reevaluate himself. No longer an adopted orphan, he now belongs.

In between June's and Lipsha's homecomings, other characters—Albertine Johnson, King Kashpaw, Nector Kashpaw, and Bev Lamartine—all come home with varying results. Albertine, a mixed blood, like Euro-Americans has left home. At the beginning of the novel, she returns home to the reservation from nursing school and tries to repair the family by planning to tell Lipsha that June is his mother (she fails to tell him), rescuing Lynette from her husband King's attempts to drown her, and attempting to reassemble the pies that King and Lynette have smashed in their abusive fight. Neither wholly Indian nor wholly assimilated, Albertine tries to act as a bridge between European and Native American societies but is unsure of her place in a changing family and culture.

King comes home from the Twin Cities to show off the new convertible he has bought with the insurance money from his mother's death. In the course of his homecoming, King is exposed as a fake. In the city, he wears a cap given him by his wife, which boasts he is the "World's Greatest Fisherman." But the real fisherman in the family is Uncle Eli, who has lived off the land with traditional skills; King yields the hat to him and admits his insufficiency in tribal ways. King winds up thudding against his car, ripping off its antenna and side-view mirrors, and kicking in the headlights in frustration, anger, and grief. Lynette urges him to "go back home" to the Cities because "you always get so crazy when you're home" on the reservation (39). He thus has no real "home."

Nector Kashpaw leaves the reservation as a teenager to work on a movie in South Dakota and eventually finds himself posing in a "diaper" (90) for a rich white female artist. He returns home, having learned that "the only interesting Indian is dead, or dying by falling backwards off a horse" (91). Under his wife Marie's guidance, he eventually rises to become tribal chairman of the reservation.

Like King, Bev Lamartine has left the reservation and found moderate success in the Twin Cities as a salesman. He returns to the reservation to claim his son, Henry; but, once home, he recognizes that Henry and his seven brothers by different fathers are a "pack" bound by "simple unquestioning belongingness" (85), a belongingness Bev lacks. He again becomes entangled with Henry's mother, Lulu, despite his marriage to a white woman in the Twin Cities. Coming home thus leads to an understanding of who one is and one's place in the family, community, and culture but also anger, estrangement, disappointment, and death.

Indeed, two characters in *Love Medicine* can never come home. Henry Jr., now an adult Vietnam War veteran and posttraumatic stress victim, commits suicide when he cannot reconnect with home because, according to James Ruppert, his actions in Vietnam destroyed Ojibwe ideals of "war, death, honor and right thinking" (*Mediation* 133). Gerry Nanapush, Ojibwe activist and fugitive from the law, can never go home, where he is known and belongs, because he will be captured. He regretfully tells his son, Lipsha, that he will not ever have what is called a home.

Another important theme related to home is that of family, its breakdown, its strength, and its survival. Crucial to the family is the mother; and Erdrich's novels abound with mothers who abandon their children, mothers who nurture their own children and those of others, and even men who act as mothers. June Kashpaw, Adelaide Adare, Fleur Pillager, and Pauline Puyat are all mothers in the novels who abandon their children for various reasons, and their children must all strive to understand why they were abandoned. But while *The Beet Queen* begins with Adelaide Adare leaving her three helpless children at a carnival and flying off with the Great Omar, the novel ends tenderly with Celestine James Adare patiently waiting for her daughter, Dot, to return from fleeing a disastrous sugar beet celebration in a skywriter's plane. Dot describes seeing Celestine: "It is my mother, and all at once I cannot stop seeing her. . . . In her eyes I see the force of her love. It is bulky and hard to carry, like a package that keeps untying. . . . It is embarrassing. I walk to her, drawn by her, unable to help myself" (337). In *Love Medicine*, Marie Kashpaw raises five children who live, loses two others in death, and takes in June, June's abandoned son, Lipsha, and others to mother.

The other mother figure in *Love Medicine* is Marie's rival, Lulu Lamartine, who, despite various sexual adventures that led to eight sons by different fathers, is an excellent mother. She keeps a neat home, takes pride in her children, and makes her younger boy obey perfectly, while her older sons adore her and demand everyone else do so, too.

Other good mothers in Erdrich's novels include Rozin in *The Antelope Wife,* who tirelessly nurses her deathly ill daughter, Cally, after another daughter accidentally dies, and the Blue Prairie Woman, who follows and reclaims her lost daughter, Matilda. In *The Bingo Palace*, Shawnee Ray Toose is a young single mother who decides she will not be the kind of mother who abandons her child and fights for his custody. But not all motherly love is patient, self-sacrificing, and pleasant. Albertine Johnson in *Love Medicine* says her relationship with her mother was "like a file we sharpened on, and necessary in that way" (10).

Furthermore, not all mothers are the women who have given birth to the children. In *The Beet Queen*, Mary Adare tries to mother her niece, Dot, with painful consequences in her birthday party giving and hilariously disastrous consequences in imprisoning Dot's teacher in a toy box and providing Dot with a wooden maul for a prop in a school play (a maul that Dot uses to cudgel her reluctant beau). But Mary is not Dot's only non–birth mother figure. There is also her godfather, Wallace Pfef, who tries to boost Dot's self-esteem first by giving her a well-orchestrated Hawaiian-themed birthday party and then by rigging the election so Dot becomes beet queen. Both attempts fail comically and miserably.

As is obvious with Wallace, males as well as females can mother. In *Love Medicine*, for example, June leaves the care of Marie because she no longer trusts even a surrogate mother after being abandoned by her own mother and is raised by Eli Kashpaw, who teaches her traditional Ojibwa ways. In *The Antelope Wife*, Scranton Roy longs so greatly to preserve the lives of first his adopted daughter, Matilda, and then his own son, Augustus, that he miraculously is able to breastfeed them. Scranton raises Matilda until she is seven, raises Augustus after his wife dies in childbirth, and then raises Augustus's son alone. Mothering is thus a difficult, daunting, and mistake-filled task but is essential for the physical and emotional health of the children and the community as a whole.

Erdrich's novels are filled with other important themes that resonate with non-Native and Native American readers. Chief among these are romantic love; marriage; the will to survive and endure; the past, especially its interaction between native and colonizing peoples; change; loss in its many forms, including death and destruction of a people and way of life; chance, fortune, luck, and Indian gambling; tricksters and storytellers; and the need for healing through love, forgiveness, and humor.

CRITICAL RECEPTION

Erdrich's first novel, *Love Medicine*, received many honors, including the aforementioned National Book Critics Circle Award, the *Los Angeles Times* Award for best novel of the year, the Janet Kaufman Award for best first novel, and the Virginia McCormack Scully Prize for best book featuring Indians or Chicanos. It has become a staple of college syllabi and remains her most acclaimed work.

Erdrich's novels have been praised for their honest portrayal of reservation life, moving family sagas, lyric prose, complex shifts in time and voice, tonal complexity, striking imagery, and characterization, especially of women. The comedy of *The Beet Queen* and *Tales of Burning Love* has particularly been singled out, as have their portrayals of small-town midwestern life. There has been some slight criticism, however, of fragmentation, a feeling that the novels are highlighted by a series of prominent scenes rather than presenting a gradual unfolding of character and plot in both *The Beet Queen* and *Tracks*. *Tracks*, because of its setting before the time of settled reservation life, has been recognized as the most political of her novels in its subject matter of loss of Native American land. Some reviewers, however, complained that the book is didactic and that her prose verges on sentimentality and too obvious attempts at myth making.

Of all the novels, *The Bingo Palace* has received the most criticism. Erdrich's work was still called rich and complex with dazzling poetic prose, but reviewers warned that this was not the work to begin reading to understand Erdrich's skill as a writer. They did not find Lipsha a sympathetic character or his romance with Shawnee believable, perhaps because of the uncertainty of his main narrative voice.

Erdrich's *The Antelope Wife*, though it revolves around an entirely new family saga, has been called "vintage Erdrich. It's absolutely terrific and also a bit disappointing" (Postlethwaite 6). As did earlier novels, it emphasizes the power of love in intertwined Ojibwa families, uses magical realism and rich images, skips around in time, and has strong female characters. But Diane Postlethwaite observes that the novel lacks freshness, that Erdrich "has done all this before" (6). Though a similar criticism of sameness was initially leveled at *The Last Report on the Miracles at Little No Horse*, it has been highly praised for turning that sameness into a powerful, wrenching, yet slyly humorous novel written in Erdrich's dream-like, poetic prose.

BIBLIOGRAPHY

Works by Louise Erdrich

Imagination. Westerville, OH: Charles Merrill, 1981.
Jacklight. New York: Holt, 1984.
Love Medicine. New York: Bantam, 1984.
The Beet Queen. New York: Bantam, 1986.
Tracks. New York: Harper, 1988.
Baptism of Desire: Poems. New York: Harper, 1989.
Erdrich, Louise, and Michael Dorris. *The Crown of Columbus.* New York: Harper, 1991.
——. *Route Two.* Northridge, CA: Lord John Press, 1991.
Ed. *Best American Short Stories 1993.* Boston: Houghton, 1993.
Love Medicine. New and expanded edition. New York: Harper, 1993.
The Bingo Palace. New York: Harper, 1994.
The Blue Jay's Dance: A Birth Year. New York: Harper, 1995.
Grandmother's Pigeon. New York: Hyperion, 1996.
Tales of Burning Love. New York: Harper, 1996.
The Antelope Wife. New York: Harper, 1998.
The Last Report on the Miracles at Little No Horse. New York: Harper, 2001.

Studies of Louise Erdrich

Baringer, Sandra. " 'Captive Woman?': The Rewriting of Pocahontas in Three Contemporary Native American Novels." *Studies in American Indian Literature* 11 (1999): 42–63.
Beidler, Peter G., and Gay Barton. *A Reader's Guide to the Novels of Louise Erdrich.* Columbia: University of Missouri Press, 1999.
Bensen, Robert. "Creatures of the Whirlwind: The Appropriation of American Indian Children and Louise Erdrich's 'American Horse.' " *Cimarron Review* 121 (1997): 173–88.
Bevis, William. "Native American Novels: Homing In." *Critical Perspectives on Native American Fiction.* Ed. Richard F. Fleck. Washington, D.C.: Three Continents Press, 1993. 15–45.
Burdick, Debra. "Louise Erdrich's *Love Medicine, The Beet Queen,* and *Tracks*: An Annotated Survey of Criticism through 1994." *American Indian Culture and Research Journal* 20 (1996): 137–66.

Catt, Catherine M. "Ancient Myth in Modern America: The Trickster in the Fiction of Louise Erdrich." *Platte Valley Review* 19 (1991): 71–81.

Chavkin, Allan, ed. *The Chippewa Landscape of Louise Erdrich.* Tuscaloosa: University of Alabama Press, 1999.

—— and Nancy Feyl Chavkin, eds. *Conversations with Louise Erdrich and Michael Dorris.* Jackson: University Press of Missouri, 1994.

Desmond, John F. "Catholicism in Contemporary American Fiction." *America* 14 May 1994: 7–11.

Farrell, Susan. "Colonizing Columbus: Dorris and Erdrich's Postmodern Novel." *Critique: Studies in Contemporary Fiction* 40 (1999): 121–35.

Ferguson, Suzanne. "The Short Stories of Louise Erdrich's Novels." *Studies in Short Fiction* 33 (1996): 541–55.

Hansen, Elaine Tuttle. *Mother without Child: Contemporary Fiction and the Crisis of Motherhood.* Berkeley: University of California Press, 1977.

Holt, Debra C. "Transformation and Continuance: Native American Tradition in the Novels of Louise Erdrich." *Entering the 90's: The North American Experience. Proceedings from the Native American Studies Conference at Lake Superior University.* Ed. Thomas E. Schirer. Sault Ste. Marie, Ontario: Lake Superior University Press, 1991. 149–61.

Kiely, Robert. *Reverse Tradition: Postmodern Fictions and the Nineteenth Century Novel.* Cambridge, MA: Harvard University Press, 1993.

Lee, Robert A. "Ethnic Renaissance: Rudolfo Anaya, Louise Erdrich, and Maxine Hong Kingston." *The New American Writings: Essays on American Literature since 1970.* Ed. Graham Clarke. New York: St. Martin's Press, 1990. 139–64.

Lincoln, Kenneth. *Indi'n Humor: Bicultural Play in Native America.* Oxford: Oxford University Press, 1993.

Manley, Kathleen. E. B. "Decreasing the Distance: Contemporary Native American Texts, Hypertext, and the Concept of Audience." *Southern Folklore* 51 (1994): 121–35.

McKinney, Karen Janet. "False Miracles and Failed Vision in Louise Erdrich's *Love Medicine.*" *Critique: Studies in Contemporary Fiction* 40 (1999): 152–60.

Postlethwaite, Diana. Rev. of *The Antelope Wife. New York Times Book Review* 12 April 1998: 6.

Ratcliffe, Krista. "A Rhetoric of Classroom Denial: Resisting Resistance to Alcohol Questions While Teaching Louise Erdrich's *Love Medicine.*" *The Languages of Addiction.* Ed. Jane Lilienfeld and Jeffrey Oxford. New York: St. Martin's Press, 1999. 105–21.

Reynolds, Susan Salter. "Playing to Her Strengths; Louise Erdrich Writes What She Knows Best: Her American Indian Heritage, the Trials of Life and Her Devotion to Her Children." *Los Angeles Times* 16 May 2001: E1.

Ruppert, James. "Mediation and Multiple Narrative in *Love Medicine.*" *North Dakota Quarterly* 59 (1991): 229–41.

——. *Mediation in Contemporary Native American Fiction.* American Indian Literary and Critical Studies 15. Norman: University of Oklahoma Press, 1995.

Sarve-Borham, Kristen. "Games of Chance: Gambling and Land Tenure in *Tracks, Love Medicine,* and *The Bingo Palace.*" *Western American Literature* 34 (1999): 277–300.

Slethaug, Gordon E. "Centrifugal Writing, Multivocal Narration, Undecidability, and a Sense of the Past: Louise Erdrich's *Tracks.*" In *Postcolonialism and Cultural Resistance.* Ed. Jopi Nyman and John A. Stotesbury. Joensuu, Finland: Faculty of Humanities, University of Joensuu, 1999. 232–43.

Stookey, Lorena L. *Louise Erdrich: A Critical Companion.* Westport, CT: Greenwood Press, 1999.

Storhoff, Gary. "Family Systems in Louise Erdrich's *The Beet Queen." Critique* 39 (1998): 341–52.

Wong, Hertha D. Sweet, ed. *Louise Erdrich's Love Medicine: A Casebook.* New York: Oxford University Press, 2000.

MARY GAITSKILL (1954–)

Robert Johnson

BIOGRAPHY

Key figure among late-1980s American women writers dubbed "Bad Girls" (Wolcott 38), Mary Gaitskill was born November 11, 1954, in Lexington, Kentucky. She grew up, however, outside Detroit. Suburban culture deeply affected her values and artistic vision. Gaitskill remarks, "Where I lived, in Livonia, Michigan, being cool was paramount, and *cool* meant being invulnerable and blasé. It was OK to be sarcastic, aggressive, or cruel (especially if you could be clever at the same time), but displays of love and tenderness were a little embarrassing" ("Does *Little Women*" 36).

Published accounts suggest that Gaitskill received institutional psychological care as a young woman and that, in her teenage years, she lived away from her immediate family. Gaitskill claims that she did not "finish high school" (Walsh 15), yet by 1981, she had graduated from the University of Michigan, where she earned the Avery Hopwood Award for her collection *The Woman Who Knew Judo and Other Stories*, which was never published.

Gaitskill has grown reticent speaking of personal issues with critics. In the mid-1990s, though, she discussed frankly having learned a good deal about women's and men's desires while working as an exotic dancer and as a prostitute. Of the former experience, she says that adolescence had not provided her with a sense of authentic female roles, so she experimented, miming traditionally seductive guises on stage. She notes of her audience: "We were . . . in on this game that was both serious and totally ridiculous and we all knew it and we could laugh at ourselves." About sex work, Gaitskill recounts that she discovered there was "a lot of choice involved, on all levels," undercutting common images of sex workers as victims or "empowered goddesses of the night" (Walsh 17, 18). Quarreling with commentaries linking her fiction directly with this background, however, Gaitskill contends, "In my 20s, I also worked as a bookstore clerk, in a restaurant, I cleaned houses. . . . It is narrow to focus so exclusively" (Macdonald 50).

Gaitskill initially faced the daunting wave of rejection shared by many new writers. Susan Walker reports that Gaitskill received an especially stinging reaction from one publisher, who cited the writer's "distinctive voice" and hoped she would find someone who enjoyed "the sound of it." Nonetheless, Gaitskill had attracted an agent by 1985 and founded her career with the publication of her story collection *Bad Behavior* (1988). The book "quickly generated critical praise and media attention" (D14), Walker adds. Gaitskill followed with a novel, *Two Girls, Fat and Thin* (1991), and another group of stories, *Because They Wanted to* (1997). She also has established herself as an essayist and book reviewer in print media and at internet sites. What is more, Gaitskill has taught creative writing on university campuses.

Explaining why she writes, Gaitskill offers that stories "mimic life like certain insects mimic leaves and twigs." They expose life's "rich, unseen" depths. "I get great satisfaction," Gaitskill sums, "from plunging my hands into that underlayer" ("Why I Write" 78).

MAJOR WORKS AND THEMES

All of Gaitskill's fiction investigates the consequences of choice and the limits of human freedom. Gaitskill reports to a popular reference series: "My experience of life as essentially unhappy and uncontrollable taught me to examine the way people, including myself, create survival systems and psychological 'safe' places for themselves in unorthodox and sometimes apparently self-defeating ways" ("Mary Gaitskill" 144). This pursuit of survival, of connection and intimacy, leads her to believe that central to human happiness is taking responsibility for assessing and pursuing one's own—not imposed—needs.

In addition, Gaitskill challenges the popular notion that particular ranges of personal concerns properly lie beyond discussion. Gaitskill believes that such problems "always made themselves felt, one way or another, but we sort of pretended they weren't there." The cure is emotional honesty: admitting that we are "responsible" for our feelings and must find ways to live with them ("Formerly Forbidden Topics"; see also "On Not Being"). Each of Gaitskill's major published works exposes the necessity of such responsibility and the painful cost of trying to live without it.

In *Bad Behavior*, carefully delineated characters stub their emotional toes, wreck and chase their lives, and experiment with wild ranges of sexual practices, their struggles usually set against big-city backdrops—outside the windows, street trash swirls; down-and-outers speak with prophetic authority. In "Daisy's Valentine," Joey falls in love with his co-worker Daisy. Trouble is, both already have live-in partners. Delving into the nature of his feelings, Joey flirts, builds Daisy an elaborate handmade valentine, and shuns the attentions of his girlfriend. Daisy recognizes the attraction but is unsure of how to react: "If you're nice to me, I'll probably make you unhappy," she warns. "I've done that to people" (18). In the end, they discover that they do not know how to make each other happy, though they do destroy their old relationships.

What do I want? How do I get it? Both questions haunt characters in this collection. Young and free when sex is said to be liberated and the emotions unwanted baggage, when cultural myths propose that success lies everywhere for the taking, Gaitskill's characters nonetheless fumble. They know all the hip theories for living but scramble at applications. "A Romantic Weekend" pairs a young woman who claims she is a masochist with a man who fantasizes berating her. He discovers, though, she is too intellectual, sentimental: "He could tell that she was trying to like being bitten, but that she did not" (41). In spite of misgivings, the woman discovers she responds to the man, somehow needs his abuse and his attentions. Why, she cannot fathom.

"Something Nice" and "Trying to Be" explore the lives of young women who dabble at "tricking" while waiting for careers to start. They strive to protect their emotional needs from the physical demands of their business. Clients, duped in return by the theater of prostitution, believe they can purchase the women themselves. Freed from having to interact, the women are thus buoyed, yet roles inevitably blur, fueling frustration. Notably, one of the girls can find great pleasure herself simply in adoring the orderliness of a local Korean market, where everything is in "organized, traditional piles" (130).

More directly a study of deception, "Secretary" narrates the ordeal of a young woman whose combination of low sense of self and poor business skills provokes her twisted boss to punish her in ugly, demeaning ways. People who lack direction and who have not been prepared honestly to know themselves, Gaitskill shows, *will* be used.

In these early stories, characters struggle, facing imposed notions of identity. *Two Girls, Fat and Thin* deepens Gaitskill's investigation of the battle to find the self and to save it. One of the two "girls," Dorothy, responds to a request for interviews with people who once had swelled the cultish ranks of writer Anna Granite's followers. Loosely based on novelist Ayn Rand, Granite preaches a gospel of "Definitism," championing strong individuals against the demands of mass culture. Dorothy never has known real affection, has, at times, stress-eaten herself to enormous proportions, and was used sexually by her paranoid, manipulative father. She finds solace in Granite's promise of individual worth through being uniquely alone.

The other "girl" in the title is the woman who posted the call for information, Justine. Perhaps named for the Marquis de Sade's character, critics argue, she, like Dorothy, has been abused as a child but is gaunt, aggressively sexual, and has pursued her own sense of identity partly masochistically, thrilling at imposed control.

The novel shifts focus, chapter by chapter, to detail each woman's life. Finally, Dorothy rescues the writer from the hands of a sadist who has taken a session of sex play beyond limits Justine finds desirable. The book ends with Justine in Dorothy's comforting arms. The pair find completion melding their experiences and points of view—thus achieving an intimacy denied characters in *Bad Behavior*. They curl around one another in Justine's troubled bed like yin and yang. Dorothy muses: "Her body against me was like a phrase of music" (304).

Because They Wanted to develops Gaitskill's concern with identity a step further, emphasizing the search for language with which effectively to name and understand one's needs. "Tiny, Smiling Daddy" recounts a man's discovering that his once rebellious daughter has found what appears to be a contented life as a lesbian and artist. Unfortunately, without warning him, she has dissected their own tense relationship in an essay published in a national magazine. While he cannot escape recognizing the legitimacy of her identities, he resents seeing his—and her—life played out in "ghastly talk-show language" (20). "Because They Wanted to" documents tough choices faced by a runaway who takes on babysitting work for a mother who does not return to reclaim her brood. The babysitter muses through painful memories and in the end decides she cannot assume another woman's role—presumably until she sorts out her own. One widely cited piece from the collection is "The Dentist," in which a young

woman misreads the kindly behavior of her dentist, becoming in the process infatu-
ated. Inverting the usual sexual stalker motif in gender while satirizing emotional self-
delusion, Gaitskill creates a story in which, she claims, friends have found a good
deal of humor ("A Literary Lone Star" 57).

The group closes with a cycle of related tales, "The Wrong Thing," which portray
a poetry teacher's making deep decisions about whether she can commit herself to
love and be wanted in return in a world where lovers can coo, "You're so sweet I
just want to tie you up and torture you" (252). How can love, Gaitskill asks, not be
ownership?

Readers seeking introductory exposure to Gaitskill's essay work will find she pursues related themes in "Modern Romance: A Lesson in Appetite Control" (1989), a
meditation separating sexual desire from myths of romantic love; "On Not Being a
Victim," probably Gaitskill's most formal statement regarding sexual responsibility;
and "A Woman's Prerogative," in which Gaitskill defines and defends her choice not
to be a mother.

CRITICAL RECEPTION

Gaitskill's fiction has garnered a range of judgments—some openly troubled. Since
the beginning, critics have praised her narrative abilities but argued with some of the
content of her fiction. One British reviewer dismisses *Bad Behavior* as featuring a
gang of "low life, Warhol-cool neurotics and self-deceivers" (Diski 38). James Wolcott
explains the book's tone as presenting the heartbeat of an era—one in which women,
he fears, live subservient roles born of "sexual Darwinism" (38). George Garrett,
however, sees in the book the arrival of "a vital and gifted new writer." He praises
the "lean and quick and spare, tightly controlled" prose and judges Gaitskill "wise
beyond her years, utterly unsentimental" (3). Michiko Kakutani adds praise for Gaitskill's "radar-perfect detail" and "reportorial candor" (17). Responding to critics' homing in on the edgy mood of her book, Gaitskill tells Deborah Stead that her characters
are "people in a little ugly world that in their own way they try to make pretty."
Sexual pain, she notes, can "feel like love, especially if love has been connected to
violence in the past" (3).

In like fashion, *Two Girls, Fat and Thin* divides critics sharply. British reviewer
Chris Savage King calls the work a "stunning debut novel" ("Double Dare" 38), and
David Gates places the book in a tradition of American tales featuring "loners"
("Clinging" 63). Roz Kaveney praises the novel's "fully realized" portrait of emotional
complexities (19).

Nonetheless, Gaitskill's novel also has attracted some powerfully negative responses. Emblematic are Pico Iyer's complaint that Gaitskill's fiction may ultimately
be man hating (94) and Elizabeth Benedict's worry that, in stepping off into the longer
rhythms demanded by novels, Gaitskill might well have "lost her bearings" (3).

Because They Wanted to was nominated for a 1998 PEN/Faulkner Award and generally has been viewed by critics as an indication that Gaitskill has now acquired a
wider canvas and vocabulary of attitudes, though she embraces many of the same
topics. Amy Sickels judges that Gaitskill's writing has become much more mature
and perceptive. Winter N. Miller notes that as the characters "stretch their own borders, Gaitskill pushes the reader's boundaries" as well (79). David Gates believes
Gaitskill's work "has gotten more intense," that her sharpened prose dominates

even "peerless descriptions of bad sex" ("Beyond" 57). Chris Savage King calls the book "a perfectly formed set of stories" (14).

Importantly, some critical concerns remain. E. J. Graff notes that while she may be left with a "writer's envious awe" at Gaitskill's technical prowess, the stories' mulling of emotional disorder evokes a kind of uncomfortable turn on the Wordsworthian: "Gaitskill's method might be called experience recollected in distress" and denies characters resolution (9). Richard Eder raises suspicions lingering among some critics of Gaitskill's negatively portraying men (C33).

Defending the collection, however, and linking the book with Gaitskill's whole production, Ann Powers writes that, at root, Gaitskill challenges lines drawn between deviant and normal behaviors. Gaitskill's stories show that the "so-called fringe" is "utterly, painfully normal." Gaitskill's theme, she argues, remains consistent: Humans hunger after "the worth of love." Powers concludes that Mary Gaitskill "sees what's worth saving in these outsiders' lives, and as much as they mourn, these stories are also jeremiads against the modern world's assault on the soul" (51).

BIBLIOGRAPHY

Works by Mary Gaitskill

Bad Behavior. New York: Poseidon, 1988.
"Modern Romance: A Lesson in Appetite Control." *Ms.* May 1989: 55–56.
Two Girls, Fat and Thin. New York: Poseidon, 1991.
"On Not Being a Victim." *Harper's* March 1994: 35–44.
"Does *Little Women* Belittle Women?" *Vogue* January 1995: 36, 38, 44.
Because They Wanted to. New York: Simon & Schuster, 1997.
"A Woman's Prerogative." *Elle* September 1999: 283ff.

Studies of Mary Gaitskill

Benedict, Elizabeth. "The Janes versus the Johns." Rev. of *Two Girls. Los Angeles Times Book Review* 24 Feb. 1991: 3, 8.
Danto, Ginger. Rev. of *Two Girls. New York Times Book Review* 17 Feb. 1991: 1, 25.
D'Erasmo, Stacey. "Of Human Bondage." Rev. of *Bad Behavior* and *Two Girls. Voice Literary Supplement* Feb. 1991: 17.
Diski, Jenny. "Mental Deserts." Rev. of *Bad Behavior. New Statesman & Society* 21 Apr. 1989: 38–39.
Eder, Richard. "The Battle of the Sexes." Rev. of *Because. Newsday* 19 Jan. 1997: C33.
Fleming, Juliet. "The Bonds of Love." Rev. of *Because. Times Literary Supplement* 12 Dec. 1991: 21.
"Formerly Forbidden Topics Pervade Public Life." Host Linda Wertheimer. *All Things Considered.* National Public Radio. 12 May 1994. (Transcript)
Garrett, George. "Fun and Games for Sadomasochists." Rev. of *Bad Behavior. New York Times Book Review* 21 Apr. 1988: 3.
Gates, David. "Clinging to the American Edge." *Newsweek* 8 Apr. 1991: 61, 63.
——. "Beyond Bad Behavior." Rev. of *Because.* Newsweek 20 Jan. 1997: 57.
Graff, E. J. "Mixed Emotions." *Women's Review of Books* 14 (1997): 8–9.
Iyer, Pico. "Are Men Really So Bad?" *Time* 22 Apr. 1991: 94.
Kakutani, Michiko. "Seedy Denizens of a Menacing Downtown World." Rev. of *Bad Behavior. New York Times* 21 May 1988: 17.

Kaveney, Roz. "Determining the Shape of Things." Rev. of *Two Girls. Times Literary Supplement* 28 June 1991: 19.

King, Chris Savage. "Double Dare." Rev. of *Two Girls. New Statesman & Society* 5 July 1991: 38.

——. Rev. of *Because. Independent* 13 Dec. 1997: 14.

Macdonald, Jenny. "Women Writers: Still Need Room to Write." *Woman Newsmagazine* Winter 1999: 50, 57.

"Mary Gaitskill." *Contemporary Authors.* Vol. 128. Detroit: Gale, 1990. 144.

McGraw, Erin. "Larger Concerns." *Georgia Review* 51 (1997): 782–92.

Miller, Winter N. Rev. of *Because. Ms.* Jan. 1997: 79–80.

Powers, Ann. "Bodies in Trouble." Rev. of *Because. Village Voice* 4 Feb. 1997: 51.

Sickels, Amy. Rev. of *Because. Literary Review* 42 (1999): 349–51.

Stead, Deborah. "Making the Best of an Ugly Little World." *New York Times Book Review* 21 Apr. 1988: 3.

Walker, Susan. "Short Stories of Intimacy." *Toronto Star* 23 Oct. 1998: D14.

Walsh, Susan. "Notes on Trick." *Voice Literary Supplement* Sept. 1995: 15ff.

Walters, Barry. "Oh, Those Nasty Joys." Rev. of *Bad Behavior. Village Voice* 14 June 1988: 64.

"Why I Write: Six Acclaimed Writers Reveal Their Primal, Intimate, and Sometimes Mercenary Motives for Putting Pen to Paper." *Utne Reader* Nov./Dec. 1998: 76–79.

Wolcott, James. "The Good-Bad Girls." *Vanity Fair* December 1988: 38ff.

KAYE GIBBONS (1960–)

Elizabeth J. Wright

BIOGRAPHY

Kaye Batts Gibbons was born in Nash County, North Carolina, on May 5, 1960. The youngest of three children born to Charles and Alice Batts, Gibbons spent her childhood on her family's farm, where her parents grew tobacco. Life changed dramatically for Gibbons in March 1970, when her mother committed suicide at age forty-seven by taking pills. After her mother's death, Gibbons lived with her alcoholic father until she was sent in 1971 to live with her mother's sister in Bailey, North Carolina. Neither Gibbons nor her aunt was satisfied with the living arrangement, and so Gibbons was sent to live in a foster home following the death of her father in May 1972. Gibbons moved again in 1973, when she went to live with her older brother and his new wife in Rocky Mount, North Carolina. Gibbons would live there until she graduated from Rocky Mount High School in 1978.

Having completed her secondary education, Gibbons began her undergraduate education at North Carolina State University, where she majored in English. In 1980 Gibbons made plans to transfer to the University of North Carolina at Chapel Hill; however, during the fall of that year, she suffered from manic depression and thus was unable to attend university. After being hospitalized in Raleigh from August 1981 until March 1982, Gibbons recovered and was able to return to class at North Carolina State University. Manic depression would again force Gibbons to withdraw from school in 1983. During this time, Gibbons met Michael Gibbons, a graduate student in landscape architecture at North Carolina State. The couple would marry in May 1984 and would eventually have three daughters: Mary (1984), Leslie (1987), and Louise (1989). They divorced in the early 1990s.

Gibbons's career as a writer got underway during 1985, when she once again enrolled at the University of North Carolina at Chapel Hill. While a student in Louis Rubin's fall 1985 course on Southern literature, Gibbons wrote the poem "June Bug." This poem, which was published in the *Carolina Quarterly* in 1986, served as the basis for a short story that, with Rubin's encouragement, became *Ellen Foster*. Published in 1987, Gibbons's novel parallels her own life as she tells the story of Ellen, a young girl whose life is thrown into turmoil after her mother's suicide. Desperate to escape her abusive father after her mother's death, Ellen, like Gibbons, finds sanctuary after going to live in a foster home. An overnight success, Gibbons's novel garnered praise from famed Southern writers Eudora Welty and Walker Percy and was eventually awarded the Sue Kaufman Prize for first fiction from the American Academy and Institute of Arts and Letters. Her reputation as a writer firmly established, Gibbons received a National Endowment for the Arts Fellowship to work on her next novel, *A Virtuous Woman* (1989). The year 1991 saw the publication of Gibbons' third novel, *A Cure for Dreams*. For this work, Gibbons was awarded both the Nelson Algren Heartland Award for fiction, given by the *Chicago Tribune*, and the PEN/Revson Foundation Fellowship.

With the publication of each novel, Gibbons's reputation as a novelist has grown. Her three most recent novels, *Charms for the Easy Life* (1993), *Sights Unseen* (1995), and *On the Occasion of My Last Afternoon* (1998), have all been national best-sellers. Indeed, by the time *Ellen Foster* and *A Virtuous Woman* were selected for Oprah Winfrey's influential book club in October 1997, she already had a loyal following. Winfrey's book club, combined with the recent broadcast of the Hallmark Hall of Fame movie, *Ellen Foster*, has served only to increase her readership. Currently, Gibbons lives in Raleigh, North Carolina, with her husband since 1993, Frank Ward, an attorney, and her three daughters.

MAJOR WORKS AND THEMES

Like other twentieth-century Southern women writers, including Ellen Douglas, Tina McElroy Ansa, Lee Smith, and Eudora Welty, Kaye Gibbons frequently uses her fiction as a space to ruminate on the workings of family. Perhaps the most poignant discussion of family comes in *Ellen Foster*, when the title character, Ellen, embarks on a search for a new family after her mother commits suicide. At first, Ellen lives with her father, an alcoholic who frequently abuses the young girl. After a teacher intervenes and arranges to have Ellen removed from her father's home, the novel traces Ellen's experiences as she is shuttled from one family to the next.

Although Ellen can envision the notion of living with a loving family, she finds it difficult to find a family that wants to accept her as their own. After living unhappily with a series of blood relatives, including her maternal grandmother and her maternal aunt, Ellen decides to select her own family. Using what she knows about family from staying with her friend, Starletta, Ellen decides that she wants to live with Mrs. Foster, who runs a foster home for unwanted children. There Ellen finds the family for which she has longed. Perhaps more significant, being part of a safe space permits Ellen to begin to think about the difficulties that other people, including Starletta, the young African American girl who befriends Ellen early in the novel, endure.

In *Ellen Foster*, Ellen's mother's suicide marks a turning point in her daughter's life. Gibbons would continue to explore the effects of parental mental illness and its impact upon families in *Sights Unseen*. In this novel, the narrator is a young girl who focuses on her mother's frequent bouts of mental illness. Unable to understand the serious nature of her mother's condition until she is an adult, the narrator recalls how she longed for her mother during the times when she would go away for extended periods of time. What the daughter did not know was that her mother was often institutionalized during these absences. While her mother endures electroshock therapy, the daughter longs for her mother to bring order back to the home. *Sights Unseen*, like *Ellen Foster*, is concerned with the way that a daughter deals with the sudden absence of her mother. In each novel, Gibbons suggests that the loss is not one that can be easily healed.

Gibbons continues to explore the complicated relationship between mothers and daughters in *A Virtuous Woman*, *A Cure for Dreams*, and *Charms for the Easy Life.* *A Virtuous Woman* tells the story of Ruby Pitt Woodrow, a sheltered upper-middle-class white girl whose relationship with her parents is strained after she marries Jack Stokes, a tenant farmer twenty years her senior. In this unconventional relationship, Ruby finds solace that she never experienced while living at home with her parents. In similar fashion, *A Cure for Dreams* focuses on the close mother-daughter bond that connects Lottie O'Cadhain Davies and her daughter, Betty Davies Randolph. Narrated by Betty's daughter, Marjorie, the novel examines how the women rely upon each other for comfort during the depression and World War II. Gibbons continues to examine the mother-daughter relationship in *Charms for the Easy Life*, a novel that traces the lives of three generations of women. The narrator, Margaret, comes from a family of strong women. Her grandmother, Charlie Kate, is a country doctor to whom formally trained doctors turn for advice. Margaret's mother, Sophia, is a widow determined to find a good man to marry. Margaret's recollection of her mother and grandmother illustrates the solace that women may find in each other's company. Gibbons's frequent portrayal of mothers and daughters illustrates how this relationship can be both productive and destructive.

Because the relationships between mothers and daughters are at the center of many of her novels, men are often minor characters in Gibbons's fiction. Yet Gibbons does have much to say about marriage in her work. In *Ellen Foster*, Gibbons uses the suicide of Ellen's mother to show how an abusive marriage may drive a woman to mental illness. Men are described as similarly controlling in *A Cure for Dreams*. When Marjorie's father refuses to give his wife money to buy anything but the most ordinary of fabric, she responds by telling him that chintz is less expensive than gingham, organdy less expensive than cotton. In *On the Occasion of My Last Afternoon*, the insults Emma Garnet Tate Lowell's father directs at her mother make her physically ill and lead to her death. Perhaps because their relationships with men prove so disappointing, many of Gibbons's female characters choose to live independently of men. Having learned that "a man will leave you," Charlie Kate, the self-made doctor in *Charms for the Easy Life*, simply decides that she will make do without one (25).

Gibbons's novels are not, however, without positive male characters. In *A Virtuous Woman*, Jack Stokes is a dedicated and loving husband who is flummoxed by the household chores he must take on after his wife's death. In *Sights Unseen*, the narrator's father deals patiently with his wife's alternating bouts of mania and depression. And in Gibbons's most recent novel, a historical novel set in antebellum and post–Civil War Virginia, the main character, Emma Garnet Tate Lowell, finds love and companionship when she marries Quincy, a New England doctor who remains devoted to her throughout his life. Such relationships, Gibbons suggests, are not found but made. Indeed, the most positive marriages occur when unlikely couples, such as Jack and Ruby Stokes and Emma and Quincy Lowell, somehow find a way to connect.

CRITICAL RECEPTION

Since the publication of *Ellen Foster* in 1987, Gibbons's work has been well received. Popular with contemporary audiences, several of Gibbons's books, including *Ellen Foster*, *A Virtuous Woman*, and *Charms for the Easy Life*, have become bestsellers. Reviews of Gibbons's novels have been, for the most part, positive. In a review of *Charms for the Easy Life*, for example, Stephen McCauley writes that he was "carried along by Ms. Gibbons's natural gift for telling stories and by her lyrical prose" (17). Gibbons has also gained mention in studies of the "new" Southern fiction writers. In 1993, for example, Julian Mason's study of Gibbons appeared in *Contemporary Fiction Writers of the South: A Bio-Bibliographical Sourcebook*.

Critical studies of Gibbons's work have focused on how her characters endure physical and psychological trauma. In " 'The Only Hard Part Was the Food': Recipes for Self-Nurture in Kaye Gibbons's Novels," Veronica Makowsky examines the importance of food in Gibbons's writing, explaining that "in their preoccupation with meals, Gibbons's narrators are all seeking the perfect recipe for happiness: how to provide nurturance for others, how to receive for themselves and, most importantly, how to nurture themselves" (103).

Other critics have examined how Gibbons's characters use storytelling to make sense of their complex lives. As Nancy Lewis explains in "Kaye Gibbons: Her Full-Time Women," Gibbons, like many other contemporary Southern writers, makes conversation the central focus of her novels. Such conversation is vital to Gibbons's characters. As Tonita Branan explains in "Women and 'The Gift for Gab': Revisionary Strategies in *A Cure for Dreams*," the women characters in Gibbons's novel use conversation to gain power in the home. Kathryn McKee also looks at the politics of conversation in *A Cure for Dreams*, arguing that the women use language to "shape the realities they otherwise find unbearable" (97). Linda Adams Barnes ascribes similar importance to the power of talk in Gibbons's novels, explaining that her characters use conversation "to tell themselves into existence" (29).

Still other critics have focused on how Gibbons's novels deal with issues of race, class, and gender. In " 'Colored Biscuits': Reconstructing Whiteness and the Boundaries of 'Home' in Kaye Gibbons's *Ellen Foster*," Giavanna Munafo uses her discussion of the novel to examine how race is systematically excluded from discussions of the American dream. Kristina K. Groover approaches *Ellen Foster* as a quest narrative, arguing that the novel rewrites the gendered quest narratives embodied in such texts as Mark Twain's *Huckleberry Finn*.

BIBLIOGRAPHY

Works by Kaye Gibbons

"June Bug." *Carolina Quarterly* 38 (1986): 37.
Ellen Foster. New York: Vintage, 1988.
"Places of Language and Time: The Surface of the Miranda Stories." *Kenyon Review* 10 (1988): 74–79.
A Virtuous Woman. New York: Vintage, 1989.
A Cure for Dreams. Chapel Hill, NC: Algonquin, 1991.
Charms for the Easy Life. New York: G. P. Putnam's, 1993.

Sights Unseen. New York: G. P. Putnam's, 1995.
On the Occasion of My Last Afternoon. New York: G. P. Putnam's, 1998.

Studies of Kaye Gibbons

Barnes, Linda Adams. "Telling Yourself into Existence: The Fiction of Kaye Gibbons." *Tennessee Philological Bulletin: Proceedings of the Annual Meeting of the Tennessee Philological Association* 30 (1993): 28–35.

Branan, Tonita. "Women and the 'Gift for Gab': Revisionary Strategies in *A Cure for Dreams.*" *Southern Literary Journal* 26 (1994): 91–101.

Groover, Kristina K. "Re-Visioning the Wilderness: *Adventures of Huckleberry Finn* and *Ellen Foster.*" *Southern Quarterly* 37 (1999): 187–97.

Hoffman, Alice. "Shopping for a New Family." Rev. of *Ellen Foster*, by Kaye Gibbons. *New York Times Book Review* 31 May 1987: 13.

Lewis, Nancy. "Kaye Gibbons: Her Full-Time Women." *Southern Writers at Century's End.* Ed. James Perkins and James H. Justus. Lexington: University Press of Kentucky, 1997. 112–22.

Makowsky, Veronica. " 'The Only Hard Part Was the Food': Recipes for Self-Nurture in Kaye Gibbons's Novels." *Southern Quarterly: A Journal of Arts in the South* 30 (1992): 103–12.

Mason, Julian. "Kaye Gibbons." *Contemporary Fiction Writers of the South: A Bio-Bibliographical Sourcebook.* Westport, CT: Greenwood Press, 1993. 156–68.

McCauley, Stephen. " 'He's Gone. Go Start the Coffee.' " Rev. of *Charms for the Easy Life*, by Kaye Gibbons. *New York Times Book Review* 11 April 1993: 17.

McKee, Kathryn. "Simply Talking: Women and Language in Kaye Gibbons's *A Cure for Dreams.*" *Southern Quarterly: A Journal of Arts in the South* 35 (1997): 97–106.

Munafo, Giavanna. " 'Colored Biscuits': Reconstructing Whiteness and the Boundaries of 'Home' in Kaye Gibbons' *Ellen Foster.*" *Women, America, and Movement: Narratives of Relocation.* Ed. Susan Roberson. Columbia: University of Missouri Press, 1998. 38–61.

Powell, Padgett. "As Ruby Lay Dying." Rev. of *A Virtuous Woman*, by Kaye Gibbons. *New York Times Book Review* 30 April 1989: 12.

Smurthwaite, Lori F. " 'Why Doesn't Anyone Tell Them Their Own Mothers Have Stories?': Representations of Mother/Daughter Relationships in Contemporary American Fiction." Dissertation, University of Southern California, 1998.

Souris, Stephen. "Kaye Gibbons's *A Virtuous Woman*: A Bakhtinian/Iserian Analysis of Conspicuous Agreement." *Southern Studies: An Interdisciplinary Journal of the South* 3 (1992): 99–115.

Wagner-Martin, Linda. "Kaye Gibbons' Achievement in *On the Occasion of My Last Afternoon.*" *Notes on Contemporary Literature* 29 (1999): 3–5.

Watts, Linda. "Stories Told by Their Survivors (and Other Sins of Memory): Survivor Guilt in Kaye Gibbons's *Ellen Foster.*" *The World Is Our Culture: Society and Culture in Contemporary Southern Writing.* Ed. Nancy Folks Summers. Lexington: University Press of Kentucky, 2000. 220–31.

GAIL GODWIN (1937–)

Lynn Domina

BIOGRAPHY

Gail Godwin was born on June 18, 1937, in Birmingham, Alabama, and grew up in Asheville, North Carolina. Her parents, Mose Winston Godwin and Kathleen Krahenbuhl Godwin, were divorced, and Gail Godwin did not meet her father until her high school graduation. Although Godwin accepted her father's invitation to live with him, this arrangement was brief because Mose Godwin committed suicide shortly thereafter. As a child, Godwin had lived with her mother, who was a journalist, and maternal grandmother. Kathleen Godwin taught writing and spent her weekends composing stories of romance; their regular publication supplemented the family income. From observing her mother, Godwin learned that writers use their imaginations to create something from nothing, that women are writers, and that writing pays.

After attending Peace Junior College and earning a BA from the University of North Carolina in 1959, she spent a year as a reporter at the *Miami Herald*. After being fired from that job, she worked in London as a travel consultant for the US Travel Service from 1962 to 1965. She married Douglas Kennedy in 1960 and was divorced from him in 1961. She subsequently married Ian Marshall, though that marriage was equally brief, lasting from 1965 to 1966. She earned an MA from the University of Iowa in 1968 as well as a PhD from that institution in 1971. By this time, she had been writing fiction seriously for a number of years, publishing her first novel before she completed her PhD. In addition to her numerous novels and collections of short stories, Godwin has collaborated as librettist for composer Robert Starer, and she has recently published a book of nonfiction. In addition to her books, she has published numerous articles and stories in such periodicals as *Atlantic*, *Ms.*, *Harper's*, *Cosmopolitan*, and *Esquire*. In the late 1970s, she taught at Vassar College and Columbia University.

Godwin has earned a number of awards for her writing, including two National Endowment for the Arts Grants, one in creative writing and one for librettists; a

Guggenheim Fellowship in creative writing; an Award in Literature from the American Institute and Academy of Arts and Letters; and nominations for the National Book Award and the American Book Award. She currently lives in Woodstock, New York.

MAJOR WORKS AND THEMES

Gail Godwin's fiction generally is realistic. While the various books feature different types of settings and characters, the themes and concerns that emerge in these books tend to be fairly consistent or to reflect upon and respond to each other. Godwin's concerns include the nature of families; the position of women as individuals as well as wives, mothers, sisters, and daughters; the demands on artists; and the role of religion in contemporary lives. Most of her protagonists and major characters are women, but male characters are also fully developed and sympathetically treated. Her characters frequently reflect her own southern background. Godwin's style does not often seem to have been influenced significantly by her postmodern or modern peers—her tone is not overarchingly ironic, for example, nor are her plot lines fractured or fragmented, nor is stream of consciousness her predominant mode. Yet her themes nevertheless reveal her position as a contemporary American writer who delves into contemporary American issues.

Family life in Godwin's work is never easy. Marriages are seldom conventional, and the successful ones succeed in part because the characters acknowledge, without accepting, critiques of their unconventionality. In *The Good Husband* (1994), for example, gender roles are reversed as the male partner permits, even encourages, his wife's career and professional goals to have priority over his own. In *Evensong* (1999), the protagonist marries a man significantly older than herself, a man who was a younger colleague of her father. In other novels, fathers die as mothers leave and children assume caretaking roles.

Perhaps Godwin's most popular novel—certainly the most popular among her earlier novels—is *A Mother and Two Daughters* (1982), set in the fictional Mountain City, North Carolina. Leonard Strickland dies of a heart attack; the novel follows the lives of his wife, Nell, and their daughters, Cate and Lydia, who are both in their late thirties. As in many novels that portray sibling relationships, the two women have chosen dramatically different lives, presumably because of their distinct temperaments. Lydia is the more conventional, having married early, had children, and identified herself primarily as a wife and mother. During the course of the novel, however, she leaves her husband without clear provocation. After beginning her college education, she achieves public success as the star of a cooking program. While this career remains to some degree within the traditionally feminine realm, it nevertheless permits her a public rather than entirely private identity.

Cate, on the other hand, has always been defined as the more radical of the sisters. A college professor, she has been divorced twice. Yet the college where she teaches is struggling financially, and because Cate is not a well-published scholar, her professional future looks uncertain. Ironically, just as her conventional sister has left her marriage, Cate begins to consider another marriage in part for its security.

Meanwhile, Nell also begins to understand herself anew, as widow rather than wife, as individual rather than fraction of a couple. While each of these characters could have been reduced to a type, Godwin develops them fully and distinctly enough so that they complement and complicate rather than simply circumscribe each other. Through their actions and interactions, the characters reveal the difficulty of making ethical choices based on self-knowledge.

In *The Finishing School* (1985), which followed *A Mother and Two Daughters* by three years, Godwin again examines family relationships, but the more prominent theme is the relationship between art and the artist. The protagonist and narrator, Justin Stokes, a forty-year-old actress, examines the events of the summer during which she turned fourteen. In this novel, the most provocative relationship is not between mother and daughter or sister and sister but between mentor and protégée. During this crucial summer, Justin meets Ursula DeVane, herself an unsuccessful actress in her forties. Ursula lives in upstate New York with her brother, a pianist who has also achieved slight success. The finishing school of the title consists of the lessons Ursula attempts to teach Justin throughout this summer. Like many individuals involved in similar relationships, Justin progresses from enchantment to disenchantment as she recognizes Ursula's own weaknesses.

As an artist and someone who would describe herself as a bohemian, Ursula's life presents an alternative to the lives of the other residents of the area, many of whom work for IBM. Ursula perceives these workers stereotypically, as clones of one another and pawns of a conformist system, but the novel transcends such reductive interpretations, especially as Justin grows less enthralled and hence more potentially critical of her mentor.

While Godwin has continued to explore interpersonal relationships in her more recent novels, she has also begun to explore an additional issue: the role of religion in the lives of contemporary Americans. Godwin is atypical among contemporary novelists in this respect for she refuses to treat conventional religion, specifically the Episcopalian branch of Christianity, with irony or sarcasm, nor does she assume the role of evangelist. Instead, she explores religion as an ordinary aspect of less-than-heroic individual lives. Religion as a significant object of exploration is most prominent in *Father Melancholy's Daughter* (1991) and its sequel, *Evensong* (1999).

The Father "Melancholy" of the title is an Episcopal priest named Walter Gower whose wife had left him many years before and was subsequently killed in an automobile accident. His daughter is Ruth, who was six when her mother left and has spent the intervening years speculating about her mother's motives and filling the role of caretaker for her father. A young adult during the time in which *Father Melancholy's Daughter* is set, Ruth finds herself falling inconveniently—some would say inappropriately—in love with Adrian Bonner, a forty-something colleague of her father. Compared with Walter, Adrian seems remarkably young, but at this point he also seems temperamentally most suited to be a bachelor. In the sequel, however, the two marry as Ruth follows her father's vocational footsteps. In these books, Godwin does not make an overt argument for the legitimacy of organized religion, nor does she engage in explicit doctrinal debate regarding the Christian ordination of women. Yet she is obviously responding to the issues of her time, since women have been ordained in the Episcopal Church only within the last generation. In this respect, however, these novels are most effective because Godwin does not present either Christianity itself or women as priests as issues to be debated but rather simply as facts to be explored.

CRITICAL RECEPTION

Gail Godwin is unusual in that she has frequently earned both critical and popular acclaim. Her novels regularly receive lengthy reviews in such prominent periodicals as *New York Times Book Review*, *Los Angeles Times Book Review*, *Washington Post Book World*, and *Christian Science Monitor*. Although some reviews of her work have been mixed, she is generally perceived as a good, if not a great, novelist and her books as accomplished works of fiction, if not masterpieces. Critics most often cite her for her ability to create characters who are convincing and engaging and her ability to construct plots that are plausible and coherent. Most notably in response to *The Good Husband*, reviewers have suggested that Godwin permits her plots to be over-burdened with symbolic resonance. That is, what action there is becomes subsumed in abstract interpretations of the events. Such a criticism can be hard to avoid in novels that are predominantly introspective.

Like many of her contemporaries, Godwin has thus far received more attention from reviewers than from scholars. Articles about her and her work are more likely to appear in the more literary of mainstream publications than in academic journals. This type of critical attention indicates that while Godwin is frequently read, she is not yet regularly taught in literature courses. Yet she has also begun to receive scholarly attention from critics working on Southern or contemporary fiction and from those interested in feminist issues. As often occurs when a writer's work approaches canonical status, these initial scholarly articles attempt to situate Godwin within a particular literary tradition, for example, Southern literature or women's literature. As these categories would indicate, many current critiques of Godwin's work assume a sociological or psychological approach. Since Godwin's more recent fiction is less likely to be set in the South than is her earlier fiction, one can speculate that future critics will be less likely to classify her as a regional writer. If Godwin remains as prolific a writer as she has been to this point, she will likely garner substantial critical attention as scholars attempt to create coherent and consistent analyses of late twentieth-century American literature.

BIBLIOGRAPHY

Works by Gail Godwin

The Perfectionists. New York: Harper, 1970.
Glass People. New York: Knopf, 1972.
The Odd Woman. New York: Knopf, 1974.
Dream Children. New York: Knopf, 1976.
Violet Clay. New York: Knopf, 1978.
A Mother and Two Daughters. New York: Viking, 1982.
Mr. Bedford and the Muses. New York: Viking, 1983.
The Finishing School. New York: Viking, 1985.
A Southern Family. New York: Morrow, 1987.
Father Melancholy's Daughter. New York: Morrow, 1991.
The Good Husband. New York: Ballantine, 1994.
Evensong. New York: Ballantine, 1999.
Heart: A Personal Journey through Its Myths and Meanings. New York: William Morrow, 2001.

Studies of Gail Godwin

Cheney, Anne. "A Hut and Three Houses: Gail Godwin, Carl Jung, and *The Finishing School*." *Southern Literary Journal* 21 (1989): 64–71.

Halisky, Linda H. "Redeeming the Irrational: The Inexplicable Heroines of 'A Sorrowful Woman' and 'To Room Nineteen.' " *Studies in Short Fiction* 27 (1990): 45–54.

Kissel, Susan S. *Moving On: The Heroines of Shirley Ann Grau, Anne Tyler, and Gail Godwin*. Bowling Green, OH: Bowling Green State University Popular Press, 1996.

Pelzer, Linda C. "Visions and Versions of Self: The Other/Woman in *A Mother and Two Daughters*." *Studies in Contemporary Fiction* 34 (1993): 155–64.

Seidel, Kathryn Lee. "Gail Godwin and Ellen Glasgow: Southern Mothers and Daughters." *Tulsa Studies in Women's Literature* 10 (1991): 287–94.

Wimsatt, Mary Ann. "Gail Godwin's Evolving Heroine: The Search for Self." *Mississippi Quarterly* 42 (1988/89): 27–45.

——. "Gail Godwin, the South, and the Canons." *Southern Literary Journal* 27 (1995): 86–95.

Xie, Lihong. *The Evolving Self in the Novels of Gail Godwin*. Baton Rouge: Louisiana State University Press, 1995.

MARY GORDON (1949–)

Cheryl D. Bohde

BIOGRAPHY

The only child of David Gordon and Anna Gagliano Gordon, Mary Catherine Gordon was born December 8, 1949, in Long Island, New York. While her mother was an Irish Catholic, her father, a Lithuanian Jew, converted to Catholicism. A polio victim at a young age, Anna worked as a legal secretary, so David raised Mary, teaching her to read at age three. Claiming a Harvard education, David Gordon contributed to various periodicals, including girlie magazines. Suffering a heart attack in the New York Public Library on January 14, 1957, David left behind an adoring daughter who never came to terms with his death until 1992, when Gordon began researching the memoir *The Shadow Man*: *A Daughter's Search for Her Father* (1996). Gordon learned that most of her father's colorful biography was false: David Gordon had not graduated from Harvard nor attended Oxford, nor lived on Paris' Left Bank; he had dropped out of school at sixteen to work as a clerk for the Baltimore and Ohio Railroad.

Growing up in the working-class neighborhood of Valley Stream, New York, Gordon attended the Holy Name of Mary parochial school, where she planned to be a nun who wrote poetry. After graduating from the Catholic Mary Louis Academy in Queens, Gordon won a scholarship to Barnard College, where she studied creative writing and worked with Elizabeth Hardwick. In an interview with M. Deiter Keyishian, Gordon lauds Barnard's atmosphere: The college draws the "women of her dreams," ones who desire an "urban situation" and a "female environment" (82). In the late 1960s, Gordon became estranged from the Catholic Church: Unhappy with its position on women and sex, she threw herself into the heady issues of the age, women's rights and the Vietnam War, participating in sit-ins and marches on Washington, D.C. However, she never lost her desire to write.

Receiving a BA degree in 1971, Gordon earned an MA from Syracuse University's writing program, where she studied with poet W. D. Snodgrass. Beginning a doctoral degree in 1973, she saw her first publication, "To a Cow," a poem in *American Review* (Bennett xiii). Gordon married anthropologist James Brian in 1974 and taught for four years at Dutchess Community College, Poughkeepsie. The short story "Now I Am Married," published in the *Virginia Quarterly Review* (1975), won the Balch Award the following year (Bennett xiii). While researching Virginia Woolf at the British Museum in 1976, Gordon wrote to Margaret Drabble, who introduced Gordon to agent Peter Matson; he remains her agent today. Separating from her husband in 1977, Gordon wrote *Final Payments*, which the *New York Times Book Review* named one of the outstanding books of 1978. The next year, *Final Payments* won the Jane Heidinger Kafka Prize for best novel written by an American woman, and Gordon divorced James Brian to marry Arthur Cash, an English professor and biographer of Laurence Sterne.

In 1980 Gordon's first child, Anna, was born; her second novel, *The Company of Women*, appeared, winning the 1981 Janet Heidinger Kafka Prize. Son David was born in 1983. The next year, Gordon received an honorary doctorate from North Carolina's Belmont Abbey College. A second honorary doctorate, one from Massachusetts' Assumption College, was awarded in 1988, after publication of the 1985 *Men and Angels,* which garnered her the New York Public Library's Literary Lion Award, and the 1987 short story collection *Temporary Shelter*. After *The Other Side* appeared in 1990, Gordon received her third honorary doctorate from State University of New York at New Paltz. Appointed the Millicent C. McIntosh Professor of Writing at Barnard College and adjunct professor at Columbia in 1990, Gordon received the Barnard Woman of Achievement Award the same year.

In the next decade, Gordon published *Good Boys and Dead Girls and Other Essays* (1991), *The Rest of Life: Three Novellas* (1993), the memoir *The Shadow Man* (1996), *Spending: A Utopian Divertimento* (1998), *Joan of Arc* (2000), and the personal memoir *Seeing through Places: Reflections on Geography and Identity* (2000). A prolific writer, Gordon also publishes fiction and nonfiction in various periodicals including *Atlantic Monthly, Harper's, Ladies' Home Journal, Redbook, Mademoiselle,* and the *New York Times*. Granted a Guggenheim Fellowship in 1993 and the Lila Wallace Reader's Digest Award in 1992, she received yet another honorary doctorate from Chicago's Saint Xavier University in 1994. Gordon was awarded the O. Henry Short Story Prize in 1997 for "City Life."

MAJOR WORKS AND THEMES

Mary Gordon's fiction, characterized by her lucid, intense prose and her moral consciousness, illuminates the complexity of establishing and maintaining human relationships. Calling herself a "woman's writer," Gordon explores the constraints of being female in a patriarchal culture; in her early novels, in particular, Gordon tackled the rigidity and sexism of the Catholic Church.

Gordon's first two novels, *Final Payments* and *The Company of Women*, are linked by their exploration of women coming of age within a Catholic culture of self-sacrifice: Protagonists Isabel Moore and Felicitas Taylor try to shed a repressive Catholic upbringing as they explore the new secular world of the 1960s.

In *Final Payments*, Isabel Moore devotes eleven years in Queens to caring for her father, a reactionary Catholic intellectual. After his death, Isabel finds a job and acquires two lovers, both married men. After the wife of the second lover denounces her, Isabel forsakes her new worldly life to resume her role as nurse: She moves in with her former housekeeper, an abusive, unforgiving nag. After an alcoholic old priest counsels that self-love is a spiritual responsibility, Isabel gives the old woman her financial inheritance and asks two friends to rescue her from her life of fruitless self-sacrifice: A spiritual, complete life, she realizes, allows beauty, pleasure, and, above all, healthy social interaction.

Like Isabel, the young protagonist of *The Company of Women*, Felicitas Taylor lives in a household dominated by rigid conservative Catholicism. In part biography, *The Company of Women* chronicles a young woman's renunciation of Church patriarchy; surrounded by a female circle of friends, whose spiritual life centers upon the conservative priest Father Cyprian, Felicitas seeks intellectual and spiritual autonomy. Attending Barnard University in the tumultuous 1960s, she falls in love with a god-like young Marxist professor. Felicitas spurns her classical studies, her mother, and her upbringing—until she becomes pregnant. The novel ends with Felicitas marrying a hardware store owner so her beloved daughter, Linda, will have a father. The novel ends in Linda's voice: She rejoices in her mother, her grandmother, and that loving circle of friends.

In her third novel, *Men and Angels*, Gordon broadens her theme of spirituality. Protagonist Laura Post embodies a perverse Christian fundamentalism that prohibits tolerance and genuine love. Hired as an *au pair* while Anne Foster works on a catalogue for an exhibition of Caroline Watson's paintings, Laura, a troubled young woman, attempts to convert the Fosters to her limited religious worldview. Devoted to her husband, who is in France on sabbatical, and to her children, Anne wrestles with guilt as her own research becomes increasingly integral to her developing sense of autonomy. After a serious incident with the children, Laura is fired; she then commits suicide in the Fosters' home.

After publishing a collection of short stories, Gordon released *The Other Side*, which continued her examination of self-sacrifice and familial obligations. Set on the eve of the Assumption, August 14, 1985, the novel entwines the lives of four generations of Irish Americans, the MacNamaras. In the novel, Gordon tackles a tenet of immigration: Assimilation into the American culture is automatic. Called from his nursing home to be with his dying wife, Ellen, whom he no longer loves, Vincent MacNamara reflects upon his hard life in the New World. Told in different voices— Vincent's, Ellen's, and two of their grandchildren's—*The Other Side* exposes the difficulties of assuming a new cultural identity.

The Rest of Life: Three Novellas questions gendered expectations about love in vignettes about middle-aged and elderly women and their romances. "Immaculate Man," "Living at Home," and "The Rest of Life" tell the story of three women and the men most important to them. As in *Men and Angels, The Rest of Life* explores the differences in loving children and loving men: While the mothers recognize their attachment to the child is absolute and inviolate, their love for a man may be intense yet transient.

Gordon's 1998 *Spending: A Utopian Divertimento* is an exuberant celebration of love, sex, art, and female autonomy: Monica Szabo is provided money and time to pursue her art by her lover, the mysterious "B.," a commodities broker. After creating a controversial series of paintings about Christ, problems abound: She is targeted by the Christian Right; one daughter wants to marry an unsuitable man; B. loses his fortune. Monica, who had worried that her capitulation to love would thwart her creativity, recognizes that B. himself—not his powers of provision—is integral to her happiness. In the fifteen years between *Final Payments* and *Spending*, Gordon has come full circle: While Isabel belatedly realizes that intimacy and self-fulfillment are not selfish needs, Monica simply expects both to be realized. Of the unabashedly sexual content of *Spending*, Gordon says, "Women have to learn to honor the animal in themselves. A lot of women just work too hard. It's time to allow ourselves pleasure and play" (Bolick 7).

CRITICAL RECEPTION

Commentary focuses upon Gordon's preoccupation with two dilemmas facing women: balancing maternity with creativity and existing within religious—especially Catholic—parameters.

Several studies analyze Gordon's portrayals of motherhood and creativity: Susan Rubin Suleiman's "On Maternal Splitting: A Propos of Mary Gordon's *Men and Angels*" explores the internal turmoil of an artistic mother; three maternal figures in the book—curator Anne, artist Caroline Watson, *au pair* Laura—offer variations on "good" and "bad" mothering (27–29). Ellen Macleod Mahon continues the discussion in "The Displaced Balance: Mary Gordon's *Men and Angels*," arguing that Anne and Laura are foils in their efforts to parent. "Mary Gordon's Mothers" admits the so-cioliterary tension in mothering: "Intense guilt" is "a central feature" of the fictional mother (Perry 208). In contrast, *Spending* playfully converges motherhood and artistic fame and fortune in a fable of the male muse: a wealthy, handsome, sexually proficient businessman who serves the middle-aged woman painter (Warren, "Painter" D5).

The difficulty of living a religious/moral life is analyzed in a number of studies. Marcia Bundy Seabury links Gordon's "feminist vision" to her "religious vision": Gordon's contemporary women are split/partitioned between the spiritual and secular worlds (39). Eleanor B. Wymward's "Mary Gordon: Her Religious Sensibility" co-gently argues that Gordon's "religious sense is basic to her vision of life" (148). Gordon's first four novels are discussed in Anita Gandolfo's *Testing the Faith: The New Catholic Fiction in America*: Built upon the theme of not only the "power of external oppression" but, more importantly, the "dangerous coercion" of "one's own compulsions," these works explore the trials Gordon's protagonists face as they attempt to reconcile faith and fulfillment (169). In "Mary Gordon's *Final Payments*: A Romance of the One True Language," John M. Neary argues that Gordon's first novel is a "religious novel about the religious value of novels": He lauds Gordon's ability to treat religious issues "metaphorically, even playfully, without freezing them into dogma" (110). Finally, Ross Labrie praises Gordon for tackling Catholic restrictions placed upon women in a world of expanded opportunity: Women's "powerless[ness]," for Gordon, resides in the "anti-intellectualism of American Catholicism" (169).

Recent criticism lauds Gordon's unblinking examination of immigration and the myth of ready assimilation. June Dwyer argues that *Temporary Shelter* fictionalizes the tribulations of three Irish women who immigrate to America: Protagonists of each of the stories find "their self-fashioning [as new American citizens] is reactive and defensive, rather than a free choice" (104).

BIBLIOGRAPHY

Works by Mary Gordon

Final Payments. New York: Random, 1979.
The Company of Women. New York: Random, 1980.
Men and Angels. New York: Random, 1985.
Temporary Shelter. New York: Random, 1987.
The Other Side. New York: Viking Penguin, 1990.
Good Boys and Dead Girls and Other Essays. New York: Viking Penguin, 1991.
The Rest of Life: Three Novellas. New York: Viking, 1993.
The Shadow Man: A Daughter's Search for Her Father. New York: Random, 1996.
Spending: A Utopian Divertimento. New York: Macmillan, 1998.
Joan of Arc. New York: Viking, 2000.
Seeing through Places: Reflections on Geography and Identity. New York: Scribner, 2000.

Studies of Mary Gordon

Bennett, Alma. *Mary Gordon*. New York: Twayne, 1996.
Bloom, Alice. "Why the Novel (Still) Matters." *Hudson Review* 43 (1990): 155–64.
Bolick, Katie. "Catholic. Woman. Writer." Interview with Mary Gordon. *Atlantic Unbound* 6 May 1999: 1–8. <http://www.theatlantic.com/unbound/factfict/ff9905.htm>
Booth, Rosemary. "A Concentration of Purpose: The Artistic Journey of Mary Gordon." *Commonweal* 115 (1988): 426–30.
Callahan, Amy. "Mary Gordon: The Art of Teaching and Writing." *Columbia University Record* 27 March 1998: 1–5.
Clemons, Walter. "Let Charity and Love Prevail." Rev. of *Men and Angels*. *Newsweek* 1 April 1985: 75.
Dwyer, June. "Unappealing Ethnicity Meets Unwelcoming America: Immigrant Self-Fashioning in Mary Gordon's *Temporary Shelter*." *MELUS* 22 (1997): 103–12.
Feeney, Joseph J. "Imagining Religion in America: Three Contemporary Novelists." *Critic* 42 (1987): 58–73.
Gandolfo, Anita. *Testing the Faith: The New Catholic Fiction in America*. New York: Greenwood Press, 1992.
Gilead, Sarah. "Mary Gordon's *Final Payments* and the Nineteenth-Century English Novel." *Critique: Studies in Modern Fiction* 27 (1986): 213–27.
Iannone, Carol. "The Secret of Mary Gordon's Success." *Commentary* 79 (1985): 62–66.
Johnston, Eileen Tess. "The Biblical Matrix of Mary Gordon's *Final Payments*." *Christianity and Literature* 44 (1995): 145–66.
Keyishian, M. Deiter. "Radical Damage: An Interview with Mary Gordon." *Literary Review* 32 (1988): 69–82.
Kolbenschlag, Madonna. "Man, Woman, Catholic." *America* 145 (1981): 4–9.
Kuebrich, David. "Apropos of a Modern Faith: Feminism, Class, and Motherhood in Mary Gordon's *Men and Angels*." *Christianity and Literature* 46 (1997): 293–316.
Labrie, Ross. "Women and the Catholic Church in the Fiction of Mary Gordon." *English Studies in Canada* 22 (1996): 167–79.
Lee, Don. "About Mary Gordon." *Ploughshares* 23 (1997): 218–25.
Mahon, Ellen Macleod. "The Displaced Balance: Mary Gordon's *Men and Angels*." *Mother Puzzles: Daughters and Mothers in Contemporary American Literature*. Ed. Mickey Pearlman. New York: Greenwood Press, 1989. 91–99.
McCormick, Patrick. "Looking for Grace in All the Right Places." *US Catholic* Nov. 1999: 26–29.

Morey, Ann-Janine. "Beyond Updike: Incarnated Love in the Novels of Mary Gordon." *Christian Century* 102 (1985): 1059–63.

Neary, John M. "Mary Gordon's *Final Payments*: A Romance of the One True Language." *Essays in Literature* 17 (1990): 94–110.

Perry, Ruth. "Mary Gordon's Mothers." *Narrating Mothers: Theorizing Maternal Subjectivities.* Ed. Brenda O. Daly and Maureen T. Reddy. Knoxville: University of Tennessee Press, 1991. 209–21.

Prose, Francine. "To Have and Have Not." Rev. of *The Rest of Life: Three Novellas. Newsday* 8 Aug. 1993: 33.

Rigney, Barbara Hill. *Lilith's Daughters: Women and Religion in Contemporary Fiction.* Madison: University of Wisconsin Press, 1982.

Seabury, Marcia Bundy. "Of Belief and Unbelief: The Novels of Mary Gordon." *Christianity and Literature* 40 (1990): 37–55.

Suleiman, Susan Rubin. "On Maternal Splitting: A Propos of Mary Gordon's *Men and Angels*." *Signs* 14 (1988): 25–41.

Toolan, David. Rev. of *The Other Side. America* 13 Jan. 1990: 15–16.

Ward, Susan. "In Search of 'Ordinary Human Happiness': Rebellion and Affirmation in Mary Gordon's Novels." *Faith of a (Woman) Writer.* Ed. Alice Kessler-Harris and William McBrien. New York: Greenwood Press, 1988. 303–8.

Warren, Colleen Kelly. "Illuminating Inner Thoughts." Rev. of *The Rest of Life: Three Novellas. St. Louis Post-Dispatch* 10 Oct. 1993: 5C.

——. "Painter Finds Male Muse with No Strings Attached." Rev. of *Spending. St. Louis Post-Dispatch.* 22 Feb. 1998: D5.

Wymward, Eleanor B. "Mary Gordon: Her Religious Sensibility." *Cross Currents* 37 (1987): 147–58.

ELIZABETH FORSYTHE HAILEY (1938–)

Kristin Brunnemer

BIOGRAPHY

The eldest of Earl and Janet Forsythe's four children, Elizabeth Forsythe Hailey was born on August 31, 1938, in Dallas, Texas. As the daughter of a lawyer who obtained his law degree from Yale and a homemaker who studied art at Vassar and in Europe, Hailey writes that her childhood was "no different from [that of] any conventional, sheltered, middle-class child coming of age in the postwar years" ("Hailey," *Contemporary Authors Autobiography Series* 226). At an early age, however, Hailey noted that she wanted a career, something the average female child of her time was not expected to obtain. Writing about this desire in the *Contemporary Authors Autobiography Series*, Hailey notes that "even at the age of ten, I loved the feeling of coming home from the workplace at the end of the day, and I knew that whatever I did with my life, I was not going to be one of those wives who stayed home putting dinner on the table and looking to her husband for news of the outside world" (225).

In third grade, Hailey's first byline was published by her elementary school newspaper, an experience that gave her the feeling that her life had really begun ("Hailey," *Contemporary Authors Autobiography Series* 225). This was not to be her last opportunity in the field of journalism either. In high school, Hailey wrote her own column for the *Bagpipe*, Highland Park High School's newspaper, and in her senior year, she was selected to write a weekly article for the *Dallas Morning News*' high school page. After graduating as valedictorian, Hailey interned at the newspaper until the end of summer, when she left Dallas for Roanoke, Virginia, and her freshman year at Hollins College.

At Hollins, Hailey received the opportunity to travel abroad to Paris, an experience that, coupled with her grandmother's journals of her own voyage, became the basis for her protagonist's European excursions in *A Woman of Independent Means* (1978). Likewise, Hailey's 1958 year abroad coincided with the Algerian struggle for independence, and her record of the political events in Paris earned her a front-page story in the Dallas newspaper. Returning from Europe and her junior year of college, Hailey spent her summer vacation as a reporter for the *Dallas Morning News*, "more determined than ever" to make a career of journalism ("Hailey," *Contemporary Authors Autobiography Series* 228). However, Hailey, who wanted to write for the city news department, was disappointed with her post in entertainment, which ran stories on local films and theater productions. Ironically, another reporter, her future husband Oliver Hailey, was equally discouraged, having been assigned to the city desk instead of the entertainment post he had requested. Meeting through the experience, the couple was soon engaged and married the summer following Hailey's graduation on June 25, 1960.

In September 1960, the Haileys moved to New Haven, Connecticut, where Oliver attended the Yale School of Drama and Elizabeth took comparative literature courses from Columbia University. In December 1960, she began an editorial position with Yale University Press, an appointment that, according to Hailey, combined her interests in journalism and literature ("Hailey," *Contemporary Authors Autobiography Series* 230). Hailey kept the position until Oliver earned his MFA, and the couple left New Haven to pursue their career interests.

Between 1963 and 1967, the Haileys made their home where Oliver's work as a playwright and screenwriter took them: New York, Texas, Connecticut, and California. On July 12, 1966, their first child, Elizabeth Kendall, was born in Hollywood. In 1967 Elizabeth and Oliver Hailey purchased a home in Studio City, a suburb of Los Angeles, where Oliver worked as a freelance writer for film and television. Elizabeth assisted with many of these projects, including *McMillan and Wife* and an eight-week position as co-head writer for the CBS soap opera *Love of Life*. Shortly thereafter, on April 24, 1970, their second daughter, Melinda Brooke, was born.

Although Hailey had written short stories and had worked on writing projects alongside her husband, she did not begin writing her first novel, *A Woman of Independent Means*, until she was thirty-five. Describing this epistolary novel based on the life and journals of her maternal grandmother, Bess Kendall Jones, for whom she herself was named, Hailey asserts that her grandmother's "courage and independence made her a better role model for me than anyone I was reading about in the pages of *Ms.* magazine" ("Hailey," *Contemporary Authors Autobiography Series* 232). Published in 1978, the book was a national best-seller and has since been adapted into a 1983 play and a 1995 NBC miniseries.

Hailey's second novel, *Life Sentences* (1982), which spans the lives of three college friends from the 1960s to the 1980s, met with equal success, maintaining a position on the *New York Times*' best-seller list for nearly three months. Commenting on the two novels, Hailey contends that she originally thought her second book would be quite different from her first; yet when she finished *Life Sentences*, she noted that it had striking parallels to her first novel: "*A Woman of Independent Means* is about a strong woman in an unliberated time asserting her independence. *Life Sentences* is about a strong woman in a liberated time acknowledging her interdependence" ("Hailey," *Contemporary Authors Autobiography Series* 233).

Hailey followed the success of her first two novels with the publication of two others: the semiautobiographical *Joanna's Husband and David's Wife* (1986), a book that follows her protagonist's journals of her marriage, and *Home Free* (1991), which addresses the larger role that women, family, and home play in the community. In

1998 Penguin released a twentieth anniversary edition of *A Woman of Independent Means* with "A New Letter to the Reader" by Hailey.

MAJOR WORKS AND THEMES

Reflecting on her novel, *Life Sentences*, Hailey remarked that it was "a fictional reflection on what Betty Friedan has called 'the second stage'—the desire for a life that includes men and children without relinquishing any of our [women's] hard-earned independence" ("Hailey," *Contemporary Authors Autobiography Series* 234). One can posit that all of Hailey's novels are engaged with these same desires and themes, for if any one phrase could summarize Hailey's work, it might be that coined by 1970s feminism: The personal is political. Indeed, Hailey's work, drawing heavily from her own experiences, centers on the various roles of women, as mothers, wives, and daughters, and how those roles interact with the world outside the family and home. Concurrently, Hailey's work might also be characterized by the notion that the political is personal as her novels also delve into the experiences of women facing such political issues as rape, abortion, homelessness, divorce, and economics. By demonstrating the ways in which the personal affects the political as well as how political issues are experienced personally, Hailey's work generates complex female characters whose lives reflect the lived experiences of women.

Hailey's first and quite possibly her most famous novel, *A Woman of Independent Means*, exemplifies this political and personal continuum through the letters of Bess Steed Garner to her relatives, friends, and business associates. Beginning with Bess's 1899 childhood letter to fourth grade sweetheart Robert Steed to her stroke-impaired 1968 letter to a granddaughter, Hailey's novel chronicles the opinions, adventures, and choices of her protagonist on such issues as children, marriage, travel, war, suffrage, and women's rights. Through Bess's epistles, Hailey is able to engage in a rich dialogue about the many and varied issues that affect women, demonstrating how women's private and public lives converge.

Hailey's second novel, *Life Sentences*, also engages the notion of women's experiences as a merging of private and public, personal and political discourses. Following the lives of three college friends, Lindsay, Meg, and Cissy, Hailey demonstrates the many ways in which life's choices "sentence" one to particular avenues of life. The book, written in the third person, begins with Lindsay's rape by an unknown assailant and her subsequent pregnancy. Lindsay has already undergone a previous abortion in her twenties to care for her husband, John Henry, whose diving accident left him unable to move or communicate with the outside world. Now forty-two, Lindsay decides to have the child but, owing to complications with the pregnancy, needs the assistance of her friends, Meg and Cissy, to help her carry to term.

Through the experiences of Lindsay, Meg, and Cissy, Hailey raises many of the issues central to feminism. Writing of Lindsay's rape, for instance, Hailey notes the ways in which the act of violence has been politicized as a dichotomy between "good" and "bad" girls: "She knew people in the city who had been mugged in the street or subway or had come home to find their apartments robbed—some more than once— but it had never happened to her, a fact Lindsay attributed to the shell of physical invulnerability she wore like armor. Later, in reconstructing the incident, she realized that until it happened to her, she was as guilty as any man of thinking that a rape victim was somehow 'asking for it.' For was not the inverse of this attitude (feeling safe precisely because she was *not* 'asking for it') just as prejudiced?" (2).

Lindsay's rape demonstrates many other issues that can be deemed both personal and political, such as medical care for rape victims, pregnancy risks, options for older women, and the difficulties in balancing professional demands with familial ones. Hailey's supporting characters, Meg and Cissy, must also reconcile their desires for family and for personal fulfillment. Meg, a lawyer who cannot have children, feels she is denied motherhood, while Cissy finds it difficult to maintain her own identity, much less a career, with three young children and a husband whose job relocates the family every few years. Thus, for all the sharp political insights interwoven into the pages of her novel, Hailey equally recognizes that such issues always have a personal side to them as well.

Describing the experience of writing *Life Sentences*, Hailey acknowledges that it "provided a fictional framework in which I could explore and clarify my attitudes toward the events of my own adulthood—and especially the changing roles and relationships of men and women" ("Hailey," *Contemporary Authors* 234). Hailey's third novel, *Joanna's Husband and David's Wife*, further explores these changing roles and relationships through the twenty-four-year marriage of Joanna and David. Attempting to depict "what marriage is like—for both the man and the woman" (11), Hailey's largely autobiographical novel is composed of Joanna's journal entries and David's italicized replies. This format results in a dialogue between husband and wife regarding their roles, the choices they have made, and their consequences.

Hailey's work is further defined by her sympathetic male characters: The men in her novels are never vilified, nor are they presented as the only source of women's problems. Rather, they are as strong, as giving, and as torn by their circumstances and their choices as Hailey's female protagonists. Even in *Life Sentences*, Lindsay's rapist, who could so easily be fashioned into a monster, is revealed, albeit problematically and unrealistically, to be a grief-stricken widower who has anonymously provided Lindsay with financial assistance for raising her child. Hailey's depiction of men as supportive but ultimately as troubled by and uncertain about their changing relationships and roles as women is mirrored by her contention that "marriage is the key to the survival of the human race. Until two individuals can learn to care for each other without trying to dominate or possess, then how can whole countries hope to live together in peace?" ("Hailey," *Contemporary Authors* 234).

Home Free presents another sympathetic portrait of both men and women through the characters of Kate, Ford, and Sunny. It is also another example of Hailey's desire to address the political by means of personal experience. Centered on the chance Christmas Eve meeting of Kate, a wealthy housewife whose husband has recently left her, and Ford, a homeless construction worker whose family resides in a downtown homeless shelter, *Home Free* utilizes these characters to explore political topics such as class, economics, and homelessness while demonstrating how equality between men and women repairs Ford and Sunny's marriage and their beliefs in their individual worth.

Home Free also moves far beyond Hailey's earlier interconnections between the personal and the political. In this novel, Kate's personal friendship with Ford motivates her to offer his family residence in her home. As Ford and Sunny slowly regain their economic footing and self-esteem, Kate discovers her own self-worth, deciding to utilize her connections and financial resources to build houses for other homeless families. Thus, it is the protagonists' friendships with one another that help them to heal personally, challenge them to act politically, and, once again, demonstrate how Hailey's writing engages both the personal and the political by means of human experience.

Hailey concludes *Joanna's Husband and David's Wife* with a note to the protagonist's daughter, telling her, "All I can leave you as a guide is the elusive truth of my own experience" (399). In utilizing the personal and political events that shape the lives of men and women, the work of Elizabeth Forsythe Hailey truly embraces "the elusive truth" of experience.

CRITICAL RECEPTION

Perhaps best known for her first novel, *A Woman of Independent Means*, Hailey and her work have been widely praised and favorably reviewed by such newspapers and magazines as *Ms.*, *Christian Science Monitor*, *New York Times Book Review*, and *Library Journal*. Hailey's second novel, *Life Sentences*, which had a fourteen-week stay on the 1983 *New York Times* best-seller list, also received favorable reviews. Outside of these occasional praise-filled commentaries, however, Hailey's work has not obtained much critical attention. This might be due to the categorizing of her novels as popular rather than literary fiction. Nevertheless, Hailey's books have garnered high sales and multiple printings, including Penguin's recent 1998 rerelease of *A Woman of Independent Means* and the distribution of all of her novels in the books-on-tape format.

BIBLIOGRAPHY

Works by Elizabeth Forsythe Hailey

A Woman of Independent Means. New York: Delacorte, 1978.
Life Sentences. New York: Delacorte, 1982.
Joanna's Husband and David's Wife. New York: Delacorte, 1986.
Home Free. New York: Delacorte, 1991.

Studies of Elizabeth Forsythe Hailey

"Elizabeth Forsythe Hailey." *Contemporary Authors Autobiography Series*. Ed. Dedria Bryfonski. Vol. 1. Detroit: Gale, 1984. 225–35.
Elsbernd, Mary Ellen. "Home Free." Rev. of *Home Free*. *Library Journal* Jan. 1991: 152.
Gindick, Tina. "Writers Lives Unchanged by Success." Interview with Elizabeth Hailey and Oliver Hailey. *Los Angeles Times* 27 Feb. 1984: 28.
"Hailey, Elizabeth Forsythe." *Contemporary Authors: A Bio-Bibliographical Guide to Current Writers in Fiction, General Nonfiction, Poetry, Journalism, Drama, Motion Picture, Television, and Other Fields*. Ed. Frances C. Locher. Vols. 93–96. Detroit: Gale, 1980. 202.
Israel, Jodi. "*Home Free*." Review of *Home Free*. *Library Journal* 15 Mar. 1992: 146.
Jacoby, Susan. "*Life Sentences*." Rev. of *Life Sentences*. *Washington Post* 11 Oct. 1982: B3.
Johnson, Nora. "Life Sentences." Rev. of *Life Sentences*. *New York Times* 14 Nov. 1982: 14.
MacDougall, Ruth Doan. "*Joanna's Husband and David's Wife*." Review of *Joanna's Husband and David's Wife*. *New York Times* 23 Feb. 1986: 22.

O'Conner, Patricia. "*Joanna's Husband and David's Wife*." Rev. of *Joanna's Husband and David's Wife*. *New York Times Book Review* 1 Mar. 1987: 34.

Peacock, Mary. "A Woman of Independent Means." Rev. of *A Woman of Independent Means*. *Ms*. July 1978: 32.

Steinberg, Sybil. "Home Free." Review of *Home Free*. *Publishers Weekly* 7 Dec. 1990: 72.

Tyler, Anne. "*A Woman of Independent Means*." Rev. of *A Woman of Independent Means*. *New York Times Book Review* 28 May 1978: 4.

SHELBY HEARON (1931–)

Elizabeth Blakesley Lindsay

BIOGRAPHY

Evelyn Shelby Reed was born January 18, 1931, in Marion, Kentucky, to geologist Charles B. Reed and Evelyn Shelby Roberts Reed. Her father's work involved prospecting for gold and oil and took the family all over the United States. Shelby and her family, including younger sisters Frances, Susan, and Linda, spent time in Kentucky, Texas, and Georgia.

Her father's career influenced her during childhood and adolescence, giving her a great deal of knowledge, a love for the natural world, and superb argumentative skills from the scientific debates her family engaged in. Hearon writes about having a normal, active social life and being one of the smartest students in high school, known for writing well, and usually being the only female student in advanced science classes ("Shelby Hearon," *Contemporary Authors* 160–61). Although she won a statewide writing competition in Texas when she was a senior in high school, writing was not initially among her career goals. Her name had caused gender confusion for years, and a newspaper headline about her victory proclaimed: "Austin Boy Wins Ready-Writing" ("Shelby Hearon," *Contemporary Authors* 161). When she took placement tests for the University of Texas, she scored exceptionally well in math and science categories but, given her gender, was counseled to pursue liberal arts ("Shelby Hearon," *Contemporary Authors* 160). Hearon notes that she was "very imprinted by having an androgynous name"; although she was the third female named Evelyn Shelby in her family, she was the first to be called Shelby (P. Bennett 115–6). Her mother was very involved with the family genealogy, and this importance of family and naming plays a large role in Hearon's fiction. Hearon has said that when she began writing, she had the idea that she "was passing down family myths, family scripts" (Levine 56).

Shortly after she graduated from the University of Texas at Austin in 1953, she married law student Robert Hearon. The couple had two children, Anne and Reed.

Divorced in 1977, she married philosophy professor Bill Lucas in 1981. This union also ended in divorce, and she is currently married to cardiovascular physiologist William Halpern and resides in Burlington, Vermont.

Hearon began writing in journals when her children were young and she had begun to feel trapped by the expectations of wives and mothers in the 1950s (Rodenberger 601). In spite of the demands on her time as a wife and mother, spending her time, as she puts it, "being Betty Crocker in the kitchen, Brigitte Bardot in the bedroom and Maria Montessori in the nursery," she began a draft of her first novel in 1961 (Levine 57). In 1964, three years after she had started writing the novel, medical emergencies impacted Hearon's life (Rodenberger 601). After facing cerebral hemorrhages and a craniotomy, Hearon threw out the draft and began anew. In 1967 the manuscript for *Armadillo in the Grass* was completed and sent unsolicited to Knopf. Retrieved from a slush pile, it was published in 1968. Knopf published her fifteenth novel, *Ella in Bloom*, in January 2001. In addition to fourteen novels and numerous short stories and essays, since 1998 she has contributed book reviews to the *Chicago Tribune*.

Throughout her career, Hearon has served as visiting professor or writer-in-residence at several universities, including the University of Houston, University of California at Irvine, University of Illinois at Chicago, Clark University, Wichita State University, Ohio Wesleyan University, Colgate University, University of Miami, and the University of Massachusetts at Amherst. In 1996 forty-two boxes of Hearon's papers became available for researchers at the Harry Ransom Humanities Research Center at the University of Texas at Austin.

Hearon has received numerous awards through her career, including Guggenheim and National Endowment for the Arts Fellowships, PEN fiction prizes, and the 1990 American Academy of Arts and Letters Literature Award for *Owning Jolene* (1989).

MAJOR WORKS AND THEMES

Hearon writes about women of all ages and their lives, work, and inner growth. Her fiction centers on how women define their roles, deal with the intricacies of love, marriage, and divorce, and cope with loss.

Hearon's characters often face a crisis that motivates their searches to define their identities. In *Owning Jolene*, nineteen-year-old Jolene is trying to break free and define herself after years of being caught in the middle of her bitterly divorced parents and an aunt and uncle, all of whom have forced her to live with them at various times. Jolene's last name shifts from Temple to Jackson throughout the novel, depending on which parent has commandeered her. Lutie Sayre, the protagonist of *Group Therapy* (1984), is a divorced Texan who moves to New York City to begin a new life. Overwhelmed by the cultural differences between the South and the Northeast, Lutie joins a self-image seminar led by two male therapists. In *Life Estates* (1994), Harriet and Sarah are lifelong friends and recent widows who seek to understand the roles they have played and to redefine how they will spend the rest of their lives.

Love, from the beginning of relationships to the bitter divorces that mark the end, is another key presence in Hearon's works. Hearon's *Hug Dancing* (1991), called by one reviewer "a comic romance of divorce" (Robb 61), involves Cile and Andy, high school sweethearts who were separated and married other people. Twelve years after high school, Andy returns to Waco, and they begin an affair that continues over several years until they finally plan to leave their spouses and begin a life together. Their plans go awry when Cile's husband begins an affair with another woman and sudden changes leave Andy in a precarious financial position. Reviewer Carolyn Banks notes that in *Group Therapy*, Lutie is "saved" by the therapeutic image seminar, which helps her on personal and psychological levels and also helps acclimate her to the differences in life in New York (quoted in "Shelby Hearon" 239). Lutie falls in love with one of the therapists, which allows Hearon to examine the cultural differences between the North and the South as well as to portray two adults beginning a new relationship.

Hearon often tackles loss and grief. In *Footprints* (1996), Nan and Douglas Mayhall face the sudden loss of their daughter, Bethany, who is killed in an accident. Hearon captures the intense grief of the couple as she portrays the ensuing disintegration of their marriage. Bethany was an organ donor, and while Nan is not interested in meeting people who benefitted from Bethany's gifts, Douglas convinces her to attend a social function for families of donors and recipients. Douglas "is desperate to find what is left of Bethany and moves through the crowd tapping his chest in hopes someone will respond to his silent signal" (McCorkle B38). In addition to such poignancy, Hearon includes moments of humor. Jill McCorkle points out that humor can be difficult in novels dealing with grief but asserts that Hearon is able to inject her witty style and portray humorous situations as Nan copes with her loss (B38).

Harriet and Sarah, the two friends recently widowed in *Life Estates*, cope with the losses of their husbands and the subsequent changes that affect their friendship. Throughout the novel, the two women come to terms not only with the loss of their husbands but also with their feelings and realizations about their marriages and deceased husbands. Harriet was trapped as a dependent in a marriage that grew more loveless each year, while Sarah had been more independent during her marriage, especially as it was failing, leaving her better prepared for widowhood. As they begin to examine their lives and consider their own mortality, their friendship undergoes major changes as they realize they may not fit the roles they have played for years. Lee Smith also points to Hearon's ability to portray characters' sense of humor, however brittle or pained, in the face of grief (724). Smith quotes several funny incidents from the novel where Harriet fears she will become a stereotypical "Widow. Capital W" (724).

Although one of her novels, *Five Hundred Scorpions* (1987), features a male protagonist, Hearon's strengths lie in her perceptive, touching, and often humorous portraits of women who face universal issues of love, loss, and identity.

CRITICAL RECEPTION

Hearon has won several awards and enjoyed a long publication history, but academic critical reception has been limited. Very few literary scholars have approached her work, although her novels are widely reviewed in newspapers and trade journals.

The literary scholars who have dealt with Hearon have focused on her identity as a Texan or Western writer. Carol Marshall looks at images of women and elements of the fairy tale in Texas fiction, comparing Hearon's *Hannah's House* (1975) with works by Dorothy Scarborough and Laura Furman. Lou Rodenberger profiles Hearon for a critical anthology on Western writers, tracing her development as a writer. Rodenberger observes that Hearon is often commended for her ability to create settings

(602). Hearon says, in "Placing Fiction" (1992), that she likes "to think of a place as having three faces: its history, its view of itself, and its significance to the people who live there" ("Placing Fiction" 17). John Blades asks Hearon about her preference for small-town settings, and Hearon replies that "to write about a place, you have to sound as if you'd lived there forever" (511A). Furthermore, Hearon notes that most big cities have professional sports teams, something she claims to know little about (Blades 511A). Without that knowledge, Hearon would feel uncomfortable writing about a native of a city. Hearon takes realistic settings quite seriously, and this may explain why so few of her novels are set outside small towns. *Group Therapy* is one of the few exceptions, but it features a transplanted Southerner struggling with life in New York City.

Many reviewers take notice of Hearon's exceptional use of setting in her novels. Kurt Tidmore's review of *Hug Dancing* commends Hearon for her "strong sense of place" and intricate plotting but asserts that she "forgot the characters" (C3). Christina Robb discusses the layered meanings of the characters' names in *Hug Dancing* but observes that the restoration of a house in the plot "overshadows the personal transformation" that Robb thinks the novel was supposed to centrally address (61). In a review of *Life Estates*, however, Lee Smith notes that Hearon "has made it her business to strip away the stereotypes" in her portrayal of two lifelong friends facing widowhood together (724). According to Smith, characters are rarely "so thoughtfully, honestly yet lovingly evoked" (724). Hearon says that she has to know where her characters stand on time, sex, and God (P. Bennett 120). While settings may be her particular strength, Hearon carefully considers the development of her characters, on physical, psychological, and spiritual levels.

Owning Jolene may be Hearon's best, or at least best-known, novel. Winner of the 1990 Academy of Arts and Letters Award, *Owning Jolene* focuses on a nineteen-year-old woman's struggle to break free from parents and relatives who have controlled her life. Tim Sandlin calls Jolene "a chronic kidnap victim," referring to various incidents in the novel when one parent snatches her from the other (10). Jolene assumes many identities and tries out several relationships as she struggles to find her true self and claim what she hopes will be a normal life. Sandlin remarks that "a lot is made of normal in this novel, maybe because no one in the book has a whiff of what the concept means" (10).

According to a prepublication review in *Publishers Weekly*, Hearon creates, in *Ella in Bloom*, another "compassionate, gently ironic tale," which focuses on a woman seeking to redefine herself (86). Overshadowed by a successful sister and a domineering mother, Ella has not realized her own strengths and charms, but through the crises that arise during the course of the novel, she comes to recognize her positive attributes, gains control of her life, and eventually finds true love. The "middle-aged woman gets a second chance at love" theme may be similar to other contemporary works, but Hearon takes this familiar subject "loftily above its usual treatment" (86).

BIBLIOGRAPHY

Works by Shelby Hearon

Armadillo in the Grass. New York: Knopf, 1968.
The Second Dune. New York: Knopf, 1973.

Hannah's House. New York: Doubleday, 1975.

Now and Another Time. New York: Doubleday, 1976.

A Prince of a Fellow. New York: Doubleday, 1978.

Barbara Jordan: A Self-Portrait. With Barbara Jordan. New York: Doubleday, 1979.

Painted Dresses. New York: Atheneum, 1981.

Afternoon of the Faun. New York: Atheneum, 1983.

Group Therapy. New York: Atheneum, 1984.

"War and Peace." *Southwest Review* 69 (1984): 379–83.

A Small Town. New York: Atheneum, 1985.

"The British Museum." *Southwest Review* 71 (1986): 383–88.

Five Hundred Scorpions. New York: Atheneum, 1987.

Owning Jolene. New York: Knopf, 1989.

"Shelby Hearon." *Contemporary Authors: Autobiography Series.* Ed. Mark Zadrozny. Vol. 11. Detroit: Gale, 1990. 157–70.

Hug Dancing. New York: Knopf, 1991.

"Placing Fiction." *Writer* 105 (1992): 17–19.

"Hall of Mirrors." *Southwest Review* 78 (1993): 72–80.

"Distressed Passenger." *Southern Review* 30 (1994): 230–44.

"Creating a Character the Reader Has Never Met." *Writer* 107 (1994): 9–12.

Life Estates. New York: Knopf, 1994.

"The Undertow of Friends." *Texas Bound.* Ed. Kay Cattarulla. Dallas: Southern Methodist University Press, 1994. 125–31.

"Fiction and the Sense of Order." *Library Chronicle of the University of Texas* 25 (1995): 100–105.

Footprints. New York: Knopf, 1996.

"Perfect-Pitch Dialogue." *Writer* 109 (1996): 3–5.

"Staying Dry." *Southern Review* 33 (1997): 713–21.

"Writing about Your Own Backyard." *Writer* 9 (1999): 7.

Ella in Bloom. New York: Knopf, 2001.

Studies of Shelby Hearon

Bennett, Charlene White. "The Influence of Libraries in the Work of Four Texas Women Writers." Thesis, Texas Woman's University, 1980.

Bennett, Elizabeth. "Shelby Hearon 'Gets It Right' in Life, 11th Novel." Rev. of *Owning Jolene. Houston Post* 22 Feb. 1989: D1ff.

Bennett, Patrick. "Shelby Hearon: Time, Sex and God." *Talking with Texas Writers: Twelve Interviews.* Ed. Patrick Bennett. College Station: Texas A&M University Press, 1980. 111–34.

Blades, John. "Urban Carpetbagger." *Chicago Tribune* 29 April 1993: 511A.

Keith, Elizabeth Anne Slay. "The Motif of the Fairy-Tale Princess in the Novels of Shelby Hearon." Thesis, University of North Texas, 1986.

Kendall, Elaine. "A Modern-Day Coming of Age in Texas." Rev. of *Owning Jolene. Los Angeles Times* 3 Feb. 1989: V8.

———. "A Witty Take on a Texas Affair." Rev. of *Hug Dancing. Los Angeles Times* 13 Dec. 1991: E19.

Levine, Beth. "PW Interviews: Shelby Hearon." *Publishers Weekly* 3 April 1987: 56–57.

Marshall, Carol. "The Fairy Tale and the Frontier: Images of Women in Texas Fiction." *The Texas Literary Tradition: Fiction, Folklore, History.* Ed. Don Graham, James W. Lee, and William T. Pilkington. Austin: University of Texas Press, 1983. 195–206.

Mayer, Pauline. "Thelma and Louise, 30 Years Later." Rev. of *Life Estates. Los Angeles Times* 6 March 1994: BR2.

McCorkle, Jill. "Still Beating . . ." Rev. of *Footprints*. *Boston Globe* 24 March 1996: B36-B38.

Parrott, Barbara Freeman. "The Vital Female in the Novels of Shelby Hearon." Thesis, University of North Texas, 1978.

Rev. of *Ella in Bloom*. *Publishers Weekly* 13 Nov. 2000: 86.

Robb, Christina. "*Hug Dancing*: A Comic Romance of Divorce." Rev. of *Hug Dancing*. *Boston Globe* 10 Dec. 1991: 61.

Rodenberger, Lou. "Shelby Hearon, Beverly Lowry and Sarah Bird." *Updating the Literary West*. Ed. Western Literature Association. Fort Worth: Texas Christian University Press, 1997. 600–7.

Sandlin, Tim. "A Normal Life, with Oven Mitts." Rev. of *Owning Jolene*. *New York Times Book Review* 22 Jan. 1989: 10.

"Shelby Hearon." *Contemporary Authors*. New rev. ser. Ed. Pamela S. Dear. Vol. 48. Detroit: Gale, 1995. 237–40.

Smith, Lee. "Widowhood Is Powerful." Rev. of *Life Estates*. *New York Times Book Review* 13 Feb. 1994: 724.

Tidmore, Kurt. "Deep in the Heart of Texas, But Shallow in Its Characterizations." Rev. of *Hug Dancing*. *Washington Post* 27 Dec. 1991: C3.

AMY HEMPEL (1951–)

Rhonda Cawthorn

BIOGRAPHY

Amy Hempel was born on December 14, 1951, in Chicago, Illinois, to Gardiner and Gloria Hempel. She spent most of her childhood in Chicago and surrounding areas. From when she was in the third grade to nearly the time she graduated from high school, she lived with her family in Denver, Colorado. She then moved to San Francisco, California. This move would have a significant effect on Hempel's fiction that is most obvious in stories from her earliest collection, *Reasons to Live* (1985). While living in California, she earned her bachelor of arts degree in journalism at California State University at San Jose. Just as writing for newspapers helped Hemingway to create his compressed, energetic prose style, training in journalistic writing helped Hempel to develop a pared-down writing style that many critics have called minimalistic. Hempel attributes much of the inspiration for the plot behind her early stories to a series of personal and family crises that she experienced before and after her move to California. Her young adult years were so full of crises and bad luck that, as Hempel states, "I went from accident to accident, hospital to hospital; I'd walk out of the house in the morning and half look up to see when the Mosler safe was going to fall out of the sky and smash me into the sidewalk" (Sapp 77). Hempel had more positive experiences in California that would influence her fiction as well, especially her dark sense of humor. One source of this dark sense of humor, Hempel admits, was her friendship with some members of an improvisational comedy group in California who helped her to see the world with a slightly "skewed vision" (Goldwater 181).

Hempel began writing when she left California and settled in New York to attend a writing workshop taught by Gordon Lish, a former editor of *Esquire* magazine. She worked with Lish for several years and remembers him as a teacher who taught her to write about her most despicable secrets, the things she "would never live down" (Sapp 81). Hempel knew immediately what she would write about: the death of her best friend whom she felt she had failed "when [she] absolutely couldn't fail her, when she was dying" (Sapp 81). The story became the much-anthologized story "In the Cemetery Where Al Jolson Is Buried," which was published in Hempel's first collection, *Reasons to Live*. The story, which blends humor with the poignant tale of her friend's death, is both heartbreaking and hilarious. Of this story and the collection as a whole, Hempel states that blending humor with the painful was one of her goals as a writer: "There's a way in which you can make the readers laugh until suddenly they're crying and they don't know what hit them" (Sapp 78). Her next short story collection, *At the Gates of the Animal Kingdom* (1990), addresses similar themes and similar characters, generally ones who are trying to cope with difficult situations in life. In her novella, *Tumble Home* (1997), Hempel tried to stake out new ground by focusing on characters who, as she states, have "everything they needed and were happy in normal ways" (Sherman 69).

Hempel's individual stories have been translated into twelve languages. She recently assembled a collection titled *Unleashed: Poems by Writers' Dogs*, which is an assemblage of poems written by famous poets—but in the voices of their pets. The collection, which Hempel edited in conjunction with poet Jim Shepherd, was published in 1999. Her stories have been anthologized in *Best American Short Stories,* the *Pushcart Prize,* and the *Norton Anthology of Short Fiction*. They have appeared in magazines and quarterlies such as *Harper's, Mother Jones, Grand Street,* and *Yale Review*. Her nonfiction has appeared in the *New York Times Magazine, Esquire, Vogue, Interview, Elle,* and other outlets. She has taught at New York University and the New School for Social Research and has conducted residencies at Sewanee, Bread Loaf, Ropewalk, the New York State Summer Writer's Institute, and elsewhere. Ms. Hempel currently lives in New York City and teaches writing at Bennington College. She is also a contributing editor of *Bomb* magazine.

MAJOR WORKS AND THEMES

Hempel once told a reviewer that she was interested in resilience and we can see how she explores the theme of resilience, the way people manage to survive unbelievable situations of pain and loss, in virtually all of her works, especially her first collection of stories, *Reasons to Live*. Of this collection, Hempel states, "If I have a motto for this particular bunch of stories," it would be what "Dr. Christian Barnard said, 'Suffering isn't ennobling, recovery is' " (O'Connor 85). This theme runs throughout *Reasons to Live* and can be especially seen in stories such as "In the Cemetery Where Al Jolson Is Buried," where a young woman must cope with not only the loss of her best friend but her own cowardice in helping her to face her death. A key figure that Hempel uses in this story, which also surfaces in her later novella, *Tumble Home*, is the chimp Koko, who learns to use sign language to communicate with human beings. In this story, Hempel uses the story of the chimp, whose pet kitten dies, to underscore the feelings of grief and loss that permeate the story. The story ends thusly: "And when the baby died, the mother stood over the body, her wrinkled hands moving with animal grace, forming again and again the words: Baby, come hug. Baby, come hug, fluent now in the language of grief" (51). The careful reader will notice the multiple resonances of the last line. The narrator, like the signing chimp, has become "fluent in the language of grief" not only because of her loss but also because of her strength to relive the memory and write the "fluent" story that we are reading (51).

Narrators in *Reasons to Live* frequently mourn a loss. In "Nashville Gone to Ashes," the narrator mourns not only the loss of her dog, Nashville, but also the death of her husband's love for her. When pondering this lost love, the narrator concludes that with love, "we give all we can, that's as far as the heart can go" (32). In another story, a young woman copes with an abortion while helping her best friend through her pregnancy. In still another, a young woman watches while a woman living in her apartment building contemplates diving from the ledge above. The narrator comforts herself from the anxiety of the situation by thinking of reassuring stories of people who have turned tragedies into their salvation. The narrator wonders, "How do we know that what happens to us isn't good?" (98). As Dawn Ann Drzal notes, "Most of the stories in *Reasons to Live* open after a crisis to find the narrator standing, shell-shocked, amidst the rubble of her life" (505). By the end of these stories, though, we feel that all of her narrators have found a way to cope, some "reasons to live."

In her second collection, *At the Gates of the Animal Kingdom*, Hempel continues to use first-person narrators who are damaged or crippled by life but who remain, in the end, survivors. In "The Harvest," the narrator is the survivor of a motorcycle accident that leaves her scarred physically, with 400 stitches in one of her legs and extremely shaken emotionally. Typical of Hempel's characters, the narrator in this story tries to mask her pain through humor, teasing her doctor, asking him if he thinks "looks are important" (10). Despite the narrator's hardened sense of humor, it is obvious that she is barely managing to cope and is still trying to figure out how to present this new scarred self to the world. In "Rapture of the Deep," the narrator tries to accept having lost her fiancé in a diving accident. The rapture of the deep of the title is the name for descending below the acceptable level for deep-sea divers, but it becomes symbolic of the nature of grief—when one feels she has descended below acceptable levels of sadness. In "The Day I Had Everything," Hempel focuses her lens on members of a self-help group of survivors of loss—loss of loved ones who have died, boyfriends who have fled, even lost pieces of themselves. Often they mask their fears and feelings of hopelessness behind hard-edged humor. One of the group members who is about to undergo a mastectomy drops a bra strap, exposes her breast, and says, "This one is for the surgeon" (63). In this collection, as in virtually all of Hempel's stories, there is some indication that the narrator will transcend whatever difficult situation she faces in the course of the story—that she will become whole again. As Suzan Sherman notes of Hempel's characters, "Her characters are damaged goods—they walk through life with the lens of loss tinting their view. These losses—whether they be the death of a best friend, an unborn baby, a mother, a house—never defeat those in mourning. They become stronger, their scars a complexity, inevitably becoming beauty" (67).

It took Hempel seven years to complete her most recently published work, *Tumble Home*, a collection of seven short stories and one novella. Critics and reviewers detected a change in tone from Hempel's previous work. Sherman notes that the work "dwells less on the losses, focusing more on the celebration of what's good, even in the simplest of terms, of being in the here and now" (67). Like Hempel's previous collections, the stories and novella in *Tumble Home* feature narrators trying to cope with difficult situations. The difference in this work, though, is that Hempel relies less on a minimalistic, humorous portrayal of characters. In the title piece of the collection, "Tumble Home," Hempel uses an extended epistolary technique, a series of letters written by a woman in a private sanitarium to a famous artist she met only once. In these letters, she describes the other people in the institution and recollections from her life. Throughout the novella, we can see both her struggle to cope with her present situation and her attempts to make the best of it, to see (which, Hempel states, is her goal for the collection) "what's good" about "being in the here and now" (67). By the end of her letters to the artist, the narrator, who is currently in an institution, recalls a church sermon called "The Blessing of Dailiness," in her effort to appreciate the fact that although her recent life has been filled with confusion and pain, she can now appreciate what is blessed in ordinary experience.

CRITICAL RECEPTION

Reasons to Live received mostly positive reviews upon its publication. Michael Schumacher, reviewing for *Writer's Digest,* states that "Hempel's compact . . . writing style only augments the almost elliptical series of incidents that transform the normal into the extraordinary" and touts "In the Cemetery Where Al Jolson Is Buried" as one of the "finest short stories written in the last decade, bar none" (62). Sheila Ballayntine, writing for the *New York Times Book Review*, states that the stories in *Reasons to Live* are "tough minded, original and fully felt. . . . They can take your breath away" (9). Other reviewers criticize Hempel's humor and spare writing style. Barbara Williamson, a reviewer for the *Nation*, states that sometimes the "revelation has a powerful impact" in Hempel's stories, while at other times "very little" (749). She also says that "when the stories work, the smooth, controlled surface cracks with real feeling; elsewhere they are merely California cool" (749). Dawn Ann Drzal notes that "while sometimes witty," Hempel's "view of the world as absurd deprives the stories of emotional power" (506).

The reception of Hempel's second collection was even more varied. Most critics had become wary of Hempel's minimalist style, as one review in the *Boston Globe* reveals, "A Little Less Minimalism Please" (Caldwell 35). Sybil Steinberg, writing for *Publishers Weekly*, states that Hempel's new collection presents stories that are "mordant and unsentimental" and that Hempel's "sharp wit sometimes shaves away too ruthlessly at characters, limiting the depth of her sympathy" (95). Ralph Novak compliments Hempel on her "wickedly vivid characters and moods" but warns that "too much compression and you end up with a black hole, which is something else altogether, but hardly literature" (33).

Reviews of Hempel's latest work, *Tumble Home*, have been mostly positive. A reviewer for *Publishers Weekly* stated that the short stories are "perfectly captured moments," but that the novella was "the standout here" with its "gentle but morbid humor" and a "tone effective and true" (47). David Gates states that in this collection, Hempel "doesn't waste a word" and called the work "stringently edited and generously imagined" (78, 79). Overall, reviewers tend to view Hempel as a writer who is constantly evolving and improving over time, and they express overwhelming eagerness to see what this inventive writer will do next.

BIBLIOGRAPHY

Works by Amy Hempel

Reasons to Live. New York: Harper, 1985.
At the Gates of the Animal Kingdom. New York: Harper, 1990.

Tumble Home. New York: Simon & Schuster, 1997.

Amy Hempel and Jim Shepherd, eds. *Unleashed: Poems by Writers' Dogs*. New York: Three Rivers Press, 1999.

Studies of Amy Hempel

Ballayntine, Sheila. "Rancho Libido and Other Hot Spots." Rev. of *Reasons to Live*. *New York Times Book Review* 28 April 1985: 9.

Begley, Adam. Rev. of *Tumble Home*. *People Weekly* 12 May 1997: 28.

Caldwell, Gail. "Amy Hempel's Stories: A Little Less Minimalism, Please." Rev. of *At the Gates of the Animal Kingdom*. *Boston Globe* 8 March 1990: 35.

Drzal, Dawn Ann. "An Assemblage of Trifles." Rev. of *Reasons to Live*. *Commonweal* 20 Sept. 1985: 505–6.

Gates, David. Rev. of *Tumble Home*. *Newsweek* 28 April 1997: 78–79.

Goldwater, Mitchell. "Amy Hempel." *Short Story Writers since World War II*. Ed. Patrick Meanor. Detroit: Gale, 1999. Vol. 218 of *Dictionary of Literary Biography*. 187–95.

Hallett, Cynthia Whitney. *Minimalism and the Short Story: Raymond Carver, Amy Hempel, and Mary Robison*. Lewiston, NY: Edwin Mellen Press, 1999.

Kakutani, Michiko. "Uphill Battles." Rev. of *Reasons to Live*. *New York Times Book Review* 13 April 1985: 14.

McCampbell, Marlene. Rev. of *Unleashed: Poems by Writers' Dogs*. *People Weekly* 25 Sept. 1999: 43.

Novak, Ralph. Rev. of *At the Gates of the Animal Kingdom*. *People Weekly* 2 April 1990: 33.

O'Connor, Patricia T. "Recovery Is Ennobling, Suffering Is Not (Amy Hempel's Motto)." Rev. of *Reasons to Live*. *New York Times Book Review* 28 April 1985: 90.

O'Laughlin, Jim. Rev. of *Tumble Home*. *Booklist* 1 May 1997: 1478.

Olson, Ray. Rev. of *Reasons to Live*. *Booklist* 15 April 1985: 1160.

————. Rev. of *Tumble Home*. *Publishers Weekly* 10 March 1997: 47.

Sapp, Jo. "An Interview with Amy Hempel." *Missouri Review* 16 (1993): 75–95.

Schumacher, Michael. Rev. of *Reasons to Live*. *Writer's Digest* 67 (1987): 62.

Sherman, Suzan. "Amy Hempel." *Bomb* 59 (1997): 66–70.

Steinberg, Sybil. Rev of *At the Gates of the Animal Kingdom*. *Publishers Weekly* 19 Jan. 1990: 95.

Williamson, Barbara Fisher. Rev. of *Reasons to Live*. *Nation* 15 June 1985: 749.

LINDA HOGAN (1947–)

Ellen L. Arnold

BIOGRAPHY

Linda Hogan was born July 17, 1947, in Denver, Colorado, the daughter of Charles Colbert Henderson, a Chickasaw, and Cleona Bower Henderson, a descendant of Nebraska Territory settlers. Hogan's father joined the military to support his family, and they relocated a great deal, but Hogan has always considered Oklahoma home. Her father's family has lived in Indian Territory since Removal, and Hogan grew up amidst a storytelling tradition, including family stories of prosperous allotment homesteads lost to the oil boom land swindles of the 1920s and bank foreclosures of the Depression. During her childhood, Hogan recalls, her Oklahoma relatives lived in poverty, without electricity or running water, and traveled by horse and buggy.

In interviews, Hogan discusses the importance of her working-class background to her sense of self. She began working full-time at age fifteen and moved at twenty to California, where she worked as nurse's aide, dental assistant, and cocktail waitress. She describes herself during that time as poorly educated and "unconscious," without words to express her inner life (Bruchac 124). Inspired by a cousin's experience in college, she began attending adult education and junior college classes and eventually received an undergraduate degree in psychology from the University of Colorado at Colorado Springs. She moved to suburban Washington, D. C., with her husband, Pat Hogan (whom she later divorced); there, while working as a teacher's aide with handicapped children, she began to write poetry as "a way of trying to define who I was in an environment that felt foreign" (Bruchac 121). In 1975 she enrolled in a creative writing class at the University of Maryland and, after returning to Colorado, received an MA degree in English and creative writing in 1978 from the University of Colorado at Boulder.

Hogan taught at the University of Colorado at Boulder from 1977 to 1979 and in 1979 adopted two daughters of Oglala Lakota heritage. She taught at Colorado Women's College in 1979 and at Rocky Mountain Women's Institute of the University of Denver from 1979 to 1980. In 1978 she published her first book of poetry, *Calling Myself Home*, followed by a play, *A Piece of Moon*, which won the Five Civilized Tribes Playwriting Award in 1980 and was produced in 1981. A second poetry book, *Daughters, I Love You*, appeared in 1981. Hogan was poet-in-residence for the Colorado and Oklahoma Arts Councils from 1980 to 1984, taught at the University of Minnesota at Twin Cities from 1984 to 1989, and returned to Colorado, where she has been associate professor in English and American Indian studies at the University of Colorado at Boulder since 1989. Hogan's eight years of experience as a volunteer in wildlife rehabilitation clinics in Minnesota and Colorado are reflected in her strong commitment to environmental causes.

Since 1981 Hogan has published four more poetry collections: *Eclipse* (1983); *Seeing through the Sun* (1985), which won the American Book Award from the Before Columbus Foundation in 1985; *Savings: Poems* (1988); and *The Book of Medicines* (1993), a National Book Critics Circle finalist and recipient of the Colorado Book Award in 1993. She has produced two collections of short fiction, *That Horse* (with co-author Charles Colbert Henderson, 1985), which includes a story by her father; and *Red Clay: Poems and Stories* (1991), which combines both stories and poems. Her short story "Aunt Moon's Young Man" (1988) was selected for *The Best American Short Stories 1989*, and her first novel *Mean Spirit* (1990) received the Oklahoma Book Award for fiction and was a finalist for the Pulitzer Prize in 1990. Her subsequent novels, *Solar Storms* (1995; recipient of the Colorado Book Award in 1996) and *Power* (1998), have also been very well received. In addition, Hogan has co-edited two collections of essays that focus on women's spiritual development and nature and published *Dwellings: A Spiritual History of the Living World* (1995), a collection of her own essays about the natural world. In 2001 Hogan published a third co-edited (with Brenda Peterson) collection of essays, *The Sweet Breathing of Plants: Women and the Green World*, about women's relationships with the natural world, and a memoir, *The Woman Who Watches over the World: A Native Memoir*. Hogan has received many additional awards, including a National Endowment for the Arts Grant in 1986, a Guggenheim Award for fiction in 1990, a Lannan Foundation Award for outstanding achievement in poetry in 1994, a Pushcart Prize, and the Lifetime Achievement Award from the Native Writers' Circle of the Americas in 1998.

MAJOR WORKS AND THEMES

Much of Hogan's work centers on the genocide and dispossession of indigenous peoples that began with the European conquest of North America, were legalized by the General Allotment Act of 1887, and persist in contemporary land and resource appropriation. Her short story "That Horse" (in *That Horse*), for example, is set amidst the grab for Indian land and mineral rights that accompanied Oklahoma statehood, and "Amen" (in *Red Clay*) describes the continuing loss of land that resulted from foreclosures during the Depression. Her first novel, *Mean Spirit*, is based on the historical "Osage Reign of Terror," a series of murders of Osage people for their land and oil rights that occurred during the Oklahoma oil boom of the 1920s. Her second and third novels are also based on historical incidents: *Solar Storms* on Cree resistance to the Canadian government's massive hydroelectric project at James Bay in the 1970s (told against the background of the devastation wrought by the fur trade) and *Power* on the killing of an endangered Florida panther by a Seminole man.

All of Hogan's writing traces in moving detail the effects of these histories in personal loss and suffering through generations of Indian lives and the devastation of place and nonhuman life that accompanies them. However, her work never slips into despair or pathos. The short story "Amen" (*Red Clay*) affirms holding to the old ways beneath a surface of conformity to white ways, while "Making Do" characteristically portrays not only the grief of loss but also the necessity to hold on to what is left. Hogan's characters "make do" with whatever is at hand, "make art out of our loss," as does Roberta when she carves the souls of her dead children into wooden birds ("Making Do" 39). For Hogan, Indians are not merely victims of history but possess "an incredible will to survival" (*Red Clay* 1), and she expresses that will in her work through themes of identity, homecoming, and interconnectedness.

Hogan's early work reveals a writer torn between her white and red halves—between awareness of the terrible loss her Chickasaw relations have experienced and the knowledge that her white great-grandfather, who married an Indian woman, "was so land hungry that he used to hire killings" (*Red Clay* 60). Her poem, "The Truth Is," in *Seeing through the Sun*, is often cited for its painful portrayal of a body divided against itself. However, Hogan's celebration of the resistance and survival of Indian people and their connection to the land moves her work toward a recognition of the special capacities of mixed bloodedness to negotiate a divided world and the power of words to heal its brokenness, a power that reaches the epitome of its expression in the exquisite language of *The Book of Medicines* and *Solar Storms*.

Solar Storms recounts the return home to the Boundary Waters area between Minnesota and Canada of a scarred and alienated mixed-blood teenage girl searching for her family and the mother who abandoned her as a baby. Angel Jensen joins four generations of her female relatives on a difficult canoe journey north through the wilderness to the site of dam protests and in the process recovers her personal history, remakes her identity with/in the natural world, and commits her life to acts of creation. In *Power*, a teen-age girl bears witness to difficult issues surrounding the rapidly disappearing Florida panther and the dwindling tribe to whom the panther is sacred. Like *Solar Storms*, a female *bildungsroman*, *Power* brings Omishto to self-definition and the strength to leave her assimilated home to join a small traditional community living deep within the Everglades. The message of both novels is the same: "Home" is a place humans must make for themselves through respect for the sacredness of life and responsible participation with it. Hogan sees herself as primarily an environmental writer: "My main work has been to find a language that expresses a care for the land and its creatures," she tells Derrick Jensen (123). Her writing is a passionate call for unity among all people in awareness that the future survival of humans and the earth itself depends on weaving new relationships with the natural world.

CRITICAL RECEPTION

Hogan's novels have been reviewed widely and generally very positively. Reviewers have emphasized the lyricism and sensuousness of her language, the depth and strength of her characters, particularly women, and her imaginative reconstruction of silenced histories. Some literary critics have objected to the alteration of historical particulars in Hogan's novels. Osage critic Robert Allen Warrior, for example, criticizes *Mean Spirit* for distorting Osage history and identities and thus failing to support tribal sovereignty (52). Others such as Betty Louise Bell and Eric Gary Anderson suggest that *Mean Spirit* explores a deeper history, one that realizes the complex processes of disorientation, resistance, and survival inherent in historical moments. In Anderson's words, Hogan "decenters" history, "exploiting the tensions between a linear-historical imperative and her own resistance to the compulsory linearity and authority of western history" (56). Hogan herself responds, "Yes, there is a problem for native writers, that we are read as voices of history. . . . This . . . serves to keep us in our literary place, not as fiction writers, not as creative people, but only as voices responding to the oppression of history" (McAdams, "Interview" 137). In her later novels, Hogan fictionalizes locations and tribes to transcend this limitation.

A great deal of attention has been given to Hogan's work among readers and critics of Native American literature. Notably two special issues of the journal *Studies in American Indian Literatures*, edited by Betty Louise Bell in 1994 and John Purdy in 1999, were devoted to critical essays on her work. Hogan is assuming a place along-side N. Scott Momaday, James Welch, Leslie Marmon Silko, and Louise Erdrich as one of the most important Native American writers in the United States. However, Hogan's work resists the tendency of critics to compartmentalize and marginalize the writing of Native Americans and is increasingly being read and studied in other contexts such as women's literature, environmental literature, and ecofeminism. Her work has been widely anthologized in collections of American literature, Native American fiction and poetry, multicultural writing, nature writing, and women's writing.

BIBLIOGRAPHY

Works by Linda Hogan

Calling Myself Home. Greenfield Center, NY: Greenfield Review, 1978.
"The 19th Century Native American Poets." *Wassaja* 13 (1980): 24–29.
"Who Puts Together." *Denver Quarterly* 14 (1980): 103–10.
Daughters, I Love You. Denver: Research Center on Women, 1981.
A Piece of Moon. Play produced at Oklahoma State University, Stillwater, October 1981.
Ed. *Native American Women*. Special Issue. *Frontiers* 6.3 (1982).
Eclipse. Los Angeles: American Indian Studies Center, University of California, 1983.
Seeing through the Sun. Amherst: University of Massachusetts Press, 1985.
Linda Hogan and Charles Colbert Henderson. *That Horse*. Acoma Pueblo, NM: Pueblo of Acoma Press, 1985.
"Making Do." *The New Native American Novel: Works in Progress*. Ed. Mary Dougherty Bartlett. Albuquerque: University of New Mexico Press, 1986. 31–39.
Linda Hogan, Carol Bruchac, and Judith McDaniel, eds. *The Stories We Hold Secret: Tales of Women's Spiritual Development*. Greenfield Center, NY: Greenfield Review Press, 1986.
"The Two Lives." *I Tell You Now: Autobiographical Essays by Native American Writers*. Ed. Brian Swann and Arnold Krupat. Lincoln: University of Nebraska Press, 1987. 233–49.
"Aunt Moon's Young Man." *Missouri Review* 11 (1988): 186–204.
Savings: Poems. Minneapolis: Coffee House Press, 1988.
Mean Spirit. New York: Atheneum, 1990.
Red Clay: Poems and Stories. Greenfield Center, NY: Greenfield Review Press, 1991.
The Book of Medicines. Minneapolis: Coffee House Press, 1993.
"Department of the Interior." *Minding the Body: Women Writers on Body and Soul*. Ed. Patricia Foster. New York: Doubleday, 1994. 159–74.
"A Different Yield." *Religion and Literature* 26 (1994): 71–80.

Dwellings: A Spiritual History of the Living World. New York: Norton, 1995.
Solar Storms. New York: Simon and Schuster, 1994.
Linda Hogan, Deena Metzger, and Brenda Peterson, eds. *Intimate Nature: The Bond between Women and Animals.* New York: Fawcett, 1998.
Power. New York: Norton, 1999.
Linda Hogan and Brenda Peterson. *The Sweet Breathing of Plants: Women and the Green World.* San Francisco: North Point Press, 2001.
The Woman Who Watches over the World: A Native Memoir. New York: Norton, 2001.

Studies of Linda Hogan

Alaimo, Stacy. "Displacing Darwin and Descartes: The Bodily Transgressions of Fielding Burke, Octavia Butler, and Linda Hogan." *Interdisciplinary Studies in Literature and Environment* 3 (1996): 47–66.

Anderson, Eric Gary. "States of Being in the Dark: Removal and Survival in Linda Hogan's *Mean Spirit.*" *Great Plains Quarterly* 20 (2000): 55–67.

Arnold, Ellen L. "Masks over the Face of God: Remapping Epistemology in Linda Hogan's *Solar Storms.*" *Paradoxa* 6.15 (2001) 49–60.

Baria, Amy Greenwood. "Review Essay: Linda Hogan's Two Worlds." *Studies in American Indian Literatures* 10 (1998): 67–73.

Bell, Betty Louise, ed. *Linda Hogan: Calling Us Home.* Special Issue. *Studies in American Indian Literatures* 6 (1994).

Blaeser, Kimberly M. "Pagans Rewriting the Bible: Heterodoxy and the Representation of Spirituality in Native American Literature." *Ariel* 25 (1994): 12–31.

Brice, Jennifer. "Earth as Mother, Earth as Other in Novels by Silko and Hogan." *Critique* 39 (1998): 127–38.

Bruchac, Joseph. "To Take Care of Life." Interview with Linda Hogan. *Survival This Way: Interviews with American Indian Poets.* Ed. Joseph Bruchac. Tucson: University of Arizona Press, 1987. 119–33.

Coltelli, Laura. "Linda Hogan." Interview with Linda Hogan. *Winged Words: American Indian Writers Speak.* Ed. Laura Coltelli. Lincoln: University of Nebraska Press, 1990. 71–86.

Fast, Robin Riley. *The Heart as a Drum: Continuance and Resistance in American Indian Poetry.* Ann Arbor: University of Michigan Press, 1999.

Gillan, Jennifer. "The Hazards of Osage Fortune: Gender and the Rhetoric of Compensation in Federal Policy and American Indian Fiction." *Arizona Quarterly* 54 (1998): 1–25.

Jahner, Elaine. "Reading All the Way down to Fire." *Feminist Measures: Soundings in Poetry and Theory.* Ed. Lynn Keller and Cristanne Miller. Ann Arbor: University of Michigan Press, 1994. 163–83.

Jensen, Derrick. "Linda Hogan." Interview with Linda Hogan. *Listening to the Land: Conversations about Nature, Culture, and Eros.* Ed. Derrick Jensen. San Francisco: Sierra Club Books, 1995. 122–29.

McAdams, Janet. "We, I, 'Voice,' and Voices: Reading Contemporary Native American Poetry." *Studies in American Indian Literatures* 7 (1995): 7–16.

——. "An Interview with Linda Hogan." *This Blood Is a Map: Voice and Cartography in Contemporary Native American Poetry.* Dissertation, Emory University, 1996.

Murphy, Patrick. *Literature, Nature, and Other: Ecofeminist Critiques.* New York: State University of New York Press, 1995.

Murray, John A. "Of Panthers and People: An Interview with Linda Hogan." *Bloomsbury Review* July/August 1998: 5ff.

Purdy, John, ed. *Linda Hogan.* Special Issue. *Studies in American Indian Literatures* 11.4 (1999).

Rainwater, Catherine. "Intertextual Twins and Their Relations: Linda Hogan's *Mean Spirit* and *Solar Storms*." *Modern Fiction Studies* 45 (1988): 93–113.

———. *Dreams of Fiery Stars: The Transformations of Native American Fiction*. Philadelphia: University of Pennsylvania Press, 1999.

Scholer, Bo. "A Heart Made out of Crickets: An Interview with Linda Hogan." *Journal of Ethnic Studies* 16 (1988): 107–17.

Shanley, Kathryn W. "Linda Hogan." *Native American Writers of the United States*. Ed. Kenneth M. Roemer. Detroit: Gale, 1997. Vol. 175 of *Dictionary of Literary Biography*. 123–30.

Smith, Patricia Clark. "Linda Hogan." Interview with Linda Hogan. *This Is about Vision: Interviews with Southwestern Writers*. Ed. William Balassi, John F. Crawford, and Annie O. Eysturoy. Albuquerque: University of New Mexico Press, 1990. 141–55.

Tarter, Jim. " 'Dreams of Earth': Place, Multiethnicity, and Environmental Justice in Linda Hogan's *Solar Storms*." *Reading under the Sign of Nature: New Essays in Ecocriticism*. Ed. John Tallmadge and Henry Harrington. Salt Lake City: University of Utah Press, 2000. 128–47.

Taylor, Paul Beekman. "Woman as Redeemer in Linda Hogan's *Mean Spirit*." *Native American Women in Literature and Culture*. Ed. Susan Castillo and Victor M. P. Da Rosa. Porto, Portugal: Fernando Pessoa University Press, 1997. 141–55.

Warrior, Robert Allen. "Review Essay of *The Deaths of Sybil Bolton*." *Wicazo Sa Review* 11 (1995): 52.

MARY HOOD (1946–)

Angela Laflen

BIOGRAPHY

Mary Hood's biography draws attention to her love of learning and her lifelong pursuit of knowledge. At every stage of her life, Hood has accepted new challenges and continues to experiment in both fiction and life. She was born September 16, 1946, in the coastal town of Brunswick, Georgia, to William Hood, an aircraft worker, and Katherine Hood (née Rogers), a teacher. Hood's parents had a significant influence on her ability and desire to become a writer. Not only did they give her support during the time that it took her to become a writer, but they also helped her to develop a unique perspective with which to look at the world. Although she is considered a Southern writer, Hood does not completely accept that designation. She has written that her father, a native New Yorker who lived in Georgia, helped her to develop "no-nonsense brevity and encompassing concatenations" ("Stubborn Sense" 36).

Hood has lived all of her life in Georgia, and it would be difficult to overestimate the impact of this state on her life and fiction. After a childhood and adolescence spent in Georgia, she attended college at Georgia State University, graduating with degrees in Spanish and mathematics in 1967. She pursued a master's degree in chemistry at Georgia Tech until she decided that she did not want a career in chemistry and left the university to pursue writing. She moved with her parents to Cherokee County, north of Atlanta, in 1970 and then to the area of Victoria in 1976. Currently, she makes her home in Woodstock, Georgia. During Hood's lifetime, she has witnessed the rural communities in which she lived become suburbanized, and she incorporates the effects of this change into her fiction. The transition from rural to suburban serves as the backdrop for many of her stories, and her characters struggle to understand the effects of this change on their communities and families.

Hood traces her decision to become a writer to her childhood, when she struggled with dyslexia to become an avid reader. Her reading history is characterized by several stages of discovery. At the age of eight, she read a book about the Quaker Whitmans,

Oregon settlers who were killed by Indians, which changed the way she viewed reading. She came to understand that reading was not only about escaping from reality but could also help readers to understand the nature of truth. She says, "You can tell from my short fiction that I was branded from that early point. I really believe that. Truth is truth. How things ought to be is not always what we get" (O'Briant, "Real Life" 8). Another discovery of importance to Hood was that women had a long history of writing fiction. When she set out to become a writer, Hood had never heard of Flannery O'Connor or Eudora Welty, two writers to whom her work is often compared. She discovered women writers when she bought a book by Elizabeth Bowen at a used paperback store, and this discovery led her to begin buying and reading books by other women authors including Virginia Woolf, Eudora Welty, and Flannery O'Connor.

Hood's interest in writing seems to stem, at least in part, from her many diverse interests. Writing allows her to study and pursue these various interests, and she has managed to incorporate into her fiction her knowledge of subjects as diverse as natural history, Spanish, philosophy, and the Southerners she interacts with daily. During the decade following 1967, while Hood experienced rejection as a writer, she took the opportunity to study, to read, and to learn about the community in which she lived; much of what she learned during this time became a part of her fiction. During these years, Hood worked in a language lab, as a librarian and substitute teacher, as a polling officer in her community, and as a visual artist, painting landscapes on everything from shovels to hand saws and even accepting commissions to paint portraits of deceased pets.

In 1984 her first collection of stories was published by the University of Georgia Press in a work called *How Far She Went*. The same year, the book won the Flannery O'Connor Award for short fiction and the *Southern Review*/Louisiana State University Short Fiction Award. Her next volume, *And Venus Is Blue*, was published by Ticknor and Fields in 1986; the title story won the Townsend Prize for fiction in 1988, and another story included in the book, "Something Good for Ginnie," won the National Magazine Award in fiction in 1986. Knopf published Hood's first novel, *Familiar Heat*, in 1995, and she is currently working on a new collection of stories, tentatively titled *Survival, Evasion, and Escape*, to be published by Knopf as well. Hood's stories and essays have also appeared in numerous journals and magazines including *Georgia Review*, *Ohio Review*, *Kenyon Review*, *Harper's Magazine*, the *Best American Short Stories 1984*, and the *Editor's Choice: New American Short Stories*.

Even after achieving success as a writer, Hood is still not content to limit herself to one profession. She joined the Southern Writer-in-Residence Program in 1996, teaching at the University of Mississippi from 1996 to 1997 and at Berry College from 1997 to 1998. Hood's work as a university instructor seems fitting given her lifelong commitment to acquiring and transmitting knowledge.

MAJOR WORKS AND THEMES

Almost all reviews of Mary Hood's work conclude that Hood is an "honest" writer who accurately portrays the lives of working-class Southerners without sentimentalizing or trivializing their lives. Not only does Hood strive to portray life truthfully in her use of language and characterization, but her works also center on characters searching for truth.

One of Hood's strengths as a writer is her ability to portray characters. Her characters are multidimensional, and the language that they speak is true-to-life. For example, it takes only the opening sentence of the story "How Far She Went" for her to create a clear image of the nature of the relationship between a grandmother and her granddaughter: "They had quarreled all morning, squalled all summer about the incidentals: how tight the girl's cut-off jeans were, the 'Every Inch a Woman' T-shirt, her choice of music and how loud she played it, her practiced inattention, her sullen look" (*How Far* 67). Hood's commitment to reality in her characterization is deliberate; she has written, "When I began to write fiction, I made a conscious decision to try to sound like the Southern talkers I had heard tell such wonderful things" ("Stubborn Sense" 36).

Hood's narrative voice always maintains an objective position and seems to report the events of the story without judging those events or the characters' involvement in them. Hood is also willing to experiment with form and style in her desire to portray life truthfully. "After Moore" (*And Venus Is Blue*) and "Doing This, Saying That, to Applause" (*How Far She Went*) might best exemplify this combination of objectivity and experimentation. In "Doing This, Saying That, to Applause," Hood uses multiple speakers who speak in sound bites, such as those heard on the evening news, to weave a suspenseful story about a nameless main character who is suspected of committing a crime. One speaker reflects, "When this happens to someone you know, you just can't explain it" (*How Far* 80). After each speaker makes an observation about the character, a short paragraph develops the story's narrative, which follows the suspect as he flees town and the law. It is impossible to completely understand the nature of the crime committed or why the main character is suspected, but Hood is effective in using the series of observations to create an impression of the character.

In "After Moore," readers share the perspective of a family counselor receiving information as various family members participate in a dialogue; the narrative perspective is introduced with " 'I guess I still love him but so what?' Rhonda told the counselor. They had sought professional help toward the bitter end. The family counselor listened and listened" (*Venus* 4). By the end, the story transcends the counselor's perspective, but like the counselor, the reader is asked only to listen without making a judgment on the characters or being given the chance to speak.

Hood most clearly explores the theme of searching for truthfulness in her first novel, *Familiar Heat*, which focuses on young Faye Rios, a woman with a "mental slate wiped clean" after she is involved in a serious car accident (186). As Faye struggles to relearn who she is and how a person must function in the world, she comes to respect facts and truth above all else: "Facts added up, or stood alone. They were what the world had and she could get—one at a time or in gulps. They were recoverable" (219). The truth helps to set Faye free and she embraces it, but this is not always the case in Hood's writing. Often the truth is very painful for Hood's characters. They become alcoholics, commit suicide, or simply deny reality rather than face a truth. Hood's writing suggests that without accepting the truth about things, people cannot grow and they cannot move past whatever truth it is that scares them. Her characters approach truth in a variety of ways, but the only successful characters are those who work to accept truth no matter how painful the consequences.

The most difficult challenges that Hood's characters face originate in their families, and she is skilled at portraying the problems that families face. This theme is prevalent in all three of her works. Some of her most powerful stories, "A Man among Men,"

"How Far She Went" (in *How Far She Went*), and "Something Good for Ginnie" (in *And Venus Is Blue*), show horribly destructive relationships between teens and their parents and grandparents. Many of her works focus on a breakdown in relationships between men and women, notable among them "Hindsight," "Inexorable Progress," "Solomon's Seal" (in *How Far She Went*), "After Moore," "The Goodwife Hawkins," "The Desire Call of the Wild Hen" (in *And Venus Is Blue*), and *Familiar Heat*.

Because she is searching for truth in family relationships, Hood allows the families in her stories a variety of ways of dealing with the problems in their lives and her stories do not have predictable outcomes, although a story's outcome is directly determined by the willingness of its characters to be loving and forgiving. "How Far She Went" ends on a positive note when a feuding grandmother and granddaughter find that they really do care about one another, all appearances to the contrary, and Rhonda and her husband, Moore, are reunited at the conclusion of "After Moore" because they are unwilling to give up on their marriage and each other. In contrast, "The Desire Call of the Wild Hen" and "Solomon's Seal" end without reconciliation between couples because the main characters cannot learn from or accept having made mistakes in the past, and so they cannot move beyond them.

CRITICAL RECEPTION

Critics usually discuss Mary Hood as a Southern writer following in the tradition of other strong Southern writers including Flannery O'Connor, Eudora Welty, and Katherine Anne Porter; however, in their reviews of her work, most critics spend more time discussing the differences between Hood's themes and those of other Southern writers rather than the similarities. Although her stories are located in the South and her characters are primarily working-class Southerners trapped in isolation, poverty, or destructive relationships, unlike many Southern writers, Hood does not find redemptive potential in the land or in love. Furthermore, her characters are not consumed by their history or by religious fervor. God factors very little into their lives. As a result, critics conclude that Hood is a transitional writer, one committed to examining "Southern" themes but conducting the examination with a fresh eye.

With the publication of Hood's first collection of short stories, *How Far She Went*, in 1984, many critics identified Hood as a great writer in the making. *How Far She Went* not only earned the Flannery O'Connor Award for short fiction and the *Southern Review*/Louisiana State University Short Fiction Award in 1984 but also won praise for its insightful characterizations, vivid imagery, and treatment of difficult themes. Even reviewers who found technical fault with the book identified Hood as a writer with enormous potential. In his review of the book, Frederick Busch nicely sums up the critical reaction to "How Far She Went" and to Mary Hood as a writer: "This slender volume . . . reveals a writer well worth reading now—and watching in the future" (203).

Consequently, critics were watching when Hood published her second collection of stories, *And Venus Is Blue*, in 1986. This book was the most favorably received of the three that Hood has published to date. David Baker describes the eight stories in the collection as "some of the finest, most powerfully written and moving pieces of fiction I've read in a long time" (142), and Alice McDermott calls the book a "marvelous collection" (11). In *And Venus Is Blue*, Hood experiments with the short story form, and critics praised this experimentation and identified it as wholly successful. Most critics agree that with *And Venus Is Blue*, Hood delivered on the promise she made in *How Far She Went* and created a collection of stories that powerfully illustrates how the American South can move "courageously into the future, carrying a diminished past on its back" (Kitchen 214).

Reviews of Hood's first novel, *Familiar Heat*, published in 1995, were mixed. Reviewers disagree on whether the structure of the book is a strength or a weakness. The novel is organized into five books, each of which contains multiple parts. Consequently, some reviewers see the book as simply another collection of short stories by Hood, only centered on one central story this time. Other reviewers, such as Malcolm Jones, Jr., praise the structure. Jones says, "This Georgia writer has made the leap to the longer form without ever looking winded" (86). As with *How Far She Went*, even those who find technical fault with the book praise its characterization, demonstrating once again that this is Hood's real strength as a writer. Perhaps most importantly, though, is the absence of any challenge to Hood's right to be called a great American writer in reviews of *Familiar Heat*. Although critics do not agree on the significance of *Familiar Heat*, they certainly seem to have accepted the importance of Mary Hood.

BIBLIOGRAPHY

Works by Mary Hood

How Far She Went. Athens: University of Georgia Press, 1984.
"A Stubborn Sense of Place." *Harper's Magazine* Aug. 1986: 35–45.
And Venus Is Blue. New York: Ticknor and Fields, 1986.
Familiar Heat. New York: Knopf, 1995.

Studies of Mary Hood

Aiken, David. "Mary Hood: The Dark Side of the Moon." *Southern Writers at the Century's End*. Ed. Jeffrey J. Folks and James A. Perkins. Lexington: University Press of Kentucky, 1997. 21–31.
Baker, David. "Time and Time Again." Rev. of *And Venus Is Blue*. *Kenyon Review* 9 (1987): 137–42.
Busch, Frederick. Rev. of *How Far She Went*. *Georgia Review* 39 (1985): 203–4.
Farmer, Joy A. "Mary Hood and the Speed of Grace: Catching Up with Flannery O'Connor." *Studies in Short Fiction* 33 (1996): 91–99.
Jones, Malcolm, Jr. "A Literary Soap Opera." Rev. of *Familiar Heat*. *Newsweek* 20 Nov. 1995: 86.
Kitchen, Judith. "The Moments That Matter." Rev. of *And Venus Is Blue*. *Georgia Review* 41 (1987): 209–14.
McDermott, Alice. "Love Was All They Knew to Call It." Rev. of *And Venus Is Blue*. *New York Times Book Review* 17 Aug. 1986: 11.
O'Briant, Don. "Mary Hood Joins Ranks of Authors She Happened On." *Atlanta Constitution* 11 Jan. 1985: C1–5.
———. "The Real Life of Mary Hood." *Atlanta Weekly* 25 Jan. 1987: 6, 8.
Peters, Joanne M. "Mary Hood." *Contemporary Authors*. Ed. Susan M. Trosky. Vol. 128. Detroit: Gale, 1990. 189–90.

Samway, Patrick H. "Mary Hood: A Fiction Writer Worth Following." Rev. of *Familiar Heat. America* 16 Nov. 1996: 21.

Scura, Dorothy M. "Southern Women Writing at the End of the Century: Five Recent Novels." Rev. of *Familiar Heat. Southern Review* 33 (1997): 859–71.

JOSEPHINE HUMPHREYS (1945–)

Bill Clem

BIOGRAPHY

Josephine Humphreys was the first of three daughters born to William Wurt and Martha (Lynch) Humphreys on February 2, 1945, in Charleston, South Carolina, where she has made her home for most of her life and which has been the setting of most of her fiction. After attending private girls schools and receiving encouragement in reading and writing from both her grandmother and her mother, Humphreys attended Duke University as an Angier B. Duke Scholar to major in English literature. While there, she studied creative writing with Reynolds Price, the man who would prove to be both an influence on Humphreys's writing and integral to her publishing. Elected to Phi Beta Kappa in 1966, Humphreys went on to graduate summa cum laude in 1967. Upon finishing the baccalaureate degree at Duke, she moved to New Haven, where she earned an MA in English at Yale as a Woodrow Wilson Foundation Fellow and was the winner of the Mary Cady Tew Prize in 1968. Although she did not complete a doctorate, she studied for the degree at University of Texas at Austin from 1968 to 1970 as a Danforth Foundation Fellow.

In 1970 Humphreys returned to Charleston with her college sweetheart and husband, Thomas Hutcheson, an attorney. From 1970 to 1977, Humphreys began a family (she has two sons) and taught English as assistant professor at Baptist College of Charleston. In 1977 Humphreys changed courses; she says, "Finally, at the age of 33, I stopped doing everything except child-care. I stopped entertaining. I stopped seeing my friends, and used all my extra time to write. It wasn't difficult to do that. I was driven to do it" (Presson 103). Nearly five years after this initial change, Humphreys completed the manuscript for her first novel, which she sent—after eight revisions—to Price nearly twenty years after having studied with him at Duke. Upon reading only fifty pages, he helped her to secure Harriet Wasserman as an agent and Viking as publisher. In 1984 Viking published *Dreams of Sleep*, which came to universal critical praise, won the PEN/Ernest Hemingway Prize for best American first novel, and secured for Humphreys a Guggenheim Fellowship and a Lyndhurst Fellowship. The monies from these fellowships helped her to finish her second novel, *Rich in Love*, published in 1987. *Rich in Love* received mostly positive reviews and led to a screenplay and movie production directed by Bruce Beresford.

Humphreys published her third novel, *The Fireman's Fair*, in 1991, after the devastation of the infamous Hurricane Hugo, which serves as a backdrop to the protagonist's crisis. Immensely popular, *The Fireman's Fair*, like Humphreys's two earlier novels, garnered favorable responses and secured the writer's place among serious contemporary novelists. Each of her three novels earned citations as *New York Times* Notable Books of the Year for 1984, 1987, and 1991, respectively, and earned their author the Hillsdale Prize for fiction from the Fellowship of Southern Writers (1993); membership to the South Carolina Academy of Authors (1994); the American Academy and Institute of Arts and Letters Literature Award (1996); the Fellowship of Southern Writers (1999); honorary doctorates from Duke, Furman University, and Lander College; and judgeships for the National Endowment for the Arts, the Lila Wallace Foundation, the Ernest Hemingway Foundation, and the Townsend Prize.

Humphreys's fourth novel, *Nowhere Else on Earth*, published in 2000, earned positive reviews and demonstrated the novelist's dexterity and versatility in the craft of fiction writing. She is a novelist from whom readers and critics alike will continue to anticipate new works.

MAJOR WORKS AND THEMES

Josephine Humphreys's first three novels all share contemporary Charleston, South Carolina, settings. As such, each reveals the trials and tribulations of disintegrating families and the loss of identity in the "New South," a place in which tradition is shunned as outsiders move in and industrial capitalism takes over. Traditional plot and character developments showcase white protagonists who all feel overwhelmed and/or saddened by the lives they lead and by change; each character attempts to come to terms with the new situation by making an effort to conserve both what once was and what is or by fleeing to shut out the horror of change. Race and gender become important issues for main characters as each assesses the world and the ways in which this new place can be negotiated.

Dreams of Sleep presents a white, middle-class, married couple, Will and Alice Reese, and a precocious white teenager, Iris Moon, all of whom desire nothing more than a stable family life in an ever-changing society. Will hates his job as an obstetrician because his patients seem not to need him: Drugs allow them to forget the pain he has worked hard to assuage. The changing nature of medicine is only one of many incomprehensible changes that Humphreys depicts. Will's mother sells real estate to outsiders, and her new husband wants to build theme parks: The "New South," a land without tradition, becomes indistinguishable from other regions of the country. Alice feels a serious discontent in the banality of her middle-class existence, but she feels powerless to do anything about it. Her melancholy results in her meeting Iris, the teenager who becomes the babysitter for Alice's children. Iris herself wants change, but simple change: She wants the family she has never had and knows that she cannot have as long as she loves her best friend, Emory, who is African American. Iris believes that a union between them could produce only more chaos than that which already exists. Racial identity and gender, in a post–civil rights and feminist era, seem to upset the equanimity of white middle-class familial identity.

The white middle-class family is central to Humphreys's second and third novels, *Rich in Love* and *The Fireman's Fair*. *Rich in Love* reads like a contemporary *bildungsroman*, with Lucille Odom, a character very much like Iris, unfolding events of her life from two years ago to the present. Lucille, like Iris, wants family; only Lucille wants to reassemble a family in which the mother has left because of her refusal to accept mundanity. Rae, Lucille's sister, returns home unhappily married, pregnant, and longing for a lost freedom, leaving Lucille to take care of her, her husband, and their needs—this combined with Lucille's father's needs leads Lucille to look to others, specifically her African American friend, Rhody, for methods to accept change. Rob Wyatt of *The Fireman's Fair* is a much older and male version of Lucille in that he wants something stable. Rob, plagued by a legacy of male domination and female subjugation in his first family, must deal with the consequences of both man-made and natural disaster. Surviving the disaster of Hurricane Hugo, which serves as the backdrop and metaphor for devastation wrought by change, Rob is plagued by self-doubt, resulting in unemployment, a desire to leave behind his parents and brother, and his humiliation over attempts at securing love with his employer's wife.

Race and gender issues become the central focus of Humphreys's fourth and latest novel, *Nowhere Else on Earth*. A departure in subject matter for the author, this fourth novel presents the story of Rhoda Strong, an infamous Lumbee woman who narrates the story of her life during the American Civil War. A researched historical novel, *Nowhere Else on Earth* displays Humphreys's ability to take on form and content beyond the traditional novel and the concerns of the white middle class of the southern United States.

CRITICAL RECEPTION

Dreams of Sleep is Humphreys's most acclaimed novel and the one on which most critics have focused. Upon publication, the novel received universal praise. Critic Jonathan Yardley, writing for the *Washington Post*, hails the novel as an "exceptional performance by a previously unknown writer" (3). Ellen Douglas in the *New York Times Book Review* calls *Dreams of Sleep* an "extraordinarily accomplished first novel," one with characters who could "be the stuff of a supermarket romance if they had been drawn to stereotype, but each is a precisely and delicately created individual" (15). Academic critics have focused on the novel's "domesticity": Elinor Ann Walker believes that "*Dreams of Sleep* may be called primarily a narrative about the family, but its story illuminates new occupations and preoccupations for family members. In this novel, Humphreys redefines both domestic space and southern place" (87). Michael A. Griffith asserts that Humphreys's first novel is one of "new domestic realism" (108).

Rich in Love and *The Fireman's Fair* both received mixed but mostly positive reviews. Writing in the *Nation*, Michael Malone believes that in *Rich in Love*, Humphreys "gives us people's responses to their own lives; that is to say, Humphreys is someone, in Henry James's phrase, on whom nothing is lost—at least, nothing at which she has chosen to look" (388). Her third novel fared well; its reception can be summarized with the brief comment of the reviewer from the *Antioch Review*: "How wonderful to find in this day and age a truly romantic novel . . . written with style and wit. . . . Humphreys has done it again, in this, her third novel" (473).

Nowhere Else on Earth, a change in subject matter, earned Humphreys further praise. Susan Dodd for the *Washington Post* exclaims that this fourth novel "is an extravagant gift to lovers of language. Along with telling a grand story, Humphreys writes a beautiful sentence. Word by perfect word, she has distilled to a splendid coherence the complexities of history and the human heart" (C3).

BIBLIOGRAPHY

Works by Josephine Humphreys

Dreams of Sleep. New York: Viking, 1984.
"My Real Invisible Self." *A World Unsuspected: Portraits of Southern Childhood.* Ed. Alex Harris. Chapel Hill: University of North Carolina Press, 1987. 1–13.
Rich in Love. New York: Viking, 1987.
"A Disappearing Subject Called the South." *The Prevailing South: Life and Politics in a Changing Culture.* Ed. Dudley Clendinen. Atlanta: Longstreet Press, 1988. 212–20.
"The Epistle of Paul to Titus: Liars and Evil Beasts." *Incarnation: Contemporary Writers on the New Testament.* Ed. Alfred Corn. New York: Viking, 1990. 247–56.
The Fireman's Fair. New York: Viking, 1991.
"Bells." *The Wedding Cake in the Middle of the Road.* Ed. Susan Stamberg and George Garrett. New York: Norton, 1992. 48–57.
Nowhere Else on Earth. New York: Viking, 2000.

Studies of Josephine Humphreys

Dodd, Susan. "In the Civil War South, a Heart Awakens." Rev. of *Nowhere Else on Earth. Washington Post* 4 Sept. 2000: C3.
Douglas, Ellen. "Charleston without Tears." Rev. of *Dreams of Sleep. New York Times Book Review* 13 May 1984: 15.
Drzal, Dawn Ann. "Casualties of the Feminine Mystique." *Antioch Review* 46 (1988): 450–61.
Rev. of *The Fireman's Fair. Antioch Review* 49 (1991): 473.
Ford, Elizabeth A. "Josephine Humphreys: 'Hope's Last Stand.' " *Southern Writers at Century's End.* Ed. Jeffrey J. Folks and James A. Perkins. Lexington: University Press of Kentucky, 1997. 201–11.
Gretlund, Jan Nordby. "Citified Carolina: Josephine Humphreys' Fiction." *Southern Landscapes.* Ed. Tony Badger, Walter Edgar, and Jan Nordby Gretlund. Tubingen: Stauffenburg Verlag, 1996. 254–65.
Griffith, Michael A. " 'A Deal for the Real World': Josephine Humphreys' *Dreams of Sleep* and the New Domestic Novel." *Southern Literary Journal* 26 (1993): 94–108.
Henley, Ann. " 'Space for Herself': Nadine Gordimer's *A Sport of Nature* and Josephine Humphreys' *Rich in Love." Frontiers: A Journal of Women Studies* 13 (1992): 81–89.
Hobson, Fred. "Richard Ford and Josephine Humphreys: Walker Percy in New Jersey and Charleston." *The Southern Writer in the Postmodern World.* Ed. Fred Hobson. Athens: University of Georgia Press, 1991. 41–72.
"Humphreys, Josephine." *Contemporary Authors.* Ed. Susan M. Trosky. Vol. 127. Detroit: Gale, 1989. 204–8.
"Humphreys, Josephine." *Contemporary Literary Criticism.* Ed. Sharon K. Hall. Vol. 34. Detroit: Gale, 1985. 63–66.

"Humphreys, Josephine." *Contemporary Literary Criticism*. Ed. Roger Matuz. Vol. 57. Detroit: Gale, 1990. 233–38.

Irons, Susan H. "Josephine Humphreys's *Dreams of Sleep*: Revising Walker Percy's Male Gaze." *Mississippi Quarterly* 47 (1994): 287–300.

Jackson, Shelley M. "Josephine Humphreys and the Politics of Postmodern Desire." *Mississippi Quarterly* 47 (1994): 275–85.

Lawson, Lewis A. "Special Section of Josephine Humphreys." *Mississippi Quarterly* 47 (1994): 273–315.

Magee, Rosemary M. "Continuity and Separation: An Interview with Josephine Humphreys." *Southern Review* 27 (1991): 792–802.

Malone, Michael. "Rich in Words." Rev. of *Rich in Love*. *Nation* 10 Oct. 1987: 388–89.

McKee, Kathryn B. "Rewriting Southern Male Introspection in Josephine Humphreys' *Dreams of Sleep*." *Mississippi Quarterly* 46 (1993): 241–54.

Millichap, Joseph. "Josephine Humphreys." *Contemporary Fiction Writers of the South: A Bio-Bibliographical Sourcebook*. Ed. Joseph M. Flora and Robert Bain. Westport, CT: Greenwood Press, 1993. 244–54.

Pate, Willard. " 'Do You Think of Yourself as a Woman Writer?': A Panel Discussion Including Ellen Gilchrist, Josephine Humphreys, Gloria Naylor, and Louise Shivers." *Furman Studies* 34 (1988): 1–13.

——. " 'The Place of Women Writers in the Literary Tradition': A Panel Discussion Including Ellen Gilchrist, Barbara Hardy, Josephine Humphreys, and Louise Shivers." *Furman Studies* 34 (1988): 14–25.

Presson, Rebekah. "The Known World: An Interview with Josephine Humphreys." *New Letters* 59 (1992): 99–107.

Rash, Tom. "All in the Family." *South Carolina Review* 22 (1990): 131–40.

Spencer, Joseph. "Josephine Humphreys." *Bulletin of Bibliography* 50 (1993): 325–29.

Summer, Bob. "PW Interviews Josephine Humphreys." *Publishers Weekly* 4 Sept. 1987: 49–50.

Vinh, Alphonse. "Talking with Josephine Humphreys." *Southern Quarterly* 32 (1994): 131–40.

Walker, Elinor Ann. " 'Go with What Is Most Terrifying': Reinventing Domestic Space in Josephine Humphreys' *Dreams of Sleep*." *Studies in the Literary Imagination* 27 (1994): 87–104.

——. "Josephine Humphreys's *Rich in Love*: Redefining Southern Fiction." *Mississippi Quarterly* 47 (1994): 275–85.

Yardley, Jonathan. "Desire under the Magnolias." Rev. of *Dreams of Sleep*. *Washington Post Book World* 6 May 1984: 3.

GISH JEN (1956–)

Cora Agatucci

BIOGRAPHY

Gish Jen is the American-born daughter of parents who emigrated from Shanghai, China. Born Lillian C. Jen in New York City in 1956, she grew up in Yonkers and Scarsdale, New York. Jen remembers being aware from an early age that they were "almost the only Asian American family in town" and that "the conscious impulse of my family was to assimilate" (Feldman 27). Jen attributes her gift of verbal humor to growing up "half Jewish" in Scarsdale (Satz 136), later observing that sometimes humor "is a way to organize your anger" as well as "transcen[d] it" (Lee, "Gish Jen" 225). Jen sees a strong "sympathy . . . between the Jewish and Chinese cultures" and cites Jewish American writers as "the biggest influence on my work" ("April Guest").

The Scarsdale community placed "a strong emphasis on education" ("April Guest"), and Jen did well in school "without too much effort" (Satz 138). Like the mother in "What Means Switch?" (1990), Jen's mother did not encourage her to "work at being any smarter" for fear that she "would have trouble getting married" (Satz 138). An avid reader, young Jen was influenced strongly by Jane Austen's novels. In fifth grade, Jen wrote her first short story for a school literary magazine and later grew to admire writers such as Alice Munro and Jamaica Kincaid.

Jen regards assimilation as "a fact of life" in the United States, for "better or worse" (Lee, "Gish Jen" 219–20). But if "all change involves loss," Jen declares (Satz 139), it can also offer rewards. Coming of age in the late 1960s, in the wake of the civil rights movement, marked Jen with a distrust of received authority ("April Guest"). During this period, Jen would set the complex, comic explorations of youthful rebellion, intergenerational conflict, unstable ethnic identity, and cross-cultural "switching" of her second novel. In *Mona in the Promised Land* (1996), Jen consciously "tried to contribute to the process of boundary crossing, to painting pictures that are a little less black and white—a little more complicated" (Lee, "Gish Jen" 229).

In the 1970s, Jen attended Harvard University, where she studied both pre-med and pre-law before becoming an English major. Although a prosody class with Robert Fitzgerald stimulated her literary aspirations, she later enrolled in the Stanford business school in a last attempt to "do something practical" (Lee, "Gish Jen" 217); however, she was primarily attracted by its writing program and spent the first year reading novels and taking writing classes. At Stanford, Jen met her future husband, David O'Connor, but by the beginning of her second year, she rejected business school and left for China.

Like the protagonist of "Duncan in China" (in *Who's Irish?: Stories,* 1999), Jen served as a "foreign expert" for a provincial coal mining institute. "Absorbing" rather than "writing" during her brief sojourn, Jen concludes that she probably could not have written *Typical American* (1991) if she had not gone to China (Lee, "Gish Jen" 218, 219). There, in a "purer form," she recognized the Chinese in herself and her family and began to know the "conflicts" among "what it means to be Chinese; what it means to be American; what it means to be Chinese American" (Lee, "Gish Jen" 218). After returning to the states, Jen joined the Iowa Writer's Workshop in the early 1980s.

At Iowa, Jen used her legal name, Lillian, when she published the short stories "Bellying-Up" (1981) and "The Small Concerns of Sparrows" (1982) in small literary magazines. Her early stories did not feature Asian American characters. But the political climate was changing, with the rise of multiculturalism during the time Jen was completing her MFA in 1983. Asian characters Callie and Mona Chang first emerge in "The White Umbrella" (1984), which Jen published under "Gish," a nickname acquired in high school. Jen changed her name when she "discovered writing to be liberating; . . . just as I could create stories, I could create this self, Gish Jen" (Matsukawa 116).

After moving with her husband back to Cambridge, Massachusetts, Jen was awarded a 1985 Bunting Fellowship, overcame lingering ambivalence about her identity as a writer, and began work on her first novel, *Typical American* (Smith 60). Jen was encouraged by the publication of several short stories, more awards and fellowships, and accolades in mainstream reviews between 1985 and 1991. The "extreme struggle" with her parents over the legitimacy of her career finally ended when a Chinese newspaper praised *Typical American.*

A tragic miscarriage ended her first pregnancy during the writing of the last sections of *Typical American* and "had a lot to do with the book taking such a dark turn," Jen states (Smith 60). A similar tragedy darkens the past of protagonist Art Woo in "Birthmates" (1994). Yet the same period gave "unbidden" rise to "other voices, other moods," Jen explains, including the "funny, buoyant voice" of Mona Chang, which Jen would "siphon . . . off into stories" (Smith 60). Jen's fiction characteristically blends comic and tragic.

A healthy son, Luke, was born to Jen and O'Connor by the time *Typical American* was published in 1991. Rave reviews greeted Jen's first novel, even as they betrayed limited expectations of ethnic writers at the controversial high tide of multiculturalism. This movement legitimized the state of being "between worlds" as a literary theme and opened up new ways of appreciating works like the widely anthologized "In the American Society" (1986) (Lee, "Gish Jen" 228). However, Jen chaffs at being "ghettoized" as an Asian American writer (Lee, "Gish Jen" 220) and at interpretations of her work limited to stereotypical themes expected of hyphenated Americans, such as "preserving one's heritage" (Matsukawa 114). *Typical American* is "an American story," Jen declares, a determinedly "antiexotic" treatment of Chinese Americans, intended to expand WASP-centered definitions of "American" tradition and experience (Lee, "Gish Jen" 220). Jen's commitment to artistic independence has also led her to treat topics considered "dangerous" and "uncomfortable" for "nice" Chinese American girls, such as "the Jews and Japanese," racism, and sex, in works like "What Means Switch?" (1990) and *Mona in the Promised Land* (1996) (Satz 140).

Jen wrote *Mona* and "Birthmates" during Luke's first five years, with a second child, Paloma, arriving by 1996, the year of *Mona*'s publication. The priorities of motherhood have reduced Jen's concern "about other people's reactions" to her writing, and the publishing explosion of diverse Asian American works has alleviated a "pressure to write something representative" (Lee, "Gish Jen" 229). Jen remains consciously committed to dismantling stereotypes and exercising "social responsibility" in representing the experiences of Asian Americans and other groups in literature (Lee, "Gish Jen" 223). In recent articles such as "Who's to Judge? Identity Politics V. Inner Lives" (1997) and "An Ethnic Trump" (1996), Jen engages in dialogues regarding the mixed blessings of multiculturalism and identity politics as well as the destructive effects of lingering racist constructions. At the same time, the new stories appearing in Jen's latest book, *Who's Irish?: Stories*, written during her pregnancy with Paloma, reflect an expanded "range of interests" (Lee, "Gish Jen" 230). After a recent interview with Jen in her Cambridge, Massachusetts, home, Wendy Smith surmises that "motherhood has extinguished neither [Jen's] intelligence nor her artistic ambition, but it's changed both in ways she could not have anticipated" (59). The influence of motherhood is most notable in "House, House, Home," experimental in its "more circular time frame," its "more contemplative mood," and its emphasis on "growth" rather than "conflict and resolution" (Smith 60). While family demands have prompted Jen to "stic[k] to short stories for now," she plans to write a third book featuring the Chang family (Lee, "Gish Jen" 230).

MAJOR WORKS AND THEMES

Gish Jen's fiction has emerged in a publishing "explosion" of Asian American writing (Wong 3), presaged by the successes of Maxine Hong Kingston's *Woman Warrior* (1976) and Amy Tan's *Joy Luck Club* (1989). In their 1974 anthology *Aiiieeeee! An Anthology of Asian American Writers*, editors Jeffery Paul Chan, Frank Chin, and Lawson Fusao Inada proposed a still-influential definition of Asian American literature: a US-born sensibility "neither Asian nor white American" (xxi). The editors selected primarily Chinese and Japanese American works representative of "non-Christian, nonfeminine, and non-immigrant" tendencies (Wong 8). Since 1974 feminist critics have contested Chan, Chin, and Inada's "masculine ethnopoetics" (Cheung, *Words Matter* 5–7), and the "rancorous backlash against multiculturalism in education" has stimulated increasingly sophisticated methodological debates over "how Asian American literature is to be read" (Wong 4) and valued.

Negotiating this conflicted literary climate, Jen has charted her own course, tempering her claims to artistic freedom with commitment to socially responsible literary representation. Jen's two novels and many of her short stories depict the tragicomic experiences of the immigrant Chang family coming to know and learning to live in post–world war America. "In the American Society" focuses on the characters' tragicomic adjustments to exclusionary mainstream suburbia. *Typical American* complicates familiar narratives of immigrant cultural dislocation by establishing the Changs as a new kind of immigrant: Shanghainese elite stranded in the United States by Mao's Communist revolution in the early 1950s (Cheung, *Interethnic Companion* 54). The middle-class Ralph, Helen, and Theresa—decidedly unexotic and ordinary, sympathetic but fallible—ultimately find themselves becoming what they initially criticize as "typical American." The parodic agent of their transformative crisis is glib, corrupt Grover Ding. This self-made millionaire forefronts the seductive distortions inherent in the American dream. National myths intersect with family dynamics and patriarchal oppressions to undermine the Changs' attempts to remake a home in America. Ralph Chang must finally accept the "bleak" but necessary realization that the American myth of boundless possibilities is delusory, and his attempts at self-making nourished by this myth have always been circumscribed by his own and America's limitations. "It's an American story," the novel declares itself in the opening line. Essential to Jen's project is to expand national narratives that exclude the rich multiplicity of its immigrant stories, to challenge restrictive ideas of what qualifies as "typical American," and to redefine Americanness in terms that embrace the Changs "as 'us' rather than 'other' " (Feldman 27).

Mona in the Promised Land focuses on the first-generation daughter of Ralph and Helen Chang, now upwardly mobile in the New York suburb of "Scarshill." Building on previous short stories featuring the characters and points of view of Callie and Mona Chang, Jen continues her project of redefining American identity by dramatizing its fluidity. Out of familiar coming-of-age episodes such as bittersweet first love and teen rebellion, Jen consciously crafts a new kind of assimilation narrative. Jen views ethnicity as "a very complicated thing, not a stable, unified thing"; it is "naïve" and reductive to believe one can preserve a "pure" Chinese American identity, for "all the groups in America have rubbed off on each other" ("April Guest"). An exuberant comedy, *Mona* is propelled by a series of ethnicity-bending transformations, with its protagonist's Jewish "switch" at the center. Her parents are appalled when Mona refashions herself into a "Changowitz": "America means being whatever you want, and I happened to pick being Jewish." No representative Chinese American or model minority, hapless but endearing Mona bursts through stereotypes, transgresses tribal enclaves, and braves intergenerational conflicts en route to claiming adulthood and asserting new paradigms of American identity.

"Birthmates" is a darker investigation of intrafamily distances traceable to the conditions of survival in a racist society. Protective emotional deadening enables Art Woo to negotiate the work world but renders him incapable of grieving the loss of his child at the cost of his marriage. The protagonist comes to this realization after a series of comic misadventures in a welfare hotel are initiated by its antic children, and the unexpected kindness of a disadvantaged black woman challenges his defenses and revitalizes buried emotions. Jens uses a complex blend of gravity and levity to elucidate her themes. "Who's Irish?" presents the blunt, stubborn, hilariously perceptive Chinese grandmother, who speaks in pidgin English her bewilderment and criticism about her daughter's assimilated American life. The comedy of cross-cultural misunderstanding is sobered by exposure of its darker consequences, in this case, child abuse.

"Duncan in China" reverses the traditional immigrant formula by following the Chinese American protagonist to the People's Republic in search of "the China of ineffable nobility and refinement" (*Who's Irish?* 49). What he finds instead is entrenched anti-intellectualism, a misbegotten romance, and a tubercular cousin who forces his son into a drunken tabletop dance to humiliate his American relative.

Jen does not limit herself to subjects and themes concentrated on the Chinese American. For example, in "The Water-Faucet Vision," young Callie Chang's ethnicity is incidental to her quest to become a Catholic martyr. At once comic and heart-breaking misadventures, defined by failed attempts to work miracles, erode her religious faith. An older Callie is left mourning her losses, "wistful for the time when religion seemed all I wanted it to be. One had only to direct the hand of the Almighty and say, Just here, Lord, we hurt here—and here, and here, and here" (*Who's Irish?* 48). New stories such as "House, House, Home" in *Who's Irish?* suggest that this fascinating and accomplished fiction writer will continue to experiment with subjects, themes, and techniques.

CRITICAL RECEPTION

In a publishing climate avid for new Asian American works, mainstream reviewers celebrated Jen's first novel in 1991. Frequently compared with Maxine Hong Kingston and Amy Tan, Jen was hailed as one of the "fresh voices above the noisy din . . . [that] splendidly illustrate the frustrations, humor and eternal wonder of the immigrant's life" (Simpson and Pico 66). Critics admired Jen's tragicomic rendering of Chinese immigrant experience, her vivid characterizations and dialogue, and her sharp descriptive detail. As Matsukawa observes, Jen's fiction challenges readers "to re-examine their definitions of home, family, the American dream, and . . . what it means to be a 'typical American' " (112). A finalist for the national Book Critics Circle Award and a *New York Times* book of the year, *Typical American* established Jen's reputation as one of the best young fiction writers of "a generation [that] seems to have found its Asian American voice" (Feldman 25).

"The Water-Faucet Vision" (1987) was selected for *Best American Short Stories 1988*. Awards from Radcliffe's Bunting Institute, the Copernicus Society, the Massachusetts' Artists' Foundation, the MacDowell Colony, and the National Endowment for the Arts supported the writing of *Typical American*. By the early 1990s, stories featuring the immigrant Chang family, such as "The White Umbrella," "In the American Society," and "What Means Switch?" were anthologized and accepted by mainstream periodicals such as *Atlantic Monthly*. In 1992 Jen was awarded a Guggenheim Foundation Fellowship. "Birthmates" (1994), selected for *Best American Short Stories 1995* and then for John Updike's *Best American Short Stories of the Century* (1999), strengthened Jen's reputation as a premier short story writer.

Most reviewers were delighted by Jen's second novel and its irreverent ethnicity-switching comedy centered in witty Mona Chang, coming of age in the upwardly mobile suburbs. *Mona in the Promised Land* was named to *New York Times* notable books of the year and *Los Angeles Times* best ten books of 1996. Among other strengths found in her works, critics appreciated *Mona*'s departure from the serious debates concerning multiculturalism and ethnic diversity that dominated ethnic American literature in the 1990s.

Manjit Bhatia welcomes the fluidity of ethnic identities and comic "explosion of transformations" represented in *Mona*, the fluidity of ethnic identity proposing an alternative "idea of the universal" with which readers can empathize (78). Bhatia explains, "Each of her characters can stand for different types of people because over time each one actually becomes different types of people" (78). Sometimes unfavorably, reviewers contrast the fast-paced comedy of *Mona* with the darker-toned *Typical American*. For example, Valerie Miner judges *Mona*'s "emotional range" limited (35) and misses "the characters' complex choices in *Typical American*," though she still finds "strength and grace" in Jen's "rueful wisdom about being an immigrant family's daughter," coping with "bifurcated identity" and intergenerational conflict (36).

The range, balanced levity and gravity, and tempered optimism of the collection *Who's Irish?* were well received. In 1999, the same year Jen received the Lannan Literary Award for fiction, Hilary Roxe introduced Jen as "one of the foremost contemporary Asian-American authors" and applauded her characters for "break[ing] the mold of the hyphenated American" (48). New and previously published stories in the collection—notably "Duncan in China," "Who's Irish?," and "Birthmates"—were praised for humorous reversals of stereotypes and situations.

Rachel C. Lee explains that because mainstream presses too often imagine Asian American literature as "appealing only to ghettoized interests, Asian American cultural producers face increased pressure to emphasize the broad value of their works" (*Americas* 3). "It's like putting us in Chinese laundries," as the title of a chapter from Cheung's *Words Matter* suggests. Jen's interview, included in this section, helps explain why many contemporary Asian American writers hold seemingly contradictory desires "to reclaim a distinctive ethnic tradition" and "to be recognized as fully American" (5). Frequently frustrations with being exoticized and "treated as perpetual foreigners in the United States" lead to ambivalence "about their Asian heritage" (Cheung, *Words Matter* 5). Unfortunately, academic schools of Asian American literary criticism can contribute to young writers' constraints by privileging literary works and readings that emphasize "exposure of America's exclusion of Asians as a group," devaluing alternative narratives and strategies (Lee, *Americas* 45).

Rachel C. Lee offers a rare extended treatment of *Typical American* in *The Americas of Asian American Literature*. She analyzes Jen's strategies for exposing "violence [to women's bodies and perspectives] within the Asian American household" (45), a "gendered critique" elided by dominant readings of "minority literature as exposes of racial oppression" (viii). For example, female characters' silence and inaction operate to interrupt "masculine narratives of self-making" (64), exposing "the racial and gendered assumptions embedded in national scripts of success" (70). Lee opens new territory for future studies in examining "suppressed tales" of family dynamics, domesticity, womanly desires, and female friendships as well as "political investments in keeping them suppressed" (15).

BIBLIOGRAPHY

Works by Gish Jen

"Bellying-Up." *Iowa Review* 12 (1981): 93–94.
"The Small Concerns of Sparrows." *Fiction International* 14 (1982): 47–55.
"The White Umbrella." *Yale Review* 73 (1984): 401–9.
"Eating Crazy." *Yale Review* 74 (1985): 425–33.
"In the American Society." *Southern Review* 22 (1986): 606–19.
"The Water-Faucet Vision." *Nimrod* 31 (1987): 25–33.
"What Means Switch?" *Atlantic Monthly* May 1990: 76–84.

"Grover at the Wheel." *New Yorker* 31 Dec. 1990: 32–37.

"Challenging the Asian Illusion." *New York Times* 11 Aug. 1991: B1ff.

Typical American. Boston: Houghton Mifflin-S. Lawrence, 1991.

"Birthmates." *Ploughshares* 20 (1994): 81–97.

"An Ethnic Trump." *New York Times Magazine* 7 July 1996: 50.

Mona in the Promised Land. New York: Knopf, 1996.

"Who's to Judge? Identity Politics V. Inner Lives." *New Republic* 21 April 1997: 18–19.

"Just Wait." *Ploughshares* 24 (1998): 141–51.

"Who's Irish?" *New Yorker* 14 Sept. 1998: 80–84.

Who's Irish?: Stories. New York: Knopf-Random House, 1999.

Studies of Gish Jen

"April Guest: Gish Jen." *Guest Speakers: Language Arts Author Spotlight.* McDougal Littell, 1999 (http://www.mcdougallittell.com/lit/guest/garchive/jen.htm) June 2000.

Bhatia, Manjit. Rev. of *Mona in the Promised Land. Quadrant* Nov. 1998: 78.

Chan, Jeffery Paul, Frank Chin, and Lawson Fusao Inada, eds. *Aiiieeeee! An Anthology of Asian American Writers.* Washington, D.C.: Howard University Press, 1974.

Cheung, King-Kok, ed. *An Interethnic Companion to Asian American Literature.* Cambridge: Cambridge University Press, 1997.

——. *Words Matter: Conversations with Asian American Writers. Intersections: Asian and Pacific American Transcultural Studies.* Ed. Russell C. Leong. Honolulu: University of Hawai'i Press, Los Angeles: UCLA Asian American Studies Center, 2000.

Feldman, Gayle. "Spring's Five Fictional Encounters of the Chinese American Kind." *Publishers Weekly* 8 Feb. 1991: 25–27.

Lee, Rachel C. *The Americas of Asian American Literature: Gendered Fictions of Nation and Transnation.* Princeton: Princeton University Press, 1999.

——. "Gish Jen." Interviews, 1993 and 1996. *Words Matter: Conversations with Asian American Writers.* Ed. King-Kok Cheung. *Intersections: Asian and Pacific American Transcultural Studies.* Ed. Russell C. Leong. Honolulu: University of Hawaii Press, Los Angeles: UCLA Asian American Studies Center, 2000. 215–32.

Matsukawa, Yuko. "*MELUS* Interview: Gish Jen" 1991. *MELUS* 18 (1993): 111–20.

Miner, Valerie. "Asian American Pancake." Rev. of *Mona in the Promised Land. Nation* 17 June 1996: 35–36.

Roxe, Hilary. "Asian Balancing Act: Gish Jen Mends Conflicting Aspects of Immigrant Culture with Candor, Humor and Poignancy." Rev. of *Who's Irish?. Time International* 9 Aug. 1999: 48.

Satz, Martha. "Writing about the Things That Are Dangerous: A Conversation with Gish Jen." *Southwest Review* 78 (1993): 132–40.

Simpson, Janice C., and Iyer Pico. "Fresh Voices above the Noisy Din: New Works by Four Chinese-American Writers Splendidly Illustrate the Frustrations, Humor and Eternal Wonder of the Immigrant's Life." *Time* 3 June 1991: 66–67.

Smith, Wendy. "Gish Jen: 'The Book That Hormones Wrote.'" *Publishers Weekly* 7 June 1999: 59–60.

Trudeau, Lawrence J., and others, eds. *Asian American Literature: Reviews and Criticism of Works by American Writers of Asian Descent.* Detroit: Gale, 1999.

Wong, Sau-ling Cynthia. *Reading Asian American Literature: From Necessity to Extravagance.* Princeton: Princeton University Press, 1993.

DIANE JOHNSON (1934–)

Stephanie Brown

BIOGRAPHY

Diane Johnson was born in Moline, Illinois, in 1934, the first child of Dolph Lain, a high school principal, and his wife, Frances. Her tranquil Midwestern childhood provided her with some of the material she would later utilize in novels set in exotic locales far from her hometown. As she told interviewer Susan Groag Bell, "In a couple of my books, I have put a middle-western protagonist, always somebody who's displaced like I am, looking at the mess of today. This person remembers an orderly society from which subsequent events seemed to depart" (124). After graduating from high school at seventeen, she spent two years at Stephens College, an academy for future flight attendants in Columbia, Missouri. She left the Midwest in the summer of 1953 "to get married [to first husband, B. Lamar Johnson, Jr., with whom she would have four children], which was the fashion then, and to have babies," she told interviewer Janet Todd (121). The Johnsons moved to the West Coast, where the young mother for the first time "tried novel writing at home when they had their naps" (121). During a year spent in Utah, where her medical student husband was interning, Johnson took courses and received her BA from the University of Utah. Returning to California, Johnson subsequently embarked upon a graduate degree in English at the University of California at Los Angeles.

The circumstances of Johnson's personal life had an obvious impact on her writing. In 1965 she received a PhD and simultaneously published her first novel, *Fair Game*; her dissertation would later become the biography *Lesser Lives: The True History of the First Mrs. Meredith* (1973), nominated for a National Book Award. Her experience of the simultaneous and sometimes conflicting responsibilities of motherhood and graduate school seems to be reflected in her early novels, all of which focus on "a central female character who is uncertain about how to conduct her life" (Baughman 220). In 1968 Johnson rewed; her second husband, John Frederic Murray, is a professor of medicine and an expert in international health. With Murray, Johnson found herself traveling the world. A three-month stint in Iran in 1978 provided the basis for what many consider her finest books, *Persian Nights* (1987), which was nominated for the Pulitzer Prize and which she wrote after taking an eight-year-long break from novel writing to concentrate on writing critical essays (ultimately published as *Terrorists and Novelists* in 1982), and another biography, *Dashiell Hammett: A Life* (1983). Her knowledge of the medical world gave *Health and Happiness* (1990), a tale of hospital intrigue, the unmistakable ring of realism, while her later travels with Murray resulted in a collection of seemingly autobiographical essays entitled *Natural Opium: Some Travelers' Tales* (1993). Johnson, who now divides her time between her residences in Paris and San Francisco, sets her most recent novels *Le Divorce* (1997) and *Le Mariage* (2000) in France, focusing on the experiences of expatriate Americans navigating the pitfalls of a mysterious foreign culture: "I can support the ambiguity of being an alien," Johnson told Bill Goldstein, explaining that she herself has "always been a kind of expatriate," whether residing in Iran, Paris, or California, itself "another alien world" (G10).

MAJOR WORKS AND THEMES

Diane Johnson is a prolific writer in several genres: Since the publication of her first novel in 1965, she has produced eight more novels, two major biographies, a book of criticism, the screenplay for a major motion picture, short stories, and travel essays and reviews for the *New York Times*, *Washington Post*, and *San Francisco Chronicle*, among others. Her work resists simple categorization; although her novels are generally written from the perspective of female protagonists, she hastens to point out that "[their] particular troubles . . . are not necessarily meant to be feminist complaints. . . . I'm not trying to write manifestos about female independence, but human lives" (Bell 127). Nevertheless, in an essay entitled "Should Novels Have a Message?" Johnson remarks that "the composing of messages, like child care, seems to be a duty that, in most societies, no one really wants. It gets left to . . . women" (*Terrorists* 128), suggesting that, for better or worse, women writers have specific responsibilities. "In writing, as in mourning," writes Johnson, "it sometimes appears that women have reserved or been assigned the duty of expressing human resentment" (*Terrorists* 4).

Her writing is also difficult to classify generically; her breakthrough novel, *The Shadow Knows* (1974), is both a psychological thriller and a woman's novel, as well, perhaps, as a parody and critique of the traditionally masculine province of the detective story. *Natural Opium* masquerades as fiction despite the fact that the unnamed characters, identified only by the initials D. and J., appear to be based on Johnson and her husband, John. Even her biographies take a somewhat unconventional approach. In his review of Johnson's 1983 biography *Dashiell Hammett*, George Stade remarks that "the novelist is far more evident in this biography than the critic. . . . Her method is . . . the method of the camera eye. . . . Her readers must decide for themselves what made Hammett tick" (G1). Her detachment results as well in a kind of deadpan tone that makes it similarly hard to determine whether or not she is a comic writer; although Johnson's work is without doubt funny, her narratives are often also littered with tragic or violent events that shock characters and readers alike out of their complacency and either catapult the plot in a wholly new direction or end it altogether.

Yet Johnson's disparate works are brought together by certain common themes.

One is the question of the reliability of perception, especially when navigating unfamiliar territory. Whether struggling with being an outsider in a tightly knit Mormon family, as Karen does in *Loving Hands at Home* (1968); desperately seeking an explanation for seemingly random acts of violence, like the terrorized N. of *The Shadow Knows*; or attempting, with Isabel, the young narrator of *Le Divorce*, to make sense of the complicated mores of Parisians, Johnson's characters almost always try to chart the waters of their surroundings, often using inadequate or compromised information and interpretations. In *Persian Nights* (1987), Chloe Fowler arrives alone in Shiraz because her husband has been detained in the United States and immediately discovers that she is ill equipped to understand an Iranian society poised on the brink of revolution that toppled the shah in 1979. Though the novel's focus initially seems to be the domestic drama of Chloe's extramarital affairs and unraveling marriage, ultimately Johnson takes on broader issues of international politics and cultural difference that link Chloe's perspective to that of American foreign policy "experts" who seem equally isolated from reality. As Johnson explains to Jayne Anne Phillips, "Being an American makes you sort of dimwitted about social unrest" (G8).

Using the domestic crisis to explicate broader social issues is another specialty of Johnson, especially in her most recent novels. In *Le Divorce*, a disintegrating marriage between an American woman and a French man provides a lens through which to examine the cultural assumptions of cisatlantic constructions of national identity. *Le Divorce* filters its observations about French culture through the perceptions of Isabel, a college-age California native who speaks only a few words of French. Isabel's general bafflement alternates with moments of insight: "I had learned that it did not ingratiate you with the French to claim to share their social problems. This challenges either their belief that their problems are worse, or that American ones are so much worse that a comparison is insulting" (118). By contrast, *Le Mariage* is told from a variety of viewpoints and features a far wider cast of characters, including reclusive filmmaker Serge Cray, modeled on Stanley Kubrick, who died while Johnson was still writing the book. Though *Le Mariage* purports to be the story of another international union, this time between an American journalist, Tim Nollinger, and a French antiques dealer, Anne-Sophie, it is really an extended meditation on the "tension between people trying to be themselves once they're out of their native context versus the obligation that is laid on every American to be an American, with all the flaws imputed to Americans by other countries" (Goldstein G10). Perhaps more firmly than any of her earlier works, *Le Mariage*, whose settings include both bourgeois Paris and the Pacific Northwest, establishes Johnson's credentials as a major contributor to the form of the international novel, along with her predecessors F. Scott Fitzgerald and Henry James, with whom she has been compared more than once, despite the fact that she told Katherine Usher Henderson in 1990 that she "was always on the opposite side from Henry James" (53).

CRITICAL RECEPTION

Although today she is a critically acclaimed and best-selling writer, Johnson was not immediately hailed as a major new talent. *Fair Game* (1965), described by Judith Baughman as "polished, sophisticated social comedy" (222) and by Johnson herself as "unsatisfactory" (Bell 125), received almost no critical attention; and Johnson's 1968 novel, *Loving Hands at Home*, which tells the story of a dissatisfied young

Mormon homemaker who leaves her husband, went similarly unremarked. In 1971 she attracted some notice with her third novel, *Burning*; however, it was criticized for what some viewed as its cliché subject matter. Like the previous two books, *Burning* features a female protagonist whose comfortable wifely existence is shattered by an event that brings her into contact with a previously unknown, unconventional reality. *Burning*'s Bingo Edwards lives a sheltered life in Bel Air with her orthopedic surgeon husband until she is forced into contact with her neighbors, an eccentric psychiatrist and his patients. Despite the complaints that the topic of neurotic Americans addicted to group therapy and self-analysis has been "done to death" as material for satire, Johnson was praised for her mastery of a coolly detached comic tone and for her sympathetic and innovative treatment of her female protagonists. Although Johnson subsequently published award-winning short stories and a biography of Mary Ellen Meredith before returning to novel writing, significant critical recognition eluded her until the publication of her fourth novel, *The Shadow Knows*. Critics called the novel "cunning," and director Stanley Kubrick was sufficiently impressed by her ability to write a taut and suspenseful psychological thriller that he chose her to write the screenplay for his movie *The Shining*. Indeed, *The Shadow Knows* remains an object of academic scrutiny decades after its initial appearance in 1974.

From this point on, Johnson's popularity grew exponentially. Her next novel, *Lying Low* (1978), the suspenseful story of four days in the lives of four secret-harboring housemates, was hailed as a minor masterpiece, and in 1988, based in part on the success of *Persian Nights* (1987), Johnson was awarded the Mildred and Harold Strauss Livings, a yearly stipend to enable her to devote her time exclusively to writing. *Le Divorce*, her best-selling 1997 comedy of manners, made Johnson, the recipient of three National Book Award nominations and two Pulitzer Prize nominations, a household name for the first time. Her most recent novel, *Le Mariage*, was published by Dutton in 2000 to mostly excellent reviews; writing in the *New York Times*, Angeline Goreau observes that *Le Mariage* is "splendid entertainment, decorated with speculations of a redeeming nature. [Johnson] offers hope that, as James observed, 'the novel remains still, under the right persuasion, the most independent, most elastic, most prodigious of literary forms.' " (G8).

BIBLIOGRAPHY

Works by Diane Johnson

Fair Game. New York: Harcourt, 1965.

Loving Hands at Home. New York: Harcourt, 1968.

Burning. New York: Harcourt, 1971.

Lesser Lives: The True History of the First Mrs. Meredith. New York: Knopf, 1973.

Edwin Broun Fred: Scientist, Administrator, Gentleman. Madison: University of Wisconsin Press, 1974.

The Shadow Knows. New York: Knopf, 1974.

Lying Low. New York: Knopf, 1978.

The Shining. Screenplay adapted from *The Shining*. Stephen King. Warner Brothers, 1980.

Terrorists and Novelists. New York: Knopf, 1982.

Dashiell Hammett: A Life. New York: Random House, 1983.

Introduction. *Frankenstein*. Mary Shelley. New York: Bantam Classics, 1984. vii–xix.

Persian Nights. New York: Knopf, 1987.

Health and Happiness. New York: Knopf, 1990.

Natural Opium: Some Travelers' Tales. New York: Knopf, 1993.

Le Divorce. New York: Dutton, 1997.

Le Mariage. New York: Dutton, 2000.

Introduction. *Jane Eyre.* Charlotte Brontë. New York: Modern Library Classics, 2000. vi–xvi.

Paris: A Tour along the Seine. Photography by Philip Trager. Santa Fe: Arena Editions, 2000.

Studies of Diane Johnson

Baughman, Judith. "Diane Johnson." *Dictionary of Literary Biography Yearbook: 1980.* Ed. Karen L. Rood, Jean W. Ross, and Richard Ziegfeld. Detroit: Gale, 1981. 220–26.

Bell, Susan Groag. Interview with Diane Johnson. *Women Writers of the West Coast: Speaking of Their Lives and Careers.* Ed. Marilyn Yalom. Santa Barbara: Capra, 1983. 123–37.

Blankley, Elyse. "Clear Cutting the Western Myth: Beyond Joan Didion." *San Francisco in Fiction: Essays in a Regional Literature.* Ed. David Fine and Paul Skenazy. Albuquerque: University of New Mexico Press, 1995. 177–97.

Chell, Cara. "Marriage as Metaphor: The Novels of Diane Johnson." *Portraits of Marriage in Literature.* Ed. Anne C. Hargrove and Maurine Magliocco. Macomb: Western Illinois University Press, 1984. 159–69.

"Diane Johnson." *Major Twentieth-Century Writers: A Selection of Sketches from Contemporary Authors.* Ed. Bryan Ryan. Vol. 4. Detroit: Gale, 1991. 1522–26.

Goldstein, Bill. "An American in . . . " Rev. of *Le Mariage. New York Times* 16 April 2000: G10.

Goreau, Angeline. "La Difference." Rev. of *Le Mariage. New York Times* 16 April 2000: G8.

Greiner, Donald J. *Women without Men: Female Bonding and the American Novel of the 1980s.* Columbia: University of South Carolina Press, 1993.

Hammer, Andrea Gale. "Poetry and Family: An Interview with Karl Shapiro (with Remarks from Diane Johnson)." Interview with Karl Shapiro and Diane Johnson. *Prairie Schooner* 55 (1981): 3–31.

Henderson, Katherine Usher. "Interview with Diane Johnson." *Inter/View: Talks with America's Writing Women.* Ed. Mickey Pearlman and Katherine Usher Henderson. Lexington: University of Kentucky Press, 1990. 49–57.

Henley, Joan. "Re-Forming the Detective Story: Diane Johnson's *The Shadow Knows.*" *Clues: A Journal of Detection* 9 (1988): 87–93.

LeClair, Thomas. "Interview with Diane Johnson." *Anything Can Happen: Interviews with Contemporary American Novelists.* Urbana: University of Illinois Press, 1983. 201–16.

Melley, Timothy. " 'Stalked by Love': Female Paranoia and the Stalker Novel." *Differences: A Journal of Feminist Cultural Studies* 8 (1996): 68–100.

Phillips, Jayne Anne. "The Shiraz Quartet." Rev. of *Persian Nights. New York Times* 5 April 1987: G8.

Ryan, Marjorie. "The Novels of Diane Johnson." *Critique: Studies in Modern Fiction* 16 (1974): 53–63.

Stade, George. "Mysteries of a Hardcase." Rev. of *Dashiell Hammett: A Life. New York Times* 16 Oct. 1983: G1.

Todd, Janet. "Interview with Diane Johnson." *Women Writers Talking.* New York: Holmes and Meier, 1983. 121–32.

GAYL JONES (1949–)

Michelle L. Taylor

BIOGRAPHY

Gayl Jones's intense tales of African American female sexuality and violence have generated intense praise from her colleagues and readers. She has been hailed as one of America's finest writers by Maya Angelou, James Baldwin, and John Updike. Such public praise would likely embarrass Jones, a highly private and humble person. Over the years, Jones has guarded her privacy fiercely. What we do know of Jones is her daring and outstanding oeuvre that challenges the role of official history by exploring African American culture, generally, and her birthplace, Lexington, Kentucky, specifically. Overall, her body of work echoes the cadences of the Southern oral tradition that she grew up with in Lexington.

Gayl Jones was born into a family of storytellers on November 23, 1949. Jones's grandmother, Amanda Wilson, wrote plays for her church. Jones's father, Franklin, was a cook, and her mother, Lucille, was a homemaker and aspiring writer who wrote and told stories to entertain Jones and her brother, Franklin, Jr., and passed on the penchant for storytelling to her daughter. Indeed, "storyteller" is the label Jones prefers for herself, which is appropriate because the term captures the nonlinear and passionate aspects of her writing.

Jones's education proved to be another factor in the development of her writing career and her style. Jones grew up in a racially segregated community in Lexington and attended an all-black high school until the tenth grade, when the school was integrated. Jones began writing in elementary school, wrote her first story in the second grade, and continued to write through her high school years at Henry Clay High School. Though Jones was painfully shy and did not talk to her teachers or classmates, some teachers were proactive and recognized Jones for her talent as a writer. One teacher in particular, Elizabeth Hardwick, helped Jones secure a scholarship to Connecticut College, where she majored in English. Jones was frequently honored for her work and received the college's award for poetry in 1969 and 1970 and the Frances

Steloff Award for fiction in 1970 for her short story "The Roadhouse." Interestingly, just as Jones's family passed on their love for language and storytelling, their family history gave her ample material. "The Roadhouse," for example, is based on her grandparents. The story tells of a woman who cares for an ill stranger who later anonymously pays her bills, which is the story of her grandparents' first meeting.

Jones graduated from Connecticut College in 1971 and later entered graduate school at Brown University. She continued to be withdrawn from both her professors and her peers, but they were nevertheless impressed with her work. Jones graduated with an MA in creative writing in 1973 and received her PhD in 1975. While at Brown, Jones met Michael Harper, an African American writer and critic, who helped Jones publish her work. In the four years that Jones attended Brown, not only had she written two unpublished plays, *Chile Woman* and *The Ancestor: A Street Play*, but she also had completed two novel manuscripts along with a collection of short stories and poetry. In the end, it was the manuscript for *Corregidora* that Harper took to Random House editor Toni Morrison, who later edited the novel, which was published in 1975. Morrison also edited Jones's second novel, *Eva's Man*, which was published by Random House in 1976.

Owing to the overwhelming critical success of *Corregidora* and *Eva's Man*, Jones was fast becoming a literary success. Throughout the 1970s, during the height of the African American feminist movement, Jones was frequently recognized for her literary accomplishments. In 1975 she received the Howard Foundation Award and accepted a position at the University of Michigan. In 1976 she received a fellowship from the National Endowment for the Arts and published a collection of short stories, *White Rat*, in 1977. From 1975 to 1988, Jones was an assistant professor of Afro-American and African studies, a position that proved to have a lasting impact on the rest of her life. While teaching at Michigan, Jones met her future husband, Bob Higgins, then a student at Michigan. When the couple married, Higgins took Jones's name, and so began an unconventional relationship. Jones continued to teach and publish, and in 1981 she published *Song for Anninho*, a long verse poem based on her unpublished novel, *Palmares*. She was granted tenure at the University of Michigan in 1982.

However, despite the professional success, Jones was suffering on the personal front. Bob Jones had a history of emotional problems, and in 1982 he threatened participants at a gay rights parade. The police interrupted a fight between Bob Jones and the protesters, but he later returned with a gun and was subsequently arrested for felonious assault. The charge carried a possible sentence of four years, but the couple fled the United States before his trial. He was later sentenced in absentia. Rumors abound regarding Jones's departure from Michigan; some say, for instance, that she did not leave without first critiquing the school for what she believed to be racist practices. Jones and her husband lived in anonymity in Paris until 1988. Jones continued to write and published two collections of poetry, *The Hermit Woman* and *Xarque and Other Poems*, in 1983 and 1985, respectively. In 1988 the couple returned to the United States, where they secretly lived in Lexington. They returned to care for Jones's mother, Lucille, who was suffering from cancer; during their stay in Lexington, Jones continued to write and published *Liberating Voices: Oral Tradition in African American Literature* (1991), a work of literary criticism. Jones's mother died in February 1998, prompting her son-in-law to accuse the hospital of kidnaping and racism. Subsequently, Jones and her husband founded the Lucille Jones Foundation to uncover any conspiracies surrounding her mother's death. In the meantime, Bob Jones began a threatening letter-writing campaign to public officials in Lexington.

In the midst of grieving for her mother, Jones published her fourth novel, appropriately titled *The Healing* (1998). *The Healing* was Jones's first novel in over twenty years and was regarded by the media as a major literary event. All of the intense media attention regarding the novel eventually led authorities to her husband for whom they had a fourteen-year-old arrest warrant from Michigan. An interview in *Newsweek* finally led authorities to her mother's home in Lexington. When the police arrived, they entered a volatile situation, in which the couple, so convinced that they were the victims of a racist conspiracy, had barricaded themselves in their home with the gas turned on. During the stand-off, Bob Jones committed suicide by slashing his throat. Gayl Jones was later institutionalized; she has since been released. In 1999 Jones published her fourth novel, *Mosquito*, to great acclaim. However, despite the accolades for this very accomplished writer, she has continued to live a very private life. In an interview, Jones suggested that she wanted to live like J. D. Salinger and Thomas Pynchon so that her work would be the lens through which the public could view her. In accordance with her own wishes, Jones has returned to her craft and is currently editing an anthology of her mother's poetry and writing a book about her late husband.

MAJOR WORKS AND THEMES

Although Gayl Jones has written extensively in other genres, she is best known for her novels, in which she creates worlds where madness, violence, and sexuality collide, often with destructive results for women. Though the characters may seem tragic at some moments, their experiences are rendered compelling because of the honesty with which they confront society. Jones is careful to let the characters speak for themselves and does not give the reader directions or offer ways to understand the characters. As a result, readers have to understand them based on their words and actions.

Jones's first novel, *Corregidora*, fits squarely within the paradigms of African American feminism, exemplifying work that reflects the multiple subject positions occupied by African American women. Furthermore, the novel examines the sometimes-tragic intersections of race, sexuality, and gender. In the novel, Jones uses the diasporic slave past to underscore the historic abuse of the black female body as well as the possibilities for female agency. Jones's combination of a nonlinear plot with raw language and poetic lyricism makes for a representation of unofficial history that is both disturbing and compelling.

The novel is narrated by blues singer Ursa Corregidora, who is haunted by her family's historical relationship to Old Man Corregidora, a wealthy Brazilian slave owner who prostituted his female slaves, except for those that he kept for himself. Among those that he turned into his personal concubines was Ursa's great-grandmother. He produced a child with Ursa's great-grandmother and then impregnated his own child. After giving birth to a female child, the daughter escaped to the United States to protect her child from Corregidora's sexual depravity. However, despite the legacy of abuse, all of the women keep the Corregidora name to remind them of the patriarchal slave system. The purpose of keeping the name is to make generations that share the name, which ensures that the story will be passed on as a cautionary tale to future generations.

The family mandate is particularly difficult for Ursa because of the injuries she sustains during an assault by her jealous husband, Mutt. Though Mutt meets Ursa while she is singing at a small club, he wants her to end her career once they are married. Despite his protestations, Ursa continues to sing, and it is during a jealous rage that he pushes her down a flight of stairs. Ultimately, the doctors can save her only by removing her womb, as well as the child she is carrying. Ursa's inability to have children suggests that the Corregidora family history will not be passed on to future generations and, hence, forgotten.

Ursa's physical recovery period is relatively brief, but her emotional recovery spans twenty years; her struggles with emotional healing constitute the bulk of the novel's flashback narrative. In telling her story, she confronts her maternal family history, personal relationships, and her career as a blues singer. Further, Ursa gains more control over her life and the narrative. By the end of the narrative, Ursa returns to the stage and to her relationship with Mutt, but she does so with a new understanding of the relationship between history, sexuality, and creation. She is therefore able to view her music as a form of creation, not only for herself but also for future generations. Thus, her music embodies the story of her own personal history and the broader history of the slave past and its continuing impact on African American life and culture.

Ursa's role as a blues singer is of special importance because of Jones's own commitment to capturing the essence of the blues in narrative form. Historically, blues music has functioned as a folk history of the African American experience, which tells of survival and transcendence in a hostile world. Jones focuses on the restorative power of the blues because it is through Ursa's singing that she is able to envision herself as a speaking subject. Furthermore, the blues serves as a metaphor for the relationships that Jones portrays in the narrative. Jones views *Corregidora* as a blues narrative insofar as it incorporates both the joy and the pain inherent in human relationships. Jones's use of the blues is particularly effective not only because it locates her in a long line of African American writers who use the blues as a narrative model but also because it is an important mechanism with which to understand the multi-layered struggles of African American women in an inhospitable environment.

The narrative of Jones's second novel, *Eva's Man*, also focuses on the themes of female agency and male domination. Unlike Ursa Corregidora, who gains more control over her life through narrating her story, Eva Medina Canada, the protagonist in *Eva's Man*, is a study in madness and loss of control. As Keith Byerman makes clear in his reading of the novel, "We know Eva is insane, not because Jones tells us, but because the time and space distortion, the obsessions and repetitions, and the increasingly confusing and obscure references within the narrative are the linguistic markers of a psychotic personality" (132). Eva's madness is not peculiar to her own individual personality; instead, it results from the collective history of sexual abuse inflicted upon and the negative stereotypes associated with the black female body.

Eva grows up believing that women have no control over their bodies, and her perceived inability to control her sexuality is the premise of the novel. Eva's abuse begins at an early age when she is victimized by a young neighbor. Throughout her life, Eva encounters several different abusers: her mother's boyfriend, a cousin who tries repeatedly to seduce her, and an ex-husband so jealous that he locks her in their apartment. After a lifetime of abuse, Eva strikes back at her lover, Davis. After being imprisoned in his apartment, Eva poisons him and orally castrates him. She then calls the police and is later imprisoned for her crime. Much to the amazement of the police, Eva refuses to explain herself and silently resists the system that attempts to define her. At the end of *Corregidora*, Ursa's new relationship with Mutt offers a possibility for redemption; however, the role of redemption is far more complicated in *Eva's Man*. Eva's only redemptive possibility comes as a result of her imprisonment in the prison psychiatric ward when she finally experiences sexual pleasure with her cell-mate, Elvira. Though *Corregidora* only hints at the possibilities for lesbian relation-ships, *Eva's Man* suggests that it is a viable alternative that is perhaps a more redemptive and healthier expression of female sexuality.

Both Jones's collection of short stories, *White Rat*, and the verse poem, *Song for Anninho*, focus on themes similar to her novels. The stories in *White Rat* focus on race, madness, and female sexuality. The stories include "The Women," in which a young girl recalls her mother's lesbian relationships while trying to understand her own heterosexual awakening; "Persona," which deals with a professor's previously unacknowledged desire for other women; and "White Rat," which focuses on the racial dilemmas faced by a black male so light-skinned that he could pass for white. *Song for Anninho* explores Jones's interest in the diasporic slave past and focuses on a husband and wife living in Palmares, a fugitive slave settlement. The poem follows the pair, Anninho and his wife, Almeyda, as they resist the institution of slavery. Unlike the characters in her novels and short stories, the two are not destroyed by their experiences but instead find opportunities for transcendence through their shared personal relationship.

Jones's return to the American literary scene was bittersweet because along with the praise for *The Healing* came tragic events that changed her life. As the title suggests, *The Healing* is not as tragic as Jones's earlier novels; instead, it presents opportunities for communal renewal. The novel follows the protagonist, Harlan Ea-gleton, as she travels throughout the United States as a faith healer. One of her first stops is a small tank town, so named because the water tank is the town's most distinguishing marker of community pride.

In *The Healing*, Jones makes good use of memory, orality, and nonlinearity. Indeed, while Harlan changes the lives of the people that she heals, her memories and mon-ologues reveal the myriad changes she has undergone. Before she became a faith healer, Harlan Jane or Harlan Truth, as she is also known, was a manager for a rock band, a horse race gambler, a photographer in Africa, and a hairdresser. In many ways, *The Healing* is reminiscent of *Song for Anninho* in that it depicts the liberating potential of human relationships and concludes with a surprisingly positive ending that celebrates rather than laments life.

In the midst of Harlan's healing and seemingly endless shape shifting is a narrative of social critique in which the characters comment on issues ranging from art and language to Afrocentrism and literature. Jones continues her emphasis on ideas and the power of social change in her fourth novel, *Mosquito*. Like *The Healing*, *Mosquito* focuses on a traveling woman, whose movements often signal momentous shifts in her life and the lives of the people whom she encounters. Ostensibly, the novel is about the efforts of an African American female truck driver, Sojuorner Nadine Jane Johnson, also known as Mosquito, to help a pregnant Mexican stowaway whom she finds in her truck. The novel is set in a small Texas border town, which metaphorically parallels the physical and emotional border crossings that take place in the novel. Through her efforts to help the stowaway, Mosquito encounters a host of memorable characters, including a revolutionary priest, activist lawyers, and refugees. By transporting refugees along the New Underground Railroad, Mosquito begins to understand her role in society. Though Mosquito speaks in the vernacular, she is hardly an uninformed narrator. Mosquito's views are thought provoking, and her wit is razor sharp. Ultimately, Mosquito is an intriguing and complex narrator who not only questions society but also invites readers to question society as well. Throughout the text, Mosquito critiques the world in which she lives and the people in it, as seen in the relationship that develops between Mosquito and Delgadina, a Mexican bartender whom she befriends during her travels. The topics of conversation between Delgadina and Mosquito are varied, and many focus on issues of multiculturalism and institutional racism. The conversations allow Jones to speak in a decidedly political voice as she speaks on behalf of African Americans and Mexicans. Just as the novel blurs the boundaries of historicity, it nevertheless brings into sharp focus Jones's skill in telling complex narratives about the relationship between self, society, and history.

The themes in Jones's work can be read as an exploration of history, trauma, and African American female subjectivity. By weaving together narratives of trauma and survival, Jones narrates stories that would otherwise go untold. Her work, then, not only examines the relationship between race, gender, and sexuality but, more importantly, allows for the articulation of multiple feminist experiences that reject narrowly defined normative ideals.

CRITICAL RECEPTION

After the publication of *Corregidora*, Jones accrued a following of distinguished writers who applauded her for her ability to write honestly and brilliantly about issues of race and gender. She was lauded for her skill in incorporating the blues and African American folklore into her work, which has since become standard reading in African American and women's studies courses. However, the publication of *Eva's Man* sparked considerable debate and criticism from African American male critics regarding Jones's depictions of black men. Jones, Alice Walker, and a number of feminist writers are criticized for what are perceived to be unrealistic and harsh representations that perpetuate stereotypes regarding black male subjectivity. However, what critics do not immediately acknowledge is that Jones's depictions are not so much gender biased as they are representations of how race and racism constitute a tragic intersection in the lives of the characters.

Despite the initial negative attention regarding Jones's depictions of race and masculinity, many critics have begun to interrogate the relationship between history and slavery that is ever present in her work. Among them is Madhu Dubey, who establishes a link between the slave past and the maternal legacy in *Corregidora*. Likewise, Stelamaris Coser considers slavery in Jones's work within the context of Brazilian slavery. Gender, violence, and sexuality are also central critical frameworks for analyzing Jones's work, most notably in *Corregidora* and *Eva's Man*. As critics have pointed out, Jones's work is a sometimes brutal but always provocative renegotiation of race, gender, and history. And it is her careful interrogation of these relationships that has established Jones as an important voice in African American literature.

BIBLIOGRAPHY

Works by Gayl Jones

Corregidora. New York: Random House, 1975.

Eva's Man. New York: Random House, 1976.

White Rat. New York: Random House, 1977.

Song for Anninho. Ann Arbor: Lotus, 1981.

The Hermit Woman. Ann Arbor: Lotus, 1983.

Xarque and Other Poems. Ann Arbor: Lotus, 1985.

Liberating Voices: Oral Tradition in African American Literature. Cambridge, MA: Harvard University Press, 1991.

The Healing. Boston: Beacon, 1998.

Mosquito. Boston: Beacon, 1999.

Studies of Gayl Jones

Bruce, Simon. "Traumatic Repetition: Gayl Jones's *Corregidora*." *Race Consciousness: African American Studies for the New Century*. Ed. Judith Jackson Fossett and Jeffrey Tucker. New York: New York University Press, 1997. 93–112.

Byerman, Keith. "Gayl Jones." *Afro-American Fiction Writers after 1955*. Ed. Trudier Harris and Thadioius Davis. Detroit: Gale, 1984. Vol. 33 of *Dictionary of Literary Biography*. 128–35.

Champion, Laurie. Rev. of *Mosquito*. *African American Review* 34 (2000): 366–68.

Coser, Stelamaris. *Bridging the Americas: The Literature of Paule Marshall, Toni Morrison, and Gayl Jones*. Philadelphia: Temple University Press, 1995. 120–63.

Dubey, Madhu. "Gayl Jones and the Matrilineal Metaphor of Tradition." *Signs* 20 (1995): 245–67.

Johnson, Patrick E. "Wild Women Don't Get the Blues: A Blues Analysis of Gayl Jones's *Eva's Man*." *Obsidian II: Black Literature in Review* 9 (1994): 26–46.

Morgenstern, Naomi. "Mother's Milk and Sister's Blood: Trauma and the Neoslave Narrative." *Differences: A Journal of Feminist Cultural Studies* 8 (1996): 101–26.

Robinson, Sally. " 'We're All Consequences of Something': Cultural Mythologies of Gender and Race in the Novels of Gayl Jones." *Engendering the Subject: Gender and Self-Representation in Contemporary Women's Fiction*. Albany: State University of New York Press, 1991. 135–88.

Wilcox, Janelle. "Resistant Silence, Resistant Subject: (Re)Reading Gayl Jones's *Eva's Man*." *Bodies of Writing, Bodies in Performance*. Ed. Thomas Foster, Carol Siegel, and Ellen Berry. New York: New York University Press, 1996. 72–96.

JAMAICA KINCAID (1949–)

Sharon Hileman

BIOGRAPHY

In 1973 Elaine Cynthia Potter Richardson changed her name to Jamaica Kincaid, thereby beginning the process of self-invention she felt was necessary in order to write. Elaine Richardson was born May 25, 1949, at St. John's, Antigua, a Caribbean island that remained a British colony until 1981. She was the illegitimate child of Annie Richardson Drew, from the French colony of Dominica, and Frederick Potter, an Antiguan. Potter never married her mother and played no role in his daughter's life as she grew up on the island of Antigua. Instead, David Drew, Kincaid's step-father, became her surrogate father.

Kincaid received a British colonial education in Antigua, steeped in the works of Milton, Shakespeare, and Wordsworth; her favorite book was Charlotte Brontë's *Jane Eyre.* When she left the islands in 1966, she had never read a book by a Caribbean author and was unfamiliar with any Caribbean literary tradition. This departure was necessitated by her family's need for financial assistance to support the three younger brothers born in rapid succession after Kincaid reached the age of nine. Her mother had already removed her from school so that she could help care for her siblings and apprenticed her to a seamstress to learn a trade. When Kincaid refused to continue the apprenticeship, her parents prevailed upon her to immigrate to the United States and become an *au pair*.

Kincaid obtained a position in Scarsdale, New York, and for a while dutifully sent money home. Eventually, though, she abandoned work as a servant and refused to continue her financial support for the siblings she had never wanted. She held a series of low-paid office jobs and attended several schools until she obtained her high school diploma. During this period, she severed her relationship with her mother, and a twenty-year separation between the two ensued.

In 1976 Kincaid began writing for the *New Yorker*, authoring "Talk of the Town" columns that described her life in Antigua and gave her impressions of New York.

These columns were recently collected and published as *Talk Stories* (2001). In 1978 the *New Yorker* published her first short story, "Girl" (*At the Bottom of the River*) a one-page litany of instructions and warnings given by a Caribbean mother to her daughter. This very short story provided the voice and subject material that would launch Kincaid's career as a writer. The conflicted mother/daughter relationship it conveyed would be more fully developed in her collection of short stories *At the Bottom of the River* (1983) and in her autobiographical novels *Annie John* (1985) and *Lucy* (1990). Later works focus on other family members and venture into new genres. *The Autobiography of My Mother* (1996) combines biography, autobiography, and fiction to create a character based in part on Kincaid's mother and maternal grandmother. The memoir *My Brother* (1997) gives an account of the AIDS-induced death of one of Kincaid's younger brothers and her return to Antigua to help nurse him. In addition to memoirs, Kincaid has also written nonfiction, ranging from *A Small Place* (1988), which is a polemical critique of colonial and postcolonial Antigua, to *My Garden (Book)* (1999), a collection of essays on gardening and its relation to memory and conquest.

Kincaid herself is an avid gardener at her home in Bennington, Vermont, where she lives with her husband, Allen Shawn, a composer and college professor, and their two children, Annie and Harold. Her first Vermont garden was constructed in the shape of the Caribbean islands.

MAJOR WORKS AND THEMES

Kincaid has said that her greatest interest is in studying the relationship of the powerful and powerless. She does so both by portraying the relationships of parents and children, especially mothers and daughters, and by considering the colonial relationship of the mother/country and daughter/colony. Frequently the themes are combined in a single work, so that the novel *Annie John*, for instance, shows the progression from closeness to separation between mother and daughter as it simultaneously chronicles the daughter's developing awareness of the need to free herself from colonial bonds. The protagonist's identity will be formed not by imitating the mother or mimicking the British but by rejecting and rebelling against the agents that seek to dominate her.

The theme of rebellion is specifically alluded to in *Lucy*, an autobiographical novel, whose protagonist's name is a form of Lucifer, the rebellious archangel. Lucy is an angry character, rebelling against her mother, her colonial heritage, her island home, and her white, American, upper-middle-class employers. Having come to the United States, Lucy confronts a different form of the imperialist and racist culture associated with British colonialism. Like Annie John, she is an adolescent still struggling with identity formation, but whereas Annie's was a coming-of-age story, Lucy's is an immigrant's account of the struggle of reconciling two worlds and two worldviews.

Most recently, Kincaid has approached themes of dominion and colonization by writing about gardening. She argues that the gardener's enterprises of uprooting, transplanting, hybridizing, and cultivating are akin to the colonizer's project. In addition, she believes that only members of a colonizing class would have originally had the leisure, wealth, and opportunity to construct the elaborate gardens of past centuries.

One of Kincaid's major literary tropes—*Paradise Lost*—also features a garden, of course, but its significance is in its loss. Kincaid's characters experience loss, both the lost paradise of childhood bliss and the lost paradise of an island home when they are exiled from it. Antigua, as well as other Caribbean islands, has also experienced loss because of its colonial experience. The British exterminated the native Carib and Arawak Indians and then imported, enslaved, and killed innumerable Africans in order to provide a labor force for their sugar plantations. In *The Autobiography of My Mother*, Kincaid inscribes these losses in her protagonist, a descendant of both Carib Indians and African slaves. Xuela Claudette Richardson, who has Kincaid's family name and represents her maternal ancestors, projects a history of dispossession, beginning with the death of her own mother in giving birth to Xuela. Later, when her father also dies, Xuela proclaims herself an orphan. In *A Small Place*, Kincaid calls residents of the Caribbean "orphans," people without a motherland or fatherland, without love, without a tongue (language) of their own.

In addition to attacking the colonizers, Kincaid also levies attacks upon the postcolonial practices that continue the exploitation and corruption they introduced. *A Small Place* is an indictment of the white tourist who sees Antigua only as a vacation resort, but it also criticizes black Antiguans for the political, social, and economic problems that plague the island. *My Brother*, a memoir chronicling the AIDS-induced death of Kincaid's brother, compares the invasion and devastation of AIDS to the operations of colonialism but also critiques Antiguans for their homophobia and insensitivity to victims' suffering.

The theme of betrayal and self-betrayal underlies Kincaid's work, for whether relationships exist between parents and children, colonizer and colonized, self and other, they will eventually be marred by an abuse of power. Betrayal may take the form of exploitation, abandonment, enslavement, or rejection, but it always causes people to suffer. Kincaid believes that "life is difficult and that's that" (Snell 31); thus, she writes stories of suffering, stories with no happy endings.

CRITICAL RECEPTION

All of Kincaid's works, regardless of genre or subject matter, have been praised for their lyrical style, described as rhythmic, hypnotic, incantatory. She is noted for constructing atmospheres or moods that predominate over plot and penetrate the consciousness of readers. By combining ordinary, commonplace events with fantasy, she creates dream-like, surrealistic worlds such as in the ten stories of *At the Bottom of the River*. This first book won the Morton Dauwen Zabel Award of the American Academy and Institute of Arts and Letters and was nominated for the PEN/Faulkner Award.

The mother/daughter relationship depicted in *At the Bottom of the River*, *Annie John*, and *Lucy* has received a great deal of critical attention. Articles based upon theories of female development explicated by Nancy Chodorow have focused on mother/daughter bonding, pre-Oedipal narrative, and merging and separation issues. *Annie John* has been called a "universal" coming-of-age novel and has become one of the most widely read books in the high school curriculum (Mistron xi). It was one of three finalists for the 1985 Ritz Paris Hemingway Award.

Annie John and *Lucy*, its successor, have also been analyzed as female *bildungsromans* since both chart the growth and development of a young girl from the Caribbean. With minor plot modifications, *Lucy* has been seen as the continuation of Annie John's story: The protagonist's name has changed, she immigrates to the United States rather than England, and she becomes an *au pair* instead of a nurse. However, it is Lucy's rebelliousness and anger that have received the most critical attention. She has been read as a postcolonial subject struggling to establish her cultural identity, an identity complicated not only by her experience of British colonial practices but also by her immersion in privileged American culture.

Although critics tried to rationalize and explain Lucy's anger in terms of colonizer and colonized, they still felt the book lacked *Annie John*'s appeal. When Kincaid went on to express her own anger at the colonizers and the legacy of corruption they left in Antigua, readers labeled *A Small Place* "a jeremiad" (Rushdie, quoted in Locke A24) and described it as "distorted" (Hill 19) and "scathing" (Simmons, "Coming of Age" 117). The *New Yorker* would not publish the piece because of its anger. Although critics had been able to discuss Kincaid's depiction of ambivalence in Annie John's feelings of love and hate for her mother, they could not understand Kincaid's own ambivalence toward Antigua. Kincaid, however, described the book as a "turning point" (Perry, "Jamaica Kincaid" 132) and believed it enabled her to develop a "voice of resistance" (Ferguson, "A Lot of Memory" 167).

If Kincaid's anger and ambivalence were criticized in her nonfiction, her next work of fiction, *The Autobiography of My Mother*, was to be negatively received for its "bitter" (Kakutani E7), "inhuman" and "almost unbearable" (Schine 5) story. Readers did not like or identify with the withdrawn and indifferent protagonist, who remained aloof in her marriage to a European and aborted her child when she became pregnant. Incapable of experiencing love, Xuela instead exercised sexual power in her relationships, reversing the traditional positions of colonizer and colonized. Although the book's nihilism and mood of sad hopelessness depressed readers, the novel was a finalist for the National Book Critics' Circle Award and the PEN/Faulkner Award.

A different sort of negativity was portrayed in Kincaid's memoir *My Brother*, described as a "frank meditation on sexuality, death, and family" (DeLombard 14). Kincaid did not really know this half-brother who was dying from AIDS. He had been a toddler when she left the island, and she had not communicated with him in twenty years. Visiting him, she discovered they did not even speak the same kind of English. Nonetheless, by returning to a story about family and reintroducing the domineering mother from *Annie John*, Kincaid regained her audience's sympathies. The *New York Times* called *My Brother* a "rich, complex book" that did not sentimentalize its subject (Quindlen 7), while the *Women's Review of Books* praised its "luminous" treatment of death (McDowell 1). It became a finalist for the National Book Award.

Kincaid's work has been compared with Merle Hodge's, Wole Soyinka's, James Baldwin's, and Toni Morrison's, but she cannot really be categorized as a Caribbean, postcolonial, black, or feminist writer. Eschewing classification, except as a self-proclaimed exile and outsider, Kincaid says she simply writes to save her own life and to make sense out of her past.

BIBLIOGRAPHY

Works by Jamaica Kincaid

At the Bottom of the River. New York: Farrar, 1983.
Annie John. New York: Farrar, 1985.
Annie, Gwen, Lilly, Pam and Tulip. New York: Whitney Museum of American Art, 1986.

A Small Place. New York: Farrar, 1988.

Lucy. New York: Farrar, 1990.

The Autobiography of My Mother. New York: Farrar, 1996.

My Brother. New York: Farrar, 1997.

"Introduction." *Generations of Women: In Their Own Words*. San Francisco: Chronicle Books, 1998. 9–11.

Ed. *My Favorite Plant: Writers and Gardeners on the Plants They Love*. New York: Farrar, 1998.

My Garden (Book). New York: Farrar, 1999.

Talk Stories. New York: Farrar, 2001.

Studies of Jamaica Kincaid

Birbalsingh, Frank. "Jamaica Kincaid: From Antigua to America." *Frontiers of Caribbean Literature in English*. New York: St. Martin's, 1996. 138–51.

Bloom, Harold, ed. *Jamaica Kincaid*. Philadelphia: Chelsea House, 1998.

Byerman, Keith E. "Anger in *A Small Place*: Jamaica Kincaid's Cultural Critique of Antigua." *College Literature* 22 (1995): 91–102.

Caton, Louis F. "Romantic Struggles: The *Bildungsroman* and Mother-Daughter Bonding in Jamaica Kincaid's *Annie John*." *MELUS* 21 (1996): 125–42.

Chick, Nancy. "The Broken Clock: Time, Identity, and Autobiography in Jamaica Kincaid's *Lucy*." *CLA Journal* 40 (1996): 90–104.

Covi, Giovanna. "Jamaica Kincaid and the Resistance to Canons." *Out of the Kumbla*: *Caribbean Women and Literature*. Ed. Carol Boyce Davis and Elaine Savory Fido. Trenton: Africa World Press, 1990. 345–54.

Cudjoe, Selwyn R. "Jamaica Kincaid and the Modernist Project: An Interview." *Callaloo* 12 (1989): 396–411.

DeLombard, Jeannine. "My Brother's Keeper: An Interview with Jamaica Kincaid." *Lambda Book Report* May 1998: 14.

Donnell, Alison. "She Ties Her Tongue: The Problems of Cultural Paralysis in Postcolonial Criticism." *Ariel* 26 (1995): 101–16.

——. "When Writing the Other Is Being True to the Self: Jamaica Kincaid's *The Autobiography of My Mother*." *Women's Lives into Print: The Theory, Practice, and Writing of Feminist Auto/Biography*. Ed. Pauline Polkey. New York: St. Martin's/Macmillan, 1999. 123–36.

Dutton, Wendy. "Merge and Separate: Jamaica Kincaid's Fiction." *World Literature Today* 63 (1989): 406–10.

Ferguson, Moira. "*Lucy* and the Mark of the Colonizer." *Modern Fiction Studies* 39 (1993): 237–59.

——. *Colonialism and Gender Relations from Mary Wollstonecraft to Jamaica Kincaid: Eastern Caribbean Connections*. New York: Columbia University Press, 1994.

——. *Jamaica Kincaid: Where the Land Meets the Body*. Charlottesville: University Press of Virginia, 1994.

——. "A Lot of Memory: An Interview with Jamaica Kincaid." *Kenyon Review* 16 (1994): 163–88.

Hill, Alison Friesinger. Rev. of *A Small Place*. *New York Times Book Review* 10 July 1988: 19.

Ismond, Patricia. "Jamaica Kincaid: 'First They Must Be Children.' " *World Literature Written in English* 28 (1988): 336–41.

Kakutani, Michiko. "Loss in the Caribbean, from Birth On." Rev. of *The Autobiography of My Mother*. *New York Times* 16 Jan. 1996: E7.

Kumin, Maxine. Rev. of *My Garden (Book)*. *Women's Review of Books* March 2000: 5.

Locke, Richard. "An Antiguan Girl in America." Rev. of *Lucy*. *Wall Street Journal* 16 Oct. 1990: A24.

MacDonald-Smythe, Antonia. "Authorizing the Slut in Jamaica Kincaid's *At the Bottom of the River*." *Macomere: Journal of the Association of Caribbean Women Writers & Scholars* 2 (1999): 96–113.

Mahlis, Kristen. "Gender and Exile: Jamaica Kincaid's *Lucy*." *Modern Fiction Studies* 44 (1998): 164–83.

McDowell, Deborah E. Rev. of *My Brother*. *Women's Review of Books* Jan. 1998: 1.

Mistron, Deborah. *Understanding Jamaica Kincaid's Annie John: A Student Casebook to Issues, Sources, and Historical Documents*. Westport, CT: Greenwood Press, 1999.

Murdoch, H. Adlai. "Severing the (M)other Connection: The Representation of Cultural Identity in Jamaica Kincaid's *Annie John*." *Callaloo* 13 (1990): 325–40.

Natov, Roni. "Mothers and Daughters: Jamaica Kincaid's Pre-Oedipal Narratives." *Children's Literature: Annual of the Modern Language Association Seminar on Children's Literature and the Children's Literature Association* 18 (1990): 1–16.

Niesen de Abruña, Laura. "Family Connections: Mother and Mother Country in the Fiction of Jean Rhys and Jamaica Kincaid." *Motherlands: Black Women's Writing from Africa, the Caribbean, and South Asia*. Ed. Susheila Nasta. London: Women's Press, 1991. 257–89.

——. "Jamaica Kincaid's Writing and the Maternal-Colonial Matrix." *Caribbean Women Writers: Fiction in English*. Ed. Mary Conde and Thorunn Lonsdale. New York: St. Martin's, 1999. 172–83.

Oczkowica, Edyta Katarzyna. "Jamaica Kincaid's *Lucy*: Cultural 'Translation' as a Case of Creative Exploration of the Past." *MELUS* 21 (1996): 153–58.

Paravisini-Gebert, Lizabeth. *Jamaica Kincaid: A Critical Companion*. Westport, CT: Greenwood Press, 1999.

Perry, Donna. "Initiation in Jamaica Kincaid's *Annie John*." *Caribbean Women Writers: Essays from the First International Conference*. Ed. Selwyn R. Cudjoe. Wellesley, MA: Calaloux, 1990. 245–53.

——. "Jamaica Kincaid." *Backtalk: Women Writers Speak Out*. New Brunswick, NJ: Rutgers University Press, 1993. 127–41.

Quindlen, Anna. "The Past Is Another Country." Rev. of *My Brother*. *New York Times Book Review* 19 Oct. 1997: 7.

Rice, Anne P. "Burning Connections: Maternal Betrayal in Jamaica Kincaid's *My Brother*." *A/B: Auto/Biography Studies* 14 (1999): 23–37.

Schine, Cathlee. "A World as Cruel as Job's." Rev. of *The Autobiography of My Mother*. *New York Times Book Review* 4 Feb. 1995: 5.

Schultheis, Alexandra. "Family Matters in Jamaica Kincaid's *The Autobiography of My Mother*." *Jouvert: A Journal of Postcolonial Studies* 5 (2001) (http://social.chass.ncsu. edu/jouvert/).

Simmons, Diane. *Jamaica Kincaid*. New York: Twayne, 1994.

——. "The Rhythm of Reality in the Work of Jamaica Kincaid." *World Literature Today* 68 (1994): 466–72.

——. "Coming of Age in the Snare of History: Jamaica Kincaid's *The Autobiography of My Mother*." *The Girl: Constructions of the Girl in Contemporary Fiction by Women*. Ed. Ruth O. Saxton. New York: St. Martin's, 1998. 107–18.

——. "Jamaica Kincaid and the Canon: In Dialogue with *Paradise Lost* and *Jane Eyre*." *MELUS* 23 (1998): 65–85.

Snell, Marilyn Berlin. "Jamaica Kincaid Hates Happy Endings." *Mother Jones* 22 (1997): 28–31.

Tapping, Craig. "Children and History in the Caribbean Novel: George Lammings' *In the Castle of My Skin* and Jamaica Kincaid's *Annie John*." *Kunapipi* 11 (1989): 51–59.

Tiffin, Helen. "Decolonization and Audience: Erna Brodber's *Myal* and Jamaica Kincaid's *A Small Place*." *SPAN: Journal of the South Pacific Association for Commonwealth Language and Literature Studies* 30 (1990): 27–38.

——. "Cold Hearts and (Foreign) Tongues: Recitation and Reclamation of the Female Body in the Works of Erna Brodber and Jamaica Kincaid." *Callaloo* 16 (1993): 909–21.

——. " 'Flowers of Evil,' Flowers of Empire: Roses and Daffodils in the Work of Jamaica Kincaid, Olive Senior, and Lorna Goodison." *SPAN: Journal of the South Pacific Association for Commonwealth Language and Literature Studies* 46 (1998): 58–71.

Timothy, Helen Pyne. "Adolescent Rebellion and Gender Relations in *At the Bottom of the River* and *Annie John*." *Caribbean Women Writers: Essays from the First International Conference*. Ed. Selwyn R. Cudjoe. Wellesley, MA: Calaloux, 1990. 233–42.

Vorda, Allan. "I Come from a Place That's Very Unreal: An Interview with Jamaica Kincaid." *Face to Face: Interviews with Contemporary Novelists*. Ed. Allan Vorda and Daniel Stern. Houston: Rice University Press, 1993. 77–106.

NANCI KINCAID (1950–)

Deborah Maltby

BIOGRAPHY

Nanci Kincaid was born in Tallahassee, Florida, on September 5, 1950, to William Henry Pierce and Lois Swingle Pierce. The family lived in a blue-collar neighborhood, in which Kincaid's parents were among the few college-educated residents. Her mother was unusual as an outspoken pro-integration champion, during that time of great tension and change in racial relations in the South. Kincaid's father operated the textbook dispensary for the state of Florida and brought home sample textbooks for Kincaid and her younger brothers and sisters. Kincaid often wrote stories on the white pages at the beginning and end of the textbooks. "The blank page has always attracted me," she says (Maltby).

In college at Virginia Tech, Kincaid was an honors English student. But instead of pursuing writing, Kincaid left college to marry a football coach. The years spent raising her two daughters but not actively writing provided her with material and a mature perspective for her fiction. She began writing again and finished her education later, with a BA at Athens State College in 1987 and an MFA in fiction writing at the University of Alabama in 1991. She has taught fiction writing at University of Alabama at Tuscaloosa, University of North Carolina at Charlotte, and University of Arizona at Tucson.

In the 1980s, Kincaid began her first novel, *Crossing Blood*, as a story about the relationship between a black family and a white family in segregation-era Tallahassee. However, she says, "The manuscript was huge. I had no idea what a novel was" (Maltby). Kincaid continued to work on the manuscript, breaking it into short stories, some of which were published in journals such as *New Letters*, *Missouri Review*, and *Carolina Quarterly*. In graduate school, she found that most other students were writing short fiction rather than novels, so she would "yank out a chapter, twist it into a short story, and take it in to workshop" (Maltby). Eventually, Kincaid restructured the story as a much tighter novel, and it was published in 1992 by Putnam.

Kincaid's second book, *Pretending the Bed Is a Raft* (1997), is a collection of eight short stories, mostly about women's lives, marriage, and family life. She polished the collection while working on her second novel, *Balls* (1998), which centers on marriages in the football world. After her first marriage ended, she began writing *Balls* for what she calls "the poorest reason: personal cleansing. I felt I was privy to an untold story—all the women in the life (football wives) know it, but don't tell it" (Maltby). She sold the concept to her first publisher, Putnam, but ended up buying back the rights and selling *Balls* to Algonquin Press, which publishes many noted Southern writers. Ironically, by the time *Balls* was published, Kincaid had married another college football coach.

Though Kincaid is a Southern writer, she has spent many of her adult years living outside the South. "I embrace my southernness," she says. "Also, I have this accent and I'm not really aware of it, but it identifies me as southern. One thing I like about the South is the power of language. You have the Scotch-Irish and the African-Americans; they're opposite in so many ways, but there's a strong oral tradition in both" (Maltby).

Kincaid says that being Southern helps her as a writer because she feels that the South is a place where the best art is organic, or at least starts out organic. "Writers write. They're self-taught," she says. "I think you can over-study your craft. I don't know all the rules. In graduate school they'd say, 'Well, you can't do that; it isn't correct,' but I did it. I broke a lot of rules because I didn't know better. Thank goodness" (Maltby).

MAJOR WORKS AND THEMES

Both Kincaid's novels, *Crossing Blood* and *Balls*, are set in the South and are deeply rooted in Southern attitudes and behaviors and in the paradoxes and pain of women's lives. Both novels, in different ways, also have female protagonists who view and attempt to interpret another culture from the outside.

While many contemporary Southern writers have explored racial issues, *Crossing Blood* takes a fresh approach by going straight to the heart of the issue: the question of what would happen if men and women of different races became acquainted. Kincaid treats the issue in a thoughtful and accessible way in *Crossing Blood* by having the attraction between a black boy and a white girl begin in childhood.

Kincaid reveals her themes while experimenting in both novels with narrative form and voice. *Crossing Blood* is told in a series of undated, mostly chronological episodes through the eyes of Lucy, the white girl, as she grows up trying to understand a series of mixed messages about love, marriage, and racial stereotypes. In the early episodes, Lucy is a little girl who tries to interpret events she witnesses but does not understand. As she grows into her teen years, her voice sounds appropriately more mature.

Lucy is fascinated with the boy next door, Skippy, who lives in the African American residential area. Both children know that any openly romantic relationship between them is forbidden by society. From her position as observer, Lucy tries to understand Skippy's world. That world, where she is unwelcome, includes his house, the "colored woods" (49), and a bar.

Marriage and the compromises women make are major themes in both *Crossing Blood* and *Balls*. Lucy's stepfather, Walter, is a kind man who provides a comfortable life for his family but is upset when his wife involves herself in political issues and especially in the lives of the black family next door. The marriage in the house next door also puzzles Lucy, who cannot understand why Skippy's mother, Melvina, tolerates her husband's constant womanizing and drinking.

Lines between the races, between men and women, between the two families, and between the sections of town repeatedly are discussed and crossed in *Crossing Blood*. Images of glass, especially in windows, also recur. Glass windows in houses and cars allow the people inside to look out but are also fragile and susceptible to shattering. Broken or opened windows provide an invasion route into the orderly, safe world within.

In *Balls*, set in the late 1960s and early 1970s, Kincaid includes a strong subtext about attraction between men and women of different ethnicities, which reflects Southern society's ongoing adjustments to integration. Primarily, however, *Balls* explores marriage and gender roles, focusing on the wives and families of college football coaches. The Southern obsession with football, along with the hero worship of star players and successful coaches, creates a men-only environment where coaches focus exclusively on their jobs. The pretty homecoming queen, Dixie, marries her boyfriend, Mac, a former football star and now a football coach. She knows how to follow socially prescribed rules for coaches' wives: Smile, look pretty, entertain well, and do not expect too much of men. Meanwhile she attempts to decode their world, where clearly she is unwelcome. Dixie's own ideas, her natural desire for some attention from her husband, her growing need to express herself as a writer, and the needs of her children are all subordinated to football. In many ways, *Balls* is Mac's story, and Mac is almost as much a victim of his situation as Dixie is. He does not seem to realize it, but Kincaid denies him a voice.

The women dominate as Kincaid tells the story of *Balls* through multiple female narrators. Dixie's voice mingles with those of the other coaches' wives, of her mother, of their maid, and of a number of other minor female characters. This multivoiced approach functions as Southern storytelling: It takes twists and turns and involves voices from many community members, building to a story. The nonlinear narrative also reflects the circular way women often communicate and adds authenticity to the story.

Authentic-sounding women's voices reveal seven of the eight stories in *Pretending the Bed Is a Raft*, Kincaid's short story collection. The stories in *Pretending the Bed Is a Raft* are edgier and more brittle than Kincaid's novels. Unhappy women appear in the stories: women who experience unfulfilled marriages, women who have extramarital affairs, and women who leave home. Some of the women even seem to have been given permission, whether by themselves or by their author, to move beyond logic, closer and closer to the edge of hysteria.

Some of the most memorable stories contain bizarre images. "Snakes," about a family's disintegration, begins in a town known for rattlesnakes. The story includes a harrowing scene in which a snake climbs up the outside of the family's house and is trapped for days between the window screen and a roll-out window. The snake does not die. Neither do huge snakes that people try to kill by running over them with their cars. Everywhere the family moves, there are snakes, which gives the story a creepy undertone of paranoia. Nearly hysterical, the wife in the story finally leaves home with three of her five children.

The hysteria continues in the darkly comic "Just Because They've Got Papers Doesn't Mean They Aren't Still Dogs." Here, three women spend a long, strange winter day transporting the ashes of Harold, the husband of one of the women, in a cardboard box. The women begin to act as if the ashes are the live husband, taking him inside a restaurant when they stop to eat. One woman whose husband is still alive begins to wish that he were dead, that she were free, and, even, that she could have a teaspoon of Harold's ashes for herself.

The themes of death and illogical, emotional behavior are strongly evident in the collection's title story, about a young woman who is diagnosed with cancer but chooses not to have treatment. Wanting to die more fulfilled than she lived, she carefully plans what she will do before she dies. She makes a list of her desires and pursues it methodically, acquiring a body wave and a lover and tape recording future birthday messages for her children. At the end of the story, she accomplishes the final item on the list, getting baptized in the bathtub while her family (and the prospective wife she's picked out for her husband) observe. The story questions whether she selfishly wants to control her fate or lovingly provides the glue that will hold her family together after her death.

CRITICAL RECEPTION

Some reviews of *Crossing Blood* categorize it as a somewhat predictable coming-of-age novel, written for young adults. Reviewers agree that Lucy's voice is strong and believable, but some object to the parts of the story about the adults and say that the story loses ground during its violent climax. Scholarly analysis points out Kincaid's portrayal of the relationship between the races and the rich symbolism present throughout the novel.

Balls received more attention, since Kincaid was already known for *Crossing Blood*. Most reviewers note that it is perceptive, authentic, and funny, but several criticize the multiple voices as an ineffective narrative approach. Some question whose story it is: Dixie's, Mac's, or football's. The female characters draw praise for their clarity. One reviewer seems to miss the obvious when commenting that the women in the story cannot seem to win.

It can be misleading to say that Kincaid's works are funny, because focusing on the humor runs the risk of trivializing them. Most reviewers of *Pretending the Bed Is a Raft* move past focusing on the humor and look instead at the heart of most of the stories: quirky, confused women seeking self-knowledge. Some reviewers find the youthful narrators more convincing than the mature ones, but most praise the collection as strong and characterize Kincaid as a major talent.

BIBLIOGRAPHY

Works by Nanci Kincaid

"Head Walking." *Rectangle* 62 (1987): 36–38.
"Spittin Image of a Baptist Boy." *Carolina Quarterly* 41 (1989): 43–50.
"This Is Not the Picture Show." *Story* 38 (1990): 70–79.
"Above the Neck." *New Letters* 57 (1991): 45–62.
"Any Crazy Body." *Southern Exposure* 19 (1991): 23–29.
Crossing Blood. New York: Putnam, 1992.
"Past Useless." *Missouri Review* 14 (1991): 189–200.

"A Sturdy Pair of Shoes That Fit Good." *Crescent Review* 9 (1991): 105–17.

"Heaven Is No Use If You're Dead When You Get There." *Shenandoah* 42 (1992): 80–93.

"Snakes." *Southern Exposure* 20 (1992): 44–49.

"Pretending the Bed Is a Raft." *Carolina Quarterly* 45 (1993): 33–69.

"As Me and Addie Lay Dying." *Southern Review* 30 (1994): 582–95.

"The Place Poe Knows." *Carolina Quarterly* 47 (1995): 41–47.

"Won't Nobody Ever Love You Like Your Daddy Does." *Southern Humanities Review* 29
    (1995): 55–69.

"Pretty Please." *DoubleTake* 6 (1996): 84–87.

"Not a Jewish Woman." *Daughters of Kings: Growing Up as a Jewish Woman in America.*
    Ed. Leslie Brody. Boston: Faber and Faber, 1997. 62–86.

Pretending the Bed Is a Raft. Chapel Hill: Algonquin, 1997.

"Total Recoil." *Oxford American* August 1997: 29–33.

Balls. Chapel Hill: Algonquin, 1998.

"How I Found Out I Was Southern." *Oxford American* March–May 1999: 27–29.

"Trish Hannah." *No Hiding Place: Uncovering the Legacy of Charlotte-Area Writers.* Ed. Frye
    Gaillard. Asheboro, NC: Down-Home Press, 1999. 50–53.

Studies of Nanci Kincaid

Rev. of *Balls. Publishers Weekly* 3 Aug. 1998: 71.

Rev. of *Balls. Atlantic Monthly* Nov. 1998: 138.

Ciresi, Rita. Rev. of *Crossing Blood. Library Journal* 1 May 1992: 118.

Rev. of *Crossing Blood. Publishers Weekly* 24 Jan. 1994: 52.

Dodge, Dennis. Rev. of *Balls. Booklist* July 1998: 1829.

Eckard, Paula. "Decoding Black and White: Race, Gender and Language in *Crossing Blood.*"
    CLA Journal 40 (1997): 174–84.

Haworth, Karla. "To a Gridiron Wife, Life Mirrors Football." *Chronicle of Higher Education*
    25 Sept. 1998: A53.

Hayward, Lana. Rev. of *Pretending the Bed Is a Raft. Bloomsbury Review* July–Aug. 1998: 10.

Maltby, Deborah. Nanci Kincaid telephone interview. 29 August 2000.

"Nanci Kincaid." *Contemporary Authors.* Ed. Scot Peacock. Vol. 174. Boston: Gale, 1999.
    256–57.

Rev. of *Pretending the Bed Is a Raft. Kirkus Reviews* 15 Sept. 1997: 1407.

Rev. of *Pretending the Bed Is a Raft. Missouri Review* 21 (1998): 213–14.

Quinn, Mary Ellen. Rev. of *Pretending the Bed Is a Raft. Booklist* 1 Oct. 1997: 308.

Sanders, Erica. "Pigskin Widow." *New York Times Book Review* 13 Dec. 1998: 35.

Stark, Stephen. Rev. of *Crossing Blood. New York Times Book Review* 31 Jan. 1993: 21.

Williams, Wilda. Rev. of *Balls. Library Journal* 1 Sept. 1998: 214.

BARBARA KINGSOLVER (1955–)

Lisa Abney

BIOGRAPHY

Barbara Kingsolver grew up in rural Kentucky. Born April 8, 1955, she lived in this rural setting until she embarked upon her college career at De Pauw University in Indiana. She spent many hours listening to the stories of those in her community and often begged her mother to tell her stories; by the time she was eight years of age, she reversed the role of listener to storyteller and began writing private journals (Fleischner 1). Though she had a great interest in writing, she never entertained the notion of writing professionally. Additionally, she had little access to the works of women writers and maintained the assumption that she could never succeed at writing because the writers she had read were "mostly old, dead men" (Fleischner 1). Further, the community in which Kingsolver was reared viewed literature as frivolous and was more committed to the daily work of survival than to the loftier activity of reading.

At De Pauw, Kingsolver enrolled in a creative writing course, though she was a biology major. She became active in a variety of social causes, particularly in the Vietnam War protest movement. Kingsolver earned her degree in 1977 and began to support herself by holding a variety of occupations: "archaeologist, copy editor, X-ray technician, housecleaner, biological researcher, and translator of medical documents" (Fleischner 2). Later, she enrolled at the University of Arizona to pursue a master of science degree in biology. Upon completion of this degree, she became a science writer for the University of Arizona and soon began to write freelance features for newspapers and periodicals. She worked as a freelance writer from 1985 to 1987 and wrote fictional pieces at night. She married a chemist in 1985, and while pregnant with her first child in 1986, she wrote *The Bean Trees*, which was published in 1988.

Following the success of *The Bean Trees,* Kingsolver continued to write both fiction and nonfiction. Her next popular work was *Homeland and Other Stories*, which was published in 1989, followed by the novels *Animal Dreams* in 1990, *Pigs in Heaven* in 1993, *High Tide in Tucson: Essays from Now and Never* in 1995, *The Poisonwood*

Bible in 1998, and *Prodigal Summer* in 2000. Along with her fiction and essays, she has also written a collection of poetry, *Another America/Otra America* (1992), and a nonfiction work called *Holding the Line: Women in the Great Arizona Mine Strike of 1983* (1989). The twelve years following the initial publication of *The Bean Trees* have heralded a great deal of success for Kingsolver. Her works have consistently been well received by critics. However, while Kingsolver's professional life prospered, her personal life experienced some turbulence during this time. By 1996 Kingsolver's first marriage had ended, and a few years later, she met and married Stephen Hopp, with whom she had her second child, Lily. She prefers spending time with her family and working for environmental and human rights causes to promoting her works and participating in press events. Kingsolver today lives primarily in Tucson, yet she spends time in both Arizona and Kentucky.

MAJOR WORKS AND THEMES

Kingsolver is a fervent believer in the adage that all writing is political, and in her works, she frequently deals with issues to which she maintains a commitment. Her novels generally include depictions of Latin Americans and Native Americans. Through the development of characters such as Mattie, Estevan, and Esperanza in *The Bean Trees* and Hallie in *Animal Dreams*, she frequently focuses upon the plight of the illegal refugee and the underground network of people who assist these refugees once they enter the United States. The depiction of the Cherokee community in *Pigs in Heaven* shows the plight of Native Americans to maintain and pass on their culture. Kingsolver's work repeatedly displays themes that focus on the importance of community, the quest for finding one's place in the world, and the preservation of traditional cultures. Clearly, Kingsolver's main point throughout her novels is that a person cannot survive without the help and support of other people.

In her first novel, *The Bean Trees*, the principal character, Taylor Greer, feeling that she has no future in the small Kentucky town in which she was reared, leaves for the west to find a new, exciting world and her place within that world. Taylor leaves behind a closely knit community that has all the problems of many small communities—an overdeveloped need to define people by their social class, a lack of economic productivity, hypocrisy, and a high level of conformity. She strikes out by herself in her old Volkswagen, and as she travels west, she has many adventures. In Oklahoma, a Native American woman shoves a baby into Taylor's car, thus giving Taylor a new responsibility. Taylor names her child Turtle because of the strength of the grip the child uses to cling to her. Turtle and Taylor grow closer as the novel progresses, and Taylor becomes a loving and caring mother. However, all is not rosy in their world; the big city of Tucson is laden with dangers for Taylor. Her car breaks down just as she rolls into Tucson—she has little money and is forced to feed Turtle vending machine food. She eludes some unsavory male characters whose motives do not seem entirely honest. Luckily, Taylor and Turtle stumble into Jesus is Lord Tires, and Mattie, the owner of the shop, seeing the pair's frightful condition, offers Taylor a job and an opportunity to find her place in the world. Taylor's discovery of Mattie and the tire shop provides her with a community in which she can find support and strength. Upon finding her job at Jesus is Lord Tires, Taylor looks for a place to live and finds a roommate, fellow Kentuckian Lou Ann Ruiz. Lou Ann, too, is misplaced. Having married a Hispanic rodeo cowboy who loses his leg in an accident and leaves her while she is pregnant with her son, Dwayne Ray, Lou Ann has suffered alone in the big city. She has no job, no friends, and nowhere to turn. Sporadically supported by Angel (her recently departed husband), she finds that she must advertise for a roommate in order to afford to keep her small, ramshackle house. Lou Ann and Taylor work together to provide for their children. Lou Ann watches the children while Taylor works. They share food, bills, and their lives. They form a micro-community.

Within this text, Kingsolver depicts the traditional ways of a variety of cultures. Lou Ann's grandmother and mother come to Tucson when Dwayne Ray is born, and the women share parenting advice with the ever-patient Lou Ann. Their folk traditions and ways become articulated within the text, as do many of Taylor's family's beliefs. Additionally, Kingsolver includes the traditions of the Guatemalans Estevan and Esperanza. Kingsolver's primary theme in this novel is that people need one another to survive and that without community, people drift with no sense of purpose or ability to survive. In doing so, she illustrates the importance of the preservation of traditional cultures.

Diverging from her first novel in terms of setting and characters, Kingsolver peoples her second novel, *Animal Dreams*, with characters who represent the Native American, Central American, and Hispanic communities found in New Mexico and Arizona. In *The Bean Trees*, Kingsolver depicts characters isolated from their communities who do not attain wholeness until they reunite with their communities. While *The Bean Trees* treats serious subjects like the sexual abuse of children, isolation from culture, class structure issues, and loss of identity with a positive and light tone, *Animal Dreams* provides a deeper and, at times, more somber depiction of the problems that occur when the quest for identity leads to a fragmented self, as shown through the character, Codi, who encounters a series of bad relationships with men and with her father while trying to find her identity. To the outside world, Codi is the daughter of the small-town doctor; she is educated, beautiful, and confident. In reality, she maintains the emotions of a young child; she feels rejected owing to the early death of her mother and her father's clinical treatment of her sister and her. When the novel begins, the reader sees that Codi has based her identity on the life of Hallie, her sister, with whom she has lived for many years. When Hallie leaves to go to Nicaragua as an agricultural advisor, Codi is left ungrounded and returns to the small town of Grace, Arizona, where she grew up. This trip home becomes a painful experience, as the town serves as a mirror to her past—much of which she has subconsciously blocked. While in Grace, she accepts the fact that her father suffers from Alzheimer's disease and is dying. She begins to learn bits and pieces of her heritage, which confuse her since her father has essentially re-created himself as an Illinois transplant to the region when, in fact, his family members are looked down upon as renegades. He married his second cousin, one of the town's highly esteemed Graciela sisters. The fictional story that he created to cover the truth about his marriage involved changing his wife's name to Alice from Althea (a family name of the Gracielas) and changing his last name from Nolina to Noline. He raised his daughters in a formal and isolated manner in the small town, and few town members went against his wishes to keep the secret from his daughters because he was the town's only physician. The novel becomes further complicated when a copper mine pollutes the local river and a plan is hatched by the mining company to dam the town's only water source. Codi becomes significant in the town's environmental movement because the high school students she teaches discover the lack of microscopic organisms that exist in healthy bodies of water. Along with environmental issues, Kingsolver addresses the cultural issues of the individuals inhabiting the region such as the Native Americans and the Hispanics who live in the village. The long-standing Hispanic Catholic tradition of the celebration of the Day of the Dead plays a significant role in the work, for it is through the practice of this tradition with her friend, Emelina, and her family that Codi finds the dead Nolinas who have no one to decorate their graves. Their tombs lay in a disarrayed and unattended state. The lack of attention to these graves indicates the family's status within this closely knit community. As Codi begins to discover her ancestors and the role that they played in the community, she begins to find her place within this town. Aiding her on this quest for self is her past lover, Loyd Peregrina, to whom she looks for comfort and protection. He helps her to realize that comfort, protection, and stability come from within, not from an association with someone else. *Animal Dreams* provides a realistic entrée into Codi's world of dispossession and pain, healing, and peace. Within this novel, like her previous work, the themes of community, quest for self, and the importance of traditional culture appear repeatedly.

Kingsolver's third novel, *Pigs in Heaven*, focuses upon the question of custody and who should be the parents of Turtle Greer, the abandoned Native American child of *The Bean Trees*. In this novel, as in her other work, the themes of community, quest for self, and the importance of traditional culture appear repeatedly. This novel opens with Turtle and Taylor at the Hoover Dam. Of all the visitors to the site that day, Turtle is the only one who sees a mentally challenged young man fall down a hole on the dam. Driving back to Tucson, Turtle mentions to Taylor what she has seen. Taylor, community-minded, as are most of Kingsolver's characters, turns the car around and the mother-daughter effort to cajole the dam personnel into looking for the lost person succeeds. The young man is rescued, and Turtle instantly becomes a hero. She appears on numerous television shows and comes to the attention of Annawake Fourkiller, a Cherokee lawyer, who has a personal reason for wanting to recover lost tribal children. The novel becomes the saga of a custody battle with some odd turns that make the ending a positive and happy resolution to this difficult issue. In fighting for custody, Taylor is forced to go into hiding and to lose the support system that she has developed in Tucson. Taylor unsuccessfully tries to live alone with Turtle, and the pair eventually returns to Oklahoma to face the custody battle. Taylor's mother becomes involved in the custody struggle, and through her involvement, the tribal customs and traditions are conveyed to the reader. Kingsolver deftly reflects the Cherokee community and the importance of maintaining tribal culture. Further, the importance of this culture to Turtle becomes clear as she reunites with her home community. In this work, Kingsolver again focuses upon the importance of a shared community and the individual's place within that community. These issues, coupled with her vivid depictions of tribal practices, indicate the significance of these traditions.

While Kingsolver's first three books depict Southwestern settings, her 1998 novel, *The Poisonwood Bible*, portrays missionary life in Africa. *The Poisonwood Bible* stands as Kingsolver's longest work. Numbering 546 pages in the hardback edition, it focuses upon the lives of the Price family—Americans who go to Africa as missionaries. The text provides a complex intertwining of narratives as the life stories of the family from the perspective of the mother, Orleanna, and her four daughters, Leah, Rachel, Adah, and Ruth May, are revealed. While the Price patriarch, Nathan, possesses no voice of his own in the text, his words and attitudes are expressed in the texts of the women who surround him. The themes of this work, like those of other Kingsolver texts, illustrate the unwanted encroachment of Anglo, Protestant ways upon cultures such as the Native American and African. Within the novel, Kingsolver includes critiques of Western economic systems such as capitalism and political systems that America and European countries hold dear, such as anonymous voting and free speech. The Price family arrives in Africa completely unprepared for the life they will experience. They lack the skills necessary to survive in Africa, and without the clandestine assistance of the villagers, the family might have perished. Again, in this novel as her others, Kingsolver brings to light the importance of the community. Throughout *The Poisonwood Bible*, the African community maintains solidarity and works collectively to avoid the onslaught of missionary religion that the Prices embrace and advocate to all around them.

Unlike their African counterparts who hold distinct places in the community, the Price family members' quests for their place in the world exact a high price from the Americans. Leah finds her place with Anatole, an African she later marries and lives with in Angola. The couple and their children work to improve the lives of those around them. Ruth May's place becomes evident when she dies and is buried in Africa—she literally becomes the continent through her death. After Nathan's family leaves him, he retreats deeper and deeper in the jungle, where he moves from one village to another and becomes disillusioned by his empty dream. Ultimately, the weight of his mistaken beliefs leads him to insanity. Like her father, who wanders, Rachel roams from man to man until she finally becomes "lucky in love" and inherits a hotel from one of her many lovers. She settles down to manage the hotel and ultimately finds her role as an American expatriate. Although she is unable to return to America, she never embraces African society. Living in an expatriate no-man's land is the best situation that she can find for herself. Adah, possessing the high moral sensitivity of Leah, wants to help others and flees Africa to return to America, where she becomes a doctor who specializes in tropical medicine. Orleanna, throughout the tale, knows that her role is the mother and wife—her identity is tied to her children's lives; when Ruth May meets her untimely death, Orleanna leaves Kilanga with Adah and returns to Georgia, where her life begins anew. As in many of Kingsolver's works, the importance of community and quest for one's place become pivotal themes.

As the characters in *The Poisonwood Bible* illustrate community and quest for self, so, too, do the characters of her most recent work, *Prodigal Summer*. This novel portrays the often parallel yet disparate lives of park ranger and zoologist Deanna Wolfe and Lusa Malof Landowski Widener, an entomologist, who forfeits her career to help her husband, Cole, tend his family farm. As in other Kingsolver novels, these characters seek a place in which they feel accepted. Deanna lives alone in the Zebulon National Forest, where she tracks animals and observes the area's vast wildlife. She views her life as thoroughly complete. She treasures her solitude and has no qualms about living in a small cabin in the middle of the forest with no electricity or indoor plumbing. When Eddie Bondo, a rakish young man, appears one day in the forest, he surprises the dowdy Deanna. Ironically, they both seek to find coyotes in the forest— he to kill them, she to preserve them. Their paths cross numerous times in the text, and ultimately they become lovers—a situation with which Deanna never feels truly at ease. While Deanna's life makes this odd turn, Lusa's life changes also. Her husband is killed in a trucking accident, and she is left to manage his family's farm. The space that she inhabits as his widow comes with a host of busybody sisters who refuse to accept her or her citified ways. Her life becomes a cycle of staving off relatives and finding a way to make the farm run without the relatives' intervention. Neither of these two intelligent and strong women feels comfortable with her identity, and this theme remains central throughout the text.

While this theme becomes central to the novel, the importance of community and the preservation of traditional ways serve as secondary themes. The community in this novel differs from that in Kingsolver's other works in that there are no Native Americans or other indigenous groups in the work. The society of the little town is formed largely by individuals of Anglo-Scot-Irish stock who have come and have settled in the small mountain town. The majority of the townspeople rely upon one another and help with crop harvesting and ranching, and, of course, they attend important community events such as Cole Widener's funeral. Even Cole's provincial sisters help Lusa when she needs assistance with canning or tending her farm. The community is composed of individuals who are independent yet who need one another to survive.

While community is an important element of the text, so, too, is the preservation of traditional ways. In this novel, the traditional ways are not just cultural ways but become ecological issues as well. Deanna Wolfe's goal is to preserve the nature that teems on Zebulon Mountain and to assist with the preservation of the habitat of nonnative coyotes who have migrated to the mountain. Her stepmother, Nannie Rawley, holds this same view. She is an organic gardener and is often at odds with her neighbor Garland Walker, who relies heavily on pesticides and herbicides to farm his land. This novel, like Kingsolver's other texts, emphasizes community, traditional culture, and ecology as primary themes.

Kingsolver's politically charged statements appear throughout her novels, yet while fervently expressing her beliefs, she manages to create characters who do not merely function as mouthpieces for Kingsolver's causes. The characters have depth and illustrate conflicts and passions common to all humans.

CRITICAL RECEPTION

Oddly, as prolific and interesting an author as Kingsolver is, few articles or book-length studies exist regarding her work. Only one book-length study exists, *Barbara Kingsolver: A Critical Companion*, issued in 1999 by Greenwood Press. Only some twenty articles critique Kingsolver's characters or themes.

Mary Jean DeMarr's book-length study of Kingsolver focuses on her works up to *The Poisonwood Bible*. DeMarr's work provides summaries of the novels and critiques many aspects of Kingsolver's work such as character development and theme. This critical piece does not include information relating to Kingsolver's short stories or to her essays. The primary focus centers on Kingsolver's novels.

Along with DeMarr's book-length study, articles concerning Kingsolver's work focus upon a variety of issues. Loretta Martin Murrey's "Loner and the Matriarchal Community in Barbara Kingsolver's *The Bean Trees* and *Pigs in Haven* [sic]" addresses the role of the loner in literature, starting with Huck Finn as the most well-known loner in literature and moving to Kingsolver's character, Taylor Greer. Murrey examines the development of matriarchal communities within *The Bean Trees* and *Pigs in Heaven* and the way in which Taylor finds her place within these communities.

In addition to the volume regarding Kingsolver's work, there have been several articles that examine in her novels issues from morality to the environment. Ruth Smith's "Negotiating Homes: Morality as a Scarce Good" examines Kingsolver's development of morality in *The Bean Trees* and *Pigs in Heaven*. Patti Capel Swartz examines the environmental and political issues that Kingsolver addresses in *Animal Dreams*. Krista Comer's essay also addresses landscape and the environment as it forms in Kingsolver's work.

Charlotte M. Wright's and Maureen Ryan's essays provide complete assessments of Kingsolver's work up to *The Poisonwood Bible*. Wright's review evaluates her writing in terms of community in the novels and provides summaries of reviews of the novels, while Ryan's work attends to the issues of political correctness that appear in the works. These essays provide general overviews and do not examine one specific work in an exhaustive manner.

Janet Bowdan's article is the single piece of critical work that dedicates itself to an analysis of Kingsolver's poetry. Her essay, "Re-Placing Ceremony: The Poetics of Barbara Kingsolver," discusses Kingsolver's poetic piece, *Another America*. Bowdan discusses the need for connections between humans displayed in Kingsolver's poetry. She additionally addresses the violence that this volume of poetry depicts.

While Kingsolver's work has not been extensively analyzed, it certainly is rife for such activity. This prolific writer's works illustrate not only her political ideas, but the novels also depict communities and individuals in a realistic and interesting manner. Kingsolver, while perhaps not as well attended to by critics as other writers, has subtly and quietly made her mark upon contemporary American literature.

BIBLIOGRAPHY

Works by Barbara Kingsolver

"Rose-Johnny: A Story." *Virginia Quarterly Review* 63 (1987): 88–109.
The Bean Trees. New York: Harper, 1988.
Holding the Line: Women in the Great Arizona Mine Strike of 1983. New York: ILR Press, 1989.
Homeland and Other Stories. New York: Harper, 1989.
Animal Dreams. New York: Harper Perennial, 1990.
Another America/Otra America. With Spanish translations by Rebecca Cartes. Seattle: Seal Press, 1992.
"The Prince Thing." *Woman's Day* 18 Feb. 1992: 26, 28, 110.
Pigs in Heaven. New York: Harper Perennial, 1993.
High Tide in Tucson: Essays from Now or Never. New York: Harper, 1995.
"Untitled." *Letters to Our Mothers: I've Always Meant to Tell You: An Anthology of Contemporary Women Writers*. Ed. Constance Warloe. New York: Pocket Books, 1997. 55–59.
The Poisonwood Bible. New York: Harper, 1998.
Prodigal Summer. New York: Harper, 2000.

Studies of Barbara Kingsolver

Aay, Henry. "Environmental Themes in Ecofiction: *In the Center of the Nation* and *Animal Dreams*." *Journal of Cultural Geography* 14 (1994): 65–85.
Bowdan, Janet. "Re-Placing Ceremony: The Poetics of Barbara Kingsolver." *Southwestern American Literature* 20 (1995): 13–19.

Comer, Krista. "Sidestepping Environmental Justice: 'Natural' Landscapes and the Wilderness Plot." *Breaking Boundaries: New Perspectives on Women's Regional Writing*. Ed. Sherrie Inness and Diana Royer. Iowa City: University of Iowa Press, 1997. 216–36.

DeMarr, Mary Jean. *Barbara Kingsolver: A Critical Companion*. Westport, CT: Greenwood Press, 1999.

Fleischner, Jennifer. "An Introduction to Barbara Kingsolver: A Brief Biography." *A Reader's Guide to the Works of Barbara Kingsolver*. New York: Harper, 1998. 1–3.

Murrey, Loretta Martin. "The Loner and the Matriarchal Community in Barbara Kingsolver's *The Bean Trees* and *Pigs in Haven* [sic]." *Southern Studies* 5 (1994): 155–64.

Newman, Vicky. "Compelling Ties: Landscape, Community, and Sense of Place." *Peabody Journal of Education* 70 (1995): 105–18.

Perry, Donna. "Barbara Kingsolver." *Backtalk: Women Writers Speak Out: Interviews*. New Brunswick, NJ: Rutgers University Press, 1993. 143–69.

Quick, Susan Chamberlain. "Barbara Kingsolver: A Voice of the Southwest: An Annotated Bibliography." *Bulletin of Bibliography* 54 (1997): 283–302.

Ross, Jean W. "Kingsolver, Barbara." *Contemporary Authors*. Vol. 134. Detroit: Gale. 284–90.

Ryan, Maureen. "Barbara Kingsolver's Lowfat Fiction." *Journal of American Culture* 18 (1995): 77–82.

Smith, Ruth. "Negotiating Homes: Morality as a Scarce Good." *Cultural-Critique* 38 (1997/98): 177–95.

Swartz, Patti Capel. " 'Saving Grace': Political and Environmental Issues and the Role of Connections in Barbara Kingsolver's Animal Dreams." *Isle: Interdisciplinary Studies in Literature and Environment* 1 (1993): 65–79.

Wright, Charlotte M. "Barbara Kingsolver." *Updating the Literary West*. Fort Worth: Texas Christian University Press, 1997. 504–11.

MAXINE (TING TING) HONG KINGSTON (1940–)

Sharon Hileman

BIOGRAPHY

Maxine Hong, whose Chinese name is Ting Ting, was born October 27, 1940, a Year of the Dragon, in Stockton, California, to Chinese immigrant parents. Her father, Tom Hong, had been educated as a scholar in China but was forced into menial positions in the United States, working as a manager of a gambling house and then as a proprietor of New Port Laundry. Her mother, Ying Lan Chew, who had been trained as a practitioner of Western medicine and midwifery in China, experienced a similar decline in professional status and was employed in the family laundry and as a fieldworker. Maxine, named after a successful blond gambler, was the first of the six Hong children born in the land of the Gold Mountain; two earlier children, born in China, did not survive.

Maxine Hong's first language was Say Yup, a Cantonese dialect spoken in Guangdong Province, the place in China from which her parents had emigrated. Other villagers from the same province had also settled in Stockton and used the laundry as a community gathering center, so Maxine had many opportunities to absorb the oral tradition and "talk story" that would eventually inform her own writing. She did not learn English until she began school but claims that the English language and written stories came to her simultaneously at about the age of eight. So steeped was she in the oral narrative of her mother and Chinese community members that she could not understand the expository essay as a form until she became a university student.

Maxine Hong received eleven scholarships to attend the University of California at Berkeley, where she began her studies as an engineering major. Eventually, she became an English major, received her BA in 1962, and then returned to obtain a teaching certificate in 1965. She married Earll Kingston, a fellow student and actor, the year she received her degree and one year later gave birth to their only child, Joseph Lawrence Chung Mei. The family traveled to Hawaii where they remained for seventeen years. At first, Kingston taught high school and business college courses.

However, with the publication of *The Woman Warrior: Memoir of a Girlhood among Ghosts* in 1976, followed by *China Men* in 1980, Kingston's fame as a writer brought her professional appointments at the University of Hawaii, Eastern Michigan University, and her alma mater, the University of California. *The Woman Warrior* received the National Book Critics Circle Award the year it was published and was named one of the top ten nonfiction works of the decade. The Modern Language Association has identified *The Woman Warrior* as "the most frequently assigned twentieth-century literary text by a living author on American high school, college, and university campuses" (Huntley 75). *China Men* received the American Book Award for nonfiction, and in the year of its publication, 1980, Kingston was proclaimed a "Living Treasure of Hawaii." This honorary Buddhist designation originated in China and is usually reserved for people whose achievements are acknowledged when they have become octogenarians.

In 1984 Kingston visited China for the first time. She had been afraid to make such a trip, worried that the China of her imagination would not correspond with the actual country. Her fears, however, were unfounded, and the Chinese Writers' Association, which had sponsored the trip, praised her for maintaining literary traditions that they had been forced to abandon during the Chinese Cultural Revolution.

In 1987 Kingston published two works in limited editions. *Hawai'i: One Summer, 1978* was a combination of essays—most of which had been published in the *New York Times*—and woodblock prints made by the son of Jade Snow Wong. *Through the Black Curtain* (1987), alluding to the stage curtain in Chinese theater, consisted of excerpts from her first two books, material from the then-unpublished *Tripmaster Monkey*, and essays on Chinese theater.

Tripmaster Monkey: His Fake Book, published in 1989, was Kingston's first novel. In it, she conflated her protagonist with the Monkey King, a Chinese trickster figure. The "fake book" of the title refers to a jazz musician's book of melodies from which new songs can be improvised. Like jazz musicians, Kingston and her protagonist play upon language and literature, both American and Chinese, to improvise puns, allusions, stories, and the epic drama that concludes the work. *Tripmaster Monkey* received the PEN West Award in fiction in 1989 and the John Dos Passos Prize for literature in 1998.

Following this exuberant, Joycean extravaganza of a novel, Kingston began work upon a totally different project, researching the three legendary Chinese books of peace in order to construct her own pacifist work, tentatively titled *The Fourth Book of Peace*. However, in 1991, an Oakland wildfire destroyed her home, her manuscript, her computer, and all her notes and research for the book. Through the help of a hypnotist and her readers, who supplied their own notes, tapes from readings she had given from the manuscript-in-progress, and even a new computer, Kingston was able to reconstruct much of the missing book. By 2001 she had written almost 2,000 pages and was in the process of editing *The Fifth Book of Peace* for publication.

A practicing Buddhist, Kingston not only writes about peace but also conducts workshops for Vietnam War veterans, enabling them to write about their experiences and work with her to create a "language of peace" (Huntley 23).

MAJOR WORKS AND THEMES

Kingston's themes emanate from her dual cultural heritage—being both Chinese and American—and the resulting issues of identity formation, discrimination, generational conflict, and coming to voice that characterize the immigrant experience. Kingston's characters must also acculturate in order to proceed beyond being hyphenated Chinese-Americans and emerge as full Americans, who are modified by their Chinese heritage but revel in their contributions to US history, culture, and language. One of her chapter titles in *China Men* alludes to Gertrude Stein's work and insists upon "The Making of More Americans." In fact, Kingston envisions her writing as the continuation of William Carlos Williams's *In the American Grain*, a literary and mythical account of American history. Her narrative begins where his ended—at the Civil War—and she goes on to recount the building of the American railroads by Chinese laborers. Believing that Walt Whitman expressed the true spirit of an all-inclusive America, Kingston incorporates lines and images from *Leaves of Grass* into *Tripmaster Monkey* and tellingly names her protagonist Wittman Ah Sing.

The problems of establishing one's identity as a Chinese American (unhyphenated) are central in all of Kingston's works. *The Woman Warrior*, a coming-of-age story, focuses on many of the conflicts a bilingual, bicultural child experiences both within the family and within the social institutions of school and community groups. The female narrator must also contend with being devalued because she is a girl in a patriarchal culture, a "maggot in the rice," according to one Chinese proverb. The narrator's conflicting images of women range from her victimized and passive Chinese aunts, who either commit suicide or have to be institutionalized, to her strong and powerful mother and the legendary woman warrior, Fa Mu Lan. In addition, she must confront the "American feminine" and determine its role in her own identity formation.

After rejecting the negative gender stereotypes from traditional China and contemporary America, the narrator learns how to integrate the positive elements of Chinese culture, such as talk story, with the powerful tools she is acquiring in the West, specifically the written English language. In so doing, she becomes a word warrior, whose writing will effect the same revenge and change as did Fa Mu Lan's weapons.

Kingston believes that the way to change people's stereotypical thinking and to change the world is one word at a time. She deliberately titled her second book *China Men* in order to reclaim and redefine her ancestors' identity, disarming the pejorative and racist slur of "Chinaman." This book, which provides the stories and myths of the men in her family, is the other half of *The Woman Warrior*. Kingston had intended to write one book but discovered that the men's stories "seemed to interfere" with the coherence and integration of myth and memory in the women's stories, so she took them out (Rabinowitz 179). *China Men*, in depicting the lives of the grandfathers, great-grandfathers, and sojourners who went to the Gold Mountain, provides an account of the racism and exploitation the Chinese experienced in America, from the sugar cane fields of Hawaii to the gold fields in Alaska. Kingston even includes eight pages of the exclusionary laws that were implemented from 1868 to 1978 to limit or prohibit the emigration of Asians, especially women, in order to prevent reproduction.

In addition to an account of how several generations of Chinese men fared historically in the United States, *China Men* is also Kingston's personal search for her own father and her attempt to give him voice. Unlike the vociferous Brave Orchid, the mother whose voice and stories filled *The Woman Warrior*, Tom Hong maintained silence and would not or could not tell his own story. Kingston attempted to construct that story in *China Men*, creating a character called "the father" and providing five different accounts of his entry into the United States. When the book was translated into Chinese, Tom Hong read it and wrote marginal comments in Chinese calligraphy, finally participating in a dialogue with his daughter.

Still confronting issues of identity and voice in her novel *Tripmaster Monkey*, Kingston creates a male protagonist significantly different from the China men. Wittman Ah Sing is the new Chinese American man of the 1960s, one who views life as performance and claims that his ancestors came to the Gold Mountain to play (in theater companies) rather than work. As a young, newly graduated English major, Wittman spends the entire novel undertaking a quest to construct his identity. His picaresque, episodic story is a reenactment of a classic Chinese narrative: *Journey to the West*. In that work, the monk Tripitaka travels to India with his companions, including Monkey, the trickster, experiencing eighty-one adventures along the way. Kuan Yin, the Chinese Goddess of Mercy, oversees the trip, and in Kingston's novel, she becomes the omniscient narrator. Wittman, like Monkey, believes he is capable of seventy-two transformations and proceeds to make changes in his clothing, appearance, and language throughout the novel. He speaks the American idiom fluently, bursting into "linguistic pyrotechnics" (Huntley 169) that include allusions, wordplay, and quotations that reflect both his Chinese and American heritage. Furthermore, by claiming that his task is "to spook out prejudice" (*Tripmaster Monkey* 332), Wittman attacks racism and its stereotypes of Chinese Americans. Kingston incorporates Wittman's lengthy monologue against racism into the novel's last chapter, where it also becomes the final performance in an epic play he has written and staged. Through this play, which includes parts for everyone he knows, Wittman's anger is transformed into community-building art.

CRITICAL RECEPTION

While lauded for its poetic descriptions and style, *The Woman Warrior: Memoir of a Girlhood among Ghosts* immediately received negative critical attention concerning its generic status. Because the work clearly mixed fiction and nonfiction, truth and fantasy, critics felt the term "memoir" in its title was misleading. Furthermore, Frank Chin, Kingston's most vehement critic, claimed that autobiography was a Western, Christian genre and any Chinese attempting to write one was "selling out" ("This Is Not" 122). He went on to attack Kingston's work as "simply a device for destroying history and literature" ("Come All Ye" 3). One form of this "destruction," according to other critics, was Kingston's revising of classical Chinese myth in her version of Fa Mu Lan, the woman warrior. Critics were also concerned because the work did not meet their expectations for ethnic autobiography, which would ordinarily present the author as a spokesperson for a positively portrayed ethnic community. Kingston, however, did not claim to speak for Chinese Americans and did not attempt to deconstruct white readers' concepts of Asians. Thus, Chin accused her of perpetuating stereotypes, and Katheryn M. Fong claimed she was misleading non-Chinese readers (67). Chin and Fong also critiqued Kingston's portrayal of patriarchal Chinese culture, Chin believing she vilified Chinese manhood and Fong thinking she overexaggerated Chinese American male chauvinism.

Shocked at the many ways *The Woman Warrior* had been misinterpreted, Kingston responded to many of her critics in "Cultural Mis-Readings by American Reviewers." In this article, she argued that *The Woman Warrior* is a book about America, portraying Chinese Americans (unhyphenated) who speak American slang and experience an American "transmutation" of Chinese myths (Skandera-Trombley 97). She believes critics are asking the wrong question when they wonder if her work is "typical" of Chinese Americans; instead, they should ask, "Is this work typical of human beings?" (Skandera-Trombley 101).

The reviews of *China Men*, Kingston's second book, often mentioned the similarities between it and *The Woman Warrior*. Linda Kauffman thought the same characters, motifs, and images appeared, and other reviewers observed that *China Men* blended myth, legend, history, and memory as had its predecessor. Critics commented on the anger and fierceness expressed in the work but felt those qualities worked positively to create narrative tension. John Leonard, writing in the *New York Times*, described *China Men* as "sheer magic," a work in which "history meets sensuality" ("Books of the Times" C9). The major criticism came from Frederick Wakeman, Jr., a sinologist, who objected to Kingston's revisions of traditional Chinese myth. He labeled this aspect of her work "jejeune" and "inauthentic" (43) and considered it a form of "self-indulgent fantasy" (42). Most critics, however, praised Kingston's fusion of imagination and history, and Mary Gordon thought all women writers would envy Kingston's "success at depicting the world of men without women" (24–25).

Perhaps because Kingston's third major work, *Tripmaster Monkey: His Fake Book*, was labeled a novel, most critics no longer raised questions about the authenticity of its Chinese myths or the representative qualities of its protagonist, Wittman Ah Sing, a fifth-generation Californian and a Berkeley graduate. Bharati Mukherjee said this was "no conventional rendering of the artist as a young man" (X1) but also considered the novel "bloated" with the jokes, talk stories, myth, history, puns, and trivia that constituted it. In more positive phraseology, Anne Tyler called it "a novel of excesses" (44), which she attributed to both the protagonist and the author. Several critics noted similarities in the linguistic inventiveness and language play in Joyce's *Ulysses*, Kingston's *Tripmaster*, and the works of Salman Rushdie. In fact, Jeanne R. Smith claimed that the "dizzying inventiveness" (337) of language overshadowed both plot and characters. Most critics, however, have been struck by Wittman Ah Sing's extraordinary character. As a poet-playwright of the 1960s, who is bright, witty, idealistic, alienated, paranoid, angry, and insecure, Wittman, in his alter ego as the Chinese Monkey King, brings energy, chaos, and transformation into the world of the novel. Anne Tyler says he is characterized by "manic energy," which makes the work "exhausting" (46) to read. John Leonard thinks Kingston has created the quintessential novel of the 1960s, expressing the social and political concerns of the decade in Wittman's lengthy and explosive monologues ("Of Thee Ah Sing" 772). Kingston acknowledges that her aggressively masculine protagonist is modeled on Frank Chin, her most hostile critic. In creating this character and giving him voice, Kingston believes she has achieved two important goals: to write a new American language and to "write the Other" (M. Chin 59). She also believes that the laughter generated by the Monkey spirit will help solve the world's problems (M. Chin 61).

BIBLIOGRAPHY

Works by Maxine Hong Kingston

The Woman Warrior: Memoirs of a Girlhood among Ghosts. New York: Knopf, 1976.
China Men. New York: Knopf, 1980.

"Cultural Mis-Readings by American Reviewers." *Asian and Western Writers in Dialogue: New Cultural Identities*. Ed. Guy Amirthanayagam. London: Macmillan, 1982. 55–65.

Hawai'i One Summer, 1978. San Francisco: Meadow Press, 1987.

Through the Black Curtain. Berkeley, CA: Friends of the Bancroft Library, 1987.

Tripmaster Monkey: His Fake Book. New York: Knopf, 1989.

Studies of Maxine Hong Kingston

Carabi, Angeles. "Special Eyes: The Chinese-American World of Maxine Hong Kingston." *Belles Lettres* 4 (1989): 10–11.

Chang, Hsiao-hung. "Gender Crossing in Maxine Hong Kingston's *Tripmaster Monkey*." *MELUS* 22 (1997): 15–34.

Cheung, King-Kok. " 'Don't Tell': Imposed Silences in *The Color Purple* and *The Woman Warrior*." *PMLA* 103 (1988): 162–74.

———. "The Woman Warrior versus the Chinaman Pacific: Must a Chinese American Critic Choose between Feminism and Heroism?" *Conflicts in Feminism*. Ed. Marianne Hirsch and Evelyn Fox Keller. New York: Routledge, 1990. 234–51.

———. "Provocative Silence: *The Woman Warrior* and *China Men*." *Articulate Silences: Hisaye Yamamoto, Maxine Hong Kingston, Joy Kogawa*. Ithaca, NY: Cornell University Press, 1993. 74–125.

———. "Talk Story: Counter Memory in Maxine Hong Kingston's *China Men*." *Tamkang Review* 24 (1993): 21–37.

Chin, Frank. "This Is Not an Autobiography." *Genre* 18 (1985): 109–30.

———. "Come All Ye Asian Writers of the Real and the Fake." *The Big Aiiieeeee!: An Anthology of Chinese American and Japanese American Literature*. Ed. Jeffery Paul Chan, Frank Chin, Lawson Fusao Inada, and Shawn Wong. New York: Meridian, 1991. 1–92.

Chin, Marilyn. "A *MELUS* Interview: Maxine Hong Kingston." *MELUS* 16 (1989/90): 57–74.

Chu, Patricia P. "*Tripmaster Monkey*, Frank Chin, and the Chinese Heroic Tradition." *Arizona Quarterly* 53 (1997): 117–39.

Chun, Gloria. "The High Note of the Barbarian Reed Pipe: Maxine Hong Kingston." *Journal of Ethnic Studies* 19 (1991): 85–94.

Cook, Rufus. "Cross-Cultural Wordplay in Maxine Hong Kingston's *China Men* and *The Woman Warrior*." *MELUS* 22 (1997): 133–46.

Feng, Pin-Chia. *The Female Bildungsroman by Toni Morrison and Maxine Hong Kingston: A Postmodern Reading*. New York: Peter Lang, 1998.

Fishkin, Shelley Fisher. "Interview with Maxine Hong Kingston." *American Literary History* 3 (1991): 782–91.

Fong, Katheryn M. "To Maxine Hong Kingston: A Letter." *Bulletin for Concerned Asian Scholars* 9 (1977): 67–69.

Furth, Isabella. "Beee-e-een! Nation and Transformation and the Hyphen of Ethnicity in Kingston's *Tripmaster Monkey*." *Modern Fiction Studies* 40 (1994): 33–49.

Gao, Yan. *The Art of Parody: Maxine Hong Kingston's Use of Chinese Sources*. New York: Peter Lang, 1996.

Garner, Shirley Nelson. "Breaking Silence: *The Woman Warrior*." *The Intimate Critique: Autobiographical Literary Criticism*. Ed. Diane P. Freedman, Olivia Frey, and Frances Murphy Zauhar. Durham: Duke University Press, 1993. 117–25.

Goellnicht, Donald C. "Tang Ao in America: Male Subject Positions in *China Men*." *Reading the Literatures of Asian America*. Ed. Shirley Geok-lin Lim and Amy Ling. Philadelphia: Temple University Press, 1992. 191–212.

Gordon, Mary. "Mythic History." Rev. of *China Men*. *New York Times Book Review* 15 June 1980: 24–25.

Hunt, Linda. " 'I Could Not Figure Out What Was My Village': Gender vs. Ethnicity in Maxine
    Hong Kingston's *The Woman Warrior*." *MELUS* 12 (1985): 5–12.

Huntley, E. D. *Maxine Hong Kingston: A Critical Companion*. Westport, CT: Greenwood Press,
    2001.

Juhasz, Suzanne. "Maxine Hong Kingston: Narrative Technique and Female Identity." *Contem-
    porary American Women Writers: Narrative Strategies*. Ed. Catherine Rainwater and
    William Scheick. Lexington: University Press of Kentucky, 1985. 173–90.

Kauffman, Linda. "*China Men*." Rev. of *China Men*. *Georgia Review* 35 (1981): 205.

Koss, Nicholas. " 'Will the Real Wittman Ah Sing Please Stand Up': Cultural Identity in
    Tripmaster Monkey: His Fake Book." *Fu Jen Studies: Literature and Linguistics* 26
    (1993): 24–50.

Lappas, Catherine. " 'The Way I Heard It Was . . . ': Myth, Memory, and Autobiography in
    Storyteller and *The Woman Warrior*." *CEA Critic* 57 (1994): 57–67.

Leonard, John. " 'Books of the Times': *China Men*." Rev. of *China Men*. *New York Times* 3
    June 1980: C9.

———. "Of Thee Ah Sing." Rev. of *Tripmaster Monkey: His Fake Book*. *Nation* 5 June 1989:
    768–72.

Li, David Leiwei. "The Naming of a Chinese American 'I': Cross-Cultural Sign/ifications in
    The Woman Warrior. *Criticism* 30 (1988): 497–515.

———. "*China Men*: Maxine Hong Kingston and the American Canon." *American Literary
    History* 2 (1990): 482–502.

Lim, Shirley Geok-Lin, ed. *Approaches to Teaching Kingston's The Woman Warrior*. New
    York: MLA, 1991.

———. "The Tradition of Chinese American Women's Life Stories: Thematics of Race and
    Gender in Jade Snow Wong's *Fifth Chinese Daughter* and Maxine Hong Kingston's
    The Woman Warrior." *American Women's Autobiography: Fea(s)ts of Memory*. Ed.
    Margo Culley. Madison: University Press of Wisconsin, 1992. 252–67.

———. " 'Growing with Stories': Chinese American Identities, Textual Identities (Maxine
    Hong Kingston)." *Teaching American Ethnic Literature*. Ed. John Maitinot and David
    Peck. Albuquerque: University of New Mexico Press, 1996. 273–91.

Lin, Patricia. "Clashing Constructs of Reality: Reading Maxine Hong Kingston's *Tripmaster
    Monkey: His Fake Book* as Indigenous Ethnography." *Reading the Literatures of Asian
    America*. Ed. Shirley Geok-Lin Lim and Amy Ling. Philadelphia: Temple University
    Press, 1992. 333–47.

Ling, Amy. *Between Worlds: Women Writers of Chinese Ancestry*. New York: Pergamon, 1990.

———. "Chinese American Women Writers: The Tradition behind Maxine Hong Kingston."
    Redefining American Literary History. Ed. A. LaVonne Brown Ruoff and Jerry W.
    Ward. New York: MLA, 1990. 219–36.

———. "Maxine Hong Kingston and the Dialogic Dilemma of Asian American Writers." *Buck-
    nell Review* 39 (1995): 151–66.

Linton, Patricia. " 'What Stories the Wind Would Tell': Representation and Appropriation in
    Maxine Hong Kingston's *China Men*." *MELUS* 19 (1994): 37–48.

Maini, Irma. "Writing the Asian American Artist: Maxine Hong Kingston's *Tripmaster Monkey*:
    His Fake Book." *MELUS* 25 (2000): 243–64.

Mukherjee, Bharati. "Wittman at the Golden Gate." Rev. of *Tripmaster Monkey: His Fake
    Book*. *Washington Post* 16 April 1989: X1.

Nishime, LeiLani. "Engendering Genre: Gender and Nationalism in *China Men* and *The Woman
    Warrior*." *MELUS* 20 (1995): 67–82.

Quinby, Lee. "The Subject of Memoirs: *The Woman Warrior's* Technology of Ideographic
    Selfhood." *De/Colonizing the Subject: The Politics of Gender in Women's Autobiog-
    raphy*. Ed. Sidonie Smith and Julia Watson. Minneapolis: University Press of Minnesota,
    1992. 297–320.

Rabine, Leslie. "No Lost Paradise: Social Gender and Symbolic Gender in the Writings of Maxine Hong Kingston." *Signs: Journal of Women in Culture and Society* 12 (1987): 471–82.

Rabinowitz, Paula. "Eccentric Memories: A Conversation with Maxine Hong Kingston." *Michigan Quarterly Review* 26 (1987): 177–87.

Shostak, Debra. "Maxine Hong Kingston's Fake Books." *Memory, Narrative, and Identity: New Essays in Ethnic American Literature.* Ed. Amritjit Singh, Joseph T. Skerrett, Jr., and Robert E. Hogan. Boston: Northeastern University Press, 1994. 233–60.

Simmons, Diane. *Maxine Hong Kingston.* New York: Twayne, 1999.

Skandera-Trombley, Laura, ed. *Critical Essays on Maxine Hong Kingston.* New York: G. K. Hall, 1998.

Sledge, Linda Ching. "Maxine Hong Kingston's *China Men*: The Family Historian as Epic Poet." *MELUS* 7 (1980): 3–22.

———. "Oral Tradition in Kingston's *China Men*." *Redefining American Literary History.* Ed. A. LaVonne Brown Ruoff and Jerry W. Ward. New York: MLA, 1990. 142–54.

Slowik, Mary. "When the Ghosts Speak: Oral and Written Narrative Forms in Maxine Hong Kingston's *China Men*." *MELUS* 19 (1994): 73–89.

Smith, Jeanne R. "Cross-Cultural Play: Maxine Hong Kingston's *Tripmaster Monkey*." *Critical Essays on Maxine Hong Kingston.* Ed. Laura E. Skandera-Trombley. New York: G. K. Hall, 1998. 334–48.

Smith, Sidonie. Maxine Hong Kingston's *Woman Warrior*: Filiality and Woman's Autobiographical Storytelling." *A Poetics of Women's Autobiography: Marginality and the Fictions of Self-Representation.* Bloomington: Indiana University Press, 1987. 150–73.

Tanner, James. "Walt Whitman's Presence in Maxine Hong Kingston's *Tripmaster Monkey: His Fake Book*." *MELUS* 20 (1995): 61–74.

Tyler, Anne. "Manic Monologue." Rev. of *Tripmaster Monkey: His Fake Book. New Republic* 17 April 1989: 44–46.

Wakeman, Frederic, Jr. "Chinese Ghost Story." Rev. of *China Men. New York Review of Books* 14 Aug. 1980: 42–44.

Wang, Alfred S. "Maxine Hong Kingston's Reclaiming of America: The Birthright of the Chinese-American Male." *South Dakota Review* 26 (1988): 18–29.

Wang, Jennie. "*Tripmaster Monkey*: Kingston's Postmodern Representation of a New 'China Man.' " *MELUS* 20 (1995): 101–14.

Williams, A. Noelle. "Parody and Pacifist: Transformations in Maxine Hong Kingston's *Tripmaster Monkey: His Fake Book.*" *MELUS* 20 (1995): 83–100.

Wong, Sau-Ling Cynthia. "Autobiography as Guided Chinatown Tour? Maxine Hong Kingston's *The Woman Warrior* and the Chinese-American Autobiographical Controversy." *Multicultural Autobiography: American Lives.* Ed. James Robert Payne. Knoxville: University Press of Tennessee, 1992. 248–79.

———. *Maxine Hong Kingston's The Woman Warrior: A Casebook.* New York: Oxford University Press, 1999.

HARPER LEE (1926–)

Catherine Cucinella

BIOGRAPHY

Nelle Harper Lee, born April 28, 1926, to Amasa Coleman Lee (A. C.) and Frances Finch Lee, grew up in Monroeville, Alabama. Harper shared her childhood with Truman Capote (often identified as the inspiration for Dill in *To Kill a Mockingbird*). Lee's fame rests on her first, and only, novel, *To Kill a Mockingbird*, published in 1960.

Lee attended Monroeville public schools, spent 1944–1945 at Huntington College in Montgomery, lived in England as an exchange student at Oxford University, entered the University of Alabama in 1945 to study law, and left in 1950 before completing the law degree. Lee's choice of law reflects familial influences (she dedicates her novel to Mr. Lee and her sister, Alice), and Atticus Finch in *Mockingbird* certainly shares many similarities with A. C. Lee. Lee's father, Amasa, descendant of Robert E. Lee, practiced law as the senior partner of Barnett, Bugg, and Lee. Alice took a law degree, practicing law throughout her life.

Besides studying law at the University of Alabama, Lee wrote satires, editorial columns, and reviews, all of which appeared in several campus publications. In early interviews, Lee herself acknowledges that law studies provided the logical thinking that she considered necessary for a good writer. Lee's familiarity with the courts and legal language underwrites the poignancy and power of the courtroom scenes in *Mockingbird*.

In 1950 Lee moved to New York to pursue a writing career. Supporting herself by working as an airline reservation clerk with Eastern Airlines and BOAC, Lee began to solicit literary agents. Following the advice of an agent, she expanded one short story into *To Kill a Mockingbird*. As Lee narrates in her essay "Christmas to Me," published in *McCall's* in December 1961, she received financial support from her closest friends in Manhattan in order to write. The handwritten Christmas card directed, "You have one year off from your job to write whatever you please. Merry

Christmas" (63). Indeed, Lee took that year and in 1957 submitted her completed manuscript to J. B. Lippincott.

Initially viewing Lee's novel as a series of short stories, the editors at Lippincott criticized the manuscript but encouraged Lee to rewrite it. Under the editorial direction of Tay Hohoff, Lee wrote a "compassionate, deeply moving novel, and a most persuasive plea for racial justice" (*Library Journal* 7). *To Kill a Mockingbird* became an immediate success, receiving the Pulitzer Prize for fiction in 1961, the Alabama Library Association Award in 1961, the Brotherhood Award Conference of Christians and Jews in 1961, and in 1962 *Bestsellers* magazine's Paperback of the Year Award. Also in 1962, Robert Mulligan directed a film version of the novel, for which Gregory Peck won the Academy Award for best actor for his portrayal of Atticus. Lee's novel has sold over 20 million copies in the United States and remains on high school reading lists throughout the country.

Lee never published a second novel, and although she has received a number of honorary doctorates, including one from the University of Alabama in 1990 and one from Spring Hill College in Mobile in 1997, the novelist does not speak publicly and grants no interviews. In the introduction to the 1995 thirty-fifth-anniversary edition of *To Kill a Mockingbird*, Lee writes, "I am still alive, although very quiet." Lee lives in New York.

MAJOR WORKS AND THEMES

Although *Mockingbird* seems to deal with two predominate issues, racial intolerance and childhood memories, the novel interweaves multiple and interconnected themes. Edgar Schuster identifies five "thematic motifs" in the novel: first, the growth motif ("Jem's physiological and psychological growth"); second, "the caste system in Maycomb"; third, the mythology of the mockingbird; fourth, education; and fifth, superstition (507). However, Lee's novel extends beyond these five thematic motifs as the first-person narrative of Scout Finch reveals a candid look at, and pointed critique of, many of America's social institutions. Education, the law, religion, the family, and patriarchal expectations all come under scrutiny in this novel through Jem's and Scout's fascination.

However, the trial of the black man Tom Robinson for the rape of a white woman provides the most disturbing and intense drama in the novel. Although, as numerous critics point out, the trial comprises "roughly fifteen percent of the total length of the novel" (Schuster 507), Tom's arrest, trial, conviction, and death bring together the multiple themes of the narrative. This coming-of-age novel confronts the myth of childhood innocence, acknowledges marginalizing class systems, examines social stagnation, and celebrates individual heroism while perilously negotiating between challenging and reinscribing sexist, racist, or classist paradigms.

Lee's thematic concerns play out within and against such paradigms as *Mockingbird* investigates the maturation of both Jem and Jean Louise (Scout) Finch. The novel questions the meaning of womanhood in a world dominated by rigid standards—standards that define both maleness and femaleness. The narrative begins and ends with Jem and elaborates his awakening to the social injustices that constrain Maycomb. Yet through Scout, the female narrator, Lee presents a careful study of how femaleness emerges in relation to patriarchy and how femaleness manifests in relation to individual males within that system. However, both of Atticus's children must come to terms with the expectations and conditions of a male-dominated world.

Lee astutely presents a range of both masculinities and femininities in *Mockingbird*, making clear that Jem and Scout must choose the man/woman he/she will become. Just as Jem must evaluate and judge the various males who populate his world, Scout must assess the females and various femininities that they represent. Calpurnia, Miss Maudie, Aunt Agatha, and the ladies of the Missionary Society present Scout with a picture of Southern womanhood—a womanhood for the most part restricted and restrained by the conventions of a small Southern town.

Despite the various depictions of women, Lee offers no representation of motherhood. Instead, Scout encounters mothering from all segments of Maycomb. Although the novel does not directly reject motherhood, it contains no biologically linked white mothers and children, thus conspicuously absenting mothers from the dominant structure of Maycomb (ironically, black mothers and children do appear—Tom Robinson's wife and children and Calpurnia and her son). Rather than mothers, the novel depicts mothering exemplified by Atticus's relationship with his children. Thus, the novel confronts the patriarchal mandate that women must mother in order to socialize children. The communal mothering that both the children receive and, more significantly, the lessons that Scout receives about femininity combine to loosen the restrictions normally associated with women.

In Scout, however, Lee constructs an active, able, and articulate girl as she interweaves the gender and education themes through Scout's experiences in school. Scout has difficulty reconciling her intellectual abilities—the ability to read and write cursive—within a system that demanded "fresh minds"—minds pliable to fitting the rigid paradigms of the prevailing educational model (*Mockingbird* 21). Lee pointedly indicts an educational program more intent on system rather than on the learning process and the place of the individual student in that process. In addition, Scout's struggles within the school system reveal the patriarchal bias of education. While Jem successfully negotiates the educational system, Scout senses that she is "being cheated out of something" (*Mockingbird* 37). Scout suffers under this system; Jem does not. While pointing to the gender equality within education, Lee simultaneously acknowledges the importance of education for girls and suggests that this education must take place outside of the formal structures of education. Both Jem and Scout learn from their father, from conversations with other adults, and from their own experiences and observations.

For the most part, the two children observe the townspeople's reaction to Atticus's defense of Tom Robinson as they experience first-hand racist behavior. Lee's major concern with racism leads to her concern with defining heroism. As the children's awareness of the prevailing racist attitudes of their neighbors emerges, they also begin to see their father from a new, and startling, perspective. Before Atticus's culminating courtroom speech and before the tribute paid to him by the black community, Atticus shoots a rabid dog, in a scene that evokes the quintessential Western hero. Jem and Scout confront their father's personal history, as Miss Maudie tells them, "Forgot to tell you the other day that besides playing the Jew's harp, Atticus Finch was the deadest shot in Maycomb County in his time" (*Mockingbird* 102). Thus, the children's perspective of their father as a man who "didn't do anything . . . that could possibly arouse the admiration of anyone" shifted to an understanding of their father's heroism (*Mockingbird* 93–94).

This episode delineates several of the major themes in *Mockingbird*: Heroism depends on individual action and character; one does not understand another until he or she walks in that individual's shoes; surface appearance often belies personal histories. Atticus and the mad dog foreshadow Atticus's role as the public defender of Tom Robinson, but they also foreshadow Boo Radley's killing of Bob Ewell.

While many critics of *Mockingbird* identify a disjunction between the Robinson narrative and the story of Boo Radley, Lee does, in fact—stylistically and thematically—connect the two stories. The trope of the mockingbird refers both to Tom Robinson and to Boo Radley: "but remember it's a sin to kill a mockingbird" (*Mockingbird* 94). This lesson—the sin of killing the innocent—propels all the lessons that Jem and Scout learn. Although Atticus proves Tom Robinson's innocence, the black man does, in fact, die—killed by the racist and classist ideology of a small Southern town. Boo Radley, although marginalized, does not die. Ironically, Boo does commit a punishable crime; however, Boo is in and of the town, and, as such, the law of Maycomb County decides to "hush it up" (279). Sheriff Tate's explanation for his decision resonates with Atticus's earlier admonition to his children about the sin of killing mockingbirds: "To my way of thinkin', Mr. Finch, taking the one man who's done you and this town a great service an' draggin' him with his shy ways into the limelight—to me, that's a sin. It's a sin and I'm not about to have it on my hands" (279). Whether this passage points to Tate's culpability in the murder of Tom Robinson or whether Tate expresses remorse over Tom's death, this passage provides the final lesson for Scout. She tells Atticus, "Mr. Tate was right. . . . Well, it'd be sort of like shootin' a mockingbird, wouldn't it?" (279). The narrative ends with some mockingbirds dead and some left to sing protected by the community.

CRITICAL RECEPTION

Upon its publication, *To Kill a Mockingbird* received generally favorable reviews. All reviews, including the mixed or unfavorable ones, tended to applaud Lee's storytelling ability and the "sweetness, humor, and compassion" of the novel (Jackson 101). *Times* reviewer Herbert Mitgang identifies Lee as "a storyteller justifying the novel as a form that transcends time and place." He continues, "The author eases the reader into the life of the town with warmth and good humor" (33). Small-town life and childhood emerge as the focus of most reviews of the novel.

All reviewers, however, did not find the novel engaging as they point to the problem with telling the story through a child's perspective and effectively conveying "the story that [Lee] wants to tell" (Hicks 15). Frank Lyell qualifies his praise for Lee and her novel, finding fault with "Scout's expository style" (18). Several reviewers find some of the scenes in *Mockingbird* too melodramatic, the narration too simple, or the characters too typical. For example, Elizabeth Lee Haselden takes Lee to task for her preoccupation with "delineating 'character types,' " for her failure to present "*people*" with whom the reader can identify, and for her inadequacy to depict an "inner struggle for an ethical answer to injustice," and Haselden notes that the book lacks "real compassion for people" (655).

The critical scholarship on *Mockingbird*, however, does identify a struggle regarding ethics, and ironically, as Claudia Durst Johnson notes, legal rather than literary scholars have produced "some of the more interesting criticism of the novel" ("Without Tradition" 485). The legal commentary tends to fall under two large rubrics: unequal judicial treatment of people of color (particularly males) and Atticus's iconic status as a lawyer. Both legal and literary scholars point to the Scottsboro case (Alabama 1931) as a model for the trial in *Mockingbird*. The Scottsboro case, however, is just one of many incidents of racial prosecution throughout the South, according to Bryan K. Fair in his introduction to the *Alabama Law Review*'s symposium on *To Kill a Mockingbird*. Fair asserts that *Mockingbird* illustrates "the injustice of White racism and how it corrupts access to criminal justice for Blacks" (406). Calvin Woodard extends this focus to argue that the novel "is . . . an attempt by a critic of the Southern legal system to deal with a serious legal problem through nonlegal means" (566). Taught in law classes, *Mockingbird* often focuses on Atticus as a model of an ethical and worthy lawyer. Indeed, much scholarship, legal and literary, investigates the novel's depiction of morality, ethics, and definitions of right and wrong as embodied in Atticus as well as in the social structure of Maycomb County.

Carolyn Jones argues that Atticus exemplifies the "moral life" (53). Many critics echo Jones's placement of Atticus as the moral center of the novel; however, Jill P. May points out that Atticus "is the typical paternalistic white man who will help blacks as well as he can but who believes that in the end little can be done to change southerners" (93). Thus, scholarship regarding heroism and ethical behavior makes clear that Lee's novel complicates these issues and presents a complex examination of right and wrong.

This examination unfolds through the voice of Scout, and as Dean Shackelford argues, a "number of significant questions about gender are raised in the novel": Scout's perception of herself as an outsider, her identification with her father, and Atticus's "androgynous nature" (108). While Shackelford raises important questions regarding Scout's socialization into womanhood, important questions remain regarding how *Mockingbird* constructs female subjectivity. Lee seems to walk a fine line between constructing a femininity challenging patriarchal expectations and one seeking to embrace patriarchal values.

Just as feminist scholarship should reexamine gender issues in *Mockingbird*, critics concerned with the racial aspects call for a rethinking of the novel. Diann L. Baecker begins this process in her work on the novel, arguing that the "Africanist presence in this novel is simultaneously illuminated and repressed by Lee" (128). Baecker, like many of the critics of *Mockingbird*, argues for Boo Radley's outsider status; she suggests that Boo aligns very closely with the Africanist presence in the novel, stressing, however, that "Boo is not like the black people" (129). This critic's work on *To Kill a Mockingbird* recenters the importance of a black presence in the novel, a presence that she sees crucial to Lee's ability "to talk about issues of gender, particularly sexuality" (131). Baecker's work moves beyond existing *Mockingbird* scholarship concerned with racial injustice and theorizes the place of blackness in the novel. This move makes clear that Lee's novel, significant in 1960, remains a valuable site of critical inquiry.

BIBLIOGRAPHY

Works by Harper Lee

To Kill a Mockingbird. New York: J. B. Lippincott, 1960.
"Love—In Other Words." *Vogue* 15 April 1961: 64–65.
"Christmas to Me." *McCall's* Dec. 1961: 63.

Studies of Harper Lee

Baecker, Diann L. "Telling It in Black and White: The Importance of the Africanist Presence in *To Kill a Mockingbird*. *Southern Quarterly* 36 (1998): 124–32.

Bloom, Harold, ed. *Modern Critical Interpretations: To Kill a Mockingbird*. Philadelphia: Chelsea House, 1999.

Bruell, Edwin. "Keen Scalpel on Racial Ills." *English Journal* 53 (1964): 658–61.

Champion, Laurie. " 'When You Finally See Them': The Unconquered Eye in *To Kill a Mockingbird*." *Southern Quarterly* 37 (1999): 127–36.

———. "Harper Lee." *American Writers: A Collection of Literary Biographies*. Ed. Jay Parini. Suppl. 8. New York: Scribner's, 2001. 113–31.

Dave, R. A. "*To Kill a Mockingbird*: Harper Lee's Tragic Vision." *Studies in American Fiction. Indian Studies in American Fiction*. Ed. M. K. Naik. Dharwar, India: Karnatak University, 1974. 311–23.

Erisman, Fred. "The Romantic Regionalism of Harper Lee." *Alabama Review* 26 (1973): 122–36.

———. "Literature and Place: Varieties of Regional Experience." *Journal of Regional Cultures* 1 (1981): 144–53.

Fair, Bryan K. "Using Parrots to Kill Mockingbirds: Yet Another Racial Prosecution and Wrongful Conviction in Maycomb." *Alabama Law Review* 45 (1994): 403–72.

Fine, Laura. "Gender Conflicts and Their 'Dark' Projection in Coming of Age White Female Southern Novels." *Southern Quarterly* 36 (1998): 121–29.

Ford, Nick Aaron. "Battle of the Books: A Critical Survey of Significant Books by and about Negroes Published in 1960." *Phylon* 22 (1961): 119–34.

Freedman, Monroe H. "Atticus Finch—Right and Wrong." *Alabama Law Review* 45 (1994): 473–82.

Going, William T. "*Store* and *Mockingbird*: Two Pulitzer Novels about Alabama." *Essays on Alabama Literature*. Tuscalusa: University of Alabama Press, 1975. 9–31.

Hall, Timothy L. "Moral Character, the Practice of Law, and Legal Education." *Mississippi Law Journal* 60 (1990): 511–54.

Haselden, Elizabeth Lee. "We Aren't in It." Rev. of *To Kill a Mockingbird*. *Christian Century* 24 May 1961: 655.

Henderson, Robert W. Rev. of *To Kill a Mockingbird*. *Library Journal* 85 (1960): 1937.

Hess, Natalie. "Code Switching and Style Shifting as Marked Liminality in Literature." *Language and Literature* 5 (1996): 5–18.

Hicks, Granville. "Three at the Outset." Rev. of *To Kill a Mockingbird*. *Saturday Review* 23 July 1969: 15–16.

Hoff, Timothy. "Influences on Harper Lee: An Introduction to the Symposium." *Alabama Law Review* 45 (1994): 389–402.

Jackson, Katherine Gauss. Rev. of *To Kill a Mockingbird*. *Harper's* Aug. 1960: 101.

Johnson, Claudia Durst. "The Secret Courts of Men's Hearts: Code and Law in Harper Lee's *To Kill a Mockingbird*. *Studies in American Fiction* 19 (1991): 129–39.

———. *To Kill a Mockingbird: Threatening Boundaries*. New York: Twayne, 1994.

———. *Understanding To Kill a Mockingbird: A Student Casebook to Issues, Sources, and Historic Documents*. Westport, CT: Greenwood Press, 1994.

———. "Without Tradition and within Reason: Judge Horton and Atticus Finch in Court." *Alabama Law Review* 45 (1994): 483–510.

Jones, Carolyn. "Atticus Finch and the Mad Dog: Harper Lee's *To Kill a Mockingbird*." *Southern Quarterly* 34 (1996): 53–63.

Lyell, Frank H. "One-Taxi Town." Rev. of *to Kill a Mockingbird*. *New York Times Book Review* 10 July 1961: 5ff.

May, Jill P. "Censors as Critics: *To Kill a Mockingbird* as a Case Study." *Cross-Culturalism*

    *in Children's Literature: Selected Papers from the 1987 International Conference of the
    Children's Literature Association.* Ed. Susan R. Gannon and Ruth Anne Thompson.
    New York: Pace University, 1988. 91–95.

Mitgang, Herbert. "Books of the Times." Rev. of T*o Kill a Mockingbird. New York Times* 13
    July 1960: 33.

Phelps, Teresa Godwin. "The Margins of Maycomb: A Rereading of *To Kill a Mockingbird.*"
    Alabama Law Review 45 (1994): 511–30.

Schuster, Edgar. "Discovering Theme and Structure in the Novel." *English Journal* 52 (1963):
    506–11.

Shackelford, Dean. "The Female Voice in *To Kill a Mockingbird*: Narrative Strategies in Film
    and Novel." *Mississippi Quarterly* 50 (1996/97): 101–13.

Shaffer, Thomas L. "The Moral Theology of Atticus Finch." *University of Pittsburgh Law
    Review* 42 (1981): 181–224.

———. "Growing Up Good in Maybomb." *Alabama Law Review* 45 (1994): 531–62.

Woodard, Calvin. "Listening to the Mockingbird." *Alabama Law Review* 45 (1994): 563–84.

URSULA K. LE GUIN (1929–)

Kate K. Davis

BIOGRAPHY

Ursula K. Le Guin's influence on science fiction writing is akin to the effect Jane Austen had on the British novel: revolutionary. Both authors feminized and, more importantly, humanized their respective genres and profoundly affected storytelling. Austen produced novels that defied convention, proving that male-oriented action plots were not essential to good novels. Le Guin's use of sociological and cultural approaches to conflict, rather than "shoot-'em-up" technological solutions, increased the literary appeal of this marginalized genre, which traditionally was anti-feminist and conservative.

Ursula Kroeber was born the youngest child of Alfred Louis Kroeber and Theodora Kracaw Brown Kroeber in Berkeley, California, on St. Ursula's Day, October 21, 1929. Young Ursula grew up in an intellectually stimulating environment surrounded by scientists, writers, students, and the subjects of her father's anthropological work— members of California's vanishing Native American tribes. The family spent summers in the forests of Napa Valley, where she says she "was not a tomboy in the sense of being brave and courageous, but my parents made no great distinctions between boys and girls, so I had the freedom of the woods" ("Dialogue" 152). Nature, interpersonal and cultural relationships, and the balance between humans and environment would become significant themes in Le Guin's short stories and novels.

Despite her love of trees and the West, Ursula Kroeber went East to study, receiving a BA from Radcliffe College in 1951 and an MA in romance languages from Columbia University in 1952, Phi Beta Kappa from both. She went in 1953 on a Fulbright Scholarship to France, where she met fellow Fulbright scholar Charles A. Le Guin, a history professor. They were married on December 22, 1953. Le Guin discontinued her doctoral studies to raise three children—Elizabeth, Caroline, and Theodore—and to pursue the creative writing she had begun in college. While Charles finished his doctorate at Emory University in Atlanta, Ursula taught French, worked as a secretary, and wrote. They have lived in Oregon since 1959.

Le Guin began writing poetry and stories at age nine and had a science fiction story rejected by the editor of *Astounding Science-Fiction* in 1942, when she was twelve. Twenty years later, her next attempt, "April in Paris" (*The Wind's Twelve Quarters,* 1975), was accepted by *Fantastic.* After several unsuccessful attempts, Le Guin reevaluated her stories and submitted them to science fiction magazines, where she found initial success as a writer; hence, she has been categorized as a science fiction writer despite publication of many realistic works. Although traditionally science fiction is not a well-respected "literary" genre, even detractors of fantasy admire Le Guin's works. For Le Guin, science fiction fulfilled her creative urges to explore other cultures: "In most fiction the author tries to get into the skin of another person; in science fiction you are often expected to get into the skin of another person from another culture" ("An Interview" 65).

Le Guin's fantastic stories resulted from many influences. Her mother was an avid mythologist, psychologist, and writer known for *Ishi in Two Worlds* (1961), the biography of the supposedly "last wild Indian" in California. Her father, Alfred Kroeber, a professor of cultural anthropology at Berkeley, was a cultural relativist. Dr. Kroeber shared stories and legends from his Native American informants with his children. Le Guin incorporates storytelling and naming as literary devices to convey cultural information about her characters. She says, "The house was always full of people with funny accents. I'm comfortable with foreign languages, and I enjoy them, so it's a lot of fun making them up. Word-making is one of the roots of fantasy" ("Dialogue" 158). In her essay "Why Are Americans Afraid of Dragons?" (*The Language of the Night: Essays on Fantasy and Science Fiction,* 1979), Le Guin observes a fear of the nonliteral and unexplained that invites the reader to share and learn the genre's language. She believes science fiction and realism both depend on observation and science to determine what is real. In 1973 Le Guin challenged the science fiction community when she criticized the genre's depiction of women, the poor, and average citizens as complying with the status quo and failing to be speculative: "All those Galactic Empires, taken straight from the British Empire of 1880 . . . the White Man's Burden all over again" ("American SF and the Other" 239). Additionally, in 1976 Le Guin withdrew a short story from the Nebula Award competition as protest for the expulsion of Stanislaw Lem from the Science Fiction Writers of America. It is difficult to single out specific works by Le Guin as "best" or "most notable." However, there is no doubt her books continue to challenge readers to question previously held notions of identity and self in this increasingly multicultural, globally oriented world.

MAJOR WORKS AND THEMES

In the mid-1960s, Le Guin published her most famous novels: *Rocannon's World* (1966), *Planet of Exile* (1966), *City of Illusions* (1967), and the critically acclaimed *Left Hand of Darkness* (1969). Later important works include *The Dispossessed* (1974), *The Word for World Is Forest* (1976), "Vaster Than Empires and More Slow" (1971), and "The Day before the Revolution" (1974). These works are referred to as the "Hainish" cycle, a group of novels and stories that chronicle the reestablishment of contact with widely varying human (Hain) colonies separated by galactic war. The protagonists often encounter humanoid colonists who have evolved biologically and culturally away from "normal." The plots explore peaceful resolutions of diplomatic and social concerns.

In 1968, while in England on a sabbatical trip with her husband, Parnassus Press asked Le Guin to write a book for young readers. This invitation eventually led to the publications of *A Wizard of Earthsea*, (1968), *The Tombs of Atuan* (1971), and *The Farthest Shore* (1972), all of which address subjects such as coming of age, sexual awareness, death, and the soul. Other popular Le Guin titles include the short story collection *Compass Rose* (1982), the essay collection *Dancing at the Edge of the World: Thoughts on Words, Women, Places* (1989), and *Steering the Craft: Exercises and Discussions on Story Writing for the Lone Navigator or the Mutinous Crew* (1998). *The Lathe of Heaven* (1971), *Very Far Away from Anywhere Else* (1976), *Orsinian Tales* (1976), and *Malafrena* (1979) are fanciful but set on Earth. Le Guin expresses her interest in Taoism, feminism, morality, and pacifism in *Always Coming Home* (with Todd Barton, 1987), *Searoad: Chronicles of Klatsand* (1991), and *Four Ways to Forgiveness* (1995).

MAJOR WORKS AND THEMES

Many of Le Guin's plots and themes explore the political and social concerns of their time. She warns, though, "If you're preaching, you're a second-class artist. But do you have to dump the morality to be a first-class artist?" ("*Progressive* Interview" 36). Nevertheless, her works reflect her Taoism, feminism, environmentalism, and liberalism. For instance, Le Guin's first novel, *Rocannon's World*, blends elements of science fiction and fantasy in a mythic quest for identity. Gaverel Rocannon, an ethnologist studying alien cultures, sets out to warn his home world about an enemy military base on the planet Formalhaut II. Rocannon learns to use mental telepathy to conquer his enemies but suffers being privy to the anguish of their deaths. The balance of opposites is central to Le Guin's Taoist concept of interrelatedness. The major themes in *Rocannon's World*—individual versus community, irrational versus rational, technology and its responsibilities, and the overcoming of cultural prejudices—are important throughout Le Guin's work.

In *Planet of Exile*, telepathic skills become a discipline taught throughout the League of All Worlds. A colony of humans from Earth, isolated for over sixty years, strives to remain culturally pure despite the natives, who are less technologically advanced and illiterate. In a reverse of the classic novel of imperialism, the native Tevarians are white and the colonists are black. Both groups are culturally stagnant: The Earthmen are losing their skills and knowledge and cannot adequately digest the planet's foods; the Tevarians have not advanced for generations. A Romeo-and-Juliet-like plot between Jakob and Rolery initiates contact between the groups. The colony's eventual success depends upon the peoples' acceptance of each other.

The next novel, *City of Illusions*, explains why that colony was isolated. The Shing had taken over the League of All Worlds, making Earth their capital. They keep humans isolated and incapable of consolidating knowledge. The amnesiac Falk journeys to the Shing's glass city through a landscape that reflects his own growth. The Shing are a confusing combination of reality and falsehood, reflection and substance, morality and immorality. Only the Shing can lie telepathically, but they are incapable of knowing truth. By meditating on a Taoist passage, Falk regains his memory, outwits the Shing, and returns home to pave the way for reestablishment of the league.

According to Le Guin, the inspiration for her best-known novel, *The Left Hand of Darkness*, came "as a vision, a scene of these two people pulling something in a great snowy wilderness" ("Dialogue" 150). The planet Gethen, known as Winter, is covered by huge, permanent ice fields. Genli Ai, an envoy from the Ekumen, formed after the league, tries to establish economic and political ties with the Gethenians, who believe they are the only sentient beings in the universe. The humanoid Gethenians are androgynous, except during "kemmer," when they assume specific male or female roles. This poses a problem for Genly Ai, who remains male and who assumes the powerful officials he encounters are also male. However, Le Guin's challenge of sexual stereotypes and gender relations is not the novel's central theme.

On Gethen, there is no war, though the two competing political states—the monarchy Karhide and the communist Orgoreyn, modeled after Cold War United States and Stalinist Russia—are on the brink of wide-scale violence. Genly Ai flees to Orgoreyn to escape persecution in Karhide. Imprisoned as a spy, Ai is rescued by Estraven, an exiled Karhidish official previously assumed an enemy. Estraven, a member of the Handdarata, is capable of brief superhuman strength and endurance, powers essential for survival as they cross the polar ice. During the flight, Ai comes to terms with Estraven's androgyny, and they learn to communicate through "mind-speech." Ultimately, the people of Gethen welcome outside contact, though Le Guin leaves the outcome of such influences ambiguous. In *The Left Hand of Darkness*, Le Guin begins her exploration of the nature of government and the role of individual freedom, choice, and responsibility that continues in *The Dispossessed*.

The Dispossessed is set in a time before mind-speech and instant, long-distance communication. The protagonist is not an alien visitor but rather a citizen of twin planets, Anarres and Urras, that share the same orbit. On desert Anarres, survival depends on cooperation between citizens. This egalitarian anarchist society is based entirely on personal responsibility and community awareness instead of law. Urras, in contrast, is a lush planet where the main society has distinct sexual and social divisions and everything or person is treated as a commodity.

The plot of *The Dispossessed* concerns Shevek's travels back and forth from Anarres to Urras. He realizes there is intellectual freedom on Urras but not on his home planet. When he discovers a theory of simultaneity, he produces the "ansible" device for instantaneous communication between worlds. The two planets compete to purchase or suppress this discovery, so Shevek gives both equal access to the information, thereby laying the groundwork for future interplanetary cooperation. *The Dispossessed*'s subtitle, "An Ambiguous Utopia," stresses binaries and balance: Both worlds are ideal yet flawed. Together they create a whole.

A Wizard of Earthsea is the story of Ged, a young wizard, who comes of age and into his powers. The second novel, *The Tombs of Atuan*, concerns the next life stage, adulthood and sexual awareness, but the protagonist is Tenar, a young woman. In *The Farthest Shore*, Ged becomes Archmage and forges a peaceful society. That society's balance and world peace is maintainable only through later surrender of male power to women in *Tehanu: The Last Book of Earthsea* (1990). These books continue to be enormously popular with adult and young adult readers. Other notable Le Guin works are set on Earth. *The Lathe of Heaven* explores the permeable boundary between waking reality and dreams. In the realistic *Very Far Away from Anywhere Else*, two high school seniors become friends and deal with sexuality as they mature. Although *Malafrena* is set in a fictional nineteenth-century Eastern European country, Charlotte Spivack believes it is about the Austrian Empire (114). The highly acclaimed *Always Coming Home,* written with Todd Barton, is an anthropological study of the Kesh, a fictional Pacific Coast people. Le Guin includes a dictionary, literature, natural history, maps, and music. Elizabeth Cummins suggests Le Guin's way of changing America's "head-long dash toward nuclear war and depletion of natural resources is to change the stories" (19).

Pacifism and environmentalism are other important themes that Le Guin explores. In the short story "Vaster Than Empires and More Slow" (*The Wind's Twelve Quarters*), expedition scientists land on an all-vegetal planet. As invading predators, they trigger a slow panic in the sentient plant life, which in turn creates terror in the visitors. A similar balanced and harmonious forest is the setting of *The Word for World Is Forest*. The invaders are Terran colonists, who exploit the forest and its people. The small, green hunter-gatherers, the Athsheans, regularly enter dream states and use visions to keep sane. The Terrans call them "Creechies," deriving from creature. Not only is this novel directly analogous to the conflict in Vietnam, but it also reflects the present-day situation of many indigenous peoples such as the Indians in the Amazon rain forest.

Le Guin escapes pigeonholing by having written several mainstream works. *Searoad: Chronicles of Klatsand* is a collection of stories about an Oregon town. Elizabeth Cummins considers this collection a revision of the Persephone myth and a celebration of older women despite the androcentric dismissal of their worth (229). Individual morality is the theme of "The Ones Who Walk Away from Omelas" (1993). In the utopian society of Omelas, collective happiness depends on the suffering of a single scapegoat. A diabolical choice pits decency and logic. *Four Ways to Forgiveness* approaches reconciliation between races from four perspectives.

In *The Telling* (2000), Sutty is a female Earthling observing a planet, where society is tightly controlled by a capitalist, religious dictatorship, the "Corporation." The Corporation wishes to become part of the interstellar community by destroying evidence of its primitive past. Sutty uncovers an extraordinarily diverse and culturally rich past in a town of traditional people whose ways are evidence of a passive political resistance. *The Telling* is a meditation on the human need for storytelling, whether oral or written, and the futility of censorship.

In 2001 Le Guin published two books: a much-anticipated collection of short stories, *Tales from Earthsea*, and *The Other Wind*, a novel with characters from Earthsea. *Tales from Earthsea* explores and extends the characters and themes of the previous Earthsea books but from a more mature and personal perspective. *The Other Wind* focuses on the boundaries between life and death. Le Guin's most recent novels attest to her dedication to writing. She continues to intrigue readers with her plots and to inspire them with her messages. Summing up Le Guin's long career, Gerald Jones notes, "At the age of 72, [she] has brought to bear on her youthful creation the hardheaded, cleareyed, ultimately optimistic view of human nature. . . . I was grateful to have before me a work of art that embodies this lesson: When the good band together, they can accomplish miracles" (19). Le Guin's artistry and messages are timeless.

CRITICAL RECEPTION

Le Guin's work has prompted more collective critical attention than that of almost any other fantasy writer. Although some critics criticize Le Guin's fiction because it defies generic conventions, others praise her works for their complex themes. For example, Harold Bloom says, "There is no purer story teller writing now in English than Le Guin" (3). He considers *The Left Hand of Darkness* "a book that sustains many readings, partly because its enigmas are unsolvable, and partly because it has the crucial quality of a great representation, which is that it yields up new perspectives upon what we call reality" (6). Similarly, George Edgar Slusser notes that Le Guin's novels and stories are "far superior" to the science fiction of their day: "There is little doubt that Le Guin is one of the best writers currently working in the science fiction and fantasy genres" (3). Darko Suvin likens Le Guin to fellow science fiction writer Philip K. Dick: "But while Dick is a 'romantic' writer, whose energy lashes out in a profusion of incandescent and interfused narrative protuberances, Le Guin is a 'classical' writer, whose energy is as fierce but strictly controlled within a taut and spare architectural system of narrative cells" (233).

Early criticism of Le Guin's works examines the Taoist and Jungian influences on her work. Slusser determines an "evolution in Le Guin's ethos—from an early existentialism through a quiet 'Taoist' period to strong political activism," but cautions that Taoism is not an interlude but "the strongest single force behind her work" (3). Dena C. Bain observes, "The importance of Le Guin's contribution to science fiction lies in her ability to use a distinctly Western art form to communicate the essence that is Tao. In many of her novels, Tao is the universal base upon which societies and individual characters act" (211).

Critics often compare the Earthsea novels with C. S. Lewis's *Chronicles of Narnia* because both authors employ myths of redemption and quest. However, according to Robert Scholes, Le Guin places these myths "in the service of a metaphysic which is entirely responsible to modern conditions of being because its perspective is broader than the Christian perspective" (36). Le Guin "works not with a theology but with an ecology, a cosmology, a reverence for the universe as a self-regulating structure" (Scholes 37). Slusser describes the Earthsea epic as "not simply 'pre-Christian'; it is quite un-Christian, un-Western, in its naturalism, its reverence for the balance of life, its refusal of transcendental values" (43). Sarah Lefanu suggests that unlike Lewis, Le Guin often writes thinly veiled parables of current events such as allusions to the My Lai massacre in *The Word for World Is Forest* (55).

Critics also observe a Taoist dialectic evident in Le Guin's Jungian psychological premises. Donna R. White notes Jung's influence is particularly evident in Le Guin's use of the Shadow archetype to represent an "individual's repressed self—the primitive, undeveloped, negative, creative, dark, animalistic part of a person" (17). Bernard Selinger notes, "Scrutiny of her work reveals a valorization of that private part of the name . . . a questioning of paternal or phallic discourse" (14). Ian Watson regards Le Guin's sentient forest, in "Vaster Than Empires and More Slow," as a blatant depiction of "the hidden unconscious area of the mind" (264).

Feminist criticism of Le Guin's works focuses mainly on her treatment of sexuality and sexual identity in *The Left Hand of Darkness*. Despite evidence that shows Le Guin imagined her protagonists as "male," this book is regarded as an important contribution to feminist literature (Lefanu 51). Lefanu observes that Le Guin's "profound antagonism to violence and her belief in social equality" have never faltered because "for her, feminism must have its political context" (64). While some feminist critics complain that the "androgyny theme fails because the inhabitants of Gethen all seem to the reader to be exclusively male, rather than bisexual" (Spivak 153), Elizabeth Cummins suggests that "most of Le Guin's protagonists, whether male or female

... displayed the characteristics of the female principle and that these characteristics (acceptance, nurture, receptivity, balance, and anarchism) are shown to be virtues" (171). Margaret Keulen specifically objects to Le Guin's use of the "he" pronoun when referring to an androgynous Gethenian as an instance of inscribed sexism in the English language (101).

Critics have looked at many other ideas expressed in Le Guin's works. Perhaps James W. Bittner captures best the essence of Le Guin's body of work: "It is possible to read each of Le Guin's novels as the quest of an artist-hero; it is also possible to read her entire body of fiction . . . as the growth of the artist's mind" (63).

In addition to the critical attention her novels have received, Le Guin's works have garnered her numerous awards and honors. For the Earthsea books, Le Guin was awarded the following: *A Wizard of Earthsea—Boston Globe* Horn Book Award, 1969; *The Tombs of Atuan*—Newbery Honor (silver), 1972; *The Farthest Shore*—National Book Award, 1973; and *Tehanu: The Last Book of Earthsea*—Nebula Award, 1991. Awards for science fiction include the following: *The Left Hand of Darkness*—Nebula Award, 1969, and Hugo Award, 1970; *The Dispossessed*—Hugo, Jupiter, Nebula, and Jules Verne Awards, 1975; *The Word for World Is Forest*—Hugo Award, 1973; "The Ones Who Walk Away from Omelas"—Hugo Award, 1974; "The Day before the Revolution"—Nebula and Jupiter Awards, 1975; and *Four Ways to Forgiveness—Asimov's* Reader's Award, 1995. Other awards include the Hugo Award in 1987 and the International Fantasy Award in 1989 for *Buffalo Gals and Other Animal Presences* and the Pushcart Prize in 1991 for *Searoad: Chronicles of Klatsand*. In 1979, when Le Guin won the Gandalf Award, she earned the title "Grand Master of Fiction," a title she still holds. She continues to produce top-quality speculative fiction eagerly awaited by her devoted fans. Her imagination provides alternative possibilities to our own troubles—solutions, or at least suggestions, for evolving toward higher consciousness and unity.

BIBLIOGRAPHY

Works by Ursula K. Le Guin

Planet of Exile. New York: Ace, 1966.
Rocannon's World. New York: Ace, 1966.
City of Illusions. New York: Ace, 1967.
A Wizard of Earthsea. Berkeley, CA: Parnassus, 1968.
The Left Hand of Darkness. New York: Ace, 1969.
The Lathe of Heaven. New York: Scribner's, 1971.
The Tombs of Atuan. New York: Atheneum, 1971.
The Farthest Shore. New York: Atheneum, 1972.
The Dispossessed. New York: Harper & Row, 1974.
Dreams Must Explain Themselves. San Bernardino, CA: Borgo, 1975.
Wild Angels. Santa Barbara, CA: Capra, 1975.
The Wind's Twelve Quarters. New York: Harper & Row, 1975.
"American SF and the Other." *Science Fiction Studies: Selected Articles on Science Fiction 1973–1975*. Ed. R. D. Mullen and Darko Suvin. Boston: Gregg Press, 1976. 238–40.
Orsinian Tales. New York: Harper & Row, 1976.
Very Far Away from Anywhere Else. New York: Atheneum, 1976.
The Word for World Is Forest. New York: Berkeley, 1976.

The Language of the Night: Essays on Fantasy and Science Fiction. Ed. Susan Wood. New York: Putnam, 1979.

Leese Webster. New York: Atheneum, 1979.

Malafrena. New York: Putnam, 1979.

The Beginning Place. New York: Harper & Row, 1980.

Hard Words and Other Poems. New York: Harper, 1981.

Adventures in Kroy. New Castle, VA: Cheap Street, 1982.

Compass Rose. New York: Harper, 1982.

The Eye of the Heron and Other Stories. London: Panther, 1982.

The Visionary: The Life Story of Flicker of the Serpentine of Telina-Na. Santa Barbara, CA: Capra, 1984.

Always Coming Home. With Todd Barton. New York: Harper, 1985.

King Dog: A Screenplay. Santa Barbara, CA: Capra, 1985.

Buffalo Gals and Other Animal Presences. Santa Barbara, CA: Capra, 1987.

Catwings. New York: Orchard, 1988.

Wild Oats and Fireweed: New Poems. New York: Perennial Library, 1988.

The Blind Geometer and The Return from Rainbow Bridge. With Peter Gudynas, Michael B'ohme, and Kim Stanley Robinson. New York: Tom Doherty, 1989.

Catwings Return. New York: Orchard, 1989.

Dancing at the Edge of the World: Thoughts on Words, Women, Places. New York: Grove, 1989.

Fire and Stone. New York: Atheneum, 1989.

Napa: The Roots and Springs of the Valley. San Francisco, CA: Linden Editions, 1989.

Way of the Water's Going: Images of the Northern California Coastal Range. With Ernest Waugh and Allan Nicholson. New York: Harper & Row, 1989.

Tehanu: The Last Book of Earthsea. New York: Atheneum, 1990.

Searoad: Chronicles of Klatsand. New York: Harper Collins, 1991.

"The Ones Who Walk Away from Omelas." New York: Creative Education, 1993.

Buffalo Gals, Won't You Come Out Tonight? San Francisco: Pomegranate, 1994.

A Fisherman of the Inland Sea: Science Fiction Stories. New York: Harper Prism, 1994.

Going Out with Peacocks and Other Poems. New York: Harper Perennial, 1994.

Wonderful Alexander and the Catwings. New York: Orchard, 1994.

Four Ways to Forgiveness. New York: Harper Prism, 1995.

Unlocking the Air and Other Stories. New York: Harper Collins, 1996.

Tao Te Ching: A Book about the Way and the Power of the Way. Boston: Shambhala, 1997.

Steering the Craft: Exercises and Discussions on Story Writing for the Lone Navigator or the Mutinous Crew. Portland, OR: Eighth Mountain, 1998.

Tom Mouse and Ms. Howe. New York: DK Publishing, 1998.

Jane on Her Own: A Catwings Tale. New York: Orchard, 1999.

Sixty Odd: New Poems. Boston: Shambhala, 1999.

The Telling. San Diego: Harcourt Brace, 2000.

The Other Wind. San Diego: Harcourt Brace, 2001.

Tales from Earthsea. San Diego: Harcourt Brace, 2001.

Studies of Ursula K. Le Guin

Bain, Dena C. "The 'Tao Te Ching' as Background to the Novels of Ursula K. Le Guin." *Ursula K. Le Guin: Modern Critical Views.* Ed. Harold Bloom. New Haven: Chelsea House, 1986. 211–24.

Bittner, James W. *Approaches to the Fiction of Ursula K. Le Guin.* Ann Arbor: University of Michigan Research Press, 1979.

Bloom, Harold. "Introduction." *Ursula K. Le Guin: Modern Critical Views.* Ed. Harold Bloom. New Haven: Chelsea House, 1986. 1–10.

——, ed. *Ursula K. Le Guin: Modern Critical Views.* New Haven: Chelsea House, 1986.

Cummins, Elizabeth. *Understanding Ursula K. Le Guin.* Columbia: University of South Carolina Press, 1993.

"Dialogue with Ursula Le Guin." Interview with George Wickes and Louise Westling. *Northwest Review* 20 (1982): 147–59.

"An Interview with Ursula Le Guin." Interview with Larry McCaffery and Linda Gregory. *Missouri Review* 7 (1984): 64–85.

Jones, Gerald. Rev. of *The Other Wind. New York Times Book Review* 7 Oct. 2001: 19.

Keulen, Margarete. *Radical Imagination: Feminist Conceptions of the Future in Ursula LeGuin, Marge Piercy, and Sally Miller Gearhart.* New York: Peter Lang, 1991.

Lefanu, Sarah. *In the Chinks of the World Machine.* London: Women's Press, 1988.

"*The Progressive* Interview: Ursula Le Guin." Interview with Jane Slaughter. *Progressive* March 1998: 36ff.

Scholes, Robert. "The Good Witch of the West." *Ursula K. Le Guin: Modern Critical Views.* Ed. Harold Bloom. New Haven: Chelsea House, 1986. 35–45.

Selinger, Bernard. *Le Guin and Identity in Contemporary Fiction.* Ann Arbor: University of Michigan Research Press, 1988.

Slusser, George Edgar. *The Farthest Shores of Ursula K. Le Guin.* San Bernardino, CA: Borgo Press, 1976.

Spivack, Charlotte. *Ursula K. Le Guin.* Boston: Twayne, 1984.

Watson, Ian. "The Forest as Metaphor for Mind: *The Word for World Is Forest* and "Vaster Than Empires and More Slow." *Science-Fiction Studies: Selected Articles on Science Fiction 1973–1975.* Ed. R. D. Mullen and Darko Suvin. Boston: Gregg Press, 1976. 261–67.

White, Donna R. *Dancing with Dragons: Ursula K. Le Guin and the Critics.* Columbia, SC: Camden House, 1999.

BEVERLY LOWRY (1938–)

Stephanie Gordon

BIOGRAPHY

Beverly Fey Lowry was born on August 10, 1938, in Memphis, Tennessee, her mother naming her for a debutante seen on the Sunday pages of the *Memphis Commercial Appeal*. Her parents, both Arkansas natives, had two more children, sons born three and twelve years after Beverly. Lowry spent her childhood in the Mississippi Delta, in Greenville, later to become the Eunola of three of her novels.

After high school, Lowry attended the University of Mississippi; however, she left Ole Miss in an effort to rebel against a system that rated young women according to their backgrounds and the sororities to which they belonged. She transferred to Memphis State and majored in drama, receiving her BA in drama/speech and English literature in 1960.

After graduation, she married Glen Lowry, who was to become a stockbroker, and the couple moved to Manhattan, where they had two sons, Colin and Peter. Here, Lowry worked for a time as an actress in children's plays; she also swam at the Coliseum in a water ballet. With her husband and sons, Lowry moved to Houston in 1965, and it is here that her writing career began. Lowry found it easier to begin writing in Houston, noting that there, "it didn't matter who your daddy was, much less your granddaddy" (Smith 51). After becoming an associate professor at the University of Houston in 1976, Lowry published her first novel, *Come Back, Lolly Ray*, in 1977. Lowry proved to be a highly productive writer, publishing her second novel, *Emma Blue*, in 1978. Her next novel, *Daddy's Girl*, was published in 1981 and won the Jesse Jones Award from the Texas Institute of Letters for the best work of fiction written that year.

Six years elapsed before her next novel was published, although Lowry had finished drafts of two new novels, *The Perfect Sonya* and *Breaking Gentle*, by 1984. However, both of her parents died in that period, and, even worse, her son Peter was killed by a hit-and-run driver in 1984. By Lowry's own admission, Peter had been a troubled young man but had tried to mend his ways. Then he was killed, and his death irrevocably changed Lowry's life, making it difficult for her to revise *The Perfect Sonya*. Finally, this book was published in 1987, although critics did not receive it as favorably as they had her previous novels. Her fifth novel, *Breaking Gentle*, was published in 1988; it was also hard for Lowry to revise because it concerned the well-meaning but inept parents of a troubled teenaged daughter. Nevertheless, the book was widely praised, some critics calling it her best novel to date.

Crossed Over: A Murder, a Memoir was published in 1992 and received critical acclaim. This nonfiction book is Lowry's most personal work, an account of her relationship with the infamous young female pick-ax murderer Karla Faye Tucker, who went to Texas death row for her crime and was later executed. *The Track of Real Desires* was published in 1994; here, Lowry returned to the Eunola of her first two novels. Her next book was the nonfiction *Her Dream of Dreams, The Rise and Triumph of Madam C. J. Walker*, slated for a late 2002 publication.

Lowry has held academic appointments at the University of Houston, Rice University, the University of Montana, George Washington University, and the University of Alabama and is currently the director of nonfiction writing in the MFA program in creative writing at George Mason University in Washington, D.C. She has also served as president of the Texas Institute of Letters and as board member for the PEN/Faulkner Foundation along with other service duties. The many awards she has received include a Guggenheim Fellowship, a Literature Grant from the National Endowment for the Arts, the Texas Institute of Letters Jesse Jones Award for fiction in both 1981 and 1987, the Mississippi Institute of Arts and Letters Fiction Award for 1994, and a Rockefeller Foundation Fellowship. Her papers are archived at both Southwest Texas University and the University of Houston.

MAJOR WORKS AND THEMES

Several of Lowry's novels center on a young single woman who, by luck, determination, and talent, finds a place for herself in the world. *Come Back, Lolly Ray*, for example, has as its polestar Lolly Ray Lasswell, a high school girl who is an ace baton twirler, so gifted that she draws large crowds and entertains them seemingly for hours by her clever maneuvers. Lolly Ray has complete confidence in her talents, even as she is suffering from the life on the edge of social acceptance she lives in a trailer with her parents—and from the lack of a solid relationship with her edgy, self-centered mother. *Emma Blue* develops the same theme but centers on Emma, Lolly Ray's illegitimate daughter. Emma is a determined and intelligent young woman who ventures into the unknown, in spite of her many disadvantages. *Daddy's Girl* reveals the idea of a woman in the public eye in a much more overt way than *Emma Blue*. This novel's main character is a young single mother named Sue who manages a large, busy household, writes songs under an alias, and sings at honky-tonks. Finally, Pauline of *The Perfect Sonya* works in New York City as an actress and supplements her income by swimming in a restaurant fish tank. In creating often financially disadvantaged female characters who nevertheless manage to forge their own identities, Lowry gives significance to the lives of young women who have an "outsider" status.

Lowry's protagonists are always explored in relation to their families—another major subject of Lowry's fiction. The family is a force to be reckoned with and then transcended in *Come Back, Lolly Ray*; *Emma Blue*; and *The Perfect Sonya*. However, in *Daddy's Girl*, *Breaking Gentle*, and *The Track of Real Desires*, the family can create both heaven and hell on Earth but ultimately shapes the lives of the characters involved for the better. Generally, the father-daughter configuration is the most important, although weak or indifferent mothers and their daughters are also important to Lowry's novels. In *Daddy's Girl*, the father Big is larger than life and presents obstacles for Sue, even while she adores him. *The Perfect Sonya* has a far more troubled father-daughter line-up. Pauline's father attempts to engage her in an incestuous act that ultimately haunts her far into adulthood, while her mother pathetically drinks, overeats, and slips frequently into depressions. The father-daughter-mother configuration is more innocuous in *Breaking Gentle*, however. Here the father is well-meaning and loving but terribly inept in helping his rampaging teenage daughter. The mother, Diana, is also inept but tries her hardest to be a good mother. In the end, the family comes together in love and understanding.

Dreams are a motif that runs through most of Lowry's novels. The female protagonists of *Come Back, Lolly Ray*; *Emma Blue*; and *Daddy's Girl* spend much of their time daydreaming of glory and a better life. Lolly Ray's tendencies to daydream show both her self-preoccupation and her essential aloofness. Emma daydreams as a way to escape the narrow confines of her life in the family trailer, while Sue daydreams in bed about the glory of singing to a rapturously applauding audience, which she says she eats "absolutely up" (10). In the same novel, Big's dreams concern the loose ends of his life—his ex-wife, various dangers—showing him to be somewhat insecure behind the swaggering bravado. Dreams turn dark and Freudian in *The Perfect Sonya*, showing Pauline's deeply submerged agitation over her relationship with her father.

Another major theme in Lowry's fiction concerns food, which is closely linked to sexuality. In *The Perfect Sonya*, food distracts the characters from their problems and provides a way of avoiding pain. One sees this idea also in *The Track of Real Desires*, a novel that centers on a sumptuous dinner party. Here, food provides a means of communion among the often-troubled characters, and it also keeps the characters occupied, too busy to worry about their own woes. In *The Track of Real Desires*, food is also a sensual experience. In this novel, Sissy loves to eat almost as much as she loves to masturbate. However, eating is also a metaphor for her essential loneliness, for she is married to a man who does not provide her with the sexual attention that she needs. In the short story "Mama's Turn," a woman cooks food for her family and lover as an act of love; sex and food are conflated again in this story when the narrator also provides a detailed account of an act of fellatio. In another short story entitled "Don't Bother to Come If You're Not Going to Stay," an oddly surrealistic tale about two lonely people who meet by chance and then begin living together, food becomes the means by which they negotiate their relationship. The female character lives to eat pies, pies, and more pies, and the man happily joins in with her; but when she is forced to eat alone, she betrays him, smashing several frozen pies onto his head while he is bathing until he drowns. In *Breaking Gentle*, the emphasis on cooking shows the importance of the domestic life to the two main characters. However, their overweight teenage daughter is addicted to food; at one point, she notes that "food definitely was the great power" (110), showing her unease with herself, her parents, and that same domestic life.

Most of Lowry's characters are highly sexed, living life with gusto and engaging in many affairs or alternative lifestyles. Pauline in *The Perfect Sonya* seeks out and has an affair with a much older man, her uncle, as well as numerous other men. She also has a fling with an older woman actor. Lolly Ray Lasswell's sexuality is a means by which she can escape boredom; her heart hardly seems in it at all, and she certainly derives no pleasure from it. Diana of *Breaking Gentle* manages to have affairs even while she leads a fairly successful marriage. Finally, *The Track of Real Desires* highlights the sexual actions of a number of characters as they have affairs, come out of the closet, or keep the act of sex within the traditional male-female married unit.

A final major theme in Lowry's novels is that of life's changes such as uncertainty, disasters, and death. In *Come Back, Lolly Ray*, the lead character gets pregnant before she leaves for college, causing the townspeople to withdraw the offer of a paid college education they had made to their town's biggest star. Emma in *Emma Blue* chances upon a dying elderly woman and through this situation comes into a relationship with a wealthy, much older husband, the grandson of the elderly woman. The book's mantra speaks to this theme of uncertainty in particular: "You never know. Girl, you just never never know" (16). The protagonist of the short story "Out of the Blue," for example, did not know that innocently hanging around the parking lot of a Target store would lead to his being abducted and very possibly murdered by two thugs. This type of story also represents Lowry's darker vision of life's uncertainties. Death comes for Sissy in *The Track of Real Desires*: A lusty woman who loves nothing more than to masturbate, Sissy is driving down a highway when the "urge" hits her. Then a rabbit jumps in front of her car. She swerves sharply and is thrown from the car, breaking her neck on impact when the car flips over.

CRITICAL RECEPTION

All of Lowry's books have been well reviewed, especially the later novels. More recently, critical articles have also begun appearing on her work. Regarding *Come Back, Lolly Ray*, Susan Horowitz of the *Saturday Review* says that it is a book of "multiple and varied pleasures" (28). The *New Yorker* calls *Emma Blue* an "elegant" and "nimble" book (147), although the reviewer for the *Virginia Quarterly* considers it a "fairy tale" (98), possibly because the female protagonist is "rescued" from her life of poverty by a much older, wealthy man. In the *Nation*, Alice Denham writes of *Daddy's Girl* as having a "marvelous" voice but being ultimately wearying because it is "wide but not deep" (25). However, Benjamin DeMott says that ultimately the "wit, energy, freshness of detail and wonderfully breezy sexuality of *Daddy's Girl* go far to outweigh its structural fuzziness" (15). Critic Merrill Maguire Skaggs devoted much of a lengthy essay to *Daddy's Girl*, calling it the most "arresting" and challenging of Lowry's books ("Eating the Moment" 69, 70).

Although reviewers have been highly favorable toward Lowry's novels, they were not as enthusiastic about *The Perfect Sonya*. Ann H. Fisher calls it "not unappealing, not altogether successful" (84), and Lynn Freed of the *New York Times* wishes that the characterization had been stronger and the book's transitions smoother (10). However, Merrill Maguire Skaggs disagrees, calling it a "startling psychological *tour de force*" ("Deprivation" 23). *Breaking Gentle* fared better with critics. In "Deprivation Makes No Desert," Skaggs notes its heart-breaking and deeply loving quality (25–26), while William H. Pritchard says that *Breaking Gentle* is a "strong and graceful performance" (9). Finally, Lowry's last novel, *The Track of Real Desires*, was also well received. Regarding the novel's characters, Judith Grossman says that Lowry "balances sympathy for these damaged lives and satire adroitly throughout" (42).

Walter Satterthwaite also praises this novel, finding it "poignant without veering into sentimentality . . . a fine, funny, altogether admirable novel" (10). All in all, Lowry's novels have received praise worthy of their complicated themes and characterizations.

BIBLIOGRAPHY

Works by Beverly Lowry

"Mama's Turn." *Bitches and Sad Ladies: An Anthology of Fiction.* Ed. Pat Rotter. New York: Harper, 1975. 225–36.
Come Back, Lolly Ray. New York: Doubleday, 1977.
Emma Blue. New York: Doubleday, 1978.
Daddy's Girl. New York: Viking, 1981.
"If You're Not Going to Stay Then Please Don't Bother to Come." *Mississippi Review* 10 (1981): 118–32.
The Perfect Sonya. New York: Viking, 1987.
Breaking Gentle. New York: Viking, 1988.
"Out of the Blue." *Southwest Review* 73 (1988): 255–72.
Crossed Over: A Murder, A Memoir. New York: Knopf, 1992.
The Track of Real Desires. New York: Knopf, 1994.
Her Dream of Dreams, The Rise and Triumph of Madam C. J. Walker. New York: Knopf. Forthcoming 2002.

Studies of Beverly Lowry

DeMott, Benjamin. "The Three Faces of Sue." Rev. of *Daddy's Girl. New York Times Book Review* 25 Oct. 1981: 15.
Denham, Alice. "Fame and Fiction." Rev. of *Daddy's Girl. Nation* 234 (1982): 25.
Rev. of *Emma Blue. New Yorker* 2 Oct. 1978: 147
Rev. of *Emma Blue. Publishers Weekly* 3 July 1978: 60.
Rev. of *Emma Blue. Virginia Quarterly* 55 (1979): 98.
Fisher, Ann H. Rev. of *The Perfect Sonya. Library Journal* 112 (1987): 84.
Freed, Lynn. "She Didn't Cheat on Chekhov." Rev. of *The Perfect Sonya. New York Times Book Review* 26 July 1987: 10.
Grossman, Judith. "Living with Dying." Rev. of *Souls Raised from the Dead, The Track of Real Desires,* and *Talk before Sleep. Women's Review of Books* July 1994: 42.
Horowitz, Susan. Rev. of *Come Back, Lolly Ray. Saturday Review* 4 (1977): 28.
Pritchard, William H. "The Unpredictable Dailiness of Life." Rev. of *Breaking Gentle. New York Times Book Review* 14 Aug.1988: 9.
Rodenburger, Lou. "Shelby Hearon, Beverly Lowry, and Sarah Bird." *Updating the Literary West.* Ed. Western Literature Association. Ft. Worth: Texas Christian University, 1997. 600–607.
Satterthwaite, Walter. "Parties Are Such Sweet Sorrow." *New York Times Book Review* 8 May 1994: 10
Skaggs, Merrill Maguire. "Eating the Moment Absolutely Up: The Fiction of Beverly Lowry." *Southern Quarterly* 21 (1983): 67–82.
——. "Deprivation Makes No Desert: Beverly Lowry's Fiction." *Mississippi Quarterly* 42 (1988/ 89): 19–26.
——. "Beverly Lowry (1938–)." *Contemporary Fiction Writers of the South: A Bio-Bibliographical Sourcebook.* Ed. Joseph M. Flora and Robert Bain. Westport, CT: Greenwood Press, 1993. 267–74.

Smith, Wendy. "*Publishers Weekly* Interviews Beverly Lowry." *Publishers Weekly* 4 April 1994: 51–52.

Wilson, Austin. "What It Means to Be a Southern Writer in the 80's: A Panel Discussion with Beverly Lowry, Reynolds Price, Elizabeth Spencer, and James Whitehead." *Southern Quarterly* 26 (1988): 80–93.

PAULE MARSHALL (1929–)

Michelle L. Taylor

BIOGRAPHY

Paule Marshall was born Valenza Pauline Burke on April 19, 1929, in Brooklyn, New York. Marshall's parents, Samuel and Ada Burke, emigrated to the United States from Barbados shortly after World War I and settled in a tight-knit West Indian community. Marshall's childhood was fertile ground for her future career as a writer. While growing up, Marshall was an avid reader and read novels by Charles Dickens, William Makepeace Thackeray, and Henry Fielding; however, it was not until she began to read the works of Paul Laurence Dunbar that she began to entertain the possibility of becoming a writer. For Marshall, reading Dunbar's poetry exposed her to experiences and a language similar to her own and thus spoke to her in a way that the writings of Dickens and Thackeray did not.

Among childhood influences that Marshall acknowledges, the events that took place in her home proved to have the most profound impact. The daily gatherings of Marshall's mother and her friends introduced her to the sights and sounds of the Bajan (Barbadian) community. By listening to the women talk at the kitchen table, Marshall began to understand the complexities of being a black female immigrant to the United States during the pre–civil rights era. Marshall also began to understand the rich heritage of the Barbadian community that her parents left behind, and such is the world that Marshall recreates in her works. Though Marshall did not visit the Caribbean until she was nine, her home life allowed her to develop a strong sense of Barbadian cultural practices and rituals. Marshall refers to these women as the "kitchen poets" and writes about them in her 1983 essay, "The Making of a Writer: From the Poets in the Kitchen," in which she credits them as being among her first literary influences: "This is why the best of my work must be attributed to them; it stands as testimony to the rich legacy of language and culture they so freely passed on to me in the wordshop of the kitchen" (35).

Marshall continued her education by moving from listening at the kitchen table to attending Brooklyn College, where she graduated cum laude in 1953. After graduation, Marshall worked briefly as a librarian at the New York Public Library. After leaving the library, Marshall worked for two years as a research assistant and full-time journalist for the African American magazine *Our World*. It is worth noting that Marshall was the only woman on the magazine staff and her presence angered some of her male colleagues. But despite the resistance, Marshall took advantage of the opportunities afforded by her position and was able to travel quite extensively throughout the Caribbean and South America. She would later use these travels for material in her collection of short stories, *Soul Clap Hands and Sing* (1961).

In 1957 Marshall married Kenneth Marshall and gave birth to her only child, Evan-Keith, in 1958. Marshall wanted desperately to devote attention to her writing career, but her pursuits were hindered by her family responsibilities. To meet both her needs and the needs of the family, Marshall hired someone to care for her young son and rented an apartment where she could write. Though Marshall's husband did not agree with her decision, this effort allowed her to complete her first novel, *Brown Girl, Brownstones*, which was published in 1959.

Marshall received considerable recognition following the publication of *Brown Girl, Brownstones*, including a Guggenheim Fellowship in 1960. In 1961 Marshall published *Soul Clap Hands and Sing*, for which she was awarded the National Institute of Arts Award. Following the publication of *Soul Clap Hands and Sing*, Marshall published a number of short stories, including "Reena" (1962), "To Da-Duh, In Memoriam" (1967), and "Some Get Wasted" (1968). Both "Reena" and "To Da-Duh, In Memoriam" are included in a later collection of short stories, *Reena and Other Stories* (1983). Marshall's public recognition continued in 1962, when she was awarded the Richard and Hinda Rosenthal Foundation Award.

During the eight years between the publication of *Soul Clap Hands and Sing* and *The Chosen Place, the Timeless People*, Marshall experienced a number of personal and professional changes. The demands of Marshall's career took their toll on the young family, and as a result, she divorced her first husband in 1963. However, Marshall's professional career continued to flourish, and in 1964 she received a Ford Foundation Grant for poets and fiction writers. She also received a National Endowment for the Arts Fellowship in 1967. Two years later, she published her second novel, *The Chosen Place, the Timeless People*. By 1970 Marshall was remarried to Haitian businessman Nourry Menard and dividing her time between the United States and Haiti.

By 1983 Marshall was well established as a prominent figure in American literature. After a fourteen-year absence from publishing, Marshall published her third novel, *Praisesong for the Widow*, in 1983, for which she won the Columbus Foundation American Book Award. She also published a collection of short stories, *Reena and Other Stories*, later in 1983. Marshall continued to garner critical praise for her work, including the American Book Award in 1984 and the John Dos Passos Award for literature in 1989.

The following decade proved to be just as fruitful for Marshall's career. In 1990 Marshall was an honoree of the PEN/Faulkner Foundation and published her fourth novel, *Daughters*, a year later. In 1992 Marshall received the prestigious MacArthur Fellowship. Marshall is currently dividing her time between teaching and writing and holds the Helen Gould Sheppard Chair of Literature and Culture at New York University. She recently published her fifth novel, *The Fisher King*, in 2000.

MAJOR WORKS AND THEMES

One of the most important unifying themes in Marshall's oeuvre is the interconnectedness of Africa-descended people throughout the diaspora. Though she takes as her primary focus the migratory journeys between the Caribbean and North America, she is nonetheless interested in the shared past represented by the African homeland. Marshall's investment in revisiting the African past grows in large part from her interest in the geographical disruption caused by the middle passage. To that end, she uses her writing as a common historical marker that will inform her readers on key historical moments and figures. Further, language and the oral tradition are also crucial to her project of creating and maintaining historically centered literary texts. The thematic influences of African and African American rituals and folklore are ever present in her works, including the ring shout, the myth of the Flying African, and Ibo Landing.

With the publication of her first novel, *Brown Girl, Brownstones*, Marshall made an important contribution to black women's writing through her rendering of two powerful and memorable female protagonists, Silla and Selina Boyce. Indeed, it is the relationship between mother and daughter, Silla and Selina, that is one of the earliest and most memorable explorations of the mother-daughter relationship in African American literature. It is precisely through the lens of the mother-daughter relationship that Marshall also examines and critiques the black immigrant experience in America, racism, and capitalism. Though the relationship between Silla and her husband, Deighton, is of crucial importance to the plot, the novel ultimately becomes Selina's story and represents one of the earliest female *bilundsgromans* to focus on the psychic development of a young black woman.

Marshall creates a vibrant Barbadian community in which Silla emerges as a strong-willed and hard-working member of the community who wants desperately to succeed in America by owning her own brownstone. Silla is constructed in marked contrast to her husband, Deighton, a romantic dreamer who entertains dreams of returning to Barbados. Marshall uses the memories of Barbados as a means of critiquing American standards and the limits of the American dream. Living in the United States, even with all of its racial injustice, is a far better life for Silla than returning to the poverty that Deighton romanticizes. That Silla is willing to nearly destroy her family to succeed problematizes the peace and prosperity usually accorded to the American dream. Caught between her parents' struggles, Selina's attempts to create a space for herself, despite the opposing forces in her home, constitute the bulk of the novel.

Selina's relationship with her parents, Silla in particular, becomes even more complex as Silla becomes more desperate to own the coveted brownstone. When Deighton inherits property in Barbados, Silla forges his name on legal documents to obtain the cash value of the property. Deighton is overwhelmed by the missed opportunity to return home and spends all of the money on a frivolous shopping spree that infuriates Silla and prompts her to alert immigration officials. As a result, Deighton is deported but dies before he reaches Barbados, though it is unclear if he commits suicide or is pushed off of the boat. By the end of the novel, Silla finally owns the brownstone but is haunted by the guilt of Deighton's death. Again, Selina is caught between the experiences of her parents as she struggles simultaneously to maintain a relationship with her mother and to cope with her father's death.

Marshall continues her exploration of West Indian experiences in *Soul Clap Hands and Sing*, a collection of four novellas published in 1961. The titles of each of the novellas—"Barbados," "Brooklyn," "British Guinea," and "Brazil"—immediately alert the reader to Marshall's commitment to exploring the relationship between the African diaspora and the residual effects of histories of oppression. Marshall breaks new ground in this collection by examining the lives of four elderly men, a treatment that is among the first of its kind in African American literature. In this vein, Marshall precedes Ernest Gaines's *Gathering of Old Men* by examining the relationship between age and black masculinity in a literary context. The men in *Soul Clap Hands and Sing* have all in some way been wounded by racial oppression, which ultimately results in failed dreams and emotional emptiness. Consider, for example, Mr. Watford in "Barbados," who spends his life making money in the United States so that he can return to Barbados to live a life of luxury. Quite interestingly, the type of life that he wants to lead in Barbados is quite similar to the lifestyle of the colonials who oppressed him. As a result, Mr. Watford, much like the other protagonists in the collection, is forced to evaluate the meaning of his life, his life's work, and finally his relationship to his homeland.

Although the four novellas in *Soul Clap Hands and Sing* focus most prominently on issues of black masculinity, Marshall is nonetheless careful to explore gender relations through the men's relationships with the women in their lives. Marshall returns to an exploration of women's lives in her later works, including the much anthologized short story "Reena," which first appeared in *American Negro Short Stories* (1966). Marshall again ventures into previously uncharted territory with her exploration of the life of a middle-aged, educated black woman. Reena is therefore among a new generation of heroines who embody the hopes of the previous generation but are nevertheless haunted by the specter of racism that also marked the lives of their ancestors. Such is the case for Reena, who returns home to Brooklyn to attend the wake of a beloved aunt who worked hard to buy her own brownstone but died before she could enjoy it. It is during the wake that Reena examines her own life, career, and family. As a result, Reena comes to terms with her role as a woman and a mother, determined to create a life for herself that is not bound by social restrictions.

As Barbara Christian points out, Reena is the woman who Selina might have become, and a forerunner to Merle Kibona, the protagonist in Marshall's second novel, *The Chosen Place, the Timeless People*. Like Reena, Merle is also torn between the past and the present and thus has to eventually come to terms with her own past in order to move ahead. The novel is set in Bournehills, a fictitious island in the Caribbean that is itself torn between the past and the present. The novel focuses on the relationship between the residents of Bournehills and a philanthropic agency, the Center for Applied Social Research. While members of the agency believe that they are helping to modernize the island, the residents are resistant to the organization's token attempts to right the wrongs of the past. Though the novel is focused on the Caribbean, it encapsulates many of the tensions faced by many Third World nations struggling to maintain a sense of their cultural heritage while also coping with the foreboding presence of the West. At the center of the struggle is Merle, a London-educated Bournehills native who returns home after a failed marriage. In her efforts to come to grips with her personal past, she is also forced to acknowledge her relationship with her cultural history. Written on the verge of the feminist movement, Merle embodies the personal as political message of the movement and is at the center of the island's struggle to overcome the injustices of the past.

Fourteen years after the publication of *The Chosen Place, the Timeless People*, Marshall published her third novel, *Praisesong for the Widow*. This novel centers on Avatara "Avey" Johnson, a middle-aged, middle-class black woman who reconnects with her West Indian past. Like Silla, Avey believes in the American dream and is seduced by all of its material comforts. However, after the death of her husband, she goes on a cruise to the West Indies that changes her life. Avey abandons the cruise and travels alone to the island of Carriacou, where she immerses herself in the cultural rituals that she had forgotten while living in New York. As a result, Avey sells her home in New York and returns to her childhood home so that she can instill in her grandchildren a sense of historical identity that she came dangerously close to losing.

Marshall's fourth novel, *Daughters*, also considers issues of self and cultural rediscovery. Like *Brown Girl, Brownstones*, this novel focuses on a young woman's attempt to cope with the expectations and personal histories of her parents. The protagonist, Ursa Beatrice Mackenzie, is the daughter of an African American mother, Estell, and an West Indian politician father, Primus. However, while *Brown Girl, Brownstones* focuses on the mother-daughter relationship, this novel emphasizes the relationship that develops between Ursa and her father, Primus. Ursa has been overwhelmed by her father's overbearing personality, and in the end, she has to disengage herself from his shadow and help him rediscover the man he was before becoming involved in the island's corrupt politics.

Marshall's fifth novel, *The Fisher King*, continues the work of *Daughters* through its emphasis on cross-generational connections and healing. *The Fisher King* marks a return to Brooklyn and tells the story of the late jazz pianist Sonny-Rhett Payne through the eyes of his lover, Hattie Carmichael. Unlike Marshall's other novels that focus quite specifically on the impact of West Indian cultural histories, this novel examines the complex nature of interpersonal and intraracial relationships within the context of an artist's struggle for creative and personal freedom. The novel centers on Hattie's return from Paris to Brooklyn, where she and Sonny fled in order to escape American racial and cultural intolerance. Hattie returns with her charge, Sonny's grandson (also named Sonny), to attend a memorial concert in Sonny's honor. However, the novel is more intimately concerned with recounting Hattie's relationship with Sonny and his wife and her best friend, Charisse. The story that develops chronicles the romantic triangulation of Hattie, Sonny, and Charisse, their exile to Paris, and the emotional void following Sonny's and Charisse's tragic deaths. Hattie's return to Brooklyn allows her to confront the past and also introduces Sonny to a family that he has never known. In the eight-year old Sonny, Marshall creates a memorable and surprisingly mature protagonist who struggles to repair the rifts in the family that he has just met. Ultimately, Hattie is forced to acknowledge the price of her past freedom and its impact on her future and her relationship with Sonny.

CRITICAL RECEPTION

Though Marshall's works have not experienced considerable commercial success, her works have garnered substantial critical attention. The continued impact of feminist scholarship, most specifically black feminist criticism, has sustained critical interest in Marshall's work. Issues central to black feminist criticism—sexuality, maternity, and self-creation—are frequently used as theoretical approaches to her work. Also of importance to critics is Marshall's investment in constructing narratives that privilege the cultural and historical significance of the black diaspora.

The interest in Marshall's work speaks not only to her obvious talent but also to the timeless quality of the stories that she creates. As Evelyn Hawthorne points out, Marshall's work, *Brown Girl, Brownstones*, in particular, has revised literary traditions. Hawthorne writes: "*Brown Girl* served to re-define the literary subject, to give validation to culture-specific values, language, histories, and traditions, and to revision literary work as a weapon of struggle" (2). As Hawthorne rightly suggests, history, language, and tradition are all crucial components of Marshall's work. And it is precisely Marshall's integration of past and present, resistance, and empowerment that makes her one of American literature's most significant voices.

BIBLIOGRAPHY

Works by Paule Marshall

Brown Girl, Brownstones. New York: Random House, 1959.
Soul Clap Hands and Sing. New York: Antheneum, 1961.
"The Negro Woman in American Literature." *Freedomways* 6 (1966): 21–25.
"Reena." *American Negro Short Stories*. Ed. John H. Clarke. New York: Hill & Wang, 1966. 264–82.
The Chosen Place, the Timeless People. New York: Harcourt, 1969.
"Shaping the World of My Art." *New Letters* Oct. 1973: 97–112.
"Some Get Wasted." *Harlem U.S.A.* Ed. John Henrik Clarke. Berlin: Seven Seas, 1974. 364–75.
"The Making of a Writer: From the Poets in the Kitchen." *New York Times Book Review* 9 Jan. 1983: 3, 34–35.
Praisesong for the Widow. New York: Putnam, 1983.
Reena and Other Stories. Old Westbury, NY: Feminist Press, 1983.
Daughters. New York: Plume, 1991.
The Fisher King. New York: Scribner's, 2000.

Studies of Paule Marshall

Christian, Barbara. "Paule Marshall." *Afro-American Writers after 1955*. Ed. Trudier Harris and Thadious Davis. Detroit: Gale, 1984. Vol. 33 of *Dictionary of Literary Biography*. 161–70.
Coser, Stelamaris. "From the Natives' Point of View: The Ethnographic Novels of Paule Marshall." *Bridging the Americas: The Literature of Paule Marshall, Toni Morrison, and Gayl Jones*. Philadelphia: Temple University Press, 1995. 27–80.
DeLamotte, Eufenia. *Places of Silence, Journeys of Freedom: The Fiction of Paule Marshall*. Philadelphia: University of Pennsylvania Press, 1998.
Denniston, Dorothy. *The Fiction of Paule Marshall: Reconstructions of History, Culture, and Gender*. Knoxville: University of Tennessee Press, 1995.
Ferguson, Moira. "Of Bears & Bearings: Paule Marshall's Diverse *Daughters*." *MELUS* 24 (1999): 177–95.
Francis, Donnette. "Paule Marshall: New Accents on Immigrant America." *Black Scholar* 30 (2000): 21–25.
Hawthorne, Evelyn. "The Critical Difference: Paule Marshall's Personal and Literary Legacy." *Black Scholar* 30 (2000): 2–6.

Olmstead, Jane. "The Pull to Memory and the Language of Place in Paule Marshall's *The Chosen Place, the Timeless People* and *Praisesong for the Widow*." *African American Review* 31 (1997): 249–67.

Pettis, Joyce. "Legacies of Community and History in Paule Marshall's *Daughters*. *Studies in the Literary Imagination* 26 (1993): 77–87.

BOBBIE ANN MASON (1940–)

Laurie Champion

BIOGRAPHY

Born in Mayfield, Kentucky, on May 1, 1940, Bobbie Ann Mason has used her hometown setting to master the art of regional writing. Although Mason left Mayfield to pursue graduate school, which prompted her writing career, her portrayals of scenes and characters from rural Kentucky have contributed to her success as a significant American short story writer and novelist. Mason's parents were dairy farmers, and she and her three siblings spent much of their childhoods helping with farm chores. From an early age, Mason developed a taste for art, spending her early adolescence listening to popular music and reading literature such as Nancy Drew and other girl sleuth mysteries.

After earning her BA from the University of Kentucky in 1962, Mason moved to New York City, where she worked for Ideal Publishing Co. and wrote for popular magazines such as *Movie Stars*, *Movie Life*, and *T. V. Star Parade*. She received her MA in English at the State University of New York at Binghamton in 1966. In 1969 she married Roger B. Rawlings, an editor and writer, and in 1972 she received her PhD from the University of Connecticut. After receiving her doctorate, Mason began teaching at Mansfield State College in Pennsylvania, where she continued to teach until 1979. While teaching, she published two scholarly books, *Nabokov's Garden: A Guide to "Ada"* (1974) and *The Girl Sleuth: A Feminist Guide to the Bobbsey Twins, Nancy Drew, and Their Sisters* (1974).

During the 1980s, Mason's short stories began to appear in distinguished magazines such as the *New Yorker* and *Atlantic*. Her short story collections *Shiloh and Other Stories* and *Love Life* also appeared in the 1980s. The success of Mason's fiction, including the film adaptation of *In Country*, enabled Mason to quit teaching and pursue a writing career full time. In 1990 Mason returned to Kentucky to live. Perhaps her return home prompted her to write the novel *Feather Crowns* (1993), which is based on a historical event that occurred in the small western Kentucky town of Hopeville, and her memoir, *Clear Springs* (1999), which celebrates many aspects of small-town life. Mason received honorary doctorates from the University of Kentucky and from Eastern Kentucky University in 1994 and 1995, respectively.

MAJOR WORKS AND THEMES

Acclaimed as both a novelist and a short story writer, throughout her works, Bobbie Ann Mason realistically portrays ordinary people, depicting working-class characters of rural western Kentucky who work at K-Mart or Rexall, drive trucks, build houses, and clip grocery coupons. Lack of economic means often intensifies characters' struggles, leading to divorce or drinking. The characters frequently lack direction for their lives, failing to recognize or act upon opportunities to improve their circumstances.

Mason's short stories exemplify minimalism, a writing technique that consists of a pared-down writing style, realism, little surface plot, open-ended resolutions, and frequent use of first-person and present-tense narrative devices. Mason's fiction is compared with those of minimalist writers such as Raymond Carver, Ann Beattie, and Frederick Barthelme.

Strained romantic relationships is one subject that recurs throughout Mason's short fiction. In "Shiloh," one of Mason's most acclaimed stories, Leroy, a truck driver, and his wife, Norma Jean, struggle to preserve their marriage, strained partially because of the death of their child that occurred years ago. While Leroy is unable to understand the changes he sees in Norma Jean after she attends college, Norma Jean contemplates leaving Leroy. Similarly, Louise, the protagonist of "Still Life with Watermelon," decides whether to remain married to Tom, who has moved out of their house. Louise shares her house with Peggy, whose husband, Jerry, has recently left her to live with their former landlord's mistress. Although their predicaments seem similar, Peggy and Louise react to their situations very differently. While Peggy struggles to restore her marriage, Louise tries to create a new identity for herself. Georgeann, the protagonist of "The Retreat," struggles with her conflicting desires to leave her husband, who is a preacher, and to remain a respected member of the community. Unlike some of Mason's other women protagonists, Georgeann remains in her marriage because she feels it is her duty.

Mason is also well known for her portrayal of popular culture, especially her allusions to pop singers and quotes from popular tunes. Mason's references to popular culture sometimes are set against the background of the Vietnam War. In her fiction that concerns the Vietnam War, Mason focuses on the psychological impact of the war on her characters. Mason's first novel, *In Country* (1985), is packed with references to pop culture, relating to the time frame of the war and to the present time frame of the novel. Among other pop cultural references, a quote from Bruce Springsteen's album *Born in the USA* serves as an epigraph, Sam and Emmett watch M*A*S*H, and references occur to the Beatles, all symbolizing the attitudes of post–Vietnam War American culture, an important background against which the novel is set. Set primarily in rural western Kentucky, *In Country* is told from the point of view of seventeen-year-old Sam Hughes, a young woman whose father was killed in Vietnam before she was born. Along with her Uncle Emmett, who was wounded physically and psychologically in the war, Sam searches for family history as well as answers about the Vietnam War. Sam, Emmett, and Sam's grandmother drive to the Vietnam Memorial in Washington D.C., and it is here that Sam, while seeing her father's name, which is the same as hers, on the wall, discovers her identity. One major theme in the novel is the search for the father, and when Sam identifies with him, she is able to break away from the alienation of her past. Sam's grandmother and Emmett also gain some sort of spiritual healing during the visit to the Vietnam Memorial. Similarly, "Big Bertha Stories" reflects a young couple's attempt to cope with the psychological effects of the Vietnam War on the husband, Donald. Years after the Vietnam War, Donald begins to experience post-traumatic stress syndrome. Donald works away from his home and returns frequently, where he experiences nightmares. He tells stories about Big Bertha, a mining machine he personifies to represent a person with supernatural abilities of strength. The stories of Big Bertha parallel Donald's memory of his battles in Vietnam. The narratives Donald tells increasingly lose their narrative structure, until finally he becomes unable to tell them sensibly. Donald eventually enters a hospital, where he remains for therapy.

Mason's themes sometimes juxtapose the present with the past, usually contrasting a lifestyle complicated by modern technology with a more simple, agrarian lifestyle. However, Mason does not necessarily criticize modern technology; rather, she seems to suggest that technology has both weaknesses and strengths. She certainly reveals that social progress, in terms of offering women more choices, has benefitted society. In her second short novel, *Spence + Lila* (1988), Mason portrays the simplistic life-style of Spence and Lila Culpepper, who live in rural Kentucky. When Lila has a mastectomy, she and Spence are forced to recognize a changing world, one full of modern technology and impersonal attitudes. The modern lifestyles of their three grown children are juxtaposed against the simple, rural existence Spence and Lila have lived all their lives. One main subject of the novel is the notion of the agrarian tradition versus industrialism, a lifestyle complicated by modern machines and corporations. Likewise, the title story of the short story collection *Love Life* depicts young Jenny and her Aunt Opal, who sips alcohol and watches TV. Both women consider their single marital status, and the story exemplifies differences between generations: the old rural way of life and the new generation who live in the modern enterprising world.

Feather Crowns is Mason's first full-length novel. The same rural Kentucky setting Mason uses in her earlier novels and many of her short stories is used in this novel. In *Feather Crowns*, Mason depicts Christie and James Wheeler, a tobacco farming couple. Spanning over sixty years, the novel begins in 1900, when Christie gives birth to quintuplets, an event that brings the couple national attention, and ends with Christie's retrospective insights about celebrity. The event brings reporters, doctors, and sightseers to the little town, demonstrating the theme of simple life versus modern industrial progress.

In 1999 Mason published a memoir, *Clear Springs*. The book covers a time span of three generations of Mason's family, who resides in Clear Spring, Kentucky. Organized into five sections, the narrative has a loose linear development. Mason's memoir reveals not only personal history but also one that relates to the culture of the baby-boom generation as a whole. At the beginning of her narrative, Mason directly poses the following questions: "What happened to me and my generation? What made us leave home and abandon the old ways? Why did we lose our knowledge of nature? Why wasn't it satisfying? Why would only rock-and-roll music do? What did we want?" (11).

In *Clear Springs*, Mason uses the memoir genre to sum up the themes and subjects of her fiction. She reveals the struggles of people who long for a simple life, uncomplicated by personal struggles such as divorce, and she shows both the consequences and the rewards of technological development. Although throughout her works Mason concentrates primarily on small-town life, most of her works transcend regional fiction, for the hopes, dreams, and often despair of her characters frequently express universal sentiments.

CRITICAL RECEPTION

Initially receiving almost unanimously favorable reviews in distinguished magazines and newspapers, Mason's work has since been the subject of numerous scholarly essays. Mason's realistic portrayals of rural Kentucky and the South, her references to popular culture, and her feminist themes are the subjects of most critical attention to Mason's works. In addition to the attention given her novels, Mason has received critical acclaim for her short stories.

Mason's works often are looked at in terms of ways they reveal conflicts between tradition and change, especially in terms of Southern tradition. Albert E. Wilhelm's "Making Over or Making Off: The Problem of Identity in Bobbie Ann Mason's Short Fiction" traces the effect of social change on rural residents in *Shiloh and Other Stories*. Similarly, in "Finding One's History: Bobbie Ann Mason and Contemporary Southern Literature," Robert H. Brinkmeyer, Jr., examines ways Mason's characters look to contemporary culture for guidance rather than asking their elders for advice. Considering Mason a female Southern writer, Harriet Pollack's "From *Shiloh* to *In Country* to *Feather Crowns*: Bobbie Ann Mason, Women's History, and Southern Fiction" demonstrates that Mason writes in the tradition of Southern women writers who reveal history in their works by portraying a "silent history" that chronicles not wars or other heroic deeds, but "lives lived on the margins of official history and culture" (96).

In both her novels and her short stories, Mason refers to many aspects of popular culture, a topic several critics address. The title of Leslie White's "Function of Popular Culture in Bobbie Ann Mason's *Shiloh and Other Stories* and *In Country*" reflects its topic, as does Robert H. Brinkmeyer, Jr.'s "Never Stop Rocking: Bobbie Ann Mason and Rock-and Roll."

Many critics examine Mason's works from a feminist perspective. G. O. Morphew, in "Downhome Feminists in *Shiloh and Other Stories*," examines Mason's working-class women to show how they become empowered to defy traditionally defined female roles through their age, economic independence, and education. Laurie Champion's "Bobbie Ann Mason's (Open-Ended) Marriages" looks at various choices concerning romantic relationships made by women in several of the stories in *Shiloh*. "'Use to, the Menfolks Would Eat First': Food and Food Ritual in the Fiction of Bobbie Ann Mason" reveals Darlene Hill's observations about the changing roles of women expressed in Mason's short stories in terms of ways they defy stereotypical roles for women that prescribe roles for cooking and eating. In "Gender Issues in Bobbie Ann Mason's *In Country*," Ellen A. Blais examines both masculine and feminine roles of various characters in the novel. She argues that although most of the characters accept a pre-1960s definition of gender roles, Emmett and Sam reject traditional roles.

Only one full-length study of Mason's works has appeared: Albert E. Wilhelm's

Bobbie Ann Mason: A Study of the Short Fiction, published as a volume in Twayne's Studies in Short Fiction Series. It is interesting to note that Mason's short stories have received as much attention as her novels, giving her prestige as both a short story writer and as a novelist.

BIBLIOGRAPHY

Works by Bobbie Ann Mason

The Girl Sleuth: A Feminist Guide to the Bobbsey Twins, Nancy Drew, and Their Sisters. Old Westbury, NY: Feminist Press, 1974.
Nabokov's Garden: A Guide to "Ada." Ann Arbor, MI: Ardis, 1974.
Shiloh and Other Stories. New York: Harper, 1982.
In Country. New York: Harper, 1985.
Spence + Lila. New York: Harper, 1988.
Love Life. New York: Harper, 1989.
Feather Crowns. New York: Harper, 1993.
Midnight Magic. Hopewell, NJ: Ecco Press, 1998.
Clear Springs: A Memoir. New York: Random, 1999.

Studies of Bobbie Ann Mason

Arnold, Edwin T. "Falling Apart and Staying Together: Bobbie Ann Mason and Leon Driskell Explore the State of the Modern Family." *Appalachian Journal* 12 (1985): 135–41.
Bakker, Dee. "Women Writers and Their Critics: A Room with a View." *Mid-American Review* 13 (1992): 80–85.
Bezner, Kevin. "Into the Darkness and Back Again: An Interview with Bobbie Ann Mason." *Washington Post Book Review* Jan. 1986: 13–14.
Blais, Ellen A. "Gender Issues in Bobbie Ann Mason's *In Country.*" *South Atlantic Quarterly* 56 (1991): 107–18.
Blythe, Hal, and Charlie Sweet. "The Ambiguous Grail Quest in 'Shiloh.' " *Studies in Short Fiction* 32 (1995): 223–26.
Booth, David. "Sam's Quest, Emmett's Wound: Grail Motifs in Bobbie Ann Mason's Portrait of America after Vietnam." *Southern Literary Journal* 23 (1991): 98–109.
Brinkmeyer, Robert H., Jr. "Finding One's History: Bobbie Ann Mason and Contemporary Southern Literature." *Southern Literary Journal* 19 (1987): 22–33.
——. "Never Stop Rocking: Bobbie Ann Mason and Rock-and-Roll." *Mississippi Quarterly* 42 (1988/89): 5–17.
Bucher, Tina. "Changing Roles and Finding Stability: Women in Bobbie Ann Mason's *Shiloh and Other Stories.*" *Border States: Journal of the Kentucky-Tennessee American Studies Association* 8 (1991): 50–55.
Champion, Laurie. "The Balance of Effects: An Interview with Bobbie Ann Mason." *Dark Horse Literary Review* 2.1 (2000): 33–40.
——. "A Bobbie Ann Mason Bibliography." *Dark Horse Literary Review* 2.1 (2000): 41–44.
——. "Bobbie Ann Mason's (Open-Ended) Marriages." *Midwest Quarterly* 43 (2001): 95–111.
Ditsky, John. " 'Following a Serpentine Brick Path': The Fiction of Bobbie Ann Mason." *Hollins Critic* 33.4 (1996): 1–15.
Durham, Sandra Bonilla. "Women and War: Bobbie Ann Mason's *In Country.*" *Southern Literary Journal* 22.2 (1990): 45–52.
Dwyer, June. "New Roles, New History and New Patriotism: Bobbie Ann Mason's *In Country.*" *Modern Language Studies* 22.2 (1992): 72–78.

Flora, Joseph M. "Bobbie Ann Mason." *Contemporary Fiction Writers of the South: A Bio–Bibliographical Sourcebook*. Ed. Flora and Robert Bain. Westport, CT: Greenwood Press, 1993. 275–85.

Gholson, Craig. "Bobbie Ann Mason." *Bomb* 28 (1989): 40–43.

Giannone, Richard. "Bobbie Ann Mason and the Recovery of Mystery." *Studies in Short Fiction* 27 (1990): 553–66.

Havens, Lila. "Residents and Transients: An Interview with Bobbie Ann Mason." *Crazyhorse* 29 (1985): 87–104.

Henning, Barbara. "Minimalism and the American Dream: 'Shiloh' by Bobbie Ann Mason and 'Preservation' by Raymond Carver." *Modern Fiction Studies* 35 (1989): 589–99.

Hill, Darlene. " 'Use to, the Menfolks Would Eat First': Food and Food Rituals in the Fiction of Bobbie Ann Mason." *Southern Quarterly* 30.2–3 (1992): 81–89.

Hill, Dorothy Combs. "An Interview with Bobbie Ann Mason." *Southern Quarterly* 31.1 (1992): 85–118.

Kinney, Katherine. " 'Humping the Boonies': Sex, Combat, and the Female in Bobbie Ann Mason's *In Country*." *Fourteen Landing Zones: Approaches to Vietnam War Literature*. Ed. Philip K. Jason. Iowa City: University of Iowa Press, 1991. 38–48.

Kling, Vincent. "A Conversation with Bobbie Ann Mason." *Four Quarters* 4.1 (1990): 17–22.

Krasteva, Yonka. "The South and the West in Bobbie Ann Mason's *In Country*." *Southern Literary Journal* 26.2 (1994): 77–90.

Lohafer, Susan. "Stops on the Way to 'Shiloh': A Special Case for Literary Empiricism." *Style* 27 (1993): 395–406.

Lupack, Barbara Tepa. "History as Her-Story: Adapting Bobbie Ann Mason's *In Country* to Film." *Vision/Re-Vison: Adapting Contemporary American Fiction by Women to Film*. Ed. Barbara Tepa Lupack. Bowling Green: Bowling Green State University Popular Press, 1996. 159–92.

Lyons, Bonnie, and Bill Oliver. "An Interview with Bobbie Ann Mason." *Contemporary Literature* 32 (1991): 449–70.

McKee, Kathryn B. "Doubling Back: Finding Bobbie Ann Mason's Present in Her Past." *Southern Literary Journal* 31.1 (1998): 35–50.

Morphew, G. O. "Downhome Feminists in *Shiloh and Other Stories*." *Southern Literary Journal* 21.2 (1989): 41–49.

Morrissey, Thomas J. "Mason's *In Country*." *Explicator* 50 (1991): 62–64.

Pollack, Harriet. "From *Shiloh* to *In Country* to *Feather Crowns*: Bobbie Ann Mason, Women's History, and Southern Fiction." *Southern Literary Journal* 28.2 (1996): 95–116.

Roberts, Nora Ruth. "Class and Gender in Nancy Drew (and My Research on Bobbie Ann Mason)." *Spectacle* 1.1 (1997): 171–88.

Ryan, Barbara T. "Decentered Authority in Bobbie Ann Mason's *In Country*." *Critique* 31.3 (1990): 199–211.

Ryan, Maureen. "Stopping Places: Bobbie Ann Mason's Short Stories." *Women Writers of the Contemporary South*. Ed. Peggy Whitman Prenshaw. Jackson: University Press of Mississippi, 1984. 283–94.

Schroeder, Eric James. "Bobbie Ann Mason: 'Eventually I Had to Confront the Subject.' " *Vietnam, We've All Been There: Interviews with American Writers*. Ed. Eric James Schroeder. Westport, CT: Praeger, 1992. 164–79.

Shomer, Enid. "An Interview with Bobbie Ann Mason." *Black Warrior Review* 12 (1986): 87–108.

Smith, Michael. "Bobbie Ann Mason, Artist and Rebel." *Kentucky Review* 8.3 (1988): 56–63.

Smith, Wendy. "*Publishers Weekly* Interviews: Bobbie Ann Mason." *Publishers Weekly* 30 Aug. 1985: 424–25.

Stewart, Matthew C. "Realism, Verisimilitude, and the Depiction of Vietnam Veterans in *In*

Country." *Fourteen Landing Zones: Approaches to Vietnam War Literature*. Ed. Philip K. Jason. Iowa City: University of Iowa Press, 1991. 166–79.

Tanzman, Lea. "Mason's 'Shiloh': Another Civil War." *Notes on Contemporary Literature* 25 (1995): 5–6.

Thompson, Terry. "Mason's 'Shiloh.' " *Explicator* 54 (1995): 54–58.

Todd, David Y. "A Conversation with Bobbie Ann Mason." *Boulevard* 4 (1990): 132–45.

Underwood, Karen. "Mason's 'Drawing Names.' " *Explicator* 49 (1990): 231–32.

White, Leslie. "The Function of Popular Culture in Bobbie Ann Mason's *Shiloh and Other Stories* and *In Country*." *Southern Quarterly* 26.4 (1988): 69–79.

Wilhelm, Albert E. "Making Over or Making Off: The Problem of Identity in Bobbie Ann Mason's Short Fiction." *Southern Literary Journal* 18.2 (1986): 76–82.

——. "Private Rituals: Coping with Change in the Fiction of Bobbie Ann Mason." *Midwest Quarterly* 28 (1987): 271–82.

——. "An Interview with Bobbie Ann Mason." *Southern Quarterly* 26.2 (1988): 27–38.

——. "Bobbie Ann Mason: Searching for Home." *Southern Writers at Century's End*. Ed. Jeffrey J. Folks and James A. Perkins. Lexington: University Press of Kentucky, 1997. 151–63.

——. *Bobbie Ann Mason: A Study of the Short Fiction*. New York: Twayne, 1998. Vol. XX of Studies in Short Fiction.

Winther, Marjorie. "M*A*S*H, Malls and Meaning: Popular and Corporate Culture in *In Country*." *Literature, Interpretation, Theory* 4.3 (1993): 195–201.

JILL McCORKLE (1958–)

Suzanne Disheroon-Green

BIOGRAPHY

Born July 7, 1958, Jill McCorkle is the author of five novels and two collections of short fiction. McCorkle was born in Lumberton, North Carolina, the daughter of secretary Melba Collins McCorkle and postal employee John Wesley McCorkle. She earned her bachelor's degree from the University of North Carolina at Chapel Hill in creative writing in 1980, taking her degree with highest honors. She then completed her MA at Hollins College in 1981, winning the Andrew James Purdy Fiction Prize during her matriculation. She also entered into a short-lived marriage to Steven Alexander, from whom she was divorced in 1984.

In an interview with Ann DeWitt Moss, McCorkle states that she "liked to write, wanted to write, and in fact, did write" from the time she was seven years old. She became seriously "hooked" on writing during her second year in college, when she enrolled in a formal writing course under Prof. Max Steele, and his encouragement of her efforts gave McCorkle "the push she needed to get started" (Moss 366). Despite Steele's reminders that, even with talent and hard work, she might never be published, McCorkle pursued a career as an author. She remarks upon the influence of other contemporary writers such as Lee Smith, who was also a student at UNC. She recalls that Smith "wrote about the kinds of things I was interested in anyway. Lee was normal in terms of her life and the way she acted. From her I learned that what I knew was important, that I could write about what I knew and make it interesting. I guess I began to realize that I had something to say. She taught me that" (Moss 366). McCorkle also studied with renowned literary critic Louis D. Rubin and has remarked that her writing has been influenced by writers such as Eudora Welty, who inspired her to feel liberated.

For several years following the completion of her studies, McCorkle held a variety of positions to support her writing career, working as a teacher, librarian, and secretary. Although she published several of her stories in college literary magazines, her first professional publications appeared shortly after the termination of her studies: "Carson" was reprinted in *Crescent Review* (1983) and "The Spell and the Beautiful Garden" appeared in *Seventeen* (1984).

In 1984 McCorkle accomplished an unprecedented feat in the publishing world: She simultaneously published her debut novels, *The Cheer Leader* and *July 7th*. This bold move by Algonquin Press—coincidentally, a press founded by McCorkle's mentor, Louis Rubin—speaks to what critic Ursula Hegi has called McCorkle's "range and versatility." The success of these two novels, and those that followed, led to invitations to teach creative writing at Duke, UNC, and Tufts.

McCorkle married Daniel Shapiro in 1987, and the couple share two children, Claudia and Robert. She currently teaches creative writing at Harvard University. She continues to write prolifically, despite the demands of teaching and family life.

MAJOR WORKS AND THEMES

Jill McCorkle most frequently deals with issues relevant to women and their relationships. While she does examine the male-female relationship, especially in works such as *Crash Diet* (1992), she focuses most acutely upon women's internal struggles with societal expectations as well as upon the negotiations inherent in successful and supportive communities of women. Further, critics have argued that McCorkle's novels may be classified as female *bildungsromans*, given their emphasis on the coming of age of young people, most often women.

McCorkle's concurrently released novels, *The Cheer Leader* and *July 7th* (1984), address the difficulties inherent in negotiating the coming of age in the contemporary South. For example, Jo, the protagonist of *The Cheer Leader*, gives every outward appearance of being a normal, well-adjusted high school student. She makes excellent grades, is extremely popular, dates the right boys, and has a bright future ahead of her. However, it rapidly becomes apparent to the reader that her life is a facade. During her adolescence, Jo questions everything about her life—her decisions, her friends, and the expectations placed upon her by her parents, friends, and society in general, simply by virtue of her looks. The pressure of conforming to these expectations finally becomes too great for Jo to bear. When she leaves home to attend college, she suffers a psychological breakdown, which manifests itself as an eating disorder that very nearly kills her. It is only by working through this crisis and learning to cope with and sort out what is expected of her—as opposed to what she expects of herself— that Jo begins moving toward psychological wholeness. By the end of the novel, Jo is on the road to recovery but is not yet a whole person. Because of Jo's fractured nature at the end of the story, the novel is "invariably compared with Sylvia Plath's *The Bell Jar*," according to Lynn Z. Bloom (297); despite the outward similarities in the novels, McCorkle's novel leaves the reader with a much more hopeful attitude toward Jo's possibilities for recovery as opposed to the relatively dark future that we expect for Plath's protagonist. As Annie Gottlieb remarked in a piece for the *New York Times Book Review*, "McCorkle's skill moves her work beyond the familiar plot" found in Plath's novel (7).

July 7th, McCorkle's "other" first novel, also demonstrates the difficulties inherent in the process of coming of age. This novel, which takes place in a small North Carolina town similar to Lumberton, deals on the surface with the aftermath of a grisly murder: A local convenience store clerk is found suffocated near a vending machine, swaddled in Saran Wrap. One witness to the events, Sam Swett, an aspiring writer en route from New York, comes of age as he "gropes toward maturity through wondering what it would be like to be each of the people he meets" (Bloom 298). Coupled with the coming-of-age motif that recurs throughout McCorkle's body of work is another theme to which she frequently returns: that of the family trying to negotiate its relationships and their boundaries and the discovery of an "atmosphere of forgiveness and reconciliation" in which "everyone gets a second—or third or fourth—chance to find shelter and succor, to live right and do well" (Bloom 299). McCorkle draws upon the Southern tradition of shared experiences that create a sense of community among an otherwise diverse group of people.

Tending to Virginia (1987) also focuses upon the growth of communal identity and specifically upon the strength of family ties in the face of adversity. Virginia Turner Ballad—Ginny Sue to her family—finds herself doubting the foundation on which her marriage is based at the worst conceivable time, as she is expecting her first child. Her growing doubts about their relationship and about her husband's love for her drive Ginny Sue back to her hometown and into the bosom of her family. She is rapidly sucked into the dysfunctionality of her family: the beloved grandmother and great-aunt who suffer from age-related memory loss; Cindy, the cousin with whom Ginny Sue has historically shared a stormy, jealous relationship, and her socially reclusive mother, Madge; and her own mother, Hannah, who, to a large extent, must tend to all of the people around her. Ginny Sue becomes ill, placing her pregnancy at risk and causing her to remain under her mother's care for several days. During this period, a ferocious storm blows in, and the entire family of women is forced to seek shelter in the same house. Their enforced confinement leads to the resolution of number of long-standing familial issues: Ginny Sue's abuse at the hands of Cindy's father, the reason for Madge's withdrawal from life, the loves and adventures of Lena and Emily Pearson. Despite the difficulties that these women experience in relating to each other, their sense of a communal identity and support system is reaffirmed, leading the novel to a satisfactory conclusion.

Another example of McCorkle's use of the *bildungsroman* is found in *Ferris Beach* (1990), which relates the story of Katie Burns, who is enamored by the fairy-tale quality of Ferris Beach. Ferris Beach exists "mostly as a nexus of illusions and fantasies" in Katie's mind, a place she associates with "huge Ferris wheels and strings of blinking lights, and cotton candy whipped and spun around a paper cone" (Loewinsohn 10). The beach itself, however, comes to represent not only a relationship that Katie's father encourages her to build with Angela, the little girl who may be his illegitimate daughter, but the "polar opposite of the closed, predictable, respectable middle-class world in which Katie grows up"—a world that is "emotionally impoverished" (Loewinsohn 10). In much the same vein as *The Cheer Leader*, *Ferris Beach* explores the coming of age of an adolescent girl who ultimately seeks liberation from the social system that would restrict her choices.

McCorkle's first collection of short stories, *Crash Diet* (1992), runs the gamut of human experience, dealing with topics such as death, grief and recovery; the death of love, relationships and marriages, and what really happens to Southern girls who reject the accepted code of conduct. Men do not fare well in this collection, being portrayed as "largely contemptible . . . but it is the world [of these stories] itself that is under indictment: the shallowness of its myths, the shoddiness of its pleasures, the cruelty of its constraints" (Butler 15). Because of the fact that it shows the only likable man found in the collection—or perhaps in spite of it—the story "Departures" is the most striking piece. "Departures" relates the story of Anna Craven, two years a widow, illustrating her gradual return to life after the death of her beloved husband and the ways in which she must negotiate this revitalization. While she misses her husband terribly, she gradually comes to defy the role of grieving widow in which her children attempt to cast her. Despite the fact that her children mean well, it is a role that ill-suits Anna, who longingly recalls the love and passion of her marriage. Rather than an ode to the dead, "Departures" celebrates life and the necessity for those left behind to continue living. Other stories detail women who are left by their husbands for younger women and the choices in men that are available to women who find themselves suddenly and unexpectedly single. According to critic Jack Butler, "The percentages feel about right. To these women, in this world, these men probably do represent the choices. Nor is it just romance that has gone bad for them. None of their other relationships work either" (15). McCorkle creates a community for each of the women who populate these stories, but the communities are unsupportive at best and dysfunctional in many cases. In other words, they offer a slice of life that is quite real to late-twentieth-century readers.

Carolina Moon (1996) once again takes place in a small North Carolina town. Queen Mary Purdy—"Quee"—opens a stop-smoking clinic, much to the surprise and horror of the town folk, owing in large part to her unorthodox methods such as massage and aromatherapy. Her venture merely scratches the surface of Fulton's unusual happenings, however, and Quee's business provides a safe venue in which many of the townspeople exorcize not only their smoking habits but their personal demons as well.

Final Vinyl Days (1998) is McCorkle's most recent offering. This collection again focuses upon relationships, coming of age, and communal identities, with the high point occurring in the story titled "Your Husband Is Cheating on Us." The framework for this piece is ostensibly provided by a conversation between two women, in which the mistress tells the wife that the husband—"Mr. Big"—is cheating on both women with a third. Readers learn the narrator's entire loveless history, her mock plans to poison the faithless lover, and the loneliness that drives her to confide in a woman who would otherwise be her natural competitor. Instead, at least from the narrator's perspective, a camaraderie develops where we might expect enmity. The pathos with which each character is drawn illustrates the innate need for connection with another human being.

CRITICAL RECEPTION

McCorkle's novels have met with high praise from critics in such prestigious sources as the *New York Times Book Review* and the *Los Angeles Times*, and her collection of short stories *Final Vinyl Days* was named a Notable Book of the Year by the *New York Times*. She has been called "funny" and "poignant" by *Publishers Weekly*, and Joanne Wilkinson has noted that McCorkle "wears her artistry lightly, casually, and she wears it well" (1855). Not only has McCorkle been well received by critics and popular readers, she has received numerous prestigious awards, including the New England Book Sellers Award, and has published stories in venues such as *Atlantic Monthly*, The *Southern Review*, The *Ladies Home Journal*, and *Cosmopolitan*.

Upon the release of *The Cheer Leader* and *July 7th*, critics were impressed by the "rare opportunity to watch her mature, because her publisher is issuing her first and second novels simultaneously. And mature she does, in one big stride" (Gottlieb 9). One of the effects of this maturation process is her ability to deliver "again and again . . . the shock of recognition. " 'That's just how it *is*,' readers across the country will say to themselves in repeated delight" (Butler 15). Throughout her career, McCorkle has been praised for the "tremendous exuberance" of her characters, for her ability to bring a diverse and rich cast of characters to life, as well as for her engaging narrative technique. Given the young age at which she began publishing her work and the success that this work has enjoyed, we should expect continued growth and prolific output from this fine writer.

BIBLIOGRAPHY

Works by Jill McCorkle

The Cheer Leader. Chapel Hill, NC: Algonquin, 1984. Reprint. New York: Penguin, 1985.
July 7th. Chapel Hill, NC: Algonquin, 1984. Reprint. New York: Penguin, 1985.
Tending to Virginia. Chapel Hill, NC: Algonquin, 1987. Reprint. Boston: G. K. Hall, 1989.
Ferris Beach. Chapel Hill, NC: Algonquin, 1990.
Crash Diet. Chapel Hill, NC: Algonquin, 1992.
Carolina Moon. Chapel Hill, NC: Algonquin, 1996.
Final Vinyl Days. New York: Fawcett, 1998.

Studies of Jill McCorkle

Bennett, Barbara. " 'Reality Burst Forth': Truth, Lies, and Secrets in the Novels of Jill Mc-Corkle. *Southern Quarterly* 36.1 (1997): 107–22.
——. "Making Peace with the (M)other." *The World Is Our Culture: Society and Culture in Contemporary Southern Writing*. Ed. Jeffrey J. Folks and Nancy Summers Folks. Lexington: University Press of Kentucky, 2000. 186–200.
——. *Understanding Jill McCorkle*. Columbia: University of South Carolina Press, 2000.
Bloom, Lynn Z. "Jill McCorkle." *Contemporary Fiction Writers of the South: A Bio-Bibliographical Sourcebook*. Ed. Joseph M. Flora and Robert Bain. Westport, CT: Greenwood Press, 1993. 295–302.
Butler, Jack. "Is There Anything Worse Than a Man?" Rev. of *Crash Diet*. *New York Times Book Review* 14 June 1992: 15–16.
Rev. of *Final Vinyl Days*. *Publisher's Weekly* 20 April 1998: 44.
Gottlieb, Annie. Rev. of *The Cheer Leader* and *July 7th*. *New York Times Book Review* 7 Oct. 1984: 9.
Hegi, Ursula. *The Cheer Leader* by Jill McCorkle. Rev. of *The Cheer Leader*. *Los Angeles Times* 15 Nov. 1984: E34.
Kane, Patricia. "When Women Tell Stories: Jill McCorkle's *Tending to Virginia*." *Notes on Contemporary Literature* 19 (1989): 7.
Lesser, Ellen. "Voices with Stories to Tell: A Conversation with Jill McCorkle." *Southern Review* 26 (1990): 53–65.
Loewinsohn, Ron. "The World across the Street." Rev. of *Ferris Beach*. *New York Times Book Review* 7 Oct. 1990: 10.
McCord, Charline R. " 'I Still See with a Southern Eye': An Interview with Jill McCorkle." *Southern Quarterly* 36.3 (1998): 103–12.

Moss, Ann DeWitt. "Jill McCorkle." *Dictionary of Literary Biography: Yearbook 1987*. Ed. J. M. Bruccoli. Detroit: Gale, 1988. 366–70.

Pierce, Todd. "Jill McCorkle: The Emergence of the New South." *Southern Studies* 5 (1994): 19–30.

Summer, Bob. "Jill McCorkle." *Publishers Weekly Interviews* 12 Oct. 1990: 44–45.

Walker, Elinor A. "Celebrating Voice and Self in Jill McCorkle's *Crash Diet*." *Notes on Contemporary Literature* 23 (1993): 11–12.

——. "Dizzying Possibilities, Plots, and Endings: Girlhood in Jill McCorkle's *Ferris Beach*." *The Girl: Construction of the Girl in Contemporary Fiction by Women*. Ed. Ruth O. Saxton. New York: St. Martin's, 1998. 79–94.

Wilkinson, Joanne. Rev. of *Carolina Moon*. *Booklist* Aug. 1996: 1855.

ELIZABETH McCRACKEN (1966–)

Roy Flannagan

BIOGRAPHY

Elizabeth McCracken was born in 1966 in Brighton, Massachusetts, to Samuel and Natalie McCracken. Her Presbyterian father was a writer and assistant to the provost of Boston University. Her mother, also a writer and editor for Boston University, was descended from a long line of rabbis including Rabbi Sharasefsky, the first to be ordained in Des Moines. Elizabeth moved with her parents and her older brother to Portland, Oregon, when she was nine months old. She then traveled to London briefly before returning to Boston at the age of seven. She describes her childhood as uneventful and uninteresting, with no great tragedies, experiences, or noticeable precocity. She liked to watch Abbott and Costello on TV and to play with her older brother. Her family took frequent trips to Des Moines, Iowa, where both families had relatives. When asked about her early life, McCracken has claimed that her family is more interesting than herself. She keeps records of her family history and documents, calling them her "Desiderata," a touchstone for her subsequent creative work.

During her teenage years, McCracken landed her first job as a librarian at the Newton Free Library in Newton, Massachusetts. She worked there for several years, shelving books and taking queries from behind the circulation desk. After not quite graduating from high school, McCracken somehow managed to study creative writing at Boston University under such mentors as Derek Walcott and George Starbuck. After graduating magna cum laude with distinction and then receiving a BA and an MA at Boston University in 1988, she went on to study creative writing at the University of Iowa with Allan Gurganus, an experience she characterized as "wanting to be a Christian and studying with Billy Sunday" (Pech 524). Earning her MFA in 1990, she undertook two year-long fellowships with the Fine Arts Work Center in Provincetown and then turned to graduate library science school at Drexel University, eventually earning an MS in library and information science in 1993.

By the time she became the circulation desk chief at the Somerville Public Library in Massachusetts, she had published her first collection of short stories, *Here's Your Hat What's Your Hurry* (1993). She was twenty-seven. Perhaps unsurprisingly, given the many librarians who appear in the collection, the American Library Association gave it the ALA Notable Book Award. McCracken continued to work at the circulation desk until 1995. The critical and popular success of her novel *Giant's House* allowed her opportunities such as being visiting writer at the Iowa Writing Festival (1997) and Western Michigan University (1998). By 1999 McCracken described herself as "unemployed, unmarried, childless, cheerful—not the stuff of riveting autobiography" (Pech 524).

MAJOR WORKS AND THEMES

Even though her fiction is usually set in Massachusetts and Iowa, Elizabeth Mc-Cracken fits loosely in the tradition of Southern gothic writers such as Carson Mc-Cullers (her favorite writer) and Flannery O'Connor. Her character-driven realist fiction often juxtaposes the grotesque and the odd with the "normal" in an attempt to fathom how bodies determine identity and the ways identity also exceeds or transcends such limits. McCracken explores how people, when looked at closely, rarely fit within normative boundaries. Individual stories in her collection, *Here's Your Hat What's Your Hurry*, often begin with a freak of some kind—a tattooed lady, a woman with no arms, a man recently released from a lifetime prison sentence—who attempt to fit in with more conformist American society. McCracken's inspirations include circus performers, old comedy acts, and the *Guinness Book of World Records*. Her interest in extremes of the physical leads her to themes similar to those in David Lynch's movie *Elephant Man*: By living on the periphery of accepted human society, freaks can help both to define what it means to be human and to bring out the inherent monstrosity of "normal" people.

Such a thematic treatment of the grotesque and the bizarre could easily lead to sensationalistic prose, but McCracken demonstrates affection for her characters' alienation and she carefully grounds her work in the quotidian concerns of middle- to lower-class small-town Americans. Critics describe her work as "romantic," and her characters often attempt to connect with others through love. In an interview, Mc-Cracken points out that "our lives are constantly transformed by love," but she qualifies this love as not physical or necessarily romantic; rather, it could just as easily be fraternal or familial (Adler 1). The librarian Peggy Cort's love for James Strickland, the giant in *The Giant's House*, is never sexually consummated. He remains cut off from her by their differing ages (she is about fifteen years older) and his huge size; consequently, her love for him, while at the center of the book, is hard to characterize. She devotes her life to James with near-obsessive fervor that sometimes borders on the erotic. She admires his attempts to transcend his abnormality through his intellectual curiosity and ambition to be more than just a giant. Otherwise fated for a kind of embittered spinsterish existence, Peggy finds in James a way to become selfless in her devotion, and James's eventual fame as the tallest man in the world seems to justify her fascination with him.

Similarly, in McCracken's collection of short stories, *Here's Your Hat What's Your Hurry*, this confluence of love and abnormality once again helps define her characters. In "It's Bad Luck to Die," Lois's abnormality is the chief sign of her husband's love. While Lois's mother bemoans the tattoos all over her daughter's body, she characterizes them as a long love letter from her deceased husband, Tiny. Thus, her freakishness is a consequence of love. In other stories, McCracken almost overloads the plots with bizarre characters. In "What We Know about the Lost Aztec Children," a child's ability to accept a circus sideshow dwarf in his household becomes a test of his acceptance of his armless mother, who once worked in the circus as well. In "Mercedes Kane," a mother admires a child prodigy from afar, but she becomes disillusioned when she invites the now-grown prodigy, Mercedes, to stay in her household with her less obviously gifted and resentful daughter, Ruthie. Naturally, Mercedes proves a big disappointment when she denies her past and pretends to be ignorant of her former knowledge. She has no place in society outside of the child's quiz shows, and so she lives in obscurity, deliberately covering up her gifts. As much as the mother wants to idolize her, her daughter, Ruthie, seeks to see through Mercedes's deceptions and fails. In the end, Mercedes recedes into the same mystery that she arrived in, becoming more a template of what others want to see in her than a fully formed character. Once again, a freak defines the limitations and the affections of the characters she encounters.

McCracken also explores the way families develop myths around themselves. McCracken's editor, Susan Kamil of Dial Press, hopes that one day McCracken will attain the exalted status of Anne Tyler, as her families often exhibit the ability of Tyler's families to create separate worlds unto themselves (6). In McCracken's short story "Some Have Entertained Angels Unaware," a father abandons his two children to a group of homeless people who have taken shelter in his home. Unaccountably, two of the homeless men adopt the two children and raise them in opposite ways. While the brother receives a strict practical upbringing with Bobby, the sister becomes educated in rebellion when her "parent" Mike teaches her how to engage in delinquent behavior without getting caught. They smoke marijuana in the balcony of a theater when she is in junior high and spend the night in a Denny's drinking coffee and writing English papers with fictionalized citations. Eventually, the homeless people form a homogenous community of their own as the children's father descends into alcoholism. Thus do new family networks form out of compassion when blood ties break apart.

In other stories, characters strive to join foster families when their actual families fall short. In the title story of the collection, Aunt Helen Beck goes from family to family, telling members that she is a relative. She is something of an emotionally isolated confidence woman, stealing one item from each household to give to the next as a housewarming present. By the end of the story, she adopts a young boy who has been largely abandoned by his mother. Their status as perpetual guests, but never actual relatives, serves as an apt metaphor for the frayed human connections throughout the collection. In *The Giant's House*, one can see James Strickland's family forming its identity on his deformity. Since Peggy Cort takes it upon herself to take care of him and organize the building of his specially designed house, the Stricklands accept her as a family member. By the end of the novel, she conceives a child with James's father and pretends it is James's, and this somewhat makeshift genetic connection cements her union with the Strickland clan. Because of this unexpected child, she becomes as much a freak in the town's eyes as James.

Another major motif in McCracken's work is the near omnipresence of libraries and librarians. When she worked in the Newton Public Library, McCracken realized at a young age that the library brought in a wider variety of humans than one would find in a sociology class, and people took books home with them, thus spurring her on to write (Pech 524). Libraries and librarians appear repeatedly in McCracken's work—they bridge the gap between books and lived experience, thereby grounding the freakishness of the stories in banal stacks of books. When a young divorcee gets stabbed ninety-six times, as she does in "Juliet," a story McCracken published in *Esquire*, the shock of knowing about that murder is filtered through the workers of the library where Judith used to frequent, muting its violence. Likewise, in *The Giant's House*, Peggy Cort can mask her misanthropy and boredom with her professional manner as a helper from behind the circulation desk. In place of the chaos and willfulness of life, the librarian seeks order and calm, the answer to anyone's question, and love becomes another form of knowledge. McCracken grounds her stories in extraordinary humility. Her incongruous depression-era sensibility, full of modesty, pragmatics, and everyday hard work, helps to temper her stories of freaks and their loves. Her affection for her characters helps her avoid the stereotyping that these kinds of characters risk.

CRITICAL RECEPTION

Elizabeth McCracken has enjoyed an uncommonly positive and generous public reception of her works. While her collection of short stories sometimes earned a B from magazines like *Publishers Weekly*, her career really gained momentum during the summer of 1996 when *The Giant's House* earned her mention as one of the "Twenty Best Young American Novelists" by *Granta* magazine. Perhaps in part because of *Granta*'s early endorsement, her novel went on to become a finalist for the National Book Award and won the Salon Book Award. Critics writing for major publications tend to praise her work effusively. Daphne Merkin, reviewing *The Giant's House* for the *New Yorker*, writes: "Somewhere in the middle of reading this book, I found myself wanting to never leave its carefully delineated, well-tended precincts" (74). *Publishers Weekly*, in its review of *Here's Your Hat What's Your Hurry*, writes that "McCracken is not merely a born raconteur; she is also an assured stylist and an astute student of human nature" (50). While professional journals have yet to provide more measured assessments of her beginning career, she has already been lauded as one of the promising authors of her generation. As Adam Mazmanian writes in *Library Journal*, "McCracken is definitely a writer to watch" (165).

BIBLIOGRAPHY

Works by Elizabeth McCracken

"Juliet." *Esquire* Jan. 1988: 88–93ff.
"Indelible Ink." *Michigan Quarterly Review* 30 (1991): 158–71.
Here's Your Hat What's Your Hurry. New York: Dial, 1993.
"The Giant of Cape Cod." *Granta* 54 (1996): 171–92.
The Giant's House. New York: Turtle Bay/Random House, 1996.
"Desiderata." *Bold Type* March 1997 (http://www.randomhouse.com/boldtype/0397/mccracken/essay.html)
"A Splendid Invention." *Salon* 17 Nov. 1997 (http://www.salon.com/feature/1997/11/cov_17mccracken.html)

"One Fiennes Day." *Elle* Dec. 1997: 152.
"Depp Charge." *Elle* June 1998: 104.
"The Road Behind." *New York Times Magazine* 8 March 1998: 54–55.
"Waters World." *Elle* Oct. 1998: 180.

Studies of Elizabeth McCracken

Adler, Laura Reynolds. "Welcome to Elizabeth McCracken's Inventive World." *Bookpage* Fiction Interview July 1996 (http://www.bookpage.com/9608bp/fiction/thegiantshouse.html).
Ermelino, Louisa. Rev. of *The Giant's House. People Weekly* 9 Sept. 1996: 31.
Rev. of *The Giant's House. Publishers Weekly* 6 May 1996: 866.
Gilbert, Matthew. "A Tall Tale." Rev. of *The Giant's House. Boston Globe* 14 July 1996: B33.
Goodman. Bob. "An Interview with Elizabeth McCracken." *Beacon Street Review* 10 (1997): 44–51.
Greenlaw, Lavinia. Rev. of *The Giant's House. Times Literary Supplement* 29 Nov. 1996: 22.
Rev. of *Here's Your Hat What's Your Hurry. Publishers Weekly* 19 April 1993: 50.
Kamil, Susan. "An Interview with Elizabeth McCracken's Editor." *Bold Type* March 1997 (http://www.randomhouse.com/boldtype/0397/mccracken/interview.html).
Kushner, Jill Menkes. "Elizabeth McCracken: Perspectives on Romance and Loss." *Literary Review* 40 (1997): 342–45.
Mazmanian, Adam. "Librarian Falls for Pituitary Giant." Rev. of *The Giant's House. Library Journal* July 1996: 162ff.
"McCracken, Elizabeth." *Contemporary Authors.* Ed. Scott Peacock. Vol. 167. Detroit: Gale, 1999. 237–38.
Merkin, Daphne. "Big: A Decade of Unlikely Happiness." Rev. of *The Giant's House. New Yorker* 29 July 1996: 74.
O'Connor, Patricia T. Rev. of *Here's Your Hat What's Your Hurry. New York Times Book Review* 4 July 1993: 17.
O'Rear, Joseph Allen. Rev. of *The Giant's House. Review of Contemporary Fiction* 17 (1997): 207–8.
Pearl, Nancy. Rev. of *The Giant's House. Booklist* 15 May 1996: 1569.
Pech, Janet. "McCracken, Elizabeth." *World Authors 1990–1995.* Ed. Clifford Thompson. New York: H. W. Wilson, 1999. 523–24.
Post, Francine. Rev. of *Here's Your Hat What's Your Hurry. Los Angeles Times Book Review* 6 June 1993: 3.
Postlethwaite, Diana. "Peggy and Goliath." Rev. of *The Giant's House. New York Times Book Review* 7 July 1996: 8.
Rendlestei, Jill E. "A Teller's Tale: Elizabeth McCracken Reveals Her Writing Inspirations." *World and I* 14 (1999): 290–95.

COLLEEN JOHNSON McELROY (1935–)

James L. Hill

BIOGRAPHY

A gifted poet, fiction and nonfiction writer, and recently folklorist, Colleen Johnson McElroy was born October 30, 1935, in St. Louis, Missouri, to Percia Purcell and Ruth Celeste Rawls. After her parents divorced in 1938, she and her mother moved in with her grandmother, Anna Belle Long, or "Mama" as she was affectionately called. Growing up in St. Louis on Kennerly Avenue in Mama's house, with its full-length boudoir mirror and wind-up Victrola, McElroy often eavesdropped on her mother and aunts while they told stories; thus, in Mama's house, she learned the rudiments of storytelling. She attended the segregated schools of St. Louis and as a teenager walked across town to attend the all-black Charles Sumner High School. In 1943 her mother married army sergeant Jesse Dalton Johnson, a Columbus, Georgia, native. As an army brat, McElroy moved often with her family, beginning her lifelong attraction to travel. She graduated from high school in 1953 and by age twenty-one had lived in St. Louis, Wyoming, Kansas, and Frankfort and Munich, Germany, where she attended college from 1953 to 1955.

When she returned to the United States in 1955, McElroy worked a variety of odd jobs, but she soon returned to college, moving home with her parents in Fort Reilly, Kansas, and enrolling in Kansas State University. In 1956 she graduated from Kansas State University and headed east with a scholarship to enter the University of Pittsburgh's Speech and Hearing Program.

From 1958 to 1966, she was a student, mother, and speech pathologist. In 1958 she married Burl Wilkinson, with whom she had two children, Kevin and Vanessa; and in 1962 she returned to Kansas State University to complete the master of science degree in speech pathology, which she received in 1963. Her multiple careers, however, took their toll, and in 1964 her marriage to Wilkinson ended. The next two years she continued working as chief clinician at a Kansas City, Missouri, rehabilitation center and managed a part-time private practice.

In 1966 McElroy migrated to the Pacific Northwest, taking a job as director of speech and hearing services at Western Washington University, Bellingham, Washington. After relocating, she was gradually seduced by the life of the academy and began taking advanced courses at Western Washington University. Under the tutelage of Colin Tweddell, professor of anthropology, she studied the relationships between language and culture, continuing her cultivation of her interests in folklore, language, and travel. Later, she entered the doctoral program at the University of Washington, where she completed her degree in 1973 in ethnolinguistic patterns of dialect differences and oral traditions. That same year, she joined the faculty of the University of Washington.

An outgrowth of her training and work as a speech therapist, McElroy's first publication was a college textbook, *Speech and Language Development for the Preschool Child: A Survey*, published in 1972. In the early 1970s, she married poet David McElroy, who adopted her two children. As an emerging writer living in Bellingham, Washington, at that time a haven for writers in the Pacific Northwest, McElroy received encouragement from Richard Hugo, John Logan, Knute Skinner, Robert Huff, and Denise Levertov. She also read for the first time black poets such as Langston Hughes, Joseph S. Cotter, Anne Spencer, Robert Hayden, Margaret Walker, and Gwendolyn Brooks and with her husband began associating with local writers. Influenced by the artistic milieu of periodic gatherings of writers, surreal theater, and experimental arts, she was drawn irretrievably into the life of a writer. Later, when she moved to Seattle, she met other writers and through the United Black Artists Guild formed relationships with Ishmael Reed, Al Young, and John Edgar Wideman. These early experiences heavily influenced her first poems, collected in a 1973 chapbook *The Mules Done Long Since Gone*. Three years later, she published *Music from Home: Selected Poems*; and in a subsequent volume in 1979, *Winters without Snow*, she detailed the pain of her 1978 divorce from David.

Although in her mid-thirties when she started writing seriously, McElroy continued to hone her poetic craft and expanded her interest to fiction, participating in a Bread Loaf Writers Workshop led by John Gardner. Subsequently in 1987 she published her first collection of short stories, *Jesus and Fat Tuesday and Other Short Stories*, and in 1990 a second volume, *Driving under the Cardboard Pines*. At the same time, she continued to write poetry. She published *Bone Flames* (1987), *Lie and Say You Love Me* (1988), and *What Madness Brought Me Here: New and Selected Poems, 1968–1988* (1990). Additionally, she became an accomplished writer of television scripts and plays, earning membership in both the Writers Guild and the Dramatists Guild. In 1982 she collaborated with Ishmael Reed on a choreopoem play, *The Wild Gardens of the Loup Garou*; and in 1987 she wrote *Follow the Drinking Gourd*, a play about Harriet Tubman. While both *Wild Gardens* and *Drinking Gourd* were performed, they were never published.

When her children reached high school age, McElroy began traveling more extensively outside the United States. Her travels took her through most of Europe, several countries in Africa, Central and South America, Japan, the Pacific, and Southeast Asia; and many images from her travels, not surprisingly, invest her fiction and poetry. Between 1977 when she completed her first Fulbright Fellowship in South America and her second Fulbright in 1993 in Madagascar, McElroy gained "a scholar's perspective" on her travels. "Each piece of writing," she concluded, "is a new port of call, full of surprises and disappointments, pleasures and intrigues"("Wherever" 143).

McElroy still lives in Seattle, where she teaches English and creative writing at the University of Washington. One of the founders of the University of Washington's highly rated MFA creative writing program, she has extended her influence beyond the academy to her mentorship of young writers in Seattle. In 1983 she also made history by becoming the first African American woman appointed full professor of English at the University of Washington.

MAJOR WORKS AND THEMES

The poetry and fiction of Colleen J. McElroy transcend the longstanding but often oversimplified black versus universal dichotomy, for while her writings embrace the African American literary tradition in all of its complexity, she often extends beyond it, exploring new subjects and links in the human continuum. In some ways, therefore, McElroy may be atypical of African American writers. Yet, in their cosmologies, themes, folklore, and origins, her writings are distinctively African American. Like many African American writers, she is intentionally autobiographical, drawing liberally on her life experiences. In some of her early poems, "Webs and Weeds," "Sidewalk Games," and "Recess" (*Music From Home*), for example, she revisits, as she often does, the locale and people of St. Louis; and in such poems as "Sweet Anna Took Time," in *Music from Home*, "Caledonia" and "Tapestries," in *Lie and Say You Love Me*, and "Ruth," in *Queen of the Ebony Isles* (1985), McElroy captures the potency of caring black family life and the strength of black people, two major themes in her writings. Additionally, she uses the dynamics of African American history and folklore to anchor her narratives. The masterful "Years That Teach What Days Don't Even Know," in *Bone Flames*, and "Foul Line—1987," in *What Madness Brought Me Here*, reveal her skillful use of history, while such poems as "Webs and Weeds" and "Amen Sister" illustrate her incorporation of folk traditions. Yet, surprisingly and perhaps uncharacteristically, she sparingly uses dialect in her fiction or poetry.

While primarily a poet, McElroy has also produced two volumes of short stories that incorporate her characteristic poetic sensibility, lyrical prose style, humor, and deftness at detailed description. In the twenty-nine stories in *Jesus and Fat Tuesday and Other Short Stories* and *Driving under the Cardboard Pines*, she presents a panorama of characters—outlaws, pimps, prostitutes, strippers, lesbians, family matrons, undertakers, losers, gang members, and futuristic lab technicians. Her fiction liberally incorporates black folk traditions; she universalizes black life in uncanny ways; and she illustrates the continua of black life, whether south to north, east to west, African American to global, or temporal to mythic. Further, some of the characters, relatives, and locales in *Jesus and Fat Tuesday* and *Driving under the Cardboard Pines* appear in more than one story, as indeed they do in her poetry. No matter what her subject matter or theme, however, McElroy interweaves the potency of African American culture into her stories.

Though McElroy's perspective may often be "A Long Way from St. Louie," her reality originates "out of a world that was segregated" (Sherman 30). Not only did the racial and social restrictions of St. Louis spawn her interest in travel, they also informed the subject matter of her fiction and poetry. Thus, in her depiction of black life, as Jennifer Margulis indicates, McElroy often focuses on the mundane or ordinary "to address more profound concerns: the lost sensual and hermetic world of childhood, the injustice of a social system prejudiced against black Americans, the loneliness of growing older" (488). In her short stories, she presents vignettes or slice-of-life glimpses of individuals coping with the realities of their lives, often circumscribed by family, community, or individual circumstance.

Set mostly in the Midwest in the early decades of the twentieth century, *Jesus and Fat Tuesday and Other Short Stories* portrays characters who do not necessarily lead exemplary lives but are admirable as they display strength and endurance in their struggles. "A Brief Spell by the River" portrays Cressy Pruitt, who is raped by Sam Packer, one of Jesse James' henchmen; but unable to negotiate the great racial divide, she must reconcile her life and move on. In "The Limitations of Jason Packard," even with the love and support of a good woman, Packard is unable to escape the setting of the sun on his way of life, while Toulouse in "Jesus and Fat Tuesday" seeks refuge in the alcohol recovery center where he works, unable to reconcile his estrangement from his family. Similarly, in the "The Return of the Apeman" in *Driving under the Cardboard Pines*, Franklin Washington cannot escape the gang life of St. Louis, while Aleeda Grace Sykes is lured back into a life of crime in "Amazing Grace and Floating Opportunity." In "Ruby-Ruby," a semiautobiographical story, the middle-class Eustacia Portugal, who is raising her sisters' children, struggles against the enduring lure of the ghetto life of the Clinton-DeWitt Projects, especially since her nieces are attracted to it. As Phillis K. Collier observes, "McElroy mostly wants us to understand how her characters operate within these states of expectation, survival, and epiphany" (110). The lives of McElroy's characters, however, often resonate beyond their personal circumstances, becoming mythic or symbolic, for like DeVeaux, Walker, and Morrison, she employs mythic dimensions to expand the meaning of her stories. In "Amazing Grace and Floating Opportunity," for example, Aleeda Sykes's struggles ultimately represent those of the black community, and Eustacia Portugal's life in "Ruby-Ruby" is emblematic of several generations of her family.

In her autobiographical essay "Wherever I Am," McElroy reveals that her interests in folk culture developed while she studied with anthropologist Colin Tweddell, and her writings reflect the blossoming of her interests. She regularly infuses African American folk culture and historical observation into her poetry and stories. In "Jeremy Franklin Simmons," for example, the protagonist is characterized as "too dumb to find his butt in the dark with a flashlight and a map" (36); and in "Amazing Grace and Floating Opportunity," Aleeda always used to remind her husband Butler that "you don't wash your feet in the same water you drink" (54). McElroy also embeds relevant and often penetrating historical observations in her stories, for when Eustacia confronts her nieces in "Ruby-Ruby," they resort to "that inherited language passed down from slavery to generations of black women who learned to speak volumes without ever saying a word" (103). Similarly, McElroy ensures that her readers are aware of the interrelatedness of cultures. Typical of such reminders is the story "Driving under the Cardboard Pines," where if Blind Birdie could see, "he would have immediately seen the similarities between that street corner Muslim and those warriors of the Sudan" (130). Thus, folk culture and history significantly enrich McElroy's narratives.

CRITICAL RECEPTION

Established as a poet long before she began writing fiction, McElroy has received most of her accolades for her poetry. She has been widely anthologized as a poet and is recognized for her lyricism, humor, rich narrative style, sense of place, and transcendence of geography. Though not as well known as other contemporary black women writers and much more critically neglected, she has received numerous awards and honors, including a National Endowment for the Arts Creative Writing Award and the Matrix Women Achievement Award for her *Queen of the Ebony Isles*. She also earned the Before Columbus American Book Award in 1985, also for *Queen of the Ebony Isles*.

In both *Jesus and Fat Tuesday and Other Short Stories* and *Driving under the Cardboard Pines*, McElroy transfers her fine poetic qualities to her narratives, and though limited, the critical reception of her fiction has been very positive. Critics believe that her fiction, like her poetry, startles but enlightens as she examines the fortitude and endurance of her characters. Additionally, she is highly praised for the dialogue and mythic dimensions of her short fiction. In recent years, too, critics have shown increased interest in McElroy's nonfiction books, *A Long Way from St. Louie: Travel Memoirs* (1997) and *Over the Lip of the World: Among the Storytellers of Madagascar* (1999), a collection of folktales. Neither as a poet nor as a fiction writer, however, has McElroy received her deserved critical attention. Her writings remain an African American treasure still unfamiliar to far too many readers.

BIBLIOGRAPHY

Works by Colleen Johnson McElroy

Speech and Language Development of the Preschool Child: A Survey. St. Louis: C. C. Thomas, 1972.

The Mules Done Long Since Gone. Seattle: Harrison-Madronna Press, 1973.

Music from Home: Selected Poems. Carbondale: Southern Illinois University Press, 1976.

Winters without Snow. San Francisco: Ishmael Reed, 1979.

Looking for a Country under Its Original Name. Yakima, WA: Blue Begonia Press, 1985.

Queen of the Ebony Isles. Middletown, CT: Wesleyan University Press, 1985.

Bone Flames. Middletown, CT: Wesleyan University Press, 1987.

Jesus and Fat Tuesday and Other Short Stories. Berkeley, CA: Creative Arts, 1987.

Lie and Say You Love Me. Tacoma, WA: Circinatum Press, 1988.

Driving under the Cardboard Pines. Berkeley, CA: Creative Arts, 1990.

What Madness Brought Me Here: New and Selected Poems, 1968–1988. Hanover, NH: University Press of New England, 1990.

"Wherever I Am." *Contemporary Authors Autobiography Series*. Ed. Joyce Nakamura. Vol. 21. Detroit: Gale, 1995. 119–44.

A Long Way from St. Louie: Travel Memoirs. Minneapolis: Coffee House, 1997.

Travelling Music. Ashland, OR: Storyline Press, 1998.

Over the Lip of the World: Among the Storytellers of Madagascar. Seattle: University of Washington Press, 1999.

Studies of Colleen Johnson McElroy

Arnold, Kyle. Rev. of *Music from Home: Selected Poems*. *Encore* 17 Jan. 1977: 46–47.

Collier, Phillis K. Rev. of *Jesus and Fat Tuesday and Other Short Stories*. *Prairie Schooner* (1989): 109–10.

Gomez, Jewelle. "Homeward Bound." Rev. of *Driving under the Cardboard Pines*. *Kenyon Review* 13 (1991): 226–30.

Hemley, Robin. Rev. of *Jesus and Fat Tuesday and Other Short Stories*. *Obsidian* 11 (1998): 82–85.

Margulis, Jennifer. "Colleen McElroy." *Oxford Companion to African American Literature*. Ed. William Andrews, Frances Foster, and Trudier Harris. New York: Oxford University Press, 1997. 488.

"McElroy, Colleen J." *Contemporary Authors*. Ed. Clare Kinsman. Vol. 49–52. Detroit: Gale, 1975. 363.

"McElroy, Colleen J." *Black Writers: A Selection of Sketches from Contemporary Authors*. Ed. Linda Metzger. Detroit: Gale, 1989. 397–98.

"McElroy, Colleen J." *Contemporary Authors New Revision Series*. Ed. Frances Locher and Ann Envory. Vol. 2. Detroit: Gale, 1989. 451.

Medea, Andra. "Colleen McElroy." *Black Women in America*. Ed. Darlene Clark Hine. Vol. 2. New York: Facts on File, 1997. 132–33.

Rhone, Shuana. "Author and Poet Colleen McElroy Takes Long Way Home." *St. Louis Post-Dispatch* 14 April 1998: D1.

Sherman, Charlotte W. "Walking across the Floor: A Conversation with Colleen J. McElroy." *American Visions* 10 (1998): 30.

Strickland, Daryl. "Seattle's Black Voices." *Seattle Times* 16 Feb. 1997: 1.

TERRY McMILLAN (1951–)

Suzanne Disheroon-Green

BIOGRAPHY

The author of five wildly successful novels, Terry McMillan enjoys success among critics and popular readers alike. The daughter of Edward McMillan and Madeline Washington Tillman, the author grew up in Port Huron, Michigan, a suburb roughly sixty miles outside of Detroit. Because of her father's alcoholism and the abuse that resulted, McMillan and her four siblings were cared for primarily by her mother, who worked in an auto factory and as a domestic.

The daughter of working-class parents who did not place a great deal of emphasis on reading—her mother was too busy earning a living—McMillan discovered the joys of reading while working in a local library shelving books as a teenager. It was not until she began working at the library that she began reading the writings of African American writers, most notably James Baldwin. She reveals that she initially was embarrassed when she encountered one of Baldwin's books, because "I was too afraid. I couldn't imagine that he'd have anything better or different to say than Thomas Mann, Henry Thoreau, Ralph Waldo Emerson. . . . Needless to say, I was not just naive, but had not yet acquired an ounce of black pride" (Trescott D1).

Following her high school years, McMillan moved to Los Angeles and began taking writing courses at Los Angeles Community College. She earned a bachelor's degree from the University of California at Berkeley in 1979. Upon the completion of her undergraduate degree, McMillan enrolled at Columbia University, where she completed the MFA degree. During this time, she lived with Leonard Welch and suffered the effects of substance abuse. After three years, she joined Alcoholics Anonymous and began recovering from her addictions. She shares a son, Solomon Welch, with her former lover and is presently married to Jonathan Plummer.

McMillan has taught writing at Stanford University, the University of Wyoming, and the University of Arizona. She has been the recipient of a fellowship from the National Endowment for the Arts (1988) and the American Book Award of the Before

Columbus Foundation (1987). McMillan is a prolific writer who has garnered a great deal of critical attention, and her work has been compared with that of Mark Twain and Zora Neale Hurston.

MAJOR WORKS AND THEMES

McMillan's body of work addresses the struggles of African American women as they attempt to find suitable lovers and/or husbands, to achieve financial success, and to raise their families. McMillan does not attempt to sanitize the experience of the African American woman, who, McMillan argues, often suffers at the hands of the African American man who cannot—or will not—accept his share of responsibility for providing for his family, rearing his children, and honoring his commitments. McMillan's characters frequently must overcome adversity in order to prosper, regardless of whether that adversity is financial or emotional.

McMillan is also credited with the (re)creation of a new genre in the American literary tradition: the urban romance novel (Porter 41–42). Rather than setting her stories of African American women in the rural South, as many writers have, Mc-Millan places her characters in urban and suburban areas and shows them negotiating the difficulties of jobs, relationships, financial obligations, and child-rearing issues in more contemporary environments than those examined by her literary predecessors. The element of place in McMillan's fiction has served as an example to other contemporary urban romance novelists such as Bebe Moore Campbell and Tina McElroy Ansa.

McMillan's first novel, *Mama* (1987), is largely autobiographical, telling the story of her mother's difficulties with a womanizing husband. Mama herself struggles with drug addiction and alcoholism, but ultimately her love for her children and her sense of responsibility to them and to herself give her the fortitude to overcome her addictions. As the title suggests, the novel is a celebration of the "resilience and ingenuity" of Mama, the central character. The novel began as a short story; as McMillan sought feedback on the piece, readers told her repeatedly that it really should be a novel rather than a story. After two stints at renowned artists' colonies, McMillan turned *Mama* from a story into a four-hundred-page manuscript. Houghton Mifflin agreed to publish the book within days of receiving it. Readers of *Mama* were impressed with the "runaway narrative pulling a crowded cast of funny, earthy characters" (Sayers 8).

Disappearing Acts (1989) departs somewhat from McMillan's standard themes, as the author chooses to deal with a romance between a successful businesswoman and a blue-collar working man. Critics praised the novel for its narrative technique, which alternates between the two star-crossed main characters. The two fall in love at first sight, move in together, and try valiantly to overcome the fears that have resulted from past loves that ended badly. *Disappearing Acts* speaks to McMillan's position that "even though a lot of 'professional' men claim to want a smart, independent woman, they're kidding themselves," pointing out that "these men do not feel secure unless they are with passive women or with women who will back down, back off, or just acquiesce until they appear to be tamed" ("Terry (L.) McMillan" par. 14). Critics credit McMillan with creating "sympathetic portraits of black men" in *Disappearing Acts* and for depicting "relationships between black men and black women as something more than the relationship between victimizer and victim, oppressor and oppressed" ("Terry (L.) McMillan" par. 16). In this regard, McMillan's work moves beyond that of African American women writers such as Zora Neale Hurston and Alice Walker, each of whom tends to depict her women characters as the "mules of the world," who are perpetually oppressed.

The subject matter of *Disappearing Acts* caused McMillan to become entangled in what has been called a landmark legal dispute with her former lover, who sued her for allegedly defaming his character. McMillan created in the character of Franklin "the voice of a deeply good person plagued with much anger" (Bronson 1). Despite the claims of her former partner that the male character in *Disappearing Acts* was recognizable as himself, his claim was dismissed by the court, to the great relief of fiction writers.

McMillan's first major success was *Waiting to Exhale* (1992), which has since been made into a motion picture for which McMillan wrote the screenplay. *Waiting to Exhale* follows the lives of four women, detailing their relationships with men as they search for the man who will allow them to "exhale"—to let down their guard and relax in the safety of a loving relationship. On the surface, these women appear to have everything, except for the love of a good man. The theme of the book speaks to "men's fear of commitment," with the narrative developing a closely related theme dealing with the fear of growing old alone. *Waiting to Exhale* is a strong example of the urban romance genre, the revival of which McMillan is credited for.

How Stella Got Her Groove Back (1996) once again returns to her theme of the trials of a successful woman as she attempts to negotiate meaningful relationships with men. *Stella* tells the story of a single, financially independent woman who has become disenchanted with her seemingly storybook life. She has a great job, a loving son, a mansion, and a sizable, if somewhat troublesome, family. When Stella loses her job, she suddenly finds herself cast adrift, unsure of what direction she should go next. She decides to take a vacation to Jamaica to clear her mind and unexpectedly falls in love with a man twenty years her junior. Initially believing their relationship to be an infatuation, Stella returns to the states at the end of her vacation but finds herself increasingly drawn to the beautiful, kind-hearted young man. Despite the obstacles to their relationship, not the least of which is the reticence of Stella herself to embrace the young man as an equal rather than as a child—a "boy toy"—the couple finally decides to embark on a life together. Stella rediscovers her "lost sense of joy and fun" and finds love in the bargain.

Many critics found *Stella* a "less than engaging" read (Coughlin 21), and much as with *Mama*, critics have pointed out its seemingly autobiographical nature. McMillan's ongoing relationship with Jonathan Plummer—similar to the Winston character in *Stella*, Plummer is substantially younger than McMillan—certainly invites this comparison. However, McMillan emphatically argues that "Stella isn't a reinvention of myself. She's only part of my persona. . . . What I give my characters are my concerns, which for the most part are grounded in reality" (Porter 41).

A Day Late and a Dollar Short (2001) has been called a tour-de-force by critics. The story of the Prices, a somewhat dysfunctional family, *A Day Late and a Dollar Short* chronicles the ebb and flow of the relationships between Viola, the mother who serves as the backbone for a family of four children with a variety of addictions and resentments, and an erstwhile husband who has left her for a younger woman after thirty-eight years. The narrative of the novel shifts frequently among each of the major characters, and critics disagree on the success of the technique in this novel. Janet Maslin has called McMillan's latest effort "pandering . . . to daytime television" (E11), while Ruth Coughlin has argued that *A Day Late and a Dollar Short* is a refreshingly rejuvenated effort by McMillan.

CRITICAL RECEPTION

McMillan's first novel received substantial critical attention—far more than is generally lavished on a first novel by an unknown writer—because of her own tireless self-promotion. Whereas publishers generally arrange public signings, readings, and book tours, these events often come along with the publication of a second or even a third successful book. McMillan, however, was determined that *Mama* would be a success and, accordingly, undertook the arrangement of a publicity tour herself. Bookstores found her approach refreshing, and she received a substantial number of positive reviews. Not surprisingly, *Mama* went into its third printing just six weeks after its initial release.

Critics have often addressed the amount of profanity and the level of violence that are present in McMillan's works. The author has remarked that using earthy language is one way of keeping her narratives fresh and realistic, of keeping her language usage accurate. As she said in *Publishers Weekly*: "That's the way we talk. And I want to know why I've never read a review where they complain about the language that male writers use" (Smith 51). McMillan seems to intuitively understand the "backlash to success, especially if you're black and female—black and/or female" (Porter 42). She sums up her attitude succinctly: "You know my mama used to say, 'Always have a thick skin, because people are gonna talk about you if you do, and talk about you if you don't. So f*** 'em' " (Porter 42).

Instead of dwelling on the opinions of critics and readers, then, McMillan focuses on "my story, and telling it, and feeling it. And that's how I write. And that's why I write" (Porter 42). McMillan uses autobiography as a tool when it is useful to the development of her narratives, with little concern for the fallout. This strategy clearly works for McMillan, whose earthy, realistic style and systematic refusal to depict African American women in stereotypical, oppressed roles have led to great success.

BIBLIOGRAPHY

Works by Terry McMillan

Mama. Boston: Houghton Mifflin, 1987.
Disappearing Acts. New York: Viking, 1989.
Ed. *Breaking Ice: An Anthology of Contemporary African-American Fiction*. New York: Viking, 1990.
Waiting to Exhale. New York: Viking, 1992.
Waiting to Exhale. Screenplay. Schindler–Swerdlow Productions. Twentieth Century Fox Films, 1995.
How Stella Got Her Groove Back. New York: Viking, 1996.
A Day Late and a Dollar Short. New York: Viking, 2001.

Studies of Terry McMillan

Bronson, Tammy J. "Terry McMillan: Overview." *Contemporary Popular Writers*. Ed. Dave Mote. Detroit: St. James Press, 1997.

Coughlin, Ruth. Rev. of *A Day Late and a Dollar Short*. *New York Times Book Review* 4 Feb. 2001: 21.

Dandridge, Rita B. "Debunking the Beauty Myth in Terry McMillan's *Waiting to Exhale*." *Language, Rhythm, and Sound: Black Popular Cultures into the Twenty-First Century*. Ed. Joseph K. Adjaye and Adrianne R. Andrews. Pittsburgh: University of Pittsburgh Press, 1997. 121–33.

——. "Debunking the Motherhood Myth in Terry McMillan's *Mama*." *CLA Journal* 41 (1998): 405–16.

——. "Terry McMillan." *Contemporary African American Novelists: A Bio-Bibliographical Critical Sourcebook*. Ed. Emmanuel S. Nelson and Deborah G. Plant. Westport, CT: Greenwood Press, 1999. 319–26.

Ellerby, Janet Mason. "Deposing the Man of the House: Terry McMillan Rewrites the Family." *MELUS* 22 (1997): 105–17.

Harris, Tina M. "Interrogating the Representation of African American Female Identity in the Films *Waiting to Exhale* and *Set It Off*." *Popular Culture Review* 10 (1999): 43–53.

—— and Patricia S. Hill. "*Waiting to Exhale* or 'Breath(ing) Again': A Search for Identity, Empowerment, and Love in the 1990's." *Women and Language* 21 (1998): 9–20.

Jackson, Edward M. "Images of Black Males in Terry McMillan's *Waiting to Exhale*." *MAWA Review* 8 (1993): 20–26.

Maslin, Janet. "Get a Grip, Girlfriend: You Can Deal with It." Rev. of *A Day Late and a Dollar Short*. *New York Times Book Review* 18 Jan. 2001: E11.

Podolsky, Marjorie. "Black Women Writers Playing the 'Dozens.' " *Pennsylvania English* 20 (1996): 3–11.

Porter, Evette. "My Novel, Myself." *Village Voice* 21 May 1996: 41–42.

Saunders, James Robert. "A Missing Brother: The Ultimate Inadequacy of the Reverend Jasper." *The Wayward Preacher in the Literature of African American Women*. New York: McFarland, 1995. 125–44.

Sayers, Valerie. Rev. of *Disappearing Acts*. *New York Times Book Review* 6 Aug. 1989: 8.

Smith, Wendy. "An Interview with Terry McMillan." *Publisher's Weekly* 11 May 1992: 50–51.

"Terry (L.) McMillan." *Contemporary Authors Online*. Detroit: Gale, 1999 (http://www.galenet.com).

"Terry McMillan." *Contemporary Literary Criticism*. Detroit: Gale, 2000.

Trescott, Jacqueline. "The Urban Author, Straight to the Point. Terry McMillan, Pulling Together the Urgent Fiction of Black Life." *Washington Post* 17 Nov. 1990: D1.

TONI MORRISON (1931–)

Julie Buckner Armstrong

BIOGRAPHY

No official biography of Toni Morrison exists to date, but future writers may note how her life story mirrors key events in African American history. Not surprisingly, her novels often take these events as themes, deepening readers' cultural knowledge of a past that, until recently, has not received the recognition that it deserves. From the 1970s to the 1980s, many writers and scholars, Morrison included, struggled to bring that cultural knowledge into American consciousness; in 1993, when she became the first African American to win the Nobel Prize for literature, that struggle reached a watershed moment.

The known facts of Toni Morrison's personal history begin near the turn of the century, with her grandparents living in the Deep South as sharecroppers and her parents later joining the great migration out, like so many African Americans during the reconstruction and Jim Crow eras. Ella Ramah Willis, Morrison's mother, left Alabama with her family to escape a legacy of racism—their land had been taken away by whites—and eventually found work in various domestic jobs. George Wofford, Morrison's father, left Georgia for the economic promise of an industrialized North, only to find that he often had to hold several jobs at once: welder, construction worker, and car washer, to name a few. The two met and married in Lorain, Ohio, and on February 18, 1931, Ramah gave birth to Toni, originally named Chloe Anthony Wofford, who was the second of their four children. The Woffords created a stable home life, emphasizing education, hard work, and self-worth and filling their children's lives with music and storytelling. In many ways, their family history encapsulates the American dream, but its undertones of economic and racial hardship also reveal the dream's limitations.

The groundwork for Morrison's writing ability was laid long before her actual career as a novelist began. She read widely as a child and was encouraged in her family's fondness for sharing supernatural tales. In college, she majored in English and minored in the classics, graduating from Howard University in 1953 and going on to complete an MA from Cornell University in 1955, where she wrote a master's thesis on William Faulkner and Virginia Woolf. Later, as a teacher and then as an editor, Morrison gained respect for her ability to recognize and foster writing talent. She did not publish her own first novel, however, until she was nearly forty years old.

Chloe Anthony Wofford transformed into Toni Morrison—teacher, editor, and writer—between 1950 and 1970, while the civil rights and black arts movements encouraged African Americans in these fields. While in college, Morrison changed her first name to Toni, she says, because people had trouble pronouncing Chloe. After receiving her MA, she taught English at Texas Southern and Howard Universities. Between 1958 and 1964, she married Harold Morrison, a Jamaican architect, had two sons, Harold Ford and Slade Kevin, divorced, and returned to Lorain. In 1965 she accepted a position with a textbook subsidiary of Random House in Syracuse, New York, where the loneliness of being a single parent in a town where she knew no one prompted her to return to a short story she had written while married and teaching at Howard—a work that later became *The Bluest Eye* (1970). A promotion to senior editor sent Morrison to New York City to work with such African American women writers as Toni Cade Bambara, Gayl Jones, and Angela Davis. During this time, Morrison also edited a scrapbook of black history, *The Black Book* (1974), compiled by Middleton Harris. During her early days with Random House, Morrison also kept working on *The Bluest Eye*, which was rejected several times before Holt, Rinehart, and Winston published it in 1970.

Encouraged by her first work, Morrison began to focus on writing and teaching, although she continued to work as an editor for Random House until 1984. Since 1971 she has served on the faculty of several universities, among them the State Universities of New York at Purchase and Albany, Yale, Bard, and, beginning in 1989, Princeton, where she is currently the Robert F. Goheen Professor of the Humanities. Her novels have received numerous awards, including the National Book Critics Circle Award and the American Academy of Arts and Letters Award for *Song of Solomon* (1977), the Robert F. Kennedy Award and Pulitzer Prize for *Beloved* (1987), and culminating in the 1993 Nobel Prize for literature. Other literary works include *Sula* (1974), *Tar Baby* (1981), *Jazz* (1992), and *Paradise* (1997).

Since the publication of *Song of Solomon*, Morrison has increasingly found herself a public figure—the subject of television documentaries and talk shows, magazine covers, and even a Swedish postage stamp—acting most frequently as a spokesperson for American race and gender relations. Her work as writer and editor has been credited with helping to establish a renaissance of African American women writers and contributing to a more culturally diverse literary canon. She has authored a critical work, *Playing in the Dark: Whiteness and the Literary Imagination* (1992), that draws attention to the previously neglected role of the Africanist presence in American literature. She has edited two books of commentary on major events of the 1990s, *Racing Justice, En-Gendering Power: Essays on Anita Hill, Clarence Thomas, and the Construction of Social Reality* (1992) and *Birth of a Nation'hood: Gaze, Script, and Spectacle in the O. J. Simpson Case* (1997). Morrison has also tried her hand at a variety of creative pieces, including *Dreaming Emmett*, a play commissioned by the New York State Writers Institute in 1986 to commemorate the first federal celebration of the birth of Martin Luther King, Jr., and the lyrics to *Honey and Rue* (1995), an operatic piece commissioned by Carnegie Hall. The twentieth century's close found her continuing to ride the crest of her creative powers as a cultural force to be reckoned with.

MAJOR WORKS AND THEMES

Morrison's novels can be said to constitute an imaginative history of African Americans, blending historical accuracy and realism with supernatural elements and folklore. In a 1986 interview with Christina Davis, Morrison describes her fictional project as one that involves recovery: "The reclamation of the history of black people in this country is paramount in its importance because while you can't really blame the conqueror for writing history his own way, you can certainly debate it. There's a great deal of obfuscation and distortion and erasure, so that the presence and the heartbeat of black people has been systematically annihilated in many, many ways, and the job of recovery is ours" (quoted in Taylor-Guthrie 224–25).

In Morrison's fiction, recovery has two meanings. The term refers primarily to the reconstruction of an insufficiently acknowledged African American past and its rich traditions in myth and storytelling. Historical recovery, in turn, can foster healing: Restoring the presence leads to restoring the soul. By producing narratives that run counter to official histories and traditional ways of knowing the past, Morrison enriches her readers' lives and redefines the American mosaic. For characters in her novels, however, healing never comes easily: The past may exist as something to recover from more than revisit, or the supernatural may be an insufficient antidote for real problems. Rather than creating panaceas, Morrison invites readers to mourn as well as celebrate and, perhaps more importantly, to question our most fundamental notions about the way American history and culture are constructed.

In three of Morrison's novels, the past is a trauma that characters must recover from, and they rely upon violent, but not fully successful, means of doing so. Morrison's most poignant work, *Beloved*, recounts the psychological horrors of slavery that linger in the mind long after physical freedom has been obtained. For Sethe, an escaped slave, those horrors reach their nadir when she murders her own baby girl rather than have the child taken back to the plantation, ironically named "Sweet Home." The daughter's ghost continues to haunt Sethe, breaking up her family, driving away the community, and eventually leading Sethe to the brink of death herself. Only when the townspeople come together to exorcise Beloved's ghost can Sethe, along with her Sweet Home friend Paul D, begin her recovery process. The novel's ending suggests, however, that while the ghost of the past may be forgotten, it is never completely gone.

Paradise and *Jazz* take African-American history forward—into the great migration of families to western and northern states from the reconstruction and Jim Crow South, where rights and freedoms enacted by federal law rarely materialized in fact. While characters in these novels seem to be functioning normally and successfully in their new locations, their premigration experiences continue to boil under the surface, leading them to destructive acts. In *Paradise*, inhabitants of an Oklahoma town find their refuge from whites unraveling under the pressure of class and skin-color prejudice. Town fathers exert an enormous amount of control trying to eliminate difference and prevent change, but their efforts result in a violent outburst that destroys a nearby commune of women. The supernatural makes an appearance in this novel's ambiguous ending: Are the women killed, do they escape, do they live on as ghosts, and, most important, does their exorcism in any way help preserve Paradise? Set during the Harlem Renaissance, *Jazz* also takes an act of violence as its central event. After Joe Trace murders his much younger lover, Dorcas, his wife, Violet, is driven by jealousy to mutilate the girl's corpse. Because of past losses, Joe and Violet cannot cope with the possibility of loss in the present; like Sethe and the townspeople of Paradise, they resort to drastic means to prevent further violence against their souls. These novels, often seen as a trilogy, offer readers important history lessons: Although recovery as a process is often complicated and incomplete, traumatic events of the past must be confronted if one is to move forward into the future.

The Bluest Eye and *Sula* cover African American experience in mid-century, where individuals lived in less fear but still felt the effects of social marginalization. In these novels, the past is not as much the problem for characters as prevailing cultural norms; however, like *Beloved, Paradise,* and *Jazz,* they show how individuals and communities can be driven to drastic means while attempting to heal. *The Bluest Eye* examines how aesthetic standards derived from white culture can be detrimental to blacks. Because the Breedlove family believe themselves physically ugly, their lives descend into existential ugliness: The mother Pauline rejects her own family in favor of her white employer's home and children, the father Cholly's misguided attempts to love his daughter Pecola result in rape, and she believes that having blue eyes will deliver her from poverty and abuse. Pecola is a child whom no one can save: not the stable, loving MacTeer family who takes her in, the prostitutes who accept her for herself, or the character named Soaphead Church, a minister and pedophile whose attempt to make her believe that she has blue eyes finally drives her over the edge of sanity. In *Sula*, residents of the Bottom inhabit the rocky hillside land rejected by white people in the valley. They look to Sula as a scapegoat for all their woes because of her unconventional lifestyle, while Sula looks to her friend Nell for comfort and stability. When Sula has an affair with Nell's husband, loses her friend, and ultimately dies alone, Bottom residents are left at a loss. The novel ends tragically with many killed inside a collapsing tunnel and their land eventually returned to whites, who decide that they prefer hillside homes after all.

While *The Bluest Eye* and *Sula* castigate white culture in general for practices and values that traumatize blacks, *Tar Baby* and *Song of Solomon* focus on two particular institutions: traditional nuclear families and middle-class respectability. Both of these novels, set in contemporary times, bring Morrison's examination of African American experience into the present moment and posit recovery of history and myth as cure for modern spiritual bankruptcy. *Tar Baby*'s Street family—white, well off, and relatively self-sufficient on their West Indian plantation—live with their servants Ondine and Sydney, characters described as well-bred "Philadelphia Negroes." The Streets' outward show of success, however, masks a dysfunctional household with a history of child abuse at its core. The novel's revelations are set in motion by the return of Jadine, Ondine and Sydney's niece, whom the Streets have helped toward a modeling career, and the arrival of Son, who stows away on Margaret Street's boat but is later invited into the Street home. Son eventually saves himself from these characters' superficial respectability through apparently supernatural means: Running from his obsession with Jadine, he becomes absorbed into the island itself—apparently joining the legendary French cavaliers who haunt it. Milkman, in *Song of Solomon*, experiences a similar fate, and his story stands as one of Morrison's clearest statements on the possibilities for historical and psychic recovery. As Milkman's last name, Dead, suggests, he is emotionally and culturally stunted. His family, although traditional and successful, are trapped in a cycle of anger and resentment. Milkman has no ties to his past or to any person, with the exception of his aunt, Pilate, who lives with her daughter, Reba, and granddaughter, Hagar, and whose immediate family offers a spiritually nourishing counterpoint to Milkman's own. (Similar multigenerational trios exist in *Sula* and *Beloved*, indicating Morrison's belief that "traditional" family may be defined differently from the father/mother/two-children norm.) Only by seeking out his family's history can Milkman grow, and the novel's end leaves him presumably learning, like his great-grandfather before him, how to fly. As in several Morrison novels, however, this ending poses problems. Is Milkman's flight literal or metaphorical? Does it represent healing or escape? In interviews, Morrison has explained that this ambiguity is deliberate. Her fictional goal is not so much to document a character's recovery as to engage readers in the process of revising our own understanding of the history, myths, and traditions we have been given. Morrison's art is that of the storyteller, who depends upon listener participation to create meaning and who transmits culture in ways often more profound than those who delineate our official versions of the past.

CRITICAL RECEPTION

Toni Morrison is one of those rare authors whose works achieve critical and commercial success. She is both Nobel Prize winner and best-selling author, the focus of dozens of recent doctoral dissertations, and a popular icon. The secret of Morrison's success lies in her writing's ability to transcend perceived oppositions. Her fiction, for example, makes ideological as well as aesthetic statements. Often probing emotionally and politically charged subject matters such as slavery and racism, Morrison has a large following of readers from diverse backgrounds. Her works can be both accessible and technically complicated, drawing upon conventions of classical literature as well as vernacular culture. Her narratives are not always organized linearly—scenes shift between the supernatural and the realistic—and her endings are frequently ambiguous. Her prose is always lyrical, filled with hypnotic sentences. Such emotional and technical difficulty, rather than turning readers off, more often seems to pull them in. Morrison tells stories that many do not want to hear, and her means of telling often leaves readers spellbound: The horrific becomes beautiful, the pitiable becomes infused with dignity, the hidden is brought into full view. Hers is an art of cultural memory that speaks to readers from a variety of perspectives.

Such blurring of boundaries leaves Morrison's work difficult to classify. She does not fit clearly into one literary tradition, but many have been eager to claim her. Harold Bloom argues that her fractured narratives and sensuous syntax place her within a modernist context, with William Faulkner and Virginia Woolf serving as literary progenitors (they are, of course, subjects of her master's thesis). Henry Louis Gates places her combination of black vernacular and poetic lyricism in an African American tradition that includes James Baldwin and Zora Neale Hurston. Early books on Morrison by Trudier Harris and Denise Heinze examine in detail how the author manipulates traditional African American fictional elements such as folklore and the theme of double-consciousness. Another early study by Elliot Butler-Evans examines Morrison more specifically as a *female* African American writer, comparing her narrative strategies with those of Alice Walker and Toni Cade Bambara. Others have placed Morrison within a female context that is not necessarily African American. Marilyn Sanders Mobley compares her use of folklore with that of Sarah Orne Jewett, and Barbara Hill Rigney calls Morrison's writing *l'écriture féminine*, as defined by French feminist critics Julia Kristeva and Hélène Cixous. Jill Matus has contextualized Morrison as a feminist postcolonial writer but notes how difficult the author is to classify under any rubric. The tendency to pigeonhole authors can be reductive in itself, and Morrison eschews all labels placed upon her writing: "I am not *like* James Joyce; I am not *like* Thomas Hardy; I am not *like* Faulkner. I am not *like* in that sense," she explained to Nellie McKay in 1983 (quoted in Taylor-Guthrie 152).

No matter what literary tradition Morrison is cast into, her influence on contemporary writing is undeniable. Even before winning the Nobel Prize, Morrison was recognized as a major force in American letters, the primary figure among a renaissance of African American women writers and a key contributor to a changing literary canon in the 1980s. Her rise to success has not been without controversy, however. In the introduction to a collection of essays, Nancy J. Peterson traces Morrison's critical reception, noting that many reviewers have criticized her writing as too emotional or unnecessarily difficult; yet this same introduction explains that such dissenting voices are soon drowned out by praise for the author. Morrison's versatility as a writer along with her role as public intellectual have contributed to this celebration of her talents. While posing a challenge to the categories that critics often try to place upon literature, Morrison has also challenged existing ideas about literary traditions in general. By asking questions about who defines those traditions and why, about who gets included using which criteria, Morrison as writer and critic has helped to expand contemporary notions of American and world literature.

BIBLIOGRAPHY

Works by Toni Morrison

The Bluest Eye. New York: Holt, Rinehart, 1970.
Ed. *The Black Book*. Compiled by Middleton Harris. New York: Random House, 1974.
Sula. New York: Knopf, 1974.
Song of Solomon. New York: Knopf, 1977.
Tar Baby. New York: Knopf, 1981.
Dreaming Emmett. Albany, NY, performed. 4 January 1986.
Beloved. New York: Knopf, 1987.
Jazz. New York: Knopf, 1992.
Playing in the Dark: Whiteness and the Literary Imagination. New York: Vintage, 1992.
Ed. *Race-ing Justice, En-Gendering Power: Essays on Anita Hill, Clarence Thomas, and the Construction of Social Reality*. New York: Pantheon, 1992.
Lyricist. *Honey and Rue*. Composed and conducted by André Previn. Performed by Kathleen Battle and the Orchestra of Saint Luke's. Deutsche Grammophon, 1995.
Morrison, Toni, and Claudia Brodsky Lacour, eds. *Birth of a Nation'hood: Gaze, Script, and Spectacle in the O. J. Simpson Case*. New York: Pantheon, 1997.
Paradise. New York: Knopf, 1997.

Studies of Toni Morrison

Bjork, Patrick Bryce. *The Novels of Toni Morrison.* New York: Peter Lang, 1992.

Bloom, Harold, ed. *Toni Morrison: Modern Critical Views.* New York: Chelsea House, 1990.

Butler-Evans, Elliot. *Race, Gender, and Desire: Narrative Strategies in the Fiction of Toni Cade Bambara, Toni Morrison, and Alice Walker.* Philadelphia: Temple University Press, 1989.

Carmean, Karen. *Toni Morrison's World of Fiction.* Troy, NY: Whitson, 1993.

Furman, Jan. *Toni Morrison's Fiction.* Columbia: University of South Carolina Press, 1996.

Gates, Henry Louis, Jr., and K. A. Appiah, eds. *Toni Morrison: Critical Perspectives Past and Present.* New York: Amistad, 1993.

Grewel, Gurleen. *Circles of Sorrow, Lines of Struggle: The Novels of Toni Morrison.* Baton Rouge: Louisiana State University Press, 1998.

Harding, Wendy, and Jacky Martin. *A World of Difference: An Inter-Cultural Study of Toni Morrison's Novels.* New York: Greenwood Press, 1994.

Harris, Trudier. *Fiction and Folklore: The Novels of Toni Morrison.* Knoxville: University of Tennessee Press, 1991.

Heinze, Denise. *The Dilemma of Double-Consciousness: Toni Morrison's Novels.* Athens: University of Georgia Press, 1993.

Holloway, Karla F. C., and Stephanie A. Demetrakopoulos, eds. *New Dimensions of Spirituality: A Biracial and Bicultural Reading of the Novels of Toni Morrison.* New York: Greenwood Press, 1987.

Jones, Bessie W., and Audrey L. Vinson. *The World of Toni Morrison: Explorations in Literary Criticism.* Dubuque, IA: Kendall-Hunt, 1985.

Kolmerten, Carol A., Stephen M. Ross, and Judith Bryant Wittenberg, eds. *Unflinching Gaze: Morrison and Faulkner Re-Envisioned.* Jackson: University of Mississippi Press, 1997.

Matus, Jill. *Toni Morrison.* Manchester, UK: Manchester University Press, 1998.

McKay, Nellie Y., ed. *Critical Essays on Toni Morrison.* Boston: Hall, 1988.

McKay, Nellie Y., and Kathryn Earle, eds. *Approaches to Teaching the Novels of Toni Morrison.* New York: MLA, 1997.

McKee, Patricia. *Producing American Races: Henry James, William Faulkner, Toni Morrison.* Durham: Duke University Press, 1999.

Middleton, David L., ed. *Toni Morrison: An Annotated Bibliography.* New York: Garland, 1987.

——. *Toni Morrison's Fiction: Contemporary Criticism.* New York: Garland, 1997.

Mobley, Marilyn Sanders. *Folk Roots and Mythic Wings in Sarah Orne Jewett and Toni Morrison: The Cultural Function of Narrative.* Baton Rouge: Louisiana State University Press, 1991.

Otten, Terry. *The Crime of Innocence in the Fiction of Toni Morrison.* Columbia: University of Missouri Press, 1989.

Page, Philip. *Dangerous Freedom: Fusion and Fragmentation in Toni Morrison's Novels.* Jackson: University of Mississippi Press, 1995.

Peach, Linden, ed. *Toni Morrison.* New York: St. Martin's Press, 1997.

Peterson, Nancy J., ed. *Toni Morrison: Critical and Theoretical Approaches.* Baltimore: Johns Hopkins University Press, 1997.

Rigney, Barbara Hill. *The Voices of Toni Morrison.* Columbus: Ohio State University Press, 1991.

Samuels, Wilfred D., and Clenora Hudson-Weems, eds. *Toni Morrison.* Boston: Twayne, 1990.

Taylor-Guthrie, Danielle, ed. *Conversations with Toni Morrison.* Jackson: University of Mississippi Press, 1994.

GLORIA NAYLOR (1950–)

Chris Ruiz-Velasco

BIOGRAPHY

Gloria Naylor, novelist and essayist, was born on January 25, 1950, in New York City. Her parents, Roberta McAlpin and Roosevelt Naylor, moved to New York in 1949, one month before the birth of Gloria, the first of their three daughters. Shortly after Naylor's birth, the army drafted Roosevelt Naylor, and he spent two years in training. Upon his discharge in 1952, the family moved to the upper Bronx and then to an apartment building in Harlem owned by Naylor's maternal grandparents, Luecilia and Evans McAlpin. The street numbers of that apartment building, 314 and 316, later found their way into Naylor's first novel, *The Women of Brewster Place* (1982). In 1963 the family moved once again, this time to Queens, where Naylor became more conscious of racism. These changes seem to have prompted Naylor's mother to present her daughter, a shy and introspective child, with a diary so the young girl could articulate her feelings.

In 1963 Naylor's mother joined the Jehovah's Witnesses, and Naylor followed suit in 1968, at the age of eighteen. This experience profoundly affected the course of Naylor's life. Abandoning her plans to attend Hunter College, Naylor dedicated herself to religious activities. For the next seven years, until 1975, the Jehovah's Witnesses served as the focus of Naylor's life. Along with the opportunity to travel, the Jehovah's Witnesses also helped Naylor overcome her shyness because she had to talk to strangers in order to persuade them of her beliefs. In addition, the Jehovah's Witnesses hold a deep reverence for the written word and for the power that the written word holds. This belief would influence Naylor's own views about language, even after she left the Jehovah's Witnesses. However, the Jehovah's Witnesses also isolated Naylor from contacts with people outside of the church as well as from writings not published by the church.

Naylor's departure from the religious group in 1975 marked another period of change in her life. Leaving behind the Jehovah's Witnesses meant that Naylor also left behind friends and support. This separation immensely affected her emotionally, eventually leading to a nervous breakdown. Undaunted, over the next six years, while working full-time as a switchboard operator, Naylor pursued an undergraduate degree. At first, she studied nursing at Medgar Evers College but soon transferred to Brooklyn College, where she majored in English. There she discovered feminism and African American literature. In 1977 Naylor read her first novel by an African American woman, Toni Morrison's *Bluest Eye*. This book had a tremendous impact on Naylor. Because of her involvement with the Jehovah's Witnesses, their isolationism, and their reading restrictions, she had never encountered any of the black literature that had exploded during the late 1960s and early 1970s. Her encounter with Morrison's novel, as well as her attendance at a reading given by Morrison, encouraged the twenty-seven-year-old Naylor to write fiction.

In 1981 Naylor completed her undergraduate degree at Brooklyn College as well as her first novel, *The Women of Brewster Place*. She then attended Yale, where she pursued an MA in Afro-American studies. Meanwhile, *The Women of Brewster Place* appeared in 1982. The following year, 1983, Naylor completed her MA and as her thesis wrote what would later become her second novel, *Linden Hills*.

In addition, Naylor received the American Book Award for best first novel as well as the Distinguished Writer Award from the Mid-Atlantic Writers Association. In 1983 she also began a teaching career. She held the position of writer-in-residence at Cummington Community of the Arts as well as visiting lecturer at George Washington University. In 1985 Naylor published her second novel, *Linden Hills*. She continued writing and teaching throughout the 1980s and held positions at several universities, including Yale, Princeton, Brandeis, and Cornell. During this period, Naylor also garnered several awards, among them a National Endowment for the Arts Fellowship, the Candace Award from the National Coalition of One Hundred Black Women, a Guggenheim Fellowship, and the Lillian Smith Award. Arguably Naylor's most acclaimed novel, *Mama Day*, appeared in 1988, followed by *Bailey's Café* in 1992. Her most recent novel, *The Men of Brewster Place*, appeared in 1998. While best known for her novels, Naylor has also published several essays, written a column in the *New York Times* during 1986, and authored the scholarly work "Love and Sex in the Afro-American Novel," which appeared in the *Yale Review* in 1989. In addition, Naylor has edited *Children of the Night: The Best Short Stories by Black Writers, 1967 to the Present* (1995).

MAJOR WORKS AND THEMES

With the appearance in 1982 of her first novel, *The Women of Brewster Place*, Gloria Naylor presented many of the major themes that she would perpetuate throughout her subsequent works. These themes include black sisterhood, community, African heritage, history, and sexuality as well as gender and class issues, especially as they pertain to the African American community. In addition, Naylor explores alternate views of reality, as evidenced in her use of dreams and magic. Importantly, none of these themes exists in isolation from each other, as Naylor weaves them with the fabric of her narratives.

As Larry R. Andrews points out, Gloria Naylor "devotes considerable attention to the special bond that can exist between women characters, including women of different generations" (2). This attention seems most tightly focused in Naylor's first novel, *The Women of Brewster Place*, which Naylor subtitles a "Novel in Seven Stories." The novel focuses on these bonds as it simultaneously paints a picture of the imagined ghetto community of Brewster Place. Each of the seven interconnected stories offers the portrait of a featured character. The foremost of these characters, Mattie Michael, appears throughout the novel, usually in a mothering and nurturing role. As Karen Castellucci Cox rightly notes, each of these characters represents specific historical periods and issues, and "each of the first six stories takes on the narrative of one of these women . . . tracing the influence upon her and shaping her as archetype for one kind of historically silenced story" (161). The novel traces the story of these women's lives and their struggles as they negotiate an urban milieu marked by racism, sexism, poverty, and crime.

Naylor continues her exploration of community in her second novel, *Linden Hills*. This novel, loosely based on Dante's *Inferno*, takes place over four days and follows two young poets, Willie and Lester. The two men literally work their way down through the seven levels of the black middle-class neighborhood, Linden Hills. As the two young men make their journey, they witness the hypocrisy and moral bankruptcy of the community. According to Catherine Ward, *Linden Hills* exhibits a "serious moral tone and gives a universalizing mythic dimension to what might otherwise be considered a narrow subject, the price American blacks are paying for their economic and social 'success' " (182). Ultimately, Willie and Lester encounter Luther Nedeed, the character who represents Dante's Satan.

In *Mama Day*, Naylor continues her exploration of community, sisterhood, familial relations, history, and magic. Set on Willow Springs, an imagined island off the coast of Georgia and South Carolina, but belonging to neither, the novel contains several allusions to Shakespeare, especially to *The Tempest*, *King Lear*, and *Hamlet*. Through the title character's relationship to her grand-niece, Ophelia "Cocoa" Day, Naylor traces the history of a family and the community in which it resides. The text's multiple narrators give *Mama Day* a multivoiced texture that invokes themes regarding community, memory, and matriarchy.

In both *Bailey's Café* and *The Men of Brewster Place*, Naylor builds upon her earlier themes and explores more closely issues surrounding masculinity. The characters who frequent the diner appear in Naylor's novel, and they each express stories, backgrounds, histories, and anxieties that propel the narrative. As in her earlier works, the imagined setting that Naylor constructs serves as an important element of her work. As Virginia C. Fowler notes, "Bailey's Café is a metaphysical setting, representing an emotional and spiritual condition" (122).

CRITICAL RECEPTION

Most of the critical work about Gloria Naylor focuses on the major themes that recur throughout her work. Since the appearance of her first novel, many critics have noted the alternative ways of knowing exemplified through the magical and mythical within Naylor's works. Larry R. Andrews argues that "Naylor has moved from the merely naturalistic to the symbolic and mythical modes as well, as she adds historical depth to the presentation of the female bond" (25). Andrews also points to another of Naylor's dominant themes and areas of concern, the relations between women: "This bond among women confers identity, purpose, and strength for survival" (2). Likewise, Virginia C. Fowler notes that Naylor's female characters share "a resilient spirit that refuses to be destroyed" (25). Importantly, these depictions of black sisterhood arise within the context of community.

Again, because Naylor so tightly interweaves her themes, discussions focusing on community or sisterhood also tend to explore other thematic threads. Thus, regarding Naylor's work, Karen Castellucci Cox can argue, "Because the communal memory exists outside historical progression in a nether-world of dreams and desires meant to shape the whole, it often constructs its stories from the materials of family secrets, folk legends, ghost tales, and the like" (159). These notions of a communal memory as well as a communal experience manifest through Naylor's use of multiple narratives and multiple narrators. As Philip Page observes regarding *Bailey's Café*, "To avoid the constrictions of a single perspective, Naylor includes the voices of nearly every character" (36). As Page further clarifies, "In addition to creating a communal narration that implies the need for all perspectives to be heard, Naylor's narrative technique tends to transform the written text into oral performance" (37). Multiple perspectives and multiple concerns predominate in both Naylor's work and the criticism that surrounds it.

The larger implications of Naylor's work also come to the surface as one examines the multiple layers of narrative, narrators, and history in her texts. Dorothy Perry Thompson comments, "Naylor constructs her text, her (re)figurations, with recursions that pay homage to the history and expressive culture of Africa and the diaspora. Mere reflection is not a stopping place for her. As she ascends to make new models, she not only revises Western tradition, but also liberates her listener/reader" (107).

BIBLIOGRAPHY

Works by Gloria Naylor

Women of Brewster Place. New York: Viking, 1982.
Linden Hills. New York: Ticknor and Fields, 1985.
Mama Day. New York: Ticknor and Fields, 1988.
"Love and Sex in the Afro-American Novel." *Yale Review* 78 (1989): 19–31.
Bailey's Café. New York: Harcourt, 1992.
He's a Russian Jew. Berkeley: Black Oak Books, 1992.
Ed. *Children of the Night: The Best Short Stories by Black Writers, 1967 to the Present*. Boston: Little Brown, 1995.
The Men of Brewster Place. New York: Hyperion, 1998.

Studies of Gloria Naylor

Andrews, Larry R. "Black Sisterhood in Gloria Naylor's Novels." *CLA* 33 (1989): 1–25.
Awkward, Michael. *Inspiring Influences: Tradition, Revision, and Afro-American Women's Novels*. New York: Columbia University Press, 1991. 97–134.
Bobo, Jacqueline, and Ellen Seiter. "Black Feminism and Media Criticism." *Screen* 32 (1991): 286–302.
Christol, Helene. "Reconstructing American History: Land and Genealogy in Gloria Naylor's *Mama Day*." *The Black Columbiad: Defining Moments in African American Literature and Culture*. Ed. Werner Sollers and Maria Diedrich. Cambridge: Harvard University Press, 1994. 347–56.
Collins, Grace E. "Narrative Structure in *Linden Hills*." *CLA* 34 (1991): 290–300.

"A Conversation: Gloria Naylor and Toni Morrison." *Conversations with Toni Morrison.* Ed. Danille Guthrie Taylor. Jackson: University Press of Mississippi, 1994. 188–217.

Cox, Karen Castellucci. "Magic and Memory in the Contemporary Story Cycle: Gloria Naylor and Louise Erdrich." *College English* 60 (1998): 150–72.

Donlon, Joycelyn Hazelwood. "Southern Racial Communities and Strategies of Story-Listening in Gloria Naylor and Lee Smith." *Twentieth Century Literature* 41 (995): 16–35.

Eckard, Paula Gallant. "The Prismatic Past in *Oral History* and *Mama Day.*" *MELUS* 20 (1995): 121–35.

Erikson, Peter. "Shakespeare's Naylor, Naylor's Shakespeare: Shakespearean Allusions as Appropriation in Gloria Naylor's Quartet." *Literary Influence and African-American Writers.* Ed. Tracy Mishkin. New York: Garland, 1996. 325–57.

Felton, Sharon, and Michelle C. Loris. *The Critical Response to Gloria Naylor.* Westport, CT: Greenwood Press, 1997.

Fowler, Virginia C. *Gloria Naylor: In Search of Sanctuary.* New York: Twayne, 1996.

Harris, Trudier. *The Power of the Porch: The Storyteller's Craft in Zora Neal Hurston, Gloria Naylor, and Randall Keenan.* Athens: University of Georgia Press, 1996.

Gates, Henry Louis Jr., and K. A. Appiah, eds. *Gloria Naylor: Critical Perspectives Past and Present.* New York: Amistad, 1993.

Kelley, Margot Anne, ed. *Gloria Naylor's Early Novels.* Gainesville, FL: University Press of Florida, 1999.

Korenman, Joan S. "African-American Women Writers, Black Nationalism, and the Matrilineal Heritage." *CLA* 38 (1994): 143–61.

Kubitschek, Missy Dehn. "Toward a New Order: Shakespeare, Morrison, and Gloria Naylor's *Mama Day.*" *MELUS* 19 (1994): 75–90.

Lynch, Michael F. "The Wall and the Mirror in the Promised Land: The City in the Novels of Gloria Naylor." *The City in African-American Literature.* Ed.

Yoshinobu Hakutani and Robert Butler. Madison, NJ: Fairleigh Dickinson University Press, 1995. 181–95.

Meisenhelder, Susan. " 'The Whole Picture' in Gloria Naylor's *Mama Day.*" *African American Review* 27 (1993): 405–19.

Montgomery, Maxine Lavon. "The Fathomless Dream: Gloria Naylor's Use of the Descent Motif in *The Women of Brewster Place.*" *CLA* 36 (1992): 1–11.

——. "Authority, Multivocality, and the New World Order in Gloria Naylor's *Bailey's Café.*" *African American Review* 29 (1995): 27–33.

O'Connor, Mary. "Subject, Voice, and Women in Some Contemporary Black American Women's Writing." *Feminism, Bakhtin, and the Dialogic.* Ed. Dale M. Bauer and Susan Jaret McKinstry. Albany: State University of New York Press, 1991. 199–217.

Page, Philip. "Living with the Abyss in Gloria Naylor's *Bailey's Café.*" *CLA* 40 (1996): 21–45.

Perry, Donna. "Gloria Naylor." *Backtalk: Women Writers Speak Out.* Ed. Donna Perry. New Brunswick, NJ: Rutgers University Press, 1993. 217–44.

Puhr, Katheleen M. "Healers in Gloria Naylor's Fiction." *Twentieth Century Literature* 40 (1994): 518–27.

Sandiford, K. A. "Gothic and Intertextual Constructions in *Linden Hills.*" *Arizona Quarterly* 47 (1991): 117–39.

Stanford, Ann Folwell. "Mechanisms of Disease: African-American Women Writers, Social Pathologies, and the Limits of Medicine." *NWSA* 6 (1994): 28–47.

Storhoff, Gary. " 'The Only Voice Is Your Own': Gloria Naylor's Revision of *The Tempest.*" *African American Review* 29 (1995): 35–45.

Thompson, Dorothy Perry. "Into the Midst of Nothing." *Gloria Naylor's Early Novels.* Ed. Margot Anne Kelly. Gainesville, FL: University Press of Florida, 1999.

Toombs, Charles. "The Confluence of Food and Identity in Gloria Naylor's *Linden Hills*." *CLA* 23 (1993): 5–7.

Traub, Valery. "Rainbows of Darkness: Deconstructing Shakespeare in the Work of Gloria Naylor and Zora Neale Hurston." *Cross Cultural Performances*: *Differences in Women's Literature*. Ed. Marianne Novy. Urbana: University of Illinois Press, 1993. 150–63.

Tucker, Lindsey. "Recovering the Conjure Woman: Texts and Contexts in Gloria Naylor's *Mama Day*." *African American Review* 28 (1994): 173–88.

Ward, Catherine. "A Modern Inferno." *Gloria Naylor: Critical Perspectives Past and Present*. Ed. Henry Louis Gates, Jr., and K. A. Appiah. New York: Amistad, 1993. 182–96.

Warren, Nagueyalit. "Cocoa and George: A Love Dialectic." *SAGE* 7 (1990): 19–25.

Whitt, Margaret Earley. *Understanding Gloria Naylor*. Columbia: University of South Carolina Press, 1999.

JOYCE CAROL OATES (1938–)

Mona M. Choucair

BIOGRAPHY

Joyce Carol Oates was born into a working-class Catholic family outside of Lockport, New York and enjoyed a childhood on her grandparents' farm. She has described her childhood as nothing out of the ordinary but said it was quite a happy one indeed. Many scholars find parallels between her fictional Eden County and the real Erie County of her youth. From such a seemingly innocent background, Oates wrote her first controversial novel at the age of fifteen.

Oates enjoyed her college years at Syracuse University, where she was named valedictorian in 1960. She then attended the University of Wisconsin, where she received her MA in English literature and met her husband, Raymond Joseph Smith, an English instructor. In 1963, while working toward her PhD and writing fictional pieces, Oates successfully published her first collection of short stories, *By the North Gate*. Between 1961 and 1967, Oates lived and worked in Detroit, where she taught at the University of Detroit and wrote about the city's turbulence; her very successful novel, *them* (1969), was born out of her time in the city. In 1967 she and her husband moved to Ontario, Canada, where she taught at the University of Windsor, and together the couple founded the *Ontario Review*. Since leaving Canada in 1977, Oates has been a writer-in-residence at Princeton University in New Jersey.

Joyce Carol Oates's first two short story collections, *By the North Gate* (1963) and *Upon the Sweeping Flood and Other Stories* (1966) launched her career as a fiction writer and a commanding voice in contemporary literature. These two collections focus on violence as Oates delves into the decay of morality, emotional instability, and abuse.

The Wheel of Love and Other Stories (1970) is often hailed as the Oates's best work. In this volume of short stories, Oates explores a gamut of emotions associated with love and relationships. Oates's most critically acclaimed short story is "Where Are You Going, Where Have You Been?," a tragic story that recounts the emotional turmoil and rape of Connie, the teenaged protagonist desperately seeking attention from the opposite sex. Here, Oates creates the demonic character of Arnold Friend while simultaneously developing Connie's ultimate nightmare. Although the afore-mentioned story is Oates's most anthologized short work, critics have often chastised the author for the very adult nature of this sexual initiation tale, most often citing its violently graphic sexual overtones. In *The Goddess and Other Women* (1974), Oates continues her theme with the sexual oppression of women.

In *Crossing the Border: Fifteen Tales* (1976), Oates begins her popular thematic approach to both physical and psychological barriers; whether they are actual borders between countries and/or cities or barriers in relationships, the author makes the topic of borders and limitations very intriguing. Renee and Evan Maynard, an American couple, appear in several of the tales; Oates traces the couple's reactions to certain obstacles in their romantic relationship as they move to various locales. Likewise, in *All the Good People I've Left Behind* (1978), Oates portrays the life of Annie Quirt, the quintessential lady seeking her knight in shining armor, who appears in five of her short works. Quirt moves from relationship to relationship before she realizes the futility of her quests. Oates has received positive critical acclaim for her candid rev-elations of vulnerability, particularly in her provocative portrayals of women.

From 1989 to 2000, Joyce Carol Oates churned out eleven novels and seven short story collections, not to mention several essays and one play. Criticism on the novels centers primarily on *We Were the Mulvaneys* (1996), *My Heart Laid Bare* (1998), and *Blonde* (2000). The most common critiques assert that Oates accosts the reader with odd tensions drawn between real-life scenarios and the macabre fantastical worlds that she evokes.

MAJOR WORKS AND THEMES

With the release of her recent works, Joyce Carol Oates has ushered in a new genre of writing, focusing on the psychological studies of human cruelty. Her characters mirror real-life names like Jeffrey Dahmer and Marilyn Monroe. Within such a range, Oates paints surreal, often horrific accounts of reality. Perhaps "obsession" best cap-tures the essence of Oates's most recent fictional works.

The idea of the motive behind the crime pervades many of Oates's stories. In a collection of short works entitled *Zombie* (1995), the author delves into the mind of serial killer Quentin P. He becomes the monster next door in Oates's horrific account of brutality and mutilation. In *Man Crazy* (1997), Oates depicts the victim of a serial killer, Ingrid Boone, otherwise known as Doll-girl for her beauty and later Dog-girl as a result of her demoralization at the hands of a crazed assailant. All of these character sketches hail back to the memorable, despicable character of Arnold Friend, who lures Connie to her death in the famous short story, "Where Are You Going, Where Have You Been?". The friend/fiend character, based on an actual serial killer known for his outlandishly decorated Volkswagen Beetle and suave, smooth talk, seems to morph into the above Quentin, a more grotesque and outwardly maniacal killer. Yet, the most puzzling, disturbing aspect of Oates's new works is the blurring of the lines between love and hate; for this author, violence "is itself a determining social condition, a tropism at the heart of the American personality" (Scott 1).

Moreover, Oates's obsession with fragmented women proves quite compelling. At-tempting to reveal the realities of normal women, Oates depicts pragmatic yet often shocking character sketches, simultaneously attracting and bewildering readers. "Joyce Carol Oates's women are stereotypical portraits of frustrated neurotic human beings," says Mary Kathryn Grant, "physically crippled by the events of their lives and the tragic frustrations with which they cannot cope. Their only redeeming quality is that they do survive; they manage to make it through these overwhelming circumstances" (25). From her short stories to her novels, illustrations of "destructive" searching women appear (Grant 28).

Perhaps the best earlier illustrations of her destructive women appear in the collection entitled *The Goddess and Other Women* (1974). From Kali to Ruth, Katherine, and Nancy, Oates's women suffer under male domination and ultimately break down, both physically and mentally. Oates proves that although the stronger women survive, they also face unbelievable obstacles. Grant continues her description of the Oates women by calling them "the antithes[es] of the liberated woman" (29).

Oates reveals a more disturbed, frightening picture of women in her newest collection of short works, *The Collector of Hearts* (1998), where she presents more of the grotesque facets of her character sketches; for instance, in "Death Mother," Oates resembles Edgar Allan Poe in her searing account of Jeanette's mother, who appears simultaneously "suicidal and murderous" (Livesey 1). And in her novel published under the pseudonym Rosamond Smith, *Starr Bright Will Be with You Soon* (1999), Oates presents a "serial mom" figure who proves as cunning and conniving as Janet Leigh from *Psycho* (Pye 29).

In a bold move for even an audacious author, Oates recently published *Blonde* (2000), "a messy, fierce . . . kaleidoscope novel of ideas . . . [a] lurid celebrity potboiler," chronicling the life of the legendary Marilyn Monroe "directly and frankly" through fiction (Miller 1). Better than any Hollywood rendition of Monroe's outward beauty and stardom, Oates explores the hidden inner, ugly world of the icon. Oates sees Monroe as "a powerful, instinctual actress sabotaged and tortured by a man's world that both coveted and despised her body" (Miller 3). Disgust and desire combine to render a novel that perpetually shocks and saddens the reader.

As an extension of her psychological studies, Oates delves into the meaning of place and time, admitting that as a young girl, she had quite an obsession with a sense of place herself: "I find myself running in a place so intriguing to me, amid houses, or the back of houses, so mysterious, I'm fated to write about these sights, to bring them to life in fiction" ("Writers on Writing" 3). In *Foxfire: Confessions of a Girl Gang* (1993), Oates presents a less horrific yet equally disturbing picture of women on a mission of vengeance; their purpose—to obliterate men. In the novel, the girls, led by Margaret (Legs) Sadovsky, take vengeance upon their men in a mythical landscape set in 1950s New York; they become warriors, vigilantes, and modern outlaws of justice for women. The novel proves outlandish, "orgiastic, incandescent, and crazy" (Crowley 1). This work melds together the disturbing female and a sense of place, implying that everyone has a sense of their place in the world.

In *A Garden of Earthly Delights* (1967), Oates reveals the too-familiar feeling of dislocation and uprootedness as she depicts the Walpoles, a family that constantly moves from locale to locale, migrants fighting against the voracious pulse of the city— the nuances, power, and luring qualities. Whether depicting Detroit, Chicago, or Cedar Grove, Oates presents the city as an uncaring, harsh, and suffocating place. Against such a backdrop, her protagonists must fight to survive. Oates personifies again that when pitted against the city, the community loses.

CRITICAL RECEPTPION

From the publication of her first collection of short stories, *By the North Gate* (1963), to her latest novel, *Blonde* (2000), Joyce Carol Oates has elicited numerous, varied criticisms of her works. While it is quite true that Oates portrays the realities of daily life through her bizarre characterization and mysterious, often troubling plots, it is her use of violence that has attracted the most critical response: "In the world of her novels, people make love, play pianos, and eat violently. Music explodes, grins shatter, grease spatters maliciously, as Oates uses every rhetorical device at her command to create an explosive atmosphere" (Grant 95).

Of all her work, *them* (1969), *Marriages and Infidelities* (1972), *Crossing the Border* (1976), and *The Collector of Hearts* (1998) have drawn the most critical attention. In countless interviews, Oates defends her stark, often disturbing subjects. She explains, "I start with intense emotion. I evoke form to contain it. . . . I rewrite constantly to keep up with the emotion until it becomes formally disciplined. . . . And I can't write a novel unless I know the precise end" (Todd 292). And when asked whether the writing process is difficult for her, Oates candidly replies, "Like crawling over broken glass. It is tormenting, but worth it" (Todd 293).

Violence in the form of perversity abounds in the Oates canon. With her early short story "Stigmata," Oates depicts a surreal image of a Christ figure as the father in the story bleeds from his hands, feet, and side on Good Friday; his ensuing suffering becomes the impetus for the storyline. In *Marya: A Life* (1986), Oates combines a woman's search for her matrilineal past with jarring, violent physical landscapes. One scene from the novel that proves most distressing involves Marya's classmates cutting her hair against her will, an act that is "both a kind of rape and a rite of passage" (Showalter 50).

In *Heat and Other Stories* (1991), Oates seems fascinated by blood and carnage. From an ax murder to a brutal beating to a harrowing stabbing, Oates serves up the sordid details of violent crimes in Hitchcock fashion (Robinson 411). Such distortion appears again in *We Were the Mulvaneys* (1996), where Oates shows a family's "fall from grace" through demonic images of abuse, ranging from verbal to sexual. Oates depicts Marianne Mulvaney's rape and her father's disabling dysfunction in a novel that "makes us glad to forgive its trespasses," according to David Gates (2). "What keeps us coming back to Oates Country," Gates continues, "is something stronger and spookier: her uncanny gift of making the page a window, with something happening on the other side that we'd swear was life itself" (3). Amid such criticism over her depictions of violence, Oates vehemently defends her works: "Artists in our society . . . draw the kind of vituperative abuse that used to be reserved for ax murderers and corrupt politicians; but since the nature of their 'crime' is unclear, they can never hope for acquittal" (Wagner 3).

BIBLIOGRAPHY

Works by Joyce Carol Oates

By the North Gate. New York: Vanguard Press, 1963.
With Shuddering Fall. Greenwich, CT: Fawcett, 1964.
Upon the Sweeping Flood and Other Stories. London: Coronet Books, 1966.

A Garden of Earthly Delights. New York: Vanguard Press, 1967.
Expensive People. New York: Vanguard Press, 1968.
Invisible Woman: New and Selected Poems. Princeton: Ontario Review Press, 1968.
Women in Love and Other Poems. New York: Albondocani Press, 1968.
them. New York: Vanguard Press, 1969.
The Wheel of Love and Other Stories. New York: Vanguard Press, 1970.
Wonderland. Princeton: Ontario Review Press, 1971.
Marriages and Infidelities. New York: Vanguard Press, 1972.
Do with Me What You Will. New York: Vanguard Press, 1973.
The Goddess and Other Women. New York: Vanguard Press, 1974.
The Hungry Ghosts: Seven Allusive Comedies. Los Angeles: Black Sparrow Press, 1974.
Where Are You Going, Where Have You Been? Stories of Young America. Greenwich, CT: Fawcett, 1974.
The Assassins. New York: Plume, 1975.
The Poisoned Kill and Other Stories from the Portuguese. New York: Vanguard, 1975.
The Seduction and Other Stories. Los Angeles: Black Sparrow, 1975.
The Childwold. New York: Plume, 1976.
*Crossing the Border: Fifteen Tale*s. New York: Vanguard, 1976.
Night Side: Eighteen Tales. New York: Vanguard, 1976.
All the Good People I've Left Behind. Santa Barbara, CA: Black Sparrow, 1978.
Son of the Morning. New York: Vanguard, 1978.
Unholy Loves. New York: Vanguard, 1979.
The Lamb of Abyssalia. Cambridge: Pomegranate, 1980.
A Sentimental Education: Stories. Los Angeles: Sylvester and Orphanos, 1981.
Mysteries of Winterthurn. New York: Dutton, 1984.
A Bloodsmoor Romance. New York: Plume, 1985.
Solstice. Princeton: Ontario Review, 1985.
Marya: A Life. New York: Duttton, 1986.
You Must Remember This. New York: Dutton, 1987.
American Appetites. New York: E. P. Dutton, 1989.
Pseud. Rosamond Smith. *Soul/Mate*. New York: Dutton, 1989.
Because It Is Bitter and Because It Is My Heart. New York: Plume, 1991.
Heat and Other Stories. New York: Plume, 1991.
Black Water. New York: Dutton, 1992.
Foxfire: Confessions of a Girl Gang. New York: Plume, 1993.
Haunted: Tales of the Grotesque. New York: Plume, 1995.
Zombie. New York, Plume, 1995.
We Were the Mulvaneys. New York: Plume, 1996.
Man Crazy. New York: Plume, 1997.
Will You Always Love Me? and Other Stories. New York: Plume, 1997.
The Collector of Hearts. New York: Plume, 1998.
My Heart Laid Bare. New York: Plume, 1998.
Broke Heart Blues. New York: Penguin, 1999.
Pseud. Rosamond Smith. *Starr Bright Will Be with You Soon*. New York: Plume, 1999.
"Writers on Writing." *New York Times* 18 July 1999: 1–3.
Blonde. New York: HarperCollins, 2000.
Faithless. New York: HarperCollins, 2000.
Middle Age. Princeton: Ontario Review, 2001.

Studies of Joyce Carol Oates

Bastian, Katherine. *Joyce Carol Oates's Short Stories: Between Tradition and Innovation*. Frankfurt: Lang, 1983.

Bender, Eileen T. "Between the Categories: Recent Short Fiction by Joyce Carol Oates." *Studies in Short Fiction* 17 (1980): 415–23.

——. *Joyce Carol Oates: Artist in Residence*. Bloomington: Indiana University Press, 1987.

Bloom, Harold, ed. *Joyce Carol Oates: Modern Critical Views*. New York: Chelsea House, 1987.

Brem, Linda M. G. "The Narrator as Alter Ego in Joyce Carol Oates's 'Heat.' " *Notes on Contemporary Literature* 28 (1998): 12.

Chauche, Catherine. "Joyce Carol Oates in Berlin: The Birth of a Myth." *Journal of the Short Story in English* 14 (1990): 9–24.

Chell, Cara. "Un-Tricking the Eye: Joyce Carol Oates and the Feminist Ghost Story." *Arizona Quarterly* 41 (1985): 5–23.

Creighton, Joanne V. *Joyce Carol Oates*. Warren French, ed. Boston: G. K. Hall, 1979.

——. *Joyce Carol Oates: Novels of the Middle Years*. New York: Twayne, 1992.

Crowley, John. Rev. of *Foxfire: Confessions of a Girl Gang*. *New York Times* 15 Aug. 1993: 1–2.

Daly, Brenda O. "An Unfilmable Conclusion: Joyce Carol Oates at the Movies." *Journal of Popular Culture* 23 (1989): 101–14.

Egan, James. " 'Romance of a Darksome Type': Versions of the Fantastic in the Novels of Joyce Carol Oates." *Studies in Weird Fiction* 7 (1990): 12–21.

Gates, David. Rev. of *We Were the Mulvaneys*. *New York Times* 15 Sept. 1996: 1–3.

Grant, Mary Kathryn. *The Tragic Vision of Joyce Carol Oates*. Durham: Duke University Press, 1978.

Gurstein, Rochelle. "Common Worlds and Violations: A Response to Joyce Carol Oates." *Salmagundi* 111 (1996): 86–85.

Harty, Kevin J. "Archetype and Popular Lyric in Joyce Carol Oates's 'Where Are You Going, Where Have You Been?' " *Pennsylvania English* 8 (1980/81): 26–28.

Hoel, Kristin, "Joyce Carol Oates: Passion and Madness: Moderne Amerika." *Vinduet* 39 (1985): 32–38.

Johnson, Greg. *Understanding Joyce Carol Oates*. Columbia: University of South Carolina Press, 1987.

——. "Joyce Carol Oates Goes to College." *Five Points* 2 (1998): 42–68.

Livesey, Margot. Rev. of *The Collector of Hearts*. *New York Times* 7 March 1999: 1–4.

Milazo, Lee, ed. *Conversations with Joyce Carol Oates*. Jackson: University Press of Mississippi, 1989.

Miller, Laura. Rev. of *Blonde*. *New York Times* 2 April 2000: 1–3.

Morris, Daniel. "Figuring and Disfiguring: Joyce Carol Oates on Boxing and the Paintings of George Bellows." *Mosaic* 31 (1998): 135–50.

Padgett, Jacqueline Olaon. "The Portugal of Joyce Carol Oates." *Studies in Short Fiction* 31 (1994): 765–82.

Petite, Joseph. "The Marriage Cycle of Joyce Carol Oates." *Journal of Evolutionary Psychology* 5 (1984): 223–36.

Pye, Michael. "Serial Mom." Rev. of *Starr Bright Will Be With You Soon*. *New York Times Book Review* 11 April 1999: 29.

Robinson, Sally. "Heat and Cold: Recent Fictions by Joyce Carol Oates." *Michigan Quarterly Review* 31 (1992): 400–14.

Rozga, Margaret. "Threatening Places, Hiding Places: The Midwest in Selected Stories by Joyce Carol Oates." *Midwestern Miscellany* 18 (1990): 34–44.

Scott, A. O. Rev. of *Man Crazy*. *New York Times* 21 Sept. 1997: 1–4.

Showalter, Elaine. "My Friend, Joyce Carol Oates: An Intimate Portrait." *Ms*. March 1986: 44–50.

Siegel, Jerrold. "Boundaries: A Response to Joyce Carol Oates." *Salmagundi* 111 (1996): 96–104.

Silet, Charles L. P. "Rosamond Smith AKA Joyce Carol Oates." *Mystery Scene* 62 (1999): 60–64.

Singh, Sushila. "Joyce Carol Oates: The Woman Question in Her Exploration of the Contemporary Human Condition." *Panjab University Research Bulletin* 19 (1988): 11–20.

Todd, David Y. " An Interview with Joyce Carol Oates." *Gettysburg Review* 6 (1993): 291–99.

Wagner, Linda W., ed. *Critical Essays on Joyce Carol Oates.* Boston: G. K. Hall, 1979.

Wesley, Marilyn C. "On Sport: Magic and Masculinity in Joyce Carol Oates's Fiction." *Lit: Literature Interpretation Theory* (1991): 65–75.

——. "Father-Daughter Incest as Social Transgression: A Feminist Reading of Joyce Carol Oates." *Women Studies* 21 (1992): 251–63.

Wilson, Mary Ann. "From Thanatos to Eros: A Study of Erotic Love in Joyce Carol Oates's 'Do with Me What You Will.' " *Studies in the Humanities* 11 (1984): 48–55.

Zapf, Hubert. "Aesthetic Experience and Ideological Critique in Joyce Carol Oates's 'Master Race.' " *International Fiction Review* 16 (1989): 104–6.

TILLIE OLSEN (1912 OR 1913–)

Ernest Smith

BIOGRAPHY

Although several sources list Tillie Lerner Olsen's year of birth as 1913, Olsen herself says that the year is uncertain owing to the absence of a birth certificate. The second of six children, Tillie Lerner was born in Omaha, Nebraska, on January 14, in either 1912 or 1913. Her parents, Samuel Lerner and Ida Berber Lerner, were Jewish immigrants who left Russia after the unsuccessful rebellion of 1905, which protested the tyrannical regime of Tsar Nicholas II. Continually under economic strain, her parents worked as laborers, her mother taking on piecework such as other people's laundry, while her father held various jobs, including tenant farming and working in a meat-packing house. Tillie was forced to leave Omaha Central High School in 1929, after her junior year, to help support the family. Among the jobs she has held are hotel maid, trimmer in a meat-processing plant, food server, solderer, and jar capper. Some of the experiences associated with such manual labor have made their way into her fiction.

Despite economic hardships, Olsen's parents passed down to her a commitment to economic and social activism and a firm belief in the value of reading and education. She made extensive use of the local library, and by all accounts, her neighborhood in Omaha was ethnically diverse. Her father served as secretary of the Nebraska Socialist Party, and among his daughter's fondest memories is one of presenting Eugene Debs, national leader of the Socialist Party, with a bouquet of roses when he visited Omaha after his release from prison for protesting the First World War. By the time she was twenty, Olsen had joined the Young People's Socialist League and Young Communist League. During the early 1930s, Olsen was twice arrested for her involvement in defending laborers. In Kansas City, in the winter of 1932, she was jailed for distributing leaflets to the meat packers, an experience recounted in her 1994 essay, "The Thirties: A Vision of Fear and Hope." Lacking bail money, she contracted pleurisy and incipient tuberculosis during the several weeks spent in jail. After returning to

Omaha to recover, she moved to Faribault, Minnesota, where she bore a daughter, Karla (in 1932), out of wedlock, and began work on the novel *Yonnondio: From the Thirties*, ultimately published over forty years later, in 1974. An excerpt of the novel's opening chapter appeared as "The Iron Throat" in *Partisan Review* in 1934. It would be twenty years before Olsen returned to the genre of fiction writing.

In 1933 Olsen relocated to southern California and then settled in San Francisco, where she has lived ever since. Her second arrest occurred in San Francisco in 1934, when she participated in a massive protest march responding to the murder of several striking longshoremen. "The Strike," first published in *Partisan Review* in 1934, chronicles the San Francisco maritime strike, a landmark event in American labor, and Olsen's subsequent arrest and arraignment are treated in two essays published in *New Republic* in 1934: "Literary Life in California" and "Thousand-Dollar Vagrant." In San Francisco, Tillie Lerner met Jack Olsen, a union printer and fellow member of the Young Communist League. They began living together in 1937, married in 1943, before Jack went away to war, and lived together until Jack Olsen died in 1989. In addition to Karla, the couple raised three of their own daughters: Julie (born in 1938), Katherine Jo (born in 1943), and Laurie (born in 1948). One of Olsen's great themes as a writer is the intertwined rewards and difficulties of motherhood, and a chief reason for her relatively small output as a writer is the fact that she raised her children without relief from daily domestic duties in addition to working at assorted jobs outside the home. She would later reflect that in the literary realm, "until very recently almost all distinguished achievement has come from childless women" (*Silences* 31).

As an activist and union organizer, Jack Olsen was among the many who were forced to testify before Senator Joseph McCarthy's House Un-American Activities Committee during the 1950s. He was blacklisted and had to undertake a new profession as a printer. The activities of the Olsen family were closely monitored by the FBI. In 1955, at the urging of her oldest daughter, Karla, Tillie Olsen enrolled in a creative writing class at San Francisco State University. Among the work she produced in the class was a draft of a story titled "Help Her to Believe," which later became "I Stand Here Ironing," the final version of which first appeared in *Best American Short Stories of 1957*. Encouraged by her instructor at San Francisco State, she chose to continue writing and earned a fellowship to Stanford University for the academic year 1956–1957. Two years later, she won a Ford Foundation Grant, and by 1961, her story "Tell Me a Riddle," which had appeared in *New World Writing* the previous year, won the O. Henry Award as best American short story of that year. The book *Tell Me a Riddle* (1961) included the title story and "I Stand Here Ironing," as well as two additional stories written during the 1950s: "Hey Sailor, What Ship?" and "O Yes."

Olsen subsequently published a novella, "Requa," in *Iowa Review* in 1970. The text appeared the following year as "Requa I" in *Best American Short Stories of 1971*, and in 1972 she published an important and influential biographical interpretation for the Feminist Press edition of Rebecca Harding Davis's 1861 serialized novel *Life in the Iron Mills*. While sorting through papers in 1972, Jack Olsen found the manuscript of his wife's abandoned novel *Yonnondio*; unable to pick up the thread of the book begun over forty years earlier, Tillie Olsen published the book with Delacorte Press in 1974, with a brief afterword beginning "Reader, it was not to have ended here." Discussing the process of putting the manuscript together, Olsen presents the novel as a work of "arduous partnership" between her younger and older selves. Olsen's most influential work, *Silences* (1978), is a collection of nonfiction essays, addresses, and reflections on the theme of hindrances to creativity, especially for women. Echoing Virginia Woolf's *Room of One's Own*, the book probes the various forces that have resulted in the "unnatural thwarting" of women's voices in the arts. Always interested in the relationships of mothers and daughters, in the 1980s, Olsen edited a book of writings on the theme by various authors, *Mother to Daughter, Daughter to Mother: Mothers on Mothering. A Daybook and Reader* (1984), and co-authored a prefatory essay for a book of photography, *Mothers and Daughters: That Special Quality. An Exploration in Photography* (1987). After living for several years in an apartment house built by the longshoremen's union in the 1930s, in San Francisco's Fillmore district, Olsen recently moved into a small house adjacent to the home of her youngest daughter, Laurie. Over the last thirty years, she has won fellowships and awards from the Guggenheim Foundation, the American Academy and National Institute of Arts and Letters, and the National Endowment for the Humanities, has held numerous visiting teaching positions at colleges and universities, and has received several honorary doctoral degrees.

MAJOR WORKS AND THEMES

Olsen's major themes revolve around the social and economic positions of the working class and of women, the silencing of the creative voice, and the perseverance of the human spirit. At the age of fifteen, in a store selling secondhand books, Olsen came across three 1861 volumes of *Atlantic Monthly* with installments of Rebecca Harding Davis's *Life in the Iron Mills; or, The Korl Woman*. Recalling her reading experience, she has said that for her, the text's message was "Literature can be made out of the lives of despised people" and "You, too, must write" (Dresdner 240). Olsen's depiction of her characters, many of whom are "despised" or simply ignored by mainstream society, reveals her essential humanism. In *Yonnondio*, Anna, the wife and mother of the desperately impoverished family, overcomes the strains of poverty, five children, and a husband who abuses alcohol and brutalizes both her and the children. After being raped by her husband and undergoing a life-threatening miscarriage, she suffers an emotional collapse, but by the end of the unfinished novel, she has recovered enough to both nurture the growing children and take in work to help the family financially. Olsen, however, does not let her reader miss what has been lost in Anna's life, the potential gone to waste. Even her husband, Jim Holbrook, is often portrayed sympathetically, a representative of the exploitation of the working class. The title of the novel is taken from a Whitman poem elegizing Native American communities swept from the continent by the white man's advance, and Deborah Silverton Rosenfelt terms the novel an elegy, not just for the families of common laborers of the 1920s and 1930s, but for Olsen's own "lost words between the mid-thirties and late fifties" (155).

The theme of lost words is taken up in Olsen's influential nonfiction work, *Silences*. Intended "to re-dedicate and encourage," the book's prefatory pages announce its concern "with the relationship of circumstances—including class, color, sex; the times, climate into which one is born—to the creation of literature" (xi). Part 2 of *Silences* consists of brief reflections and specific examples of writers who have struggled against the forces that thwart creativity. Olsen lays out her theme in the three major essays that begin the book: "Silences in Literature," "One out of Twelve: Writers Who Are Women in Our Century," and "Rebecca Harding Davis." The second of these essays, originally delivered for a 1971 panel organized by the Women's Commission of the Modern Language Association, points out that only one of every twelve writers taught and anthologized is a woman and calls for increased attention to texts written by women. The essay is a landmark early text that helped to open the literary canon to many heretofore-neglected women writers.

The book that first drew attention to Olsen's writing was *Tell Me a Riddle*, which opens with her frequently anthologized story "I Stand Here Ironing." An interior monologue narrated by the mother of a nineteen-year-old daughter, the story explores not just the dynamics of the mother-daughter relationship but, more specifically, the difficult circumstances of a working-class, single mother attempting to raise a child during the depression and the Second World War. Lisa Fry Dresdner contends that "by emphasizing the material conditions that shape lives and relationships," Olsen "emphasizes that possibility for change emerges from understanding our past and our situation" (236). The book's next two stories treat the theme of exclusion from a community. In "Hey Sailor, What Ship?" a sailor becomes estranged from his oldest friends owing to the incommensurability of his alcoholic, vagabond behavior and the more domesticated rhythms of his friends' family lifestyle. "O Yes" deals with racism through the story of a disintegrating friendship between two junior high school girls, one black and one white. The title story, "Tell Me a Riddle," is the book's longest and deals with the intertwined themes of aging, Jewishness, memory, and family. Jewish immigrants married for nearly fifty years, the aging couple in the story is locked in a battle of wills until Eva, the wife, is found to be terminally ill. The remainder of the story involves her family's attempt to connect with her during her final months and her own reconciliation with a past that has involved social activism, unceasing domestic duties, and her own struggle to maintain personal independence and a spiritual connection with her heritage.

CRITICAL RECEPTION

The critical response to Olsen's work has been overwhelmingly positive. Reviewing *Silences* in 1978, Margaret Atwood offered what stands as a summation of the critical consensus: "Few writers have gained such wide respect based on such a small body of published work. . . . Among women writers in the United States, 'respect' is too pale a word: 'reverence' is more like it" (1). When Olsen published *Tell Me a Riddle* in 1961, reviewers tended to note her age and the fact that her writing career had been put on hold while she raised a family and speculated on similarities between the author's life and that of the mother in "I Stand Here Ironing." On the whole, the stories were widely praised, with one particularly noteworthy review by Irving Howe in the *New Republic* commenting on the depth of feeling in Olsen's fiction, in particular the "remarkable" title story (22). Ten years later, Olsen's "Biographical Interpretation," her afterword to Rebecca Harding Davis's *Life in the Iron Mills*, drew praise for its ability to understand and analyze the plight of the woman writer. While *Silences* has become Olsen's most noted work because of its role in the women's movement, the expansion of the canon, and the rise of feminist criticism, some responses were less laudatory than Atwood's, who found the book's patchwork style to be effective. Joyce Carol Oates, writing in the *New Republic*, expressed concern with the book's style and organization and found it marred by omissions, inconsistencies, and anger while at the same time finding strength in the book's "polemical passages" (33). Olsen's only novel, *Yonnondio*, found favor with most reviewers upon its publication in 1974. Catharine R. Stimpson's review noted that "Olsen's compelling gift is her ability to render lyrically the rhythms of consciousness of victims" (565). In his review for the *Washington Post Book World*, Jack Salzman termed it the best novel to emerge from the proletarian movement of the 1930s but added that Olsen's style and gift for characterization so distinguish the novel that discussion and analysis of it cannot be confined to any historical period. *The Critical Response to Tillie Olsen* (1994), edited by Kay Hoyle Nelson and Nancy Huse, is an invaluable and inclusive compendium of critical writing on Olsen.

As historical and cultural interpretations of literature have flourished, book-length critical studies of Olsen's work have accelerated in recent years. Of particular note are studies such as those by Mara Faulkner, Constance Coiner, and Nora Ruth Roberts, all of which discuss Olsen's work within the context of her political and cultural surroundings. As literature, history, and politics cease to be regarded as independent of one another, we can assume that Olsen's work will continue to be vital to future generations of readers and critics.

BIBLIOGRAPHY

Works by Tillie Olsen

"The Iron Throat." *Partisan Review* 1 (1934): 3–9.
"I Want You Women up North to Know." *Partisan* 1 (1934): 4.
"The Strike." *Partisan Review* 1 (1934): 3–9. Reprinted in *Years of Protest: A Collection of American Writings of the 1930's*. Ed. Jack Salzman. New York: Pegasus, 1967. 138–44.
"There Is a Lesson." *Partisan* 1 (1934): 4.
"Thousand-Dollar Vagrant." *New Republic* Aug. 1934: 67–69.
Tell Me a Riddle. Philadelphia: Lippincott, 1961.
"Requa." *Iowa Review* 1 (1970): 54–74.
"A Biographical Interpretation." Afterword. *Life in the Iron Mills; or, The Korl Woman*. By Rebecca Harding Davis. Old Westbury, NY: Feminist Press, 1972. 67–174.
Yonnondio: From the Thirties. New York: Delacourt, 1974.
Silences. New York: Delacourt, 1978.
Ed. *Mother to Daughter, Daughter to Mother: Mothers on Mothering. A Daybook and Reader*. Old Westbury, NY: Feminist Press, 1984.
Ed. Tillie Olsen, Julie Olsen Edwards, and Estelle Jussim. *Mothers and Daughters: That Special Quality. An Exploration in Photography*. New York: Aperture, 1987.
"The Thirties: A Vision of Hope and Fear." *Newsweek* 3 Jan. 1994: 26–27.

Studies of Tillie Olsen

Atwood, Margaret. "Obstacle Course." Rev. of *Silences. New York Times Book Review* 30 July 1978: 1, 17.
Cantwell, Robert. "Literary Life in California." *New Republic* 22 Aug. 1934: 49.
Coiner, Constance. " 'No One's Private Ground': A Bakhtinian Reading of Tillie Olsen's *Tell Me a Riddle*." *Listening to Silences: New Essays in Feminist Criticism*. Ed. Elaine Hedges and Shelley Fisher Fishkin. New York: Oxford University Press, 1994. 71–93.

——. *Better Red: The Writing and Resistance of Tillie Olsen and Meridel Le Sueur*. New York: Oxford University Press, 1995.

Dresdner, Lisa Fry. "Tillie Olsen." *Twentieth-Century American Western Writers*. Ed. Richard H. Cracroft. Detroit: Gale, 1999. Vol. 206 of *Dictionary of Literary Biography*. 234–42.

Faulkner, Mara. *Protest and Possibility in the Writing of Tillie Olsen*. Charlottesville: University Press of Virginia, 1993.

Fishkin, Shelley Fisher. "Reading, Writing, and Arithmetic: The Lessons *Silences* Has Taught Us." *Listening to Silences: New Essays in Feminist Criticism*. Ed. Elaine Hodges and Shelley Fisher Fishkin. New York: Oxford University Press, 1994. 23–48.

Frye, Joanne S. *Tillie Olsen: A Study of the Short Fiction*. New York: Twayne, 1995.

Gelfant, Blanche H. "After Long Silence: Tillie Olsen's 'Requa.' " *Studies in American Fiction* 12 (1984): 61–69.

Howe, Irving. "Stories: New, Old, and Sometimes Good." Rev. of *Tell Me a Riddle*. *New Republic* 13 Nov. 1961: 22.

Nelson, Kay Hoyle, and Nancy Huse, eds. *The Critical Response to Tillie Olsen*. Westport, CT: Greenwood Press, 1994.

Oates, Joyce Carol. Rev. of *Silences*. *New Republic* 29 July 1978: 32–34.

Orr, Elaine Neil. *Tillie Olsen and a Feminist Spiritual Vision*. Jackson: University Press of Mississippi, 1987.

Orr, Lisa. " 'People Who Might Have Been You': Agency and the Damaged Self in Tillie Olsen's *Yonnondio*." *Women's Studies Quarterly* 23 (1995): 219–28.

Pearlman, Mickey, and Abby H. P. Werlock. *Tillie Olsen*. Boston: Twayne, 1991.

Roberts, Nora Ruth. *Three Radical Women Writers: Class and Gender in Meridel Le Sueur, Tillie Olsen, and Josephine Herbst*. New York: Garland, 1996.

Rosenfelt, Deborah Silverton, ed. *"Tell Me a Riddle": Tillie Olsen*. New Brunswick, NJ: Rutgers University Press, 1995.

Salzman, Jack. "Fragments of Time Lost." Rev. of *Yonnondio*. *Washington Post Book World* 7 Apr. 1974: 1.

Stimpson, Catharine R. "Three Women Work It Out." Rev. of *Yonnondio*. *Nation* 30 Nov. 1974: 565–68.

CYNTHIA OZICK (1928–)

Laurie Champion

BIOGRAPHY

Cynthia Ozick was born in New York City on April 17, 1928, the second child of William and Celia (Regelson) Ozick. From 1933 to 1941, she attended PS 71 in Bronx, New York. Her parents owned a drugstore, and Ozick helped the family business by delivering prescriptions when she was a child. In grade school, she sometimes was taunted for being a Jew. For example, she was shamed for not singing Christmas carols and called anti-Semitic names. However, during her childhood, she also read seriously and vowed to become a writer someday. Her childhood commitment to becoming a writer was inspired partially because her uncle, Abraham Regelson, was a Hebrew poet, a role she envisioned for herself.

After Ozick graduated from Hunter College High School in Manhattan, which she attended from 1942 to 1946, she attended New York University, where she received a BA in English in 1949. A year later, she received an MA in English from Ohio State University. In 1952 she married Bernard Hallote, a lawyer, and during the 1950s, she worked in Boston as an advertising copywriter. She taught composition at New York University between 1964 and 1965. Her only child, a daughter, Rachel, was born on September 24, 1965.

Ozick's success as a writer began in 1966 with the publication of her first novel, *Trust*, and the publication in *Hudson Review* of "The Pagan Rabbi," one of her most anthologized short stories. Her success as a writer continues. She has published novels, collections of short stories, and collections of essays as well as shorter pieces of fiction and nonfiction in distinguished magazines such as *New Yorker*, *Harper's*, *Commentary*, and *Partisan Review*. She has also won numerous prestigious awards including the National Book Critics Award (2001), Distinguished Artist-in-Residence at City College (1982), a Guggenheim Fellowship (1982), a Jewish Theological Seminary Distinguished Service in Jewish Letters Award (1984), and the 1983 Strauss Living Award that provided her with $35,000 a year for five years, which enabled her to pursue her writing without having to work for economic support. She has also received honorary doctorates from the Hebrew Union College in Cincinnati, Yeshiva University of New York, and Hunter College in New York.

MAJOR WORKS AND THEMES

A significant Jewish American writer, Cynthia Ozick's works frequently exemplify her belief that "stories ought to judge and interpret the world" (*Bloodshed* 4). Ozick's Jewish characters struggle to preserve traditions, search for personal and cultural heritage, and attempt to cope with various forms of anti-Semitism, both personally and culturally. As pointed out in her critical essays, Ozick believes that art becomes idolatrous for Jews unless it serves moral purposes. Sometimes, she argues, imagination and freedom can be "dangerous," as the artistic gift is both a blessing and an encumbrance. As she says, "Being a Jew is something more than being an alienated marginal sensibility with kinky hair. Simply: to be a Jew is to be covenanted; . . . or, at the very minimum, to be aware of the covenant itself. . . . If to be a Jew is to be covenanted then to write of Jews without taking this into account is to miss the deepest point of all" ("Ethnic Joke" 113–14). Even critics such as Harold Bloom who take issue with Ozick's claims about the purpose of art and scholars who debate Ozick's works in terms of the intentional fallacy agree that she is one of America's most significant contemporary writers.

Understanding Ozick's works requires reading beyond the surface level of the plot. Sometimes, her plots violate a straightforward, chronological approach, which demands that readers assemble the incidents to find ways incidents are connected. Her first novel, *Trust* (1966), serves as a good example of the sorts of narrative structures Ozick frequently employs. *Trust* is divided into four sections: "Part One: America" begins in 1957 and is set in New York, where the narrator contemplates her college commencement, attended by neither of her parents. "Part Two: Europe" moves to 1946 and is set in Paris, where the narrator first meets her father. "Part Three: Brighton" moves back in time a decade before the time frame of part two and is set in Brighton, England, where the narrator was born. The final section of the novel, "Part Four: Duneacres," set in Duneacres, an island estate in Westchester County, continues the time frame and action of the end of part one. The various sections of *Trust* explore the narrator's relationship with each of her three "fathers": William, her mother's first husband; Enoch, her mother's second husband; and Gustave Nicholas Tilbeck, her biological father. Although in some ways Tilbeck seems least likely among the narrator's father figures to gain her affection, ultimately he receives her loyalty, her "trust."

More linear in structure than *Trust*, Ozick's second novel, *The Cannibal Galaxy* (1983), centers on Joseph Brill, who is the principal for an American school he founds. The focus of the school is the idea of a "Dual Curriculum," based on Jewish tradition and European secular education. He devotes his life to pursing his dream of this sort of education. He longs for a *wunderkind* student and develops a test designed to determine which students will succeed; however, the student Hester Lilt scores low on the test yet gains recognition as an artist, while Brill's own son scores high on the exam yet becomes an administrator at a junior college. Presenting Talmudic wisdom tales and using parables to provide suggestions for the dual approach to teaching,

Hester gives a lecture that could inspire Joseph; however, because he arrives late to her lecture and is unable to concentrate, he is unable to comprehend her message.

Another technique found in Ozick's writing is the use of an open-ended conclusion, which invites multiple interpretations. For example, *The Messiah of Stockholm* (1987) gives a fictional account of the allegedly lost manuscript of Bruno Schulz, a Polish Jewish writer who was shot by Nazis in 1942. Bruno's two collections of stories were published, but many believe Schulz wrote another manuscript, *Messiah*, which remains lost. The protagonist of *The Messiah of Stockholm*, Lars Andemening, believes he is Bruno Schulz's son and studies Polish to understand his father's voice. In the four years spent searching for Schulz's lost manuscript, Lars has accumulated pieces of information about Schulz in the form of related documents such as photos and letters. One day, a woman who claims to be Schulz's daughter brings the manuscript of *Messiah* to Lars. Believing the manuscript has been counterfeited by Eklund, who also authenticates the manuscript with elaborate handwriting analysis, Lars reads the manuscript in front of the Eklunds and their daughter, realizes the futility of his search, and burns the manuscript. *The Messiah of Stockholm* invites readers to ponder whether the manuscript Lars burns is authentic. In addition to creating a fictional account of a historical event, Ozick subtly comments on different types of value placed on art. In some ways, *The Messiah of Stockholm* refers to itself as a text and is representative of the sort of metafiction Ozick frequently utilizes in her fiction.

Some of Ozick's works can be classified as stories of magical realism. For example, her most recent novel, *The Puttermesser Papers* (1997), which derives from "Puttermesser and Xanthippe" and "Puttermesser: Her Work History, Her Ancestry, Her Afterlife," which appear in *Levitation: Five Fictions* (1982), is a Kafka-esque story. The novel portrays the adventures of Ruth Puttermesser, who creates the golem Xanthippe after her demotion from a bureaucratic job in New York City. Ruth's golem helps her become mayor of New York, but this status is short-lived. A compassionate liberal with artistic sensibilities, Ruth identifies with George Eliot, but her own lover re-creates Metropolitan Museum paintings instead of creating original works of art. After Ruth is killed and raped after her death, she goes to Paradise, where she marries the philosophy major she had been in love with when she was nineteen. She also gives birth in Paradise and is "happy—in her brain and in her heart, in her womb and in all her sexual parts" (233). However, as is typical in Ozick's works, all does not end well in *The Puttermesser Papers*, for happiness fades even in Paradise, where one discovers that "the secret meaning of Paradise is that it too is hell" (234). Boundaries between the real and the imitation and between the real universe and unknown worlds are blurred in *The Puttermesser Papers*. As in some of her other magical realism stories, the blurred distinctions in *The Puttermesser Papers* invite readers to consider philosophical issues such as the meaning of art, the purpose of religion, distinctions between truth and fallacy, and the significance of both life and death.

Although Ozick has received substantial acclaim for her novels and essays, she is perhaps most recognized for her achievement in the short story. *The Pagan Rabbi and Other Stories* (1971) was nominated for a National Book Award and received the B'nai B'rith Jewish Heritage Award, the Jewish Book Council Award, and the Edward Lewis Wallant Award. Her stories have been chosen for inclusion in the prestigious volumes *Best American Short Stories* and *Prize Stories: The O. Henry Awards*. One of Ozick's best-known short stories is "The Shawl," which she published together with "Rosa" in *The Shawl* (1981). "The Shawl" is told from Rosa's point of view, as she recalls the death of her infant daughter, who was thrown into an electric fence by Nazis during the Holocaust. The infant had sucked on the shawl, which comforted her and kept the Nazis from noticing her; however, one day, the shawl was missing and the infant's cries were heard. After her infant's death, Rosa uses the shawl to stifle her own cries. The sequel, "Rosa," depicts Rosa years later in Miami, where she receives a letter from a sociologist who wants to interview her as a Holocaust survivor. Rosa is frustrated because American customers who frequent her business cannot relate to the story of her daughter's death. In a laundromat, she finally meets Simon Persky, who listens to her story. However, she thinks he steals her underwear, and while looking for them, she wanders into a hotel. When she is thrown out of the hotel, Simon is waiting for her. Ironically, the behaviors she sees that bother her about the man are the very habits she possesses. For example, she mocks his broken English, while realizing her own English is limited. The story ends with her getting her telephone reconnected and her acceptance of Persky; thus, some healing of the trauma caused by the death of her daughter occurs.

Like "Rosa" and some of Ozick's other stories, the title story of *Levitation: Five Fictions* concerns a Holocaust survivor. "Levitation" involves a party given by two novelists. The party is dull and boring, except when one of the guests begins to tell about his experiences as a Holocaust survivor. The Holocaust survivor and those listening to his story float in the air.

Other well-known short stories by Ozick include "The Pagan Rabbi" and "Envy; or, Yiddish in America," both in *The Pagan Rabbi and Other Stories*. "The Pagan Rabbi" uses magical realism to reveal the spiritual conflict Rabbi Isaac Kornfeld experiences. The conflict concerns the battle between Kornfeld's soul, Judaic law, and his flesh, tempted by a spirit in a tree, or nature. "Envy; or, Yiddish in America" concerns the Yiddish poet Edelshtein who goes to New York seeking a translator. Instead of finding fame, he becomes obsessed with Ostrover, a successful Yiddish writer, whose fame Edelshtein envies.

"Usurpation (Other People's Stories)," which appears in *Bloodshed and Three Novellas* (1976), is also about an aspiring writer. This story concerns an obscure writer who hears a well-known writer read his latest story "The Magic Crown." She hears elements of the story that remind her of her own writings, so she wants to "usurp" the tale and write it in her own style and voice. Coincidentally, at the end of the presentation, another writer in the audience approaches the narrator and claims he is kin to the characters in the story that has just been presented. He gives the narrator a manuscript, and she usurps both stories, rewriting both into her own story. In addition to fictionalized writers as characters, "Usurpation" alludes to writers and poets such as Bernard Malamud, S. Y. Agnon, Solomon Ibn Gabirol, and Saul Tchernikhovsky. But "Usurpation" is more than metafiction that shows how writers build on and allude to the works of other writers. Packed with references to Jewish culture and tradition, "Usurpation," as Joseph Lowin points out, parallels the midrashic mode and is "about rewriting oneself, continually and continuously mulling over the metaphysical problem of writing as a proper Jewish activity" (*Cynthia Ozick* 105).

In both her fiction and her nonfiction, Ozick comments on the artistic process itself. The purpose of art is important to Ozick both in theory and in practice. Also, history, culture, and religion are significant subjects Ozick explores throughout her works. From her first publication in 1966 to her recently published collection of essays *Quar-*

rel and Quandary (2000), Ozick continues to contribute significantly to the American literary canon.

CRITICAL RECEPTION

Victor Strandberg points out in his 1983 essay "The Art of Cynthia Ozick" that the critical response to Ozick's works "has been highly favorable but scanty" (266). In order to bring critical attention to Ozick's works, Stranberg provides an analysis of each of Ozick's publications. After providing an overview of the central ideas Ozick expresses in her essays, he examines *Trust, The Pagan Rabbi and Other Stories, Bloodshed and Three Novellas*, and *Levitations: Five Fictions* in chronological order of publication. Stranberg's essay is a seminal analysis of Ozick's works: He moves beyond simplistic interpretation to look at her body of work as a whole in relation to her ideas about art, culture, and religion.

Since Stranberg's seminal essay, Ozick's works have begun to receive well-deserved critical attention. Most of this critical attention has centered on Ozick's role as Jewish writer. The titles of the following essays reveal various approaches to Ozick as a Jewish writer: "Cynthia Ozick, Jewish Writer," by Joseph Epstein; "American Jewish Writing, Act II," by Ruth R. Wisse; "The Jewish-American Woman as Artist: Cynthia Ozick and the 'Paleface' Tradition," by Arlene Fish Wliner; "Triangles of History and the Slippery Slope of Jewish American Identity in Two Stories by Cynthia Ozick," by Janet L. Cooper; "Cynthia Ozick, Pagan vs. Jew (1966–1976)," by Deborah Heiligman Weiner; "Covenanted to the Law: Cynthia Ozick," by Ruth Rosenberg; "Cynthia Ozick and Grace Paley: Diverse Visions in Jewish and Women's Literature," by Jeanne Salladé Criswell; "Jewish-American Literature's Lost-and-Found Department: How Philip Roth and Cynthia Ozick Reimagine Their Significant Dead," by Sanford Pinkser; "Cynthia Ozick and the Jewish Fantastic," by Joseph Lowin; "The Jewish Stories of Cynthia Ozick," by Josephine Z. Knopp; "Cynthia Ozick as the Jewish T. S. Eliot," by Mark Krupnick; and "Reading Cynthia Ozick: Imagining Jewish Writing," by Murray Baumgarten.

Sarah Blacher Cohen continues an earlier critical approach of looking at Ozick as a Jewish writer in her full-length study, *Cynthia Ozick's Comic Art: From Levity to Liturgy*, while Elaine M. Kauvar departs from approaches that look at Ozick as a Jewish writer in her book *Cynthia Ozick's Fiction: Tradition and Invention*. Kauvar reassesses Ozick's works to demonstrate her a significant writer of contemporary American literature, thus situating Ozick as a central American mainstream writer. Similar to Kauvar's approach, Andrew Lakritz's assessment, in "Cynthia Ozick at the End of the Modern," looks at Ozick in broader contexts than some earlier critics. Lakritz examines *The Messiah of Stockholm* as a postmodern text and discusses Ozick as a significant postmodern writer.

Fortunately, since Stranberg's 1983 essay, Ozick has begun to receive the critical attention her fiction and nonfiction deserve. While some critics continue to contextualize Ozick specifically as a Jewish or as a woman writer, others examine her in broader contexts. In any case, it is apparent that Ozick is among the most important contemporary writers. Her works continue to break new ground for writers, both building on and departing from earlier traditions.

BIBLIOGRAPHY

Works by Cynthia Ozick

Trust. New York: New American Library, 1966.

"Ethnic Joke." Rev. of *Bech: A Book*. By John Updike. *Commentary* Nov. 1970: 106–14.

The Pagan Rabbi and Other Stories. New York: Knopf, 1971.

Bloodshed and Three Novellas. New York: Knopf, 1976.

Levitation: Five Fictions. New York: Knopf, 1982.

The Cannibal Galaxy. New York: Knopf, 1983.

Art and Ardor: Essays. New York: Knopf, 1987.

The Messiah of Stockholm. New York: Knopf, 1987.

Metaphor and Memory. New York: Knopf, 1989.

The Shawl. New York: Knopf, 1989.

Epodes: First Poems. Columbus, OH: Logan Elm, 1992.

Portrait of the Artist as a Bad Character and Other Essays on Writing. London: Pimlico, 1996.

Fame and Folly. New York: Knopf, 1996.

The Puttermesser Papers. New York: Knopf, 1997.

Quarrel and Quandary: Essays. New York: Knopf, 2000.

Studies of Cynthia Ozick

Aatlin, Linda. "Cynthia Ozick's *Levitation: Five Fictions*." *Studies in American Jewish Literature* 4 (1985): 121–23.

Baumgarten, Murray. "Reading Cynthia Ozick: Imagining Jewish Writing." *Contemporary Literature* 37 (1996): 307–14.

Bloom, Harold, ed. *Modern Critical Views: Cynthia Ozick*. New York: Chelsea House, 1986.

Borchers, Hans. "Of Suitcases and Other Burdens: The Ambiguities of Cynthia Ozick's Image of Germany." *Centennial Review* 35 (1991): 607–24.

Brown, Erella. "The Ozick-Bloom Controversy: Anxiety of Influence, Usurpation as Idolatry, and the Identity of Jewish American Literature." *Studies in American Jewish Literature* 11 (1992): 62–82.

Burstein, Janet Handler. "Cynthia Ozick and the Transgressions of Art." *American Literature* 59 (1987): 85–101.

Cahill, Daniel J., and Susan Currier. "A Bibliography of Writings by Cynthia Ozick." *Texas Studies in Literature and Language* 25 (1983): 313–21.

Chartok, Haim. "Ozick's Hoofprints." *Yiddish* 6 (1987): 5–12.

Cohen, Sarah Blacher. "The Fiction Writer as Essayist: Ozick's *Metaphor and Memory*." *Judaism* 39 (1990): 276–81.

——. *Cynthia Ozick's Comic Art: From Levity to Liturgy*. Bloomington: Indiana University Press, 1994.

Cole, Diane. "Cynthia Ozick." *Twentieth-Century American-Jewish Fiction Writers*. Ed. Daniel Walden. Detroit: Gale, 1984. Vol. 28 of *Dictionary of Literary Biography*. 213–25.

Cooper, Janet L. "Triangles of History and the Slippery Slope of Jewish American Identity in Two Stories by Cynthia Ozick." *MELUS* 25 (2000): 181–95.

Criswell, Jeanne Salladel. "Cynthia Ozick and Grace Paley: Diverse Visions in Jewish and Women's Literature." *Since Flannery O'Connor: Essays on the Contemporary American Short Story*. Ed. Loren Logsdon and Charles W. Mayer. Macomb: Western Illinois University, 1987. 93–100.

Epstein, Joseph. "Cynthia Ozick, Jewish Writer." *Commentary* Mar. 1984: 64–69.

Finkelstein, Norman. "The Struggle for Historicity in the Fiction of Cynthia Ozick." *Lit: Literature, Interpretation, and Theory* 1 (1990): 291–302.

Fishman, Sylvia Barack. "Imagining Ourselves: Cynthia Ozick's *The Messiah of Stockholm.*" *Studies in American Jewish Literature* 9 (1990): 84–92.

Friedman, Lawrence S. *Understanding Cynthia Ozick.* Columbia: University of South Carolina Press, 1991.

——. "A Postcolonial Jew: Cynthia Ozick's Holocaust Survivor." *Journal of the South Pacific Association for Commonwealth Literature and Language Studies* 36 (1993): 436–43.

Gitenstein, Barbara R. "The Temptation of Apollo and the Loss of Yiddish in Cynthia Ozick's Fiction." *Studies in American Jewish Literature* 3 (1983): 194–201.

Gottfried, Amy. "Fragmented Art and the Liturgical Community of the Dead in Cynthia Ozick's *The Shawl.*" *Studies in American Jewish Literature* 13 (1994): 39–51.

Greenstein, Michael. "The Muse and the Messiah: Cynthia Ozick's Aesthetics." *Studies in American Jewish Literature* 8 (1989): 50–65.

——. "Ozick, Roth, and Postmodernism." *Studies in American Jewish Literature* 10 (1991): 54–64.

Harap, Louis. "The Religious Art of Cynthia Ozick." *Judaism* 33 (1984): 353–63.

Hellerstein, Kathryn. "Yiddish Voices in American English." *The State of the Language.* Ed. Leonard Michaels and Christopher Ricks. Berkeley: University of California Press, 1979. 182–201.

Hornung, Alfred. "The Transgression of Postmodern Fiction: Philip Roth and Cynthia Ozick." *Affirmation and Negation in Contemporary American Literature.* Ed. Gerhard Hoffmann and Alfred Hornung. Heidelberg: Universitatsverlag C. Winter, 1994. 229–49.

Johnson, Stuart. "Germinal James: The Lesson of the Apprentice." *Modern Fiction Studies* 31 (1985): 233–47.

Kauvar, Elaine M. "Cynthia Ozick's Book of Creation: Puttermesser and Xanthippe." *Contemporary Literature* 26 (1985): 40–54.

——. "An Interview with Cynthia Ozick." *Contemporary Literature* 26 (1985): 375–401.

——. *Cynthia Ozick's Fiction: Tradition and Invention.* Bloomington: Indiana University Press, 1993.

——. "An Interview with Cynthia Ozick." *Contemporary Literature* 34 (1993): 359–94.

——. *A Cynthia Ozick Reader.* Bloomington: Indiana University Press, 1996.

Kielsky, Vera Emuna. *Inevitable Exiles: Cynthia Ozick's View of the Precariousness of Jewish Existence in a Gentile Society.* New York: Peter Lang, 1989.

Klingenstein, Susanne. "Destructive Intimacy: The Shoah between Mother and Daughter in Fictions by Cynthia Ozick, Norma Rosen, and Rebecca Goldstein." *Studies in American Jewish Literature* 11 (1992): 162–73.

Knopp, Josephine Z. "The Jewish Stories of Cynthia Ozick." *Studies in American Jewish Literature* 1 (1975): 31–38.

Kremer, S. Lillian. "Cynthia Ozick (1928–)." *Jewish American Women Writers: A Bio-Bibliographical and Critical Sourcebook.* Ed. Ann R. Shapiro. Westport, CT: Greenwood Press, 1994. 265–77.

Krupnick, Mark. "Cynthia Ozick as the Jewish T. S. Eliot." *Soundings* 74 (1991): 351–68.

Lakritz, Andrew. "Cynthia Ozick at the End of the Modern." *Chicago Review* 40 (1994): 98–117.

Lowin, Joseph. "Cynthia Ozick and the Jewish Fantastic." *Identity and Ethos.* Ed. Mark H. Gelber. New York: Peter Lang, 1986. 311–23.

——. "Cynthia Ozick, Rewriting Herself: The Road from 'The Shawl' to 'Rosa.' " *Since Flannery O'Connor: Essays on the Contemporary American Short Story.* Ed. Loren Logsdon and Charles W. Mayer. Macomb: Western Illinois University, 1987. 101–12.

——. *Cynthia Ozick.* Boston: Twayne, 1988.

Malcolm, Cheryl Alexander. "Compromise and Cultural Identity: British and American Perspectives in Anita Brookner's *Providence* and Cynthia Ozick's 'Virility.' " *English Studies* 5 (1997): 459–71.

Martin, Margot L. "The Theme of Survival in Cynthia Ozick's 'The Shawl.' " *RE: Artes Liberales* 14 (1988): 31–36.

Meyers, Judith. "Double Otherness: Woman as Holocaust Survivor in Cynthia Ozick's 'Rosa.' " *Selected Essays from the International Conference on The Outsider 1988.* Ed. John Micheal Crafton. Carrollton: West Georgia College, 1990. 141–51.

New, Elisa. "Cynthia Ozick's Timing." *Prooftexts* 9 (1989): 288–94.

Pifer, Ellen. "Cynthia Ozick: Invention and Orthodoxy." *Contemporary American Women Writers: Narrative Strategies.* Ed. Catherine Rainwater and William J. Scheick. Lexington: University Press of Kentucky, 1985. 109–16.

Pinsker, Sanford. *The Uncompromising Fiction of Cynthia Ozick.* Columbia: University of Missouri Press, 1987.

——. "Jewish-American Literature's Lost-and-Found Department: How Philip Roth and Cynthia Ozick Reimagine Their Significant Dead." *Modern Fiction Studies* 35 (1989): 223–35.

Powers, Peter Kerry. "Disruptive Memories: Cynthia Ozick, Assimilation, and the Invented Past." *MELUS* 20 (1995): 78–97.

Rainwater, Catherine, and William J. Scheick. "An Interview with Cynthia Ozick." *Texas Studies in Literature and Language* 25 (1983): 255–65.

Rose, Elisabeth. "Cynthia Ozick's Liturgical Postmodernism: The Messiah of Stockholm." *Studies in American Jewish Literature* 9 (1990): 93–107.

Rosenberg, Ruth. "Covenanted to the Law: Cynthia Ozick." *MELUS* 9 (1982): 39–44.

——. "The Ghost Story as Aggada: Cynthia Ozick's 'The Pagan Rabbi' and Sheindel's Scar." *Haunting the House of Fiction: Feminist Perspectives on Ghost Stories by American Women.* Ed. Lynette Carpenter and Wendy K. Kolmar. Knoxville: University of Tennessee Press, 1991. 215–28.

Rovit, Earl. "The Two Languages of Cynthia Ozick." *Studies in American Jewish Literature* 8 (1989): 34–49.

Scrafford, Barbara. "Nature's Silent Scream: A Commentary on Cynthia Ozick's 'The Shawl.' " *Critique* 31 (1989): 11–15.

Sokoloff, Naomi B. "Interpretation: Cynthia Ozick's *Cannibal Galaxy.*" *Prooftexts* 6 (1986): 239–57.

Strandberg, Victor. "The Art of Cynthia Ozick." *Texas Studies in Literature and Language* 25 (1983): 266–312.

——. *Greek Mind/Jewish Soul: The Conflicted Art of Cynthia Ozick.* Madison: University of Wisconsin Press, 1994.

Weiner, Deborah Heiligman. "Cynthia Ozick, Pagan vs. Jew (1966–1976)." *Studies in American Jewish Literature* 3 (1983): 179–83.

Wilner, Arlene Fish. "The Jewish-American Woman as Artist: Cynthia Ozick and the 'Paleface' Tradition." *College Literature* 20 (1993): 119–32.

Wisse, Ruth R. "American Jewish Writing, Act II." *Commentary* June 1976: 40–45.

GRACE (GOODSIDE) PALEY (1922–)

Lisa María Burgess Noudéhou

BIOGRAPHY

Poet, mother, teacher, and activist, Grace Paley was born Grace Goodside on December 11, 1922, in the Bronx to Russian Jewish parents. Manya Ridnyick (1885–1944) and Isaac Gutseit (1885–1973) had emigrated from the Ukraine in 1906. Paley grew up with English, Yiddish, and Russian as home languages and socialism as home politics. Home included her older brother Victor (1906–) and sister Jeanne (1908–1999) as well as her father's mother (Natasha) and one of his sisters (Mira).

Despite the family's high expectations given her intellect, Paley dropped out of high school and then left Hunter College in New York after one year (1938–1939). A poet since she was a child, Paley then took a course with W. H. Auden at the New School for Social Research in New York (about 1940). She never completed any formal degrees.

Grace Goodside became Grace Paley when she married Jess Paley in 1942. Soon after their marriage, they traveled across the United States, as Jess had joined the Signal Corps. During this time, Paley's mother died of breast cancer in 1944. Jess Paley served in the South Pacific for 18 months of active duty in World War II. Upon his return, he worked as a freelance photographer and filmmaker. Grace and Jess had two children: Nora in 1949 and Danny in 1951. After being separated from 1967 to 1972, Paley divorced Jess and married Robert Nichols, a writer and landscape architect. The following year, in 1973, Paley's father died. In 1974 Paley and Nichols toured China for three weeks. The two collaborated on "Chilean Diary," published in *WIN* in 1973. Paley and Nichols have lived together in both New York and Vermont.

To earn a bit of money, Paley started teaching creative writing in 1966 at Sarah Lawrence College in New York. While continuing to teach at Sarah Lawrence until 1988, Paley has also taught at Columbia University, Dartmouth College, Syracuse University, and City College of New York. Her much-sought-after courses have been important occasions for Paley to interact with, teach, and inspire youthful writers.

Known as much for her political activism as for her writing, Paley has worked for world peace since the 1950s. During the Vietnam War, for instance, Paley worked through the group Support in Action to educate young men about their options when faced with the draft, visited Vietnam in 1969 as part of a peace movement delegation to bring home first-hand knowledge of the decimation of war and of the situation of both U.S. and Vietnamese prisoners of war, helped to organize public demonstrations against the war, and wrote articles in an effort to convince Americans to end the war. During the Cold War, Paley, a delegate of the War Resisters League, attended the World Peace Congress in Moscow in 1972. She spoke with Russian dissidents such as Aleksandr I. Solzhenitsyn and Andrei D. Sakharov, exchanging information so that both nations' dissidents would know what issues and obstacles faced their peers. With regard to feminist issues, Paley has worked, through both her writings and various political organizations, to call attention to women's issues and goals. Like Adrienne Rich, Paley developed her feminism through her own descriptions of the particular pressures of women's lives in the 1950s. Paley cites Ruth Herschberger's *Adam's Rib* (1948) as one of the first books that she read that addressed the issue of women's sexuality (Bolinsky). Paley has supported feminism within wider movements to gain respect for the individual and the environment. She has been an important member of the Greenwich Village Peace Center (1960), Support in Action (1960s), Women's Pentagon Action (1981), Seneca Women's Peace Encampment, War Resisters League, PEN (Poets, Essayists and Novelists), RESIST, and the Jewish Women's Committee to End the Occupation of the Left Bank and Gaza (1987), to name just a few of the organizations through which Paley has worked for world peace.

Currently, Paley lives in both Vermont and New York. She continues as engaged as ever, publishing her prose and poetry and offering talks and interviews.

MAJOR WORKS AND THEMES

Paley began writing stories in 1952. Her first two stories were "Goodbye and Good Luck" and "The Contest," both of which were published in *Accent: A Quarterly* (1956, 1958). These stories were later collected in Paley's first collection, *The Little Disturbances of Man: Stories of Men and Women at Love*. Since then, she has published stories in numerous journals and has produced three collections of stories: *The Little Disturbances of Man: Stories of Men and Women at Love* (1959), *Enormous Changes at the Last Minute* (1974), and *Later the Same Day* (1985). In general, Paley's stories are known for their wit, irony, character voices, and poetic precision. Key themes that run through her stories include listening and storytelling, women's lives from teen to grandmother, men versus women, what it means to be Jewish in US society, aging and dying, responsibility for others and the world, and motherhood.

The Little Disturbances of Man already demonstrates these qualities and themes. In "Goodbye and Good Luck," Rosie Lieber speaks to her niece in a Russian-Jewish-Yiddish-American voice about her life and relationships with men, closing with the message to be passed to her sister that she is finally getting married and going away. This early story deals with the themes of listening and storytelling, women's lives, men versus women, and being Jewish in the United States. "The Loudest Voice" is a much-loved humorous story told in the voice of Shirley Abramowitz, the daughter of first-generation immigrants. The school's ironic choice of Shirley to narrate the Christmas pageant touches on the problems of assimilation into U.S. society when one is not Christian, addressing the theme of what it means to be Jewish in U.S. society. But even while dealing with this serious theme, Paley entertains the reader with the wit of a loud, self-confident young girl who closes her story with a prayer "for everybody: my talking family, cousins far away, passersby, and all the lonesome Christians. I expected to be heard. My voice was certainly the loudest (63)." In contrast, Paley takes on the voice of a twenty-nine-year-old Jewish man being interviewed by an Army psychologist in "The Contest." The man tells the story of Dotty Wasserman, whom he describes as "a medium girl, size twelve, a clay pot with handles—she could be grasped" (67). But, in fact, Dotty turns out to be a woman who cannot be grasped, a woman who uses the narrator to win a contest and enjoy a tour of Palestine and Europe, leaving him with $100 and a case of slides. In this story, Paley again deals with being Jewish in the United States, men versus women, and listening and storytelling. These stories, like the other stories in the collection, demonstrate the wit and control of voice that are characteristic of Paley's writing.

Paley's second collection, *Enormous Changes at the Last Minute*, and third collection, *Later the Same Day*, continue to develop these themes. The book *Later the Same Day* is marked by its sorrow and celebration, mourning people's inability to communicate or save each other and celebrating people's attempts to be saviors. "Lavinia: An Old Story," for instance, is told by a mother to her daughter's suitor. The mother mourns how marriage and motherhood have focused Lavinia's laughter and "good cheer" on the domestic rather than on astonishing achievements. But the story, in the telling, celebrates the mother's appreciation of her daughter and her attempts to protect her daughter. This last collection develops the themes of listening and story telling, women's lives from teen to grandmother, men versus women, what it means to be Jewish in U.S. society, aging and dying, responsibility for others and the world, and motherhood primarily through the Faith story cycle.

Paley uses the story cycle, telling numerous self-contained stories about the same group of characters, to enable the reader to understand different characters and their perspectives. The Ginny story cycle, which Paley develops in her first two collections, begins with "An Interest in Life" (1959), which is told by Virginia about her experiences as a mother of four deserted by her husband and helped by John, a former boyfriend. "Distance" (1974), in contrast, is told by Mrs. Raftery, who had originally prevented her son, John, from proposing marriage to Ginny. Reading the two stories together enables the reader to understand characters that do not necessarily understand each other.

Paley's primary story cycle focuses on Faith, a liberal, politically active mother of two, who is often read as an alter ego to Paley. The characters of Faith, her family (parents, sons Richard and Anthony/Tonto, ex-husband, boyfriends, husband Jack), and friends (Selena, Susan, Ann, Ruth, Edie, Louise, Cassie) make up a cycle that consists of at least thirteen stories. Readers met Faith in "Two Short Sad Stories from a Long and Happy Life," published in the first collection of stories. These two stories are narrated by Faith and deal with a woman's relationships to her husbands and to her sons. The ending of the second story, in which Faith begs her son Anthony to give her some time to herself and he assures her that he will never leave her and will always love her, illustrates the tension between independence as a woman and love and responsibility as a mother. The second collection developed the cycle through such stories as "Faith in the Afternoon," "Faith in a Tree," and "The Long Distance Runner," which are told either from Faith's perspective or in her voice. The third collection includes such stories as "Dreamer in a Dead Language" told in the third person and focusing on Faith's parents, "Friends" told by Faith about the death of her friend Selena, and "Zagrowsky Tells." This last story is spoken by the pharmacist Iz Zagrowsky primarily to Faith, telling how her demonstrations against his racism in front of his store triggered his daughter's insanity and led to the birth of his black grandson. This story focuses on the insensitivity of Faith and her friends and enables the reader to understand Zagrowsky's point of view. Using different voices of characters that the reader has come to know enables Paley to provide a social critique that encompasses all sides of an issue, thus making it possible for the reader to attain a level of awareness that the characters never achieve.

How Paley develops the link between personal and political conflicts, between the mundane and the historical, and between present choices and the future of the world and of children can be seen, in particular, in the poetic precision of her imagery. Paley clearly developed her imagery through writing poetry. Although she had been writing poetry since she was a child, she began to publish her poetry late in life. She published her first collections of poetry as limited editions: *16 Broadsides* (1980) and *Goldenrod* (1982). *Leaning Forward: Poems* (1985), *New and Collected Poems* (1992), and *Begin Again: Collected Poems* (2000) are the key collections of her poetry. Paley's poems explore similar themes to those found in the short stories.

Paley's political writing includes stories and poems as well as speeches and reports and even a calendar (*365 Reasons Not to Have Another War: Peace Calendar 1989*). The collection of stories and poems titled *Long Walks and Intimate Talks* (1991), beautifully illustrated by Vera B. Williams, develops the reader's political awareness through depictions of individual acts of resistance. The collection *Just As I Thought* (1998) presents stories, speeches, and political reports in thematic groups that follow a roughly chronological order, moving from the 1950s to the Vietnam War era to teaching to activism in the 1990s to her father. This directly political writing embodies the way that Paley has been able to link her concerns as a mother, teacher, and writer with her concerns about the world's future.

CRITICAL RECEPTION

Paley's stories, poetry, essays, and speeches should be read in the general context of post–World War II US authors. During this time period, authors as diverse as those identified with the Beats or the Harlem Renaissance sought to expand the horizons of US literature. But Paley should also be read in the more specific context of Jewish authors that includes Bernard Malamud, Tillie Olsen, and Cynthia Ozick, who are similarly able to represent the particularities of Jewish characters and Jewish voices. In addition, Paley should be read in the specific context of feminist authors such as Toni Morrison, Alice Walker, and Adrienne Rich, who use fiction to address social wrongs. Like these women, Paley has developed new ways of writing that express social critique and represent the realities and fantasies of women's lives in the later twentieth century. Considered in these three contexts, Paley's contribution of the voice of a twentieth-century, New York Jewish woman is revealed both as part of a general movement toward humane literature that rejects the bounds of literary bigotry and as the development of a distinct voice that enables the enjoyment and understanding of everyday, yet unique, characters.

The numerous awards that Paley has received indicate the esteem with which her readers and peers hold her literary achievements. These awards include, among others, the Guggenheim Fellowship (1961), a National Endowment for the Arts Grant (1966), National Institute of Arts and Letters Literary Award for short fiction (1970), election to the American Academy and Institute of Arts and Letters (1980), the PEN/Faulkner Prize for fiction (1986), the Edith Wharton Citation of Merit for fiction writers (1986), a National Endowment for the Arts Senior Fellowship (1987), declaration as the first official New York State Writer by Governor Mario Cuomo (1989), the REA Award for Short Stories (1992), the Vermont Award for Excellence in the Arts (1993), the Jewish Cultural Achievement Award for Literary Arts (1994), and the National Book Award for *The Collected Stories* (1994).

Like her readers, literary critics have generally reacted to Paley's publications with praise. From the 1950s through the 1970s, most criticism came in the form of interviews or book reviews. Kathleen Hulley put together the first collection of essays to focus on Grace Paley's work in 1982. This special issue of *Delta* includes both essays and interviews that focus on "Paley's formal structures and strategies of resistance to traditional forms" (7). Faced with a style of writing that resists criticism by means of its directness, the critics generally found that "her narrative form refuses the murderous struggle for logo-centric dominance and provides grounds for reopening the issue of modernist writing from a disseminating perspective" (18). Other critics of Paley's writings in the 1980s focused on what it means to be Jewish in U.S. society (Mandel, Sorkin), narrative techniques (Klinkowitz, Schleifer, Taylor), and social criticism (Eckstein, Kamel) or compared Paley's writing with that of Cynthia Ozick (Criswell).

The 1990s brought key developments in the critical analysis of Paley's work. Jacqueline Taylor's *Grace Paley: Illuminating the Dark Lives* (1990) is one of the first full-length literary studies published. Taylor writes that distinctive aspects of Paley's writings include how she writes about the mundane lives of people, uses a comic voice, and develops a "resistance to all forms of oppression" (2). But, she argues, the most important aspect of her writing is her language. Using the "muted group theory" to frame the problem of speaking the language of the dominant class when one belongs to a marginalized group, Taylor writes that Paley's short stories challenge forced silence: "Refusing mutedness and the denials and distortions of dominant language, Paley claims the power to repossess language and subvert conventional forms [through] semantic encoding and narrative structures" (8).

In the same year, Neal D. Isaacs's *Grace Paley: A Study of the Short Fiction* was published as part of Twayne's Studies in Short Fiction. In the three sections of the book, Isaacs provides analysis of Paley's three story collections, thematically and chronologically organized excerpts from Paley's interviews and comments, and an overview of criticism from 1956 to 1988. While providing his own readings of the stories in the first section, the book as a whole takes a very broad view of Paley's fiction.

Two years later, Judith Arcana's *Grace Paley's Life Stories: A Literary Biography* (1993) provided a reading of Paley's biography that is interwoven with a reading of her writings. Even though the book is based on extensive interviews with Paley and Paley's family and friends, Taylor maintains a literary focus as she studies "the relationship between the life and the texts by examining the transitional space—that peculiar set of personal, socio-historical circumstances—in which the author chooses to render an actual room or boy or woman or tree *into* the room or boy or woman or tree in a story" (2).

The fourth major development in the 1990s was the publication of a collection of interviews with Grace Paley. Edited by Gerhard Bach and Blaine Hall, *Conversations with Grace Paley (Literary Conversation Series)* (1997) brings together interviews that took place between 1978 and 1995. Bach and Blaine write that Paley's main concerns, as revealed in the interviews, are "family and generational relationships; personal background and educational impact; women, their need for communication and the public's need to redefine women's roles; the process of finding her 'voice' and seeing it as representative of women's voices of her generation; her early life as a writer of poetry, the fictional voice not developing until her social identity was more clearly defined; the interrelatedness of politics, environmentalism, feminism, and immensely personal and local issues; the art of teaching; the importance of friendship as well as the importance and moral impact of community" (viii). Paley continues to provide interviews. Some of the more extensive ones have been conducted by *RESIST* (Bolinsky), *Salon* (Homes), and Al Filreis. These interviews provide important insights into Paley's own sense of the distinctions between fiction and life, of the purposes of writing, and of her various roles in the later half of the twentieth century.

During the 1990s, numerous essays have also been published in literary journals. These essays generally demonstrate a continued concern with what it means to be Jewish in US society (Baumgarten, Goffman), narrative techniques (Taylor), and social criticism (Levy, Aarons). In the case of social criticism, critics have added the analysis of the relationship between Jews and blacks in the United States (Budick, Meyer). Other topics include motherhood (Arcana, Burstein) and a comparison of Ozick and Paley (Lyons).

Jane Cooper's afterword to *Leaning Forward: Poems* (1985) provides one of the few critical considerations of Paley's poetry. Cooper denies that the poetry derives from the stories, as Paley had been writing poetry long before she ever wrote a short story. Cooper argues, instead, that Paley's poems might be considered "conversations with herself about whatever she sees, suffers, invents, suddenly wants to point out in an excess of delight, crying 'Look! Look!' Or they are brief, truthful melodies that are the pure distillation of an instant's widest view" (88).

Criticism in the twenty-first century will surely bring further consideration of Paley's short stories and will, it is hoped, begin to address her poetry, essays, and speeches as well.

BIBLIOGRAPHY

Works by Grace Paley

The Little Disturbances of Man: Stories of Men and Women at Love. Garden City: Doubleday, 1959.
Grace Paley with Robert Nichols. "Chilean Diary." *WIN* 17 May 1973: 6–8; 24 May 1973: 10–12; 31 May 1973: 9–10; 7 June 1973: 12–13.
Enormous Changes at the Last Minute. New York: Farrar, 1974.
16 Broadsides. St. Paul, MN: Bookslinger, 1980.
Goldenrod. Penobscot, ME: Granite Press, 1982.
Later the Same Day. New York: Farrar, 1985.
Leaning Forward: Poems. Afterword by Jane Cooper. Penobscot, ME: Granite Press, 1985.

Enormous Changes at the Last Minute. Screenplay by John Sayles and Susan Rice. ABC Video Enterprises. Vidmark Entertainment, 1987.

365 Reasons Not to Have Another War: Peace Calendar 1989. Paintings by Vera B. Williams. Philadelphia: New Society, 1989.

Long Walks and Intimate Talks. Paintings by Vera B. Williams. New York: Feminist Press at City University of New York, 1991.

New and Collected Poems. Gardiner, ME: Tilbury House, 1992.

The Collected Stories. New York: Farrar, 1994.

Just As I Thought. New York: Farrar, 1998.

Begin Again: Collected Poems. New York: Farrar, 2000.

Studies of Grace Paley

Aarons, Victoria. "A Perfect Marginality: Public and Private Telling in the Stories of Grace Paley." *Studies in Short Fiction* 27 (1990): 35–43. Reprint. *Contemporary American Women Writers: Gender, Class, Ethnicity.* Ed. Louis Parkinson Zamora. London: Longman, 1998: 204–13.

——. "Talking Lives: Storytelling and Renewal in Grace Paley's Short Fiction." *Studies in American Jewish Literature* 9 (1990): 30–35.

——. "Selves and 'Other Shadows': Grace Paley's Ironic Fictions." *Speaking the Other Self: American Women Writers.* Athens: University of Georgia Press, 1997.

Arcana, Judith. "Truth in Mothering: Grace Paley's Stories." *Narrating Mothers: Theorizing Maternal Subjectivities.* Ed. Brenda O. Daly and Maureen Reddy. Knoxville: University of Tennessee Press, 1991. 195–208.

——. *Grace Paley's Life Stories: A Literary Biography.* Urbana: University of Illinois Press, 1993.

Bach, Gerhard, and Blaine Hall, eds. *Conversations with Grace Paley (Literary Conversations Series).* Jackson: University Press of Mississippi, 1997.

Baumgarten, Murray. "Urban Rites and Civic Premises in the Fiction of Saul Bellow, Grace Paley, and Sandra Schor." *Contemporary Literature* 34 (1993): 397–427.

Bolinsky, Eileen, and Robin Carton. "Interview with Grace Paley on Activism and Writing." 1997 (http://www.resistinc.org/newsletter/issues/1997/12/paley.html).

Budick, Emily Miller. " 'The Anguish of the Other': On the Mutual Displacements, Appropriations, and Accommodations of Culture." *Blacks and Jews in Literary Conversation.* New York: Cambridge University Press, 1998: 200–17.

Burstein, Janet Handler. "Centering the Devalued Mother: Re-Vision and Re-Valuation." *Writing Mothers, Writing Daughters: Tracing the Maternal in Stories by American Jewish Women.* Urbana: University of Illinois Press, 1996.

Criswell, Jeanne Sallade. "Cynthia Ozick and Grace Paley: Diverse Visions in Jewish and Women's Literature." *Since Flannery O'Connor: Essays on the Contemporary American Short Story.* Ed. Loren Logsdon and Charles W. Mayer. Macomb: Western Illinois University Press, 1987.

Eckstein, Barbara. "Grace Paley's Community: Gradual Epiphanies in the Meantime." *Politics and the Muse: Studies in the Politics of Recent American Literature.* Bowling Green: Popular, 1989. 124–41.

Filreis, Al. "Interview with Grace Paley." University of Pennsylvania. 15 February 2000 (http://www.english.upenn.edu/~wh/paley.html).

Gelfant, Blanche H. "Grace Paley: Fragments for a Portrait in Collage." *New England Review* 3 (1980): 276–93. Reprint. *Women Writing in America.* Ed. B. H. Gelfant. University Press of New England, 1984. 11–29.

Goffman, Ethan. "Grace Paley's Faith: The Journey Homeward, the Journey Forward." *MELUS* 25 (2000): 197–208.

Homes, A. M. "Interview with Grace Paley: All My Habits Are Bad." 26 October 1998 *Salon* (http://www.salon.com/books/int/1998/10/26int.html).

Hulley, Kathleen, ed. *Grace Paley*. Special Issue. *Delta: Revue du Centre d'Etudes et de Recherche sur les Ecrivains du Sud aux Etats-Unis* 14 (May 1982).

Isaacs, Neal D. *Grace Paley: A Study of the Short Fiction*. Studies in Short Fiction. Boston: G. K. Hall/Twayne Series, 1990.

Kamel, Rose Yalow. "To Aggravate the Conscience: Grace Paley's Loud Voice." *Journal of Ethnic Studies* 11 (1983): 29–49. Reprint. *Aggravating the Conscience: Jewish American Literary Foremothers in the Promised Land*. New York: Peter Lang, 1989. 115–49.

Klinkowitz, Jerome. "Grace Paley: The Sociology of Metafiction." *Literary Subversions: New American Fiction and the Practice of Criticism*. Carbondale, IL: Southern Illinois University Press, 1985: 70–76.

Levy, Barbara. "Grace Paley: 'The Ear Is Smarter than the Eye.' " *Ladies Laughing: Wit as Control in Contemporary American Women Writers*. Amsterdam, Netherlands: Gordon and Breach, 1997: 91–112.

Lyons, Bonnie. "Faith and Puttermesser: Contrasting of Two Jewish Feminists." *Talking Back: Images of Jewish Women in American Popular Culture*. Hannover, NH: Brandeis University Press, 1998. 139–49.

Mandel, Dena. "Keeping Up with Faith: Grace Paley's Sturdy American Jewess." *Studies in American Jewish Literature* 3 (1983): 85–98.

Meyer, Adam. "Faith and the 'Black Thing': Political Action and Self-Questioning in Grace Paley's Short Fiction." *Studies in Short Fiction* 31 (1994): 79–89.

Park, Clara Claiborne. "Faith, Grace, and Love." *Hudson Review* 38 (1985): 481–88.

Schleifer, Ronald. "Grace Paley: Chaste Compactness." *Contemporary American Women Writers: Narrative Strategies*. Ed. Catherine Rainwater and William J. Scheik. Lexington: University of Kentucky Press, 1985. 31–49.

Sorkin, Adam J. "What Are We, Animals? Grace Paley's World of Talk and Laughter." *Studies in American Jewish Literature* 2 (1982): 144–54.

Taylor, Jacqueline. *Grace Paley: Illuminating the Dark Lives*. Austin: University of Texas Press, 1990.

SARA PARETSKY (1947–)

Elizabeth Blakesley Lindsay

BIOGRAPHY

Sara Paretsky was born June 8, 1947, in Ames, Iowa, to college professor David Paretsky and librarian Mary Edwards Paretsky. The only daughter of their five children, Paretsky grew up in a family she has described as one "where girls became secretaries and wives, and boys became professionals" (Shapiro 67).

She wrote constantly during high school and college, but she was never encouraged to attempt to publish any of her works (Rozan 44). The gender bias present in her family life spilled over into her education as well. In discussing her desire to write a strong female character, she notes that she recalls only one book written by a woman, George Eliot's *Silas Marner*, as being included in the secondary school curriculum (Ross 336). After earning a bachelor's degree from the University of Kansas in 1967, Paretsky went to graduate school at the University of Chicago to earn a PhD in history. The study of history was not her top priority, however, as she comments that she read twenty-four mysteries in the month before her oral examinations for the doctoral degree (Shapiro 67). In 1976 she married S. Courtenay Wright, a widowed father of three and a professor of physics at the University of Chicago. Although she finished her PhD in 1977, she decided against university teaching as a career. She quickly earned an MBA degree from the University of Chicago and entered the business world. She was quite successful as a marketing manager in the insurance industry, but her love remained with reading and writing. Even after her first novel was published, though, she stayed with her job for several years before devoting herself to writing full-time.

Paretsky had always read and enjoyed mystery fiction, and the decision to write a detective novel was an easy one. She was quite interested in writing about a female detective and worked on a manuscript for several years. As a New Year's resolution, she set a goal for herself to complete the novel in 1979. She wanted to write a novel about a female working in the Raymond Chandler tradition, a woman who would be "a success in a field traditionally dominated by men" (Ross 335); and during 1979, V. I. Warshawski was born. Paretsky has said that Warshawski was born while she was saying one thing to her boss but thinking another (Evans G1). For Paretsky, Warshawski has qualities Paretsky herself does not, such as speaking without concern for what others think and acting without worrying about consequences (Evans G1).

To help achieve her goal, Paretsky enrolled in a continuing education course in mystery writing taught by Stuart Kaminsky; this experience helped her hone the manuscript and gain access to the publishing world. Within eighteen months of her New Year's resolution, she finished *Indemnity Only* and began searching for a publisher, eventually signing with Dial Press, which published the novel in 1982.

Social issues have long been a concern of Paretsky's, and her character, V. I. Warshawski, shares these concerns. Paretsky's grandparents met on a union picket line, and although her parents' gender-based inequities toward Paretsky and her brothers were problematic, the family was quite liberal politically (Rozan 44). Her first experiences in Chicago were as a college student volunteering for community service projects during a summer. As for the gender bias she suffered, Paretsky says that "the women's movement of the '60's changed my life," allowing her to move beyond doubts she had about herself and "make a difference in the public sphere" (Rozan 45).

In addition to being a prolific participant in the mystery genre, Paretsky also is one of the founding members of Sisters in Crime, a group organized in 1986 to increase the visibility and status of women writing in the mystery field with reviewers, readers and publishers. Paretsky served as the first president of the group. The group is also concerned with graphic violence toward women in crime fiction and works to correct imbalances in the treatment of women (Herbert 31).

Paretsky was selected as *Ms.* magazine's Woman of the Year in 1987 and also won an award from the Friends of American Writers for *Deadlock* (1984) and a Crime Writers Association Silver Dagger Award for *Blood Shot* (1988).

MAJOR WORKS AND THEMES

Except for one novel, *Ghost Country* (1998), Paretsky's body of work consists of a detective series featuring the female investigator Victoria Iphigenia Warshawski. Known as V. I. to most, Vic to her friends, she is a lawyer-turned-private-investigator who was born and raised, and lives and works, in Chicago. The only child of a Polish police officer and an Italian opera singer, Warshawski represents a unique blend of cultures, languages, and religions. Her mother died when she was fifteen, her father ten years later, and these events have greatly shaped Warshawski. The novels are best described as hard-boiled and do feature a good amount of violence, both meted out and received by Warshawski. The cases draw on Warshawski's expertise in finance and law, often involving fraud in various industries and political settings.

Indemnity Only, the first Warshawski novel and one of the first detective novels written by a woman about a woman investigator, features Warshawski tracking down a missing woman and becoming entangled with a fraudulent scheme involving union leaders, gangsters, and crooked insurance executives. In *Deadlock*, Warshawski takes on the investigation of the death of her cousin, again uncovering corruption and fraud, this time in the shipping business. The third Warshawski novel, *Killing Orders* (1985), tackles fraud and corruption among the powerful elite of the Catholic Church.

With *Bitter Medicine* (1987), Paretsky begins to tackle even more social issues. *Bitter Medicine* involves the death of a young woman mistreated at a hospital because of her race. Medical malpractice is the major area of fraudulent activities uncovered by Warshawski, but there is an extra layer of social commentary presented here. *Blood Shot* (1988) involves a chemical company that covered up evidence that its products were harming the workers, while *Burn Marks* (1990) centers on arson and corruption in the building industry and also features Warshawski's aunt, who is alcoholic and semi-homeless. *Guardian Angel* (1992) looks at the plight of the elderly and focuses on corrupt schemes involving bankers and lawyers who prey on the elderly. *Tunnel Vision* (1994) draws attention to the homeless, child abuse, and racially motivated funding decisions regarding social services. A year after *Tunnel Vision*, Paretsky published *Windy City Blues* (1995), a collection of short stories featuring Warshawski. *Ghost Country*, Paretsky's only non-Warshawski novel to date, followed this. Some reviewers and critics thought that *Tunnel Vision*, with its ambiguity about the aging Warshawski's situation, might be the last novel of the series (Porsdam 145). Paretsky herself invited readers to visit her web site and share speculations about Warshawski's future (Evans G1). Four years after *Tunnel Vision*, though, *Hard Time* (1999) appeared, returning Warshawski to the investigative scene. *Hard Time* focuses on the exploitation and experience of immigrants and brings to light a corrupt prison system. As mentioned previously, social issues are of great concern to Paretsky and, by extension, also to the Warshawski character. Elaine Budd notes that "the 'whydunnit' in Ms. Paretsky's books is often embedded in the fabric of problems that confront us all. . . . This extra dimension adds an immediacy that is not found in many private eye novels" (quoted in "Paretsky" 443). Some readers beg to differ, though. Paretsky received an angry letter from a reader who wanted to know why the Warshawski novels were "infested" with social and political issues ("Storyteller" E1). Paretsky's response is that mysteries are by definition political (E1). Paretsky notes that she does not intend to write social or political commentary, that what matters is the story; the fact is that the stories that matter most to her are those of people who are powerless and voiceless (E1).

Feminism seems to be a driving force in Paretsky's work, and many feminist critics have embraced Warshawski as a feminist icon. In response to one interviewer's question about whether she was trying to change people's opinions of how women are viewed in society, she replied that she was just trying to tell a story (Shepherdson 38). Although she seems to want to distance herself from ideology, Paretsky's works do feature an independent, strong female character willing to take on any institution or individual in the fight for justice. As Alice Yeager Kaplan notes, Paretsky writes fiction in which "a woman claims her right to the city, her right to her body, her right to feel" (28).

Among the other important themes found in the Warshawski novels is Chicago itself. Paretsky has said that she often begins with the idea for the crime plot, but that the setting is crucial, noting that "when you live in a place and it really gets into your blood, it takes over your imagination. The reason I write about Chicago is because I know and I love this city really passionately" (Herbert 31).

In addition to the Warshawski series, Paretsky has published one nonmystery novel entitled *Ghost Country*. In this work, Paretsky tackles similar themes of corruption, homelessness, and life in Chicago. This novel interweaves the stories of several characters, including an alcoholic, washed-up opera singer, a young woman who chooses to live on the street, a homeless woman who sees a miraculous vision of the Virgin Mary, and a psychologist assigned to treat that woman. Use of multiple points of view allows all of these characters to serve as narrators at various points in the novel. Paretsky has mentioned that she has plans to write other non-Warshawski novels, including one about V. I.'s friend, Dr. Lotty Herschel (Rozan 45; Evans G1). Interestingly, she has said that before writing *Ghost Country*, she would not have called herself a writer, but the accomplishments and the process of writing this novel have rejuvenated her attitude toward writing and toward herself as a writer (Rozan 45).

CRITICAL RECEPTION

In addition to a myriad of favorable book reviews, Paretsky's works have been considered in several scholarly venues, ranging from *Journal of Popular Culture* to *Yale French Studies*.

Patricia E. Johnson examines Paretsky's *Bitter Medicine* in conjunction with Sue Grafton's *A is for Alibi*, novels that share the plot device of having the female detective become sexually involved with a man who becomes implicated in the crime. Johnson looks at the characters as women within the male-dominated arena of violence and crime in examining the women's roles in society and the effects of sex and betrayal on these characters. She addresses the debate in feminist criticism regarding female hard-boiled detectives: the concern that in writing female characters who function in a stereotypically male world, more harm than good is done. Kathleen Gregory Klein is one of the most often cited sources for this, positing that "adopting the hard-boiled formula traps their authors" (Johnson 98). On the other hand, Jane S. Bakerman and Maureen T. Reddy see female hard-boiled detective fiction as a rewriting and powerful transformation of the traditional genre (Johnson 98). As Bakerman puts it, "Sara Paretsky has reformulated and reenergized an old literary pattern by recognizing the value of combining the hard-boiled detective novel with feminist fiction" (135).

Helle Porsdam focuses on feminism and legal issues in her study of Paretsky's works and other feminist detective fiction. She also examines the issue of whether fiction involving violence and victimization can advance a feminist agenda (131–32). Porsdam provides a valuable overview of French and American feminist theory and then applies these theoretical views in analyzing Warshawski's development from "autonomous selfhood to a selfhood embedded within relationships" (133).

Richard E. Goodkin's ambitious article compares *Killing Orders* with Racine's *Iphigénie*. Goodkin starts by contrasting two critics, one who views the Oedipus story as a "classical analytical detective story" and another who makes a strong distinction between "mythic crime" and "profane crime" (81). He examines intertextual links between Racine's work and Paretsky's; it should be noted that *Killing Orders* is the novel in which readers learn that the "I" in V. I. stands for Iphigenia. Goodkin contends the two works are both readings of a shared source: Euripides's *Iphigenia in Aulis*. He focuses on incidents such as the attempt to blind Warshawksi and the recurring images of fire, including the fire that destroys her apartment (88–91).

Margaret Kinsman, a Chicago native who is a permanent resident of London, brings a mix of personal and academic outlooks to her study of Paretsky. In addition to her nostalgia for Chicago, Kinsman recognizes the coping mechanisms Warshawski uses in managing her environment as similar to ones Kinsman herself employs (16). In terms of content and conviction, Kinsman sees Paretsky and Warshawski as "Jane

Addams and Nancy Drew rolled into one" (16). Kinsman examines Warshawski as a feminist character and Paretsky as a feminist writer via a brief historiography of Chicago, literary history, and sociology (18–22). In turning to the Warshawski novels, Kinsman focuses on two prevalent symbols of the works: cars and restaurants. Cars are important to Warshawski, and, like her, her cars take a lot of physical abuse. Also, as Kinsman points out, the automobiles allow her to go places she should not go (23). Warshawski is always able to find a restaurant, no matter where she is, and she never hesitates to dine alone, which Kinsman finds interesting as a feminist action against traditional expectations and roles (24–25).

BIBLIOGRAPHY

Works by Sara Paretsky

Indemnity Only. New York: Dial, 1982.
Deadlock. New York: Dial, 1984.
Killing Orders. New York: Morrow, 1985.
Bitter Medicine. New York: Morrow, 1987.
Blood Shot. New York: Delacorte, 1988.
Burn Marks. New York: Delacorte, 1990.
Guardian Angel. New York: Delacorte, 1992.
Tunnel Vision. New York: Delacorte, 1994.
Windy City Blues. New York: Delacorte, 1995.
Ghost Country. New York: Delacorte, 1998.
Hard Time. New York: Delacorte, 1999.
"A Storyteller Stands Where Justice Confronts Basic Human Needs: Mysteries, like Life, Have to Be Political." *New York Times* 25 Sept. 2000: E1.

Studies of Sara Paretsky

Bakerman, Jane S. "Living 'Openly and with Dignity': Sara Paretsky's New-Boiled Feminist Fiction." *Midamerica: The Yearbook of the Society for the Study of Midwestern Literature* 12 (1985): 120–35.
Crawford, Brad. "Sara Paretsky's Immortal Character." *Writer's Digest* Sept. 1999: 8–9.
Decure, Nicole. "V. I. Warshawski, a 'Lady with Guts': Feminist Crime Fiction by Sara Paretsky." *Women's Studies International Forum* 12 (1989): 227–38.
Evans, Judith. "V. I. Warshawski Goes behind Bars in Sara Paretsky's Latest Novel." *St. Louis Post-Dispatch* 9 Sept. 1999: G1.
Goodkin, Richard E. "Killing Order(s): Iphigenia and the Detection of Tragic Intertextuality." *Yale French Studies* 76 (1989): 81–107.
Green, Michelle. "Sara Paretsky's Cult Heroine Is a Woman's Woman—V. I. Warshawski, the Funky, Feminist Private Eye." *People Weekly* 14 May 1990: 132–34.
Herbert, Rosemary. "Aiming Higher." *Publishers Weekly* 13 April 1990: 30–32.
Johnson, Patricia E. "Sex and Betrayal in the Detective Fiction of Sue Grafton and Sara Paretsky." *Journal of Popular Culture* 27 (1994): 97–106.
Jones, Louise Conley. "Feminism and the P. I. Code: Or, Is a Hard-Boiled Warshawski Unsuitable to Be Called a Feminist?" *Clues: A Journal of Detection* 16 (1995): 77–87.
Kaplan, Alice Yaeger. "Critical Fictions: The New Hard-Boiled Woman." *Artforum* Jan. 1990: 26–28.
Kinsman, Margaret. "A Question of Visibility: Paretsky and Chicago." Ed. Kathleen Gregory

Klein. *Women Times Three: Writers, Detectives, Readers*. Bowling Green: Bowling
    Green State University Popular Press, 1995. 15–27.

Klein, Kathleen Gregory. "Watching Warshawski." Ed. William Reynolds and Elizabeth Trem-
    bley. *It's a Print!: Detective Fiction from Page to Screen*. Bowling Green: Bowling
    Green State University Popular Press, 1994. 145–56.

"Paretsky, Sara." Ed. Judith Graham. *1992 Current Biography Yearbook*. New York: H. W.
    Wilson, 1992. 441–44.

Pope, Rebecca A. " 'Friends Is a Weak Word for It': Female Friendship and the Spectre of
    Lesbianism in Sara Paretsky." Ed. Glenwood Irons. *Feminism in Women's Detective
    Fiction*. Toronto: University of Toronto Press, 1995. 157–70.

Porsdam, Helle. "Embedding Rights within Relationships: Gender, Law and Sara Paretsky."
    American Studies 39 (1998): 131–51.

Reddy, Maureen T. *Sisters in Crime: Feminism and the Crime Novel*. New York: Continuum,
    1988.

Ross, Jean W. "*CA* Interview: Sara Paretsky." Ed. Susan M. Trosky. *Contemporary Authors*.
    Vol. 129. Detroit: Gale, 1990. 335–38.

Rozan, S.J. "Sara Paretsky: A Gun of One's Own." *Publishers Weekly* 25 Oct. 1999: 44–45.

"Sara Paretsky." *Contemporary Authors New Revision Series*. Ed. Daniel Jones and John D.
    Jorgenson. Vol. 59. Detroit: Gale, 1998. 306–10.

Shapiro, Laura. "Interview with Sara Paretsky." *Ms*. Jan. 1988: 66–67ff.

Shepherdson, Nancy. "The Writer behind Warshawski." *Writer's Digest* Sept. 1992: 38–41.

Szuberla, Guy. "The Ties That Bind: V. I. Warshawski and the Burdens of Family." *Armchair
    Detective* 27 (1994): 146–53.

ANN PETRY (1908–1997)

Michelle L. Taylor

BIOGRAPHY

Ann Lane Petry was born on October 12, 1908, the youngest of three children, into a prominent African American family in the predominantly white community of Old Saybrook, Connecticut. Both Petry's father, Peter C. Lane, and her mother, Bertha James Lane, had professional careers, as did three preceding generations of Petry's family. Her grandfather had been a chemist, and in 1890 her father became a licensed pharmacist and owned drugstores in Old Saybrook and the nearby community of Old Lyme. One of her aunts and an uncle were also pharmacists. Her mother was a licensed chiropodist, who graduated from the New York School of Chiropody and began practice in 1915. Petry's mother also worked as a hairdresser, barber, and manufacturer. Although Ann grew up in a racially segregated community, her parents' status in the community shielded her from blatant cases of racial abuse and hatred. To a large extent, Petry's decidedly middle-class upbringing proved to be a rich vein from which to mine the creative material for her writing, including *Country Place* (1947), *The Narrows* (1953), and *Miss Muriel and Other Stories* (1971).

Petry entered the Old Saybrook school system by the age of four and graduated from Old Saybrook High School in 1929. While growing up, Petry worked in the family drugstores, where she listened to stories about her family history, which inspired her to write her own versions. She began writing in high school, and by the time she graduated, she had published in various genres. Her writing appeared as a slogan for a perfume company, and she had also completed a number of one-act plays and short stories.

When Petry entered college, she had not yet decided on a career in letters but instead chose to follow family tradition and pursue a career in pharmacy. Petry graduated from the University of Connecticut School of Pharmacy in 1931. After graduation, she worked in the family drugstores in Old Saybrook and Old Lyme for several years. Though Petry's primary focus was the management of her father's stores, she continued to write short stories during the period, none of which have been published.

When Petry married mystery writer George D. Petry in 1939, the couple moved to New York for the start of their new life. Petry's time in New York changed her life as well as her perspective on writing and the world around her. Petry was eager to experience a new environment and began by immersing herself in New York's most celebrated African American community, Harlem. In 1938 she began work as a reporter for two Harlem newspapers, *Amsterdam News* and *People's Voice*. Just as Connecticut provided the backdrop for her novels, the poverty and tenor of post-Depression era urban life gave her ample material for her most successful and well-known novel, *The Street* (1946). However, it was not until 1939 that Petry published her first creative piece, a short story entitled "Marie of the Cabin Club," in the Baltimore paper *Afro-American*. The story was set in a Harlem nightclub and was published under the pseudonym Arnold Petry because she wanted to save her name for more serious work.

Petry had come to love her new home and used her experiences in the area not only for her fiction but also for her journalistic work. From 1941 to 1943, she edited the Woman's Page for *People's Voice*, where she also wrote a column that chronicled Harlem's elites, titled "The Lighter Side." In an effort to better craft her first-hand experience of urban life, Petry enrolled in a creative writing class and writing workshop at Columbia University. She credited both her five years in journalism and her classes at Columbia as having a great impact on her career.

Petry continued to write short stories, and throughout the 1940s, her stories appeared in various magazines and journals, including *Crisis*. But despite her burgeoning literary career, Petry still devoted much of her time to civic endeavors. Harlem continued to be the center of her attention and also the place where she became involved with Negro Women, Inc., a consumer watch group for working-class women, and designed programs for problem children in a local middle school. During this period, Petry taught a business letter writing course for the Harlem chapter of the National Association for the Advancement of Colored People and still found time to study painting and play the piano. She also acted in *On Striver's Row*, an American Negro Theater Production performed at Harlem's Schomburg Center.

Perhaps the most important moment in Petry's career came in 1944 when an editor for Houghton Mifflin read her short story, "On Saturday the Sirens Sound at Noon." The story, published in *Crisis*, focuses on children left home alone in Harlem. The editor urged Petry to apply for Houghton's fiction fellowship. Petry applied for and received the $2,400 fellowship, which she used to support herself while writing her best-selling novel, *The Street*. Petry's second novel, *Country Place*, was published in 1947. After her second novel, Petry and her family, which now included one daughter, Elisabeth Ann, returned to Old Saybrook. Despite the move, Petry continued to write and her third novel, *The Narrows*, was published in 1953. Petry never wrote another adult novel, but she did write frequently for children and young adults. *The Drugstore Cat* (1949), a parable for children on the value of good citizenship, was dedicated to her daughter. Both *Harriet Tubman, Conductor on the Underground Railroad* (1955) and *Tituba of Salem Village* (1964) were designed to teach young readers about key moments in African American history. She also published a collection of short stories for adult readers, *Miss Muriel and Other Stories*, in 1971.

Petry's life in Old Saybrook was relatively quiet. Though she continued to write, she devoted much of her time to her family. Petry was frequently recognized for her literary and civic accomplishments with honorariums, citations, and lectureships at the

University of Ohio and the University of Suffolk. She also received honorary degrees from Suffolk University (1983), the University of Connecticut (1983), and Mount Holyoke College (1989). Petry lived in Old Saybrook, where she died on April 18, 1997, following a brief illness.

MAJOR WORKS AND THEMES

Petry's literary influences are complex and incorporate her New England upbringing as well as her connection to African American women's writing and naturalism. So influential was the New England way of life that of her three adult novels, only her first novel, *The Street*, is not set in New England. *The Street* also proved to be the novel that confirmed Petry's place in the American literary canon. Indeed, the novel made history because it marked the first time that a novel by an African American woman sold over a million copies. Like many of the works by African American women writers, Petry's novel considers the intersection of race, class, and gender. While the works of her literary foremothers, including Zora Neale Hurston and Jessie Fauset, discuss the intersection of race and gender, *The Street*'s Lutie Johnson is the first African American female protagonist to battle an openly hostile urban environment. Though Petry's contemporaries Richard Wright and Chester Himes had written extensively on masculinity and the urban experience, Petry's novel offered a feminist perspective to the literary politics of urban social protest literature. Her novels also reflect her use of straightforward, quotidian plots characteristic of naturalist novels. Her background in journalism and keen eye for detail inform the text, and like other naturalist writers, including Theodore Dreiser and Stephen Crane, her novels reveal the myriad ways in which society and environment can destroy the human spirit. Here again, Petry signifies an established naturalist tradition by depicting the life of an African American female immersed in a hostile urban environment.

The Street chronicles Lutie Johnson and her son, Bub, as they attempt to rebuild their lives following the departure of Lutie's husband, Jim. Petry uses flashbacks to recount Lutie's early years in Long Island and Connecticut, but the primary setting of the novel is 116 Street in Harlem. The Harlem that Petry writes about in *The Street* lacks the glamour and allure commonly associated with Harlem and the Jazz Age, instead portraying this part of the city as dangerous and unforgiving. Like Wright's depiction of Chicago in *Native Son*, Harlem is a threat to both personal safety and aspirations.

Lutie is enchanted by the American dream, and her personal tragedy is that she fails to realize that as an African American woman in pre–civil rights America, the American dream is difficult to attain. Though she tries desperately to eke out a living for herself and her son, she is met only with pain and sexual violence. As seen in slave narratives and early African American novels, beauty can often prove to be a dangerous liability. Such is the case for Lutie, who not only resists the advances of white male employers but must also reject repeated offers to engage in prostitution. The tension in the novel builds as Lutie unsuccessfully tries to find safety and opportunity. To save herself from a brutal attack, Lutie must kill the assistant of a powerful white businessman who has tried to seduce her. The conclusion of the novel is a grim reminder of the pervasiveness of oppression, in which Petry indicates that Bub's entrance into a life of crime will lead him to reform school. Lutie's fate is no better because she is forced to abandon Bub and flee to Chicago, mistakenly believing that she can make a better life for herself.

Petry's second novel, *Country Place*, is set in Connecticut and is often regarded as her raceless novel because the narrative action does not focus entirely on the lives of African Americans. However, the novel does explore racism's effects on other minority groups, including Jews, Irish, and Portuguese, thus underscoring the idea that tragedy and discrimination cannot be read entirely and simply in terms of black and white.

The novel centers on the tragic post–World War II homecoming of Johnny Pearce and his confrontations with rumors regarding his wife's alleged adultery. The narrative tension increases as a host of minor characters attempt to prove to Johnny the truth of his wife's affair. After the discovery, Johnny flees to New York. The characters in a secondary plot line also come to a tragic end, and like *The Street*, this novel ends with a sense of loss and overwhelming sorrow in which many of the characters are dead or emotionally bankrupt.

It was while living in Old Saybrook that Petry wrote her final, and possibly most complex, novel, *The Narrows*. Like *Country Place*, *The Narrows* is set in a small, racially segregated town in Connecticut. The main story centers on a love affair between Link Williams, a Phi Beta Kappa graduate of Dartmouth, and Camilo Treadway, a rich, white heiress. The relationship is doomed from the start owing both to Link's indecisive nature and to Camilo's failure to tell Link that she is married. By the end of the novel, Camilo capitalizes on the myth of the black male rapist and accuses Link of sexual assault. Though her accusations are false, Link is eventually murdered by Camilo's husband and mother.

The love affair is the most commonly remarked upon aspect of the novel, but Petry adds dimension to the text by creating a host of intriguing secondary characters, all of whom participate in Link's upbringing. Chief among them are Link's adoptive mother, Abbie Crunch, the prototypical lady figure, and her best friend and entrepreneur, F. K. Jackson. In contrast to Abbie's strict and reserved parenting style, is Link's father figure, the local pub owner Bill Hod. Abbie and Bill are not related, but they are nevertheless connected through their love for Link. Bill's employee, Weak Knees, is also a constant source of support for Link. These characters supplement the text not only by shoring up Link's personality but also by offering a panoramic view of black New England. Link's death is a tragic reminder that, despite breeding and education, there were still social activities in 1950 that America would not tolerate. To a large extent, Petry used the novel to reinforce the tenuous position of black masculinity in America; however, the depictions of Abbie, F. K., and a less than desirable minor character, Mamie Prowther, explore alternative expressions of African American female identity. Like Petry's other novels, *The Narrows* reveals the importance of the novel as a mode of social protest; however, this particular novel ends on a note of hope as Abbie prepares to continue with her life in the face of seemingly unbearable loss.

The remainder of Petry's literary endeavors includes works for young readers and a collection of short stories, *Miss Muriel and Other Stories*. The stories in this collection also provide a diverse view of African American life in New England. The characters range from a pharmacist and his family to a group of migrant workers and a sensitive twelve-year old girl trying desperately to understand the dynamics of race.

Overall, the stories in this collection are not as tragic as the novels, but Petry never-theless underscores the difficulty of traversing the boundaries of race and inequality.

CRITICAL RECEPTION

Generally speaking, critics have responded favorably to Petry's work, and she has been widely reviewed in journals as varied as the *New Yorker*, *New York Times Book Review*, and *New Republic*. With the reviews came the inevitable comparisons with Richard Wright and Chester Himes. To some extent, attention to Wright and Himes eclipsed Petry's literary contributions because Wright and Himes were male and their works more closely paralleled the tenets of the naturalist tradition. Despite the gender restrictions that may have marginalized Petry's novels, *The Street* is now considered a classic in African American literature. The novel was out of print for several decades but was reissued as part of the Beacon Press Black Women Writers Series in 1985 and issued again in 1992 by Houghton Mifflin.

Though *Country Place* and *The Narrows* did not achieve the same best-seller status of *The Street*, both were fairly successful. Of the two, *The Narrows* generated more critical conversation. Contemporary reviewers find the novel interesting but not rep-resentative of her finest work. However, current reviewers believe *The Narrows* to be her finest novel. The renewed interest is due in large part to the continued investment in African American feminist studies. In the introduction to the most recent edition of the novel, Nellie McKay applauds Petry for her feminist vision: "In 1953—in the pre-contemporary feminist days of the 1940s and 1950s, when deliberate black fiction and black feminist interpretations of fiction were ideas whose time had not come—it was revolutionary" (xvii).

The current reevaluation of Petry's oeuvre contributes to African American women's literary history by underscoring the many ways in which female writers explore their particular relationship to America. Indeed, Petry's work is visionary for its time, and it holds important lessons for readers still grappling with the complex intersection of race, gender, and class.

BIBLIOGRAPHY

Works by Ann Petry

Pseud. Arnold Petry. "Marie of the Cabin Club." *Afro-American* Aug. 1939: 14.
"On Saturday the Siren Sounds at Noon." *Crisis* Dec. 1943: 368–69.
The Street. Boston: Houghton, 1946.
Country Place. Boston: Houghton, 1947.
The Drugstore Cat. New York: Crowell, 1949.
"Harlem." *Holiday* April 1949: 110–16, 163–66.
"The Novel as Social Criticism." *The Writer's Book*. Ed. Helen Hull. New York: Harper, 1950.
    32–39.
The Narrows. Boston: Houghton, 1953.
Harriet Tubman, Conductor on the Underground Railroad. New York: Crowell, 1955.
Tituba of Salem Village. New York: Crowell, 1964.
"The Common Ground." *Horn Book* April 1965: 147–51.
Legends of the Saints. New York: Crowell, 1970.
Miss Muriel and Other Stories. Boston: Houghton Mifflin, 1971.

"A Purely Black Stone." *A View from the Top of the Mountain: Poems after Sixty*. Ed. Tom Koontz and Thom Tammaro. Daleville, IN: Barnwood Press, 1981. 75.

"A Real Boss Black Cat." *A View from the Top of the Mountain: Poems after Sixty*. Ed. Tom Koontz and Thom Tammaro. Daleville, IN: Barnwood Press, 1981. 76.

"Ann Petry on Langston Hughes' 'Sweet Flypaper of Life.'" *Rediscoveries II*. Ed. David Madden and Peggy Bach. New York: Carroll & Graf, 1988. 203–7.

Studies of Ann Petry

Alexander, Sandra. "Ann Petry." *Afro-American Writers, 1940–1955*. Ed. Trudier Harris and Thadious M. Davis. Detroit: Gale, 1988. Vol. 76 of *Dictionary of Literary Biography*. 140–47.

Andrews, Larry. "The Sensory Assault of the City in Ann Petry's *The Street*." *The City in African American Literature*. Ed. Yoshinobu Hakutani and Robert Butler. Madison, NJ: Fairleigh Dickinson University Press, 1995. 196–211.

Barrett, Lindon. *Blackness and Value: Seeing Double*. Cambridge: Cambridge University Press, 1999.

Barry, Michael. " 'Same Train Be Back Tomorrer': Ann Petry's *The Narrows* and the Repetition of History." *MELUS* 24 (1999): 141–59.

Drake, Kimberly. "Women on the Go: Blues, Conjure, and Other Alternatives to Domesticity in Ann Petry's *The Street* and *The Narrows*." *Arizona Quarterly* 54 (1998): 65–90.

Holladay, Hilary. *Ann Petry*. New York: Twayne, 1996.

McKay, Nellie. Introduction. *The Narrows*. By Ann Petry. Boston: Beacon, 1988. vii–xx.

——. "Ann Petry's *The Street* and *The Narrows*: A Study of the Influence of Class, Race, and Gender on Afro-American Women's Lives." *Women and War: The Changing Status of American Women from the 1930s to the 1950s*. Ed. Maria Deidrich and Dorothea Fischer-Hornung. New York: Berg, 1990. 127–40.

JAYNE ANNE PHILLIPS (1952–)

Andrea Adolph

BIOGRAPHY

Born in Buckhannon, West Virginia, Jayne Anne Phillips has geographic roots in common with many of her fictional characters. Her childhood and adolescence in small-town Appalachia have been fertile ground for her work. Like Danner in *Machine Dreams* (1984), Lenny and Alma of *Shelter* (1994), and *MotherKind*'s (2000) Kate, Phillips "grew up on a rural road in a ranch-style brick house" built by her father (Homes 46). If her characters share elements of place and time with their creator, though, it is for Phillips a necessary union: "Any family a writer creates is going to come in some way from what the writer experienced. . . . That is how you learn what family is" (Ross 366). Phillips's connection to her characters stems from an empathic understanding: "I don't think that it's important to write from a strictly autobiographical standpoint. It's more a question of compassion" (Douglass 189).

After Phillips received a BA degree in English from West Virginia University in 1974, her father envisioned his daughter taking "a job in a local insurance agency as a secretary." But, she says, "I had to leave West Virginia" (Douglass 184). Phillips headed west and lived through a variety of experiences, working "in schools, in restaurants, [selling] bathrooms door-to-door" in California and Colorado ("Mystery" 163). After early literary successes in small press markets as a poet and as a fiction writer, Phillips enrolled in the writer's workshop at the University of Iowa and earned the MFA degree in creative writing in 1976. Stories from her MFA thesis soon became the highly acclaimed *Black Tickets* (1979), which was awarded the American Academy and Institute of Arts and Letters Sue Kauffman Prize for first fiction.

Since the appearance of *Black Tickets*, Phillips has been viewed as a major voice in contemporary American letters. Her efforts have been acknowledged with Pushcart Prizes, a fellowship from the National Endowment for the Arts, and a nomination for the National Book Critics Circle Award. Phillips has also been a resident at Yaddo, the Provincetown Fine Arts Center, and the MacDowell Colony. Though she was a

Bunting Fellow at Radcliffe (1981) and has taught at a number of academic institutions, including Boston University and Brandeis, Phillips most often prefers to remove herself from an academic career. She works to balance her family and writing lives and sees her personal life as something quite separate from her writing. Married to Mark Stockman since 1985, Phillips mothers two sons and two step-sons: "I seem to have been so successful," she comments, "at making my kids think they're the center of the world . . . they're almost unaware that I work, that I'm writing" (Homes 51). What comes out of this secluded vocation, however, has captured the attention and admiration of many others outside her family circle.

MAJOR WORKS AND THEMES

Evocative language and distinct, moving imagery mark all of Phillips's fiction. In her short stories and her novels, Phillips's lyrical prose is key to the strength of her work. Early pieces, such as the linked sections that make up *Counting* (1978, winner of the St. Lawrence Award for fiction), demand more from language to convey meaning than from content. These vignettes are as much prose poems as they are building blocks of an elliptical tale and can be viewed as bridges between Phillips's early attempts at poetry and her longer, more fluid stories and novels. When connected, the pieces tell the story of two lovers; separate, each brief movement makes an eerie statement. A build-up of action and resonance of sound create a depth to the sections that defies their brevity and surface simplicity. Always, deep emotion shimmers beneath Phillips's description of simple movements and quotidian activities. The complicated interior world of the human psyche is enhanced by the poetic quality of Phillips's style. *MotherKind*, with its use of third-person narration and mostly linear chronology, is perhaps the farthest removed, formally, from her early work but relies upon language just as heavily in order to convey the breadth and depth of human experience.

Phillips's work expresses an interest in the limits of such experience but also dwells on the way our waking lives can be extended through dreams and other effects of interiority. Stories from *Black Tickets* (1979) and *Fast Lanes* (1987), especially those with gritty urban settings, imitate dreamscape through fragmented thought and almost fantasy-like narration, but Phillips makes good use of similar technique in her longer works. The hyper-real language of dreams and psychological monologues enhances what might otherwise become too-familiar narrations of family sagas. Both *Machine Dreams* and *Shelter* are constructed from several points of view, and such narratives can run the risk of sacrificing character development to experimentation. Phillips exposes deeper layers than her characters' surfaces, though, and manipulates the thin line between waking thought and subconscious expression.

Buddy Carmody, one of the young protagonists in *Shelter*, is a fine example of Phillips's ability to use dream language to move beyond the facts of a character. Buddy's abuse at the hands of his stepfather could be viewed as the defining mark of his character, but his strong imagination extends his character beyond the position of victim. Trapped in a lightless cave with and tied to his abuser, Buddy appears to be completely subjected to the will of the older man. Phillips moves Buddy beyond his immediate physical experience through empowering visions from within: "In his dream the rolling air was Mam. . . . She was too big to get in, so she put her hands on either side of the rock wall and threw her mind inside to fill it all until she found

Buddy.... She didn't even need to say his name, he didn't have a name, he was like the marks on the high wall and the ceiling of the cave, older than names" (213). Through envisioning his mother, Buddy projects his own power to save not only himself but ultimately others as well. Phillips considers Buddy "the moral center of the book ... so young, so supposedly unformed, already a failure in the outside world. And yet ... the total master of his own world" (Homes 46). Shifting readers' focus from the exterior facts of Buddy's life to his internal existence allows Phillips to create in Buddy an unlikely but believable redeeming force at the heart of *Shelter*.

The concept of redemption is central to Phillips's use of memory in her writing. She has equated writing with religion and the understanding of the past with the spiritual. For her, craft is as much a part of the spirit as is that psyche explored by fiction: "The way a writer works with memory is almost religious," she explains ("Mystery" 166); "It has to do with redemption, really.... If you are dealing with the elements of a past ... you are basically trying to redeem that past" (Douglass 187). Though some critics have pointed to political elements in her work, often it is the absence of the political that suggests a stronger sense of the past. *Shelter* is set in the summer of 1963, just before the assassination of John F. Kennedy: "His assassination was the first of a string of murders of American heroes," she muses. "After that, the country had to face reality.... Things were not what they seemed" (Homes 46). The novel's imminent shift from teenage innocence to sexual awakening parallels the sleepy security of a country on the brink of sudden change. Though *Machine Dreams* examines the effects of war on the United States (both the Second World War and Vietnam), it also remains silent with regard to the assassinations of the 1960s, moments that otherwise tend to define national identity. In *MotherKind*, Kate becomes the first of Phillips's protagonists to discuss the place of Kennedy in her personal past. Visiting the Kennedy Library, Kate and her husband, Matt, suggest the impact of the era on the present day. Kate imagines, "He might have done more. Everything might have been different." Matt's reply, though, presents a different view: "Isn't that a bit of a myth? ..." (21). The tension between what is remembered, redeemed, and what is left behind here helps to explain the difficulties of any shared mythology.

The myths that best serve Phillips, though, are familial stories that attempt to capture the ways parents, children, and siblings both love and betray each other. The ways in which the family unit is part of each individual's history is perhaps the most common thread running through Phillips's works. *Machine Dreams* is the work most focused upon generations of family, and characters from the novel find their ways into other pieces: "Bess" and "Blue Moon" (*Fast Lanes*) are related narratives. "1934" (*Black Tickets*), too, seems to be an early beginning to Jean's story of growing up in a disbanding and downwardly mobile family. The connections in Phillips's work are not only between family members but also between texts. Though each story and novel is distinctly its own, the works build upon each other to create a larger idea of what it is like to belong to others, even when those others are removed emotionally or geographically. Generations of texts contain characters related by a sense of loyalty and of love, especially between mothers and daughters.

The mother-child relationship is an important one in Phillips's work. From early stories like "Bluegill" (*Fast Lanes*), in which a mother narrates her feelings to her unborn child, motherhood emerges as pivotal in the lives of all Phillips's characters. Buddy Carmody's "Mam" is his shelter from the ugliness of sexual abuse, and the girls away at summer camp experience effects of living in a motherless world, if only a temporary one. Maya Koreneva reads the mother-daughter relationship in "Home" as displaying "mutual love" between characters who are "almost ashamed of" their feelings for one another (269). But it is *MotherKind* that brings the multiple facets of mothering into view. While becoming a mother and learning how to parent another woman's children, Kate also "mothers" Katherine, her own mother who is battling terminal cancer. The reciprocity of feeling between mothers and children, but especially between mothers and daughters, in this novel transcends the sometimes ambivalent nature of relationships between mothers and children in Phillips's other works. In *MotherKind*, Phillips unites the reality and the mythology of families and ultimately exposes the essence of what her lyric style has always suggested: our capacity to understand, to feel, to love.

CRITICAL RECEPTION

Since her successful *Black Tickets*, Phillips has been a widely and well-reviewed writer. In recent years, she has also become the subject of literary scholarship both within the United States and abroad. The subject of war, especially of Phillips's rendering of the effects of the Vietnam War, has gained much of this critical attention, and even when not the main thesis of their scholarship, most critics acknowledge the impact of that war on Phillips's fiction. Joanna Price understands the mourning of wartime loss in *Machine Dreams* to be "marked by a sense of lost optimism . . . memories which are inscribed with both a nostalgia for, and a recognition . . . of the fictive nature of lost origins" (174). Catherine Houser, too, understands Phillips's first novel as about war and sees Danner as one of those who are "missing in action": "walking through lives they think . . . they should be living, looking for meaning and feeling lost" (33). For Houser, Danner is more radically affected by Vietnam than her brother Billy, a supposed casualty of the Vietnam epoch.

Meredith Sue Willis has investigated Phillips's use of memory as a technique in her writing and carefully separates the real landscape of West Virginia from Phillips's version, especially that of *Shelter*. For her, Phillips's settings are "mythic," "the forest of European fairy tales where children get lost and devoured" (48). She also understands characters such as Carmody and Parson to be "stereotypes" with roots not in Appalachian history but "in literature and psychology" (48). Others critics have examined the strong sense of place in Phillips's work, with varying results. Elisabeth Bronfen, a German critic, takes Phillips more to task and finds the quest for home in *Machine Dreams* to be the "retrogressive act of ultimately falling back on conservative values . . . the idea of an ahistorical timelessness of myth" that contradicts her "critical discussion of American political and social reality" (20).

In addition to work by Bronfen, other international criticism of Phillips has been included in anthologies of scholarship by former Soviet scholars. Phillips has been studied comparatively with that of her Russian contemporary Elena Makarova as representative of a generation of writers. Aleksei Zverev notes that the "emphasized triteness" of *Machine Dreams* "contrasts sharply with its inner dramatic tension" (276). He also sees in that novel "ties between different times . . . the age-old repetition of human experience" (276). Cross-cultural studies such as Zverev's underscore the essence of Phillips's work: the idea of a human experience that reaches beyond generational or regional borders and brings people closer to where shared experiences might be uncovered if looked for closely.

BIBLIOGRAPHY

Works by Jayne Anne Phillips

Sweethearts. Carrboro, NC: Truck Press, 1976.
Counting. New York: Vehicle Editions, 1978.
Black Tickets. New York: Delacorte, 1979.
How Mickey Made It. St. Paul: Bookslinger Editions, 1981.
The Secret Country. Winston-Salem, NC: Palaeman, 1982.
Machine Dreams. New York: Dutton, 1984.
Fast Lanes. New York: Vehicle Editions, 1985.
Shelter. New York: Houghton, 1994.
"Second Thoughts (What I'd Be If I Were Not a Writer)." *Brick* 51 (1995): 26–29.
"The Mystery of Language." *Passion and Craft: Conversations with Notable Writers*. Ed. Bonnie Lyons and Bill Oliver. Urbana: University of Illinois Press, 1998. 157–70.
MotherKind. New York: Knopf, 2000.

Studies of Jayne Anne Phillips

Barker, Adele Marie. "The World of Our Mothers." *Dialogues/Dialogi: Literary and Cultural Exchanges between (Ex)Soviet and American Women*. Ed. Susan Hardy Aiken, Adele Marie Barker, Maya Koreneva, and Ekaterina Stetsenko. Durham: Duke University Press, 1994. 253–65.
Bronfen, Elisabeth. "Between Nostalgia and Disenchantment: The Concept 'Home' in Jayne Anne Phillips' Novel *Machine Dreams*." *Arbeiten aus Anglistik und Amerikanistik* 13 (1988): 17–28.
Douglass, Thomas E. "Interview with Jayne Phillips." *Appalachian Journal* 21 (1994): 182–89.
Gainey, Karen Wilkes. "Jayne Anne Phillips's *Machine Dreams*: Leo Marx, Technology, and Landscape." *Journal of the American Studies Association of Texas* 21 (1990): 75–84.
Hill, Dorothy Combs. "Jayne Anne Phillips." *Contemporary Fiction Writers of the South*. Ed. Joseph M. Flora and Robert Bain. Westport, CT: Greenwood Press, 1993. 348–59.
Homes, A. M. "Jayne Anne Phillips." *BOMB* 49 (1994): 45–51.
Houser, Catherine. "Missing in Action: Alienation in the Fiction of Award-Winning Women Writers." *Mid-American Review* 14 (1994): 33–39.
Koreneva, Maya. "Hopes and Nightmares of the Young." *Dialogues/Dialogi: Literary and Cultural Exchanges between (Ex)Soviet and American Women*. Ed. Susan Hardy Aiken, Adele Marie Barker, Maya Koreneva, and Ekaterina Stetsenko. Durham: Duke University Press, 1994. 266–78.
Lassner, Phyllis. "Jayne Anne Phillips: Women's Narrative and the Recreation of History." *American Women Writing Fiction: Memory, Identity, Family, Space*. Ed. Mickey Pearlman. Lexington: University Press of Kentucky, 1989. 194–206.
Nichols, Capper. "Jayne Anne Phillips: An Annotated Primary and Secondary Bibliography 1976–1989." *Bulletin of Bibliography* 47 (1990): 177–85.
Pierce, Constance. "Contemporary Fiction and Popular Culture." *Michigan Quarterly Review* 26 (1987): 663–72.
Price, Joanna. "Remembering Vietnam: Subjectivity and Mourning in American New Realist Writing." *Journal of American Studies* 27 (1993): 173–86.
Ross, Jean W. "Interview with Jayne Phillips." *Contemporary Authors: A Bio-Bibliographical Guide to Current Writers in Fiction, General Nonfiction, Poetry, Journalism, Drama, Motion Pictures, Television, and Other Fields*. Ed. Deborah A. Straub. Detroit: Gale Research, 1988. Vol. 24 of New Revision Series. 363–67.

Squier, Susan M. "Fetal Voices: Speaking for the Margins within." *Tulsa Studies in Women's Literature* 10 (1991): 17–30.

Stanton, David R. "An Interview with Jayne Anne Phillips." *Croton Review* 9 (1986): 41–44.

Willis, Meredith Sue. "Witness in Nightmare Country." *Appalachian Journal* 24 (1996): 44–51.

Zverev, Aleksei. "The Prose of the 1980s: Three New Names." *Russian Eyes on American Literature*. Ed. Sergei Chakovsky and Inge M. Thomas. Jackson: University of Mississippi Press, 1992. 272–83.

FRANCINE PROSE (1947–)

J. P. Steed

BIOGRAPHY

In 1971 Francine Prose went to Bombay for ten months, where she spent most of her time in the Bombay University Library immersing herself in the works of Dostoevsky, Tolstoy, Proust, and Dickens. Prose had been writing since she was a child but felt no early inclination to be a writer. She had earned her BA in English from Radcliffe College in 1968 and her MA in English from Harvard University in 1969, thinking she "could just go on reading books and writing about them" (Baker 38), but she soon realized she did not want an academic life. "I looked at a globe," she says, "and India looked as far away as I could get" (Baker 38). It was during her trip to Bombay that she became seriously interested in pursuing the art of storytelling. Her first novel, *Judah the Pious*, was written during that year. She gave it to a former professor of hers, who passed it on to Harry Ford, an editor at Atheneum, and the novel was published in 1973, when Prose was just twenty-five.

Since that time, Prose has published ten novels, three collections of short fiction, a collection of Jewish folktales, and four children's books. She has also published a staggering number of articles (about 500 over the last ten years alone; Asirvatham 30) for periodicals such as *Mademoiselle, Redbook, Harper's, Atlantic Monthly, Village Voice, Commentary*, and *New York Times Book Review*. These include profiles, book reviews, travel writing, and other essays on various topics. In a particularly controversial essay titled "I Know Why the Caged Bird Cannot Read" (1999), Prose questions the literary merit of many of the works of literature being read in American high schools. And she has written other controversial essays on the unacknowledged quality of serious literary fiction by women and on the poor quality of popular culture aimed at women.

Prose married Howard Michels, an artist and sculptor, on September 24, 1976, and has been involved in the art world as well as the literary one, often writing art reviews for the *Wall Street Journal, Washington Post*, and others. Prose is also the translator of several works by Ida Fink, the Polish fiction writer.

Prose was born in Brooklyn, New York, on April 1, 1947, and grew up in a household that was, according to Prose's description, culturally rather than religiously Jewish. She attended the Brooklyn Friends School for her elementary and secondary education and as a child was "a big reader, obsessive and morbid" (Baker 38). Her parents, Philip and Jessie (maiden name, Rubin) Prose, were physicians; her father died in 1986 and her mother, at eighty-two, still practices as a dermatologist. After returning from her trip to Bombay, Prose taught creative writing at Harvard from 1971 to 1972. Following the publication of *Judah the Pious* were several years of bohemian existence, and according to Prose, she still "didn't have any idea of a writer's career" (Baker 38). Nevertheless, she continued to write and to publish, her second novel, *The Glorious Ones*, appearing only a year after the first. Prose's first son, Bruno, was born in 1978 and her second, Leon, in 1982. She was a visiting lecturer in fiction at the University of Arizona from 1982 to 1984, and in the summer of 1984, she was an instructor at the Bread Loaf Writers' Workshop in Vermont.

Prose continues to teach creative writing on occasion, and her fiction continues to be well received critically. In addition to winning the Jewish Book Council Award for *Judah the Pious*, she was given the MLLE. Award from Mademoiselle in 1975 and the Edgar Lewis Wallant Award from the Hartford Jewish Community Center in 1984 for *Hungry Hearts* (1983). She has also received a Pushcart Prize. In 1989 she received a Fulbright Fellowship and traveled to the former Yugoslavia, and in 1991 she received a grant from the Guggenheim Foundation. Most recently, in September 1999, Prose was awarded $50,000 and a one-year appointment to a private work space in the New York Public Library's new Center for Scholars and Writers; and her latest novel, *Blue Angel* (2000), was a finalist for the 2000 National Book Award. Prose's current project, for which she used her time at the New York Public Library, is a collection of biographical essays called *The Lives of the Muses: Nine Women and the Artists They Inspired*, examining the relationships between male writers and artists and their female sources of inspiration. Prose calls the collection a combination of literary criticism, art criticism, biography, and essay. Prose presently lives in upstate New York with her husband.

MAJOR WORKS AND THEMES

Although Prose is Jewish and some of her works fit well within the tradition of American Jewish literature (e.g., *Judah the Pious*, *Hungry Hearts*, "Guided Tours of Hell"), Judaism per se is not a central theme of her oeuvre, nor is Jewishness. But its influence is clear: Many of her stories have Jewish characters; the Jewish folk tradition is mined frequently; and the influence of Jewish mysticism—specifically an interest in the supernatural and the fantastic—is prevalent, especially in her earlier works. Many readers have noted and admired Prose's interweaving of the magical and the real, of the irrational and the rational, especially in the early novels; and it might be said that at its root is the examination of the relationship between art and life, which has continued from the early fiction through her most recent novel, *Blue Angel*. Indeed, many of Prose's characters are themselves artists—writers, actors, storytellers of some kind—and questions about the nature of art and language are often raised and explored.

Prose's oeuvre can be effectively divided in two, with the proliferation of her short fiction from 1987 to 1992 marking the division and the beginning of the latter half.

The strong presence of fantasy and folklore characterizes Prose's early work, eliciting from some reviewers the comparison of Prose with Isaac Bashevis Singer. Each of the first four novels is set in a far-off place or a far-off time or both, and these settings lend an exotic or mysterious, even mythic quality to the stories. The folk-legend staple of the story within a story is often employed, and the relationship between art and life is central. *The Glorious Ones* (1974), for example, is set in seventeenth-century Italy and focuses on a group of *commedia dell'arte* actors whose roles in life and on stage are subtly interfused. *Animal Magnetism* (1978), Prose's fourth novel, is set in nineteenth-century New England and focuses on the fad of animal magnetism, which might be defined as self-improvement through self-hypnosis; thus, the novel (a work of art, based on factual history, or life) is about the ways in which art (the creative practice of self-hypnosis) affects life (the reality of self-improvement).

Perhaps the most enduring of Prose's early works, however, and perhaps the best example of her characteristic blend of the real and the fantastic, is her first novel, *Judah the Pious*. Set in Poland and concerning the efforts of a rabbi to have traditional Jewish burial rites reinstated as part of modern custom, the novel is "a sophisticated pastiche of the tales of Jewish folklore" (Cruttwell 421), and the conclusion is "at once reversal and consummation," as "God and Judah . . . are found to be mountebanks and finaglers of a kind: yet their fraudulence only serves somehow to confirm holiness" (Mano 2). God and the rabbi both are artist figures who create and struggle with, and against, their realities.

Into the 1980s, Prose's fiction continues to explore the relationship between the rational and the irrational and to utilize supernatural elements interwoven with reality, but her novels gradually move to a more contemporary American setting. *Household Saints* (1981), Prose's fifth novel, takes place in the 1940s and is the story of three generations of Italian American women; it interweaves legend, religious beliefs and superstitions, and fantastical chance happenings into the everyday lives of these family members. *Hungry Hearts* (1983), set in the 1920s, becomes perhaps the most forthright in its examination of art versus life of all her works to date. It follows the adventures of the Yiddish Art Theatre—a troupe of actors who witness, during the course of their production of a play in which the lead character is possessed by a *dybbuk* (a spirit of Jewish folk legend), their lead actress experiencing what seems to be an authentic instance of life imitating art. Prose's forthright treatment of her central theme then continues in her next novel, *Bigfoot Dreams* (1986), in which reality collides with storytelling as a zany story made up by a tabloid writer is discovered to be an accidental and scandalous truth.

In addition to the theme of art versus life and the interspersion of fantasy with reality, what characterizes all of these early works is also a certain optimism, "a note of hopefulness, a sense that human beings' spiritual yearning for transcendence exists in a pure place untouched by the flaws and disappointments of real life" (Asirvatham 28). However, *Bigfoot Dreams* marks the end of Prose's early period. From 1987 to 1992, she published only short fiction, and most readers have acknowledged that with these stories, Prose enacted an abrupt shift in attitude, toward pessimism. With this shift in attitude came a shift in focus; many of the earlier works attend to the theme of marriage or human relationships, but do so secondarily and somewhat idealistically. Marriage represents a secret and special bond, as in *Hungry Hearts*, and it assumes an almost magical quality reminiscent of its religious ideal. But in the later works, the once-primary focus on the magical and the fantastic is almost nonexistent, and the focus on human relationships moves to the foreground and is cast in a new, more secular and cynical light. *Primitive People* (1992), for example, set in the suburban present day, is "a tale of stolen childhood and divorce, nanny problems, racial tensions, infidelity, and asexuality" (Potok 308).

This shift begins in the short fiction, with *Women and Children First: Stories* (1988), Prose's first story collection. These stories are about disintegrating marriages, decomposing relationships, and disillusionment. In *The Peaceable Kingdom: Stories* (1993), Prose "chronicles compromise and loss" and her families are "invariably fractured" (Mitchell 158). And the title novella of *Guided Tours of Hell: Novellas* (1997) is an examination of the bitterness, jealousy, and grotesque pompousness present among a group of scholars touring a Holocaust concentration camp. Throughout her fiction, Prose often uses the comic and the humorous as means for exploring her themes, and in the later works this comedy sharpens itself into satire.

Her latest novel, *Blue Angel*, is not only an example of this satirical edge; it also marks an ostensible return to the exploration of the relationship between art and life. The novel uses as its template the 1930 film by the same title (art imitating art), and it is the story of a creative writing teacher and failing novelist, who once wrote a successful autobiographical novel (art imitating life), but who is ruined by a bumbling affair with one of his students—a repetition of the plot of the movie, with which he is familiar (life imitating art). Along the way, Prose satirizes writing workshops, mid-life crises, and campus and sexual politics while focusing still on the other central theme of her later work—namely, human relationships and their various failures.

CRITICAL RECEPTION

Overall, the response to Prose's work has been extremely positive, and the amount of attention her work has received has increased steadily throughout her career. Her work has been reviewed extensively, and reviews of *Blue Angel* are ubiquitous. Yet, surprisingly little has been written about her work outside the pale of the review, despite the fact that Prose has been publishing novels now for nearly thirty years.

Most reviewers of Prose's early works are impressed with her ability to write in a simple style about fantastical events and with her skill in interweaving the magical with the real. Prose's novels are accepted and praised as worlds "whose dimensions are flexible and whose boundaries are fluid" (Potok 310). Thomas Lask, writing about *Judah the Pious*, says the author "navigates serenely between the real and the fantastic" and that "the hand of God can be felt hovering over all that occurs" (29). D. Keith Mano, reviewing the same novel, writes that Prose, then twenty-five years old, "appears to perceive more than a writer of that age decently should" and concludes that "she may well be a prophet" (3). Donna L. Nerboso calls *Household Saints* a "simple but powerful tale, rich in the texture of a narration that juxtaposes the ordinary with the supernatural" (1244). Prose's early writing has been compared with the writings of Chaucer, Isaac Bashevis Singer, Isak Dinesen, Nathaniel West, and Voltaire, among others.

Critics have also responded to the folk elements of Prose's work and to the evocation of legend and myth. Patrick Cruttwell and Faith Westburg note that *Judah the Pious* "appears to be sophisticated pastiche of the tales of Jewish folklore" (421), while Stephen Harvey says of *Hungry Hearts* that Prose "recreates the momentum of a picaresque fable, in which any number of primal issues simmer beneath its anecdotal, folksy manner" (3).

Critical attention is also given to Prose's use of humor—specifically, with regard to her later works, to her use of satire. Lask notes the "mocking humor" of *Judah the Pious* (29). Jan Hoffman writes that *Bigfoot Dreams* is "funny as all get-out, quippy and chock-full of cleverness"(3); and Michiko Kakutani, writing about the same novel, notes the "quirky humor" but says that the "feeling of comic superiority is leavened by an insistent sense of kinship, just as the impulse toward sentimentality is undercut by an awareness of the absurd"(12). Regarding the later works, Michael Dorris praises the humor and irony of *Primitive People* (9–10), and of *Guided Tours of Hell*, B. A. St. Andrews says, "the reader's funny bone is hammered into bits" (788). Also noted in reviews of the later works is Prose's focus on American society and her increased pessimism in her approach to her subject matter.

Most of the critics agree that Prose is a skillful storyteller, and her numerous awards and fellowships attest to this. With these awards, including her nomination for the 2000 National Book Award, critical interest in her work has been rejuvenated, and scholarly articles have begun to appear in recent years.

BIBLIOGRAPHY

Works by Francine Prose

Judah the Pious. New York: Atheneum, 1973.
The Glorious Ones. New York: Atheneum, 1974.
Marie Laveau. New York: Berkley Publishing, 1977.
Animal Magnetism. New York: G. P. Putnam's Sons, 1978.
Household Saints. New York: St. Martin's, 1981.
Hungry Hearts. New York: Pantheon, 1983.
Bigfoot Dreams. New York: Pantheon, 1986.
Women and Children First: Stories. New York: Pantheon, 1988.
Primitive People. New York: Farrar, 1992.
The Peaceable Kingdom: Stories. New York: Farrar, 1993.
Hunters and Gatherers. New York: Farrar, 1995.
Dybbuk: A Story Made in Heaven. Greenwillow Books, 1996.
The Angel's Mistake: Stories of Chelm. Greenwillow Books, 1997.
Guided Tours of Hell: Novellas. New York: Metropolitan/Henry Holt, 1997.
You Never Know: A Legend of the Lamedvavniks. Greenwillow Books, 1998.
"I Know Why the Caged Bird Cannot Read." *Harper's* Sept. 1999: 76.
Blue Angel. New York: Harper, 2000.
The Demon's Mistake: A Story from Chelm. New York: HarperCollins, 2000.
Scent of a Woman's Ink: Essays. Contentville, 2000 (www.contentville.com).
The Lives of the Muses: Nine Women and the Artists They Inspired. New York: HarperCollins.
      (Forthcoming, Fall 2002).

Studies of Francine Prose

Aarons, Victoria. "Responding to an Old Story: Susan Fromberg Schaeffer, Leslea Newman, and Francine Prose." Ed. Jay L. Halio and Ben Siegel. *Daughters of Valor: Contemporary Jewish American Women Writers*. Newark: University of Delaware Press, 1997. 112–25.

Asirvatham, Sandy. "Tipping Sacred Cows." *Poets & Writers* 28 (2000): 28–32.

Baker, Aaron, and Juliann Vitullo. "Mysticism and the Household Saints of Everyday Life." *VIA: Voices in Italian Americana* 7 (1996): 55–68.

Baker, John E. "PW Interviews: Francine Prose." *Publishers Weekly* 13 April 1992: 38–39.

Cruttwell, Patrick, and Faith Westburg. Rev. of *Judah the Pious. Hudson Review* 26 (1973): 421.

Dorris, Michael. Rev. of *Primitive People. New York Times Book Review* 5 April 1992: 9–10.

Evans, Nancy H. "Francine Prose." *Contemporary Authors*. Ed. Hal May. Vol. 112. Detroit: Gale, 1985. 402–3.

"Francine Prose." *Contemporary Literary Criticism*. Ed. Daniel G. Marowski and Roger Matuz. Vol. 45. Detroit: Gale, 1987. 322–28.

Harvey, Stephen. Rev. of *Hungry Hearts. VLS* 15 (1983): 3.

Hoffman, Jan. Rev. of *Bigfoot Dreams. VLS* 44 (1986): 3.

Jefferson, Margo. Rev. of *Judah the Pious. Newsweek* 18 Feb. 1974: 94.

Jones, Malcolm. "Smart Book, Dumb Guy: Updating *Blue Angel*." Rev. of *Blue Angel. Newsweek* 3 April 2000: 81.

Kakutani, Michiko. "Stranger than Fiction." Rev. of *Bigfoot Dreams. New York Times* 12 April 1986: 12.

Lask, Thomas. "The Sage and the Gentleman." Rev. of *Judah the Pious. New York Times* 17 Feb. 1973: 29.

——. "Tale of a Noble Blackmailer." Rev. of *Marie Laveau. New York Times* 15 Sept. 1977: C22.

Mano, D. Keith. Rev. of *Judah the Pious. New York Times Book Review* 25 Feb. 1973: 2–3.

Mitchell, Eleanor. Rev. of *A Peaceable Kingdom. Library Journal* Aug. 1993: 158.

Nerboso, Donna L. Rev. of *Household Saints. Library Journal* 106 (1981): 1244.

Potok, Rena. "Francine Prose." *Jewish American Women Writers: A Bio-Bibliographical and Critical Sourcebook*. Ed. Ann R. Shapiro. Westport, CT: Greenwood Press, 1994. 306–13.

"Prose, Francine 1947–." Ed. Pamela S. Dear. *Contemporary Authors*. Detroit: Gale, 1995. Vol. 46 of New Revision Series. 305–7.

Shapiro, Laura. Rev. of *Guided Tours of Hell. Newsweek* 10 Feb. 1997: 66.

St. Andrews, B. A. Rev. of *Guided Tours of Hell. World Literature Today* 71 (1997): 788.

MARILYNNE ROBINSON (1944–)

Catherine Rainwater

BIOGRAPHY

Marilynne (Summers) Robinson was born November 26, 1944, in Sand Point, Idaho, a small town approximately seventy miles northeast of Spokane, Washington. Sand Point is the prototype for Fingerbone, the setting of her first novel, *Housekeeping* (1980). Like the fictional Fingerbone, Sand Point is a railroad town, the switching yard for three lines that travel over wide lakes spanned by long bridges. Growing up in Idaho and western Washington, Robinson found her youthful imagination aroused, never thwarted, by the majestic, unpopulated expanses traversed by trains at the temporal and spatial edges of the closing American frontier. As a child, she read voluminously and reveled in the soul-expanding solitude that books and the "lonesome" landscape fostered. Robinson fondly recalls her love of "old, thick, hard" books that came her way, especially histories ("My Western Roots" 165).

A receptive student at Coeur d'Alene High School, Robinson nevertheless admits that her Latin teacher had to force her through Cicero; here was a bit of tough love that would set Robinson ahead of peers at Brown University, when they and other Northeasterners inquired how, since she was from Idaho, she had managed admission to an Ivy League school and, later, how she has been able to write books. Robinson's Thoreauvian rejoinders frequently assign the blame for intellectual impoverishment more to the particular intellect than to its regional origins. Also reminiscent of Thoreau, whom she greatly admires, Robinson believes that the comparative lack of social class consciousness in the West of her youth honed her academic competitive edge; having little sense of either high or low culture or of her own social status relative to such categories, she was free to discover the wonder of great books, thought, and art in her own way and to imagine herself in any role she chose.

Indeed, for Robinson, the best parts of life appear to be those limned by imagination rather than defined by material splendor. In a passage from her essay "My Western Roots," the author describes an ordinary evening from her childhood in details suggesting the young girl's intense inner life: "I remember the evenings at my grandparents' ranch, at Sagle, and how in the daytime we chased the barn cats and swung on the front gate and set off pitchy, bruising avalanches in the woodshed, and watched my grandmother scatter chicken feed from an apron with huge pockets in it, suffering the fractious contentment of town children rusticated. And then the cows came home and the wind came up and Venus burned through what little remained of atmosphere, and the dark and the emptiness stood over the old house like some unsought revelation" (168).

Despite "rustication," or perhaps enlivened by it, Robinson earned a degree in American literature at Brown University, where her love of nineteenth-century American writers such as Poe, Whitman, Melville, Emerson, Dickinson, and Thoreau was doubtless nurtured. Later, she earned a PhD at the University of Washington with a dissertation on Shakespeare. Following the publication of her highly acclaimed first novel, *Housekeeping*, Robinson began contributing articles and reviews to a variety of periodicals including *Salmagundi* and the *Wilson Quarterly*. In 1987 Robinson served as the "About Books" columnist for the *New York Times Book Review*. She has also written in the genre of the investigative report. Her book *Mother Country* (1989), an exposé of environmental politics in Britain, recounts the history of Sellafield, a plutonium-reprocessing plant in England that for years dumped two tons of nuclear waste per day into the ocean. Most recently, she has published a collection of philosophical essays, *The Death of Adam: Essays on Modern Thought* (1998).

Marilynne Robinson is married and has two grown children. For many years, she has lived in Northampton, Massachusetts. Since her debut as a fiction writer, she has frequently traveled, presenting papers and reading from her works.

MAJOR WORKS AND THEMES

Robinson has so far published only one novel—*Housekeeping*—a lyrical narrative exploring the lives of several eccentric, memorable women. When the mother of two young girls, Ruth and Lucille, commits suicide by sinking her car into the same lake that claimed the life of her own father in a train wreck, the children live with a series of relatives: first, their grandmother, who cares for them until she dies; next, two nervous, maiden great-aunts who decide they are not suited for child rearing; and finally, their mother's sister, Sylvie Foster. Sylvie is a transient who rides freight trains back and forth across the country and who maintains only the most tenuous connections with mainstream society. Though she dutifully returns to her mother's house in Fingerbone and tries hard to play mother to her nieces, Ruth and Lucille, Sylvie is simply too strange, too unique, to fulfill such a mundane domestic role; the girls grow wild, the house deteriorates, and the townspeople judge Sylvie unfit, even crazy. She and Ruth (the narrator) flee authority and Fingerbone one dark night as flames consume the last remnants of their domesticated life. Lucille, who has longed to be ordinary, stays behind, but Ruth's narration portrays her as, nevertheless, shaped by their absence.

Robinson's novel explores the effects on people's lives of absence, transience, disconnection, and abandonment. She suggests that prolonged disconnection from family and society creates a unique sort of present-oriented but memory-haunted consciousness. Robinson's train-hopping protagonists Sylvie and Ruth always move on when the place where they have temporarily settled begins to include them, to threaten them with the pain of its remembered loss. Ruth especially avoids human attachments, for she believes that people we attempt to hold on to "walk ahead of us, and walk too fast, and forget us. . . . The only mystery is that we expect it to be otherwise" (*Housekeeping* 184). Ruth and Sylvie allow even Lucille to fade from their lives, which are, ironically, both full and empty; they travel through the world, seeing everything, but taking and giving nothing, renouncing all ties.

This troubling narrative, which Robinson describes as a kind of female version of Melville's *Moby Dick*, dares readers to find the Ishmael—the outcast, the orphan, the disconnected "lonesome" spirit—that dwells within us all. Frequently reiterating her fondness for American writers of the nineteenth century, such as Melville, Robinson says that in her own writing, she tries to pick up the dropped parts of their conversation. She explores, for instance, what happens when a person such as her character, Sylvie, becomes the ultimate transcendentalist, opening her house to the elements and dining by starlight as flood waters rise in the parlor. Especially admiring the American romantics' use of metaphor to explore epistemological questions, Robinson joins their conversation by developing her own startling, evocative metaphors in *Housekeeping*. Not only the flooded house but also the wrecked train lying submerged at the bottom of the lake where Sylvie's father, sister, and many others have died suggests some primal, ontological mystery to which we, the "survivors," return, "picking among flotsam, among the small, unnoticed, unvalued clutter that was all that remained [and that] . . . only catastrophe made notable" (100). We sense this primal catastrophe of being, and in our bewildered loss we all resemble Ruth, who tries, in telling her story, to put things back together again in some way that makes sense.

About her deliberately metaphorical style, Robinson tells Thomas H. Schaub in an interview that she sometimes tests the limits of her metaphors to remind her readers, and herself, of the ultimate inadequacies of language, despite its evocative powers. However, she does not sympathize with modernist or postmodernist views of language as merely illusory or deceptive gamesmanship. She deplores what she considers reductive, anti-human views of art along with contemporary, politicized interpretive agendas. For instance, reductive feminist readings of *Housekeeping* annoy her. Though Robinson admits that she meant to write a novel about a specifically female American hero, she also says she hoped *Housekeeping* would be a book that male readers could enjoy as a novel about women but not hostile toward men. Interest in female perspectives and experience does not, for Robinson, automatically imply disdain for male authors or their art. Like her unique, boundary-crossing characters, Robinson deliberately resists categorization. Proudly independent, she declares that she feels no obligation to think like her contemporaries about either art or politics.

Unsurprisingly, Robinson laments what she sees as a contemporary disdain for American individualism and a concomitant loss of interest in the American West, one of her consuming interests. She rejects the popular suspicion that eccentric, introverted people are necessarily dangerous or ill, needing counseling or mood-altering drugs. On the contrary, Robinson believes that individualism, even extreme eccentricity, and the love of solitude that frequently defines them are the wellsprings of creativity. Such oddity also characterizes many visionary figures in the Bible, another admitted source of inspiration for her own writing. Indeed, Robinson points out both the aesthetic and the spiritual dimensions of American individualism that inform so much of the nineteenth-century literature that she admires.

CRITICAL RECEPTION

Housekeeping won the PEN/Hemingway Award for first fiction and the Richard and Hinda Rosenthal Award from the American Academy and Institute of Arts and Letters; it was also nominated for the PEN/Faulkner Fiction Award and for the Pulitzer Prize. From the beginning, critics praised Robinson's poetic language. Expressing great surprise that *Housekeeping* was a first novel, many described the narrative as "precise," "skilled," and "beautiful." The novel has been the focus of a substantial body of academic criticism since it first appeared nearly twenty years ago. In 1987 *Housekeeping* was made into a film directed by Bill Forsyth.

Literary criticism concerned with *Housekeeping* has emphasized Robinson's style, her connections to other writers (especially to nineteenth-century American writers but to some of her contemporaries, as well), and her treatment of specifically women's issues such as motherhood, domesticity, and coming of age as a female. Important to Robinson herself is her status as a writer about the American West, and a variety of critics have taken this regional focus. The novel also invites intense scrutiny of its profound psychological and biblical themes, the territory of a variety of critical approaches to *Housekeeping*. Judging this novel on its own merits, it is obviously a major work of literature; the steady stream of serious, academic attention it receives only confirms such a judgment.

BIBLIOGRAPHY

Works by Marilynne Robinson

Housekeeping. New York: Farrar, 1980. Bantam, 1989.
"Language Is Smarter Than We Are." *New York Times Book Review* 11 Jan. 1987: 8.
"Beyond the Pale with Edgar Allan Poe." *New York Times Book Review* 8 Feb. 1987: 11.
"A Nasty, Empty, Dangerous Word." *New York Times Book Review* 15 March 1987: 10–11.
"Let's Not Talk Down to Ourselves." *New York Times Book Review* 5 April 1987: 11.
Mother Country. New York: Farrar, 1989.
"My Western Roots." *Old West—New West: Centennial Essays.* Ed. Barbara Howard Meldrum. Moscow: University of Idaho Press, 1993. 165–72.
"Puritans and Prigs: An Anatomy of Zealotry." *Salmagundi* 101/102 (1994): 36–54.
"The New Puritanism." A Roundtable Discussion with Robert Boyers, Rochelle Gurstein, and Andrew Delbanco. *Salmagundi* 106/107 (1995): 194–256.
"The Fate of Ideas: Consequences of Darwinism." *Salmagundi* 114/115 (1997): 13–47.
The Death of Adam: Essays on Modern Thought. Boston: Houghton, 1998.
"Delivering Darwin: II. Signs of Struggle." *Salmagundi* 118/119 (1998): 319–27.
"Surrendering Wilderness." *Wilson Quarterly* 22 (1998): 60–64.
"The Way We Work, the Way We Live." *Christian Century* 115 (1998): 823–31.
"The Fate of Ideas: Moses." *Salmagundi* 121/122 (1999): 23–46.

Studies of Marilynne Robinson

Burke, William. "Border Crossings in Marilynne Robinson's *Housekeeping.*" *Modern Fiction Studies* 37 (1991): 716–24.
Caver, Christine. "Nothing Left to Lose: *Housekeeping*'s Strange Freedoms." *American Literature* 68 (1996): 11–37.

Foster, Thomas. "History, Critical Theory, and Women's Social Practices: Women's Time and *Housekeeping*." *Signs* 14 (1988): 73–99.

Geyh, Paula E. "Burning Down the House? Domestic Space and Feminine Subjectivity in Marilynne Robinson's *Housekeeping*." *Contemporary Literature* 34 (1993): 103–22.

Kaivola, Karen. "The Pleasures and Perils of Merging: Female Subjectivity in Marilynne Robinson's *Housekeeping*." *Contemporary Literature* 34 (1993): 670–90.

King, Kristin. "Resurfacings of the Deeps: Semiotic Balance in Marilynne Robinson's *Housekeeping*." *Studies in the Novel* 28 (1996): 565–80.

Kirby, Joan "Is There Life after Art?: The Metaphysics of Marilynne Robinson's *Housekeeping*." *Tulsa Studies in Women's Literature* 5 (1986): 91–109.

Mallon, Anne-Marie. "Sojourning Women: Homelessness and Transcendence in *Housekeeping*." *Criticism* 30 (1989): 95–105.

Ravits, Martha. "Extending the American Range: Marilynne Robinson's *Housekeeping*." *American Literature* 61 (1989): 644–66.

Schaub, Thomas. "An Interview with Marilynne Robinson." *Contemporary Literature* 35 (1994): 231–51.

——. *Lingering Hopes, Faltering Dreams: Marilynne Robinson and the Politics of Contemporary American Fiction*. Newark: University of Delaware Press, 1995.

Tyan, Maureen. "Marilynne Robinson's *Housekeeping*: The Subversive Narrative and the New American Eve." *South Atlantic Review* 56 (1991): 79–86.

MARY ROBISON (1949–)

Cynthia Whitney Hallett

BIOGRAPHY

Mary Robison was born in Washington, D.C., on January 14, 1949, but grew up in the Midwest, specifically Ohio, with her seven siblings. The daughter of psychologist F. Elizabeth Waldkoetter Reiss and attorney Anthony Cennamo, Robison was raised a Catholic. A self-described "child of the sixties," Robison ran away from home twice, the first time at sixteen to Florida, "to find and speak with Jack Kerouac before he died," and a second time, at eighteen, to San Francisco to make "the pilgrimage; it was the Haight-Ashbury, '67 or something like that" (Simpson 156). In an interview with Mona Simpson for *Vogue*, Robison describes that period of her life between San Francisco and college: "I fell in and out of marriage; I had children. I was bad and wild and had to be kept sedated a good deal of the time" (156). Robison has two daughters, Jennifer and Rachel. In the latter part of the 1970s, Robison would meet and marry fellow writer James N. Robison; this marriage, too, ended in divorce.

By 1977 Mary Robison had earned her MA degree at Johns Hopkins University in Baltimore, where she studied with John Barth. According to Robison, both the place and the person were vital components in her evolution as a writer: "I would have simply done something else; I would not have taken my fiction writing seriously had it not been for Johns Hopkins University and John Barth. Barth charged a dead battery in me" (Ross 400). Significantly, Robison comes to identify Barth as "mentor"; equally important to her style and success is the fact that she becomes a regular contributor to *New Yorker* magazine.

Robison's early literary awards include fellowships from the Yaddo Writers and Artists Colony in 1978, the Bread Loaf Writers' Conference in 1979, and the Guggenheim Foundation in 1980–1981, plus both PEN and Authors Guild Awards in 1979. Twenty years later, Robison continues to garner honors and awards. On May 17, 2000, her story "Seizing Control" (*Believe Them*) was featured in New York's Yaddo Centennial Arts Tribute in honor of a century of creativity in America. In addition, Robison was awarded a summer 2000 residency at the Yaddo Writers and Artists Colony in New York.

At the beginning of the twenty-first century, Robison published book-length texts totaling six. Her newest novel, *Why Did I Ever?*, was published in October of 2001. Her short fiction is published in three collections: *Days* (1979), *An Amateur's Guide to the Night* (1983), and *Believe Them* (1988). Her work is included in numerous anthologies, including *Best American Short Stories* (1982) and *Matters of Life and Death* (*1983*); the two most anthologized stories are "Coach" and "Yours." Her work appears in popular and academic periodicals such as the *New Yorker*, *Esquire*, and *Mississippi Review*. To date her novels are *Oh!* (1981) and *Subtraction* (1991).

While writing, publishing and reviewing fiction, Mary Robison has continued to teach creative writing at Ohio University, Harvard, Oberlin College, and the University of Houston. Additionally, throughout the 1980s, she was the writer-in-residence at the University of Southern Mississippi, the University of North Carolina at Greensboro, the College of William and Mary, and Bennington College in Vermont. In 1990 she returned to the University of Southern Mississippi as a permanent faculty member, teaching creative writing, directing dissertations, and working closely with the USM Center for Writers and *Mississippi Review*. In addition to reviewing new works of fiction, Robison remains in professional demand, consistently invited to participate in national and local academic and artistic conferences, symposia, and workshops featuring creative writing in general and often the short story in particular.

MAJOR WORKS AND THEMES

In the majority of her fiction, Robison focuses on small, insignificant events that engage the lives of ordinary persons, yet she emphasizes characterization and, with a maestro's touch, underscores the whole with humor. Consequently, irony is an essential chord as well; for although her stories are minimal in form and often somewhat bleak in subject matter, they almost always contain an infusion of humor. Robison is an astute observer and critic of the American middle class, whose stories are relevant to current social conditions in the United States. Not overtly autobiographical, the majority of Robison's stories appear to reflect some influence of her middle-class, Catholic upbringing as well as striking parallels between her fiction and her own observations about her five brothers as reported in her 1983 *Esquire* article, "The Brothers: Memories of Being Buried Alive in Boys."

Responding to Robison's particular stylistic traits, most literary critics associate her with other contemporary authors who are regularly identified as minimalist, most especially Raymond Carver, Bobbie Ann Mason, Ann Beattie, Amy Hempel, and Frederick Barthelme. Susan Mernit credits minimalist writers, including Robison, with the late twentieth-century revival of the short story as well as with writing stories that are "distinct in style [and] restrained in tone, [and that] describe the dislocations and disappointments of modern life with irony and whimsy" (303). Ultimately, Patrick Meanor insists that Robison "captures, simultaneously, the stark banality and the comic irony of the late stages of the American Dream in the last quarter of the twentieth century" (2010).

In 1979, just two years after she finished at Johns Hopkins, Robison published her first collection of short fiction, *Days*, consisting of twenty stories, of which eight had already appeared at different times in the *New Yorker* and two in *Viva*. Individually, these brief narratives address certain small adjustments that people make to keep from plummeting from the safety of their marginal existence into the abyss that is their lives; they seem able to withdraw to the very edges of their own lives, looking in, watching but not participating—as if able to exist on the frame of their own pictures (lives). The dialogue is spare and stylistically abrupt. Placing Robison's fiction squarely within prevailing social and philosophic parameters, writer and critic Ann Tyler suggests that these "are not so much stories as splinters of contemporary life, set under a microscope. . . . Their bleakness is a natural part of the modern sense of disengagement. . . . [Yet] there is humor here, as well as a deadpan exactitude" (13). In the opening story, "Kite and Paint," Robison establishes the waiting mode that recurs throughout the collection. In spite of an impending hurricane, the main characters, two men in their sixties, are too exhausted by life to evacuate their beach house—their performance echoing Samuel Beckett's *Waiting for Godot.* Sometimes Robison allows a dramatic event to intrude into the otherwise routine matters and ordinary events of these stories, as in "May Queen," in which a seventeen-year-old girl's dress catches fire from a candle during a Roman Catholic religious ceremony that seems vaguely to resemble a medieval vegetation-myth ritual—pagan myth fused with Christian rite. In these brief narratives, Robison continues to explore the theme of damaged or defective relationships, especially those of failed or failing marriages. In these stories, Robison also portrays the disorder and emotional numbness that often result from heavy drinking.

Robison also appears to draw on her Roman Catholic background for several stories that manifest a loss of faith in the sustaining power of religion. In the story "Sisters," for instance, one of the main characters is a Sister Mary Clare, a nun who is unhappy with her chosen life; rather than confronting the problem, however, she chooses to avoid it by entering a cloister and taking a vow of silence, yet another metaphor for the problems these characters have with voicing their pain. Others of these stories expand with gentle amusement to address the general incompetence and occasional insensitivity of parents, yet another recurring theme in *Days.*

The surfaces of these stories appear to wear many of the trappings of anomie. Such is "Independence Day," which features Helen, thirtyish and undirected, still living in her father's house. Helen keeps a journal of her life's adventures; it is mostly filled with notes on the movies and television shows that she watches. Brief as they may be, in all the stories of *Days,* there seems something complex and essential at work deep beneath trivial surface details.

In her first novel, *Oh!* (1981), displaying what David Leavitt calls her "wild, baroque humor" ("Book Review" 117), Robison deals satirically with the problems of a Midwestern family living under the eccentric protection of a singular father—a band of clever survivors who ultimately find a way of staying happy in a world gone crazy. In 1989, *Twister,* an independent, low-budget, comedy film, based on Robison's novel, was released. Much like the Robison novel that spawned it, *Twister* (not to be mistaken for the stormy 1996 special-effects blockbuster of the same name) is a kaleidoscope of absurd conversations, oddball characters, and events that seem to happen for no reason at all.

Two years after the publication of *Oh!* (1981), in which she had further developed her comic talents and continued to explore the state of the middle-class American family, Robison published her second volume of short fiction, *An Amateur's Guide to the Night* (1983). In these stories, Robison presents people and situations so quietly familiar to readers that while reviewing them Sarah E. Lauzen was moved to declare, "All traces of surface tension have been bleached out, and the result is as comfortable as a favorite old bathrobe" (118). In this collection, Robison continues to address mere glimpses of domestic life, most especially close-ups of middle-class young people undergoing the pangs of growing up. Addressing the continued timeliness of Robison's themes, David Leavitt appraises these stories as "flawless," and remarks on Robison's "perfect eye for detail and ear for dialogue," claiming that "no American short-story writer speaks to our time more urgently or fondly" than Robison ("Brief Encounters" 44).

Once again, Robison's dialogue captures the special texture, cadence, and jargon of contemporary young Americans, whose metaphors many parents found as lyrical as fingernails stroking a blackboard. Some of these thirteen stories retrace familiar territory in Robison's fiction. For example, in "You Know Charles," Robison explores the fear of change as well as the fear of relationships. As in Robison's first collection, the characters of this second set of stories appear to suffer from a sense of dislocation. One woman hears voices in her head; another complains about a brain tumor; an accident-prone man totals the family car and then catches on fire while cooking dinner on the hibachi. Others are simply afflicted with a heavy, nameless ennui. By the end of this collection, readers are keenly aware of the stasis and pessimism about the possibility of change that underscore so many of Robison's stories.

Although with many stories in *Days*, Robison examines numerous conflicts between parents and children, in "The Dictionary in the Laundry Chute" from *An Amateur's Guide to the Night*, she explores more fully the unhealthy consequences of disaffection with the world as created by some parents. Robison's world of wisecracking couch potatoes and phobic homebodies comes to life enjoyably in the title story of the second collection, "An Amateur's Guide to the Night," in which she reverses the roles of parent and child: An immature mother who likes to pass herself off as her daughter's sister, Harriet corrupts her mature, hardworking child into various forms of irresponsible behavior. Robison does not seem to hold out false hope for the young people in her stories; most of them seem destined to fail as dismally as their elders have. Yet through them, Robison appears to introduce a note of optimism into an otherwise bleak landscape; their overall vigor and enthusiasm brighten these stories.

In contrast, "Coach" is a relatively lengthy exploration of the down-to-earth problems of an apparently average American family. While the life of the title character centers on his job as a football coach, his wife struggles to create her own identity as an amateur artist. The cunning, if not sinister, theme of this story is that the virtues that go with coach's role are not enough to meet the requirements of life and that he may be the chief victim of his reliance on them. The bulwark of the family, this coach is flexible enough to go along with his wife's whim of setting up a studio away from home and having her fling as an artist, but he is neither shrewd nor skeptical enough to anticipate the outcome of her experiment. As one of Robison's two most anthologized stories, "Coach" is a masterpiece of reflection, quietly but progressively weighted with suggestions of a subsurface flaw of catastrophic proportions. What the reader hears at the end of the narrative is the cracking of a pane of glass as an earthquake announces its arrival. This eruption functions as both actual and metaphorical resolution.

The story "In Jewel" marks a departure in terms of setting for Robison. Here, she explores a teacher's ambiguous feelings about leaving the blue-collar coal town where she has lived most of her life. This story stands as one of the most comprehensible examples of Robison's stylistic method of employing a single moment to evoke an entire lifetime and using the part as proxy for the whole.

Also compared with the protagonists of Robison's first collection, the main characters of the stories in *An Amateur's Guide to the Night* appear to have many more triumphs. In both "Look at Me Go" and "Yours," the reader finds a genuine belief in the possibilities of love. Robison's most acclaimed story is "Yours." Roger Angell, of the *New Yorker* relates, "Mary Robison's story 'Yours' seemed to have some missing manuscript pages when it turned up in the mail in 1980, but after I'd read its seven hundred and ninety words it was plain that a single line more would be much less" (108). In this brief, poignant narrative, Robison establishes all the necessary data of time, place, and event, suggests the depth of companionship and love between Allison and her husband, and provokes the reader to a profound comprehension of being. Filling fewer than four pages, this perfect, little story is typical of many in this collection in which characters often deflect pain through mundane, often repetitive activities—rituals as ordinary as carving Halloween pumpkins.

Believe Them is both mandate and title of Robison's third collection of stories published in 1988. Robison is scrupulous at immediately establishing the varied and deliberate settings: children driving a car in a snowstorm; a woman on horseback in midsummer; a painfully intelligent teenage girl in a convent school; a young widow trying to get through winter. In her charting of human frailties, Robison seems determined to represent America coast to coast, including such cities as Providence, Baltimore, and Washington, D.C., as well as small towns in Pennsylvania, Ohio, North Carolina, and Indiana. Many of the themes of these eleven stories are familiar—family relationships, strained emotions, how people "get by"—and all of Robison's characteristic literary strengths are in evidence: her descriptive power, her skill with dialogue, her sense of humor, and her intelligent insights into the condition of middle-class America.

The title *Believe Them* comes from a litany of admonitions recited by a retarded child in the book's opening story: "Stand still in line," she says, "don't pet strange animals. . . . Whatever Father and Mother tell you, believe them" (8). Like the child in the ironically named story "Seizing Control," many of Robison's characters are only tenuously connected to reality. While many of Robison's stories are concerned with identity and self-awareness, the characters often muddle through a variety of clichéd perspectives, leading to scenes that are flat and uninspiring. Not all of these eleven stories move along as relentlessly as they might, either. What compensates most of the time is that Robison "maintains a linguistic simplicity and spare wit that shrink-wrap her work in a bright sort of irony" (Peterson 34).

In her second novel, *Subtraction* (1991), in addition to her now familiar themes of angst-ridden relationships, willful alienation, unbridled alcoholism, and epiphanic slivers, Robison creates one of her first, fully defined characters, Paige Deveraux, the female protagonist and narrator, with both a family history and an emotional past. Paige is a poet and a teacher of creative (poetry) writing at Harvard who finds herself in Houston on a mission to fetch her errant husband, but she then ends up staying months rather than days for utterly, unpredictable reasons. One has to believe that at least the corners of this work have been frayed by autobiography. In an interview for *Contemporary Authors* in the late 1980s, Robison responds to the *CA* query, "How does the combination of teaching and writing work for you?" with a simple, "It doesn't work at all," continuing, "For me, it's simply an impossible combination" (Ross 399). Robison, who wrote poetry throughout her adolescence, has taught creative writing both at Harvard and at the University of Houston. Her (now former) husband, James Robison, taught creative writing at the University of Houston from 1988 to 1999. Without a doubt, this information is not meant to imply that *Subtraction* in any way reflects the Robisons' marriage but rather is offered as proof that Mary Robison has been where she takes her characters, geographically and metaphorically.

Robison's second novel is a positive stylistic evolution through which she parlays her acute power of observation into potent, lyric descriptions; for example, soon after arriving in Texas, Paige observes, "Houston wasn't desert and cacti. Houston was magnolia and swamp, jungle heat and jungle humid, and Raymond's ice house was in a neighborhood of shotgun shacks" (5). Like all the best of Robison, *Subtraction* is a tragicomedy; self-indulgent but generous, surely ironic, filled with somewhat exaggerated but certainly recognizable people and situations.

CRITICAL RECEPTION

Mary Robison's fiction consistently meets with positive responses from both critics and fellow writers alike. Low keyed and economical, Robison's prose style places her squarely among the best American writers of the twentieth century. Her quietly penetrating writing yields an uncanny accuracy of vision. The back cover of Robison's first collection *Days* is rife with high praise, including this endorsement from her mentor, John Barth: "Mary Robison's hard-edged, fine-tooled, enigmatic super-realism is a joy." Although Robison's style falls squarely within the realm of minimalism, rarely do reviewers or literary critics draw the connection in negative terms.

Author Frederick Barthelme's comments stand alone on the back of Robison's 1991 novel: "There isn't a writer working today who sees the world, or hears it, or tastes it, or inhabits it more fearlessly than Mary Robison. Reading *Subtraction* is falling in love with her—her voice, her verbs, the peculiar squinted view she has. . . . I can scarcely imagine anyone writing a novel half as stunning anytime soon." Barthelme's words encapsulate both the professional and the literary responses to Robison's fiction. Nevertheless, in spite of having garnered high critical praise and numerous literary awards, Robison's works remain relatively unknown to the general reader. Few, if any, students find either of her novels on a reading list, and of her numerous short stories, only "Yours" and "Coach" are anthologized. Readers who are new to Mary Robison's fiction should prepare themselves for a writer whose peers consider her a genius.

Ten years later, Mary Robison published her third novel *Why Did I Ever* (2001), a brilliant soliloquy on the absurdity of life. Written as 536 snippets that reflect narrator Monica "Money" Breton's ADD syndrome, *Why Did I Ever* registers a captivating and hilarious version of what could otherwise be construed as, at least to some extent, one person's tragic existence. Certainly, it is a story about one person's method of surviving. Several articles in the *New York Times Book Review* characterize this work as, "Ritalin and lots of rules for living" (Notable 63).

In this novel, Robison blends her razor-sharp wit, dark comedic vision, superb talent, and propensity for terse prose to create a work that writer Barry Hannah labels "pure grim poetry." In fact, but for its length, *Why Did I Ever* could be mistaken for a poem. Its staccato structure of numbered stanzas occasionally punctuated with subtitles bears a striking resemblance to certain epic poetry; whereas its content echoes confessional verse. Within the conflict between content and structure only gradually do the facts of Money Breton's life emerge—much like the conflict between Money and the events that define her life. *Why Did I Ever* garnered Mary Robison the *Los Angeles Times* book prize in fiction. Announcing the book prize awards Sunday, April 28, 2002, editors of the *LA Times* reported that, "Robison rebels against form, challenges stifling social orders, and paints a dark and moving portrait of a woman whose mere survival is nothing short of miraculous" (Guccione). Notable quotes by reviewers on the dust jacket of the hard cover edition of *Why Did I Ever* include Richard Ford, "[This novel] is startling, deft, extremely attractive and smart-very smart"; Amy Hempel, "In this new novel the stakes are higher, [Robison's] mordant wit more necessary, her appeal more encompassing than ever before"; and Frederick Barthelme, "You marvel at the deftness of language and the suppleness of the thought. Seemingly offhand remarks make you laugh out loud and then stick you in some way you don't quite get."

BIBLIOGRAPHY

Works by Mary Robison

Days. New York: Knopf, 1979.
Oh! New York: Knopf, 1981.
An Amateur's Guide to the Night. Knopf, 1983.
"The Brothers: Memories of Being Buried Alive in Boys." *Esquire* Jan. 1983: 100–103.
Believe Them. New York: Knopf, 1988.
Subtraction. New York: Knopf, 1991.
Why Did I Ever. Washington, D.C.: Counterpoint, 2001.

Studies of Mary Robison

"And Bear in Mind." Rev. of *Why Did I Ever. New York Times Book Review*. 9 Dec. 2001: 30.
Angell, Roger. "Storyville: Onward and Upward with the Arts." *New Yorker* June 27 (1994): 104–9.
Bannon, Barbara A. "PW Forecasts. [*An Amateur's Guide to the Night*]." *Publishers Weekly* 30 Sept. 1983: 106–7.
Barth, John. "A Few Words about Minimalism." *New York Times Book Review* 28 Dec. 1986: 1–2, 25.
Bauer, Douglas. " 'New Scars, New Stories, No Excuses': *Subtraction* by Mary Robison." *New York Times Book Review* 24 Feb. 1991: 10.
Bawer, Bruce. "The Literary Brat Pack." *Diminishing Fictions: Essays on the Modern American Novel and Its Critics.* St. Paul, MN: Graywolf, 1988. 314–23.
Birkerts, Sven. "The School of Gordon Lish: The New American Writing and Its Mentor." *New Republic* 13 Oct. 1986: 28, 30–33.
Bolonik, Kera. "Regretfully Yours: Mary Robison's Minimalist Return." Rev. of *Why Did I Ever. Village Voice* 25 Dec. 2001: 67.
"Briefly Noted." Rev. of *Why Did I Ever. New Yorker* 12 Nov. 2001: 127.
Broyard, Anatole. "Affirmative Actions." Rev. of *Days. New York Times* 2 June 1979: 21.
——. " 'Books of the Times: A Gourmet of Collapse': *Oh!* by Mary Robison." *New York Times Supplement* 6 June 1981: 13.

Dunn, Robert. "Books: The New Kids on the Block." Rev. of *Days*. *Mother Jones* May 1983: 56–58.

——. "After Minimalism." *Mississippi Review* 40/41 (1985): 52–56.

Eder, Richard. "Pain on the Face of Middle America." *Los Angeles Times Book Review* 2 Oct. 1983: 3, 8.

Gates, David. "Less Is More, More Than Ever." Rev. of *Why Did I Ever*. *Newsweek* 3 Dec. 2001: 72

Guccione, Jean. "10 Authors Honored with Times Book Prizes." CalendarLive on latimes.com 28 Apr. 2002. http://www.calendarlive.com/top/1,1419,L-LATimes-Books-X!Article Detail-57458,00.html (20 Jun 2002).

Hallett, Cynthia Whitney. "Minimalism and the Short Story." *Studies in Short Fiction* 33 (1996): 487–95.

——. *Minimalism & the Short Story: Raymond Carver, Amy Hempel, and Mary Robison*. Lewiston, NY: Edwin Mellen Press, 1999.

Inness-Brown, Elizabeth. "Mary Robison, *Days*." *Fiction International* 12 (1980): 281–83.

Kakutani, Michiko. "Books of the Times." Rev. of *An Amateur's Guide to the Night*. *New York Times* 15 Nov. 1983: C17.

——. "Books of the Times: People Who Talk but Don't Connect." Rev. of *Believe Them*. *New York Times* 8 June 1988: C21.

Lauzen, Sarah E. "Rev. of *An Amateur's Guide to the Night*." *Chicago* Aug. 1984: 117–18.

Leavitt, David. "Brief Encounters." Rev. of *An Amateur's Guide to the Night*. *Village Voice* 10 Jan. 1984: 44.

——. "The Book Review: The Unsung Voices." *Esquire* Feb. 1986: 117–18.

McCaffery, Larry. "Errant Mom Hits the Road." Rev. of *Believe Them*. *New York Times Book Review* 31 July 1988: 12.

McKenna, Michael. "Mary Robison." *American Short-Story Writers since World War II*. Ed. Patrick Meanor. Detroit: Gale, 1993. 276–81.

Meanor, Patrick. "Mary Robison." *Critical Survey of Short Fiction*. Ed. Frank N. Magill. Vol. 5. Englewood Cliffs, NJ: Salem Press, 1993. 2010–17.

Mernit, Susan. "The State of the Short Story." *Virginia Quarterly Review* 62 (1986): 302–11.

"Notable Books." Rev. of *Why Did I Ever*. *New York Times Book Review* 2 Dec. 2001: 63.

"Notes on Current Books." Rev. of *Why Did I Ever*. *Virginia Quarterly Review* 78 (Spring 2002): 60.

Peterson, V. R. "People, Picks & Pans." Rev. of *Believe Them*. *People Weekly* 30 (1988): 34.

Pollitt, Katha. "Family and Friends." Rev. of *Oh! New York Times Book Review* 23 Aug. 1981: 14, 29.

Robison, James Curry. "1969–1980: Experiment and Tradition." *American Short Story 1945–1980: A Critical History*. Ed. Gordon Weaver. Boston: Twayne, 1983. 77–109.

Ross, Jean. W. "Interview with Mary Robison [October 26, 1984]." *Contemporary Authors*. Ed. Hal May. Vol. 116. Detroit: Gale, 1986. 397–400.

Schine, Cathleen. "Days of Wine and Ritalin." Rev. of *Why Did I Ever*. *New York Times Book Review* 25 Nov. 2001: 7.

Seaman, Donna. Rev. of *Why Did I Ever*. *Booklist* 1 Oct. 2001: 300.

Simpson, Mona. "Books in *VOGUE*: Interview: Mary Robison." *Vogue* June 1984: 156, 158.

Smith, Sarah Harrison. "Fragments of Tragedy and Pleasure." Rev. of *Why Did I Ever*. *The New Leader* 84.6 (Nov-Dec 2001): 35.

Steinberg, Sybil. "Forecasts: Fiction." Rev. of *Believe Them*. *Publishers Weekly* 15 April 1988: 76.

Tyler, Anne. "Two Seats of Bleak Lives." Rev. of *Days*. *New York Times Book Review* 29 July 1979: 13.

LESLIE MARMON SILKO (1948–)

Catherine Rainwater

BIOGRAPHY

Leslie Marmon Silko was born March 5, 1948, in Albuquerque, New Mexico, the eldest of three daughters of Virginia Leslie Marmon and Lee Howard Marmon. She grew up in a Laguna Pueblo community among Laguna, Anglo, and Mexican members of an extended family. They have been prominent in reservation politics since the Marmons, the Anglo branch of the family, first arrived in the Southwest from Ohio after the Civil War. Lee Marmon, a notable photographer, still runs the Marmon Trading Post, the old family business located about fifty miles southwest of Albuquerque.

Silko attended a Bureau of Indian Affairs elementary school and later parochial schools in Albuquerque, but probably the most essential part of her early education took place at home. As a child, she learned to love wandering the Laguna mesas alone, and she credits her father with teaching her to feel comfortable in nature, to sense her kinship with the land and the creatures inhabiting it. Also at home, her grandmother (A' mooh in Silko's fiction) taught her many of the Keresan oral stories that inform her works.

Silko began writing as a little girl, perhaps at first as a self-therapeutic means of dealing with her complicated social status as a mixed-blood Indian. She realized early that she was simultaneously both outsider and insider to each of the three cultures composing her ethnic identity. Silko vividly recalls, for example, sometimes being singled out as an Indian and other times being asked by tourists to stand aside while they took photographs of "real" Indian children. Unsurprisingly, Silko's art reveals her concern with the myriad barriers separating diverse cultures; her works examine an array of literal and conceptual borderlands.

Silko graduated in 1969 from the honors program of the University of New Mexico, where she also briefly attended law school before enrolling in graduate studies in creative writing. She writes (and often combines) poetry, essays, and fiction. She has also been involved in filmmaking. Silko founded the Laguna Film Project and once starred in a video as herself, a Laguna storyteller, in *Running on the Edge of the Rainbow* (1978). She also assisted in the production of a video version of one of her stories, "Estoy-eh-muut and the Kunideeyahs," titled *Arrowboy and the Witches*. Perhaps to some extent owing to her photographer father's influence, Silko is intrigued by the combination of verbal and visual texts, including drawings and her own and Lee Marmon's photography.

A recipient of numerous awards dating from the earliest years of her career, in 1974 alone she won a Chicago Review Award for poetry, a National Endowment for the Arts Grant, and a Rosewater Foundation Grant that freed her for the next two years to live and write in Ketchikan, Alaska. Here, she wrote much of *Ceremony* (1977), but her Alaskan experience most obviously informs *Storyteller* (1981). In 1981, with her reputation as an outstanding American writer already well established, Silko received a $176,000 award from the MacArthur Foundation. Off and on throughout her career, Silko has taught literature and writing at the University of California at Los Angeles, the University of New Mexico, the University of Arizona, Navajo Community College, and elsewhere. In 1994 the New Mexico Humanities Council named her a Living Cultural Treasure, and she received the Native Writers' Circle of the Americas Lifetime Achievement Award.

The author has been married and divorced twice; she has one son, Robert, from her first marriage to Richard Chapman and a second son, Cazimir, from her marriage to John Silko. Leslie Marmon Silko currently lives and writes near Tucson, where she continues to enjoy her childhood penchant for wandering alone in the southwestern landscape, nowadays frequently with her camera in tow.

MAJOR WORKS AND THEMES

Silko's early short stories figure among her major works—*Ceremony, Storyteller, Almanac of the Dead, Gardens in the Dunes*—partly because of the profound intertextual relationship between them and her later works. Some of these early stories appear revised and incorporated into the texts of such longer compositions as *Ceremony* and *Storyteller*. Moreover, though all of her works differ significantly from one another in ways revealing the breadth of Silko's creative talent, each also comprises a part of a self-proclaimed, larger story of indigenous Americans' 500-year resistance against colonial and postcolonial oppression. This thematic and semiotic concern with cultural resistance is identified overtly in *Almanac of the Dead* (1991) and more subtly implied in *Storyteller, Ceremony,* and *Gardens in the Dunes* (1999).

Perhaps the earliest version of Silko's core story of resistance occurs in the title piece of *Storyteller*. This complex narrative features a young female protagonist who assumes the regenerative role of storyteller after an old "grandfather" dies; presumably having likewise inherited this role from an elder, the old man has kept alive the story of a hunter (a European colonial invader) and a polar bear (representing nature and precontact native life). During the old man's life, the hunter had pursued the elusive bear, but under the young girl's control, the story intimates the bear's ascendant power portending the end of Eurocentric domination.

Silko's message is clear in this lead-off story and reiterated in various ways throughout the collection of poems, short stories, photographs, and autobiographical sketches that comprise *Storyteller*. Aesthetic forms such as poems and narratives carry formidable world-altering power to build up or tear down lived realities. As the narrator declares at the opening of *Ceremony*, realities begin in thought; the narrator tells us the world-transformative story as Thought Woman thinks it.

Silko's ongoing story of Eurocentric oppression and native resistance assumes disparate forms in her novels. *Ceremony* confronts the reader with ugly, postnuclear realities of the twentieth century that result when a group of egomaniacal C'ko'yo witches set loose the evil story of uranium mining that eventually becomes the story of the atomic bomb. The witches are a multicultural group of destructive entities, a fact underlining Silko's often-repeated message that every culture (not just European) contains evil people; the murderous, suicidal, spirit-killing, and environmentally exploitative actions of those she calls the Destroyers must be continually "balanced" by those who live responsibly, who tell and live ethical, spiritually healthy "stories." Tayo, Silko's spiritually and mentally ailing protagonist in *Ceremony*, heals himself of the effects of the witches' stories partly by fulfilling his tribal identity and responsibility and partly by participating in healing rituals. All aspects of his healing journey are facilitated by Laguna and Navajo stories that attempt to repair the damaged world set in motion by the C'ko'yo magicians.

All of Silko's works thematically explore this creative and destructive potential of spoken and written language. Like *Ceremony*, which overtly proclaims itself a ceremonial story, Silko's other novels may be viewed as verbal ceremonial acts designed to change readers and the world that her texts enter as semiotic phenomena. The story of Tayo's physical, spiritual, and emotional healing thus becomes only one layer of the narrative, which the author invites us to accept as an "offering" that, rightly received, might lead to our own and society's improved well-being.

Underlying the darker, less overtly benevolent message of *Almanac of the Dead* is the same ceremonial intent to galvanize the "500-year resistance" that will ultimately separate not Indian people from non-Indian people but the benign creators from the vicious "Destroyers" of humanity and the earth. Likewise, *Gardens in the Dunes* projects a ceremonial ethos as a Ghost Dance novel. If *Ceremony* is both about a ceremony and itself a ceremonial work designed to heal, *Gardens* is both about the Ghost Dance and itself a verbal ritual designed, like the original spiritual movement of the late nineteenth century, to realize Wovoka's prophecy of the end of colonial oppression.

Supporting her countercolonial purpose, another important part of Silko's apparent mission as a storyteller is to foster cross-cultural communication, not simply between herself as an Indian author and her diverse, primarily mainstream readership but also between Indian and non-Indian people in general. Consequently, many of her works subtly instruct the reader concerning Southwestern tribal information that underlies her narratives and concerning the requisite interpretive strategies for decoding her (and much other Native American) writing. Indeed, Silko frequently stresses the need for improved communication between cultures. Her first published short story, "The Man to Send Rain Clouds" (1969), for example, traces a Catholic priest's lack of insight into the ways of a people he has lived among for years; a clear message to Eurocentric readers of this story is that they risk being like Father Paul, obtuse and condescending toward people of unperceived complexity. The equation of sprinkled holy water and falling rain at the end of the story potentially elevates the alert reader to a more informed status; a careful reader understands what Father Paul cannot quite "remember" about the mystical relationship to water and the elements of earth that unite all cultures, however otherwise different.

Another of Silko's concerns, treated most overtly in *Ceremony* but informing all of her works, is the experience of the half-blood or mixed-blood Indian who, despite a strong traditional bent, learns to survive in Euro-American reality. Tayo in *Ceremony* must meet his traditional Laguna responsibilities as well as cope with the mainstream reality that consigns his Indian world to the past and his spiritual reality to superstition. One of Silko's earliest works, "Tony's Story" (incorporated into *Storyteller*) likewise explores this theme. A young man stalked by a sinister highway patrolman must decide whether his nemesis is a witch or merely an Indian-hating white man with a badge, or perhaps both. *Almanac of the Dead* and *Gardens in the Dunes* also feature characters struggling, like Tayo and Tony, to negotiate such dual realities; Sterling in *Almanac* and Indigo in *Gardens* ultimately learn to distinguish people of good heart from the "Destroyers," and they find ways to preserve Indian realities.

A pan-Indian environmental ethic that equates respect for the earth with respect for the female also receives heavy emphasis in nearly all of Silko's writings. For Silko, the destruction of the earth and the degradation of women are manifestations of the same underlying violence. In the frequently anthologized short story, "Lullaby" (in *Storyteller*), for instance, Silko depicts cultural violence against Indian mothers whose tubercular children found their Indian identity, as well as their disease, to be the target of the white man's "rehabilitative" efforts. Native people, however, may also be guilty of disrespect toward women and the earth. Tayo in *Ceremony* insults Corn Woman and her sister when he curses the rain, and female characters are most centrally powerful in his healing quest. In *Almanac,* the drug-dealing, gun-running Destroyers are a cultural mix of primarily male characters, and in *Gardens in the Dunes*, a botanist epitomizes Eurocentric proprietorship over females, animals, and plants. Buying and selling orchids, Edward Palmer unwittingly becomes involved in the illegal trade of rubber trees, activities that commodify the earth and potentially exploit indigenous ecosystems and peoples. Most comfortable in the abstract, intellectual worlds of horticultural science and business, Edward nurtures greenhouse orchids while starving his wife of love and affection. Impotent from a wound sustained while collecting orchids in the jungle, he cannot conceive a child with his wife, who instead plays mother to Indigo, a Sand Lizard girl whom Hattie rescues from an Indian school. Hattie, Indigo, and various other female characters in the novel, including Sister Salt, inhabit their space on the earth in ways very different from the domineering males powering turn-of-the-century society.

Enlivened through contact with the spiritually vital child and through reconnections with her own ancient, European spiritual traditions, Hattie thrives as her husband withers away under the killing influences of ruthless capitalism and his quack-physician business partner. After Edward dies and Indigo is reunited with Sister Salt, Hattie decides to live in England with her aunt, who also left America for the land of her own ancestors. For the alert reader, their departure recalls the Ghost Dance prophecy implied, but never directly stated, in the novel: a prophecy of the disappearance of all things European from the Americas, which are returned at last to their native inhabitants.

These and other thematic concerns informing Silko's art are reinforced by structural features of her texts. Essentially a Laguna storyteller at heart, Silko in her own non-traditional writing observes a Southwestern (and pan-Indian) tribal aesthetic of ceremonial form, with its power potentially to achieve desired effects in the reader. In *Ceremony*, for example, the prose and verse portions of the text are formally crafted to serve complementary functions; as Tayo seeks knowledge of how all the parts of his own personal story and the story of the world come together to make sense, the reader also seeks to discover how the parts of Silko's novel come together under one design. This design suggests the balanced, symmetrical, and beautiful form that American Indian cosmologies attribute to creation itself. Likewise, in *Almanac of the Dead*, the participatory reader actively pursues textual clues to how the world of contemporary, lived reality conforms to the story limned in Yoeme's fragmentary, prophetic codex. Such readers also negotiate interpretive cues provided by the author to suggest how they might best comprehend the unity behind the various strands of the text.

Gardens in the Dunes develops a similar but slightly more understated structural relationship between the two plots comprising the narrative. The story of Indigo and Sister Salt and the story of Edward and Hattie gradually meld into one as the plots come together, suggesting the merger of native and European peoples; but even more significantly, as the two stories separate in the end, Silko thematically and structurally intimates the fulfillment of Ghost Dance prophecy.

Leslie Marmon Silko is an author with a mission. Her cultural and political purposes, however, are not served by any conventional didacticism. Silko summons and controls her artistic energies in shamanic fashion: She generates mind-, heart-, spirit-, and world-altering stories. Like Tayo's healing Laguna stories resisting C'ko'yo witchery, Silko's art aims to counter the disastrous effects of past and present "stories" behind the violence, environmental decay, and spiritual impoverishment of the present era.

CRITICAL RECEPTION

Silko achieved early recognition for her work in the form of numerous grants and awards, but her most widespread attention followed the publication of *Ceremony* in 1977. This novel was the first by an American Indian writer to appear (nearly ten years) after N. Scott Momaday's Pulitzer Prize–winning *House Made of Dawn*, with which *Ceremony* shares some common concerns and aesthetic features. Soon after the appearance of *Ceremony*, a wealth of Native American writers began to appear on the mainstream literary horizon, many of them indebted to Silko and Momaday for helping to create an audience for their works.

Silko has not eluded controversy, however. During the 1980s, as other Indian writers began to appear on the American literary horizon, she became briefly entangled in a publicized argument with Louise Erdrich that originated with Silko's abrasive review of Erdrich's *Beet Queen* (1986). Silko praised Erdrich's lyrical style and several other features of her writing but lambasted the author for an allegedly academic, postmodern representation of Indians and Indian reality that, in Silko's view, sanitizes American history and obscures the truth about contemporary Indian life in the Dakotas. Silko's remarks seemed uncharacteristically harsh; from the author of *Ceremony*, many had apparently come to expect a more conciliatory voice. Over the next couple of years, critical commentary on Silko's works sometimes remarked her allegedly restricted notions of ethnicity and Eurocentrically contaminated, essentialist poetics. Such charges do not stand up under careful examination of her art, however.

Silko's work has also been the focus of another controversy. Some of her Indian readers expressed concern over the amount of privileged ceremonial knowledge exposed to the reading public in *Ceremony*; today, however, this objection seems moot in light of proliferating numbers of written works by Momaday, Anna Lee Walters, and others. These works frequently reveal much about native cosmology and spiritual systems that once would have been more carefully concealed from the less sympathetic, non-Indian audiences of earlier generations.

Attracting mixed reviews when it first appeared in 1991, *Almanac of the Dead* perhaps also revealed too much of a different sort of information, at least for skittish readers threatened (as the novel intends) by radical indigenous politics. The novel's comparatively hostile stance shocked some who may have expected Silko always to sound like her narrator in *Ceremony*. However, such readers almost certainly must have overlooked the less blatant but identical message concerning Eurocentric domination that *Ceremony* shares with *Almanac* (and with *Gardens*) and that even an early piece such as "Storyteller" so clearly conveys. In any case, during the decade of the 1990s, readers have learned to entertain even more aggressive Indian stories than *Almanac* from younger writers such as Sherman Alexie. Overall, Silko's critical reception, both popular and academic, has become even more enthusiastic than it began in the 1970s. She continues to merit her reputation as an American as well as a Native American writer of major significance.

Silko's works have been extensively anthologized, beginning in 1974 with Kenneth Rosen's *Man to Send Rain Clouds*, which takes its title from Silko's story of that name (first published in 1969 in the *New Mexico Quarterly*) and in which several of her other stories also appear. Her works are included in *Carriers of the Dream Wheel* (1975), *Best Short Stories of 1975* (1976), *The Remembered Earth* (1979), *Earth Power Coming* (1983), *Spider Woman's Granddaughters* (1989), and *The Heath Anthology of American Literature* (1990).

BIBLIOGRAPHY

Works by Leslie Marmon Silko

"Bravura," "A Geronimo Story," "From Humaweepi, the Warrior Priest," "The Man to Send Rain Clouds," "Tony's Story," "Uncle Tony's Goat," "Yellow Woman." *The Man to Send Rain Clouds*. Ed. Kenneth Rosen. New York: Vintage, 1974.

Laguna Woman. Greenfield Center, NY: Greenfield Review, 1974.

Ceremony. New York: Viking, 1977.

Arrowboy and the Witches. Video Tape Co., Hollywood, CA, 1978.

Running on the Edge of the Rainbow: Laguna Stories and Poems. With Leslie Silko. *Words and Place: Native Literature from the American Southwest*. Project director Larry Evers. New York: Clearwater, 1978.

Storyteller. New York: Seaver, 1981.

The Delicacy and Strength of Lace: Letters between Leslie Marmon Silko and James Wright. Ed. Anne Wright. Saint Paul, MN: Graywolf, 1986.

"The Fourth World." *Artforum* 27 (1989): 125–26.

Almanac of the Dead. New York: Simon and Schuster, 1991.

Yellow Woman. Ed. Melody Graulich. New Brunswick, NJ: Rutgers University Press, 1993.

Yellow Woman and a Beauty of the Spirit: Essays on Native American Life Today. New York: Simon and Schuster, 1996.

Sacred Water: Narratives and Pictures. Tucson: Flood Plain, 1997.

Gardens in the Dunes. New York: Simon and Schuster, 1999.

Studies of Leslie Marmon Silko

Arnold, Ellen L., ed. *Conversations with Leslie Marmon Silko*. Jackson: University of Mississippi Press, 2000.

Barnett, Louise K., and James L. Thorson, eds. *Leslie Marmon Silko: A Collection of Critical Essays*. Albuquerque: University of New Mexico Press, 1999.

Chavkin, Allan. *Leslie Marmon Silko's Ceremony: A Casebook*. Oxford University Press, 2000.

Coltelli, Laura. "Leslie Marmon Silko." *Winged Words: American Indian Writers Speak*. Lincoln: University of Nebraska Press, 1990. 135–50.

Jaskoski, Helen. *Leslie Marmon Silko: A Study of the Short Fiction*. New York: Twayne, 1998.

Nelson, Robert M. *Place and Vision: The Function of Landscape in Native American Fiction*. New York: Peter Lang, 1993.

Rainwater, Catherine. *Dreams of Fiery Stars: The Transformations of Native American Fiction*. Philadelphia: University of Pennsylvania Press, 1999.

Salyer, Gregory. *Leslie Marmon Silko*. New York: Twayne, 1997.

Seyersted, Per. *Leslie Marmon Silko*. Boise, ID: Boise State University Press, 1980.

Stein, Rachel. *Shifting the Ground: American Women Writers' Revisions of Nature, Gender, and Race*. Charlottesville: University of Virginia Press, 1997.

Velie, Alan R. *Four American Indian Literary Masters: N. Scott Momaday, James Welch, Leslie Marmon Silko, and Gerald Vizenor*. Norman: University of Oklahoma Press, 1982.

Wilentz, Gay Alden. *Healing Narratives: Women Writers Curing Cultural Disease*. New Brunswick, NJ: Rutgers University Press, 2000.

JANE SMILEY (1949–)

Jesse Cohn

BIOGRAPHY

Jane Smiley was born on September 26, 1949, in Los Angeles, California, to Frances Smiley, a journalist, and James LaVerne Smiley, a World War II veteran working as an engineer. After the breakup of her parents' marriage when she was four years old (three years after her father sought treatment for psychological problems), she moved with her mother to St. Louis, Missouri, where she grew up in an extended family. While she reports this phase of her life in a tone of warmth and humor, it seems that her writerly knowledge of the micropolitics of the family—the "domestic" realm as a scene of power plays as well as nurturance and affection—begins here.

At age twenty, Smiley met John Whiston, a student radical from Yale with whom she lived in a New Haven commune that summer; they married the following year. Of this time, Smiley remarks that subjects like "class warfare," "endangered species," and "whether Marxist analysis was appropriate to the history of the Merovingian period" were "the only things my boyfriend and I talked about" ("Shakespeare in Iceland" 46). During her first marriage (1970–1975), many of the determining political and intellectual interests of her later fiction were first defined. Books such as John H. Storer's *Web of Life: A First Book of Ecology* (1953) and Barry Commoner's *Closing Circle: Nature, Man, and Technology* (1971) made lasting impressions on Smiley, as did brief stints as a factory worker in Connecticut and Iowa and her early encounters with the women's liberation movement.

Through engagements with "feminism, environmentalism, and a vaguely Marxist materialism" ("Shakespeare in Iceland" 52), Smiley discovered her other great passion: history, particularly medieval history, Whiston's field of graduate study. After joining a medieval archaeological dig in Winchester, England, in 1971, she became enamored of Old English and Old Norse writings. She began studying these writings at the University of Iowa in 1972, completing an MFA in 1975. Her passion for history outlasted her marriage to Whiston: During the 1976–1977 academic year, she traveled to Iceland on a Fulbright to study the medieval sagas.

After her year in Iceland, Smiley returned to the University of Iowa and completed a creative dissertation ("Harmes and Feares: Nine Stories") in 1978. That year, she married historian William Silag and gave birth to a daughter, Phoebe. Before giving birth to her second daughter, Lucy, in 1982, Smiley had published seven short stories in magazines ranging from *Redbook* to *Playgirl* as well as her first two novels, *Barn Blind* (1980) and *At Paradise Gate* (1981), both to some critical acclaim; she also began teaching literature and creative writing at Iowa State University in Ames. In 1984, already experiencing dissatisfaction with her marriage, she undertook an expedition to England, Denmark, and Greenland to gather more material for *The Greenlanders* (1988), a novel whose central character, Margret Asgeirsdottir, engages in a doomed adulterous affair—a leitmotif also appearing in *The Age of Grief* (1987), *Ordinary Love & Good Will* (1989), and *A Thousand Acres* (1991). She divorced Silag in 1986, remarrying the following year to Stephen Mortensen, with whom she had a third child, A. J., in 1992. In 1997 she divorced Mortensen, and she has since moved to California, leaving the academy for her other great love: raising horses (the subject of *Barn Blind* and *Horse Heaven*, 2000).

It was toward the end of the 1980s that her writing took its most explicitly political turn with her work on *A Thousand Acres*, which was awarded the Pulitzer Prize for fiction in 1992. In years to come, she would make more vocal political statements outside the literary arena, particularly on the environmental and social costs of big agribusiness. At the same time, Smiley does not see a separation between her political activism and her literary work: "Every novel I write is political," she insists (Kanner).

MAJOR WORKS AND THEMES

What Susan Strehle says of Smiley's most acclaimed work, *A Thousand Acres*, could be said of most of her oeuvre: It seems stylistically "quite conventional—securely affiliated, in its form and style, to the Great Tradition of realistic narrative" and more specifically to the genre of "domestic realism" (211, 218). Smiley is, according to Neil Nakadate, "devotedly anti-postmodernist and anti-poststructuralist" (24); as Ryan Simmons puts it, "her institutional critique does not extend to challenging the institution of language" (332). Her novels and stories often treat such subjects as parent-child conflict (*At Paradise Gate*, *Ordinary Love & Good Will*, *A Thousand Acres*), marital infidelity (*At Paradise Gate*, "The Age of Grief," *Ordinary Love*, *The Greenlanders*, *A Thousand Acres*, *Moo*), and farming life (*Barn Blind*, *At Paradise Gate*, *The Greenlanders, Good Will*, *A Thousand Acres*). However, her seemingly conventional style and range of subject matter mask a subtler repertoire of narrative devices and a seriously ambitious thematic agenda.

The primary theme of Smiley's body of work emerges most clearly when her fiction is read against her nonfiction writing. Essays like "Farming and the Landscape" (1997), an attack on market-driven agriculture, and "Say It Ain't So, Huck: Second Thoughts on Mark Twain's 'Masterpiece' " (1996), which questions Mark Twain's place in the American literary canon, illuminate her political and philosophical concerns. These concerns are strikingly captured by a single word used in parallel ways by both of the protagonists of her paired novellas, *Ordinary Love* and *Good Will* (1989). Rachel remembers the care with which she remodeled their house, before the breakup of her marriage, in order "to give our life a suitable domestic container" (40). Surveying the landscape of the farm he has built up with his own hands, Bob says,

"The valley that is our home is soothingly beautiful, safe, and self-contained" (114). The shared impulse toward "containment" that defines the trajectory of these two lives is about a search for security in a hostile world but also the desire for property and power—in Smiley's words, "the attempt to possess other persons and call that love" ("Shakespeare in Iceland" 56).

From *Barn Blind*, the story of a woman's destructive attempt to breed and train not only her horses but her children, to *The Greenlanders*, chronicling the slow, agonizing collapse of the first European colony in the New World after generations of environmental degradation and warfare, Smiley's thematic focus is on the dream of "containing" a wild and untamable world. Smiley locates one of the less obvious meanings of "domestic" life in its etymological twin: "domination." *At Paradise Gate* explores the struggles of three generations of women to negotiate independence, selfhood, and agency for themselves within patriarchal relationships and marriages and their attempts to fill this gap with other, often more self-destructive projects. In *A Thousand Acres*, the stakes are even higher: The sexual violence with which Larry presides over his patriarchal family is duplicated in the ecological damage he wreaks on the land he farms.

Smiley also indicts the violence implicit in a traditional Western literary canon whose unquestioned authority has too often served to justify social injustices by naturalizing the social conventions that underwrite them. *A Thousand Acres* is a feminist revision of *King Lear* in which the "unnatural" daughters Regan and Goneril appear more victims than villains. Likewise, her critique of Twain's failure to confront the injustice of slavery in *Huckleberry Finn* is issued in her own *All-True Travels and Adventures of Lidie Newton* (1998), a historical novel set in the "bleeding Kansas" of the antebellum. Whereas Twain avoids moral questions in favor of "adventure," Smiley turns an adventure into a moral question. Rather than simply heroize her protagonist (Lidie, a young abolitionist woman), Smiley undermines Lidie's moral certainties while removing the option of disengagement. Together with *The Greenlanders*, which retells the narrative of the Icelandic sagas with twentieth-century ecological hindsight, and *Moo*, a satire on academic life in the corporate era, Smiley has adapted four traditional literary genres (tragedy, romance, epic, and comedy) to the demands of a contemporary critical perspective. Another of her early novels, *Duplicate Keys* (1984), subverts the more modern genre of the detective story: Although a murder investigation is the nominal subject, the detective's search for a solution to the puzzle is sidelined, and the emotions and relationships of the other characters occupy center stage.

A type of dramatic irony is Smiley's signature technique. In her fictions, projects of containment render characters unable to see themselves and their situation accurately. "Had I faced all the facts?" Ginny wonders early on in *A Thousand Acres*. "It seemed like I had, but actually, you never know, just by remembering, how many facts there were to have faced. Your own endurance might be a pleasant fiction" (96–97). The desire for "complete" control leads to the delusion that one's self-knowledge is likewise "complete" and that the "domestic container" or "pleasant fiction" in which one lives really *is* the world. Projects of domination and resistance make life into a meta-fictional hall of mirrors, what Smiley calls a "mystery." "There is something I have noticed about desire," remarks Dave, the protagonist of "The Age of Grief": "It opens the eyes and strikes them blind at the same time . . . perfect sight and perfect mystery at the same time" (*Age of Grief* 176–77). Even Larry in *A Thousand Acres* is "wrapped in an impenetrable fog of self that must have seemed . . . like the very darkness" (399). The domesticator is himself "contained."

Perhaps this is why the "lust to run things" typically ends in a catastrophe like those that befall Larry and Bob. The ultimate dramatic irony is that those in power are not in control (*A Thousand Acres* 371).

CRITICAL RECEPTION

Critical attention to Jane Smiley's work has been prolific outside the academy, but of low quality, and it has been more sparse within the academy. Newspaper reviews of her work have typically been friendly but inattentive, praising her sensitive characterization but oblivious to the political subtexts. In a favorable *New York Times* review, Michiko Kakutani discovers that *Ordinary Love & Good Will* is about "ordinary familial love" ("Pleasures" C25). When reviewers acknowledge the presence of a political subtext, they tend to reduce this subtext to a "message." For instance, in a *Time* review of *A Thousand Acres*, Martha Duffy remarks that Smiley "is a believer in the radical agriculture movement" and suggests that she has found an "imaginative [way] to express [her] convictions" (92). Readings of this sort fragment Smiley's multidimensional social critique into a collection of isolated "beliefs" that her fiction "expresses."

More recently, some academic critics have analyzed Smiley's fiction (particularly *A Thousand Acres*) in greater depth. Essays by Mary Paniccia Carden (1997), Susan Strehle (2000), and Ryan Simmons (2000) turn the critical instruments French theorists honed on the poetry of Mallarmé to the analysis of Smiley's narratives. Often these analyses are motivated by a sympathy with the feminist impulse running through her work. At the same time, this sympathy may merely obscure other dimensions of the text. For instance, Carden argues for a reading of *A Thousand Acres* as a demonstration of postmodern *écriture feminine*—a discontinuous, disruptive language of the body. Smiley's own jabs at postmodernism, for example, via the persona of Margaret Bell in *Moo*, call this reading into question. Margaret, a black professor of English at Moo University, is suspicious of "recent fashions in literary theory" that conveniently announce the death of the author just as certain "formerly silent voices" attain the privilege of literary authorship (134–35). Other ironic references to postmodern theory throughout *Moo* (chapter forty, "A Little Deconstruction," relates the demolition of a building and a tragic death) are hard to square with a reading of Smiley's writing style as triumphantly "deconstructed."

Perhaps a close reading of *Moo* supports Simmons's interpretation of Smiley as a writer who is not quite postmodern *enough*. For Simmons, the ironic and comic moments of *Moo* depend on our occupying the detached and mobile position of a narrator who is not implicated in the world of the narrative. This would seem to ratify Nakadate's assessment of Smiley as an "anti-postmodernist" devoted to the tradition of the nineteenth-century social novel of Emile Zola and George Eliot, with its liberal humanist commitment to understanding the lives of individuals via a knowledge of the societal whole. It remains to be seen whether Smiley's work can be so read without ignoring the revisionary and even the meta-fictional aspects of her work or without forgetting that, as Carden points out, whatever "knowledge" is visible at the end of her narratives comes not in the form of a commanding, panoptical overview of some whole, but that of Ginny's "gleaming obsidian shard" (*A Thousand Acres* 399) or the unassimilably alien "fragments" left to Bob in the final chapter of *Good Will*, at "the utter empty-handed end of knowledge" (196, 194). Smiley's works would seem to remain open to exploration—perhaps especially through some sophisticated ecocritical approach that would be sensitive to Smiley's complexification of the matters of "voice," "knowledge," and "wholeness."

BIBLIOGRAPHY

Works by Jane Smiley

"And Baby Makes Three." *Redbook* May 1977: 231–34.
Harmes and Feares: Nine Stories. Dissertation, University of Iowa, 1978.
"I in My Kerchief and Mama in Her Cap." *Redbook* May 1978: 157–61.
Barn Blind. New York: Harper & Row, 1980.
At Paradise Gate. New York: Simon & Schuster, 1981.
Duplicate Keys. New York: Knopf, 1984.
The Age of Grief. New York: Knopf, 1987.
Catskill Crafts: Artisans of the Catskill Mountains. New York: Crown, 1988.
The Greenlanders. New York: Knopf, 1988.
Ordinary Love & Good Will. New York: Knopf, 1989.
The Life of the Body: A Story. Minneapolis: Coffee House Press, 1990.
A Thousand Acres. New York: Knopf, 1991.
Moo. New York: Knopf, 1995.
"Say It Ain't So, Huck: Second Thoughts on Mark Twain's 'Masterpiece.' " *Harper's* Jan. 1996: 61–67.
"Farming and the Landscape." *Placing Nature: Culture and Landscape Ecology.* Ed. Joan Iverson Nassauer. Washington, D.C.: Island Press, 1997. 33–43.
The All-True Travels and Adventures of Lidie Newton. New York: Knopf, 1998.
"Shakespeare in Iceland." *Shakespeare and the Twentieth Century: The Selected Proceedings of the International Shakespeare Association World Congress, Los Angeles, 1996.* Ed. Jonathan Bate, Jill L. Levenson, and Dieter Mehl. Newark: University of Delaware Press, 1998. 41–59.
Horse Heaven. New York: Knopf, 2000.

Studies of Jane Smiley

Bakerman, Jane S. " 'The Gleaming Obsidian Shard': Jane Smiley's *A Thousand Acres.*" *Midamerica: Yearbook of the Society for the Study of Midwestern Literature* 19 (1992): 127–37.
Berne, Suzanne. "Interview with Jane Smiley." *Belles Lettres: A Review of Books by Women* 7 (1992): 36–38.
Carden, Mary Paniccia. "Remembering/Engendering the Heartland: Sexed Language, Embodied Space, and America's Foundational Fictions in Jane Smiley's *A Thousand Acres.*" *Frontiers: A Journal of Women's Studies* 18 (1997): 181–202.
Cohn, Jesse. "Fiction and Domestication: Jane Smiley." *"I Have Set My Affair on Nothing": Literary Theory, Fiction, and the Politics of Antirepresentation.* Dissertation, Binghamton University, State University of New York, 1999.
Cooperman, Jeannette Batz. *The Broom Closet: Secret Meanings of Domesticity in Postfeminist Novels by Louise Erdrich, Mary Gordon, Toni Morrison, Marge Piercy, Jane Smiley, and Amy Tan.* New York: Peter Lang, 1999.
Deutsch, Stephanie. "At Home on the Range." Rev. of *The All-True Travels and Adventures*

of Lidie Newton. Washington Times 26 Apr. 1998: B22.

Duffy, Martha. "The Case for Goneril and Regan." Rev. of *A Thousand Acres. Time* 11 Nov. 1991: 92.

Kakutani, Michiko. Review of *The Age of Grief. New York Times* 26 Aug. 1987: C21.

——. "Pleasures and Hazards of Familial Love." Rev. of *Ordinary Love & Good Will. New York Times Book Review* 31 Oct. 1989: C25.

Kanner, Ellen. "Interview with Jane Smiley." Internet. *BookPage* April 1998 (http://www.bookpage.com/9804bp/janesmiley.html).

Nakadate, Neil. *Understanding Jane Smiley.* Columbia: University of South Carolina Press, 1999.

Sheldon, Barbara. *Daughters and Fathers in Feminist Novels.* Frankfurt am Main: Peter Lang GmbH, 1997.

Simmons, Ryan. "The Problem of Politics in Feminist Literary Criticism: Contending Voices in Two Contemporary Novels." *Critique: Studies in Contemporary Fiction* 41 (2000): 319–34.

Strehle, Susan. "The Daughter's Subversion in Jane Smiley's *A Thousand Acres.*" *Critique: Studies in Contemporary Fiction* 41 (2000): 211–26.

LEE SMITH (1944–)

Cathy Downs

BIOGRAPHY

Lee Smith was born in Grundy, Virginia, in 1944, the daughter of Virginia Marshall Smith, a schoolteacher, and Ernest Lee Smith, owner of the town's five-and-dime. These circumstances of Smith's upbringing find particular and vibrant life in the novels and stories that Smith came to write as she matured: the small town in Virginia; the dime store through which all of the citizenry of the town, high and low, might pass and in which all the town's news was discussed; the schoolteacher, who, because of her education, was a kind of stranger in her own community.

Lee Smith began writing while still quite young. Notable early writings include a novel, written at age eight, and a newspaper called the *Small Review*, which she published at age eleven. The teenage character of Karen in the short story "Tongues of Fire" (*Me and My Baby View the Eclipse*, 1990), who seeks grace in evangelical Christian churches, including those in which snake handling was practiced, and of Charlene Christian, the narrator in "The Bubba Stories" (*News of the Spirit*, 1997), who wants to be a dark, tormented writer, are so truly written and so poignantly full of that adolescent longing to be someone that they could easily be the young Lee Smith herself.

Smith gained her bachelor's degree in 1967 from Hollins College in Roanoke, Virginia, where she was mentored by Louis D. Rubin and where novelist and essayist Annie Dillard was also a student. According to John D. Kalb, Rubin taught Smith to start always with characters and to make stories be *about* something. In college, Smith continued writing seriously: She sent a draft of a novel to a contest sponsored by the Book-of-the-Month-Club and was one of twelve other writers to win. In 1968, when she was just twenty-four, the rewritten version became *The Last Year the Dogbushes Bloomed*.

In 1967 Smith married poet James Seay, and the couple moved to Tuscaloosa, Alabama, where Smith became a journalist for the *Tuscaloosa News*. In the next few years, Smith bore two boys, taught seventh grade at Harpeth High School in Nashville, Tennessee (1971–1973), taught Language Arts at the Friend's School in Durham, North Carolina (1974–1977), and wrote three more novels, *Something in the Wind* (1971), *Fancy Strut* (1973), and *Black Mountain Breakdown* (1980). After Smith published *Fancy Strut*, her editor at Harper, Cass Canfield, retired. He had been her advocate against those who sought to publish only happy novels with prospects for quick sales. At this juncture, Harper would not publish *Black Mountain Breakdown*— which is about rape and mental (not musical) breakdown—and Smith began a seven-year hiatus in novel publishing and turned to short story writing instead. Her early short stories appeared in the magazine *Redbook* and were collected in a 1981 volume called *Cakewalk*. Sometimes, Smith uses the short story form to explore ideas for novels. For example, *Black Mountain Breakdown* began as the short story "Paralyzed."

The years 1980–1981 mark a kind of turning point. Smith ended her marriage to Seay and joined the English department faculty at North Carolina State University, where she stayed until her retirement in 1999. Also in 1980, Smith found a new advocate in Faith Sale, editor at Putnam, and she began, once more, to publish novels. During the 1980s, she gained national fame for *Oral History* (1983) and *Fair and Tender Ladies* (1988). Her personal life changed once more when, while teaching at Duke University's evening college, she met journalist Hal Crowther, whom she married in 1985.

As Lee Smith became a public figure in the late 1980s and into the 1990s, she stepped into her role with grace. Charitable organizations such as Habitat for Humanity, literacy advocates, and small presses found her to be their ally, as she gave readings and offered short stories for various causes. In 1994 she won the Lila Wallace Reader's Digest Fund Award, which enabled her to take a sabbatical from NCSU. With her free time, she taught at the Hindman Settlement School in Kentucky. By encouraging writers there, including older writers, to record their own histories, she has helped historically silenced communities—the farmers and miners of Appalachia—to gain a public voice. During the 1990s, Smith continued her dedication to her own art, publishing novels *Devil's Dream* (1992) and *Saving Grace* (1995), and two collections of short stories, *Me and My Baby View the Eclipse* (1990) and *News of the Spirit* (1997).

Smith has won recognition that—judging from her tour schedule—is national in scope, since she is in demand in places like Indiana and California as well as southern locales. She has won many awards, among them the O. Henry Award for her short stories in 1979 and 1981 and the PEN/Faulkner Award in 1991, and in 1999 she was recognized by the National Academy of Arts and Letters. Smith's own reflections on the writer's craft may be found in the collections *Books of Passage* and *Why I Write*.

MAJOR WORKS AND THEMES

These are the main attributes of a Lee Smith work of fiction: A closed community or family, with its insular traditions and particular history, is the world in which the work unfolds; Smith experiments with narrative voice, and those experiments highlight issues of the "truth" or "falsehood" of stories and histories; those histories, both "real" and invented, often concern passion and passion's place in the psyche, families, and communities; Lee Smith's novels and stories include characters who are "outsiders" or "strangers" to everyday life, and those "outsider" characters can comment on or highlight "insider" or "normal" culture; finally, Lee Smith writes movingly and well of the interior lives of women.

On her well-designed web site (www.leesmith.com), Smith's own list of her major works skips her first three novels. Those three early works show the hallmarks of her later writing, lacking the emotional depths a more mature writer might handle with skill. In the early novels such as *Dogbushes*, however, the young writer finds her voice.

In *The Last Day the Dogbushes Bloomed*, narrated by Susan, a nine-year-old girl, Susan is thrust rudely from the world of make-believe into the world of adult desire. The novel's—and Smith's—strength is the innocent and deadpan voice of Susan. Susan, looking at her sister's mascara (applied before a date with her "boring" beau), says: "You've got your hair all bent . . . and doesn't that stuff on your eyes make them all heavy and you can't hardly open them at all? Doesn't it hurt?" (38). Later she decides that it would be nice to be a boy because "it would even be fun to have little tiny hairs that came out of my face every night like magic" (39). Susan tells all she observes without editing. She discusses her mother's lover (whom she calls "the Baron"; her mother is "the Queen"), her sister's escape to the boyfriend (and one assumes, an unsatisfying marriage) in order to escape her family's difficulties, her rape. The prepubescent narrator, by virtue of her innocence, can discuss "impolite" topics. Susan's story is precisely about those censored topics that most need to be spoken of and understood.

Those novels of the 1980s and 1990s that critics have called "major works"—*Oral History, Fair and Tender Ladies*, and *Saving Grace*—are peopled with "Southern types," including the educated schoolteacher and the owner of the five-and-dime, fictional counterparts to her parents. However, Smith creates depth by sympathetically entering the worlds of some of those who, on the surface, might be easily "written off," the world, say, of a crone who is a traditional healer, of an ex-convict, of a single teen mother. By asking readers to encounter such marginalized characters with sympathy, Smith's *Oral History* asks the question, "Who is allowed to create reality?"

Oral History is "about" family and local history whose "truth" is held by and revealed in a teller. In this case, the history is of a family cursed by the love between a young man come newly from prison and a beautiful woman who is rumored to be a witch. The family curse is blamed for disastrous happenings in subsequent generations of the family. Having a curse, ironically, creates a kind of order or sense out of chaos, even when it becomes revealed to readers that some family members who appear to be cursed are not really related to the accursed family at all. *Oral History*'s real story is the poignant one of how people must make sense out of their lives and deaths.

The fair and tender ladies of Smith's 1988 novel are sisters in the Rowe family; their stories are told by Ivy Rowe in her letters to various correspondents. Ivy's fresh perspective, which is similar to that of Susan in *Dogbushes*, reveals the inconsistencies in what people say and what they do; however, Ivy is too sympathetic a narrator for the reader to remain long outside her hardscrabble mountain farm life. Ivy Rowe, and Florida Grace Shepherd, Smith's first-person narrator in *Saving Grace*, are tour-de-force narrators. Life on a mountain farm (*Ladies*) and life as a snake-handling evangelist's daughter (*Grace*) are interesting to read about; when told by Ivy and Grace, the stories become compelling narrations in whose spiritual tests many readers will share.

Smith is a master of the short story form; readers may compare her work with that of Bobbie Ann Mason, Anne Tyler, William Faulkner, and Flannery O'Connor. Smith's greatest strengths—creating strong characters with compelling narrative voices, finding the humanly funny or the humanly poignant in modern life, trapping human beings with their unruly passions on banal suburban landscapes—all conspire to create narratives that are funny, true, and moving. Among the best are "The Bubba Stories" (*News of the Spirit*), "The Happy Memories Club" (*News of the Spirit*), "Mom" (*Me and My Baby View the Eclipse*), and "Tongues of Fire" (*Me and My Baby View the Eclipse*).

Perhaps one of Smith's greatest contributions to the art of fiction is that she creates sympathetic middle-aged and old female characters with passionate minds. Passionate women in these two age groups have been stock comic figures since Mistress Quickly walked Shakespeare's stage and before. By writing into existence an Ivy Rowe or a Grace Shepherd, Smith has asked us to consider passion as the equal of reason in shaping human landscapes.

CRITICAL RECEPTION

Serious critical commentary came early in Lee Smith's life as a writer: Her third novel, *Fancy Strut*, garnered a *New York Times Book Review* article. Her short stories published in *Redbook* in the early 1980s probably helped gain for her a national female reading audience. Lee Smith's very "placed" novels—set in the South, present and past—gained loyal support from Southerners who showed their admiration in an outpouring of interviews, scholarly articles, book reviews, and dissertations. When *Oral History* became a Book-of-the-Month Club selection after its publication in 1983, Smith gained a national audience and her popular and scholarly acclaim began to grow. At this writing, she is fully part of the Southern canon, anthologized in small press anthologies ("Christmas Letters" is mentioned in the bibliography as only one example of many). Both Norton and Oxford have anthologized Smith's work in volumes concerning the American South. Smith appears in Kalb's *Dictionary of Literary Biography* article and has been extensively reviewed, studied, and interviewed both locally and nationally. Owing to limited space, the bibliography appearing at the end of this work samples only scholarly works about Smith, concentrating particularly on several scholars who, by their close attention to Smith's work, have helped make Smith's reputation in the academic world.

Scholarly attention toward Smith's works began in the 1980s. In 1982 her friend Lucinda MacKethan published an essay about high and low art in Smith's fiction. Dorothy Combs Hill (in her book-length biography published by Twayne), Debbie Wesley, Katherine Kearns, and Elizabeth Pell Broadwell have studied the figure of the female artist in Smith's fiction as well. MacKethan and particularly Wesley note that traditional women's arts—household arts such as cooking, healing, or beautifying the body—have been typed as "low" art forms, but nevertheless they perform an essential function: the creation of order in their communities. Other feminist scholars explore female sexuality in Smith's characters. Linda Bird's article explores how Dory Cantrell in *Oral History* gains a kind of sacred, creative power over others through her sexuality.

Several themes are uniquely Southern. One of Lee Smith's most compelling themes is that of the Southern storyteller's voice (see Buchanan); the vigor of that theme has led to fruitful scholarship. Jocelyn Hazelwood Donlon's essay about oral tales in insular communities uses speech act theory very successfully to show how tale telling creates and maintains a sense of order and belonging in a community. Anne Goodwyn Jones, in her essay that deconstructs the word "oral," notes how "oral," "orifice," and "oracular" are related in stories. Southern writers often create meaning through describing space. Critic Parks Lanier, Jr., considers the poetics of space in his essay. Southern fiction often concerns itself with the intrusion of outsiders, with the idea of the foreign, and with grotesques. William M. Teems IV's work labels some Lee Smith characters in Edward Said's words as The Other and notes how outsiders, transgressing bounds, gain power through their outsiderhood. A final theme of note is discussed in Conrad Oswalt's very knowledgeable essay concerning Appalachian religions. As Oswalt notes, Appalachian worship celebrates the passionate moment in which the soul is saved, not works or guilt. To understand how Southern writers dialogue with their birthplace, readers may wish to consult volumes by Brown and McDonald, Stephens, Magee, and Ketchim.

Lee Smith has granted many interviews, particularly to Southern publications (see Arnold and Parrish, McDonald, and Virginia Smith). As interviewee, Lee Smith has been forthcoming about why she writes; thus, her interviews are valuable for the scholar. Two reviews, that by Fred Chappell and that by Dorothy Scura, deserve special mention. These two long-time writers and scholars have placed Smith in the history of Southern letters and in the history of women writers.

Many resources are now available on Lee Smith; this listing can only suggest the breadth of coverage. Elizabeth Pell Broadwell's bio-bibliographical essay is excellent. Michelle Manning's annotated bibliography is current up to 1995. Two Southern periodicals have dedicated issues to Lee Smith (*Iron Mountain Review* and *Southern Quarterly*). Lee Smith is very active in charitable and artistic works in her community; the extent of her involvement is best traced in local newspapers (see, e.g., Rice and Townley) and in her extensive connections with small presses such as Algonquin— despite the fact that she is published nationally and does not need to go a-begging. Smith's papers are being collected at the North Carolina Historical Collection, University of North Carolina at Chapel Hill; UNC's libraries have extensive holdings by and about Smith as well.

BIBLIOGRAPHY

Works by Lee Smith

The Last Day the Dogbushes Bloomed. New York: Harper, 1968.
Something in the Wind. New York: Harper, 1971.
Fancy Strut. New York: Harper, 1973.
"Paralyzed." *Southern Exposure* 4 (1977): 36–42.
Black Mountain Breakdown. New York: Putnam, 1980.
Cakewalk. New York: Putnam, 1981.
Oral History. New York: Putnam, 1983.
Family Linen. New York: Putnam, 1985.
Fair and Tender Ladies. New York: Putnam, 1988.
Me and My Baby View the Eclipse. New York: Putnam, 1990.
The Devil's Dream. New York: Putnam, 1992.
Good Ole Girls. Musical adaptation of the writings of Lee Smith and Jill McCorkle. Director

Paul Ferguson. Theatre in the Park, Raleigh, North Carolina. Performed Sept. 18–26, 1999.

Saving Grace. New York: Putnam, 1995.

The Christmas Letters. Chapel Hill, NC: Algonquin, 1996.

"Christmas Letters." *Twelve Christmas Stories by North Carolina Writers, and Twelve Poems, Too*. Ed. Ruth Moose. Ashboro, NC: Downhome Press, 1997. 131–34.

News of the Spirit. New York: Putnam, 1997.

Excerpt from *Oral History*. *The Oxford Book of the American South: Testimony, Memory, Fiction*. Ed. Edward L. Ayers and Bradley C. Mittendorf. New York: Oxford University Press, 1997. 407–16.

"Between the Lines." *The Literature of the American South: A Norton Anthology*. Ed. William L. Andrews. New York: Norton, 1998. 1002–11.

"Everything Else Falls Away." *Why I Write: Thoughts on the Practice of Fiction*. Ed. Will Blythe. Boston: Little, Brown, 1998. 128–39.

Studies of Lee Smith

Arnold, Edwin T., and Nancy Parrish. "Lee Smith." *Interviewing Appalachia: The Appalachian Journal Interviews, 1978–1992*. Ed. J. W. Williams and Edwin T. Arnold. Knoxville: University of Tennessee Press, 1994. 341–62.

Broadwell, Elizabeth Pell. "Lee Smith (1944–)." *Contemporary Fiction Writers of the South: A Bio-Bibliographical Sourcebook*. Ed. Joseph Flora and Robert Bain. Westport, CT: Greenwood Press, 1993. 420–31.

——. "Lee Smith: Ivy Rowe as Woman and Artist." *Southern Writers at Century's End*. Ed. Jeffrey J. Folks and James A Perkins. Lexington: University Press of Kentucky, 1997. 247–61.

Brown, Fred, and Jeanne McDonald. *Growing Up Southern: How the South Shapes Its Writers*. Greenville, SC: Blue Ridge, 1997.

Buchanan, Harriet C. "Lee Smith: The Story-Teller's Voice." *Southern Women Writers: The New Generation*. Ed. Tonette Bond Inge. Tuscaloosa: University of Alabama Press, 1990. 324–45.

Byrd, Linda. "Emergence of the Sacred Sexual Mother in Lee Smith's *Oral History*." *Southern Literary Journal* 31 (1998): 119–42.

Chappell, Fred. Rev. of *The Devil's Dream*. *Southern Review* 28 (1992): 937–43.

Donlon, Jocelyn Hazelwood. "Hearing Is Believing: Southern Racial Communities and Strategies of Story-Listening in Gloria Naylor and Lee Smith." *Twentieth-Century Literature* 41 (1995): 16–35.

Hill, Dorothy Combs. *Lee Smith*. New York: Twayne, 1992.

Jones, Anne Goodwyn. "The Orality of Oral History." *Iron Mountain Review* 3 (1986): 15–19.

Kalb, John D. "Lee Smith." *American Novelists since World War II*. Ed. James R. Giles and Wanda H. Giles. Detroit: Gale, 1994. Vol. 143 of *Dictionary of Literary Biography*. 206–16.

Kearns, Katherine. "From Shadow to Substance: The Empowerment of the Artist Figure in Lee Smith's Fiction." *Writing the Woman Artist: Essays on Poetics, Politics, and Portraiture*. Ed. Suzanne W. Jones. Philadelphia: University of Pennsylvania Press, 1991. 175–95.

Ketchim, Susan. *The Christ-Haunted Landscape: Faith and Doubt in Southern Fiction*. Jackson: University Press of Mississippi, 1994.

Lanier, Parks, Jr. "Psychic Space in Lee Smith's *Black Mountain Breakdown*." *The Poetics of Appalachian Space*. Ed. Parks Lanier, Jr. Knoxville: University of Tennessee Press, 1991. 58–66.

Lee Smith. Special Issue. *Iron Mountain Review* 3.1 (1986).

Lee Smith. Special Issue. Ed. Peggy Whitman Prenshaw. *Southern Quarterly* 28 (1990).

MacKethan, Lucinda. "Artists and Beauticians: Balance in Lee Smith's Fiction." *Southern Literary Journal* 15 (1982): 3–14.

Magee, Rosemary M. *Friendship and Sympathy: Communities of Southern Women Writers.* Jackson: University Press of Mississippi, 1992.

Manning, Michelle. "The Southern Voice of Lee Smith: An Annotated Bibliography." *Bulletin of Bibliography* 53 (1996): 161–72.

McDonald, Jeanne. "Lee Smith: At Home in Appalachia." *Poets and Writers* 5 (1997): 32–41.

Oswalt, Conrad. "Witches and Jesus: Lee Smith's Appalachian Religion." *Southern Literary Journal* 31 (1998): 98–118.

Parrish, Nancy Clyde. *Lee Smith, Annie Dillard, and the Hollins Group.* Baton Rouge: Louisiana State University Press, 1998.

Rice, Marcy Smith. "Lee Smith: A Writer in Service to Women." *Raleigh News and Observer* 22 Aug. 1999: 3I.

Scura, Dorothy. Rev. of *Saving Grace. Southern Review* 33 (1997): 859–71.

Smith, Virginia. "On Regionalism, Women's Writing, and Writing as a Woman: A Conversation with Lee Smith." *Southern Review* 26 (1990): 784–95.

Stephens, Robert O. *The Family Saga in the South: Generations and Destinies.* Baton Rouge: Louisiana State University Press, 1995.

Teems, William M., IV. "Let Us Now Praise the Other: Women in Lee Smith's Short Fiction." *Studies in the Literary Imagination* 27 (1994): 63–73.

Townley, Emily. "North Carolina State University Marathon Raises $1,310 for Charity." *NCSU Technician* 27 Sept. 1999: 1.

Wesley, Debbie. "A New Way of Looking at an Old Story: Lee Smith's Portrait of Female Creativity." *Southern Literary Journal* 30 (1997): 88–101.

ELIZABETH ANN TALLENT (1954–)

Laurie Champion

BIOGRAPHY

Contemporary fiction writer and critic Elizabeth Ann Tallent is best known for her short stories. Tallent was born August 8, 1954, in Washington, D.C., the daughter of William and Joy (Redfield) Tallent. After spending her childhood in the Midwest, she received a BA from Illinois State University at Normal in 1975, the same year she married Barry Smoots. In 1976 she moved to Santa Fe, the setting of much of her fiction. In 1987 her son, Gabriel, was born.

In the early 1980s, Tallent participated in a writing workshop in Berkeley, California, and later presented readings in England with noted short story writers Raymond Carver, Richard Ford, and Tobias Wolff. In 1986 she launched her creative writing teaching career and has taught at the University of California at Irvine and Davis, University of Nevada at Reno, University of Southern Mississippi, and the Iowa Writers Workshop. She currently teaches at Stanford University, where she directed the creative writing program from 1994 to 1996. For her creative works, she has received distinguished awards, including a National Endowment for the Arts Grant, an O. Henry Award, and a Pushcart Prize. Her short stories have appeared in *Best American Short Stories*, and her fiction frequently appears in distinguished literary magazines such as the *New Yorker*, *Esquire*, and *Paris Review*. She regularly reviews books for distinguished newspapers such as the *New York Times*.

MAJOR WORKS AND THEMES

Tallent is well known for her poetic style and her depictions of images. Representative of the minimalist writing tradition, her works do not rely strongly on plot. Typically, little action occurs on the surface of her stories, but under the surface, Tallent's stories raise complex issues. Throughout her works, she depicts romantic relationships and family struggles, frequently in the form of divorced couples who get remarried and try to build new families in spite of the consequences of previous failed attempts. Most of her fiction is set in the Southwest, and she is acclaimed for her depictions of mountain and desert landscape, settings that frequently symbolize themes expressed in her fiction and her characters' emotions.

Although she has published works in other genres, Tallent's writing forte is the short story. In her short stories, Tallent creates vivid settings and characters and exhibits a remarkably poetic style that allows her stories to reveal complex themes with tightly managed prose. *In Constant Flight* (1983), Tallent's first published collection, contains eleven short stories. The stories are set in Colorado and are frequently told from the first-person point of view. Throughout the collection, failed romantic relationships are portrayed. The stories rely on poetic images more than plot to reveal themes. Often Tallent's subjects involve people faced with a crisis, a time when important decisions must be made; yet the characters often make poor decisions or become passive, making no decisions at all.

After the publication of *In Constant Flight*, Tallent began to create characters and situations that she would continue to build upon in future short stories. Her second short story collection, *Time with Children* (1987), contains thirteen stories written as a short story cycle. The stories are set primarily in Santa Fe, and some of the same characters are presented in several stories. One sequence, a set of three stories, portrays the characters Jenny and Sam. Four stories concern the characters Charlie and Kyra. In the title story, Charlie and Kyra stay in London to try to rebuild their relationship after Charlie commits adultery. Ironically, in London, Kyra becomes romantically attracted to a man who volunteers to babysit her son, spend time with her child. Two stories depict Hart and Caro, a married couple who were involved in an adulterous affair before he divorced his wife. Marital infidelity is a recurring theme in the collection, often demonstrated as the emotional consequences of failed love and parental responsibilities that arise from divorce and remarriage.

In *Honey* (1993), a collection of nine stories, Tallent continues the short story cycle she began in *Time with Children*. Characters Hart and Caro and Jenny and Sam, who all appear in *Time with Children*, appear again in *Honey*, and both *Time with Children* and *Honey* are set in the Southwest. In both collections, Tallent portrays relationships, divorces, and parental responsibilities. Hart and Caro appear in "Black Dress," "Honey," and "The Minute I Saw You," a story that portrays the birth of Caro's and Hart's baby. Caro's mother, who is visiting to help with the new baby, hears Hart talking on the telephone to his ex-wife. Hart's mother-in-law hears him tell his ex-wife that he does not want the new baby. Jenny and Sam appear in "Kid Gentle," a story that portrays their strained relationship shortly after Jenny's miscarriage. Throughout the stories, broken families, former spouses, and children from previous marriages raise demanding responsibilities. In "Prowler" and "James Was Here," two stories that do not portray characters from *Time with Children*, men sneak in their ex-wives homes, literally returning to their former spouses. Throughout the stories in *Honey*, characters symbolically return to previous relationships. Repeatedly, characters use the word "honey" as an endearment, as when Hart calls his son "honey," embarrassing him in front of a used car salesman.

Tallent's only published novel, *Museum Pieces* (1985), is set in Santa Fe and involves the separation of Clarissa and Peter Barnes and their reaction to their daughter, Tara, who faces emotional crises because of her parents' separation. Peter is an archeologist, who sleeps in the museum basement where he is employed, and Clarissa is an artist, who seeks professional therapy and paints portraits. The novel offers a superb portrayal of the desert and mountains of the Southwest, and Tallent uses geographical setting, the museum, and Peter's occupation as metaphors for characters' attempts to cope with the past. The adolescent friendship between Tara and her friend, Natalie, is another subject presented in the novel.

In addition to her novel and her short stories, Tallent also wrote a critical study of John Updike, *Married Men and Magic Tricks: John Updike's Erotic Heroes*, which was published in 1982. This collection of essays examines the theme of male sexuality in John Updike's novels. She suggests that Updike portrays men who struggle between their desires for marital domestic security and adulterous freedom, resulting in their irresponsible behavior.

CRITICAL RECEPTION

Elizabeth Tallent has received national acclaim for her short stories. Three previously published stories from *In Constant Flight* have received prestigious awards: "Ice" was reprinted in *Best American Short Stories 1981*; "Why I Love Country Music" appeared in *The Pushcart Prize VI* (1981); and "The Evolution of Birds of Paradise" was included in *Prize Stories 1984: The O. Henry Awards*. The story "Prowler" (published in *Time with Children*) appeared in *Best American Short Stories 1990*.

Although no critical studies have been written about Tallent's works, her short story collections and her novel have been reviewed widely. For the most part, she has received favorable reviews. Many critics praise Tallent's writing style and her ability to create powerful images in her fiction. Andrea Barnet, reviewing *In Constant Flight*, says that Tallent's stories "are shaped less by plot than by immaculately precise imagery" (56). Jay Parini says that Tallent's stories move beyond mere plot as "she revels in language itself, capturing the minute flickers of feeling that register as her characters fall in, or out, of love" (12). Reviewing *Honey*, Steven Boyd Saum says, "The language is precise, the structures artful, the stories working with an awareness of just how finely crafted they are" (13). Comparing the writing style of her first two short story collections with that of her novel, *Museum Pieces*, Michiko Kakutani notes, "The somewhat annoying tendency of her prose to constantly coagulate into self-consciously important metaphors" is present in the first part of the novel but diminished later in the book ("Geometry" 13).

Reviewers also recognize Tallent for her realistic portrayal of the Southwest. Elaine Kendall, in a review of *Museum Pieces*, says, "In Tallent's hands, the entire city of Santa Fe becomes a museum, a place where fragmented lives are preserved and sometimes restored" (3). Also reviewing *Museum Pieces*, William H. Pritchard says, "Miss Tallent is superb on the New Mexico landscape, especially its archaeology" (647).

Tallent's depiction of characters is another topic reviewers discuss. In a review of *Honey*, Dean Flower says that Tallent represents "with scrupulous attentiveness how her characters think" (498). On the other hand, Michael Gorra says her characters have "no public dimension" and notes the lack of "connection between these characters and the national life" (405), which he suggests makes *Time with Children* bland.

Some reviewers look at Tallent's short stories as short story cycles; for example, Isabel Fonseca says that one of Tallent's strengths emerges "only when her stories are read by a group," which allows them to be read as "companion pieces" that enrich the reading (759). Contrastingly, Kakutani criticizes the intertwined stories and hopes Tallent will "broaden her fictional territory with her next book," adding that "the tales not only reinvent situations delineated in earlier collections, but echo one another as well" ("Families" C29).

Whether favorable or not, the reviews Tallent has received, especially those in distinguished newspapers such as the *New York Times*, attest to Tallent's acclaim as a writer. Although she is known for her Southwestern settings, her works move beyond regional literature to express universal themes.

BIBLIOGRAPHY

Works by Elizabeth Tallent

Married Men and Magic Tricks: John Updike's Erotic Heroes. Berkeley, CA: Creative Arts, 1982.
In Constant Flight. New York: Knopf, 1983.
Museum Pieces. New York: Knopf, 1985.
Time with Children. New York: Knopf, 1987.
Honey. New York: Knopf: 1993.

Studies of Elizabeth Tallent

Barnet, Andrea. Rev. of *In Constant Flight*. *Saturday Review* May-June 1983: 56–58.
Clemens, Lori R. "Tallent, Elizabeth (Ann)." *Contemporary Authors*. Ed. Hal May. Vol. 117. Detroit: Gale, 1986. 426–28.
Eder, Richard. "Measuring the Tolerances in American Love." Rev. of *Time with Children*. *Los Angeles Times Book Review* 15 Nov. 1987: 3ff.
"Elizabeth (Ann) Tallent." *Contemporary Literary Criticism*. Ed. Daniel G. Marowski and Roger Matuz. Vol. 45. Detroit: Gale, 1987. 386–90.
Erdrich, Louise. "Life in Shards and Fragments." Rev. of *Museum Pieces*. *New York Times Book Review* 7 Apr. 1985: 10.
Flower, Dean. "Fiction." Rev. of *Honey*. *Hudson Review* 47 (1994): 497–98.
Fonseca, Isabel. "Detective Houses." Rev. of *Time with Children*. *Times Literary Supplement* 8 July 1988: 759.
Gorra, Michael. "Fiction." Rev. of *Time with Children*. *Hudson Review* 41 (1988): 404–5.
Kakutani, Michiko. "Geometry of Emotions." Rev. of *Museum Pieces*. *New York Times* 30 March 1985: 13.
——. "Families Bound by Ties That Stifle." Rev. of *Honey*. *New York Times* 10 Dec. 1993: C29.
Kendall, Elaine. "*Museum Pieces*." Rev. of *Museum Pieces*. *Los Angeles Times Book Review* 21 Apr. 1985: 3.
Moran, Patricia. "Elizabeth Tallent." *American Short-Story Writers since World War II*. Ed. Patrick Meanor. Detroit: Gale, 1993. Vol. 130 of *Dictionary of Literary Biography*. 296–301.
Parini, Jay. "Torn between Two Exes." Rev. of *Honey*. *New York Times Book Review* 7 Nov. 1993: 11–12.
Pritchard, William H. "Fictional Places." Rev. of *Museum Pieces*. *Hudson Review* 39 (1987): 647–48.

Saum, Steven Boyd. "Short Stories That Expand with Detail." Rev. of *Honey*. *Christian Science Monitor* 2 Dec. 1993: 13.

See, Carolyn. "Fooling Around and Other Family Habits." Rev. of *Time with Children*. *New York Times Book Review* 15 Nov. 1987: 11.

Wellenbrock, David. Rev. of *Museum Pieces*. *Western American Literature* 21 (1986): 163–64.

AMY TAN (1952–)

Carman C. Curton

BIOGRAPHY

The middle child of Daisy and John Tan, Amy Tan, whose Chinese name, Anmei, means "blessing from America," was born in 1952 in Oakland, California, only three years after her mother immigrated to the United States from China. Amy's brothers, Peter and John, were born in 1950 and 1954, respectively. Her father, trained as an engineer in Beijing, worked for the United States during World War II and, after immigrating to the United States, became a Baptist minister. In 1967 Peter died of a brain tumor. Within a year, Amy's father died, too, also of a brain malignancy. These deaths opened a door for Amy into her mother's past, for it was only then that Daisy Tan revealed that she had three more daughters living in China, who had remained in the custody of an abusive first husband after her divorce. Following the deaths of her husband and son, Daisy moved what was left of her family across the United States and Europe, finally settling in Switzerland, where Amy finished high school.

After returning to America, Tan attended Linfield College in Oregon and San Jose City College and earned a BA in English and linguistics from San Jose State University in 1973. She followed this with an MA in linguistics, also from San Jose State, the next year. Tan married Lou DeMattei in 1974.

Tan pursued a variety of careers after graduation, working as a consultant for programs serving developmentally disabled adults and children, writing and editing a medical journal, and freelancing as a technical writer. In 1985, pressured by self-imposed overwork on her business writing projects, Tan began to write fiction as a form of therapy. Her short story "Endgame" gained her admittance into the Squaw Valley Community of Writers workshop. The story was published the next year in *Seventeen* and eventually became the chapter "Rules of the Game" in *The Joy Luck Club* (1989).

The now-famous story of the publication of her first novel, *The Joy Luck Club*, began as Tan traveled to China in October of 1987 with her mother to meet two of her half-sisters, with whom Daisy Tan had not been reunited until 1978, after twenty-nine years of separation. Before the trip, Amy Tan had developed a relationship with literary agent Sandra Dijkstra, who sold the as-yet-unwritten book to G. P. Putnam's Sons for an initial contract of $50,000 while Tan was out of the country. Upon returning, Tan learned that her book had been sold and reported saying, "What book?" (Hubbard 150).

The Joy Luck Club was an enormous success, receiving both popular and critical acclaim. It remained on the *New York Times* best-seller list for nine months and sold more than 250,000 hardcover and more than 2 million paperback copies as well as earning awards from the Bay Area Book Reviewers and the American Library Association.

Although not strictly autobiographical, many of the stories from Tan's novels are inspired by anecdotes from the lives of her mother and other female relatives as well as by incidents from her own life. Tales of the abuse Daisy Tan suffered during her first marriage in China found their way into the books, as did the trauma Daisy suffered observing as her mother, Jingmei, used her own flesh to make a healing soup, learning that she had been forced into an unwanted second marriage by a wealthy man who raped her and then took her as a third concubine, and finally watching as she killed herself by swallowing opium. In an essay for *Life*, Amy Tan shares a photo from her family album, accompanied by an explanation that the picture, taken in Hangzhou, China, in 1922, came with warnings and stories of the tragic fates the women in the photo had endured. One was married to a man who mocked his wife's cooking and once spilled a pot of boiling soup onto his niece's neck, seriously injuring her. Another killed herself, and a third had to become a second concubine as the only means of supporting herself after divorcing her first husband ("Lost Lives" 90–91). Each of these tales made its way into Tan's books in one form or another.

Tan acknowledges mining her life and the lives of others for inspiration, saying that the plot of *The Joy Luck Club* is "true emotionally" to her life (Somogyi 28). In the foreword to a collection of fiction by Chinese writer Ai Bei, Tan asserts that truth is "what makes fiction so believable" (ix). Responding to her mother's assertion that people thought all of the mothers in *The Joy Luck Club* were really her, Daisy, Amy wrote *The Kitchen God's Wife*, which was partly based on events in Daisy's life before she came to America. Published in 1991, this book was also a popular and critical success and became an editor's choice selection in *Booklist*.

Despite a busy schedule of public appearances and interviews to promote her first two books, Tan produced two children's books in the next few years, *The Moon Lady* in 1992 and *The Chinese Siamese Cat* in 1994. Tan followed these publications with her third novel, *The Hundred Secret Senses* (1995). This story takes place in America and China, and, while less directly autobiographical than her previous novels, it is both more concretely detailed and more mystical.

Tan has also published two essays on the uses of language, "The Language of Discretion" (1990) and "Mother Tongue" (1990). She currently resides in San Francisco, California.

MAJOR WORKS AND THEMES

Amy Tan's publishing success echoes that of Maxine Hong Kingston's *Woman Warrior* and is part of the blossoming popularity of Asian American women writers that began in the mid-1990s. These writers include Meena Alexander, Marilyn Chin, Jessica Hagedorn, Gish Jen, Cynthia Kadohata, Joy Kogawa, Bharati Mukherjee, Faye Myenne Ng, and Cathy Song. Contributing to the availability and popularity of these writers is the growing realization that they are part of a small, oft-overlooked succession of Asian American women writers in American literature of the last century. Scholars such as Annette White-Parks and Amy Ling have contributed to the recovery and republication of works by Asian American writers such as Sui Sin Far (Edith Maude Eaton), Onoto Watanna (Winnifred Eaton), and Chuang Hua (also a pseudonym of a writer who wishes to remain anonymous). The increasing awareness, availability, and popularity of these writers have made room in the American literary tradition for works that address generation, gender, culture, class, and assimilation conflicts that Asian Americans face. Tan's *Joy Luck Club* and *Kitchen God's Wife* address all of these issues, but they focus primarily on intergenerational clashes between the Chinese mothers in the novels and their Chinese American daughters.

The Joy Luck Club presents a series of interwoven stories about four pairs of mothers and daughters who experience cultural and intergenerational conflicts due to widely differing expectations of social achievement and accomplishments. They compete via power struggles made even more complicated by communication difficulties that are caused only partly by language barriers. Though they come from widely varied backgrounds, all of the mothers express high hopes for their daughters' independence, success, and happiness in America. The daughters, on the other hand, feel constrained by their difficulties in understanding either their mothers' backgrounds or their apparent refusals to appreciate and approve of the daughters' personal and professional choices. The sixteen stories, narrated by three mothers and four daughters (Jing-mei "June" Woo tells her stories and her late mother's, too), express the disappointment the women feel in their inability to communicate with each other. The mothers, raised in China, are silenced as much by cultural gaps as by language barriers. All of the mothers are also constrained in part by the decades-old traumas and tragedies of their lives in pre–World War II China.

In *The Kitchen God's Wife*, Tan again addresses the social, cultural, gender, and generational issues that express themselves through mother-daughter relationships, though for this novel she focuses on only one pair of women, Winnie Louie and her daughter, Pearl. In both *The Joy Luck Club* and *The Kitchen God's Wife*, Tan portrays daughters who are emotionally estranged from their mothers because they feel distanced from and embarrassed by their mothers' cultural traditions. Class and assimilation issues also arise in Tan's novels, as the daughters often express exasperation over mothers who brag about saving pennies at the grocery market or wear unmatched or brightly colored clothing only because it is cheap. Intergenerational conflicts are primarily expressed, however, in the daughters' power struggles as they work to separate themselves from their mothers and their embarrassing cultural habits while simultaneously wishing for the possibility of reconciliation. The difficulty often lies in the daughters' conflicting desires for independence and acceptance.

In each of her works of fiction, including her two children's books, Tan uses a frame story format. The closely interwoven tales of *The Joy Luck Club* begin and end with the story of Jing-mei Woo learning about her late mother's life in China and of Jing-mei's trip to China to be united with her two half-sisters, the twins her mother had been separated from while fleeing Japanese soldiers during World War II. In both *The Kitchen God's Wife* and *The Hundred Secret Senses*, two related female characters explore their troubled relationships. In the course of attempting a reconciliation, characters in both novels reveal hidden histories, long-kept secrets, and a sometimes-reluctant attachment to one another. When Pearl tries to tell her mother that she has an incurable disease in *The Kitchen God's Wife*, Winnie uses the occasion to tell her daughter of her abusive first marriage and of her three children who died before she left China. After the two women have shared their secrets, Winnie creates a goddess that she gives to Pearl both to honor the memory of Winnie's long-dead children and to empower Pearl to face the future with hope, even when Winnie cannot shelter her. Just as all of Winnie's story is embedded in Pearl's narrative, Kwan's stories of her history in China, her dreams, and her past life as Nunumu, servant to missionaries, are all contained within Olivia Bishop's story of her search for self-esteem and self-knowledge in the *The Hundred Secret Senses*.

Tan also uses the frame story format in her two children's books, *The Moon Lady* and *The Chinese Siamese Cat*. The narrator of *The Moon Lady* uses the occasion of a rainy afternoon to tell her three granddaughters a story about wishes and lost hope and of how she learned the myth of the Moon Lady when she was a very young girl. This embedded narrative very closely resembles Ying-ying St. Clair's *Joy Luck Club* story, "The Moon Lady," and the narrator of the children's story is also named Ying-ying. In *The Chinese Siamese Cat*, a mother cat explains their heritage to her litter, in a story that is essentially about how a mischievous kitten restores freedom and happiness to an ancient Chinese village by rewriting a grumpy magistrate's proclamations.

In her nonfiction essays, Tan underscores her understanding of language and translation difficulties as barriers to mutual respect and understanding. In "The Language of Discretion," she warns against making simple cultural distinctions based on misunderstandings of the Chinese language and indirect styles of communication. Tan emphasizes that destructive stereotypes arise from such inaccurate distinctions, a topic she also addresses in "Mother Tongue." Admitting that, as a child, she was embarrassed by her mother's "broken" English, Tan reveals that she once thought her mother's imperfect language skills meant she had little meaningful to say, a mistake people who do not know Daisy Tan still make. Recognition of such slights and oversights has spurred Tan, she asserts, to pursue the "power of language" as well as to evoke all manners of perfect and imperfect languages in her work in order to represent the entire palette of emotions and images available to her characters as they tell their stories (7).

CRITICAL RECEPTION

The Joy Luck Club appeared on the American literary scene in 1989 as a huge popular and marketing success. Reviews were almost universally favorable. However, critical appraisal of all of Tan's novels has been mixed. While many critics point out the importance of works that address mother-daughter relationships, as do Tan's *Joy Luck Club* and *Kitchen God's Wife*, some, such as Lisa Lowe, in "Heterogeneity, Hybridity, Multiplicity: Marking Asian American Differences," assert that it is too simplistic to read these books as only stories of intergenerational conflict. Lowe argues that a less reductive reading would combat the belief that Tan's first novel presents the only acceptable interpretation of the Asian American experience. Although European Americans tend to see all Asians as alike primarily in being "other" than the majority, Lowe argues, a more accurate understanding of the complex themes of *The Joy Luck Club* would highlight the diversity of Asian Americans as a group. It would further demonstrate that clashes between the mothers and daughters in this book are more a result of differences in class and cultural expectations than of simple family conflict (36–37).

Most critical assessments of Tan's novels address her use of closely interwoven narratives and frame stories, representing points of view of two or more characters. In "Born of a Stranger: Mother-Daughter Relationships and Storytelling in Amy Tan's *The Joy Luck Club*," Gloria Shen says the apparently fragmented narrative style of *The Joy Luck Club* highlights the importance of storytelling as meaning making, since the daughters cannot attempt reconciliations with their mothers until they actually hear and understand their mothers' stories (233, 242). Yuan Yuan presents a similar assessment of *The Joy Luck Club* by describing the mothers as using their experiences from life in China to create narratives of "self-empowerment," narratives that grant them authority and that they use to shape their daughters' identities (295–96). Writing for a special issue of *Paintbrush* featuring Amy Tan, E. Shelley Reid says Tan's incorporation of a narrative style that switches from past to present and from character to character emphasizes the necessity of incorporating all parts of a self or community into a coherent whole (21). Rocio C. Davis makes a very similar argument in a chapter of *Ethnicity and the American Short Story*, concluding that short story cycles such as the one contained in *The Joy Luck Club* simultaneously represent the importance of having an identity of one's own as well as an identity firmly ensconced in one's community (8).

Qun Wang also addresses the multiple-narrator technique in Tan's works by arguing that this approach demonstrates how characters create and re-create their own identities through dialogue and storytelling (83). Another critic, Stephen Souris, also contends that, thematically, Tan's interwoven dialogues focus on the importance of "finding oneself" (105). In *Amy Tan: A Critical Companion*, E. D. Huntley, on the other hand, holds that one reading of Tan's use of layered narratives in *The Kitchen God's Wife* can demonstrate how imposed and self-imposed silences shape women's lives. This method can utilize a form of feminist criticism to show how narrators Winnie and Pearl break these silences to reclaim both their individual selves and their relationship (103–11).

In her book *Between Worlds: Women Writers of Chinese Ancestry*, Amy Ling contends that Tan's characters achieve reconciliations by learning to balance the demands of their dual cultural heritage. Critic Victoria Chen takes a similar analysis a step further to propose that by representing characters who are constantly struggling to hold a position between two languages and two cultures, Tan is also writing stories of Chinese Americans who have to work to be included in American society, which presents itself as valuing diversity, while actually privileging uniformity (5–6).

Finding a new sense of empowerment and self is another of Tan's themes that critics often address. Both Wenying Xu and M. Marie Booth Foster focus on how mothers in Tan's novels (and a grandmother in one of her children's books) actively work to rewrite goddess myths, such as those about the Moon Lady or the Kitchen God's Wife, to create both a new reality through a stronger sense of self and to model a strong woman figure for their daughters. Foster additionally contends that the mothers in *The Joy Luck Club* and *The Kitchen God's Wife* are very much like goddesses, themselves, in that it is their "altars their daughters are invited to come to for nurturance, compassion, empathy, inspiration, and direction" (214). Although not Olivia's mother, Kwan Yee, in *The Hundred Secret Senses*, is a much older sister and a mother figure in the light of the nearly total absence of their mother, Louise Laguni. Although Kwan acts the part of a "fool" in the first half of the novel, according to Linda Unali, writing on "Americanization and Hybridization," she says Kwan later acquires nearly mythical attributes (140). In the latter part of the book, Kwan acts as interpreter, guide, and inspiration for Olivia's journey of self-discovery and even as a sort of fertility goddess. Her role, according to Unali, is that "of medicine woman with a shaman's powers" (142). Readers and critics alike recognize that it is Tan's acknowledgment of the wisdom and knowledge of her older female characters, subtly represented through layers of nested stories, which makes her stories unique and her characters compelling (Braendlin 114; Heung 599).

BIBLIOGRAPHY

Works by Amy Tan

"Rules of the Game." *Seventeen* Nov. 1986: 160–64.

"Fish Cheeks." *Seventeen* Dec. 1987: 99.

The Joy Luck Club. New York: Putnam, 1989.

"Two Kinds." *Atlantic Monthly* Feb. 1989: 53–57.

"Foreword." *Red Ivy, Green Earth Mother.* By Ai Bei. Trans. Howard Goldblatt. Salt Lake City: Peregrine Smith, 1990. vii–xii.

"The Language of Discretion." *The State of the Language.* Ed. Christopher Ricks and Leonard Michaels. Berkeley: University of California Press, 1990. 25–32.

"Mother Tongue." *Threepenny Review* Fall 1990: 7–8.

The Kitchen God's Wife. New York: Putnam, 1991.

"Lost Lives of Women." *Life* April 1991: 90–91.

"Peanut's Fortune." *Grand Street* 10 (1991): 11–22.

The Moon Lady. New York: Macmillan, 1992.

Amy Tan and Ronald Bass. *The Joy Luck Club.* Screenplay. Director Wayne Wang. Hollywood Pictures, 1993.

The Chinese Siamese Cat. New York: Macmillan, 1994.

The Hundred Secret Senses. New York: Putnam, 1995.

"Young Girl's Wish." *New Yorker* 2 Oct. 1995: 80–89.

Studies of Amy Tan

Braendlin, Bonnie. "Mother/Daughter Dialog(ic)s in, around, and about Amy Tan's *The Joy Luck Club*." *Private Voices, Public Lives: Women Speak on the Literary Life.* Ed. Nancy Owen Nelson. Denton: University of North Texas Press, 1995. 111–24.

Caesar, Judith. "Patriarchy, Imperialism, and Knowledge in *The Kitchen God's Wife*." *North Dakota Quarterly* 62 (1994–95): 164–74.

Chen, Victoria. "Chinese American Women, Language, and Moving Subjectivity." *Women and Language* 28 (1995): 3–7.

Davis, Rocio G. "Identity in Community in Ethnic Short Story Cycles: Amy Tan's *The Joy Luck Club*, Louise Erdrich's *Love Medicine*, Gloria Naylor's *The Women of Brewster Place*." *Ethnicity and the American Short Story.* Ed. Julie Brown. New York: Garland, 1997. 3–23.

Foster, M. Marie Booth. "Voice, Mind, Self: Mother-Daughter Relationships in Amy Tan's *The*

Joy Luck Club and *The Kitchen God's Wife.*" *Women of Color: Mother-Daughter Relationships in 20th-*Century Literature. Ed. Elizabeth Brown-Guillory. Austin: University of Texas Press, 1996. 208–27.

Hamilton, Patricia L. "Feng Shui, Astrology, and the Five Elements: Traditional Chinese Belief in Amy Tan's *The Joy Luck Club.*" *MELUS* 24 (1999): 125–45.

Heung, Marina. "Daughter-Text/Mother-Text: Matrilineage in Amy Tan's *Joy Luck Club.*" *Feminist Studies* 19 (1993): 597–616.

Hubbard Kim. "*The Joy Luck Club* Has Brought Writer Amy Tan a Bit of Both." *People* 10 Apr. 1989: 149–50.

Huntley, E. D. *Amy Tan: A Critical Companion.* Westport, CT: Greenwood Press, 1998.

Ling, Amy. *Between Worlds: Women Writers of Chinese Ancestry.* New York: Pergamon, 1990.

Lowe, Lisa. "Heterogeneity, Hybridity, Multiplicity: Marking Asian American Differences." *Diaspora: A Journal of Transnational Studies* 1 (1991): 24–44.

McAlister, Melanie. "(Mis)Reading *The Joy Luck Club.*" *Asian America: Journal of Culture and the Arts* 1 (1992): 102–18.

Reid, E. Shelley. " 'Our Two Faces': Balancing Mothers and Daughters in *The Joy Luck Club* and *The Kitchen God's Wife.*" *Paintbrush* 22 (1995): 20–38.

Schueller, Malini Johar. "Theorizing Ethnicity and Subjectivity: Maxine Hong Kingston's *Tripmaster Monkey* and Amy Tan's *The Joy Luck Club.*" *Genders* 15 (1992): 72–85.

Shear, Walter. "Generational Differences and the Diaspora in *The Joy Luck Club.*" *Critique* 34 (1993): 193–99.

Shen, Gloria. "Born of a Stranger: Mother-Daughter Relationships and Storytelling in Amy Tan's *The Joy Luck Club.*" *International Women's Writing: New Landscapes of Identity.* Ed. Anne E. Brown and Marjanne E. Gooze. Westport, CT: Greenwood Press, 1995. 233–44.

Somogyi, Barbara, and David Stanton. "Interview with Amy Tan." *Poets & Writers* Sept./Oct. 1991: 24–32.

Souris, Stephen. "Only Two Kinds of Daughters: Inter-Monologue Dialogicity in *The Joy Luck Club. MELUS* 19 (1994): 99–123.

Unali, Linda. "Americanization and Hybridization in *The Hundred Secret Senses* by Amy Tan." *Hitting Critical Mass* 4 (1996): 135–44.

Wang, Qun. "The Dialogic Richness of *The Joy Luck Club.*" *Paintbrush* 22 (Autumn 1995): 76–84.

Wong, Sau-Ling Cynthia. " 'Sugar Sisterhood' Situating the Amy Tan Phenomenon." *The Ethnic Canon: Histories, Institutions, and Interventions.* Ed. David Palumbo-Liu. Minneapolis: University of Minnesota Press, 1995. 174–210.

Xu, Ben. "Memory and the Ethnic Self: Reading Amy Tan's *The Joy Luck Club.*" *Memory, Narrative, and Identity: New Essays in Ethnic American Literatures.* Ed. Amritjit Singh, Joseph T. Skerrett, Jr., and Robert E. Hogan. Boston: Northeastern University Press, 1994. 261–77.

Xu, Wenying. "A Womanist Production of Truths: The Use of Myths in Amy Tan." *Paintbrush* 22 (1995): 56–66.

Yuan, Yuan. "The Semiotics of China Narratives in the Con/texts of Kingston and Tan." *Critique* 40 (1999): 292–303.

MELANIE RAE THON (1957–)

Kate K. Davis

BIOGRAPHY

In 1996 Melanie Rae Thon (pronounced "tone") was recognized by *Granta* magazine as one of twenty best young American novelists. Her short stories have been included in the 1988, 1994, 1995, and 1996 editions of *Best American Short Stories*. Thon's powerful stories, often termed "gritty" and "stark," dare to push the definitions of genre as well as characterization. Thon expresses her deep need to understand others' experiences by creating fictional characters vastly different from herself and then exploring "the extraordinary states of mind of ordinary people" (Silverblatt). One might say that all fiction writers strive for such endeavors, but Thon's style lays bare her characters' existences in unique, profound, and somewhat disturbing ways.

Thon was born August 23, 1957, to Raymond Albert Thon, architect, and Lois Ann Lockwood in Kalispell, Montana. Thon's complex religious influences (Calvinist Presbyterianism and Christian Science) spawned a fascination with individuals attempting to define their own moralities based on intuition and not law. Thon is an avowed lover of the great outdoors and is fond of all animals, especially mountain goats and crows and a certain mule deer that became a friend in Montana.

Thon received a bachelor of arts in English from the University of Michigan (1980) and a master of arts in creative writing from Boston University (1982). She has taught at Emerson College, Harvard University extension and summer schools, and Syracuse University. In an interview with Caryl Phillips, Thon notes that nothing she wrote as a graduate student has become part of her published work; however, she does credit the programs with building her skills and tolerance for revision (62). From 1996 to 2000, Thon was associate professor for the Department of English and graduate creative writing program at Ohio State University, Columbus, and is currently professor at the University of Utah, Salt Lake City. Thon has also been an active instructor at writing workshops including Yellow Bay, Montana, University of Wyoming, University of Idaho, Vermont Studio Center, and California State University at Fresno.

In an effort to create or perhaps re-create her characters, Thon literally follows their journeys by visiting the places she uses as settings. Thon cites another Montana writer, Norman Maclean, author of *Young Men and Fire*, as influencing her dedication to her characters. At seventy, Maclean was driven to know the suffering of the firefighters who died on August 5, 1949, in Mann Gulch, Montana. Similarly, Thon visited the Montana State Prison in Deer Lodge to research the physical details of prison life for her novel *Sweet Hearts* (2001). Thon believes an author's relationship with her characters verges upon the sacred: "We make a covenant with the people we invent to serve and love them as honestly as possible, to bear witness to their lives without sentimentality or prejudice" ("Writing Life" 8).

MAJOR WORKS AND THEMES

Thon has published three novels, all of which involve the struggles of young adults or teenagers. Her first, *Meteors in August* (1990), lays the groundwork for the themes common throughout her works. The protagonists live in a hardscrabble town in rural Montana. Lizzie Macon's older sister, Nina, has eloped with a Native American boy, a social taboo in racist Willis. Lizzie misses her sister and compensates by falling in and out of love with both boys and girls, gaining and losing religious faith, and coming to terms with herself. Lizzie is reunited with her sister, Nina, a desperate alcoholic. Lizzie's father attacks Nina's lover, further inciting racism in an already intolerant town; but it is the compassion of a Native American man that redeems Willis and its residents.

The 1993 novel *Iona Moon* is set in White Falls, Idaho, in the mid-1960s. The title character, a teenage girl, hitchhikes to Seattle to escape the torpor of small-town life— a mother dead from cancer, a bad reputation, sexual abuse, and no prospects. Iona becomes involved with a one-legged, married Indian man but finds this affair no solution to her problems when she realizes she cannot escape herself and her past. Back in White Falls, Iona's high school friend, who has lost the use of his legs in an accident, becomes involved with his best friend's drunken mother. Their story is a compendium of the miseries unavoidable for people whose lives seem beyond their control; however, Alexandra Johnson notes, "It is Thon's considerable achievement that she is able to lay bare the scarred psyches of both men and women, lives collapsed in on themselves, hearts haunted by hope but riddled by guilt."

Sweet Hearts is the story of sixteen-year-old Flint Zimmer's escape from the Landers School for Boys. Flint and his sister, Cecile, steal their mother's car and journey to the Crow Indian Reservation to find relatives. They commit several crimes, but no one is sure whether Cecile has been kidnapped or is a willing accomplice. The entire family is confounded, except Marie, the children's deaf aunt. She understands the children's devotion to each other and the reasons behind their behaviors. It is through the narrative imagination of Marie that the family's past and present are interwoven and the violence that has plagued Flint and Cecile's family is finally illuminated.

Thon is recognized primarily as a short story writer. Her first collection, *Girls in the Grass* (1991), includes many coming-of-age stories and continues her exploration of ordinary people coping with the vicissitudes of everyday life. The title story describes the sexual awakening of three young girls who play truth-or-dare as a way of expressing their feelings toward boys and themselves; however, Thon's characters do not define themselves through their sexual encounters; her characters' bodies are not instruments of pleasure but conduits of others' desires and/or battlegrounds of survival.

Nowhere are these concepts more fully developed than in Thon's second collection of stories, *First, Body* (1997), the book that has established her reputation as a writer. In this collection, Thon's trademark characters—tenderhearted, tough kids in trouble—move to the city to grapple with urban life. But their problems are still the same. They have to survive somehow on nothing but their own bodies. The hard hitting *First, Body* is a cohesive collection of stories linked by common themes. Here Thon's style has been honed to a razor's edge, not unlike the scalpels used to autopsy the bodies in the title story. "First, Body" is the provocative story of Sid Elliot, a Vietnam vet working in a hospital morgue. Sid violates the unwritten code of the emergency room ("first, body, then brain—stop the blood, get the heart beating" 5) when he attempts to rescue the emaciated, drug-addicted Roxanne, believing his devotion will save her rather than addressing her physical state. Thon implies Roxanne's drug use will affect Sid's health. Sid is injured when he attempts to tenderly treat the cadaver of Gloria Luby, an enormously fat woman, whose body will later be used in a teaching autopsy. Ultimately it is the bodies of these two extreme women that become Sid's downfall.

Another provocative story, "Xmas, Jamaica Plain," details the lives of two young prostitutes, Emile and Nadine, as they seek shelter in a family's unoccupied home. Emile is a beautiful boy who wishes he were female. He tries on the woman's clothes and imagines himself in her place. In this story, Thon imagines the conflicting emotions of a person trapped in the wrong body. Emile's eventual overdose forces Nadine to question why she is spared.

Another character that elicits compassion, or at least sympathy, is the older black man in "Little, White Sister." Torn between contemplating what is the right thing to do and considering his past experience, he refuses to help a white woman in distress. The moral implications of this choice haunt him. His characterization personifies the balancing act people must perform when they make decisions that might have unknown and far-reaching implications. Similarly, Ada and her father, in "Father, Lover, Deadman, Dreamer," are scarred by their coverup of the daughter's hit-and-run homicide of a drunken Indian man. No matter how many men Ada sleeps with, she cannot ease her guilty feeling that some crimes are unforgivable. Both stories dwell upon the pervasive racism that seethes just below the thin veneer of society.

CRITICAL RECEPTION

In general, the reviews and critiques of Melanie Rae Thon's works are favorable. The stories are often described as Faulknerian—gritty, unsentimental, and hard-edged as well as lyrical, poignant, and beautiful. Thon is praised for her ability to cross race and gender boundaries. As Christopher Tilghman notes, "What is finally most distinctive about this work is the author's willingness to become each one of her characters. Character, narrator, and author are the same person" (209). Joyce H. Brusin believes Thon's best stories are those that stay close to her home in Montana (E12); others find her characters and plots either too contrived or too ordinary, but Sally Eckhoff observes, "Thon could probably write anything she puts her mind to" (C36). Regardless of stance, almost every critic acknowledges Thon's creative powers and skill.

Thon's novel *Iona Moon* delineates "the difference between self-pity and grief, and the distance between individual despair and common hope" (Hearon 14). Stephen Amidon considers Thon "able to tap that rich blend of American fiction that seeks salvation from deprivation in the lyrical" (15). Despite the somewhat ordinary characters and plots, T. M. McNally notes, "The novel exploits metaphors of incest and the fall; in a world haunted by the maimed, guilt and complicity have become universal conditions" (3).

Thon's most daring book, *First, Body*, justly received a wide variety of critical responses. As her style has evolved and her stories have become increasingly hard hitting, so has the criticism. Eckhoff alternately lauds Thon's writing style as "style to burn" and "musical" and decries her subject matter: "What kills *First, Body* is that Thon's gruesome, out-there subject matter and her blunt yet clever approach are fast becoming contemporary fiction's No. 1 clichés" (C36). Similarly, Stephanie Zacharek, in *Salon*, considers these stories "well-crafted," but with "another problem: They're all edges and sharp corners . . . as if recurring metaphors of cracked bone and shattered glass were all a writer needed to make a story difficult and deep."

Noting that a major theme of 1990s' women's literature is "the body," Susan Balée observes that Thon makes "a good showing in literature proper. The title story of *First, Body* cuts to the gut of the genre," but "the rest of the stories seem torpid and portentous" (341). For James Polk, *First, Body* indicates the author is "particularly drawn to the connection between victim and victimizer[;] she evokes a kind of hard-edged tenderness that is at once sensual and incapacitating" (C1). Betsy Willeford describes Thon's style as "compressed," lacking "ameliorating cosmetic touches," and "nouveau hard-boiled" (20).

Interestingly, many reviewers have likened Thon's prose to either jazz and blues music or cinematic arts. For example, Geri Gourley observes, "An undercurrent of jazz and blues rhythms is evident in the craft of these tales" (1). Sally Eckhoff notes, "The events she depicts seem to happen all at once, as if fiction could be a kind of slide show in which each successive transparency stays on the screen the whole time, bleeding into the final picture" (C36).

It is difficult to describe Thon's eclectic writing in essentialist terms. Most critics straddle the line between adulation of her skill and revulsion for her subject matter. Separately, the short stories are powerful and the characters memorable; combined, however, the myriad unfortunate characters in Thon's novels are often overwhelming and resistant to emotional involvement by the reader. Yet, everyone admires Thon's writing style and craftsmanship. Regarding *First, Body*, Christopher Tilghman suggests, "Young writers and graduate students ought to read this book and ask themselves whether they might have the courage to take their careers into a place like this" (209).

BIBLIOGRAPHY

Works by Melanie Rae Thon

Meteors in August. New York: Random, 1990.
Girls in the Grass. New York: Random, 1991.
Iona Moon. New York: Poseidon, 1993.

"The Image Notebook." *What If?* Ed. Anne Bernays and Pamela Painter. New York: Harper Collins, 1995. 30–31.

First, Body. Boston: Houghton, 1997.

"Letter to a Young Fiction Writer." *Letters to a Fiction Writer.* Ed. Frederick Busch. New York: Norton, 1999. 226–30.

"The Writing Life." *Washington Post Book World* 17 Dec. 2000: 8.

Sweet Hearts. Boston: Houghton Mifflin, 2001.

Studies of Melanie Rae Thon

Amidon, Stephen. "All Lyrical about Dirty Realism." Rev. of *Iona Moon. Financial Times* 14 Aug. 1993: 15.

Balée, Susan. "Days of Whine and Posers." *Hudson Review* 50 (1997): 340–46.

Brusin, Joyce H. "Thon's 'Girls' Filled with 'Deceptively Simple' Tales." Rev. of *Girls in the Grass. Missoulian* 9 Aug. 1991: E12.

Cameron, Julia. "Missing the Broad Skies; *Iona Moon,* by Melanie Rae Thon. Rev. of *Iona Moon. Los Angeles Times* 25 July 1993: E9.

Eckhoff, Sally. "When Worlds Collide." *Newsday* 5 Jan. 1997: C36.

Gourley, Geri. "Trying to Only Connect." Rev. of *First, Body. Bergen Record* 16 Feb. 1997: 1.

Harris, Michael. "How Tragic History Can Lie Just Beneath the Starkest Crime; *Sweet Hearts* by Melanie Rae Thon." Rev. of *Sweet Hearts. Los Angeles Times* 23 Jan. 2001: E3.

Haynsworth, Leslie. "Fighting for Solace: *PW* Interview." *Publisher's Weekly* 29 Jan. 2001: 60–61.

Hearon, Shelby. "His Kind and Her Kind." Rev. of *Iona Moon. Chicago Tribune Book World* 6 June 1993: 14ff.

Johnson, Alexandra. Rev. of *Iona Moon. Boston Review* 3 Mar. 2000 (http://bostonreview.mit.edu/ BR18.5/briefreviews.html).

McNally, T. M. "A Western Gothic Nightmare." Rev. of *Iona Moon. Washington Post* 25 July 1993: X3.

Meloy, Maile. Rev. of *Sweet Hearts. New York Times Book Review* 11 March 2001: 24.

Phillips, Caryl. "Interview with Melanie Rae Thon." *Bomb* 44 (1993): 62–65.

Polk, James. "Taut Tales of a World Where No Place Is Safe." Rev. of *First, Body. Philadelphia Inquirer* 19 Jan. 1997: C1.

Silverblatt, Michael. "Interview with Melanie Rae Thon." *Bookworm* National Public Radio KCRW, Santa Monica, 17 Jan. 1997.

Tilghman, Christopher. Rev. of *First, Body. Ploughshares* (1997): 208–9.

Willeford, Betsy. "A Short Story Writer Takes a Trip to the Emergency Room." Rev. of *First, Body. Star-Ledger* 23 Feb. 1997: 20.

Zacharek, Stephanie. Rev. of *First, Body. Salon* 22 Jan. 1997 (http://208.178.101.41/sneaks/ sneakpeeks970122.html).

ANNE TYLER (1941–)

Donna Buchanan Cook

BIOGRAPHY

Anne Tyler was born into a Quaker family on October 25, 1941. Her parents, Lloyd Parry and Phyllis Mahon Tyler, wanted to rear their children in a safe community conducive to living a simple life. After several trial-and-error moves, the Tylers re-located to the Celo Community in North Carolina. The area provided the kind of setting the Tylers sought as well as an opportunity for Lloyd Tyler, a research chemist, to continue his association with the Celo Laboratories, a lab that developed natural vitamins and drugs. The Tyler family contributed to the shared labor of the commu-nity, whose population aimed for economic freedom from the outside world, yet still maintained their own autonomy as homeowners. The Tylers planted a small organic garden that yielded much of their food, and for a time, they home-schooled Anne and her brother. Anne later began to attend the local public school but still occasionally visited the community's art classes that were provided for the children of Celo. Before Tyler turned seven, she had already written a collection of stories with illustrations.

Early on, Tyler was most influenced by *The Little House* by Virginia Lee Burton, a book read to Anne and her brothers by their mother. Tyler has said that the book her provided her with her first glimpse of how all things continually change. *The Little House* is a story about how the city grew up around a little country house, leaving it cut off from the fields of flowers, the apple orchard, and the light of the moon. The city closes in around it and it remains unused and unloved until eventually the original owner's great-great-great-great-granddaughter discovers the house and moves it out of the city to the country. Tyler's fascination with these elements of life and how circumstances change whether the change is welcome or not is apparent throughout her works.

When the Tylers moved to Raleigh, North Carolina, in 1953, they unknowingly provided twelve-year-old Anne an opportunity to gain material for her future novel *Tin Can Tree* (1965), a story born of her experiences working on a tobacco farm. In

Raleigh, the Tylers pursued their social activism—taking a stand against such issues as the death penalty and the production of the B-1 bomber. Anne Tyler's sensitivity to the individual human experience is likely a result of her parents' values and can be found throughout her novels and short stories.

During Tyler's high school years, her English teacher and literary magazine sponsor, Phyllis Peacock, encouraged her to pursue writing. Mrs. Peacock had also taught Reynolds Price, who years later mentored Tyler at Duke University. Upon graduation from high school at sixteen, Tyler was awarded a full scholarship to Duke University, where she chose to major in Russian. However, her talent and dedication to fiction writing while at Duke were rewarded with two Anne Flexner Creative Writing Awards. She won the first award for her submission of two chapters of a novel and the second for "The Saints in Caesar's Household," a short story that became her fifth publication in the *Archive*, the school's literary journal.

While attending Duke, Tyler performed in *The Glass Menagerie* and *Our Town* as well as working for the *Archive*. Having grown up in a socially conscious family, Anne Tyler found the 1960s full of issues that beckoned her involvement, especially the civil rights movement.

Tyler completed her first novel, *I Know You, Rider*, the same year she graduated Phi Beta Kappa from Duke University at the age of nineteen. Although the novel was never published, it foreshadowed a future writing style in the Southern tradition as well as a narrative structure that Tyler employed in several novels. The following year, 1962, Tyler studied Russian at Columbia University.

After she left Columbia, she wrote "The Baltimore Birth Certificate," a short story that would eventually be published in the *Critic*—her first national exposure. Tyler followed her successful first publication with the publication of another short story, "I Play Kings," in *Seventeen*, which also appeared in 1963 (Croft 17).

In 1962 Tyler moved to Camden, Maine, where she worked a part-time summer job as a proofreader for a local newspaper. However, it was the experience of her other part-time job, scrubbing fishing boat decks, that found its way into several short stories as well as the novel *Celestial Navigation* (1974). At the end of her summer in Camden, Tyler returned to Duke to work as a Russian bibliographer at the Perkins Library.

The following year, Tyler met and married Taghi Modaressi, an Iranian medical student at Duke University. Tyler and Modaressi soon moved to Montreal in order for him to conclude a residency program in child psychiatry. While living in Montreal, Tyler completed *If Morning Ever Comes* (1964), her first published novel. She then took a job at the McGill University Law Library, a position that gave her the kind of work environment that she believed would be less stressful and therefore afford her more time to write. During this time, she wrote *The Tin Can Tree* (1965). In order to devote more time to her daughters, Tezh and Mitra, born in 1965 and 1967, respectively, Tyler wrote very little until Mitra entered school in 1970.

While Tyler is most known for her novels, she also writes short stories, essays, and reviews. To date, none of her short stories has been published in a collection.

MAJOR WORKS AND THEMES

Themes concerning family, home, and identity are common in Anne Tyler's fiction. There are no complex plots in Tyler's stories, but layered into her characters' lives are complex issues that Tyler manages under the thematic rubric of relationships. In order to explore the themes she finds most interesting, Anne Tyler creates husband-wife, mother-daughter, father-son, nuclear family, and extended family relationships and conflicts. The complexities of establishing individual identities while attempting to keep family and friend relationships intact are major issues for Tyler's characters to resolve. Whether teenage as Ian Bedloe in *Saint Maybe* (1991) or past middle age as both Rebecca Davitch in *Back When We Were Grownups* (2001) and Maggie Moran in *Breathing Lessons* (1988), family, home, and identity are the infrastructure on which Tyler constructs her plots.

The opening line of *Back When We Were Grownups* represents the conflict experienced by several of Tyler's female protagonists: "Once upon a time there was a woman who discovered she had turned into the wrong person" (3). The search for identity propels many of Tyler's characters to action; a few resolve relationship issues. In *Back When We Were Grownups*, Rebecca Davitch ponders how she lost her dignified manner and became a party planner. Rebecca, like many of Tyler's female protagonists, is past middle age and worries that her life is not meaningful or that she is someone whom no one takes seriously. Family relationships have defined Rebecca's entire adult life; having raised her deceased husband's children and one of their own since his death only six years after their marriage, she has run the family's party-planning business. Rather than confront family members about thoughtless remarks or ask why they take her for granted, Rebecca tries to ignore them, but that approach only makes her feel taken advantage of and resentful. While pondering this dilemma, Rebecca eventually discovers that both her image of herself and the one her family has formed make up the real Rebecca.

Delia Grinstead in *Ladder of Years* (1995) walks away from a family beach party and disappears to "find herself." And she does. She discovers that *self* is mostly self-made, no matter where she lives. Her impulsive behavior is precipitated by a gnawing fear that her husband, Sam, married her to gain her father's medical practice. Delia is unable to get any perspective on their marriage relationship until she establishes her own independent identity. Ironically, her pilgrimage to another town eventually leads to the same life she left behind—mother (surrogate) and housekeeper. How to make relationships work and still emerge with a separate identity is a life struggle many of Tyler's characters have in common.

Tyler constructs family members that support and care for one another, yet their relationships reflect a struggle to break free and develop individuality. Sometimes it works for them; sometimes it does not. In *A Slipping-Down Life* (1970), Evie realizes that breaking away from husband Drum Casey is the first step to a new, more positive self-identity. Before she leaves, she renounces her earlier action of cutting Drum's name into her forehead, saying, "I didn't do that," creating a new identity that rejects the past and claims a better future for her baby.

In Tyler's novels *The Clock Winder* (1972), *Earthly Possessions* (1977), and *Ladder of Years*, returning home is as common as leaving home. Elizabeth Abbott, Charlotte Emory, and Delia Grinstead are real people who, in choosing to return, discover a measure of self-determinism that assists them with renewed relationships. And for those who leave and do not return, like Justine Peck in *Searching for Caleb* (1976) and Morgan Gower in *Morgan's Passing* (1980), no significant changes take place in their lives. The irony of Justine's marriage is that she reconnects to the Peck family—the family she resisted—and as a result, she remains tethered to fortune telling. Morgan Gower only changes wives, never himself. Tyler writes narratives with real-life themes; her characters experience real-life conflicts.

In her 1998 novel *Patchwork Planet,* Tyler explores the positive relationship between Barnaby Gaitlin and his elderly clients and the negative one with his family. Often Tyler's work reveals the human need for positive reinforcement and success. Kindness and good will cover a multitude of past sins for Barnaby Gaitlin, who demonstrates that it is not teenage, youthful mistakes that count, but one's whole life. Often Tyler writes themes that serve to remind the reader of the basics of human decency and respect.

In *Accidental Tourist* (1985), Macon Leary learns to cope with the loss of his son, wife, and marriage, first by embracing a lifestyle bound up by strict time-saving rules and then by letting go of them when he embarks on a relationship with Muriel Pritchett. Macon and Muriel give new meaning to "opposites attract," but the relationship allows Macon to discover that the sense of fun, wit, and even strength that Muriel brings to his life is what he needs to return to the experience of life.

In Anne Tyler's Pulitzer Prize–winning *Breathing Lessons,* characters Ira and Maggie Moran explore how a man and woman relate differently to the loss of relationships. The loss of contact with the Moran's ex-daughter-in-law, Fiona, and granddaughter, Leroy, is only one of many relationships explored. Maggie's insistence on going unannounced to Fiona's house is a ploy by Maggie to reestablish a relationship with Fiona and Leroy. Ira is bothered by the whole idea, but Maggie is convinced that it is the right decision and thus reveals how Maggie's interference in all their lives has caused estrangement and ambivalence toward maintaining contact with one another. Doris Betts views Maggie and Ira as having typical male/female attitudes. She writes, "Maggie [tries] to tinker with and repair life [while Ira meditates] more abstractly on the wastes of immortality and time" ("Tyler's Marriage" 12).

Whether relationships are a negative experience or a positive one for Tyler's protagonists, they often explore their own place and importance to those people around them. In *Saint Maybe*, Ian Bedloe spends a great part of his life agonizing over the death of his brother, Danny, and the subsequent death of Danny's wife, Lucy. Eventually Ian finds a redemptive path to overcoming his self-imposed guilt regarding their deaths. He returns to the family to help raise the children. Ian eventually realizes that his last words with Danny were not the ultimate cause of Danny's death or the beginning of Lucy's. In the end, Ian feels he has reconnected to his brother and Lucy, the family that he lost years earlier through the ongoing cycle of life—his new baby son.

Tyler's characters may be eccentric, whimsical, or plodding; they may be funny, sarcastic, or rude; they may be depressed, dependent, or delightful—but none of her characters is unbelievable. They, their families, their adventures, and their sorrows are all created because Anne Tyler finds them interesting.

CRITICAL RECEPTION

Discussions of Tyler's work range from evaluations of simplistic subjects to analyses of complex themes. C. Ralph Stephens comments that the early critical response overlooked the author's talent while craning to find social and political issues (xi). Yet, in *The Fiction of Anne Tyler,* Susan Gilbert acknowledges that *The Accidental*

Tourist (nominated for the Pulitzer Prize) and *Breathing Lessons* (winner of the Pulitzer Prize) involve issues of gun control, crime, education, and abortion (137).

Many critics comment on Tyler's characterization. Although Brooke Allen finds many of Tyler's characters "boring," she admits that these "unreflective, inarticulate characters" are among Tyler's finest (28). Allen states that *Celestial Navigation*'s story about Jeremy Pauling is "narrated with a balance and restraint that is as good as anything that Tyler has yet produced" (29). John Updike defends Tyler from accusations that her *Dinner* characters are implausible, finding them "familiar and American . . . [with] real psychologies, which make their next moves excitingly unpredictable" (299). Doris Betts compares Tyler's ability to create characters to that of Eudora Welty ("Fiction" 27). Tyler is the first to agree with the many critics that find her characters stronger than her plots, saying "Character is everything. I never did see why I have to throw in a plot, too" (Allen 34). While most critics view Tyler's realistic portrayal of characters as a strength, Cathleen Shine, in her review of *Ladder Years*, notes the contrary: "Tyler's dissociated characters have always been in danger of becoming annoying and a little boring—just like real unresponsive people. One sometimes has an urge to poke them—hard" (12). Wendy Lamb observes that Tyler seems very confident with her characters and Tyler agrees, saying that she is "always confident about" and "fond of" her characters (54).

Tyler is frequently compared with other Southern women writers, mostly Carson McCullers and Eudora Welty. Tyler cites Welty as the writer who most influenced her work, and Betts recognizes that Welty's "definition of plot as the 'why' aptly fits any of Tyler's plots ("Fiction" 27). Paula Gallard Eckard and Barbara A. Bennett make comparisons between Carson McCullers and Tyler, noting similarities in the overall style and specifically the narrative style in *Dinner*. While Brooke Allen finds Tyler's early work "a soggy imitation of Carson McCullers" (28), Updike compares Tyler with Eudora Welty, John Cheever, Flannery O'Connor, and Carson McCullers as a "remarkable talent" with "power to see and guess and know . . . with a tolerance and precision unexcelled among contemporary writers" (quoted in Stephens ix).

Tyler's most recent novels, *A Patchwork Planet* and *Back When We Were Grownups*, continue to survey familial landscapes. The response to Tyler's most recent novels overwhelmingly praises the author's talent for creating characters that readers love getting to know. As in her earlier novels, Tyler continues to depict real life. Ron Charles, reviewing *Planet*, echoes similar sentiments as other critics and reviewers when he states that Tyler "is our national specialist at portraying and healing the pain of middle-class misfits" and "is a master at bitter-sweet comedy" (B1). In *Grownups*, Tyler continues to reveal complicated relationships within families. Also, this novel confirms that Tyler's favorite setting remains Baltimore, her characters continue to model real life, and she again allows her protagonist to resolve with dignity the crisis of identity and worthiness.

BIBLIOGRAPHY

Works by Anne Tyler

"Laura." *Archive* Mar. 1959: 36–37.
"The Lights on the River." *Archive* Oct. 1959: 5–6.
"The Bridge." *Archive* Mar. 1960: 10–15.

"I Never Saw Morning." *Archive* Apr. 1961: 11–14.

If Morning Ever Comes. New York: Knopf, 1964.

The Tin Can Tree. New York: Knopf, 1965.

"Who Would Want a Little Boy?" *Ladies Home Journal* May 1968: 132ff.

"The Common Courtesies." *McCall's* June 1968: 62ff.

A Slipping-Down Life. New York: Knopf, 1970.

"With All Flags Flying." *Redbook* June 1971: 88ff.

"The Bride in the Boatyard." *McCall's* June 1972: 92ff.

The Clock Winder. New York: Knopf, 1972.

"The Base-Metal Egg." *Southern Review* 9 (1973): 682–86.

"Spending." *Shenandoah* 24 (1973): 58–68.

Celestial Navigation. New York: Knopf, 1974.

"Half-Truths and Semi-Miracles." *Cosmopolitan* Dec. 1974: 264ff.

"The Artificial Family." *Southern Review* 11 (1975): 615–21.

"A Knack for Languages." *New Yorker* 13 Jan. 1975: 32–37.

"The Geologist's Maid." *New Yorker* 28 July 1975: 29–33.

"Some Sign That I Ever Made You Happy." *McCall's* Oct. 1975: 90ff.

Searching for Caleb. New York: Knopf, 1976.

"Your Place Is Empty." *New Yorker* 22 Nov. 1976: 45–54.

Early Possessions. New York: Knopf, 1977.

"Holding Things Together." *New Yorker* 24 Jan. 1977: 30–35.

"Average Waves in Unprotected Waters." *New Yorker* 28 Feb. 1977: 32–36.

"Foot-Footing On." *Mademoiselle* Nov. 1977: 82ff.

"Linguistics." *Washington Post Magazine* 12 Nov. 1978: 38ff.

Morgan's Passing. New York: Knopf, 1980.

"Still Just Writing." *The Writer on Her Work: Contemporary Women Writers Reflect on Their Art and Situation.* Ed. Janet Sternburg. New York: Norton, 1980. 3–16.

"Laps." *Parents* Aug. 1981: 66ff.

"The Country Cook." *Harper's* Mar. 1982: 54–62.

Dinner at the Homesick Restaurant. New York: Knopf, 1982.

"Teenage Wasteland." *Seventeen* Nov. 1983: 144–45.

The Accidental Tourist. New York: Knopf, 1985.

Breathing Lessons. New York: Knopf, 1988.

"Rerun." *New Yorker* 4 July 1988: 20–32.

"A Woman like a Fieldstone House." *Ladies Home Journal* Aug. 1989: 86ff.

"People Who Don't Know the Answers." *New Yorker* 26 Aug. 1991: 26–36.

Saint Maybe. New York: Knopf, 1991.

Tumble Tower. New York: Orchard Press, 1993.

Ladder of Years. New York: Knopf, 1995.

A Patchwork Planet. New York: Knopf, 1998.

Back When We Were Grownups. New York: Knopf, 2001.

Studies of Anne Tyler

Allen, Brooke. "Anne Tyler in Mid-Course." *New Criterion* 13 (May 1995): 27–34.

Bennett, Barbara A. "Attempting to Connect: Verbal Humor in the Novels of Anne Tyler." *South Atlantic Review* 60 (1995): 57–75.

Betts, Doris. "The Fiction of Anne Tyler." *Southern Quarterly* 21 (1983): 23–37.

——. "Tyler's Marriage of Opposites." *The Fiction of Anne Tyler.* Ed. C. Ralph Stephens. Jackson: University Press of Mississippi, 1990. 1–15.

Binding, Paul. "Anne Tyler." *Separate Country: A Literary Journey through the American South.* New York: Paddington Press, 1979. 198–209.

Bowers, Bradley R. "Anne Tyler's Insiders." *Mississippi Quarterly* 42 (1988): 47–56.

Carroll, Virginia Schaefer. "The Nature of Kinship of the Novels of Anne Tyler." *The Fiction of Anne Tyler*. Ed. C. Ralph Stephens. Jackson: University Press of Mississippi, 1990. 16–27.

Carson, Barbara Harrell. "Art's Internal Necessity: Anne Tyler's Celestial Navigation." *The Fiction of Anne Tyler*. Ed. C. Ralph Stephens. Jackson: University Press of Mississippi, 1990. 47–54.

——. "Complicate, Complicate: Anne Tyler's Moral Imperative." *Southern Quarterly* 31 (1992): 24–34.

Charles, Ron. "A Middle Class Misfit's Search for Self-Respect." *Christian Science Monitor* 30 April, 1998. B1.

Crane, Gwen. "Anne Tyler, 1941– ." *Modern American Women Writers*. Ed. Lea Baechler and A. Walton Litz. New York: Scribners, 1991. 499–510.

Croft, Robert W. *Anne Tyler: A Bio-Bibliography*. Westport, CT: Greenwood Press, 1995.

Eckard, Paula Gallant. "Family and Community in Anne Tyler's *Dinner at the Homesick Restaurant*." *Southern Literary Journal* 22 (1990): 33–44.

Eder, Richard. "Trying on a New Life." *Los Angeles Times Book Review* 7 May 1995: 3.

Elkins, Mary J. "*Dinner at the Homesick Restaurant*: Anne Tyler and the Faulkner Connection." *Atlantis* 10 (1985): 93–105.

Evans, Elizabeth. *Anne Tyler*. New York: Twayne, 1993.

Gilbert, Susan. "Private Lives and Public Issues: Anne Tyler's Prize-Winning Novels." *The Fiction of Anne Tyler*. Ed. Ralph C. Stephens. Jackson: University Press of Mississippi, 1990. 136–45.

Jones, Anne G. "Home at Last, and Homesick Again: The Ten Novels of Anne Tyler." *Hollins Critic* 23 (1986): 1–14.

Kissel, Susan S. "Anne Tyler's 'Homeless at Home.' " *Moving On*. Bowling Green: Bowling Green University Press, 1996. 69–98.

Koppel, Gene. "Maggie Moran, Anne Tyler's Madcap Heroine: A Game-Approach to *Breathing Lessons*." *Essays in Literature* 18 (1991): 267–87.

——. "Jane Austen and Anne Tyler, Sister Novelists under the Skin: Comparison of *Persuasion* and *Saint Maybe*." *Persuasions* 15 (1993): 164–69.

Lamb, Wendy. "An Interview with Anne Tyler." *Critical Essays on Anne Tyler*. Ed. Alice Hall Petry. New York: G. K. Hall, 1992. 53–58.

Linton, Karin. *The Temporal Horizon: A Study of the Theme of Time in Anne Tyler's Major Novels*. Uppsala, Sweden: Acta Universitatis Upsaliensis, 1989.

Petry, Alice Hall. *Understanding Anne Tyler*. Columbia: University of South Carolina Press, 1990.

——."Bright Books of Life: The Black Norm in Anne Tyler's Novels." *Southern Quarterly* 31 (1992): 7–13.

——, ed. *Critical Essays on Anne Tyler*. New York: G. K. Hall, 1992.

Robertson, Mary F. "Medusa Points and Contact Points." *Contemporary American Women Writers: Narrative Strategies*. Ed. Catherine Rainwater and William J. Scheik. Lexington: University of Kentucky Press, 1985. 19–42.

Salwak, Dale, ed. *Anne Tyler as Novelist*. Iowa City: University of Iowa Press, 1994.

Shine, Cathleen. "New Life for Old." *New York Times Book Review* 7 May 1995: 12.

Stephens, C. Ralph, ed. *The Fiction of Anne Tyler*. Jackson: University Press of Mississippi, 1990.

Sutherland, John. "Lucky Brrm." *London Review of Books* 12 March 1992: 23–24.

Updike, John. *Hugging the Shore: Essays and Criticism*. New York: Knopf, 1983.

Voelker, Joseph C. *Art and the Accidental in Anne Tyler*. Columbia: University of Missouri Press, 1989.

ALICE WALKER (1944–)

Lisa Abney

BIOGRAPHY

During her relatively short life, Alice Walker has played many roles—activist, spiritualist, speaker, mother, daughter, and writer. She has become one of America's foremost writers, yet her humble origin would not have necessarily ensured the successes that she has attained. Walker was born in Eatonton, Georgia, on February 9, 1944, to Minnie Tallulah Grant Walker and Willie Lee Walker. Her family was poor, and sharecropping was the primary occupation of her father and of the other families with which Walker had contact while growing up in rural Georgia. Walker was reared with seven other siblings—five boys and two other girls—of whom she was the youngest. When she was eight years of age, one of Walker's brothers accidentally shot her in the eye with a BB gun. Walker lost the use of her right eye, and this event drastically changed Walker's life. The eye became a source of embarrassment and shame for her. She has come to terms with this visual impairment only as an adult (*In Search* 392).

After enduring the traumatic events of her childhood, Walker attended Spellman College from 1961 to 1963, and after a trip to Africa and a stint of involvement in the civil rights movement, she earned her BA degree in 1965 from Sarah Lawrence College. While at Sarah Lawrence, she found a mentor in writer Muriel Rukeyser. Rukeyser showed a sample of Walker's writing to her editor, and this editor later became Walker's editor, as well (Winchell 279). From 1965 to 1968, Walker worked actively in the civil rights movement in both Georgia and New York. In 1967 she married Melvyn Roseman Levanthal, an attorney. From 1967 to 1970, she taught at several universities in Mississippi, and in the 1970s, she taught at Wellesley College, the University of Massachusetts at Amherst, the University of California at Berkeley, and Brandeis. Walker and Levanthal had one daughter. While married, Walker worked on her first novel, *The Third Life of Grange Copeland*, which was published in 1970, and her second novel, *Meridian*, which was published in 1976. In 1974 Walker took a position as an editor at *Ms.* magazine. In 1977 her marriage to Levanthal ended, and she began teaching at Yale University. In 1978 she, along with a friend and fellow writer, Robert Allen, moved to San Francisco, where they lived comfortably on her Guggenheim Fellowship funds and a retainer from *Ms.*; after a short time, the pair moved to Mendocino County, where Walker concentrated on her writing. She continues to live in northern California and has produced many of her works while living in the region. Like her character Meridian Hill, Walker's life has been a journey. She has questioned organized religion, politics, sexual preference, and her purpose in life (*Anything* 3–25). Walker has lived through some of the most turbulent times in American history. She has experienced the rise of suburbia, the Red Scare, the tumultuous civil rights and anti-war movements, the Vietnam War, the legalization of abortion, the emergence of conservative politics in America during the 1980s, the death of apartheid, and a variety of personal tragedies, including the death of her parents and a serious illness of her own (*Same River* 24–31). Today, Walker lives in northern California, writes, and works for a variety of social and political causes.

MAJOR WORKS AND THEMES

The work of Alice Walker generally needs little introduction, particularly, her novel *The Color Purple* (1982). Her novels, poetry, short stories, and essays have made her name well known. Walker's other novels, *The Third Life of Grange Copeland, Meridian* (1976), *The Temple of My Familiar* (1989), and *Possessing the Secret of Joy* (1992) have drawn academic reviews but have not captured the public's interest as widely as has *The Color Purple*. Walker's works, as disparate in characters, plots, and settings as they are, set forth the themes of oppression, love, healing, survival, the consequences of choices, and the disparity of power in American society.

In the *Third Life of Grange Copeland*, her first novel, Walker creates complex characters who endure in the world of the Southern sharecropper of the Depression era. The novel's story line stems from actual events that occurred in Walker's hometown of Eatonton, Georgia. The mother of Walker's classmate was shot by her husband in the same fashion as the character, Mem, in the *Third Life of Grange Copeland*. Walker's sister worked as a cosmetologist at the local funeral home, and she allowed the impressionable Alice to see the dead woman who was being prepared for burial. The image of the dead woman haunted Walker, as did the notion that her husband might be released to wreak more havoc on the town (*Third Life* 342–43). The novel spans a thirty-year period in the life of a family. It illustrates the disparity of power in America and the ways in which narrative is suppressed because of the inequality of power. The violence in Walker's text indeed amplifies this motif. The novel graphically portrays the oppressive conditions that the sharecropper faced during the time; characters lack even the most basic human necessities. All the characters in the novel illustrate the oppressed state of African Americans in the South during the 1940s to 1960s. The title character, Grange Copeland, lives a life of oppression until he leaves his wife and children and escapes to the North, where he realizes that the freedom of which he has dreamed over the last twenty years is an illusion. He finds freedom from oppression only when he returns to the South and learns to build a life outside mainstream society. He uses Josie, a prostitute and his former lover, to procure land and a modest home. He forces her to leave since she cannot embrace his grandchild who is her grand-niece and Brownfield's daughter, Ruth. Indeed, Grange avoids oppression, yet in turn he must oppress Josie in order to secure the life he desires. Josie's choice of husband, in Grange, carries with it the consequence of losing her independence, financial power, and self-respect. The goal of Grange's existence is for Ruth to "survive whole" (Christian, *Black Women Writers* 87). Grange's life becomes a series of journeys that ultimately lead him to the idea that he can survive, can love, and can be loved, but that this love comes at a high price, for he loses his immediate family, endures hatred, and ultimately must kill his son, Brownfield, to protect Ruth. Few works deal with this aspect of rural America, and this novel captures the society and culture of the Depression-era underclass. This novel, like most of Walker's works, shows that power influences narrative.

In *Meridian*, the issues of power disparity and narrative become apparent in a slightly different way. Meridian Hill struggles to find her voice to speak on a number of occasions: When she is asked to speak in church as a child, she is struck dumb, and later, as an adult, when asked if she could kill for the civil rights cause, again she is left grasping for words. Meridian, naive about the facts of life, becomes pregnant at age seventeen and is forced to marry Eddie, who begins to have affairs with other women shortly after Meridian marries him. Eddie leaves her and their child to pursue his own interests. Meridian, knowing that she cannot endure living under the eyes of Eddie and her parents, leaves her son behind with relatives and seeks an education. During this time, she fights against racism, sees the misguided efforts of her well-meaning intentions fail when her involvement with the Wild Chile leads to the indigent woman's death, and falls in love with her soul mate, Truman Held, who repeatedly embraces and rejects her. As her doubts about the purpose of her life emerge, she becomes physically ill. Additionally, Meridian begins to see the negative aspects of the civil rights movement. The abuse of women within the movement and the lack of power that she experiences lead her to live a transient existence. During the final portion of the novel, Truman's mixed blood daughter, Camara, is killed, and Camara's mother, Carol, and Truman approach Meridian for healing and for comfort. Truman and Carol drain her last energy, and she sees that she must leave all of her past connections and move on to find a place for herself so that she can survive. Again, Walker sets forth the themes of oppression, love, survival, and consequences of choices in this text. Carol, Truman's white wife, chooses to work for civil rights and to become involved with someone outside her culture. She loses her place within white culture, yet she is never fully invited into the black culture. Ultimately, Tommy Odds, a friend of Truman and Carol, rapes her. After this attack and the subsequent death of her daughter, Carol realizes her folly and seeks a new life, though marginalized and never fully comfortable with her existence. Meridian, like Carol, must find her place outside mainstream society in order to escape oppression and pain.

The Color Purple, Walker's best-known book, again illustrates these themes of love, oppression, and the need to live beyond the mainstream in order to exist successfully. Celie, the main character of this work, which is set in the earlier part of the twentieth century, struggles to overcome incest, spousal abuse, and her relegation to a lesser position because of her gender. She fights to establish her own voice against her odious husband, Mister, or Albert, as he is sometimes called. After finding, with Shug Avery's help, the letters of her sister, Nettie, which Albert has kept from her over the years, she becomes angry. This anger, which Shug encourages her to channel into a new business, pants making, reinforces Celie's attempt to find the place in the world that she needs in order to "survive whole" (Christian, *Black Women Writers* 87). The discovery of Nettie's letters spurs her quest to be reunited with Nettie and Olivia and

Adam, who are Celie's children by her stepfather. Celie, like other of Walker's characters, struggles to find a place for herself, and ironically, the death of her incestuous stepfather enables her to find this place since she inherits the land of her biological parents through his death. Ultimately, Celie's house becomes a refuge for her family and hence heals the deep wounds of loss, which she has endured through much of her life. This touching and vivid novel illustrates Walker's commitment to the illustration of consequences of choices and the overarching power of love.

Walker's next work, *The Temple of My Familiar*, departs from the settings and linear narratives of her other novels to depict a transgenerational existence of goddesses. Walker employs the "transmigration of the soul" (Winchell, *Alice Walker* 290) in order to tell the tale of three couples who have lived a variety of lives during their existence on earth. This complex novel becomes a novel of ideas in which Walker sets forth many of her ideas regarding the history of oppression and sexism. Again, the themes of love, oppression, and consequences of choices appear in this text as in her other works.

Walker's novel, *Possessing the Secret of Joy*, which was published in 1992, again takes on political and ideological issues about which Walker feels intensely passionate. In this novel, Tashi, an African character who has appeared in both *The Color Purple* and in *The Temple of My Familiar*, undergoes therapy to come to terms with the female genital mutilation that she endures while with her tribe in Africa. The subsequent murder of a tribal circumciser, M'Lissa, by Tashi and the trial and conviction of Tashi that follow drive home Walker's message regarding the horrors of female genital mutilation.

In 1998 Walker published *By the Light of My Father's Smile*, which chronicles the lives, fragmentation, and deaths of a family. Walker makes many strong comments in this novel about families, sexuality, and the role of Christianity in societies, particularly in non-Christian cultures. The work, which is innovatively written, spins the tale of the Robinson family through the family members at various stages of their lives and deaths. Indeed, the work contains strong political, racial, and sexual statements, yet Walker's strong and interesting characters are not overshadowed by her views. The work has drawn praise from many for its innovative narrative structure, interesting characters, and powerful themes. Walker's tale in this work does not end in a trite, "happily-ever-after" fashion. The novel, like other of Walker's works, depicts many human tragedies and frailties.

Walker's fiction has drawn the most critical acclaim of her writing, yet her career as a poet and essayist has also been prolific. Walker's collections of essays such as *In Search of Our Mother's Gardens* (1983), *The Same River Twice: Honoring the Difficult* (1996), and her latest, *Anything We Love Can Be Saved* (1997), contain thought-provoking and challenging essays. Topics include politics, sexism, female genital mutilation, the place of women in society, and the need for people to find practical ways to survive intact in the face of the fast-paced, often out-of-control, twentieth century.

CRITICAL RECEPTION

Many of Walker's works have been well received by both popular and scholarly audiences. Her early works, especially *The Color Purple*, found more favor than have her later novels, which have been criticized for their overly political message and strident tone, but in all, Walker's works have been embraced by many readers.

Walker's first work, *The Third Life of Grange Copeland*, was hailed by some as a brilliant start and masterfully developed work. Critic Robert Coles in a 1971 *New Yorker* review states, "Alice Walker is a fighter as well as a meditative poet and lyrical novelist. She has taken part in the struggles her people have waged. . . . Toward the end of his third life, Grange Copeland can at last stop being hard on himself and look with kindness upon himself—and one wonders whether an achievement can be more revolutionary" (106). Other critics, however, took a less favorable approach to the book. For some, the book's publication became an opportunity for Walker's life-style to be attacked and scrutinized. For example, Hendin asserts that Walker's novel deteriorates into a series of tired political clichés (5). Walker, however, did not waver in the face of criticism about her choice to write the work. Several scholarly pieces address a variety of issues in this early work: Some examine the abuse of women, and others focus upon the development of the narratives in the work. Other pieces address religion in the work, such as "Visions of Southern Life and Religion in O'Connor's *Wise Blood* and Walker's *The Third Life of Grange Copeland*" by Robert Butler. Several articles address this work in terms of the civil rights movement, such as Onita Estes-Hicks's "The Way We Were: Precious Memories of the Black Segregated South." While Walker's first work attained positive reviews from academics and popular audiences, her second work, *Meridian*, also drew positive acclaim from critics.

Marge Piercy in a 1976 review calls *Meridian* "a fine, taut novel" (9). Many critics have discussed the element of political rebellion and have analyzed the work in terms of its political commitment. Susan Danielson's "Alice Walker's *Meridian*, Feminism and the 'Movement' " and Lynn Pifer's "Coming to Voice in Alice Walker's *Meridian*: Speaking Out for the Revolution" focus on the text in terms of the civil rights movement. Walker's interpretation of race has been addressed in articles such as Jace Anderson's "Re-Writing Race: Subverting Language in Anne Moody's *Coming of Age in Mississippi* and Alice Walker's *Meridian*." Most critics, however, address the struggle for Meridian to survive whole, which emerges as a major theme in the novel. Barbara Christian's book-length work, *Black Women Novelists: The Development of a Tradition, 1892–1976,* and Arunima Ray's article, "The Quest for 'Home' and 'Wholeness' in *Sula* and *Meridian*: Afro-American Identity in Toni Morrison and Alice Walker," discuss this major theme in *Meridian* and secondary theme in other Walker novels.

The theme of the quest for wholeness appears again in *The Color Purple*. This novel, Walker's most popular work, received much attention from critics after the film version of the novel was released. One of the primary negative comments about the work was the depiction of men in the novel as hard-hearted and brutal abusers. Walker, however, defended her work by referring to many actual examples of spouse abuse contemporary to the work's time period and to the condition of battered women in American society today. Some critics have chosen to address the narrative aspects of the work in relation to the main character, Celie, who develops her voice and begins to define herself as she progresses within the novel. Pieces such as "Errant Narrative and *The Color Purple*" by Steven C. Weisenburger; "A Womanist Way of Speaking: An Analysis of Language in Alice Walker's *The Color Purple*, Toni Morrison's *Tar Baby*, and Gloria Naylor's *Women of Brewster Place*" by Cheryl Johnson; and "The Making of Celie in Alice Walker's *The Color Purple*" by Daniel Ross deal with the issue of narrative voice. *The Color Purple* has been the subject of many dissertations, articles, and discussions in academia.

Walker's next work, *The Temple of My Familiar*, sparked controversy because of its nonlinear narrative structure and its departure from Walker's usual narrative form. Ursula LeGuin praised the work, stating that "the rhythms of Alice Walker's prose are beautiful and characteristic" (24). For some, the novel presents too many interconnected story lines and too much information to sort through. Though the novel was a *New York Times* best-seller, it lacks the popular appeal of Walker's other works; many critics, however, have written about the work. Bonnie Braendlin discusses the work in "Alice Walker's *Temple of My Familiar* as a Pastiche." Madelyn Jablon examines the role of recursive narrative in "Rememory, Dream History, and Revision in Toni Morrison's *Beloved* and Alice Walker's *The Temple of My Familiar*." The *Temple of My Familiar* has drawn much attention in terms of narrative structure. Walker's next work, *Possessing the Secret of Joy*, has also become a topic for critical attention.

As Walker's life and writing have progressed, her commitment to political causes has grown. *Possessing the Secret of Joy* has been hailed by social activists as a much needed work that draws attention to the practice of female genital mutilation, while literary critics have often regarded the work as too political and less literary than Walker's other works. Others have written with admiration of Walker's courage to write about a taboo subject such as this one. Susana Vega deals with the role of tradition in her article, "Surviving the Weight of Tradition: Alice Walker's *Possessing the Secret of Joy*." Additionally, Lale Demiturk has discussed the novel in a similar manner in "The Black Woman's Selfhood in Alice Walker's *Possessing the Secret of Joy*." Walker herself calls this book the hardest one that she has ever written, and indeed, its graphic depictions of the consequences of female genital mutilation are difficult to read. She has achieved her goal with this work, graphic though it is, for now the terrifying and difficult world of these African women has been brought to the public eye with the hope that their plight to end this mutilation will be recognized and assisted. Some critics have examined the book in terms of Western values as they influence the observation of this practice; Angeletta Gourdine addresses this in "Postmodern Ethnography and the Womanist Mission: Postcolonial Sensibilities in *Possessing the Secret of Joy*."

Walker's fiction works illustrate a wide variety of social and political themes, yet she crafts her novels well enough so that these themes, while present, do not overpower the characters that she creates. Grange, Meridian, and Celie remain distinctive in the reader's memory, yet the reader inadvertently finds him/herself pondering wholeness, abuse, love, and survival repeatedly after reading Walker's texts.

BIBLIOGRAPHY

WORKS BY ALICE WALKER

Once: Poems. New York: Harcourt, 1968.
The Third Life of Grange Copeland. New York: Harcourt, 1970.
In Love and Trouble: Stories of Black Women. New York: Harcourt, 1973.
Revolutionary Petunias and Other Poems. New York: Harcourt, 1973.
Langston Hughes: American Poet. New York: Crowell, 1974.

Meridian. New York: Harcourt, 1976.

Good Night, Willie Lee, I'll See You in the Morning. New York: Dial, 1979.

Ed. *I Love Myself When I Am Laughing . . . : A Zora Neale Hurston Reader.* By Zora Neale Hurston. New York: Feminist Press, 1979.

You Can't Keep a Good Woman Down. New York: Harcourt, 1981.

The Color Purple. New York: Harcourt, 1982.

In Search of Our Mothers' Gardens. New York: Harcourt, 1983.

Horses Make a Landscape Look More Beautiful: Poems. New York: Harcourt, 1984.

To Hell with Dying. San Diego: Harcourt, 1988.

Living by the Word: Selected Writings, 1973–1987. New York: Harcourt, 1988.

The Temple of My Familiar. New York: Harcourt, 1989.

Finding the Green Stone. San Diego: Harcourt, 1991.

Her Blue Body Everything We Know: Earthling Poems, 1965–1990 Complete. New York: Harcourt, 1991.

Possessing the Secret of Joy. New York: Harcourt, 1992.

Alice Walker and Pratibha Parmar. *Warrior Marks: Female Genital Mutilation and the Sexual Blinding of Women.* New York: Harcourt, 1993.

The Same River Twice: Honoring the Difficult. New York: Scribners, 1996.

Anything We Love Can Be Saved. New York: Random House, 1997.

By the Light of My Father's Smile. New York: Ballantine, 1998.

Studies of Alice Walker

Anderson, Jace. "Re-Writing Race: Subverting Language in Anne Moody's *Coming of Age in Mississippi* and Alice Walker's *Meridian.*" *Autobiography Studies* 8 (1993): 33–50.

Bloom, Harold, ed. *Alice Walker.* New York: Chelsea, 1989.

Bradley, David. "Telling the Black Woman's Story." *New York Times Magazine* 8 Jan.1984: 24–37.

Braendlin, Bonnie. "Alice Walker's *The Temple of My Familiar* as a Pastiche." *American Literature: A Journal of Literary History, Criticism, and Bibliography* 68 (1996): 47–67.

Butler, Robert. "Visions of Southern Life and Religion in O'Connor's *Wise Blood* and Walker's *The Third Life of Grange Copeland.*" *CLA Journal* 36 (1993): 349–70.

Christian, Barbara. "Novels for Everyday Use: The Novels of Alice Walker." *Black Women Novelists: The Development of a Tradition, 1892–1976.* Westport, CT: Greenwood Press, 1980. 180–238.

——. "Alice Walker: The Black Woman Artist as Wayward." *Black Women Writers 1950–80: A Critical Evaluation.* Ed. Mari Evans. New York: Anchor/Doubleday, 1984. 457–77.

——. *Black Women Writers 1950–80: A Critical Evaluation.* Ed. Mari Evans. New York: Anchor/Doubleday, 1984.

——. "The Contrary Women of Alice Walker: A Study of Female Protagonists in *In Love and Trouble.*" *Black Feminist Criticism: Perspectives on Black Women Writers.* New York: Pergamon, 1985. 31–46.

Coles, Robert. Rev. of *The Third Life of Grange Copeland. New Yorker* 27 Feb. 1971: 104–6.

Danielson, Susan. "Alice Walker's *Meridian*, Feminism and the 'Movement.' " *Women's Studies* 16 (1989): 317–30.

Davis, Thaddious. "Alice Walker's Celebration of Self in Southern Generations." *Southern Quarterly* 21 (1983): 38–53.

Demiturk, Lale. "The Black Woman's Selfhood in Alice Walker's *Possessing the Secret of Joy.*" *Journal of American Studies of Turkey* 2 (1995): 33–36.

Erickson, Peter. "Cast Out Alone/to Heal/and Recreate/Ourselves': Family-Based Identity in the Work of Alice Walker." *CLA Journal* 23 (1979): 71–94.

Estes-Hicks, Onita. "The Way We Were: Precious Memories of the Black Segregated South."
    African-American Review 27 (1993): 9–18.

Gaston, Karen. "Women in the Lives of Grange Copeland." *CLA Journal* 24 (1981): 276–86.

Gates, Henry Louis, and K. A. Appiah, eds. *Alice Walker: Critical Perspectives Past and
    Present.* New York: Amistad, 1993.

Gourdine, Angeletta. "Postmodern Ethnography and Womanist Mission: Postcolonial Sensibil-
    ities in Possessing the Secret of Joy." *African American Review* 30 (1996): 237–44.

Harris, Trudier. "On The Color Purple, Stereotypes, and Silence." *Black American Literature
    Forum* 18 (1984): 155–61.

——. "From Victimization to Free Enterprise: Alice Walker's *The Color Purple*." *Studies in
    American Fiction* 14 (1986): 1–17. Hendin, Josephine. Rev. of *The Third Life of Grange
    Copeland. Alice Walker: Critical Perspectves: Past and Present*. Ed. Henry Louis Gates,
    Jr. and K. A. Appiah. New York: Amistad, 1993. 3–5.

Jablon, Madelyn. "Rememory, Dream History, and Revision in Toni Morrison's *Beloved* and
    Alice Walker's *The Temple of My Familiar*." *CLA Journal* 37 (1993): 136–44.

Johnson, Cheryl. "A Womanist Way of Speaking: An Analysis of Language in Alice Walker's
    The Color Purple, Toni Morrison's *Tar Baby*, and Gloria Naylor's *Women of Brewster
    Place*." *The Critical Response to Gloria Naylor*. Ed. Sharon Felton and Michelle C.
    Loris. Westport, CT: Greenwood Press, 1997. 23–26.

Le Guin, Ursula. Rev. of *The Temple of My Familiar. Alice Walker: Critical Perspectives: Past
    and Present*. Ed. Henry Louis Gates, Jr. and K. A. Appiah. New York: Amistad, 1993.
    22–24.

McDowell, Deborah E. "The Self in Bloom: Alice Walker's *Meridian*." *CLA Journal* 24 (1981):
    262–75.

Parker-Smith, Bettye. "Alice Walker's Women: In Search of Some Peace of Mind." *Black
    Women Writers (1950–80): A Critical Evaluation*. New York: Pergamon, 1985.
    478–93.

Piercy, Marge. Rev. of *Meridian. Alice Walker: Critical Perspectves: Past and Present*. Ed.
    Henry Louis Gates, Jr. and K. A. Appiah. New York: Amistad, 1993. 9–11.

Pifer, Lynn. "Coming to Voice in Alice Walker's *Meridian*: Speaking Out for the Revolution."
    African-American Review 26 (1992): 77–88.

Ray, Arunima. "The Quest for 'Home' and 'Wholeness' in Sula and *Meridian*: Afro-American
    Identity in Toni Morrison and Alice Walker." *Indian Journal of American Studies* 23
    (1993): 59–65.

Ross, Daniel. "The Making of Celie in Alice Walker's *The Color Purple*." *Teaching American
    Literatures: Nineteen Essays*. Albuquerque: University of New Mexico Press, 1996.
    159–74.

Stein, Karen F. "*Meridian*: Alice Walker's Critique of Revolution." *Black American Literature
    Forum* 20 (1986): 129–41.

Vega, Susana. "Surviving the Weight of Tradition: Alice Walker's *Possessing the Secret of
    Joy*." *Journal of American Studies of Turkey* 5 (1997): 19–26.

Wall, Wendy. "Lettered Bodies and Corporeal Texts in *The Color Purple*." *Studies in American
    Fiction* 16 (1988): 83–97.

Washington, Mary Helen. "An Essay on Alice Walker." *Sturdy Black Bridges: Visions of Black
    Women in Literature*. Ed. Roseann P. Bell. New York: Anchor/Doubleday, 1979.
    133–49.

Winchell, Donna Haisty. *Alice Walker*. New York: Twayne, 1992.

——. "Alice Walker." *American Novelists since World War II*. Ed. James R. Giles and Wanda
    H. Giles. New York: Twayne, 1994. Vol. 143 of *Dictionary of Literary Biography*.
    277–92.

Weisenburger, Stephen C. "Errant Narrative and *The Color Purple*." *Journal of Narrative Tech-
    nique* 19 (1989): 257–75.

JOY WILLIAMS (1944–)

J. Elizabeth Clark

BIOGRAPHY

"I am not an articulate person," announced Joy Williams in a 1990 interview with Molly McQuade. "That's one reason why I became a writer—you sit there, you shape, you form, you twist, you wait, and then you've got this thing. Talk is just words. In a story, they become something else" (400). How better to describe this novel, short story, and travel writer's exquisite relationship with language and writing? Since the publication of her first novel, *State of Grace* (1973), Williams has established herself as a writer with an intense love of language and dedication to her characters. In her character-driven stories and novels, Williams presents a world slightly off-kilter through a surrealistic lens. "In the world of Joy Williams's fiction," Peter Catapano writes, "life is truly precarious. Her characters persist through an instinct for survival and a fascination with the mystery of existence" (9).

An only child born in Chelmsford, Massachusetts, on February 11, 1944, to William Lloyd and Elisabeth (Thomas) Williams, Joy Williams grew up in Cape Elizabeth, Maine. For entertainment, she often rode the Chappaquiddick Island ferry, reading and keeping notebooks about those books. The Bible proved to be an important influence in these early years. While Williams's father and grandfather were both Congregational ministers, her own interest in the text stemmed from exploring the myriad levels of mystery.

Williams left home to attend school at Marietta College in Ohio, graduating with a BA in 1963. She attended the prestigious Iowa Writers' Workshop at the University of Iowa, where she worked with R. V. Cassill. After earning an MFA in 1965, Williams made a pivotal move to Florida, a landscape that would come to dominate her work. In 1966 she won the first of many literary recognitions for her work, a third-place O. Henry Prize for "The Roomer."

The late 1960s and early 1970s marked several important critical successes. Her early work caught the attention of two important editors: George Plimpton, editor of the *Paris Review*, and Gordon Lish, fiction editor of *Esquire* magazine. Plimpton, in particular, guided Williams onto the literary scene, editing and publishing *State of Grace*, which was a National Book Award nominee in the same year. With the success of her debut novel, Williams won a National Endowment for the Arts Grant (1973) and a Guggenheim Fellowship (1974).

Her early work was followed by five more books before further major recognition for her work: *The Changeling* (1978), *Taking Care* (1982), *The Florida Keys: A History and Guide* (1987), *Breaking and Entering* (1988), and *Escapes: Stories* (1990). Williams's career speaks to her success as a writer popular with readers and with the contemporary US literary establishment. In addition to wide publication, she has received considerable critical attention for her novels and short stories, winning a National Magazine Award in 1980 for "The Farm" (*Taking Care*) and a literature citation from the American Academy of Arts and Letters (1989).

In 1993, however, Williams received one of the most prestigious awards for a contemporary writer: the Mildred and Harold Strauss Living Award (1993–1997). The Strauss Living Award provides its recipients with $50,000 annually for five years so that writers, like Williams, can devote their time exclusively to writing. Following this honor, Williams published two more major works: *The Quick and the Dead* (2000) and *Ill Nature: Meditations on Humanity and Other Animals* (2001). During this time, she also received the Rea Award for the Short Story (1999).

While Williams maintained an active teaching career in the 1980s and early 1990s as a visiting and adjunct professor at several universities including the University of Houston (1982), the University of Florida (1983), the University of California at Irvine (1984), the University of Iowa (1984), and the University of Arizona (1987–1992), she took a hiatus from teaching in 1992 according to the provisions of the Strauss Living Award.

In addition to her prolific publication of book-length collections, Williams's work has regularly appeared in publications such as *Antioch Review*, *Paris Review*, *Esquire*, *Tri–Quarterly*, *Granta*, *New Yorker*, *Grand Street*, and *Ms*. Her work has been widely anthologized in collections including the prestigious *O. Henry Prize Story Collection* (1966), *Best American Short Stories* (1978, 1985, 1986, 1987), *Norton Anthology of Short Fiction* (1978), *Great Esquire Fiction* (1983), and *American Short Story Masterpieces* (1987).

Williams lives in Arizona and Florida with her husband, Rust Hills, fiction editor for *Esquire*.

MAJOR WORKS AND THEMES

State of Grace set the tone for Williams's future work. In Williams's typically dark, almost hysterical humor and evasive language, she renders Kate Jackson's desire to capture reality. In coming to know Kate, through a novel that refuses commonsense chronology, readers meet the first of many strong women characters in Williams's work who present in their thoughts and actions a juxtaposition of living in internal, psychological ruminations and the physical outside world.

Kate cannot move psychologically or physically away from her father, a clergyman who follows her with his prophecies. Each time Kate thinks she has found reality—in photography, in a pregnancy, in her husband Grady's love, in her sorority sisters' company—something disastrous occurs, leaving Kate alone with only her father to depend on. "I am swinging in the dreadful hammock of a dream," she laments (51). Ultimately, she and her baby daughter return to the father, and Kate, in a surrealistic turn, becomes her own daughter.

Mother-child relationships also dominate two other novels, the much-berated *Changeling* (1978) and *The Quick and the Dead* (2000). *The Changeling's* Pearl shares much in common with Kate as she waits, kidnapped by a man named Walker, for the birth of her child on an island. Pearl runs away with her child, Sam, but Walker finds her. On their way back to the island, the plane crashes. Walker is dead, and we presume Sam is also. However, Pearl leaves the crash with a baby of the same age and size as Sam. The new Sam is the changeling; Pearl's relationship with the changed child reveals much about her as she distances herself from the child. Both Kate and Pearl distance themselves from the physical child, Pearl through drink and Kate through a psychological state that allows her to become, or believe she has become, her own child.

This distance between mother and child is equally apparent in the three motherless girls of *The Quick and the Dead*, Alice, Corvus, and Annabel. All three mothers are dead, but Annabel's mother haunts her and the novel, skimming through the pages as an external monitor of all situations. None of the girls is connected to her dead mother; instead, the very landscape of the novel is forbidding and alienating. The dead are everywhere, from the living dead in the nursing home to the nurse in the nursing home who is obsessed with death: " 'Birth is the cause of death,' Nurse Daisy liked to say, which is why they didn't allow her to fill out the death certificates either, although she once had scribbled, 'The set trap never tires of waiting,' and, since no one could decipher her handwriting, it sailed on through" (170). Alice, an animal activist, finds the dead animals in museums the most offensive. In the harsh Arizona desert, animals roam free, attack, and are celebrated by Alice.

Arizona is a tragic and doleful landscape, the product of aggressive land development, signified by deer jumping into swimming pools, interrupting the peace of suburban living. Corvus's parents drown. A game hunter wanders through the novel, attempting to control the wild nature desperately trying to grow back where society has established itself. The harsh reality of nature extends to the other novels as well. Kate Jackson's sorority sister is mauled by a leopard, and Pearl is obsessed by the unnatural sexual acts of the island's residents, which she compares to, and in drunken states sometimes believes are, animals'. Pearl's new child bites her savagely. In each case, nature is wild, unable to be tamed, and ultimately wins out against humanity.

These novels present life as slightly off-kilter. The unexpected always happens in Williams's world. While comic, these events also carry with them a dark undertone. In her two collections of short stories, *Taking Care* (1982) and *Escapes*, Williams brings this juxtaposition to the forefront of her writing. Unencumbered by extended plot lines, Williams's short stories avoid the biggest criticism of her writing: that her plots unfold in complicated, often seemingly impossible, chronological order. The short stories, in contrast, expose a seemingly quiet moment of domestic order and turn that moment around. Rand Richards Cooper explains of *Escapes*: "The pervasiveness of the ominous and the grotesque in Ms. Williams's modified minimalism makes for a curious combination—as of, say, Ann Beattie and Roman Polanski. . . . Indeed, the dread is somewhat too pervasive. Milk cartons at the breakfast table feature requests for organ donations. A junked television set in the back of a pickup truck has a bullet hole in the center of its screen" (10). Joy Williams's short stories and her novels are filled with such incongruities. It is as if each random and unusual event in a person's life has ended up in page after page of Williams's books.

Add to this the dramatic irony Williams interposes on her characters. In "Health," (*Escapes*) a burglar dies of asphyxiation from an exterminator's chemicals. Meanwhile, the vacationing family's Pammy, infected with TB, feels like Snow White while sunning herself at a tanning salon. The burglar, and not Pammy, dies of asphyxiation, but Pammy is the character most in touch with her ebbing health.

Williams's work often presents death—as the characters wrestle with the loss of loved ones—as an ever-looming subtext. Characters die in freak accidents, plane crashes, of diseases, and of crimes like being in the proverbial wrong place at the wrong time. Death, for Williams, is both a comic and a tragic moment. Many of her characters, like Pammy, contemplate the realities of death and do not immediately die, while other unsuspecting characters meet untimely and horrible deaths. Also, many characters, like Pearl and Corvus, live as though they are dead already, alienating themselves from the world at large.

Breaking and Entering strays from this formula. Instead of turning the world upside down for her characters, Williams assigns Willie and Liberty the task of finding the world already upside down. In Williams's most amusing book, and the one that offers its characters a redemptive moment, Willie and Liberty travel through Florida, breaking into vacation homes of wealthy people who need such material goods as a dial-a-sermon telephone service, a ceramic dildo, and toilets with deodorant sticks. Much as Kate sought to capture reality to make sense of her life, Willie and Liberty seek order. In the final scene, Willie ruminates, "You can only stay longer, maybe. You could have stayed here longer yourself. You could have been a middle-aged lady, intense but friendly, like middle-aged ladies are, with a collection of glass balls you shake and there's snow. We could sit, you and I, of an evening turning and watching. This could have been ours" (278). Ultimately, all of Williams's characters suffer from an inability to reconcile the world as they think it with the world as it exists.

CRITICAL RECEPTION

Williams's early entry to the literary scene was smooth. *State of Grace* received wide critical acclaim. From mainstream publications like the *New York Times Book Review* to smaller literary publications like the *Antioch Review*, Williams's first book was seen by critics as a major literary contribution and the promise of novels yet to be written. Gail Godwin offers a "most grateful welcome to a first-rate new novelist," observing that Williams's Kate Jackson is "no simple 'slice-of-despair' character; her sad story becomes, through the author's skill and intention, transubstantiated into significant myth" (2). Reviews and celebrations like Godwin's led to Williams's National Book Award nomination.

Imagine Williams's surprise, then, when *The Changeling* met with inimical reviews. Alice Adams wrote, "The evidence suggests that Miss Williams could and probably will write an excellent novel, which *The Changeling*, unfortunately, is not" (6). Adams also observes of Williams's intense psychological exploration of Pearl: "This border-land between psychosis and reality, the land of private mythology of the 'grotesque,' is dangerously tempting to writers: so easy to do badly, almost impossible to do well" (6). Williams discussed the deeply negative reviews of *The Changeling* with Molly

McQuade: "The reviews of that book were such that you felt they wanted you to die—or if you refused to die, then you could at least stop writing" (401).

Williams did not bow to critical pressure, however. Her subsequent short story collections led to more favorable reviews. Rand Richards Cooper writes of the "quirky and ominous" fates the characters meet in *Escapes*: "Ms. Williams proves heroically resourceful as a cataloguer of those ways and means" (9). Cooper appreciates Williams's collection as risky, "making ominousness a kind of reflex, a pose," and compares the title story of the collection, "Escapes," with Delmore Schwartz's "In Dreams Begin Responsibilities" (10). Cooper's quiet praise for the book appreciates Williams's writing for her intense examination of ordinary lives and the entry she allows readers to those characters' thoughts and feelings.

Jennifer Schuessler, in a *New York Times Book Review* of *The Quick and the Dead*, suggests Williams's clashing critical reviews emanate from the stylistic differences in Williams's novels and short stories: "Frustrated admirers have faulted her novels for their disjointed structures and increasingly wild leaps into fantasy and satire. Indeed, today her reputation rests largely on her taut, brilliantly controlled short stories written squarely in the realist mode. Read together, Williams the short–story writer and Williams the novelist sometimes seem to be writing from different planets" (7). Schuessler contradicts her own analysis, giving *The Quick and the Dead*, an "odd, intelligent, unsettling and sometimes spectacularly uningratiating" novel, a largely favorable review (7). She writes, "This strange, discomfiting novel captures, in flashes and flickers, the infinite, inconsequential mystery of the endangered human soul that's always on its way toward winking out in the dark" (7). Schuessler's comments echo Cooper's and Godwin's in paying homage to Williams's ability to create characters readers care about.

Alice, in *The Quick and the Dead*, provides a metaphor for reading Williams's intense psychological entries into her characters. She longs for a day when she will wake up and "four animals arrive to carry you off." Alice thinks "in their jaws you are carried so effortlessly, with such great care that you think it will never end, you long for it not to end, and then you wake and know that, indeed, they have not brought you back" (308). Once you enter Williams's world, she does not bring you back.

BIBLIOGRAPHY

Works by Joy Williams

"The Roomer." *Prize Stories 1966: The O'Henry Awards*. Eds. William Abrahams and Richard Poirer. Garden City, NY: Doubleday, 1966: 171–79.
State of Grace. Garden City, NY: Doubleday, 1973.
The Changeling. Garden City, NY: Doubleday, 1978.
Taking Care. New York: Random House, 1982.
The Florida Keys: A History and Guide. New York: Random House, 1987.
Breaking and Entering. New York: Vintage, 1988.
Escapes: Stories. New York: Atlantic Monthly Press, 1990.
Florida. Portland, OR: Graphic Arts Center Publishers, 1999.
The Quick and the Dead. New York: Knopf, 2000.
Ill Nature: Meditations on Humanity and Other Animals. New York: Lyons, 2001.

Studies of Joy Williams

Abel, Carol Jackson. "The Idea of Florida in Contemporary American Literature: A Study of Four Florida Writers." Thesis, Florida State University, 1991.

Adams, Alice. "Someone Else's Dream." Rev. of *The Changeling*. *New York Times Book Review* 2 July 1978: 6.

Bannon, Barbara A. "Taking Care." Rev. of *Taking Care*. *Publishers Weekly* 22 Jan. 1982: 59.

Catapano, Peter. "A Story Should Break Your Heart." Rev. of *Escapes*. *New York Times Book Review* 21 Jan. 1990: 9.

Cooper, Rand Richards. "Escapes." Rev. of *Escapes*. *New York Times Book Review* 21 Jan. 1990: 9–10.

Ellis, Bret Easton. "Breaking and Entering." Rev. of *Breaking and Entering*. *New York Times Book Review* 5 June 1988: 26.

Flanagan, Mary. "Escapes." Rev. of *Escapes*. *New Statesman & Society* 22 June 1990: 51.

Gates, David. "Escapes." Rev. of *Escapes*. *Newsweek* 26 Feb. 1990: 64.

Godwin, Gail. "State of Grace." Rev. of *State of Grace*. *New York Times Book Review* 22 April 1973: 2–3.

Hamburger, Susan. "The Florida Keys: A History and Guide." Rev. of *The Florida Keys*. *Library Journal* 1 April 1987: 148.

Huntley, Kristine. "The Quick and the Dead." Rev. of *The Quick and the Dead*. *Booklist* 1 Oct. 2000: 324.

Jenks, Tom. "How Writers Live Today." *Esquire* Aug. 1985: 123–28.

Kaganoff, Penny. "Breaking and Entering." Rev of *Breaking and Entering*. *Publishers Weekly* 6 May 1988: 104.

McQuade, Molly. "Joy Williams; A Gum–Chewing Puritan, She Writes 'Teeming, Chaotic Fiction about 'The Ever–Approaching Nothing.' " *Publishers Weekly* 26 Jan. 1990: 400–401.

Nelson, Sara. "The Best American Short Stories 1995." Rev. of *The Best American Short Stories 1995*. *People Weekly* 15 Jan. 1996: 35.

Schuessler, Jennifer. "Virtue Is Its Own Punishment." Rev. of *The Quick and the Dead*. *New York Times Book Review* 22 Oct. 2000: 7.

Steinberg, Sybil. "Escapes." Rev. of *Escapes*. *Publishers Weekly* 3 Nov. 1989: 82.

SELECTED BIBLIOGRAPHY

Adams, Katherine H. *A Group of Their Own: College Writing Courses and American Women Writers, 1880–1940*. Albany: State University of New York Press, 2001.

Adler, Ruth. "Mothers and Daughters: The Jewish Mother as Seen by American Jewish Women Writers." *Yiddish* 6 (1987): 87–92.

Baker, Houston A., Jr. *The Workings of the Spirit: The Poetics of Afro-American Women's Writing*. Chicago: University of Chicago Press, 1991.

Bakker, Dee. "Women Writers and Their Critics: A Room with a View." *Mid-American Review* 13 (1992): 80–85.

Baym, Nina. "Between Enlightenment and Victorian: Toward a Narrative of American Women Writers Writing History." *Critical Inquiry* 18 (1991): 22–41.

Bendixen, Alfred, ed. *Haunted Women: The Best Supernatural Tales by American Women Writers*. New York: Ungar, 1985.

Berlant, Lauren. "Cultural Struggle and Literary History: African-American Women's Writing." *Modern Philology* 88 (1990): 57–64.

Bilbija, Ksenija. "Spanish American Women Writers: Simmering Identity over a Low Fire." *Studies in Twentieth Century Literature* 20 (1996): 147–65.

Billingslea-Brown, Alma Jean. *Crossing Borders through Folklore: African-American Women's Fiction and Art*. Columbia: University of Missouri Press, 1999.

Bloom, Harold, ed. *Asian-American Women Writers*. Philadelphia: Chelsea House, 1997.

——, ed. *Native American Women Writers*. Philadelphia: Chelsea House, 1998.

Bono, Francesca de. "Communicating Heritage: Regional Characteristics of Some American Women Writers." *Swansea Review* (1994): 139–46.

Bower, Anne L. "Our Sisters' Recipes: Exploring 'Community' in a Community Cookbook." *Journal of Popular Culture* 31 (1997): 137–51.

Browdy de Hernandez, J. "Writing (for) Survival: Continuity and Change in Four Contemporary Native American Women's Autobiographies." *Wicazo SA Review* 10 (1994): 40–62.

Burstein, Janet. "Jewish-American Women's Literature: The Long Quarrel with God." *Studies in American Jewish Literature* 8 (1989): 9–25.

Butler, Deborah A. *American Women Writers on Vietnam: Unheard Voices: A Selected Annotated Bibliography*. New York: Garland, 1990.

Candelaria, Cordelia Chavez, and Mary Romero, eds. "Las Chicanas." Special Issue. *Frontiers* 11.1 (1990).

Carr, Irene Campos. "A Survey of Selected Literature on la Chicana." *NWSA Journal* 1 (1988–89): 253–73.

Carr, Pat. "American Women Writers and the Missed Opportunity." *Mid-American Review* 12 (1992): 105–10.

Champion, Laurie, ed. *American Women Writers, 1900–1945: A Bio-Bibliographical Critical Sourcebook.* Westport, CT: Greenwood Press, 2000.

Cheung, King-kok. "Reflections on Teaching Literature by American Women of Color." *Pacific Coast Philology* 25 (1990): 19–23.

Connor, Kimberly Rae. *Conversions and Visions in the Writings of African-American Women.* Knoxville: University of Tennessee Press, 1994.

Cortina, Lynn Ellen Rice. *Spanish-American Women Writers: A Bibliographical Research Checklist.* New York: Garland, 1983.

Cota-Cardenas, Margarita. "The Chicana in the City as Seen in Her Literature." *Frontiers* 6 (1981): 13–18.

Craft, Linda J. "Goddesses at the Borderlands: Mexican-American Women's Narrative and the Rediscovery of the Spiritual." *Language & Literature* 24 (1999): 31–42.

Dandridge, Rita B., ed. *Black Women's Blues: A Literary Anthology, 1934–1988.* New York: G. K. Hall, 1992.

D'Aponte, Mimi Gisolfi. "Native American Women Playwrights: Transmitters, Healers, Transformers." *Journal of Dramatic Theory & Criticism* 14 (1999): 99–108.

Dixson, Barbara. "Family Celebration: Portrayals of the Family in Fiction Published in the 1980s by Southern Women." *Southern Quarterly* 26 (1988): 5–14.

duCille, Ann. *The Coupling Convention: Sex, Text, and Tradition in Black Women's Fiction.* New York: Oxford University Press, 1993.

Ewell, Barbara C. "Changing Places: Women, the Old South; or, What Happens When Local Color Becomes Regionalism." *Amerikastudien/American Studies* 42 (1997): 159–79.

Faust, Langdon Lynne, ed. *American Women Writers: A Critical Reference Guide from Colonial Times to the Present.* New York: Ungar, 1988.

Fernandez, Roberta. "Abriendo Caminos in the Brotherland: Chicana Writers Respond to the Ideology of Literary Nationalism." *Frontiers* 14 (1994): 23–50.

Fetterley, Judith. *Commentary: Nineteenth-Century American Women Writers and the Politics of Recovery."* American Literary History* 6 (1994): 600–11.

Fishburn, Evelyn, ed. *Short Fiction by Spanish-American Women.* Manchester: Manchester University Press, 1998.

Ghymn, Esther Mikyung. *The Shapes and Styles of Asian American Prose Fiction.* New York: Peter Lang, 1992.

———. *Images of Asian American Women by Asian American Women Writers.* New York: Peter Lang, 1995.

Giunta, Edvige, ed. "Italian/American Women Authors." Special Issue. *Via: Voices in Italian Americana* 7.2 (1996).

Glazer, Miriyam, ed. "Contemporary Women Writers." Special Issue. *Studies in American Jewish Literature* 11.2 (1992).

Graulich, Melody, ed. "Western Women Writers." Special Issue. *Legacy* 6.1 (1989).

Green, Rayna. "Native American Women." *Signs* 6 (1980): 248–67.

Griffin, Farah Jasmine. " 'Sister, Sister?': Recent Writings on Black and White Southern Women." *NWSA Journal* 3 (1991): 98–109.

Groover, Kristina K. *The Wilderness Within: American Women Writers and Spiritual Quest.* Fayetteville: University of Arkansas Press, 1999.

Hall, Jacquelyn Dowd. " 'To Widen the Reach of Our Love': Autobiography, History, and Desire." *Feminist Studies* 26 (2000): 231–47.

Holloway, Karla F. C. "Revision and (Re)membrance: A Theory of Literary Structures in Literature by African American Women Writers." *African American Review* 24 (1990): 617–31.

——. *Moorings & Metaphors: Figures of Culture and Gender in Black Women's Literature.* New Brunswick, NJ: Rutgers University Press, 1992.

Howard, Rebecca. "The Native American Women Playwrights Archive: Adding Voices." *Journal of Dramatic Theory & Criticism* 14 (1999): 109–16.

Johnson, Yvonne. *The Voices of African American Women: The Use of Narrative and Authorial Voice in the Works of Harriet Jacobs, Zora Neale Hurston, and Alice Walker.* New York: Peter Lang, 1998.

Jordan, Shirley, ed. *Broken Silences: Interviews with Black and White Women Writers.* New Brunswick, NJ: Rutgers University Press, 1993.

Kahn, Lisa. "American Women Writers Who Write in German." *MELUS* 5 (1978): 63–70.

Kafka, Phillipa. *The Great White Way: African American Women Writers and American Success Mythologies.* New York: Garland, 1993.

Kaminsky, Amy K. *Reading the Body Politic: Feminist Criticism and Latin American Women Writers.* Minneapolis: University of Minnesota Press, 1993.

Kilcup, Karen L., ed. *Nineteenth-Century American Women Writers: An Anthology.* Oxford, UK: Blackwell, 1997.

——, ed. *Nineteenth-Century American Women Writers: A Critical Reader.* Malden, MA: Blackwell, 1998.

——, ed. *Soft Canons: American Women Writers and Masculine Tradition.* Iowa City: University of Iowa Press, 1999.

Klingenberg, Patricia. "Latin American Women Writers: Into the Mainstream (at Last)." *Tulsa Studies in Women's Literature* 6 (1987): 97–107.

Knight, Denise D., ed. *Nineteenth-Century American Women Writers: A Bio-Bibliographical Critical Sourcebook.* Westport, CT: Greenwood Press, 1997.

Korenman, Joan S. " African-American Women Writers, Black Nationalism, and the Matrilineal Heritage." *CLA Journal* 38 (1994): 143–61.

Lee, Sang Ran. "Asian-American Women Writers: A Discourse of the 'Other.' " *Journal of English Language & Literature* 40 (1994): 333–62.

Lee, Valerie. *Granny Midwives and Black Women Writers: Double-Dutched Readings.* New York: Routledge, 1996.

Levy, Barbara. *Ladies Laughing: Wit as Control in Contemporary American Women Writers.* Amsterdam, the Netherlands: Gordon and Breach, 1997.

Lichtenstein, Diane. *Writing Their Nations: The Tradition of Nineteenth-Century American Jewish Women Writers.* Bloomington: Indiana University Press, 1992.

Lindberg-Seyersted, Brita. "The Color Black: Skin Color as Social, Ethical, and Esthetic Sign in Writings by Black American Women." *English Studies* 73 (1992): 51–67.

Lockert, Lucia. "Protagonists of Latin American Women Writers." *Michigan Academician* 25 (1992): 59–65.

Logan, Shirley Wilson, ed. *With Pen and Voice: A Critical Anthology of Nineteenth-Century African-American Women.* Carbondale: Southern Illinois University Press, 1995.

Lopez, Helen. "An Introduction to Asian American Women's Fiction." *Philippine American Studies Journal* 3 (1991): 9–15.

Madsen, Deborah L. *Understanding Chicana Literature.* Columbia: University of South Carolina Press, 2000.

Magee, Rosemary M., ed. *Friendship and Sympathy: Communities of Southern Women Writers.* Jackson: University Press of Mississippi, 1992.

Mannino, Mary Ann Vigilante. *Revisionary Identities: Strategies of Empowerment in the Writing of Italian/American Women.* New York: Peter Lang, 2000.

Marchant, Elizabeth A. *Critical Acts: Latin American Women and Cultural Criticism.* Gainesville: University Press of Florida, 1999.

McCracken, Ellen. *New Latina Narrative: The Feminine Space of Postmodern Ethnicity.* Tucson: University of Arizona Press, 1999.

McDowell, Deborah E. *"The Changing Same": Black Women's Literature, Criticism, and Theory.* Bloomington: Indiana University Press, 1995.

Miller, Press Andrew, and Daniel A. Clark. "Variations on the Plantation Romance: Five Stories by Southern Women Writers." *Studies in Popular Culture* 19 (1996): 105–18.

Ordonez, Elizabeth J. "Chicana Literature and Related Studies: A Selected and Annotated Bibliography." *Bilingual Review/La Revista Bilingue* 7 (1980): 143–64.

Perez, Laura Elisa. *Reconfiguring Nation and Identity: U.S. Latina and Latin American Women's Oppositional Writings of the 1970's–1990's.* Berkeley: University of California Press, 1995.

Pollack, Sandra, and Denise D. Knight, eds. *Contemporary Lesbian Writers of the United States: A Bio-Bibliographical Critical Sourcebook.* Westport, CT: Greenwood Press, 1993.

Pratt, Mary Louise. " 'Yo Soy La Malinche': Chicana Writers and the Poetics of Ethnonationalism." *Callaloo* 16 (1993): 859–73.

Quintana, Alvina E. *Home Girls: Chicana Literary Voices.* Philadelphia: Temple University Press, 1996.

Rainwater, Catherine, and William J. Scheick, eds. *Contemporary American Women Writers: Narrative Strategies.* Lexington: University Press of Kentucky, 1985.

Rebolledo, Tey Diana. "Narrative Strategies of Resistance in Hispana Writing." *Journal of Narrative Technique* 20 (1990): 134–46.

——. *Women Singing in the Snow: A Cultural Analysis of Chicana Literature.* Tucson: University of Arizona Press, 1995.

Redfern, Bernice. *Women of Color in the United States: A Guide to the Literature.* New York: Garland, 1989.

Reid, E. Shelley. "Beyond Morrison and Walker: Looking Good and Looking Forward in Contemporary Black Women's Stories." *African American Review* 34 (2000): 313–28.

Rowell, Charles H., ed. "Emerging Women Writers." Special Issue. *Callaloo* 19.2 (1996).

Royster, Jacqueline Jones. *Traces of a Stream: Literacy and Social Change among African American Women.* Pittsburgh: University of Pittsburgh Press, 2000.

Ryan, Maureen. "The Other Side of Grief: American Women Writers and the Vietnam War." *Critique* 36 (1994): 41–57.

Sanchez, Rosaura. "Deconstructions and Renarrativizations: Trends in Chicana Literature." *Bilingual Review/La Revista Bilingue* 21 (1996): 52–58.

——. "Reconstructing Chicana Identity." *American Literary History* 9 (1997): 350–63.

Shapiro, Ann R., ed. *Unlikely Heroines: Nineteenth-Century American Women Writers and the Woman Question.* Westport, CT: Greenwood Press, 1987.

——. *Jewish American Women Writers: A Bio-Bibliographical and Critical Sourcebook.* Westport, CT: Greenwood Press, 1994.

Shimakawa, Karen. "Swallowing the Tempest: Asian American Women on Stage." *Theatre Journal* 47 (1995): 367–80.

Sitesh, Aruna. *Her Testimony: American Women Writers of the 90s in Conversation with Aruna Sitesh.* New Delhi, India: Affiliated East-West, 1994.

Sochen, June. "Identities within Identity: Thoughts on Jewish American Women Writers." *Studies in American Jewish Literature* 3 (1983): 6–10.

Stefanko, Jacqueline. "New Ways of Telling: Latinas' Narratives of Exile and Return." *Frontiers* 17 (1996): 50–69.

Stein, Rachel. *Shifting the Ground: American Women Writers' Revisions of Nature, Gender, and Race.* Charlottesville: University Press of Virginia, 1997.

Stuecher, Dorothea. *Twice Removed: The Experience of German-American Women Writers in the Nineteenth Century.* New York: Peter Lang, 1990.

Tate, Claudia. "Reshuffling the Deck; or, (Re)Reading Race and Gender in Black Women's Writing." *Tulsa Studies in Women's Literature* 7 (1988): 119–32.

——. *Domestic Allegories of Political Desire: The Black Heroine's Text at the Turn of Century.* New York: Oxford University Press, 1993.

Taumann, Beatrix. *"Strange Orphans": Contemporary African American Women Playwrights.* Wurzburg, Germany: Konigshausen & Neumann, 1999.

Tran, Qui-Phiet. "Contemporary Vietnamese American Feminine Writing: Exile and Home." *Amerasia Journal* 19 (1993): 71–83.

Uffen, Ellen Serlen. *Strands of the Cable: The Place of the Past in Jewish Women's Writing.* New York: Peter Lang, 1992.

Villanueva, Margaret. "Ambivalent Sisterhood." *Latina Feminism and Women's Studies Discourse* 21 (1999): 49–76.

Wade-Gayles, Gloria. *No Crystal Stair: Visions of Race and Sex in Black Women's Fiction.* New York: Pilgrim, 1984.

Wagner-Martin, Linda. "Ethnicity and Women's Literature." *Contemporary Literature* 31 (1990): 392–96.

—— and Cathy N. Davidson. *The Oxford Book of Women's Writing in the United States.* Oxford, UK: Oxford University Press, 1995.

Walker, Nancy. Agelaste or Eiron: American Women Writers and the Sense of Humor." *Studies in American Humor* 4 (1985): 105–25.

White, Barbara A. *American Women Writers: An Annotated Bibliography of Criticism.* New York: Garland, 1977.

Wilentz, Gay. "Affirming Critical Difference: Reading Black Women's Texts." *Kenyon Review* 13 (1991): 146–51.

Williams, Dana A., comp. *Contemporary African American Female Playwrights: An Annotated Bibliography.* Westport, CT: Greenwood Press, 1998.

Wolfe, Margaret Ripley. *Daughters of Canaan: A Saga of Southern Women.* Lexington: University Press of Kentucky, 1995.

Yamamoto, Traise. *Making Selves, Making Subjects: Japanese American Women, Identity, and the Body.* Berkeley: University of California Press, 1999.

Yarbro-Bejarano, Yvonne. "Chicanas' Experience in Collective Theatre: Ideology and Form." *Women & Performance* 2 (1985): 45–58.

Zamora, Lois Parkinson, ed. *Contemporary American Women Writers: Gender, Class, Ethnicity.* New York: Longman, 1998.

INDEX

The pages in **bold** indicate the location of the main entry

ABOUT THE EDITORS AND CONTRIBUTORS

LISA ABNEY is Director of the Louisiana Folklife Center and is an Assistant Professor of English at Northwestern State University. She holds a PhD from the University of Houston and an MA and BA from Texas A&M University. Dr. Abney's research interests include sociolinguistics, dialectology, folklore, Southern literature, and American and British Modernists. She has completed, with her co-editor, Dr. Suzanne Disheroon-Green, a compilation of works about Louisiana writers called *Songs of the New South: Writing Contemporary Louisiana*. Abney has authored several critical articles and recently completed a multimedia project which includes written text, audio, photographs, and video, entitled "The Natchitoches/NSU Folk Festival" for the Local Legacies Program of the American Folklife Center, Library of Congress.

ANDREA ADOLPH, a doctoral candidate at Louisiana State University, is currently completing a dissertation on representations of food and eating in twentieth-century British women's fiction. She holds degrees from California State University, Fresno, and from Mills College. Her work as a poet and essayist has appeared in numerous literary journals, and she co-edited *Bite to Eat Place: An Anthology of Contemporary Food Poetry and Poetic Prose* (Redwood Coast, 1995). A critical essay on Virginia Woolf and Bernard Shaw is forthcoming.

CORA AGATUCCI teaches writing, women's studies, African and Asian cultures and literatures at Central Oregon Community College in Bend. She earned her PhD in literature at the University of California, San Diego, and has published on Michelle Cliff, Eric Walrond, contemporary African-American literature, and Doris Lessing. Her African Studies instructional website has earned *Scout Report* and *Los Angeles Times* LaunchPoint selections. Current research interests include pedagogies for teaching multicultural and global literatures, and writing for the World Wide Web.

JULIE S. AMBERG is Assistant Professor of English and Humanities at York College of Pennsylvania where she teaches American literature and autobiography, women's literature, advanced writing, linguistics, and women's studies. Her current research interests are early American women's novels and the printing trade in colonial America, topics that she has written on and presented at national conferences.

JULIE BUCKNER ARMSTRONG is Assistant Professor of English at the University of South Florida, St. Petersburg, where she teaches African-American and women's literature. She is editor of *Teaching the Civil Rights Movement* (forthcoming, Routledge, 2002) and author of articles on Toni Morrison, Flannery O'Connor, and Carson McCullers. Her current research focuses on literary and artistic representations of a 1918 south Georgia lynching that also plays a role in her novel-in-progress, *Seminole Still*.

ELLEN L. ARNOLD has a PhD in Interdisciplinary Studies from Emory University. She is an Assistant Professor in the Department of English at East Carolina University, where she specializes in Native American literatures and also teaches in the Ethnic Studies and Women's

RHONDA AUSTIN holds an MA in English from Sul Ross State University in Alpine, Texas, where she teaches English composition, technical writing, and literature. She has published several short stories and is currently developing and teaching online courses. Her current project, "The U.S.–Mexico Borderlands," is a writing-intensive, team-taught multicultural literature course developed with proceeds from an NEH grant. Her interests include writing across the curriculum and computer-assisted writing instruction. Austin is also a freelance commercial writer.

JOELLE BIELE received her BA from Tufts University and her MFA in poetry and PhD in English from the University of Maryland, College Park. She is the recipient of a Fulbright Senior Scholar Award to Germany, where she taught at the University of Oldenburg. She currently teaches at the University of Maryland.

CHERYL D. BOHDE, professor of English at McLennan Community College, teaches composition and literature. Her publications and presentations reflect her interest in nineteenth-century American periodicals, Waco's David Koresh, and computer-assisted writing instruction.

AUSTIN BOOTH is Director, Collections & Research Services, Arts & Sciences Libraries, University at Buffalo (SUNY). Her recent publications focus on gender and cyberculture–she is the co-editor of *Reload: Rethinking Women & Cyberculture*, forthcoming from MIT Press in 2002.

STEPHANIE BROWN received a PhD in American literature at Columbia University in 2002. She has published articles on feminist theory and popular culture, as well as on African-American literature and film. She is currently a lecturer in English and American Studies at the *Technische Universitaet* in Chemnitz, Germany.

KRISTIN BRUNNEMER is a PhD graduate student in English at the University of California, Riverside. Her areas of interest include minority discourse, Twentieth-Century American literature, film, and visual culture and feminist theory.

JOY CASTRO is Assistant Professor of English at Wabash College in Indiana, where she teaches Twentieth-Century American literature, British modernism, and creative writing. Her fiction has appeared in such journals as *Quarterly West*, *Chelsea*, and *Mid-American Review*.

RHONDA CAWTHORN is currently a PhD candidate in English at the University of South Carolina. Her publications include an interview with National Book Award winner Tim O'Brien, and two articles "Turning Massacres into Gold: The Alchemic Power of Joy Harjo's Poetry" and "A Promise Made to Bubba: The Legacy of Sonia Sanchez's Poetry." Her current projects are a book-length study on Eudora Welty and articles on the work of Beth Nugent and Joy Williams.

LAURIE CHAMPION is Assistant Professor of English at San Diego State University, Imperial Valley. Essays on American literature have appeared in *Southern Literary Journal*, *Southern Quarterly*, *Mississippi Quarterly*, *Studies in Short Fiction*, *Journal of the Short Story in English*, and other journals. Dr. Champion is co-editor of *Blacks in the West: A Century of Short Stories* and editor of *The Critical Response to Huckleberry Finn*, *The Critical Response to Eudora Welty's Fiction*, and *American Women Writers, 1900–1945: A Bio-Bibliographical Critical Sourcebook*.

MONA M. CHOUCAIR teaches English composition at Baylor University where she received her PhD in August, 2000. Her area of concentration is Twentieth-Century literature and teaching and research interests include women minority writers of the Twentieth Cntury, women's studies, and the works of Toni Morrison.

J. ELIZABETH CLARK is an Assistant Professor of English at Fiorello H. LaGuardia Community College in New York City. She received her PhD in American Literature from Binghamton University in 2000. Her primary research interests include the poetry of AIDS, Twentieth-Century American political poetry, Latina/o Literature, and pedagogy. She serves as part of the editorial collective for the magazine *Radical Teacher*. Her poetry has appeared in *RiverSedge*, *The Comstock Review*, *The New Writer*, *Perceptions*, and *A&U: Arts and Understanding*. She is currently working on a critical manuscript about post-protease AIDS poetry.

BILL CLEM is a doctoral student in English with an emphasis in Multicultural American literatures (particularly African American), Women's Studies, and Shakespeare at Northern Illinois University. He is preparing articles for publication on Chaucer's Prioress, Shakespeare's *Titus Andronicus*, and on the novels of Toni Morrison. He is currently instructor of English at Waubonsee Community College.

JESSE COHN is working on a book about questions of literature, culture, and representation in anarchist theory. His interests include contemporary fiction, urban planning, utopian studies, and the development of avant-garde aesthetics and poetics in the Nineteenth and Twentieth Centuries. He is Assistant Professor of English at Purdue University North Central, and lives in Valparaiso, Indiana.

DONNA BUCHANAN COOK is currently writing a thesis for a Master of Arts degree in English at Sul Ross State University in Alpine, Texas. She works as a graduate assistant in the Writing Center and teaches freshman composition. Recently she read from her short stories and life writings at the IV Colloquium on Creative Writing by Women; the First International Gathering of Women Writers in West Texas, and the Center for Big Bend Studies 8th Annual Conference, 2001. Her short story "Changing Hats" was recently published in *New Texas*, 2001. Cook co-edited *The Sage* literary magazine in 2000. She plans to continue a teaching and writing career.

CATHERINE CUCINELLA teaches literature, writing, humanities, and women's studies at California State University, San Marcos. She edited *Contemporary American Women Poets: An A-to-Z Guide* (Greenwood, 2002) and has articles on women poets and writers in journals and reference volumes.

CARMAN C. CURTON is Assistant Professor of Literature and Languages at Lewis-Clark State College in Lewiston, Idaho. She has degrees from Michigan State University and University of North Texas. Professor Curton has published previously on Sui Sin Far (Edith Maude Eaton) as well as on a variety of news and feature topics for Dallas newspapers. Current research subjects include a study of Asian American women's writings and the canon as well as representations of frontier mythology in American literature anthologies.

KATE K. DAVIS is a Teaching Fellow at the University of North Texas. She has several short stories published and is pursuing postcolonial studies in British and ethnic American literature.

SUZANNE DISHEROON-GREEN serves as assistant professor of American literature at Northwestern State University in Natchitoches, Louisiana. She received her PhD in English from the University of North Texas in 1997. She is co-author of *Kate Chopin: An Annotated Bibliography of Critical Works* and *At Fault by Kate Chopin: A Scholarly Edition with Background Readings* with David J. Caudle and *Songs of the New South: Writing Contemporary Louisiana* with Lisa Abney. She has published and presented numerous articles on Kate Chopin and other southern writers. She is presently editing an anthology of Southern literature, entitled *Voices of the American South*, which will be published by Longman Publishers and co-editing a volume in the Dictionary of Literary Biography series entitled *Twenty-First Century American Novelists*. She is also working on a book-length study of the fiction of Kaye Gibbons

LYNN DOMINA is the author of a collection of poetry, *Corporal Works*, and a reference book, *Understanding A Raisin in the Sun*. She has written critical articles on Mary McCarthy, N. Scott Momaday, Zora Neale Hurston, Elizabeth Keckley, and others. She currently teaches at the State University of New York at Delhi.

CATHY DOWNS is Assistant Professor of English at Texas A&M University, Kingsville, where she teaches freshman writing and American literature courses. Her intellectual biography of Willa Cather is called *Becoming Modern*. Downs is working on a novel as well as a study of how scientific theories influenced the writing of Twentieth-Century American literary women.

ANN ENGAR is an award-winning instructor in the Honors and LEAP Programs at the University of Utah. She has written numerous articles on women authors, teaching, the practice of biography, and Eighteenth-Century British literature. She is also a senior bibliographer for the *MLA International Bibliography*.

ROY FLANNAGAN has interests in European modernism, contemporary fiction, and film. He has written about John Hawkes for *The Review of Contemporary Fiction* and Geoffrey Moorhouse for the *Dictionary of Literary Biography*. He lives in Florence, South Carolina, and teaches at Francis Marion University.

STEPHANIE GORDON is a doctoral student in English at the University of Georgia. She has had poems, reviews, and author interviews published in *The Southern Poetry Review*, *Columbia: A Journal of Art and Literature*, *Studies in American Indian Literature*, and *AWP Chronicle*, among others. She is currently working on her first book, a memoir entitled *Strange Fires*.

CYNTHIA WHITNEY HALLETT is a Professor of English at Bennett College, Greensboro, North Carolina. Her articles on a variety of authors, including Ernest Hemingway, Amy Hempel, Zora Neale Hurston, Mary Robison, and Alice Walker, have been published in diverse journals and collections of criticism. Professor Hallett began her scholarship on the short story with her undergraduate thesis at New College, Sarasota, Florida. She received her PhD from the University of South Florida, Tampa.

ROXANNE HARDE is a doctoral candidate at Queen's University in Kingston, Ontario. She is currently finishing her dissertation on American women's poetry and feminist theology. She has articles in *Contemporary Verse II*, *Mantis*, and *Critique* (forthcoming), and various collections.

SHARON HILEMAN is Professor of English and Chair of the Department of Languages and Literature at Sul Ross State University in Alpine, Texas. She co-edits the *Journal of International Women's Studies* and teaches British, postcolonial, and women's literature. Most of her publications and research interests focus on forms of women's lifewriting. Currently, she is working on a National Endowment for the Humanities project concerning women writers in the U.S.–Mexico Borderlands.

JAMES L. HILL is Assistant Vice President for Academic Affairs and Professor of English at Albany State University, Albany, Georgia. A graduate of Fort Valley State University, Atlanta University, and the Univeristy of Iowa, where he received his doctorate in American Civilization/African American Studies, Professor Hill is formerly Dean of the College of Arts and Sciences and Chair of the Department of English and Modern Languages at Albany State University. Professionally active, he is also Past Chair of the Conference on College Composition (CCCC) and the College Section of the National Council of Teachers of English (NCTE). Professor Hill has published in a number of journals and contributed to such reference collections as the

Oxford Companion to African American Literature and *African American Writers Before the Harlem Renaissance*.

ROBERT JOHNSON teaches at Midwestern State University in Wichita Falls, Texas. His latest placements have been critical studies in *American Indian Quarterly* and *Journal of the Short Story in English*, as well as short stories in *Argestes* and the yearly anthology, *New Texas*.

ANGELA LAFLEN is currently a graduate student at Purdue University with concentrations in Contemporary American Literature and Women's Literature.

ELIZABETH BLAKESLEY LINDSAY is the Languages, Literature and Cultural Studies Librarian at the University of Massachusetts, Dartmouth.

DEBORAH MALTBY earned a BA in journalism from the University of South Carolina and an MA in English from the University of North Carolina at Charlotte, where she was a student of Nanci Kincaid. Maltby teaches college English in Missouri and writes for various newspapers and magazines. Her literary research interests include the works of contemporary Southern women writers and Thomas Hardy.

CLAUDIA MILSTEAD is an instructor in the Department of English at the University of Tennessee, where she earned her PhD She teaches poetry and American literature.

LISA MARIÁ BURGESS NOUDÉHOU grew up in Mexico and the United States. She earned her Bachelor's degree at Brandeis University and her doctorate in English at the University of Pennsylvania. She has taught literature at Tsinghua University (China), Howard University (DC), Rhodes University (South Africa), and Churchill High School (MD). Her critical interests include colonial American literature and women's literature.

CATHERINE RAINWATER, Professor of English, has taught literature and writing at St. Edward's University since 1985. She is the author and/or co-editor of numerous publications. These include books as well as articles and reviews in journals such as *American Literature, American Journal of Semiotics, Philological Quarterly, Texas Studies in Literature and Language, Canadian Literature, Modern Fiction Studies, Southern Literary Journal*, and others. In 1990, she was awarded the Norman Foerster Prize by the Modern Language Association for her work on American Indian author, Louise Erdrich. Her name appears in biographical references including *Contemporary Authors, International Authors and Writers Who's Who, Who's Who in American Education*, and *Who's Who in the South and Southwest*. Currently, she is president of the Ellen Glasgow Society and editor of The Ellen Glasgow Newsletter. Her most recent work is *Dreams of Fiery Stars: The Transformations of Native American Fiction* (University of Pennsylvania Press, 1995).

CHRIS RUIZ-VELASCO is an assistant professor of English at California State University, Fullerton. His interests include minority discourse, postmodern theory, and twentieth-century American literature.

BEVERLY G. SIX is Assistant Professor of English at Sul Ross State University, Alpine, Texas, where she teaches composition and literature. Her areas of specialization include medieval literature, folklore and multicultural literature, and Native American literature, with a particular interest in literary portrayals of Native American spirituality.

ERNEST SMITH is an Associate Professor of English at the University of Central Florida. He is the author of a book-length study of *White Buildings*, Hart Crane's first volume of poetry, and several articles on modern American literature, particularly in the area of modern poetry.

J. P. STEED holds an MFA in Creative Writing from the University of Idaho and is a PhD candidate in contemporary American literature at the University of Nevada, Las Vegas. His dissertation is on "Humor and Identity in the American Jewish Novella," and one of the chapters focuses on Francine Prose's "Guided Tours of Hell."

MICHELLE L. TAYLOR graduated with a Bachelor of Arts in English and Politics from Mount Holyoke College. She is a PhD candidate in the English Department at Rice University. Her dissertation explores issues of resistance among non-elite African American women in nineteenth-century African American and American literature. She is currently an Erskine Peters Dissertation Fellow at the University of Notre Dame.

ELIZABETH J. WRIGHT is a graduate student in English at the University of New Mexico, where she is writing a dissertation on Twentieth-Century American women writers and the politics of literacy.